Betty Crocker's

COOKBOOK

PRENTICE HALL

New York ♦ London ♦ Toronto ♦ Sydney ♦ Tokyo ♦ Singapore

PRENTICE HALL GENERAL REFERENCE
15 Columbus Circle
New York, NY 10023

Library of Congress Cataloging-in-Publication Data
Crocker, Betty.
[Cookbook]
Betty Crocker's cookbook.
p.   cm.
ISBN: 0-13-073768-2; ISBN: 0-671-85039-3 (pbk.)
1. Cookery.   I. Title.
TX714.C754   1990
641.5—dc20   89-78152
CIP

Manufactured in the United States of America

10 9 8 7 6 5 4 3 2

Seventh Edition

Front cover: Oven-fried Chicken (page 283), Lemon-Chive Potatoes (page 391), Sautéed Peppers (page 390), Baking Powder Biscuits (page 38), Orange-glazed Lattice Cherry Pie (page 93), Lemon-Berry Tart (page 95), Mixed Berry Jam (page 362)

Preceeding page: Shrimp-Pesto Salad (page 316), Italian Flatbread (page 52), Crème Brûlée (page 153), Iced Coffee (page 28)

CREDITS

GENERAL MILLS, INC.

Senior Editors: Jean E. Kozar, Maureen P. Fischer
Test Kitchen Home Economists: Diane Undis,
    Mary H. Johnson, Mary E. Petersen
Nutrition Department Consultant: Nancy
    Holmes, R.D.
Recipe Copy Editor: Judy Lund
Editorial Assistant: Phyllis Weinbender
Food Stylists: Cindy Lund, Mary Sethre, Kate
    Courtney
Food Styling Assistant: Betty Bordwell
Photographer: Nanci E. Doonan
Photography Assistants: Valerie J. Bourassa,
    Matthew A. Miller
Director, Betty Crocker Food and Publications
    Center: Marcia Copeland
Assistant Manager, Publications: Lois Tlusty

CONTENTS

INTRODUCTION

Welcome to the 40th anniversary edition of *Betty Crocker's Cookbook*! We have revised and updated our cookbook to be sure that it is comprehensive, helpful and as easy to use as possible. To celebrate the forty years that *Betty Crocker's Cookbook* has been a mainstay in American homes, we've put back the intriguing food history and recipe tips you've always loved.

We have also kept many of the features you liked in the previous editions. Of course, every recipe is fully tested in the Betty Crocker Kitchens to guarantee success in *your* kitchen. You'll find helpful sections called "Cooking with Confidence" and "Special Helps" that cover all aspects of cooking, while each recipe chapter begins with basic information and useful tips.

Step-by-step instructions with photographs and easy-to-follow line drawings simplify new procedures, while identification photographs make it easy to recognize a wide variety of foods, from pastas to herbs to meats. And you'll find the beautiful food photography gives you new and varied serving ideas.

The recipes reflect the changes in American eating habits. You'll find more information on—and recipes for—fish and shellfish, pasta, grains and legumes. The nutrition information for every recipe has been expanded and is easily found at the end of each chapter. Whenever possible, we reduced the fat, sugar and sodium in the recipes and used more fresh ingredients than ever before.

There's more information on microwaving and grilling in this edition. We've also expanded our food safety information across the board, including the newest guidelines on how to prepare and cook meats and eggs safely. At the end of every chapter there's another new, helpful feature—Fix-It-Fast. Gathered here are terrific tips for quick recipes to help you beat the time crunch that all cooks seem to face today.

Throughout the cookbook you'll find two symbols: the clock ⏱ means this recipe can be completed in thirty minutes or less. The sheaf of wheat 🌾 identifies a Betty Crocker heritage recipe, one that has been consistently popular, constantly in demand and featured in a previous edition of *Betty Crocker's Cookbook*.

The 40th anniversary edition of *Betty Crocker's Cookbook* is a tribute to you who depend on Betty Crocker for great food and confidence in the kitchen. We are proud to present this exciting new edition, combining the delicious recipes, modern cooking techniques and unique heritage of Betty Crocker.

THE BETTY CROCKER EDITORS

THE HERITAGE OF BETTY CROCKER

Betty Crocker's Cookbook has been helping cooks, beginning and experienced alike, for forty years. Since the publication of *Betty Crocker's Picture Cook Book* in 1950, Americans have come to trust and rely on the fully tested recipes, helpful tips and information and advice on meal planning and nutrition. In fact, this cookbook sold a million copies in its first year. It's no wonder that Betty Crocker has been called the "First Lady of Food."

For the past four decades, *Betty Crocker's Cookbook* has kept pace with technology, new trends and changes in our lifestyle. The book was updated first in 1956. The subsequent revisions—and this current 40th anniversary edition—continue the tradition of offering the best of contemporary cooking techniques as well as the wisdom and practical skills for which the Betty Crocker experts are known.

While this cookbook has a forty-year tradition, Betty Crocker has been a valued spokesperson for much longer. She was created in 1921 by the Washburn-Crosby Flour Co., which later became General Mills. The executives at Washburn-Crosby felt that a woman's signature should be used when answering requests for baking and cooking information. Betty was selected for its friendly sound, and Crocker was the last name of a well-liked director—William G. Crocker. A contest for the most distinctive Betty Crocker signature was held among the female employees of Washburn-Crosby, and the signature remains very much the same today.

Betty Crocker's popularity soared between 1924 and 1948 with NBC radio's "Betty Crocker's Cooking School of the Air," in which more than a million people enrolled. Betty Crocker became familiar coast to coast, and during World War II joined with NBC and the War Food Administration to give listeners advice on cooking with rationed food supplies. In one survey at that time, Betty Crocker was voted one of America's best-known women, second only to Eleanor Roosevelt!

The first Betty Crocker portrait was commissioned in 1936 and introduced to celebrate the 15th anniversary of the creation of Betty Crocker. This version was based on features of several employees in the Home Services Department. In 1955, a contest was held to select a new portrait with entries from several artists, and some sixteen hundred women across the country helped pick the favorite.

In 1965 and 1968 the Betty Crocker portrait was updated to be in step with the times. In 1972 a new portrait reflected the movement of American women from the home to the workplace. The image was updated in 1980, and in 1986 the current portrait was painted, both indicative of the changing role of modern women. Throughout all her portraits, Betty Crocker has maintained her look of friendly competence.

Today, the Betty Crocker tradition of quality and dependability is stronger than ever. Home economists create, test and write recipes, and perfect cooking techniques for American homes. Nutritionists provide nutritional data and through the consumer response department, thousands of consumers receive cooking help.

Because we continually review and evaluate the material in *Betty Crocker's Cookbook*, you can be sure it's up-to-date and reliable. It's a book you can always count on to give you the best—from old-fashioned favorites to the latest trends—and everything in between.

Top: *Betty Crocker portraits: 1965, 1955, 1980, 1986.* Middle: *Cookbooks–1961, 1950, 1969; portraits—1936, 1972.* Bottom: *Cookbooks—1978, 1956, 1986; portrait—1968.*

COOKING WITH CONFIDENCE

KITCHEN SETUP AND EQUIPMENT BASICS

If you're starting out and aren't quite sure how to put your kitchen together, here are some guidelines that will get your kitchen up and running:

- Select pieces that serve a dual purpose, such as freezer-to-oven-to-table baking dishes and casseroles and ovenproof skillets.

- Choose saucepans and skillets that have tight-fitting covers. Check to be sure that knobs and handles are insulated to prevent them from conducting heat.

- Purchase the best quality equipment you can afford. Quality equipment and utensils will last longer. Make sure equipment is durable and easy to clean.

- The size and amount of cooking in your household will determine how many pieces of equipment and utensils you'll need in your kitchen. Purchase only basic equipment first, then add extra equipment as the need arises.

MEASURING AND PREPARATION EQUIPMENT AND UTENSILS

Assorted sizes of mixing bowls
Nested dry measuring cups
Measuring spoons
Glass measuring cup
Metal spatula
Rubber spatulas
Wooden spoons
Cutting boards, plastic and wood
Assorted sizes of knives
Long-handled spoon
Long-handled fork
Tongs
Vegetable peeler
Kitchen scissors
Pastry brush
Can opener/bottle opener
Shredder or grater
Strainer

Colander
Kitchen timer
Rotary beater or electric mixer

BAKEWARE

Cookie sheet or jelly roll pan
Wire rack
Pie plate
Muffin pan
Custard cups
Tube pan or bundt cake pan
Loaf pan
Assorted sizes of baking pans
Assorted sizes of casseroles
Roasting pan and rack
Pot holders
Meat thermometer

COOKWARE

Assorted sizes of saucepans (with lids)
Assorted sizes of skillets (with lids)
Dutch oven or kettle (with lid)

STORAGE

Assorted sizes of storage containers
Aluminum foil
Waxed paper
Plastic wrap
Canisters

EQUIVALENT MEASURES

3 teaspoons = 1 tablespoon
4 tablespoons = ¼ cup
5 tablespoons + 1 teaspoon = ⅓ cup
8 tablespoons = ½ cup
12 tablespoons = ¾ cup
16 tablespoons = 1 cup
2 cups = 1 pint
4 cups (2 pints) = 1 quart
4 quarts = 1 gallon

MEASURING INGREDIENTS

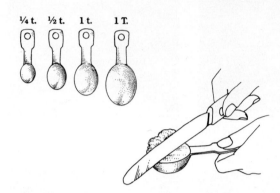

Graduated Measuring Spoons: These spoons range from ¼ teaspoon to 1 tablespoon. Some sets have a ⅛ teaspoon spoon. Use spoons to measure small amounts of liquids and dry ingredients. For thin liquids, pour into spoon until full. For thick liquids and dry ingredients, pour or scoop into spoon until full, then level.

Nested Graduated Measuring Cups: These cups range in size from ¼ cup to 1 cup. Some sets have a ⅛ cup measure (2 tablespoons) as well. Graduated cups are used to measure dry ingredients and such solid fats as shortening.

For all-purpose flour, variety baking mix, sugar and cake flour, spoon ingredient lightly into cup, then level with a straight-edged spatula or knife. Do not sift flour to measure or combine with other ingredients. Sift powdered sugar only if lumpy.

Glass Measuring Cup: These cups can be purchased in 1-, 2-, 4- and 8-cup sizes. They are used to measure liquids. Always read the measurement at eye level for an accurate reading. For sticky liquids like honey, molasses and corn syrup, lightly oiling the cup first with a vegetable oil will make removing liquid easier.

For cereal and dry bread crumbs, pour into cup.

For solid fats and brown sugar, spoon into cup and pack down firmly with spatula or spoon.

For shredded cheese, chopped nuts, coconut, cut-up dried fruit and soft bread crumbs, spoon into cup and pack down lightly.

PREPARATION TERMS

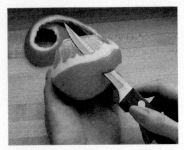

Pare: Cut off outer covering with a knife or vegetable parer.

Peel: Strip off outer covering with your fingers.

Slice: Cut food into same-size flat pieces.

Julienne: Stack thin slices; then cut into matchlike sticks.

Cube: Cut into ½-inch or wider strips; cut across into cubes.

Dice: Cut into ½-inch or narrower strips; cut across into cubes.

Chop: Cut food into irregular-size pieces.

Cut up: Cut into small pieces with kitchen scissors.

Snip: Cut into very small pieces with kitchen scissors.

Shred: Cut into long thin pieces by rubbing food across the large holes of a shredder or using a knife.

Grate: Cut into tiny particles by rubbing food across the small rough holes of a grater.

Crush: Press with side of knife, mallet or rolling pin to break into small pieces.

FOOD TERMS YOU SHOULD KNOW

BAKE: Cook in oven.

BASTE: Spoon a liquid over food during cooking to keep it moist.

BEAT: Mix ingredients vigorously with spoon, hand beater or electric mixer until smooth.

BLANCH: Plunge food briefly into boiling water to preserve color, texture and nutritional value or to remove skins from fruits or nuts.

BLEND: Mix ingredients until they are very smooth and uniform.

BOIL: Heat until bubbles rise continuously and break on the surface; for rolling boil, the bubbles form rapidly.

CARAMELIZE: To melt sugar slowly over low heat until it becomes brown in color.

CHOP: Cut into irregular pieces; a knife, food chopper or food processor may be used.

COAT: To cover food evenly with crumbs or a sauce.

COOL: Allow hot food to come to room temperature.

CRISP-TENDER: Food cooked until it is tender but still retaining some of the crisp texture of the raw food.

CRUSH: Grind into fine particles; for example, crush clove of garlic using chef's knife or garlic press.

CUBE: Cut into three-dimensional squares ½ inch or larger with knife.

CUT IN: Distribute solid fat in dry ingredients by cutting with pastry blender with a rolling motion or cutting with two knives until particles are desired size.

DASH: Less than ⅛ teaspoon of an ingredient.

DICE: Cut into cubes smaller than ½ inch.

FINELY CHOPPED: Cut into very tiny pieces.

FLAKE: To separate into pieces with fork, as in flaking fish.

FOLD: Combine ingredients lightly using two motions. First, cut vertically through mixture with rubber spatula. Next, slide spatula across bottom of bowl and up the side, turning the mixture over. Continue down-across-up-over motion while rotating bowl ¼ turn with each series of strokes.

GARNISH: To decorate the food served with additional foods that have distinctive color or texture, such as parsley, fresh berries or carrot curls.

GLAZE: To brush or drizzle a mixture on a food to give it a glossy appearance, hard finish or decoration.

GRATE: Cut into tiny particles using small holes of grater or food processor.

JULIENNE: To cut fruits, vegetables or meats into thin, matchlike strips using knife or food processor.

MARINATE: Let food stand in a savory (usually acidic) liquid for several hours to add flavor or to tenderize; marinade is the savory liquid in which the food is marinated.

MIX: Combine ingredients in any way that distributes them evenly.

PANFRY: Beginning with a cold skillet, to fry in little or no fat.

PARE: Cut off outer covering with knife or vegetable parer, as for apples or pears.

PEEL: Strip off outer covering using fingers, as for bananas or oranges.

POACH: Cook in hot liquid kept just below the boiling point.

REDUCE: Boil liquid uncovered to evaporate liquid and intensify flavor.

REFRIGERATE: Place food in refrigerator to chill or store.

ROAST: Cook meat in oven uncovered on rack in shallow pan without adding liquid.

SAUTÉ: Foods cooked in hot oil or margarine over medium-high heat with frequent tossing and turning motion.

SCALD: Heat liquid to just below the boiling point. Tiny bubbles form at the edge.

SCORE: Cut surface of food about ¼ inch deep with knife to facilitate cooking, flavoring or tenderizing.

SHRED: Cut into long, thin pieces using large holes of grater, knife or food processor.

SIMMER: Usually done after reducing heat from boiling point, continue to heat to just below boiling. Bubbles will rise slowly and break just below the surface.

SLICE: Cut into uniform flat pieces.

SOFT PEAKS: Egg whites beaten until peaks are rounded or curl when beaters are lifted from bowl, but are still moist and glossy.

SOFTEN: Let food such as margarine, butter or cream cheese stand at room temperature or microwave at medium-low (30%) until soft.

STIFF PEAKS: Egg whites beaten until peaks stand up straight when beaters are lifted from bowl, but are still moist and glossy.

STIR: Mix ingredients with circular or figure-eight motion until of uniform consistency.

STIR-FRY: A Chinese method of cooking uniform pieces of food in small amount of hot oil over high heat, stirring constantly.

TEAR: Break into pieces using fingers.

TOSS: Tumble ingredients lightly with a lifting motion.

FOOD PREPARATION BASICS

Bread Crumbs (dry): Place bread in 200° oven until dry. Place dry bread in heavy plastic bag or between sheets of waxed paper. Crush with rolling pin or mallet into very small pieces. You can also place in blender or food processor to make fine bread crumbs.

Bread Crumbs (soft): Tear soft bread into small pieces.

Coating Chicken or Fish: Place desired seasonings and bread crumbs or flour in a paper or plastic bag. Add a few pieces of chicken or fish at a time; shake until each piece is evenly coated.

Croutons: Cut bread into ½-inch slices; spread one side with softened margarine or butter. Cut into ½-inch cubes. Sprinkle with chopped herbs, grated Parmesan cheese or spices if desired. Place in ungreased heavy skillet. Cook over medium heat, stirring frequently, 4 to 7 minutes or until golden brown.

Melting Chocolate: Place chocolate in heavy saucepan. Heat on low heat until chocolate is melted, stirring frequently.

Peeling Tomatoes and Peaches: Place tomato or peach in boiling water for 30 seconds; remove with a slotted spoon and plunge into iced water. The skin will slip off easily.

Sectioning Citrus Fruits: Pare fruit down to the flesh. Cut segments from between walls of membrane.

Separating Eggs: Allow cold eggs to come to room temperature (they will be easier to separate). Crack egg. Slip egg back and forth between shell halves over a bowl, allowing the white to drop into the bowl. Place yolk in separate bowl.

Tinting Coconut: Add a few drops of food color to ½ cup coconut in a jar; cover and shake until evenly tinted.

Toasting Coconut: Sprinkle ½ cup coconut in ungreased heavy skillet. Cook over medium-low heat 6 to 14 minutes, stirring frequently until coconut begins to brown, then stirring constantly until golden brown (watch carefully; time varies greatly between gas and electric range).

Toasting Nuts: Sprinkle ½ cup nuts in ungreased heavy skillet. Cook over medium heat 5 to 7 minutes, stirring frequently until nuts begin to brown, then stirring constantly until golden brown.

UNDERSTANDING NUTRITION INFORMATION FOR RECIPES

Nutrition information is calculated for each recipe and variation. The calories per serving or unit are listed with each recipe, while complete analyses are listed alphabetically at the end of each chapter in the Nutrition Information charts.

Calculations have been done for calories, protein, carbohydrates, fat, cholesterol and sodium. The U.S. Recommended Daily Allowance (USRDA) percentage is indicated for protein, vitamin A, vitamin C, thiamine, riboflavin, niacin, calcium and iron. The USRDAs are set by the Food and Drug Administration and are based on body needs for most healthy adults.

♦ If ingredient choices are given, the first ingredient in the ingredient list is that used to calculate the nutrition information.

♦ When a range is given for an ingredient, or more than one serving size is indicated, the first amount or first serving size listed is that used for the calculation.

♦ "If desired" ingredients are not included in the nutrition calculations, whether they appear in the ingredient listing or the recipe text as a suggestion.

MICROWAVE TESTING FOR THIS BOOK

The microwave recipes in this book were tested using countertop microwaves with 600 to 700 watts. If your microwave has a rating of less than 600 or more than 700 watts, cooking time must be lengthened or shortened accordingly.

APPETIZERS & BEVERAGES

APPETIZERS & BEVERAGES

Appetizers—or hors d'oeuvres—were originally intended to whet the appetite for dinner, but they do much more than that today. Appetizers can be the start of a sit-down dinner, food to nibble less formally while dinner is cooking or a snack to tide us over to the next meal. Put together a varied selection of appetizers, add your favorite beverages, and you've created an easy party. However you use appetizers and beverages, they are sure-fire crowd pleasers, and with the variety of recipes here, you will be sure to suit every appetite and occasion.

APPETIZER BASICS

♦ Try appetizers as a first course for a special dinner. Oysters Rockefeller (page 15) is elegant and fast, or try a cold refreshing soup, such as Chilled Pear-Mint Soup (page 347).

♦ A cheese board makes party preparation easy and is great for a light meal with fruit. Use three or four different types of cheese—see the Varieties of Natural Cheese chart on page 179 for ideas—and plan on about 2 ounces of cheese per person. Serve with thinly sliced breads and crackers—pumpernickel, Italian or French baguettes, water biscuits, Scandinavian flatbreads and rice cakes are all good choices.

♦ Crudités (raw vegetables) are always an excellent addition to a selection of appetizers, colorful as well as healthy. Use cherry tomatoes, mushrooms, sugar peas, broccoli, cauliflower, jicama, fennel or other favorite vegetables.

♦ Party sandwiches can be impressive appetizers. Cut bread—white, whole wheat, rye and multigrain —into interesting shapes with cookie or canapé cutters. Spread the bread thinly with butter or margarine so the fillings won't make bread soggy. Try your favorite sandwich fillings (page 354), cream cheese spreads or items from the deli. Garnish with tiny shrimp, vegetable slices, nuts or fresh herbs.

♦ When planning a party menu, choose a variety of appetizers—hot, cold, hearty and low calorie—to satisfy the preferences of all your guests. Also, look for recipes that can be prepared in advance, so you'll have time to enjoy your guests.

♦ Leftover appetizers are great snacks. In fact, if you have appetizers in your refrigerator, you have the makings of an easy, light meal!

Preceding page: Spinach Dip (page 21), Basil Brie in Pastry (page 17), Cheese Straw Twists (page 19)

DEVILED EGGS

Deviled Eggs are not eggs with bad character. They are spicy stuffed eggs that get their name from the term "to devil," meaning to season with warming spices and condiments, making them devilishly good. These eggs are great at the buffet table and always welcome at picnics, sports events and anywhere else people want easy, portable food. With their mayonnaise binding, be sure to keep Deviled Eggs chilled—in a cooler on very long trips—or in the refrigerator until just before serving at home.

6 hard-cooked eggs, peeled
3 tablespoons mayonnaise, salad dressing or half-and-half
½ teaspoon dry mustard
⅛ teaspoon salt
¼ teaspoon pepper

Cut eggs lengthwise in half. Slip out egg yolks and mash with fork. Mix in mayonnaise, mustard, salt and pepper. Fill egg whites with egg yolk mixture, heaping it lightly. Arrange eggs on large serving plate. Cover and refrigerate up to 24 hours. 12 APPETIZERS; 70 CALORIES PER APPETIZER.

PARTY DEVILED EGGS: Garnish each deviled egg half with caviar, finely chopped parsley, scallions, capers, cooked shrimp, rolled anchovy fillet or sliced pimiento-stuffed olive. 70 CALORIES PER APPETIZER.

ZESTY DEVILED EGGS: Mix ½ cup finely shredded cheese (2 ounces) and 2 tablespoons chopped fresh parsley or 1 teaspoon prepared horseradish into egg yolk mixture. 80 CALORIES PER APPETIZER.

Snappy Stuffed Tomatillos, Southwestern Tortilla Wedges (page 17)

SNAPPY STUFFED TOMATILLOS

With more people discovering the zesty food of the Southwest every day, tomatillos are becoming popular throughout the country. These tangy fruits grow in papery husks that are easily peeled away, revealing the bright green, sticky skins. Tomatillos keep in the refrigerator as long as 2 or 3 weeks, so you can stock up on them.

> 20 tomatillos or cherry tomatoes (1¼ to 1½ inches in diameter)
> ⅔ cup shredded Cheddar cheese
> ½ cup whole kernel corn
> 2 packages (3 ounces each) cream cheese, softened
> 2 green onions (with tops), sliced
> 1 teaspoon ground red chilies
> Ground red chilies

Cut thin slice from stem ends of tomatillos. Remove pulp and seeds with melon baller or spoon. Mix Cheddar cheese, corn, cream cheese, onions and 1 teaspoon ground red chilies. Fill tomatillos with cheese mixture. Sprinkle with ground red chilies. Cover and refrigerate until serving time. Garnish with cilantro and green onions if desired.   20 APPETIZERS; 55 CALORIES PER APPETIZER.

MELON AND PROSCIUTTO

Prosciutto is a type of Italian ham cured by a special drying process, usually sold very thinly sliced. For even more flavor, sprinkle the melon with fresh lemon or lime juice before wrapping it with prosciutto.

> 1 large cantaloupe, casaba, honeydew or Spanish melon (about 3 pounds)
> ¼ pound thinly sliced prosciutto,* cut into 1-inch strips

Cut melon in half. Scoop out seeds and fibers. Cut each half lengthwise into 6 wedges and remove rind. Cut crosswise slits 1½ inches apart in each melon wedge. Place several strips of prosciutto over each wedge. Push prosciutto into slits using blade of table knife.   12 SERVINGS; 25 CALORIES PER SERVING.

*¼ pound thinly sliced ham can be substituted for the prosciutto.

MELON AND PROSCIUTTO BITES: Cut each melon wedge into 6 pieces. Wrap each piece in strips of prosciutto. Secure with wooden picks. 72 APPETIZERS; 4 CALORIES PER APPETIZER.

COCKTAIL MEATBALLS

These were first featured in our 1956 Betty Crocker's Picture Cook Book as "Silver Dollar Hamburgers, Meatballs," because they are miniature.

When pressed for time, use meatballs that you have made ahead and frozen (just be sure they are thawed before you start the recipe). You can also make these meatballs with ground turkey for a delicious, lower-fat change.

> Meatballs (page 227)
> 1 tablespoon chopped fresh parsley
> 1 bottle (12 ounces) chili sauce
> 1 jar (10 ounces) grape jelly

Prepare Meatballs—except add parsley before mixing ingredients and shape into 1-inch balls. Cook meatballs in 12-inch skillet over medium heat about 15 minutes, turning occasionally, until brown. Remove meatballs from skillet; drain. Heat chili sauce and jelly in skillet, stirring constantly, until jelly is melted. Add meatballs and stir until coated. Simmer uncovered 30 minutes. Serve hot with wooden picks. ABOUT 5 DOZEN APPETIZERS; 40 CALORIES PER APPETIZER.

To Microwave: Prepare Meatballs—except add parsley before mixing ingredients and shape into 1-inch balls. Arrange half of the meatballs in microwavable pie plate, 9 × 1¼ inches. Cover loosely and microwave on high 6 to 8 minutes, rearranging meatballs after 4 minutes, until no longer pink inside. Let stand 3 minutes; drain. Repeat with remaining meatballs.

Mix ½ cup chili sauce and ½ cup grape jelly in 2-quart microwavable casserole. Cover tightly and microwave on high 3 minutes or until jelly is melted. Stir in meatballs. Cover tightly and microwave 2 to 4 minutes longer or until meatballs are hot.

COCKTAIL SAUSAGES: Substitute 1 pound tiny cooked smoked sausages, cut crosswise in half, for the meatballs. Decrease simmering time to 20 minutes. 50 CALORIES PER APPETIZER.

GLAZED CHICKEN WINGS

Five-spice powder gives these wings a special Asian punch. See page 322 for directions to make your own five-spice powder. You can prepare these chicken wings a day in advance. Just cook as directed, then cover and refrigerate. Heat uncovered at 375° about 15 minutes or until piping hot.

> 3 pounds chicken wings (about 15)
> ⅔ cup soy sauce
> ½ cup honey
> 2 tablespoons five-spice powder
> 2 tablespoons vegetable oil
> 2 cloves garlic, crushed

Cut each chicken wing at joints to make 3 pieces; discard tips. Place chicken wings in shallow glass or plastic dish. Mix remaining ingredients. Pour over chicken. Cover and refrigerate at least 1 hour, turning occasionally.

Heat oven to 375°. Place chicken on rack in aluminum foil–lined broiler pan and reserve marinade. Brush chicken with reserved marinade. Bake 30 minutes. Turn chicken and bake 30 minutes longer, brushing occasionally with marinade, until juices run clear. ABOUT 30 APPETIZERS; 95 CALORIES PER APPETIZER.

To Microwave: Marinate chicken in rectangular microwavable dish, 11 × 7 × 1½ inches; drain. Cover tightly and microwave on high 10 to 13 minutes, rotating dish ½ turn after 5 minutes, until juices run clear.

RUMAKI

> ¼ cup soy sauce
> 2 tablespoons packed brown sugar
> 2 thin slices gingerroot or ⅛ teaspoon ground ginger
> 1 clove garlic, crushed
> 10 chicken livers, cut in half
> 10 water chestnuts, cut in half
> 10 slices bacon, cut in half

Mix soy sauce, brown sugar, gingerroot and garlic in glass or plastic bowl. Stir in chicken livers and water chestnuts. Cover and refrigerate at least 2 hours, stirring occasionally; drain.

Heat oven to 400°. Wrap a piece of bacon around a piece of liver and water chestnut. Secure with wooden pick. Place on rack in broiler pan. Bake 25 to 30 minutes, turning once, until bacon is crisp. 20 APPETIZERS; 45 CALORIES PER APPETIZER.

OYSTERS ROCKEFELLER

Rock salt
12 medium oysters in shells
2 tablespoons margarine or butter
2 tablespoons finely chopped onion
2 tablespoons chopped fresh parsley
2 tablespoons finely chopped celery
½ cup chopped fresh or frozen (partially thawed and drained) spinach
⅓ cup dry bread crumbs
⅛ teaspoon salt
7 drops red pepper sauce

Fill two pie plates, 9 × 1¼ inches, ½ inch deep with rock salt (about 2 cups each). Sprinkle with water. Scrub oysters in shells in cold water. Break off thin end of shell with hammer. Force a table knife or shucking knife between halves of the shell at broken end and twist to force apart. Cut oyster at muscle to separate from shell. Remove any bits of shell. Place oyster on deep half of shell and discard other half. Arrange filled shells on rock salt.

Heat oven to 450°. Heat margarine in 10-inch skillet over medium heat. Cook onion, parsley and celery in margarine about 2 minutes, stirring occasionally. Mix in remaining ingredients. Spoon about 1 tablespoon spinach mixture onto each oyster. Bake 10 minutes.   2 SERVINGS; 205 CALORIES PER SERVING.

To Microwave: Open scrubbed oysters by arranging 6 at a time with hinges toward outside on microwavable paper towel–lined microwavable plate. Cover tightly and microwave on high 1 minute to 1 minute 30 seconds or until shells open slightly. Remove oysters as they begin to open. Discard any oysters that do not open. Prepare as directed. Microwave one plate at a time uncovered 2 minutes 30 seconds to 3 minutes 30 seconds, rotating plate ½ turn after 1 minute, until oysters are hot and bubbly. Oysters can be microwaved without rock salt if desired. Decrease time by 1 minute.

OYSTERS PARMESAN: Omit spinach and remaining ingredients. Spoon 1 teaspoon sour cream onto oyster in each shell. Mix ½ cup grated Parmesan cheese, ¼ cup cracker crumbs, ¼ cup margarine or butter, melted, and ½ teaspoon dry mustard. Spoon about 2 teaspoons cheese mixture onto each oyster.   425 CALORIES PER SERVING.

Oysters Rockefeller

OYSTERS ROCKEFELLER

Oysters Rockefeller is a classic, created in 1899 with inspired ingenuity. When Antoine Alciatore, founder of Antoine's restaurant in New Orleans, was faced with a shortage of imported snails, he turned to the oyster, which was in plentiful supply. One enchanted diner reportedly named the new dish when he took a taste and exclaimed, "Why, this is as rich as Rockefeller!" Why do we use rock salt? It keeps the shells from tipping and holds the heat nicely around them.

Jarlsberg Crepe Horns

JARLSBERG CREPE HORNS

Parsley Crepes (below) or 10 to 12 six-inch crepes
About 2 tablespoons margarine or butter, softened
1½ cups finely shredded Jarlsberg or aged Swiss cheese (6 ounces)

Prepare Parsley Crepes. Heat oven to 350°. Cut each crepe in half. Spread with margarine. Fold each crepe half, margarine side out, to form funnel. Fill each funnel with about 1 tablespoon cheese. Place seam side down on ungreased cookie sheet. Bake 10 to 12 minutes or until hot. 20 TO 24 APPETIZERS; 90 CALORIES PER APPETIZER.

Parsley Crepes

¾ cup all-purpose flour*
1 cup milk
2 tablespoons chopped fresh parsley
¼ teaspoon baking powder
¼ teaspoon salt
1 egg
Margarine or butter

Mix all ingredients except margarine. Beat with hand beater until smooth. For each crepe, heat 1 to 2 teaspoons margarine in 7-inch crepe pan over medium-low heat until bubbly. Measure 2 tablespoons batter into small cup and pour into pan. Immediately rotate pan until thin film of batter covers bottom. Cook until light brown. Run narrow spatula around edge to loosen. Turn and cook other side until light brown. Stack crepes, placing waxed paper between each. Keep crepes covered to prevent them from drying out. 10 TO 12 CREPES.

If using self-rising flour, omit baking powder and salt.

PITA PIZZA BITES

2 pita breads (6-inch diameter)
2 cups sliced mushrooms* (about 5 ounces)
1 small red onion, thinly sliced
¼ cup chopped green bell pepper
2 tablespoons chopped fresh or 2 teaspoons dried basil leaves
1 cup finely shredded mozzarella cheese (4 ounces)
1 tablespoon grated Parmesan cheese

Heat oven to 425°. Split each bread in half around edge with knife to make 4 rounds. Place rounds, cut sides up, on ungreased cookie sheet. Place mushrooms on bread rounds. Top with onion and bell pepper. Sprinkle with basil and cheeses. Bake 8 to 10 minutes or until cheese is melted. Cut each round into 8 pieces. 32 APPETIZERS; 25 CALORIES PER APPETIZER.

1 can (4 ounces) mushroom stems and pieces, drained, can be substituted for fresh mushrooms.

MEXICAN RICE MORSELS

2 cups cooked brown or regular long grain rice (page 267)
½ cup all-purpose flour
½ teaspoon salt
¼ teaspoon pepper
2 eggs, beaten
2 ounces Monterey Jack cheese with jalapeño chilies
¾ cup crushed tortilla chips (about 3 cups)
Vegetable oil

Mix rice, flour, salt, pepper and eggs. Cut cheese into twenty-four ½-inch cubes. With wet hands, shape about 1 tablespoon rice mixture around each cheese cube. Roll rice balls in tortilla chips.

Heat oil (2 to 3 inches) in deep fryer or Dutch oven to 375°. Fry rice morsels 4 to 6 at a time 3 to 3½ minutes or until golden brown. Remove with slotted spoon. Drain on paper towels; keep warm. Repeat with remaining rice balls. Serve with salsa, guacamole and sour cream if desired. 2 DOZEN APPETIZERS; 85 CALORIES PER APPETIZER.

BASIL BRIE IN PASTRY

This elegant and impressive appetizer looks like a lot of work. It's easy, though, because you use frozen puff pastry.

> 2 tablespoons grated Parmesan cheese
> 2 tablespoons finely chopped fresh or 2 teaspoons dried basil leaves
> 1 round Brie cheese (14 ounces)
> ½ package (17¼-ounce size) frozen puff pastry, thawed

Heat oven to 400°. Grease cookie sheet. Mix Parmesan cheese and basil. Cut cheese round horizontally into 2 layers. Sprinkle basil mixture evenly over cut surface. Reassemble cheese round.

Roll puff pastry into rectangle, 15 × 9 inches, on lightly floured surface. Cut out 2 circles, 8½ and 6 inches. Place 8½-inch circle on cookie sheet. Place cheese in center. Bring pastry up and over cheese. Press to make smooth and even. Brush top edge of pastry lightly with water. Place 6-inch circle on top and press gently around edge to seal. Cut decorations from remaining pastry if desired. Moisten pastry with water to attach.

Bake about 25 minutes or until golden brown. Cool on wire rack 30 minutes before serving. Serve with assorted crackers or fruit if desired. 12 SERVINGS; 205 CALORIES PER SERVING.

SOUTHWESTERN TORTILLA WEDGES

> ½ cup Fresh Tomato Salsa (page 20) or prepared salsa
> ½ cup sour cream or plain yogurt
> ¼ cup chopped red bell pepper
> ½ cup finely chopped cooked chicken
> 8 flour tortillas (about 8 inches in diameter)
> ¼ cup Guacamole (page 20) or frozen (thawed) guacamole
> ½ cup refried beans
> 1 cup shredded Cheddar or Monterey Jack cheese (4 ounces)

Heat oven to 350°. Mix Fresh Tomato Salsa and sour cream. Reserve half of the salsa mixture. Mix the remaining salsa mixture, half of the bell pepper and the chicken. Place 2 tortillas on ungreased cookie sheet and spread with chicken mixture. Spread 2 tortillas with Guacamole and place on chicken mixture. Spread 2 more tortillas with refried beans and place on Guacamole. Top each stack with remaining salsa, a tortilla, bell pepper and cheese.

Bake about 15 minutes or until cheese is melted and filling is hot. Cut each stack into 8 wedges. 16 APPETIZERS; 95 CALORIES PER APPETIZER.

Place cheese in center of 8½-inch pastry circle on cookie sheet. Bring pastry up and over cheese. Press to make smooth and even.

Brush top edge of pastry lightly with water. Place 6-inch circle on top and press gently around edge to seal.

Vegetable Kabobs with Marinara Dip

VEGETABLE KABOBS WITH MARINARA DIP

Marinara Dip (right)
8 ounces whole mushrooms
1 medium bell pepper, cut into 6 strips, then cut in half (about 12 pieces)
1 medium zucchini, diagonally cut into ½-inch slices
6 large cherry tomatoes
2 tablespoons olive or vegetable oil

Prepare Marinara Dip. Set oven control to broil. Thread vegetables separately on 4 metal skewers. Brush vegetables with oil. Place skewers of bell pepper and zucchini on rack in broiler pan. Broil with tops about 4 inches from heat 2 minutes. Add skewers of mushrooms and cherry tomatoes. Broil 4 to 5 minutes, carefully turning every 2 minutes, until vegetables are tender. Serve with dip. 6 SERVINGS; 110 CALORIES PER SERVING.

Marinara Dip

2 tablespoons olive or vegetable oil
1 clove garlic, finely chopped
2 large tomatoes, skinned, seeded and cut into fourths
1 tablespoon finely chopped fresh or 1 teaspoon dried oregano leaves
1 tablespoon finely chopped fresh parsley
½ teaspoon salt
⅛ teaspoon pepper

Heat oil over medium heat in 2-quart saucepan. Cook garlic in oil about 2 minutes, stirring occasionally. Add remaining ingredients. Cook uncovered over medium heat about 5 minutes, stirring occasionally. Pour into blender or food processor. Cover and blend on medium speed, or process, about 15 seconds, until smooth. Serve warm.

GRILLED VEGETABLES: Prepare vegetables as directed. Place bell pepper and zucchini skewers on grill 5 to 6 inches from medium-hot coals. Grill 2 minutes. Add skewers of mushrooms and cherry tomatoes. Grill 4 to 5 minutes, carefully turning every 2 minutes, until vegetables are tender.

CHEESE STRAW TWISTS

These are party favorites, and you can "double" the recipe easily by cutting each twist in half before baking.

> 1 package (17¼ ounces) frozen puff pastry
> ⅔ cup grated Parmesan cheese
> 1 tablespoon paprika
> 1 egg, slightly beaten

Thaw pastry as directed on package. Heat oven to 425°. Cover 2 cookie sheets with parchment or heavy brown paper. Mix cheese and paprika. Roll 1 sheet of pastry into rectangle, 12 × 10 inches, on lightly floured surface with floured cloth-covered rolling pin.

Brush pastry with egg. Sprinkle with 3 tablespoons of the cheese mixture. Press cheese mixture gently into pastry. Turn pastry over. Repeat with egg and cheese mixture. Fold pastry lengthwise in half.

Cut pastry crosswise into ½-inch strips. Unfold strips and roll each end in opposite directions to twist. Place twists on cookie sheet. Bake 7 to 8 minutes or until puffed and golden brown. Repeat with remaining sheet of pastry, egg and cheese mixture. ABOUT 4 DOZEN APPETIZERS; 48 CALORIES PER APPETIZER.

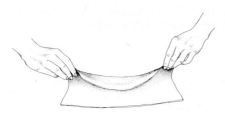

Fold pastry lengthwise in half. Cut pastry crosswise into ½-inch strips.

Unfold strip and roll each end in opposite directions to twist.

STUFFED MUSHROOMS

Golden turmeric adds zip in both flavor and color.

> 1 pound medium mushrooms
> 2 tablespoons margarine or butter
> 1 small onion, chopped (about ¼ cup)
> ½ small green bell pepper, chopped (about ¼ cup)
> 1½ cups soft bread crumbs
> 2 teaspoons chopped fresh or ½ teaspoon dried thyme leaves
> ¼ teaspoon salt
> ¼ teaspoon ground turmeric
> ¼ teaspoon pepper
> 1 tablespoon margarine or butter

Heat oven to 350°. Remove stems from mushrooms. Finely chop enough stems to measure ⅓ cup. Heat 2 tablespoons margarine in skillet over medium heat. Cook chopped mushroom stems, onion and bell pepper in margarine about 4 minutes, stirring occasionally; remove from heat. Stir in bread crumbs, thyme, salt, turmeric and pepper.

Heat 1 tablespoon margarine in shallow baking pan in oven until melted. Fill mushroom caps with bread crumb mixture. Place mushrooms, filled sides up, in pan. Bake 15 minutes. Set oven control to broil. Broil with tops 3 to 4 inches from heat 2 minutes. Serve hot. ABOUT 3 DOZEN APPETIZERS; 15 CALORIES PER APPETIZER.

To Microwave: Mix 2 tablespoons margarine, the chopped mushroom stems, onion and bell pepper in microwavable casserole. Microwave uncovered on high 2 to 3 minutes or until onion is tender. Continue as directed—except omit 1 tablespoon margarine. Arrange mushrooms, filled sides up with smallest mushrooms in center, on two 10-inch microwavable plates. Microwave one plate at a time uncovered on high 3 to 4 minutes, rotating plate ½ turn after 2 minutes, until hot.

MUSTARD DIP

> ½ cup sour cream
> ½ cup plain yogurt
> 1 tablespoon finely chopped fresh parsley
> 1 teaspoon onion powder
> ½ teaspoon garlic salt
> 1 tablespoon Dijon mustard

Mix all ingredients. Cover and refrigerate at least 1 hour. Serve with meatballs, cocktail sausages or fresh vegetables if desired. ABOUT 1 CUP DIP; 20 CALORIES PER TABLESPOON.

FRESH TOMATO SALSA

This fresh, piquant tomato-based sauce adds excitement to everything it touches—taco chips, fish, eggs, meat—and it's a staple of southwestern cooking. Also, when you make Fresh Tomato Salsa, you have a delicious dip that's low in calories.

3 medium tomatoes, seeded and chopped (about 3 cups)
½ cup sliced green onions (with tops)
½ cup chopped green bell pepper
2 to 3 tablespoons lime juice
2 tablespoons chopped fresh cilantro
1 tablespoon finely chopped jalapeño chilies
½ teaspoon salt
3 cloves garlic, finely chopped

Mix all ingredients. Serve with tortilla chips, crackers or vegetables if desired. ABOUT 3½ CUPS; 2 CALORIES PER TABLESPOON.

GUACAMOLE

2 large ripe avocados, mashed
2 medium tomatoes, finely chopped (about 1½ cups)
1 medium onion, chopped (about ½ cup)
2 jalapeño chilies, seeded and finely chopped
1 clove garlic, finely chopped
2 tablespoons finely chopped fresh cilantro
1 tablespoon vegetable oil
Juice of ½ lime (about 2 tablespoons)
½ teaspoons sallt
Dash of pepper

Mix all ingredients in glass or plastic bowl. Cover and refrigerate at least 1 hour. Serve with tortilla chips if desired. ABOUT 2½ CUPS DIP; 25 CALORIES PER TABLESPOON.

CREAMY GUACAMOLE: Stir ¼ cup mayonnaise or salad dressing into avocado mixture before adding tomatoes. ABOUT 2¾ CUPS DIP; 40 CALORIES PER TABLESPOON.

 # MEXI-DIP

½ pound ground beef
½ teaspoon dry mustard
¼ to ½ teaspoon chili powder
1 small onion, finely chopped (about ¼ cup)
½ medium green bell pepper, finely chopped (about ¼ cup)
1 can (16 ounces) refried beans
1 can (8 ounces) tomato sauce
1 package (1¼ ounces) taco seasoning mix
Sour Cream Topping (below)
Finely shredded lettuce
Shredded Cheddar cheese

Cook ground beef in 10-inch skillet, stirring occasionally, until brown; drain. Stir in mustard, chili powder, onion, bell pepper, beans, tomato sauce and seasoning mix (dry). Heat to boiling, stirring constantly. Spread in ungreased pie plate, 9 × 1¼ inches.

Spread Sour Cream Topping over ground beef mixture. Sprinkle with lettuce and cheese. Serve with tortilla chips or fresh vegetable slices if desired. ABOUT 3½ CUPS DIP; 30 CALORIES PER TABLESPOON.

Sour Cream Topping

1 cup sour cream
2 tablespoons shredded Cheddar cheese
¼ teaspoon chili powder

Mix all ingredients.

To Microwave: Crumble ground beef into 2-quart microwavable casserole. Cover tightly and microwave on high 2 to 4 minutes, stirring after 2 minutes, until no longer pink; drain. Stir in mustard, chili powder, onion, bell pepper, beans, tomato sauce and seasoning mix (dry). Cover tightly and microwave 4 to 6 minutes, stirring after 2 minutes, until boiling. Continue as directed.

FRUIT AND YOGURT DIP

1 cup vanilla yogurt
¼ cup flaked coconut, toasted if desired
1 can (8 ounces) crushed pineapple in juice, drained
2 tablespoons packed brown sugar

Mix all ingredients. Cover and refrigerate at least 1 hour. Serve with fresh fruit or cheese cubes if desired. ABOUT 2 CUPS DIP; 15 CALORIES PER TABLESPOON.

Party Cheese Ball (page 22), Dilled Yogurt Cheese

SPINACH DIP

Here's a popular serving idea: Hollow out a round loaf of sourdough or Italian bread. Fill the bread "bowl" with Spinach Dip and surround it with the bread you hollowed out, cut or torn into bite-size pieces. When the dip is gone the "bowl" can be eaten too.

2 packages (10 ounces each) frozen chopped spinach, thawed and drained
1 can (8 ounces) water chestnuts, drained and finely chopped
1 cup sour cream
1 cup plain yogurt
1 cup finely chopped green onions (with tops)
½ teaspoon salt
2 teaspoons chopped fresh or ½ teaspoon dried tarragon leaves
½ teaspoon dry mustard
¼ teaspoon pepper
1 clove garlic, crushed

Mix all ingredients. Cover and refrigerate 1 hour. Serve with rye crackers, rice crackers or fresh vegetables if desired. ABOUT 4½ CUPS DIP; 15 CALORIES PER TABLESPOON.

DILLED YOGURT CHEESE

This cheese is very close to the consistency of cream cheese, but has fewer calories. You can use a coeur à la crème mold to make an attractive heart-shaped cheese. Because these molds have fewer drainage holes than a strainer, refrigerate the shaped cheese for at least 24 hours, draining off the liquid (whey) occasionally. Serve with crackers and vegetable slices.

4 cups plain yogurt
¼ cup chopped fresh or 1 tablespoon dried dill weed
1 teaspoon salt
2 cloves garlic, finely chopped

Line 6-inch strainer with paper coffee filter or double thickness cheesecloth. Place strainer over bowl. Mix all ingredients. Pour into strainer. Cover strainer and bowl. Refrigerate at least 12 hours.

Unmold onto plate. Garnish with freshly ground pepper and additional dill weed if desired. ABOUT 1¼ CUPS SPREAD; 30 CALORIES PER TABLESPOON.

YOGURT CHEESE: Prepare as directed—except omit dill weed and garlic. 30 CALORIES PER TABLESPOON.

SHRIMP AND PISTACHIO SPREAD

1 cup creamed cottage cheese
2 tablespoons lemon juice
½ teaspoon onion powder
1 cup chopped cooked shrimp*
½ cup chopped pistachio nuts

Place cottage cheese, lemon juice and onion powder in blender or food processor. Cover and blend on high speed about 2 minutes, stopping blender occasionally to scrape sides, or process, 30 seconds or until smooth. Pour into small bowl. Stir in shrimp and nuts. Cover and refrigerate at least 1 hour. Serve with assorted crackers or ruffled potato chips if desired.   ABOUT 2 CUPS SPREAD; 20 CALORIES PER TABLESPOON.

*1 can (4¼ ounces) tiny shrimp, rinsed and drained, can be substituted for the cooked shrimp.

Shrimp and Pistachio Spread, Orange-glazed Nuts (page 24)

NUTTY FRUIT SPREAD

This spread highlights the zesty sweetness of honey-roasted nuts.

2 tablespoons orange-flavored liqueur or orange juice
1 tablespoon honey
1 package (8 ounces) cream cheese, softened
½ cup diced dried fruits and raisins
¼ cup chopped honey-roasted nuts

Mix all ingredients. Spoon into serving dish. Cover and refrigerate about 1 hour or until firm. Serve with fruit slices or assorted crackers if desired.   ABOUT 1½ CUPS SPREAD; 55 CALORIES PER TABLESPOON.

PARTY CHEESE BALL

When you make a Party Cheese Ball, you open a world of sculpting possibilities. You can shape the mixture into 3 cheese balls or logs for smaller groups or to give as gifts. Consider molding the mixture to complement the event at which it is to be served: a football, wreath, Christmas tree, bunny, whatever strikes your fancy.

2 packages (8 ounces each) cream cheese
¾ cup crumbled blue cheese (4 ounces)
1 cup shredded sharp Cheddar cheese (4 ounces)
1 small onion, finely chopped (about ¼ cup)
1 tablespoon Worcestershire sauce
¼ cup finely chopped fresh parsley or sunflower nuts

Place cheeses in bowl and let stand at room temperature until softened. Beat in onion and Worcestershire sauce on low speed. Beat on medium speed, scraping bowl frequently, until fluffy. Cover and refrigerate at least 8 hours.

Shape mixture into ball or log. Roll in parsley. Place on serving plate. Cover and refrigerate about 2 hours or until firm.   ABOUT 3½ CUPS SPREAD; 30 CALORIES PER TABLESPOON.

To Microwave: Place cheeses in microwavable bowl and microwave uncovered on medium (50%) 2 minutes 30 seconds to 3 minutes 30 seconds, stirring every minute, until softened. Continue as directed.

APPLE-LIVER PÂTÉ

2 tablespoons margarine or butter
1 medium onion, chopped (about ½ cup)
1 clove garlic, finely chopped
¼ cup apple-flavored brandy or chicken broth
1 medium cooking apple, pared and coarsely chopped
1 pound chicken livers, cut into fourths
1½ teaspoons chopped fresh or ½ teaspoon dried thyme leaves
½ teaspoon salt
¼ teaspoon pepper
2 tablespoons margarine or butter, softened

Heat 2 tablespoons margarine in 10-inch skillet over medium heat. Cook onion and garlic in margarine about 2 minutes. Stir in brandy, apple and chicken livers. Cover and simmer 12 to 15 minutes, or until apples are soft and livers are no longer pink in center. Cool about 15 minutes.

Place liver mixture in blender or food processor. Add remaining ingredients. Cover and blend on high speed about 1 minute, stopping blender occasionally to scrape sides, or process, 30 seconds or until smooth. Pour into crock or bowl. Cover and refrigerate at least 4 hours. Garnish with fresh thyme and serve with apple slices and assorted crackers if desired.   ABOUT 2½ CUPS SPREAD; 25 CALORIES PER TABLESPOON.

To Microwave: Place margarine, onion and garlic in microwavable 2-quart casserole. Cover tightly and microwave on high about 2 minutes or until onion is tender. Stir in brandy, apple and chicken livers. Cover tightly and microwave on high 10 to 12 minutes, stirring after 3 minutes, until apples are soft and livers are no longer pink in centers. Cool about 15 minutes. Continue as directed.

 POPCORN

½ cup popcorn
¼ cup vegetable oil

Pour popcorn and oil into Dutch oven. Tilt pan to distribute evenly. Cover and cook over medium-high heat until 1 kernel pops; remove from heat. Let stand 1 minute and return to heat. Cook, shaking pan occasionally, until popcorn stops popping.   ABOUT 12 CUPS POPCORN; 85 CALORIES PER CUP.

SAVORY SNACK MIX

3 cups unsalted popped popcorn or Popcorn (left)
3 cups crisy corn puff cereal
1 cup salted peanuts
1 cup thin pretzel sticks
⅓ cup margarine or butter
½ teaspoon seasoned salt
½ teaspoon ground cinnamon
¼ teaspoon red pepper sauce

Heat oven to 350°. Mix popcorn, cereal, peanuts and pretzel sticks in ungreased rectangular pan, 13 × 9 × 2 inches. Heat margarine over low heat until melted; remove from heat. Stir in remaining ingredients. Pour over cereal mixture and mix until well coated. Bake 15 minutes, stirring twice. Turn into bowl; cool. Store loosely covered.   ABOUT 9 CUPS SNACK; 300 CALORIES PER CUP.

To Microwave: Place margarine, seasoned salt, cinnamon and red pepper sauce in 3-quart microwavable casserole or bowl. Microwave uncovered on high about 1 minute or until margarine is melted; stir. Stir in popcorn, cereal, peanuts and pretzel sticks. Toss until well coated. Microwave uncovered on high 6 to 8 minutes, stirring every 2 minutes, until toasted; cool.

═ POPCORN ═

Popcorn has been a mainstay of snacking since Native Americans brought it to the first settlers. Some say that it was Quadequina, the brother of Chief Massasoit, who brought popcorn to the first Thanksgiving dinner in 1621. Natives made "poppers" out of clay, but settlers preferred forged sheet-iron poppers with long handles, keeping their hands comfortably away from the fire.

Popcorn continued to grow in popularity as it was an easy and convivial snack to make around the fireplace, and in Victorian days it was made into strings to decorate Christmas trees. In 1896 the company F. W. Rueckheim and Brother of Chicago combined peanuts, popcorn and molasses to make "Cracker Jack," a slang expression of the time that meant "excellent." Try our Caramel-Nut Corn (page 24) for your own kitchen-fresh confection. Popcorn remains a favorite—whether it's made in a conventional or hot-air popper, or by the newest method, the microwave.

CARAMEL-NUT CORN

One of our staff members brought this grass-roots recipe to us from her home state of Iowa. Delicious!

12 cups unsalted popped popcorn or Popcorn (page 23)
3 cups walnut halves, pecan halves and/or unblanched whole almonds
1 cup packed brown sugar
½ cup margarine or butter
¼ cup light corn syrup
½ teaspoon salt
½ teaspoon baking soda

Heat oven to 200°. Divide popcorn and nuts between 2 ungreased rectangular pans, 13 × 9 × 2 inches. Cook brown sugar, margarine, corn syrup and salt over medium heat, stirring occasionally, until bubbly around edges. Continue cooking 5 minutes; remove from heat. Stir in baking soda until foamy. Pour over popcorn and nuts. Toss until well coated. Bake 1 hour, stirring every 15 minutes.   ABOUT 15 CUPS SNACK; 290 CALORIES PER CUP.

CARAMEL CORN: Increase popcorn to 15 cups and omit nuts.   170 CALORIES PER SERVING.

ORANGE-GLAZED NUTS

1 cup sugar
½ teaspoon grated orange peel
½ cup orange juice
2 cups pecan or walnut halves, toasted

Grease cookie sheet lightly. Heat sugar, orange peel and orange juice in 2-quart saucepan over medium heat, stirring frequently, until sugar is dissolved. Stir in pecans. Heat to boiling; reduce heat. Simmer about 30 minutes, stirring frequently, until pecans are completely coated and no syrup remains. Spread on cookie sheet to cool. Break apart if necessary.   ABOUT 2¼ CUPS SNACK; 265 CALORIES PER ¼ CUP.

MARSHMALLOW BARS

32 large marshmallows or 3 cups miniature marshmallows
¼ cup margarine or butter
½ teaspoon vanilla
5 cups crispy corn puff, toasted oat, cornflake or whole wheat flake cereal

Butter square pan, 9 × 9 × 2 inches. Heat marshmallows and margarine in 3-quart saucepan over low heat, stirring constantly, until marshmallows are melted and mixture is smooth; remove from heat. Stir in vanilla. Stir in half of the cereal at a time until evenly coated. Press in pan; cool. Cut into about 2 × 1-inch bars.   36 BARS; 35 CALORIES PER BAR.

To Microwave: Cut margarine into 4 pieces. Place on marshmallows in 3-quart microwavable bowl or casserole. Microwave uncovered on high 1 minute 30 seconds to 2 minutes 30 seconds, stirring every minute, until marshmallows can be stirred smooth. Continue as directed.

CHOCOLATE-MARSHMALLOW BARS: Heat 1 package (6 ounces) semisweet chocolate chips over low heat, stirring frequently, until melted. Spread over cereal mixture in pan.   60 CALORIES PER BAR.

COCONUTTY-MARSHMALLOW BARS: Substitute ½ cup flaked coconut and ½ cup coarsely chopped nuts for 1 cup of the cereal.   50 CALORIES PER BAR.

PEANUT BUTTER–MARSHMALLOW BARS: Stir ½ cup peanut butter into marshmallow-margarine mixture until melted.   55 CALORIES PER BAR.

BAGEL CHIPS

For easy slicing, use day-old bagels and a serrated or very sharp knife. You can cut the bagel vertically or horizontally, whichever seems more comfortable to you.

3 bagels, each cut horizontally into 6 slices
⅓ cup margarine or butter, melted
Garlic powder

Heat oven to 350°. Brush each bagel slice on one side with margarine. Sprinkle with garlic powder. Cut each slice into fourths. Bake on ungreased cookie sheet about 15 minutes or until light brown and crisp. Serve warm or cool. Store in airtight container up to 3 days.   6 DOZEN CHIPS; 12 CALORIES PER CHIP.

CHOCOLATE-CARAMEL APPLES

The classic caramel apple is made with a sweet eating apple such as a Red Delicious. You'll also enjoy using tart Granny Smith apples—you'll love the sweet-tart combination.

6 wooden skewers or ice-cream sticks
6 medium apples
½ cup chopped nuts
¼ cup semisweet chocolate chips
2 tablespoons water
1 package (14 ounces) vanilla caramels

Insert skewer in stem end of each apple. Divide nuts into 6 mounds on waxed paper. Heat chocolate chips, water and caramels over low heat, stirring occasionally, until caramels are melted and mixture is smooth. Keep mixture over very low heat. Dip each apple into chocolate mixture, spooning mixture over apple until completely coated. (If chocolate mixture hardens while coating apples, heat over low heat.) Roll each in nuts. Let stand until coating is firm. 6 SERVINGS; 460 CALORIES PER SERVING.

To Microwave: Prepare apples and nuts as directed. Place chocolate chips, water and caramels in 4-cup microwavable measure. Microwave uncovered on high 3 to 4 minutes, stirring after 2 minutes, until caramels can be stirred smooth. Continue as directed. (If mixture thickens, microwave on high about 30 seconds.)

Caramel-Nut Corn (page 24), Chocolate-Caramel Apples

CARAMEL APPLES: Omit chocolate chips and nuts. Dip each apple into caramel mixture, spooning mixture over apple until coated. Place on waxed paper. Refrigerate until coating is firm. 360 CALORIES PER SERVING.

BEVERAGE BASICS

Beverages can be cool and refreshing or warm and soothing. Whatever you prefer, there are many from which to choose, and most can be made quickly and easily with little advance preparation. When you select beverages consider the occasion, the foods you are serving and the weather, so you'll be guaranteed to have the right drinks on hand.

♦ For parties, it's always a good idea to have a selection of both alcoholic and nonalcoholic beverages. Punch, fruit juices, carbonated beverages (including sugar-free), bottled sparkling water (flavored and unflavored), beer, wine or wine coolers as well as both caffeinated and decaffeinated coffee and tea are all good choices. If you like, let guests make their own drinks.

♦ Don't forget to set out compatible garnishes such as wedges of lemon or lime, celery sticks and so forth.

♦ For chilled punches, chill all ingredients before mixing. Fruit juices may be mixed ahead and refrigerated, but carbonated beverages and alcohol should be added just before serving. An ice ring will last longer in a punch bowl than ice cubes—be sure to make it the right size for your punch bowl. To keep a rich flavor and not dilute the punch, make the ice ring from the same ingredients used in the punch, adding pretty fruits if desired.

♦ For hot punches, be sure the punch bowl is heat-resistant. Carefully warm it with hot water before adding the punch. Hot punches can also be served in an attractive pan right from the stove or even in a fondue pot, chafing dish or slow cooker.

🌾 LEMONADE

Tastes vary as to how sweet lemonade should be, so you may want to increase or decrease the amount of sugar in this recipe to your personal taste.

    3 cups cold water
    1 cup lemon juice (about 4 lemons)
    ½ cup sugar

Mix all ingredients. Serve over ice. 6 SERVINGS (ABOUT ¾ CUP EACH); 70 CALORIES PER SERVING.

LIMEADE: Substitute lime juice (about 10 limes) for the lemons and increase sugar to ¾ cup. 105 CALORIES PER SERVING.

MINTED LEMONADE: Bruise about 6 mint leaves with back of spoon in each glass before pouring lemonade. Garnish with mint leaves. 70 CALORIES PER SERVING.

PINK LEMONADE: Add 2 tablespoons grenadine syrup, if desired, and 2 or 3 drops red food color. 70 CALORIES PER SERVING.

CHOCOLATE COLA COOLER

    2 cups crushed ice
    1 can (12 ounces) cola-flavored carbonated
      beverage, chilled
    2 tablespoons chocolate-flavored syrup

Divide ice between 2 tall glasses. Mix carbonated beverage and syrup. Pour over ice. Serve with straws if desired. 2 SERVINGS (ABOUT ¾ CUP EACH); 115 CALORIES PER SERVING.

CHERRY COLA COOLER: Substitute 2 tablespoons maraschino cherry syrup for the chocolate-flavored syrup. 115 CALORIES PER SERVING.

STRAWBERRY-GRAPEFRUIT DRINK

    1 package (10 ounces) frozen strawberries
      in syrup, partially thawed
    3 cups chilled grapefruit juice

Break up strawberries. Place strawberries and 1 cup grapefruit juice in blender. Cover and blend on high speed about 30 seconds or until smooth. Add remaining grapefruit juice. Cover and blend until mixed. Serve over ice. 4 SERVINGS (ABOUT ¾ CUP EACH); 155 CALORIES PER SERVING.

🌾 CHOCOLATE MILK SHAKES

You can personalize your milk shake by using a favorite ice-cream flavor. Peppermint, chocolate and cherry are all good with chocolate, or try another flavor that strikes your fancy. Chocolate Milk Shakes appear in our first Betty Crocker's Picture Cook Book with a chocolate syrup recipe made from scratch.

    ¾ cup milk
    ¼ cup chocolate-flavored syrup
    3 scoops vanilla ice cream

Place milk and syrup in blender. Cover and blend on high speed 2 seconds. Add ice cream. Cover and blend on low speed about 5 seconds longer or until smooth. 2 SERVINGS (ABOUT 1 CUP EACH); 350 CALORIES PER SERVING.

BERRY MILK SHAKES: Substitute strawberry or cherry ice-cream topping or frozen strawberries or raspberries in syrup, thawed, for the syrup. 355 CALORIES PER SERVING.

CANDY BAR SHAKES: Omit syrup. Add ¼ cup chopped candy bar (any flavor) with the ice cream. 330 CALORIES PER SERVING.

CHOCOLATE MALTS: Add 1 tablespoon natural instant malted milk (dry) with the syrup. 365 CALORIES PER SERVING.

PEACHY YOGURT COOLER

    1 cup chilled peach nectar
    ½ cup milk
    1 container (6 ounces) peach yogurt
    Ground nutmeg

Place nectar, milk and yogurt in blender. Cover and blend on high speed about 30 seconds or until smooth. Sprinkle with nutmeg. 2 SERVINGS (ABOUT 1¼ CUPS EACH); 180 CALORIES PER SERVING.

HOT CHOCOLATE

3 ounces unsweetened chocolate
1½ cups water
⅓ cup sugar
Dash of salt
4½ cups milk

Heat chocolate and water in 1½-quart saucepan over medium heat, stirring constantly, until chocolate is melted and mixture is smooth. Stir in sugar and salt. Heat to boiling; reduce heat. Simmer uncovered 4 minutes, stirring constantly. Stir in milk. Heat just until hot (do not boil). Beat with hand beater until foamy or stir until smooth. Serve immediately. 6 SERVINGS (ABOUT 1 CUP EACH); 210 CALORIES PER SERVING.

HOT COCOA: Substitute ⅓ cup cocoa for the chocolate. Mix cocoa, sugar and salt in saucepan. Stir in water. Heat to boiling, stirring constantly. Boil and stir 2 minutes. Continue as directed. 155 CALORIES PER SERVING.

ORANGE CAFÉ AU LAIT

½ cup powdered nondairy creamer
½ cup sugar
¼ cup instant coffee (dry)
1 teaspoon dried orange peel
¼ teaspoon ground cinnamon

Place all ingredients in blender or food processor. Cover and blend on high speed 30 seconds, stopping blender after 15 seconds to stir, or process, 5 to 10 seconds or until well mixed. Store in tightly covered container at room temperature no longer than 6 months.

For each serving, place 2 teaspoons mix in cup. Add ⅔ cup boiling water. For 6 servings, place ¼ cup mix in heatproof container and add 4 cups boiling water. 24 SERVINGS (2 TEASPOONS EACH); 30 CALORIES PER SERVING.

DESSERT ORANGE CAFÉ AU LAIT: Stir 1 tablespoon orange-flavored liqueur into each serving and top with whipped cream. 40 CALORIES PER SERVING.

COFFEE

The best coffee is made from fresh-roasted coffee beans, preferably ground just before brewing. Actually, coffee beans are not true beans, but rather the twin seeds of the cherry-red fruit produced by the tropical coffee plant. Roasting brings out the flavor of the bean, and the heat and length of roasting time determine the richness and smoothness of the coffee. The longer the bean is roasted, the darker and more richly flavored the coffee.

The strength of coffee depends directly on the ratio of coffee to water when brewing. Many coffees are blended, a combination of different beans, lighter and darker roasts, and even beans of varying quality. From whole beans to flaked coffee, the selection of flavors and grinds is vast.

♦ Regular grind is an intermediate grind size used in automatic percolator-type coffee makers and range-top percolators. As the water boils, it continually washes through the ground coffee.

♦ Drip or fine grind is used in drip coffee makers and espresso machines in which the water passes through the ground coffee only once.

♦ Electric perk and flaked are designed especially for electric percolators and automatic drip coffee makers.

Store whole beans and ground coffee in airtight containers in the freezer to slow oxidation and loss of flavor. Because coffee is naturally oily, freezing will keep it from becoming rancid. Store for six months in the freezer or for a month in the refrigerator.

SPECIAL COFFEE

Coffee has traditionally been celebrated and enhanced in a variety of ways. Café au lait, popular in France at breakfast, is classically a combination of equal parts of hot coffee and hot milk poured simultaneously into the cup from two pots, one held in each hand. Irish coffee can follow—or replace—the dessert course at dinner. It is a mixture of Irish whiskey (1 jigger) and 1 or 2 teaspoons sugar stirred into hot coffee (roughly 6 ounces) and topped with whipped cream. Espresso is made under pressure of steaming hot water, and cappuccino is espresso topped with steamed hot milk or cream. Turkish coffee is strong, black coffee served very sweet with the grounds in the cup. Café brûlot is coffee spiced with cloves, allspice and cinnamon, to which sugar and brandy are added; it is generally served after a meal.

A variety of commercial instant coffee mixes are available in many flavors, such as chocolate minted coffee.

PREPARATION METHOD

♦ Start with a thoroughly clean coffee maker. Wash after each use with hot, soapy water and rinse well with hot water. Never scour with an abrasive pad. When cleaning an automatic coffee maker, follow the manufacturer's directions.

♦ Always use fresh coffee and fresh cold water—except when making drip coffee, when you need to use boiling water. If you use hot water, especially in automatic coffee makers, it changes the percolating time.

♦ Serve steaming hot coffee as soon as possible after brewing. If coffee must stand any length of time, remove grounds and hold coffee at serving temperature over very low heat, or place in an insulated container. Coffee can be covered and refrigerated, and gently reheated later in the day. Microwaving is a quick and easy way to heat up individual cups of coffee.

COFFEE CHART*

Strength of Brew	Ground Coffee	Water
Weak	*1 level tablespoon*	*¾ cup*
Medium	*2 level tablespoons*	*¾ cup*
Strong	*3 level tablespoons*	*¾ cup*

*Best general recommendation for each serving, for drip coffee makers, automatic coffee makers and percolators.

 ## ICED COFFEE

Prepare coffee as directed—except double the proportion of coffee to water. Pour over ice in a pitcher or into ice-filled glasses.

Note: If leftover coffee is used to make ice cubes, regular strength coffee may be used. Serve with cream and powdered sugar if desired.

 ## TEA

From the celebrated high tea of the English to the tea ceremony of the Japanese, the Russian glass of tea served with a spoonful of berry preserves and the minted tea of the Middle East, a cup of tea is a cultural rite. Many of the teas you buy are blends of as many as thirty varieties. The quality of tea leaves varies according to the growing conditions: climate, altitude and the soil in which it is grown. The age and size of the leaves when they are picked are factors in flavor, too.

Broadly classified, there are four types of tea:

Black tea derives its amber color and aromatic flavor from fermentation. The leaves are then processed to preserve their fragrant oils.

Blended tea is usually a combination of various grades of tea from different countries and tea estates. Some of the best known are Earl Grey, English breakfast, Russian-style and spiced blends.

Oolong tea is partially fermented and a cross between green and black teas; it is amber in color.

Green tea, a favorite in eastern countries, is pale green in color. The flavor is slightly bitter, and the lightest color leaves produce the best brew.

PREPARATION METHOD

Whether you use loose tea or tea bags, the preparation method is the same:

♦ Start with a spotlessly clean teapot made of glass, china or glazed earthenware. Add rapidly boiling water and allow to stand a few minutes to warm the pot. Pour out just before brewing the tea.

♦ Heat cold water to a rolling boil. (Hot water from the faucet may contain mineral deposits from water pipes that can affect the flavor.)

♦ Add loose tea, a tea ball (not packed) or tea bags to the warm pot, allowing 1 teaspoon of loose tea or 1 tea bag for each cup of tea. Some people like to add one more teaspoon of tea—"one for the pot," but that is a matter of personal taste. Pour rapidly boiling water over the tea (¾ cup for each cup of tea); let stand 3 to 5 minutes to bring out the full flavor. Stir the tea once to ensure uniform strength. Do not judge the strength of tea by its color; you must taste it. Pour through a tea strainer into cups or remove the tea bags. Serve with sugar and milk or lemon if desired.

ICED TEA

Prepare tea as directed—except double the proportion of tea to water. Strain over ice in a pitcher or into ice-filled glasses.

Prepare instant tea, a concentrate, as directed on the jar.

Note: Tea that has been steeped too long or refrigerated will become cloudy. Pour a small amount of boiling water into cloudy tea to make it clear.

Eggnog (page 30), Wassail

SPARKLING PINEAPPLE PUNCH

½ cup sugar
½ cup water
2 three-inch sticks cinnamon
¼ cup lime juice
1 can (46 ounces) pineapple juice, chilled
1 bottle (1 liter) sparkling water, chilled
1 bottle (750 milliliters) champagne or sparkling white wine, chilled*

Heat sugar, water and cinnamon to boiling; reduce heat. Cover and simmer 15 minutes. Cover and refrigerate at least 2 hours or until chilled.

Remove cinnamon from syrup. Just before serving, mix syrup with remaining ingredients in punch bowl.   26 SERVINGS (ABOUT ½ CUP EACH); 65 CALORIES PER SERVING.

1 bottle (1 liter) ginger ale can be substituted for the champagne.

WASSAIL

Wassail *combines Old English and Old Icelandic phrases meaning "good health and fortune." It's customary to serve this robust punch at Christmas and salute your friends and family with the toast "Wassail."*

6 cups dry red wine*
10 cups apple cider
½ cup granulated or packed brown sugar
2 teaspoons whole cloves
2 teaspoons whole allspice
2 three-inch sticks cinnamon
2 oranges, studded with cloves

Heat wine, cider, sugar, cloves, allspice and cinnamon to boiling; reduce heat. Cover and simmer 20 minutes. Strain punch into punch bowl. Float clove-studded orange slices in bowl.   32 SERVINGS (ABOUT ½ CUP EACH); 75 CALORIES PER SERVING.

Apple cider can be substituted for the wine.

 **EGGNOG**

Eggnog is a lovely, rich and creamy drink that most people associate with the Christmas season. However, think about serving it any time of the year. You can make it with light or dark rum, with blended whiskey or bourbon or without alcohol at all. A favorite of ours, it was first featured in the 1950 Betty Crocker's Picture Cook Book.

Soft Custard (below)
1 cup whipping (heavy) cream
2 tablespoons powdered sugar
½ teaspoon vanilla
½ cup rum
1 or 2 drops yellow food color, if desired
Ground nutmeg

Prepare Soft Custard. Just before serving, beat whipping cream, powdered sugar and vanilla in chilled bowl until stiff. Stir 1 cup of the whipped cream, the rum and food color gently into custard. Pour eggnog into small punch bowl. Drop remaining whipped cream in mounds onto eggnog and sprinkle with nutmeg. Serve immediately. 10 SERVINGS (ABOUT ½ CUP EACH); 195 CALORIES PER SERVING.

Soft Custard

3 eggs, slightly beaten
⅓ cup sugar
Dash of salt
2½ cups milk
1 teaspoon vanilla

Mix eggs, sugar and salt in heavy 2-quart saucepan. Gradually stir in milk. Cook over medium heat 15 to 20 minutes, stirring constantly, until mixture just coats a metal spoon; remove from heat. Stir in vanilla. Place saucepan in cold water until custard is cool. (If custard curdles, beat vigorously with hand beater until smooth.) Cover and refrigerate at least 2 hours.

SANGRIA PUNCH

⅔ cup lemon juice
⅓ cup orange juice
¼ cup sugar
1 bottle (750 milliliters) dry red wine

Strain juices. Add sugar, stirring until dissolved. Mix juice mixture and wine. Add ice. Garnish each serving with twist of lemon peel if desired. 8 SERVINGS (ABOUT ½ CUP EACH); 95 CALORIES PER SERVING.

——— FIX-IT-FAST ———

♦ Serve small portions of such leftover main dishes as Quiche Lorraine (page 181) or pasta dishes as appetizers.

♦ Top a block of cream cheese with salsa, pepper jelly or chutney and serve with crackers.

♦ Purchase prepared vegetables and fruits at the deli for dipping.

♦ Mix salsas, chutneys or preserves into sour cream, plain yogurt or softened cream cheese and serve as a dip or spread.

♦ Turn leftover breads and rolls into snacks. Split if thick, brush lightly with melted margarine or butter and bake at 400° about 5 minutes or until light brown.

♦ Top tortillas with your choice of shredded cheese, chopped tomatoes, chopped onion, sour cream, salsa, leftover meats or vegetables, peanut butter or cream cheese. Roll up and enjoy or first microwave or heat in conventional oven until warm.

♦ Fix a quick mini pizza using tortillas, bagels, English muffins, crackers, rice cakes or hard rolls as the crust. Top with pizza sauce and your favorite toppings, then microwave or broil.

♦ Split leftover biscuits, popovers or croissants and top with shredded cheese and chopped green chilies. Broil or bake until cheese is melted.

♦ Spread peanut butter or softened cream cheese on fruit and vegetable slices.

♦ Spread graham crackers or plain cookies with ready-to-spread or leftover frosting and/or marshmallow cream and top with chopped nuts, raisins or coconut if desired.

♦ Brush saltine crackers or tortilla chips with melted margarine or butter and sprinkle with cinnamon-sugar. Bake until bubbly; cool slightly before eating.

♦ Try fruit or vegetable juices mixed with sparkling water or light, flavored carbonated beverages.

♦ Add diluted frozen fruit juice concentrate to packaged, hydrated fruit-flavored drink mixes or canned fruit drinks. For more intense flavor, add undiluted juice concentrate to drink mixes.

♦ Mix hot chocolate with hot coffee for a delicious mocha drink.

♦ Make your own flavored coffees by adding extracts, spices or ground nuts to the ground coffee before brewing.

♦ Mix iced tea with fruit juices such as orange, apple or white grape juice.

♦ Mix hot or iced coffee and teas with sweetened condensed milk for an especially rich treat.

NUTRITION INFORMATION

PER SERVING OR UNIT

PERCENT U.S. RECOMMENDED DAILY ALLOWANCE

RECIPE, PAGE

Recipe, Page	Servings per recipe	Calories	Protein (grams)	Carbohydrate (grams)	Fat (grams)	Cholesterol (milligrams)	Sodium (milligrams)	Protein	Vitamin A	Vitamin C	Thiamine	Riboflavin	Niacin	Calcium	Iron
APPETIZERS															
Apple-Liver Pâté, 23	40	25	2	1	2	45	55	2	24	0	0	6	0	0	2
Bagel Chips, 24	72	12	0	1	1	0	35	0	0	0	0	0	0	0	0
Basil Brie in Pastry, 17	12	205	8	6	17	35	310	12	4	0	4	12	2	6	2
Caramel Apples, 25	6	360	0	73	0	0	0	0	0	6	2	0	0	0	0
Caramel Corn, 24	15	170	1	28	7	0	190	2	4	0	0	0	0	0	4
Caramel-Nut Corn, 24	15	290	4	29	19	0	190	6	4	0	4	2	2	2	8
Cheese Straw Twists, 19	48	55	1	3	4	5	65	0	2	0	0	0	0	0	0
Chocolate-Caramel Apples, 25	6	460	2	80	9	0	2	2	0	6	6	2	2	0	2
Chocolate-Marshmallow Bars, 24	36	60	0	8	3	0	45	0	2	0	2	2	2	0	4
Cocktail Meatballs, 14	60	40	2	5	1	10	105	2	0	0	0	0	2	0	0
Cocktail Sausages, 14	60	50	1	6	2	10	175	2	0	2	2	0	0	0	0
Coconutty-Marshmallow Bars, 24	36	50	1	6	3	0	40	0	2	0	2	2	2	0	4
Creamy Guacamole, 20	44	40	0	1	4	0	40	0	2	8	0	0	0	0	0
Deviled Eggs, 12	12	70	3	1	6	140	80	6	2	0	0	4	0	0	2
Dilled Yogurt Cheese, 21	20	30	2	3	2	5	130	2	0	0	0	2	0	6	0
Fresh Tomato Salsa, 20	56	2	0	1	0	0	10	0	0	4	0	0	0	0	0
Fruit and Yogurt Dip, 20	32	15	0	2	0	0	5	0	0	0	0	0	0	0	0
Glazed Chicken Wings, 14	30	95	6	6	6	25	380	8	0	0	0	2	8	0	2
Guacamole, 20	40	25	0	2	2	0	30	0	2	8	0	0	0	0	0
Jarlsberg Crepe Horns, 16	20	90	3	4	6	25	105	4	4	0	0	4	0	10	0
Marshmallow Bars, 24	36	35	0	5	1	0	45	0	2	0	2	2	2	0	4
Melon and Prosciutto, 13	12	25	2	3	1	2	110	2	30	28	6	2	2	0	0
Melon and Prosciutto Bites, 13	72	4	0	1	0	0	20	0	4	4	0	0	0	0	0
Mexican Rice Morsels, 16	24	85	2	9	5	25	160	2	0	0	2	2	0	2	2
Mexi-Dip, 20	56	30	1	1	2	5	40	2	2	2	0	0	0	0	0
Mustard Dip, 19	16	20	1	1	2	5	90	0	0	0	0	0	0	2	0
Nutty Fruit Spread, 22	24	55	1	4	4	10	30	0	2	0	0	0	0	0	0
Orange-glazed Nuts, 24	9	265	2	28	18	0	0	2	0	6	14	2	0	0	2
Oysters Parmesan, 15	2	425	14	10	37	50	780	20	28	10	4	12	6	36	16
Oysters Rockefeller, 15	2	205	6	15	13	20	440	10	34	16	6	8	10	8	20
Party Cheese Ball, 22	56	30	1	0	3	10	55	0	2	0	0	0	0	2	0
Party Deviled Eggs, 12	12	70	3	1	6	140	80	6	2	0	0	4	0	0	2
Peanut Butter–Marshmallow Bars, 24	36	55	1	6	3	0	60	0	2	0	2	2	4	0	4
Pita Pizza Bites, 16	32	25	1	3	1	2	40	2	0	0	0	0	0	2	0

NUTRITION INFORMATION

PER SERVING OR UNIT

RECIPE, PAGE

	Servings per recipe	Calories	Protein (grams)	Carbohydrate (grams)	Fat (grams)	Cholesterol (milligrams)	Sodium (milligrams)	Protein	Vitamin A	Vitamin C	Thiamine	Riboflavin	Niacin	Calcium	Iron
								PERCENT U.S. RECOMMENDED DAILY ALLOWANCE							

APPETIZERS (continued)

RECIPE, PAGE	Servings per recipe	Calories	Protein (grams)	Carbohydrate (grams)	Fat (grams)	Cholesterol (milligrams)	Sodium (milligrams)	Protein	Vitamin A	Vitamin C	Thiamine	Riboflavin	Niacin	Calcium	Iron
Popcorn, 23	12	85	1	9	5	0	0	2	0	0	0	0	0	0	0
Rumaki, 14	20	45	3	4	2	65	240	4	32	0	2	10	2	0	6
Savory Snack Mix, 23	9	300	8	33	16	0	730	12	10	2	8	6	20	2	14
Shrimp and Pistachio Spread, 22	32	20	2	1	1	5	35	2	0	0	0	0	0	0	0
Snappy Stuffed Tomatillos, 13	20	55	2	2	4	15	55	2	12	8	0	2	0	2	0
Southwestern Tortilla Wedges, 17	16	95	4	8	6	15	180	6	6	2	2	2	4	8	4
Spinach Dip, 21	72	15	1	1	1	0	25	0	12	4	0	0	0	0	0
Stuffed Mushrooms, 19	36	15	0	1	1	0	35	0	0	0	0	2	2	0	0
Vegetable Kabobs with Marinara Dip, 18	6	110	2	7	9	0	190	2	20	40	6	12	10	0	6
Yogurt Cheese, 21	20	30	2	3	2	5	130	2	0	0	0	2	0	6	0
Zesty Deviled Eggs, 12	12	80	4	1	7	140	110	8	4	0	0	4	0	4	3

BEVERAGES

RECIPE, PAGE	Servings per recipe	Calories	Protein (grams)	Carbohydrate (grams)	Fat (grams)	Cholesterol (milligrams)	Sodium (milligrams)	Protein	Vitamin A	Vitamin C	Thiamine	Riboflavin	Niacin	Calcium	Iron
Berry Milk Shakes, 26	2	355	7	55	13	50	145	10	14	2	4	22	0	24	4
Candy Bar Shakes, 26	2	330	8	39	17	50	210	12	10	2	4	24	4	24	2
Cherry Cola Cooler, 26	2	115	1	29	0	0	15	0	0	0	0	0	0	0	2
Chocolate Cola Cooler, 26	2	115	1	29	0	0	15	0	0	0	0	0	0	0	2
Chocolate Malts, 26	2	365	8	55	13	50	170	12	12	2	4	24	0	24	4
Chocolate Milk Shakes, 26	2	350	8	52	13	50	160	12	12	0	4	22	0	24	4
Dessert Orange Café au Lait, 27	24	40	0	6	2	5	5	0	0	0	0	0	0	0	0
Eggnog, 30	10	195	4	12	12	120	90	6	10	0	2	8	0	8	2
Hot Chocolate, 27	6	200	7	24	11	15	140	10	6	0	4	18	0	22	6
Hot Cocoa, 27	6	150	7	21	4	15	140	10	6	0	2	18	0	22	4
Lemonade, 26	6	70	0	19	0	0	10	0	0	16	0	0	0	0	0
Limeade, 26	6	105	0	28	0	0	0	0	0	20	0	0	0	0	0
Minted Lemonade, 26	6	70	0	19	0	0	10	0	0	16	0	0	0	0	0
Orange Café au Lait, 27	24	30	0	5	1	0	5	0	0	0	0	0	0	0	0
Peachy Yogurt Cooler, 26	2	180	6	24	2	10	85	8	8	12	2	14	2	18	0
Pink Lemonade, 26	6	70	0	19	0	0	10	0	0	16	0	0	0	0	0
Sangria Punch, 30	8	95	0	10	0	0	10	0	0	16	0	0	0	0	2
Sparkling Pineapple Punch, 29	26	65	0	11	0	0	0	0	0	8	0	0	0	0	0
Strawberry-Grapefruit Drink, 26	4	155	1	39	0	0	5	0	0	100	4	2	2	2	2
Wassail, 29	32	85	0	13	0	0	5	0	0	0	0	0	0	0	2

BREADS

BREADS

Baking bread has one of the most delicious and inviting aromas. Almost nothing says "home" more clearly or creates such a cozy feeling. We have gathered breads for every baker—muffins, coffee cakes, quick breads, pancakes and biscuits. Dumplings, popovers, spoon bread, corn bread and scones also add delicious options to meal planning. And, of course, we have recipes for yeast breads. You'll agree that baking bread is fulfilling as well as delicious.

QUICK BREAD BASICS

Quick breads range from pancakes to tender, flaky biscuits to moist, rich nut breads—and all are fast and easy to make.

Quick-acting baking powder rather than slower-acting yeast is the leavening agent for quick breads. It consists of an acid, such as cream of tartar, and an alkali, such as baking soda, which react with one another in the presence of moisture to form a gas. In batter or dough this gas forms tiny bubbles that expand quickly, lifting the batter to create the structure of the quick bread. To be sure it is always fresh, purchase only a small quantity of baking powder at a time and stir before using.

Use shiny pans and cookie sheets, which reflect heat, for golden, delicate and tender crusts on muffins, coffee cakes and nut breads. If pans with dark nonstick coating are used, watch carefully so foods don't overbrown, and follow manufacturers' directions, as many suggest reducing the oven temperature by 25°.

MUFFINS

♦ Muffins need very little mixing—just until the flour is moistened; if you stir until smooth, the batter will be overmixed. Overmixing can result in a less-tender muffin with an uneven texture and pointed, rather than slightly rounded, pebbly tops.

♦ Grease only the bottoms of muffin cups for nicely shaped muffins that have no rim around the edge. Some recipes, however, require greasing the entire cup to prevent sticking.

Preceding page, clockwise from top left: *Corn Sticks (page 39), Crusty Hearth Bread (page 57), Caramel Sticky Rolls (page 57), Pesto Swirl Bread (page 51)*

♦ For evenly shaped muffins, use a spring-handled ice-cream scoop when distributing batter among cups. These are sold in different sizes and are referred to by number (number of level scoops per quart of ice cream). We recommend No. 20 or 24.

♦ Medium muffin cups, 2½ × 1¼ inches, are the standard size found in most kitchen cupboards. However, mini or jumbo muffins can be made from any batter. Use the following temperatures and times as a guide to make small and large muffins from our recipes that make 12 medium muffins.

Muffin Cup Size	Oven Temperature	Time	Yield
Small muffin cups, 1¾ × 1 inch	*400°*	*10 to 15 minutes*	*24*
Large muffin cups, 3½ × 1½ inches	*375°*	*About 25 minutes*	*4*

BISCUITS

♦ Cut in shortening with a pastry blender when making biscuits. If a pastry blender is not available, use the side of a fork, a sturdy wire whisk or two knives. "Cutting in" results in tiny lumps of shortening that produce a flaky texture throughout the biscuits.

♦ Roll or pat biscuit dough to an even thickness for attractive biscuits and even baking. A clever way to roll dough evenly is between two wooden sticks ½ inch high and 14 inches long; anyone who works with wood can make a pair. If a biscuit cutter is not available, cut biscuits with an opened 6-ounce juice can or other narrow can or glass dipped in flour.

NUT BREADS

♦ Grease only the bottoms of loaf pans for fruit or nut breads. Ungreased sides allow the batter to cling while rising during baking, which helps form a gently rounded top.

♦ Cool nut breads completely (preferably storing, tightly covered, twenty-four hours) before slicing to prevent crumbling. Cut with a sharp, thin-bladed knife, using a light sawing motion.

PANCAKES AND FRENCH TOAST

♦ Heat the griddle or skillet on medium heat or set at 375° about 10 minutes before cooking pancakes or French toast. The griddle will be evenly heated, ensuring more even browning. Because pan materials and thicknesses vary, as do cooktops, adjust heat as necessary.

MICROWAVE REHEATING

Reheating in the microwave is a great way to give leftover quick breads the warmth of fresh baked. They heat in a very short time—but the key to success is the use of medium (50%) power to avoid overheated breads. Use of the lower setting warms breads gently and more evenly than heating on higher power, which can produce dry, tough breads.

Serving sizes for muffins and biscuits are 2 to 3 inches in diameter; for coffee cake pieces, about 2½ inches square; and from bundt or ring-shaped pans, 2-inch wedges. See chart below for specific times.

Servings	Room Temperature	Frozen
1	15 to 30 seconds	45 seconds to 1 minute
2	25 to 40 seconds	60 seconds to 1 minute 30 seconds
3	35 to 60 seconds	1 minute 15 seconds to 1 minute 30 seconds
4	45 seconds to 1 minute 15 seconds	1 minute 30 seconds to 3 minutes

Pancakes can be refrigerated or frozen for a quick microwave breakfast another time. Spread the pancakes with a thin layer of margarine or butter to help them reheat evenly. Tightly wrap packets of two or four or place in sealed plastic bag. Label and freeze no longer than three months or refrigerate no longer than forty-eight hours. Unwrap pancakes and place stack on plate. Cover loosely to microwave.

Pancakes	Room Temperature	Frozen
2	1 minute to 1 minute 30 seconds	2 to 3 minutes
4	2 to 3 minutes	3 to 4 minutes

OAT BRAN MUFFINS

2 cups Oat Bran Muffin Mix (below)
¾ cup milk
⅓ cup vegetable oil
1 egg
½ cup chopped nuts
½ cup raisins or snipped pitted dried apricots or prunes, if desired

Prepare Oat Bran Muffin Mix. Heat oven to 400°. Grease bottoms only of 12 medium muffin cups, 2½ × 1¼ inches, or line with paper baking cups. Beat all ingredients except Oat Bran Muffin Mix. Stir in Mix just until moistened (batter will be lumpy). Divide batter evenly among muffin cups. Bake about 15 minutes or until golden brown. Immediately remove from pan.   1 DOZEN MUFFINS; 150 CALORIES PER MUFFIN.

Oat Bran Muffin Mix

4¼ cups all-purpose flour*
4 cups oat bran
3 cups regular or quick-cooking oats
1 cup sugar
3 tablespoons baking powder
1 tablespoon salt

Mix all ingredients in large bowl. Cover, label and store in airtight container at room temperature no longer than 6 months.

If using self-rising flour, decrease baking powder to 1 tablespoon and omit salt.

To Microwave: Prepare batter as directed. Spoon batter into 6 paper baking cups in microwavable muffin ring, filling each three-fourths full. Sprinkle with ground cinnamon. Microwave uncovered on high 2 minutes to 3 minutes 30 seconds, rotating ring ¼ turn every minute, until wooden pick inserted in center comes out clean (edges of muffins may appear slightly moist). Cool 1 minute; remove from ring. Repeat with remaining batter.

NO-CHOLESTEROL OAT BRAN MUFFINS: Substitute 2 egg whites or ¼ cup cholesterol-free egg product for the egg and skim milk for the milk. 145 CALORIES PER MUFFIN.

Blueberry Streusel Muffins (page 37), Molasses-Bran Muffins, Wine-and-Cheese Muffins

WINE-AND-CHEESE MUFFINS

Delicious served with wine and light foods such as fish and salads that don't hide the delicate flavors.

    2 cups variety baking mix
    ⅔ cup white wine or apple juice
    2 tablespoons vegetable oil
    1 egg
    1 cup shredded Swiss, Gruyère or Ched-
      dar cheese (4 ounces)
    2 teaspoons chopped fresh or freeze-dried
      chives

Heat oven to 400°. Line 12 medium muffin cups, 2½ × 1¼ inches, with paper baking cups, or grease entire cups generously. Mix baking mix, wine, oil and egg with fork. Beat vigorously 30 strokes. Stir in remaining ingredients. Divide batter evenly among cups. Bake about 20 minutes or until golden brown. 1 DOZEN MUFFINS; 150 CALORIES PER MUFFIN.

To Microwave: Prepare batter as directed. Spoon batter into 6 paper baking cups in microwavable muffin ring, filling each about three-fourths full. Microwave uncovered on high 2 to 3 minutes, rotating ring ¼ turn every minute, until wooden pick inserted in center comes out clean (edges of muffins may appear slightly moist). Cool 1 minute; remove from ring. Repeat with remaining batter.

MOLASSES-BRAN MUFFINS

    ¾ cup milk
    1½ cups shreds of wheat bran cereal
    1 egg
    ½ cup vegetable oil
    ⅓ cup molasses
    1¼ cups all-purpose* or whole wheat flour
    3 teaspoons baking powder
    1 teaspoon salt

Heat oven to 400°. Grease bottoms only of 12 medium muffin cups, 2½ × 1¼ inches, or line with paper baking cups. Pour milk on cereal in medium bowl and let stand 1 minute. Beat in egg, oil and molasses. Mix remaining ingredients. Stir into cereal mixture all at once just until flour is moistened (batter will be lumpy). Divide batter evenly among muffin cups. Bake about 20 minutes or until golden brown. Immediately remove from pan. 1 DOZEN MUFFINS; 190 CALORIES PER MUFFIN.

**If using self-rising flour, omit baking powder and salt.*

DATE-NUT MUFFINS: Stir in ½ cup pitted chopped dates and ⅓ cup chopped nuts with the oil. 230 CALORIES PER MUFFIN.

BLUEBERRY STREUSEL MUFFINS

This blueberry muffin recipe was a winner at the Illinois State Fair in the 1930s. A special streusel topping is our little contribution to this old-fashioned favorite.

Streusel Topping (below)
1 cup milk
¼ cup vegetable oil
½ teaspoon vanilla
1 egg
2 cups all-purpose* or whole wheat flour
⅓ cup sugar
3 teaspoons baking powder
½ teaspoon salt
1 cup fresh or drained canned blueberries or ¾ cup frozen blueberries, thawed and well drained

Heat oven to 400°. Prepare Streusel Topping. Grease bottoms only of 12 medium muffin cups, 2½ × 1¼ inches, or line with paper baking cups. Beat milk, oil, vanilla and egg. Stir in flour, sugar, baking powder and salt all at once just until flour is moistened (batter will be lumpy). Fold in blueberries. Divide batter evenly among muffin cups. Sprinkle each with about 2 teaspoons Streusel Topping. Bake 20 to 25 minutes or until golden brown. Immediately remove from pan.   1 DOZEN MUFFINS; 185 CALORIES PER MUFFIN.

*If using self-rising flour, omit baking powder and salt.

Streusel Topping

¼ cup all-purpose flour
2 tablespoons packed brown sugar
2 tablespoons firm margarine or butter
¼ teaspoon ground cinnamon

Mix all ingredients until crumbly.

To Microwave: Prepare batter and Streusel Topping as directed. Spoon batter into 6 paper baking cups in microwavable muffin ring, filling each three-fourths full. Sprinkle with Streusel Topping. Microwave uncovered on high 2 minutes to 3 minutes 30 seconds, rotating ring ¼ turn every minute, until wooden pick inserted in center comes out clean (edges of muffins may appear slightly moist). Cool 1 minute; remove from ring. Repeat with remaining batter and Streusel Topping.

APPLE MUFFINS: Omit blueberries. Stir in 1 cup grated apple with the milk and add ½ teaspoon ground cinnamon with the flour. Bake 25 to 30 minutes.   190 CALORIES PER MUFFIN.

CRANBERRY-ORANGE MUFFINS: Omit blueberries. Stir in 1 cup halved cranberries and 1 tablespoon grated orange peel with the milk.   190 CALORIES PER MUFFIN.

FRENCH PUFFS: Omit blueberries and Streusel Topping. Mix ½ cup sugar and 1 teaspoon ground cinnamon. Immediately roll hot muffins in about ½ cup margarine or butter, melted, and then in sugar mixture.   215 CALORIES PER MUFFIN.

OATMEAL-RAISIN MUFFINS: Omit blueberries. Stir in 1 cup raisins with the milk. Decrease flour to 1 cup. Stir in 1 cup quick-cooking oats, ½ teaspoon ground nutmeg and ¼ teaspoon ground cinnamon with the flour.   200 CALORIES PER MUFFIN.

DUMPLINGS

3 tablespoons shortening
1½ cups all-purpose flour*
2 teaspoons baking powder
½ teaspoon salt
¾ cup milk

Cut shortening into flour, baking powder and salt with pastry blender until mixture resembles fine crumbs. Stir in milk. Drop dough by spoonfuls onto hot meat or vegetables in boiling stew (do not drop directly into liquid). Cook uncovered 10 minutes. Cover and cook 10 minutes longer.   10 DUMPLINGS; 105 CALORIES PER DUMPLING.

*If using self-rising flour, omit baking powder and salt.

To Microwave: Prepare dumplings as directed. Drop dough by spoonfuls onto hot meat or vegetables in boiling stew in 3-quart microwavable casserole only around edge (do not drop dough in center). Cover tightly and microwave on high 5 to 7 minutes, rotating casserole ½ turn after 3 minutes, until dumplings are no longer doughy.

CHEESE DUMPLINGS: Add ¼ cup shredded sharp cheese (1 ounce) with the flour.   115 CALORIES PER DUMPLING.

HERB DUMPLINGS: Add ½ teaspoon dried herbs (such as sage leaves, celery seed or thyme leaves) with the flour.   105 CALORIES PER DUMPLING.

PARSLEY DUMPLINGS: Add 3 tablespoons chopped fresh parsley or chives with the flour.   105 CALORIES PER DUMPLING.

BISCUIT BASICS

Cut shortening into flour mixture until the mixture resembles fine crumbs.

Stir in enough milk until dough leaves side of bowl (dough will be soft).

Roll or pat the dough ½-inch thick. Cut with floured 2½-inch round cutter.

BAKING POWDER BISCUITS

The South is justifiably proud of its biscuits. That's why our home economists traveled in the South during the mid-1960s, baking more than 5,000 biscuits in a comparison between scratch biscuits and those made from variety baking mix. This was everyone's favorite scratch recipe!

¼ cup shortening
2 cups all-purpose* or whole wheat flour
1 tablespoon sugar, if desired
3 teaspoons baking powder
1 teaspoon salt
¾ cup milk

Heat oven to 450°. Cut shortening into flour, sugar, baking powder and salt with pastry blender until mixture resembles fine crumbs. Stir in just enough milk so dough leaves side of bowl and rounds up into a ball. (Too much milk makes dough sticky; not enough makes biscuits dry.)

Turn dough onto lightly floured surface. Knead lightly 20 to 25 times, about 30 seconds. Roll or pat ½ inch thick. Cut with floured 2½-inch biscuit cutter. Place on ungreased cookie sheet about 1 inch apart for crusty sides, touching for soft sides. Bake 10 to 12 minutes or until golden brown. Immediately remove from cookie sheet. ABOUT 10 BISCUITS; 185 CALORIES PER BISCUIT.

If using self-rising flour, omit baking powder and salt.

BUTTERMILK BISCUITS: Decrease baking powder to 2 teaspoons and add ¼ teaspoon baking soda with the salt. Substitute buttermilk for the milk. (If buttermilk is thick add slightly more than ¾ cup.) 185 CALORIES PER BISCUIT.

CORNMEAL BISCUITS: Substitute ½ cup cornmeal for ½ cup of the flour. Sprinkle cornmeal over biscuits before baking if desired. 150 CALORIES PER BISCUIT.

DROP BISCUITS: Increase milk to 1 cup. Drop dough by spoonfuls onto greased cookie sheet. 190 CALORIES PER BISCUIT.

Spicy Fruit Scones (page 40), Baking Powder Biscuits (page 38), Corn Bread, Rosy Grape Jelly (page 362)

CORN BREAD

Native Americans taught settlers to parch corn, mix it with boiling water and make thin cakes. They traveled well and soon earned the name journey cakes and later johnny cakes.

1½ cups cornmeal
½ cup all-purpose flour*
¼ cup vegetable oil or shortening
1½ cups buttermilk
2 teaspoons baking powder
1 teaspoon sugar
1 teaspoon salt
½ teaspoon baking soda
2 eggs

Heat oven to 450°. Grease round pan, 9 × 1½ inches, square pan, 8 × 8 × 2 inches, or 10-inch ovenproof skillet. Mix all ingredients. Beat vigorously 30 seconds. Pour into pan. Bake round or square pan 25 to 30 minutes, skillet about 20 minutes or until golden brown. Serve warm.   12 PIECES; 100 CALORIES PER PIECE.

If using self-rising flour, decrease baking powder to 1 teaspoon and omit salt.

To Microwave: Mix 2 tablespoons cornmeal and ½ teaspoon paprika. Grease 8-cup microwavable ring dish. Sprinkle evenly with cornmeal mixture. Prepare batter as directed. Pour into dish. Elevate dish on inverted microwavable dinner plate in microwave oven. Microwave uncovered on medium (50%) 11 to 14 minutes, rotating dish ½ turn after 8 minutes, until wooden pick inserted in center comes out clean. (Parts of surface may appear moist but will continue to cook while standing.) Let stand on flat, heatproof surface (not wire rack) 5 minutes. Invert on heatproof serving plate.

CORN MUFFINS: Grease bottoms only of 14 medium muffin cups, 2½ × 1¼ inches. Fill cups about ⅞ full. Bake about 20 minutes. 14 MUFFINS; 85 CALORIES PER MUFFIN.

CORN STICKS: Fill 18 greased corn stick pans about ⅞ full. Bake 12 to 15 minutes. 18 CORN STICKS; 65 CALORIES PER CORN STICK.

MEXICAN DOUBLE CORN BREAD: Decrease buttermilk to 1 cup. Stir in 1 can (8 ounces) cream-style corn, 1 can (4 ounces) chopped green chilies, well drained, and 1 teaspoon chili powder. 110 CALORIES PER PIECE.

ONION-CHEESE CORN BREAD: Stir in ½ cup shredded process sharp American cheese (2 ounces) and 3 medium green onions, chopped (about ¼ cup). 115 CALORIES PER PIECE.

SCONES

⅓ cup margarine or butter
1¾ cups all-purpose* or whole wheat flour
3 tablespoons sugar
2½ teaspoons baking powder
¼ teaspoon salt
1 egg, beaten
½ cup currants or raisins
4 to 6 tablespoons half-and-half
1 egg, beaten

Heat oven to 400°. Cut margarine into flour, sugar, baking powder and salt with pastry blender until mixture resembles fine crumbs. Stir in 1 egg, the currants and just enough half-and-half so dough leaves side of bowl.

Turn dough onto lightly floured surface. Knead lightly 10 times. Roll or pat ½ inch thick. Cut with floured biscuit cutter, or pat dough into rectangle and cut into diamond shapes with sharp knife. Place on ungreased cookie sheet. Brush dough with 1 egg. Bake 10 to 12 minutes or until golden brown. Immediately remove from cookie sheet; cool. Split scones. Spread with margarine and serve with preserves if desired.   ABOUT 15 SCONES; 130 CALORIES PER SCONE.

If using self-rising flour, omit baking powder and salt.

LEMON-OAT SCONES: Substitute ½ cup quick-cooking oats for ½ cup of the flour and toasted chopped almonds for the currants. Add 2 teaspoons grated lemon peel with the salt.   120 CALORIES PER SCONE.

SPICY FRUIT SCONES: Add ¾ teaspoon ground cinnamon and ⅛ teaspoon ground cloves with the salt. Substitute ½ cup diced fruits, chopped figs or dates for the currants.   130 CALORIES PER SCONE.

FRENCH TOAST

½ cup all-purpose flour*
1½ cups milk
1 tablespoon sugar
½ teaspoon vanilla
¼ teaspoon salt
6 eggs
Margarine, butter or shortening
18 slices French bread, each 1 inch thick

Beat flour, milk, sugar, vanilla, salt and eggs with hand beater until smooth. Heat griddle or skillet over medium heat or to 375°. Grease griddle with margarine if necessary. (To test griddle, sprinkle with few drops water. If bubbles skitter around, heat is just right.)

Dip bread into egg mixture. Cook about 4 minutes on each side or until golden brown.   18 SLICES; 130 CALORIES PER SLICE.

If using self-rising flour, omit salt.

CUSTARDY OVERNIGHT FRENCH TOAST: Prepare as directed—except arrange bread slices just to fit in single layer in glass baking dishes. Pour egg mixture over bread slices. Turn to coat both sides. Cover and refrigerate overnight. Cook as directed—except increase cooking time to 6 to 8 minutes on each side.   130 CALORIES PER SLICE.

PANCAKES

Pancakes are easy to personalize. Simply stir in ½ cup fresh or frozen (thawed and well drained) berries or chopped fruit— bananas, apples, peaches or pears. Serve with syrup, honey, jelly or jam to complement the fruit flavors. For crunch, you can stir in trail mix, granola or chopped nuts.

1 egg
1 cup all-purpose* or whole wheat flour
¾ cup milk
1 tablespoon granulated or packed brown sugar
2 tablespoons vegetable oil
3 teaspoons baking powder
¼ teaspoon salt
Margarine, butter or shortening

Beat egg with hand beater in medium bowl until fluffy. Beat in remaining ingredients except margarine just until smooth. For thinner pancakes, stir in additional 1 to 2 tablespoons milk. Heat griddle or skillet over medium heat or to 375°. Grease griddle with margarine if necessary. (To test griddle, sprinkle with few drops water. If bubbles skitter around, heat is just right.)

For each pancake, pour scant ¼ cup batter onto hot griddle. Cook pancakes until puffed and dry around edges. Turn and cook other sides until golden brown.   NINE 4-INCH PANCAKES; 100 CALORIES PER PANCAKE.

If using self-rising flour, omit baking powder and salt.

Nut Waffles

BUTTERMILK PANCAKES: Substitute 1 cup buttermilk for the milk. Decrease baking powder to 1 teaspoon and beat in ½ teaspoon baking soda.   75 CALORIES PER PANCAKE.

CINNAMON-OATMEAL PANCAKES: Substitute ½ cup quick-cooking oats for ½ cup of the flour. Stir in ½ teaspoon ground cinnamon with the flour.   85 CALORIES PER PANCAKE.

CORNMEAL PANCAKES: Substitute ½ cup cornmeal for ½ cup of the flour.   90 CALORIES PER PANCAKE.

 WAFFLES

Waffle irons come in many shapes and sizes, and this batter works well in all of them.

2 eggs
2 cups all-purpose* or whole wheat flour
½ cup vegetable oil or margarine or butter, melted
1¾ cups milk
1 tablespoon granulated or brown sugar
4 teaspoons baking powder
¼ teaspoon salt

Heat waffle iron. Beat eggs with hand beater in medium bowl until fluffy. Beat in remaining ingredients just until smooth. Pour batter from cup or pitcher onto center of hot waffle iron. Bake about 5 minutes or until steaming stops. Remove waffle carefully.   TWELVE 4-INCH WAFFLE SQUARES (THREE 9-INCH WAFFLES); 185 CALORIES PER SQUARE.

*If using self-rising flour, omit baking powder and salt.

CHEESE-AND-BACON WAFFLES: Omit salt. Stir 1 cup shredded sharp cheese (4 ounces) and 8 slices bacon, crisply cooked and crumbled, into batter.   265 CALORIES PER SQUARE.

CORN WAFFLES: Omit salt. Substitute 1 cup cornmeal for 1 cup of the flour and 1 can (8 ounces) cream-style corn for ¾ cup of the milk. Stir in few drops red pepper sauce.   165 CALORIES PER SQUARE.

NUT WAFFLES: Pour batter onto center of hot waffle iron. Immediately sprinkle about 2 tablespoons coarsely chopped or broken nuts, toasted, if desired, over batter.   210 CALORIES PER SQUARE.

POPOVERS

Popovers are a special favorite in the Betty Crocker Dining Room, and we've been partial to them since they appeared in the 1910 Gold Medal Flour Cook Book. After baking, popovers can be frozen. Pierce each popover with the point of a knife to let the steam out, then cool on wire rack, wrap tightly and freeze. Heat the frozen popovers in a 350° oven for about 10 minutes or until piping hot.

2 eggs
1 cup all-purpose flour*
1 cup milk
½ teaspoon salt

Heat oven to 450°. Grease 6-cup popover pan or six 6-ounce custard cups generously. Beat eggs slightly in medium bowl. Beat in remaining ingredients just until smooth (do not overbeat). Fill cups about one-half full. Bake 20 minutes. Decrease oven temperature to 350°. Bake 20 minutes longer or until deep golden brown. Immediately remove from cups and serve hot. 6 POPOVERS; 115 CALORIES PER POPOVER.

*Do not use self-rising flour in this recipe.

Popovers, Raspberry Butter (page 361)

Opposite page, clockwise from top left: Cranberry Bread (page 44), Rhubarb-Pear Bread (page 44), Chocolate-Peanut Banana Bread, Zucchini Bread (page 44)

BANANA BREAD

Ripe bananas freeze easily. Mash, adding 1 tablespoon lemon juice for each cup of bananas to prevent darkening. For this recipe, freeze in 1½-cup quantities.

1¼ cups sugar
½ cup margarine or butter, softened
2 eggs
1½ cups mashed ripe bananas (3 to 4 medium)
½ cup buttermilk
1 teaspoon vanilla
2½ cups all-purpose flour*
1 teaspoon baking soda
1 teaspoon salt
1 cup chopped nuts, if desired

Place oven rack in lowest position. Heat oven to 350°. Grease bottoms only of 2 loaf pans, 8½ × 4½ × 2½ inches, or 1 loaf pan, 9 × 5 × 3 inches. Mix sugar and margarine in large bowl. Stir in eggs until well blended. Add bananas, buttermilk and vanilla. Beat until smooth. Stir in remaining ingredients except nuts just until moistened. Stir in nuts. Pour into pans. Bake 8-inch loaves about 1 hour, 9-inch loaf about 1¼ hours or until wooden pick inserted in center comes out clean. Cool 5 minutes. Loosen sides of loaves from pans; remove from pans. Cool completely before slicing. Wrap tightly and store at room temperature up to 4 days, or refrigerate up to 10 days. 2 LOAVES (24 SLICES EACH); 85 CALORIES PER SLICE.

*If using self-rising flour, omit baking soda and salt.

To Microwave: Grease 12-cup microwavable bundt cake dish generously. Prepare batter as directed. Pour into dish. Microwave uncovered on high 12 to 14 minutes, rotating dish ¼ turn every 4 minutes, until top springs back when touched lightly. Let stand on heatproof surface (not on wire rack) 10 minutes. Remove from dish; cool.

CHOCOLATE-PEANUT BANANA BREAD: Substitute ½ cup semisweet chocolate chips and ½ cup chopped peanuts for the chopped nuts. 85 CALORIES PER SLICE.

MACADAMIA-COCONUT BANANA BREAD: Substitute 1 can (5 ounces) macadamia nuts, chopped and toasted, and ½ cup flaked coconut for the chopped nuts. 95 CALORIES PER SLICE.

MINI BANANA BREADS: Grease bottoms only of 10 miniature loaf pans, 4½ × 2¾ × 1¼ inches. Divide batter among pans (about ½ cup each). Bake 30 to 35 minutes. 10 LOAVES (8 SLICES EACH, 4 SLICES PER SERVING); 205 CALORIES PER SERVING.

ZUCCHINI BREAD

You can make almost all of your favorite nut breads with this versatile recipe.

3 cups shredded zucchini (about 3 medium)
1⅔ cups sugar
⅔ cup vegetable oil
2 teaspoons vanilla
4 eggs
3 cups all-purpose* or whole wheat flour
2 teaspoons baking soda
1 teaspoon salt
1 teaspoon ground cinnamon
½ teaspoon ground cloves
½ teaspoon baking powder
½ cup coarsely chopped nuts
½ cup raisins, if desired

Heat oven to 350°. Grease bottoms only of 2 loaf pans, 8½ × 4½ × 2½ or 9 × 5 × 3 inches. Mix zucchini, sugar, oil, vanilla and eggs in large bowl. Stir in remaining ingredients. Pour into pans. Bake 50 to 60 minutes or until wooden pick inserted in center comes out clean. Cool 10 minutes. Loosen sides of loaves; remove from pans. Cool completely before slicing. Wrap tightly and store at room temperature up to 4 days, or refrigerate up to 10 days. 2 LOAVES (24 SLICES EACH); 95 CALORIES PER SLICE.

*If using self-rising flour, omit baking soda, salt and baking powder.

To Microwave: Grease 12-cup microwavable bundt cake dish generously. Prepare batter as directed. Pour into dish. Microwave uncovered on high 11 to 14 minutes, rotating dish ¼ turn every 4 minutes, until top springs back when touched lightly. Let stand on heatproof surface (not wire rack) 10 minutes. Remove from dish; cool.

CRANBERRY BREAD: Substitute fresh or frozen (thawed) cranberries for the zucchini. Add ½ cup milk with the oil. Omit cinnamon, cloves and raisins. Add 2 teaspoons grated lemon or orange peel with the vanilla. Increase bake time to 60 to 70 minutes. 100 CALORIES PER SLICE.

PUMPKIN BREAD: Substitute 1 can (16 ounces) pumpkin for the zucchini. 100 CALORIES PER SLICE.

RHUBARB-PEAR BREAD: Omit raisins. Substitute 1½ cups finely chopped rhubarb and 1½ cups finely chopped pears for the zucchini. 100 CALORIES PER SLICE.

ZUCCHINI MUFFINS: Grease bottoms only of 24 medium muffin cups, 2½ × 1¼ inches. Fill cups about ¾ full. Bake 20 to 25 minutes or until tops spring back when touched lightly. 2 DOZEN MUFFINS; 200 CALORIES PER MUFFIN.

GOLDEN RAISIN PUFF

½ cup margarine or butter, softened
1 cup all-purpose flour*
2 tablespoons cold water
½ cup margarine or butter
1 cup water
½ cup golden raisins
1 teaspoon vanilla
1 cup all-purpose flour*
3 eggs
Lemon Glaze (below)

Heat oven to 350°. Cut ½ cup margarine into 1 cup flour until particles are size of small peas. Sprinkle 2 tablespoons cold water over flour mixture. Mix with fork. Gather pastry into ball and divide in half. Pat each half into rectangle, 12 × 3 inches, about 3 inches apart on ungreased cookie sheet.

Heat ½ cup margarine, 1 cup water and the raisins to boil; remove from heat. Quickly stir in vanilla and 1 cup flour. Stir vigorously over low heat about 1 minute or until mixture forms a ball; remove from heat. Add eggs. Beat until smooth and glossy. Spread half of the topping over each rectangle.

Bake 45 to 50 minutes or until topping is crisp and brown; cool. (Topping will shrink and fall, forming a custardy layer.) Spread with Lemon Glaze. 2 COFFEE CAKES (6 SLICES EACH); 325 CALORIES PER SLICE.

*Self-rising flour can be used in this recipe.

Lemon Glaze

1½ cups powdered sugar
2 tablespoons margarine or butter, softened
½ teaspoon vanilla
1 to 2 tablespoons lemon juice

Mix all ingredients until of spreading consistency.

DANISH PUFF: Omit raisins. Substitute almond extract for the vanilla. For glaze, substitute warm water for the lemon juice. Sprinkle coffee cakes with ½ cup chopped almonds or walnuts. 335 CALORIES PER SLICE.

✼ SOUR CREAM COFFEE CAKE

Apple-Nut Filling (below) or Brown Sugar
    Filling (right)
1½ cups sugar
¾ cup margarine or butter, softened
3 eggs
1½ teaspoons vanilla
3 cups all-purpose* or whole wheat flour
1½ teaspoons baking powder
1½ teaspoons baking soda
¾ teaspoon salt
1½ cups sour cream
Glaze (right)

Heat oven to 350°. Grease tube pan, 10 × 4 inches, 12-cup bundt cake pan or 2 loaf pans, 9 × 5 × 3 inches. Prepare one of the fillings; reserve. Beat sugar, margarine, eggs and vanilla in large bowl on medium speed 2 minutes, scraping bowl occasionally. Beat in flour, baking powder, baking soda and salt alternately with sour cream on low speed.

For tube or bundt cake pan, spread ⅓ of the batter (about 2 cups) in pan. Sprinkle with ⅓ of the filling. Repeat 2 times. For loaf pans, spread one-fourth of the batter (about 1½ cups) in each pan. Sprinkle each with ¼ of the filling. Repeat layers.

Bake about 1 hour for tube pan or bundt cake pan, about 45 minutes for loaf pans, or until wooden pick inserted near center comes out clean. Cool slightly; remove from pan. Cool 10 minutes. Drizzle with Glaze.   ONE COFFEE CAKE (16 SLICES); 355 CALORIES PER SLICE.

*If using self-rising flour, omit baking powder, baking soda and salt.

Apple-Nut Filling

1½ cups chopped apples
⅓ cup packed brown sugar
1 tablespoon all-purpose flour
2 tablespoons margarine or butter
¼ teaspoon ground nutmeg
⅛ teaspoon salt
½ cup finely chopped nuts

Cook all ingredients except nuts over medium heat, stirring constantly, until apples are tender. Stir in nuts.

Brown Sugar Filling

½ cup packed brown sugar
½ cup finely chopped nuts
1½ teaspoons ground cinnamon

Mix all ingredients.

Glaze

½ cup powdered sugar
¼ teaspoon vanilla
1 to 2 teaspoons milk

Mix all ingredients until smooth.

BISQUICK® BAKING MIX

In 1930 Carl Smith, an executive at General Mills, took a Southern Pacific train from Portland to San Francisco. Entering the dining car well after the dinner hour, he included an order for biscuits with his dinner and settled down for a long wait. Smith was surprised when his fresh hot biscuits arrived in record time, and he asked the chef what his secret was. The chef gave him the secret—the biscuit mix of lard, flour, baking powder and salt was mixed ahead of time and stored in the icebox.

Smith was intrigued, and on his return to General Mills he discussed the idea of developing the first baking mix with the company's chief chemist. At this time there were no prepared baking mixes on the market. General Mills worked to overcome the challenges of preparing a mix that wouldn't need refrigeration, keeping the baking powder active and developing the exact blend of ingredients that would produce biscuits as good as—or better than—homemade. It soon became clear that Bisquick variety baking mix advertised under the slogan "Makes Anybody a Perfect Biscuit Maker," could be used for much more than biscuits. Recipes were developed for meat pies, coffee cakes, pancakes, nut breads, shortcakes, dumplings, cookies, waffles, muffins and cobblers.

Orange-Cheese Braid, Raspberry-Marzipan Coffee Cake (page 47)

ORANGE-CHEESE BRAID

1 package (3 ounces) cream cheese
¼ cup firm margarine or butter
2½ cups variety baking mix
½ cup orange juice
1 package (8 ounces) cream cheese, softened
⅓ cup orange marmalade
Chocolate Glaze (right)

Heat oven to 400°. Cut 3-ounce package cream cheese and the margarine into baking mix. Stir in orange juice. Turn dough onto surface well dusted with baking mix. Roll gently in baking mix to coat. Knead 10 times. Roll into rectangle, 15 × 9 inches. Place on large cookie sheet.

Beat 8-ounce package cream cheese and the marmalade until smooth. Spread lengthwise down center of rectangle. Make cuts 2½ inches long at 1-inch intervals on each 15-inch side of rectangle. Fold strips over filling, overlapping and crossing in center. Bake about 20 minutes or until golden brown; cool 10 minutes. Carefully place on wire rack and cool completely. Drizzle with Chocolate Glaze. Refrigerate any remaining coffee cake. 1 COFFEE CAKE (12 SLICES); 280 CALORIES PER SLICE.

Chocolate Glaze

½ cup powdered sugar
2 tablespoons cocoa
¼ teaspoon vanilla
3 to 4 teaspoons milk

Mix all ingredients until smooth.

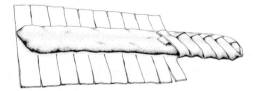

Fold 1-inch strips over filling, overlapping and crossing in center.

RASPBERRY-MARZIPAN COFFEE CAKE

You may find the almond paste easier to chop if you put it into the freezer for 1 to 2 hours.

> Streusel (below)
> 2 cups all-purpose flour*
> ¾ cup sugar
> ¼ cup margarine or butter, softened
> 1 cup milk
> 2 teaspoons baking powder
> 1 teaspoon vanilla
> ½ teaspoon salt
> 1 egg
> 1 package (3½ ounces) almond paste, finely chopped
> 1 cup fresh or unsweetened frozen (thawed) raspberries

Heat oven to 350°. Prepare Streusel. Grease square pan, 9 × 9 × 2 inches. Beat all ingredients except almond paste, raspberries and Streusel in medium bowl on low speed 30 seconds. Beat on medium speed 2 minutes, scraping bowl occasionally.

Spread half of the batter in pan. Sprinkle with half each of the almond paste, raspberries and Streusel. Repeat layers. Bake about 50 minutes or until wooden pick inserted in center comes out clean. ONE COFFEE CAKE (12 PIECES); 290 CALORIES PER PIECE.

*If using self-rising flour, omit baking powder and salt.

Streusel

> ¼ cup firm margarine or butter
> ⅓ cup all-purpose flour
> ¼ cup sugar
> ⅓ cup slivered almonds

Cut margarine into flour and sugar until crumbly. Stir in nuts.

RASPBERRY-CHOCOLATE COFFEE CAKE: Substitute 1 package (6 ounces) semisweet chocolate chips for the almond paste. 330 CALORIES PER PIECE.

YEAST BREAD BASICS

INGREDIENTS

Flour: All-purpose flour is the most widely used flour. It is made from a blend of selected wheats and is suitable for all kinds of baking. Flour contains a protein called "gluten," the structure builder of bread. When mixed with liquid and kneaded or beaten, gluten stretches and gives elasticity to dough by trapping bubbles of gas, which are formed when yeast is added. The amount of protein in flour varies with the wheat crop, as does the moisture within the flour itself. This is why most kneaded dough recipes give a range for the amount of flour.

Some flours, such as rye and whole wheat, develop insufficient gluten and usually are used in combination with all-purpose flour. Self-rising flour, which already contains leavening and salt, is not always recommended for yeast breads. However, all the recipes here were tested with self-rising flour; adjustments are indicated when necessary.

Yeast: Yeast is a live plant. Supplied with a little sugar for "food," it gives off gas, which makes dough rise. Very sensitive, too much heat will kill it, but cold will impede its growth. Yeast is available in two forms: regular or quick-acting active dry yeast and compressed yeast. Always check the expiration date on commercial yeast packages before using.

All of our recipes have been tested with dry yeast. Most of the recipes follow the "quick-mix" method of mixing the yeast with part of the flour, then beating in very warm liquid (120° to 130°). However, some recipes yield better results with the traditional method of dissolving the yeast in warm water (105° to 115°). The water temperature is higher for the quick-mix method because the flour and other ingredients dilute the yeast. Follow the correct temperatures for liquids as stated in each recipe, because using the wrong temperature for either method causes poor results.

Liquids: Water and milk are the most commonly used liquids. Water gives bread a crisper crust; milk, a velvety texture and added nutrients.

Sweeteners: Sugar, honey or molasses provide "food" for the yeast to help it grow, enhance flavor and help brown the crust.

Salt: A flavor agent that is needed to control the growth of the yeast and prevent overrising, which can cause bread to collapse.

Fat: Margarine, butter, shortening or vegetable oil are added to contribute tenderness and flavor.

Eggs: Added for flavor, richness and color.

YEAST DOUGH BASICS

1. After first addition of flour has been beaten in, the dough will be very soft and will fall in "sheets" off rubber spatula.

2. The second addition of flour makes the dough stiff enough to knead. Mix in only enough flour so dough leaves side of the bowl.

3. To knead, fold dough toward you. With heels of hands, push dough away with short rocking motions. Give dough a quarter turn; repeat.

4. When the dough is properly kneaded, it will feel elastic and the top will be smooth with some blisters appearing on the surface.

5. Dough should rise until double. Test by pressing fingertips ½ inch into dough. If impression remains, the dough has risen enough.

6. Punch down center of dough with your fist. Fold dough over and form into a ball. This releases large air bubbles to produce a finer texture.

YEAST DOUGHS

Bread making is a skill worth learning, whether you bake for economy, as a hobby or for the pleasure of the aroma. The secret to making good yeast bread is a reliable recipe and plenty of practice!

There are two basic kinds of yeast dough—batter and kneaded. Batter breads are really shortcut no-knead yeast breads. Kneaded breads require more time as well as energy for kneading the dough. Both kinds need to rise before shaping and baking to allow the yeast to activate. To let dough rise, cover and keep in a warm, draft-free place. If necessary, place covered bowl of dough on a wire rack over a bowl of warm water.

Batter Dough: Because less flour is used, the dough is stickier; instead of being kneaded, it is beaten with an electric mixer with the first addition of flour. The batter is generally not shaped but spread in the pan. There is usually only one rising time. The bread has a coarser texture and pebbled surface.

Kneaded Dough: A good loaf of kneaded bread is symmetrical and has an evenly browned crust with a smooth, nicely rounded top. It is slightly moist and soft with a tender crust, even texture, a fresh, tempting aroma and a pleasant wheaten flavor. Kneading develops the gluten and results in the even texture and smooth, rounded top. If dough is not sufficiently kneaded, the bread will be coarse, heavy, crumbly and dry. To knead, follow the Yeast Dough Basics (page 48). A standard countertop electric mixer with dough hook attachment mixes dough well enough, although the loaves may have slightly less volume than those kneaded by hand. A heavy-duty mixer yields loaves of higher volume. Be sure to follow manufacturers' directions for size of recipe the mixer can handle, as well as mixing time.

Shaping the perfect loaf of bread can be achieved by several methods. We find the method in Shaping Breads (page 50) one of the best. This method is used in Traditional White Bread (page 51), and Honey–Whole Wheat Bread (page 54). As an alternate shaping method, and for breads with an even spiral appearance, like Cinnamon-Raisin Bread (page 51) and Pesto Swirl Bread (page 51) you may wish to try the following: roll each half into rectangle, 18 × 9 inches. (If dough shrinks, gently stretch into rectangle.) Roll up tightly, beginning at 9-inch side. Press with thumbs to seal after each turn. Pinch edge firmly to seal. Press each end with side of hand to seal. Fold ends under loaf.

When making kneaded yeast breads, practice is the best teacher and will help you individualize your technique.

REFRIGERATING YEAST DOUGH

Yeast dough made with water (except plain bread dough) can be refrigerated up to five days. However, if milk and at least ¼ cup sugar are used, refrigerate no longer than three days because it could sour. After mixing dough, grease top well. Cover with moistureproof wrap, then a damp cloth. Keep cloth damp during storage. When ready to bake, shape dough; let rise until double, 1½ hours. Bake as directed.

BAKING TIPS

♦ Use loaf pans of anodized aluminum, darkened metal or glass for bread with well-browned crusts. If pans with dark nonstick coating are used, watch carefully so bread doesn't overbrown. Follow manufacturers' directions, because reducing the oven temperature by 25° is often recommended.

♦ Use shiny cookie sheets and muffin cups, which reflect heat, for tender, golden brown crusts on sweet rolls.

♦ Stagger loaf pans on a lower shelf of the oven so they do not touch sides of the oven or each other.

♦ The top of each pan should be level with, or slightly above, the middle of the oven.

♦ If baking round loaves on a cookie sheet, place the sheet on a rack in the center of the oven.

♦ Doneness is determined by tapping the crust. The loaf will have a hollow sound when done.

♦ Remove loaves from pans immediately so sides remain crusty and place on wire racks away from draft to cool.

♦ For a shiny, soft crust, brush just-baked bread with margarine, butter or shortening.

STORING

Bread and rolls can be stored in airtight containers in a cool, dry place no longer than five days. Refrigerate only in hot, humid weather. Breads can be stored, tightly wrapped in moistureproof or vaporproof material, labeled and dated, in the freezer for two to three months. To thaw, let stand wrapped at room temperature for two to three hours.

SHAPING BREADS

1. Flatten or roll dough into rectangle, 18 × 9 inches. Fold crosswise into thirds, overlapping the sides.

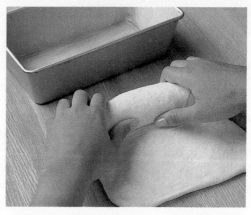

2. Flatten or roll into square, 9 × 9 inches. Roll dough up tightly toward you, beginning at one of the open ends.

3. After rolling dough up tightly, pinch edge of dough into roll to seal firmly.

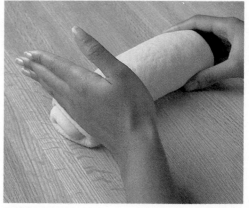

4. Press each end with side of hand to seal; fold ends under loaf.

French Bread: Make ¼-inch deep slashes across loaf at 2-inch intervals.

Caramel Sticky Rolls: To cut even slices, place a piece of dental floss or heavy thread under roll. Bring ends of floss up and crisscross at top of roll. Pull strings in opposite directions.

TRADITIONAL WHITE BREAD

Practice is the key to kneading and shaping yeast breads. Try the alternate shaping method on page 49. You will be amply rewarded when you take the heavenly smelling loaf out of the oven. This truly is the staff of life!

    6 to 7 cups all-purpose* or unbleached flour
    3 tablespoons sugar
    1 tablespoon salt
    2 tablespoons shortening
    2 packages regular or quick-acting active
        dry yeast
    2¼ cups very warm water (120° to 130°)

Mix 3½ cups of the flour, the sugar, salt, shortening and yeast in large bowl. Add warm water. Beat on low speed 1 minute, scraping bowl frequently. Beat on medium speed 1 minute, scraping bowl frequently. Stir in enough remaining flour, 1 cup at a time, to make dough easy to handle.

Turn dough onto lightly floured surface. Knead about 10 minutes or until smooth and elastic. Place in greased bowl and turn greased side up. Cover and let rise in warm place 40 to 60 minutes or until double. (Dough is ready if indentation remains when touched.)

Grease 2 loaf pans, 9×5×3 or 8½×4½×2½ inches. Punch down dough and divide in half. Flatten dough for each loaf with hands or rolling pin into a rectangle, 18×9 inches. Fold crosswise into thirds, overlapping the two sides. Flatten or roll into square, 9×9 inches. Roll dough tightly, beginning at one of the open (unfolded) ends, to form a loaf. Press with thumbs to seal after each turn. Pinch edge firmly to seal. Press each end with side of hand to seal. Fold ends under loaf. Place seam side down in pan. Brush loaves lightly with margarine. Cover and let rise in warm place 35 to 50 minutes or until double.

Place oven rack in low position so that tops of pans will be in center of oven. Heat oven to 425°. Bake 25 to 30 minutes or until loaves are deep golden brown and sound hollow when tapped; remove from pans. Brush loaves with margarine if desired. Cool on wire rack. 2 LOAVES (16 SLICES EACH); 105 CALORIES PER SLICE.

*If using self-rising flour, omit salt.

CINNAMON-RAISIN BREAD: Stir in 1 cup raisins with the second addition of flour. Mix ¼ cup sugar and 2 teaspoons ground cinnamon. After flattening dough into rectangles, sprinkle each with 1 tablespoon water and half of the sugar mixture. 130 CALORIES PER SLICE.

FRESH HERB BREAD: Stir in 2 tablespoons chopped fresh chives, 2 tablespoons chopped fresh sage leaves and 2 tablespoons chopped fresh thyme leaves just before the second addition of flour. 105 CALORIES PER SLICE.

LOW-SALT TRADITIONAL WHITE BREAD: Decrease sugar to 2 tablespoons and salt to 1 teaspoon. Substitute vegetable oil for the shortening. Each rising time will be 10 to 15 minutes shorter. 105 CALORIES PER SLICE.

PESTO SWIRL BREAD: After flattening dough into rectangles, spread each with ½ cup Pesto (page 359) or prepared pesto. Do not fold dough into thirds. Roll up tightly, beginning at 9-inch end. 130 CALORIES PER SLICE.

FLOUR

In 1880 Cadwallader C. Washburn of Minneapolis won the Gold Medal for "Superlative" Flour at the Miller's International Exhibition, held in Cincinnati, Ohio. His company, Washburn, Crosby and Company, also won the Silver Medal as well as the Bronze Medal. The company continued its pioneering excellence, introducing Gold Medal self-rising flour, with baking powder and salt added, in 1920. Beginning in 1925 our home economists began testing Gold Medal flour in typical baked products to verify its quality before shipping, and the phrase "Kitchen-tested" was added to Gold Medal flour. In 1928 Washburn Crosby consolidated all its mills, and our company of General Mills was formed.

FRENCH BREAD

The food processor method is terrific for those of us who bake frequently.

1 package regular or quick-acting active dry yeast
1 cup warm water (105° to 115°)
1 tablespoon sugar
1 teaspoon salt
3 to 3½ cups all-purpose flour*
2 tablespoons vegetable oil
Cornmeal
1 egg white
1 tablespoon cold water
Poppy seed or sesame seed, if desired

Dissolve yeast in warm water in large bowl. Stir in sugar, salt, 2 cups of the flour and the oil. Beat until smooth. Stir in enough remaining flour to make dough easy to handle (dough will be soft). Turn dough onto lightly floured surface. Knead about 5 minutes until smooth and elastic.

Place dough in greased medium bowl and turn greased side up. Cover and let rise in warm place 1½ to 2 hours or until double. (Longer rising gives typical French bread texture.)

Grease large cookie sheet and sprinkle with cornmeal. Divide dough in half. Roll each half into rectangle, 15 × 8 inches, on lightly floured surface. Roll up tightly, beginning at 15-inch side. Pinch edge of dough into roll to seal well. Roll gently back and forth to taper ends. Place both loaves on cookie sheet. Make ¼-inch-deep slashes across loaves at 2-inch intervals. Brush loaves with cold water. Let rise uncovered in warm place about 1 hour or until double.

Heat oven to 375°. Mix egg white and 1 tablespoon cold water. Brush over loaves. Sprinkle with poppy seed. Bake 25 to 30 minutes or until loaves are golden brown and sound hollow when tapped. 2 LOAVES (ABOUT 12 SLICES EACH); 65 CALORIES PER SLICE.

Do not use self-rising flour in this recipe.

Food Processor Directions: Place warm water and yeast in food processor. Cover and process, using quick on-and-off motions, until yeast is dissolved. Add flour, sugar and salt. Process about 30 seconds or until dough forms ball. (If dough is too sticky, add flour, 1 tablespoon at a time.) Do not knead dough. Continue as directed.

SOFT BREADSTICKS: Grease 2 cookie sheets and sprinkle with cornmeal. Prepare dough as directed— except add 2 teaspoons dried rosemary leaves, crushed, and 1 teaspoon dried oregano leaves with the salt. After punching down dough, divide into 24 equal parts. Roll and shape each part into rope, about 9 inches long, sprinkling with flour if dough is too sticky. Place on cookie sheet. Mix egg white and 2 tablespoons cold water. Brush over breadsticks. Sprinkle with poppy seed. Heat oven to 400°. Bake about 20 minutes or until crust is deep golden brown and crisp. Immediately remove from cookie sheets. Store loosely covered. 2 DOZEN BREADSTICKS; 65 CALORIES PER BREADSTICK.

ITALIAN FLATBREAD

2½ to 3 cups all-purpose* or unbleached flour
2 teaspoons sugar
¼ teaspoon salt
1 package regular or quick-acting active dry yeast
¼ cup olive or vegetable oil
1 cup very warm water (120° to 130°)
Olive or vegetable oil
2 tablespoons grated Parmesan cheese

Mix 1 cup of the flour, the sugar, salt and yeast in large bowl. Add ¼ cup oil and the warm water. Beat on medium speed 3 minutes, scraping bowl occasionally. Stir in enough remaining flour until dough is soft and leaves side of bowl. Turn onto lightly floured surface.

Knead 5 to 10 minutes or until dough is smooth and elastic. Place in greased bowl and turn greased side up. Cover and let rise in warm place 1 to 1½ hours or until double.

Heat oven to 425°. Grease 2 cookie sheets. Punch down dough and divide in half. Shape each half into flattened 12-inch round on cookie sheet. Cover and let rise in warm place 20 minutes. Prick centers and 1 inch in from edge thoroughly with fork. Brush with oil. Sprinkle each with 1 tablespoon cheese. Bake 12 to 15 minutes or until golden brown. 2 FLATBREADS (12 PIECES EACH); 75 CALORIES PER PIECE.

Do not use self-rising flour in this recipe.

RED PEPPER FLATBREAD: For each flatbread, cook and stir 1 medium red bell pepper, cut into ¼-inch rings, and 1 small onion, sliced, in 1 tablespoon olive or vegetable oil in 10-inch skillet over medium heat until softened. Arrange on flatbreads. 85 CALORIES PER SLICE.

Clockwise from top left: *Soft Breadsticks, Hearty Dark Rye Bread (page 54), French Bread, Red Pepper Flatbread*

HONEY–WHOLE WHEAT BREAD

In the late 1800s milling technology advanced to the point of removing the bran from whole wheat flour, creating white flour. While white flour makes a lovely, light loaf of bread, we also enjoy the heartier whole wheat loaf.

> 3 cups stone-ground whole wheat or graham flour
> ⅓ cup honey
> ¼ cup shortening
> 1 tablespoon salt
> 2 packages regular or quick-acting active dry yeast
> 2¼ cups very warm water (120° to 130°)
> 3 to 4 cups all-purpose* or unbleached flour
> Margarine or butter, melted

Mix whole wheat flour, honey, shortening, salt and yeast in large bowl. Add warm water. Beat on low speed 1 minute, scraping bowl frequently. Beat on medium speed 1 minute, scraping bowl frequently. Stir in enough all-purpose flour, 1 cup at a time, to make dough easy to handle.

Turn dough onto lightly floured surface. Knead about 10 minutes or until smooth and elastic. Place in greased bowl and turn greased side up. Cover and let rise in warm place 40 to 60 minutes or until double. (Dough is ready if indentation remains when touched.)

Grease 2 loaf pans, 9 × 5 × 3 or 8½ × 4½ × 2½ inches. Punch down dough and divide in half. Flatten dough for each loaf with hands or rolling pin into a rectangle, 18 × 9 inches. Fold crosswise into thirds, overlapping the two sides. Flatten or roll into square, 9 × 9 inches. Roll dough tightly, beginning at one of the open (unfolded) ends, to form a loaf. Press with thumbs to seal after each turn. Pinch edge firmly to seal. Press each end with side of hand to seal. Fold ends under loaf. Place seam side down in pan. Brush loaves lightly with margarine. Cover and let rise 35 to 50 minutes or until double.

Place oven rack in low position so that tops of pans will be in center of oven. Heat oven to 375°. Bake 40 to 45 minutes or until loaves are deep golden brown and sound hollow when tapped; remove from pans. Cool on wire rack. 2 LOAVES (16 SLICES EACH); 115 CALORIES PER SLICE.

*If using self-rising flour, decrease salt to 1 teaspoon.

LOW-SALT HONEY–WHOLE WHEAT BREAD: Decrease honey to ¼ cup and salt to 1 teaspoon. Substitute vegetable oil for the shortening. Each rising time will be 10 to 15 minutes shorter. 115 CALORIES PER SLICE.

APRICOT-CASHEW ROUNDS: Grease cookie sheet. Stir in ½ cup finely chopped dried apricots and 1 cup finely chopped cashews with the second addition of flour. Divide dough into fourths. Shape each into round loaf. Place on cookie sheet. Let rise 35 to 50 minutes or until double. Just before baking, make ¼-inch crosscut slashes across tops. Bake 35 to 40 minutes. 4 LOAVES (12 SLICES EACH); 100 CALORIES PER SLICE.

HEARTY DARK RYE BREAD

> 3 packages regular or quick-acting active dry yeast
> 1½ cups warm water (105° to 115°)
> 2½ cups all-purpose flour*
> ½ cup shreds of wheat bran cereal
> ½ cup dark molasses
> ¼ cup cocoa
> 1 tablespoon salt
> 1 tablespoon caraway seed
> 2 tablespoons vegetable oil
> 2 to 2½ cups dark rye flour
> Cornmeal
> ¼ cup cold water
> ½ teaspoon cornstarch

Dissolve yeast in warm water in large bowl. Add all-purpose flour, cereal, molasses, cocoa, salt, caraway seed and oil. Beat on low speed until moistened. Beat on medium speed 3 minutes, scraping bowl occasionally. Stir in enough rye flour to make dough easy to handle.

Turn dough onto lightly floured surface. Cover and let rest 15 minutes. Knead about 10 minutes or until smooth and elastic. Place in greased bowl and turn greased side up. Cover and let rise in warm place about 1 hour or until double. (Dough is ready if indentation remains when touched.)

Grease cookie sheet and sprinkle with cornmeal. Punch down dough and divide in half. Shape each half into round, slightly flattened loaf. Place loaves in opposite corners of cookie sheet. Cover and let rise in warm place 40 to 50 minutes or until double.

Heat oven to 375°. Bake 30 minutes. Meanwhile, heat cold water and cornstarch to boiling, stirring constantly. Brush over loaves. Bake 10 to 15 minutes longer or until loaves sound hollow when tapped. Cool on wire racks. 2 LOAVES (12 SLICES EACH); 120 CALORIES PER SLICE.

*If using self-rising flour, decrease salt to 1 teaspoon.

☘ HERB BATTER BREAD

3 cups all-purpose flour*
1 tablespoon sugar
1 teaspoon salt
1 package regular or quick-acting active
    dry yeast
1¼ cups very warm water (120° to 130°)
2 tablespoons chopped fresh parsley
2 tablespoons shortening
1½ teaspoons chopped fresh or ½ teaspoon
    dried rosemary leaves
½ teaspoon chopped fresh or ¼ teaspoon
    dried thyme leaves
    Margarine or butter, softened

Mix 2 cups of the flour, the sugar, salt and yeast in large bowl. Add warm water, parsley, shortening, rosemary and thyme. Beat on low speed 1 minutes, scraping bowl frequently. Beat on medium speed 1 minute, scraping bowl frequently. Stir in remaining flour until smooth. Scrape batter from side of bowl. Cover and let rise in warm place 35 to 40 minutes or until double.

Grease loaf pan, 9 × 5 × 3 inches. Stir down batter by beating about 25 strokes. Smooth and pat batter in loaf pan with floured hands. Cover and let rise in warm place about 30 minutes or until double. (Do not let overrise.)

Heat oven to 375°. Bake 40 to 45 minutes or until loaf sounds hollow when tapped. Brush top with margarine. Remove loaf from pan; cool on wire rack. 1 LOAF (ABOUT 16 SLICES); 100 CALORIES PER SLICE.

If using self-rising flour, omit salt.

FOUR-GRAIN BATTER BREAD

3½ cups all-purpose flour*
2 tablespoons sugar
1 teaspoon salt
¼ teaspoon baking soda
2 packages regular or quick-acting active
    dry yeast
2 cups very warm milk (120° to 130°)
½ cup very warm water (120° to 130°)
½ cup whole wheat flour
½ cup wheat germ
½ cup quick-cooking oats
1 to 1¼ cups all-purpose flour*
Cornmeal

Mix 3½ cups all-purpose flour, the sugar, salt, baking soda and yeast in large bowl. Add warm milk and warm water. Beat on low speed until moistened. Beat 3 minutes on medium speed, scraping bowl occasionally. Stir in whole wheat flour, wheat germ, oats and enough remaining all-purpose flour to make a stiff batter.

Grease 2 loaf pans, 8½ × 4½ × 2½ inches and sprinkle with cornmeal. Divide batter evenly between pans. Round tops of loaves by patting with floured hands. Sprinkle with cornmeal. Cover and let rise in warm place about 30 minutes or until batter is about 1 inch below top of pan.

Heat oven to 400°. Bake about 25 minutes or until loaves are light brown; remove from pans. Cool on wire rack. 2 LOAVES (16 SLICES EACH); 110 CALORIES PER SLICE.

If using self-rising flour, omit salt and baking soda.

WHOLE WHEAT BATTER BREAD: Increase whole wheat flour to 2 cups. Omit wheat germ and oats. Stir in 1 cup raisins with second addition of all-purpose flour. 85 CALORIES PER SLICE.

Honey Almond-Apple Puffs, Coconut-Praline Coffee Cake (page 60)

ANGEL BISCUITS

1 package regular or quick-acting active dry yeast
2 tablespoons warm water (105° to 115°)
1 cup shortening
5 cups all-purpose flour*
¼ cup sugar
3 teaspoons baking powder
2 teaspoons salt
1 teaspoon baking soda
2 cups buttermilk

Dissolve yeast in warm water. Cut shortening into flour, sugar, baking powder, salt and baking soda with pastry blender in large bowl until mixture resembles fine crumbs. Stir in buttermilk and yeast mixture until dough leaves side of bowl (dough will be soft and sticky).

Turn dough onto generously floured surface. Roll gently in flour to coat. Shape into ball. Knead lightly 25 to 30 times, sprinkling with flour if dough is too sticky. Roll or pat ½ inch thick. Cut with 2½-inch round cutter. Place about 1 inch apart on ungreased cookie sheet. Cover and let rise in warm place 1 to 1½ hours or until double.

Heat oven to 400°. Bake 12 to 14 minutes or until golden brown. Immediately remove from cookie sheet. ABOUT 2½ DOZEN BISCUITS; 145 CALORIES PER BISCUIT.

If using self-rising flour, omit baking powder and salt.

HONEY ALMOND-APPLE PUFFS

½ package (17¼-ounce size) frozen puff pastry, thawed
1 large pared cooking apple, cut into 6 wedges
Ground nutmeg
¼ cup honey
¼ cup sliced almonds

Heat oven to 425°. Unfold pastry and cut into 9 squares. Cut apple wedges crosswise in half (only 9 apple pieces are needed). Place 1 apple piece on each pastry square and sprinkle with nutmeg. Moisten corners of pastry with water. Gather corners over apple and pinch to seal well. Place on ungreased cookie sheet. Bake 15 to 20 minutes or until deep golden brown and puffed. Heat honey until thin. Brush honey over warm puffs. Sprinkle with almonds. Serve warm. 9 PUFFS; 180 CALORIES PER PUFF.

Place apple piece on each pastry square and sprinkle with nutmeg. Moisten corners with water. Gather corners over apple and pinch edges to seal well.

CARAMEL STICKY ROLLS

Fragrant, tender Caramel Sticky Rolls will entice even the sleepiest person out of bed.

> 3½ to 4 cups all-purpose flour*
> ⅓ cup granulated sugar
> 1 teaspoon salt
> 2 packages quick-acting or regular active dry yeast
> 1 cup very warm milk (120° to 130°)
> ⅓ cup margarine or butter, softened
> 1 egg
> 1 cup packed brown sugar
> ½ cup margarine or butter
> ¼ cup dark corn syrup
> ¾ cup pecan halves
> 2 tablespoons margarine or butter, softened
> ½ cup chopped pecans
> 2 tablespoons granulated sugar
> 2 tablespoons packed brown sugar
> 1 teaspoon ground cinnamon

Mix 2 cups of the flour, ⅓ cup granulated sugar, the salt and yeast in large bowl. Add warm milk, ⅓ cup margarine and the egg. Beat on low speed 1 minute, scraping bowl frequently. Beat on medium speed 1 minute, scraping bowl frequently. Stir in enough remaining flour to make dough easy to handle.

Turn dough onto lightly floured surface. Knead about 5 minutes or until smooth and elastic. Place in greased bowl and turn greased side up. Cover and let rise in warm place about 1½ hours or until double. (Dough is ready if indentation remains when touched.)

Heat 1 cup brown sugar and ½ cup margarine to boiling, stirring constantly; remove from heat. Stir in corn syrup. Pour into ungreased rectangular pan, 13 × 9 × 2 inches. Sprinkle with pecan halves.

Punch down dough. Flatten with hands or rolling pin into rectangle, 15 × 10 inches, on lightly floured surface. Spread with 2 tablespoons margarine. Mix chopped pecans, 2 tablespoons granulated sugar, 2 tablespoons brown sugar and the cinnamon. Sprinkle evenly over margarine. Roll up tightly, beginning at 15-inch side. Pinch edge of dough into roll to seal. Stretch and shape until even. Cut roll into fifteen 1-inch slices. Place slightly apart in pan. Let rise in warm place about 30 minutes or until double.

Heat oven to 350°. Bake 30 to 35 minutes or until golden brown. Immediately invert on heatproof tray or serving plate. Let stand 1 minute so caramel will drizzle down; remove pan. 15 ROLLS; 385 CALORIES PER ROLL.

*If using self-rising flour, omit salt.

JUMBO CARAMEL STICKY ROLLS: Prepare dough as directed—except roll dough, beginning at 10-inch side. Cut into eight 1¼-inch slices. 8 ROLLS; 720 CALORIES PER ROLL.

OVERNIGHT CARAMEL STICKY ROLLS: Prepare dough as directed—except do not let dough rise after placing rolls in pan. Wrap pan tightly with heavy-duty aluminum foil. Refrigerate at least 12 hours but no longer than 48 hours. Bake as directed.

CRUSTY HEARTH BREAD

Try the Maple-Nut variation with black walnuts.

> 1 package regular or quick-acting active dry yeast
> ¼ cup warm water (105° to 115°)
> 3 cups all-purpose* or unbleached flour
> 1 cup buttermilk
> ¼ cup shortening
> 2 tablespoons sugar
> 1 tablespoon baking powder
> ¾ teaspoon salt

Dissolve yeast in warm water in large bowl. Stir in 1½ cups of the flour, the buttermilk, shortening, sugar, baking powder and salt until smooth. Stir in remaining flour until dough forms. Turn dough onto floured surface. Knead gently about 1 minute or until smooth. Cover and let rise 10 minutes.

Grease cookie sheet. Shape dough into round loaf, about 8 inches in diameter. Place on cookie sheet. Cover and let rise in warm place 30 minutes.

Heat oven to 350°. Cut an X shape about ½ inch deep in top of bread. Bake about 35 minutes or until golden brown; cool slightly. Tear bread into pieces, or cut into slices. 1 LOAF (ABOUT 12 SLICES); 160 CALORIES PER SLICE.

*If using self-rising flour, omit baking powder and salt.

MAPLE-NUT BREAD: Substitute packed brown sugar for the granulated sugar and ⅓ cup maple-flavored syrup for ⅓ cup of the buttermilk. Stir in 1 cup coarsely chopped walnuts, toasted if desired, with the remaining flour. 235 CALORIES PER SLICE.

SPICY CORN ROLLS: Substitute ½ cup cornmeal for ½ cup of the flour. Stir in ¼ teaspoon ground cumin, ⅛ teaspoon ground allspice and ⅛ teaspoon ground red pepper (cayenne). Divide dough into 12 equal parts. Shape each part into ball and place 1 inch apart on greased cookie sheet. Let rise. Cut an X shape about ½ inch deep in top of each. Bake 15 to 20 minutes or until golden brown. 1 DOZEN ROLLS; 150 CALORIES PER ROLL.

TRADITIONAL ROLL DOUGH

This basic dough lets you make a cornucopia of rolls, from Fan Tans to Parker House Rolls. You can make a whole wheat version of the dough by substituting 1½ to 1¾ cups whole wheat flour for the second addition of all-purpose flour.

> 3½ to 3¾ cups all-purpose* or unbleached flour
> ¼ cup sugar
> ¼ cup shortening or margarine or butter, softened
> 1 teaspoon salt
> 1 package regular or quick-acting active dry yeast
> ½ cup very warm water (120° to 130°)
> ½ cup very warm milk (120° to 130°)
> 1 egg
> Margarine or butter, softened

Mix 2 cups of the flour, the sugar, shortening, salt and yeast in medium bowl. Add warm water, warm milk and egg. Beat on low speed 1 minute, scraping bowl frequently. Beat on medium speed 1 minute, scraping bowl frequently. Stir in enough remaining flour to make dough easy to handle.

Turn dough onto lightly floured surface. Knead about 5 minutes or until smooth and elastic. Place in greased medium bowl and turn greased side up. Cover and let rise in warm place about 1 hour or until double. (Dough is ready if indentation remains when touched.)

Punch down dough. Cut or roll as directed for any of the variations below. Brush with margarine. Cover and let rise about 30 minutes or until double.

Heat oven to 400°. Bake 12 to 18 minutes or until golden brown.

*If using self-rising flour, omit salt.

CLOVERLEAF ROLLS: Cut half of Traditional Roll Dough into 36 pieces. Shape into balls. Place 3 balls in each of 12 greased medium muffin cups, 2½ × 1¼ inches. Continue as directed.   1 DOZEN ROLLS; 90 CALORIES PER ROLL.

CRESCENT ROLLS: Roll half of Traditional Roll Dough into 12-inch circle on floured surface. Spread with margarine or butter, softened. Cut into 16 wedges. Roll up, beginning at rounded edge. Place rolls, point sides down, on greased cookie sheet and curve slightly. Continue as directed.   16 ROLLS; 70 CALORIES PER ROLL.

FAN TANS: Roll half of Traditional Roll Dough into rectangle, 12 × 9 inches, on floured surface. Spread with margarine or butter, softened. Cut

Clockwise from top left: *Fan Tans, Pan Rolls, Square Rolls, Parker House Rolls, Cloverleaf Rolls, Crescent Rolls*

lengthwise into 6 strips, each about 1½ inches wide. Stack strips evenly. Cut into 12 pieces, each about 1 inch wide. Place cut sides down in 12 greased medium muffin cups, 2½ × 1¼ inches. Continue as directed. 1 DOZEN ROLLS; 90 CALORIES PER ROLL.

PAN ROLLS: Cut half of Traditional Roll Dough into 24 pieces. Shape into balls. Place close together in greased round pan, 9 × 1½ inches. Continue as directed. 2 DOZEN ROLLS; 45 CALORIES PER ROLL.

PARKER HOUSE ROLLS: Roll half of Traditional Roll Dough into rectangle, 12 × 9 inches, on floured surface. Cut with floured 3-inch round cutter. Brush each circle with margarine or butter, softened. Make crease across each circle and fold so top half slightly overlaps bottom half. Press edges together. Place close together in greased square pan, 9 × 9 × 2 inches. Continue as directed. 1 DOZEN ROLLS; 90 CALORIES PER ROLL.

SQUARE ROLLS: Roll half of Traditional Roll Dough into rectangle, 13 × 9 inches, on floured surface. Place in greased rectangular pan, 13 × 9 × 2 inches. Cut dough with sharp knife ¼ inch deep to make 15 rolls. Continue as directed. 15 ROLLS; 75 CALORIES PER ROLL.

OVERNIGHT DANISH PASTRIES

2 packages regular or quick-acting active dry yeast
½ cup warm water (105° to 115°)
4 cups all-purpose flour*
⅓ cup sugar
2 teaspoons salt
1 cup cold butter,** cut into small pieces
4 eggs
1 cup milk
Jam or preserves
Powdered Sugar Glaze (right)

Dissolve yeast in warm water in large bowl. Mix in flour, sugar and salt. Cut in butter with pastry blender until mixture resembles fine crumbs. Separate eggs and refrigerate egg whites for use when shaping and baking pastry. Stir egg yolks and milk into flour mixture until soft dough forms. Cover bowl with plastic wrap and refrigerate at least 8 hours but no longer than 24 hours.

Punch down dough and divide into 3 equal parts. Shape 1 part dough at a time, let stand and bake as directed in the variations below. If dough becomes too sticky while shaping, refrigerate 5 to 10 minutes.

Powdered Sugar Glaze

1½ cups powdered sugar
¾ teaspoon vanilla
2 to 3 tablespoons water or milk

Mix all ingredients until smooth. If necessary, stir in additional water, ½ teaspoon at a time, until spreading consistency.

Do not use self-rising flour in this recipe.
**We do not recommend margarine for this recipe.*

DANISH TWISTS: Grease cookie sheet lightly. Roll 1 part dough into rectangle, 9 × 7 inches, on lightly floured surface. Cut crosswise into nine 1-inch strips. For each twist, pinch ends of strip together to form ring, stretching strip slightly. Twist to form figure 8. Place at least 2 inches apart on cookie sheet. Brush with egg white. Let rise uncovered at room temperature about 25 minutes or until puffy and loops fill in.

Heat oven to 350°. Make an indentation in center of each loop. Fill with ½ to 1 teaspoon jam. Brush dough with egg white. Bake about 15 minutes or until light golden brown; cool slightly on wire rack. Drizzle with one-third of the Powdered Sugar Glaze. 9 TWISTS; 190 CALORIES PER TWIST.

LATTICE COFFEE CAKE: Grease cookie sheet lightly. Roll 1 part dough into rectangle, 12 × 8 inches, on lightly floured surface. Place on cookie sheet. Spread ½ cup jam in 3-inch strip across center of rectangle. Make 4-inch diagonal cuts on each 8-inch side of rectangle at 1-inch intervals. Fold strips from alternating sides over jam, overlapping strips to cover jam completely. Press ends to seal. Brush with egg white. Let rise uncovered at room temperature about 25 minutes or until puffy.

Heat oven to 350°. Brush dough with egg white. Bake about 20 minutes or until light golden brown. Cool slightly on wire rack. Drizzle with one-third of the Powdered Sugar Glaze or make only one-third of the recipe. 8 SLICES; 200 CALORIES PER SLICE.

COCONUT-PRALINE COFFEE CAKE

When twisting this coffee cake, try not to stretch the dough too much to keep a pretty shape with the filling inside.

> ½ cup flaked coconut
> ½ cup chopped pecans
> ½ cup packed brown sugar
> 2 tablespoons milk
> 2 tablespoons margarine or butter, melted
> 1 teaspoon ground cinnamon
> 1 loaf (about 1 pound) frozen white bread dough, thawed
> ¼ cup margarine or butter, softened
> Powdered sugar

Grease jelly roll pan, 15½ × 10½ inches. Mix coconut, pecans, brown sugar, milk, 2 tablespoons margarine and the cinnamon. Roll dough into rectangle, 15 × 10 inches, on lightly floured surface. Spread with ¼ cup margarine. Sprinkle with coconut mixture and press into dough. Roll up as for jelly roll, beginning at 15-inch side. Cut roll lengthwise in half. Place strips, filling sides up and side by side, on pan. Twist together gently and loosely. Cover and let rise about 45 minutes or until double.

Heat oven to 350°. Bake 25 to 30 minutes or until golden brown. Immediately remove from pan; cool slightly. Sprinkle with powdered sugar.   1 COFFEE CAKE (16 SLICES); 170 CALORIES PER SLICE.

QUICK COCONUT-PRALINE FILLING COFFEE CAKE: Substitute 1 package (9.9 ounces) coconut pecan frosting mix (dry) for the coconut, pecans and brown sugar. Omit ¼ cup margarine or butter. Continue as directed.   215 CALORIES PER SLICE.

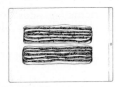

1. Cut roll lengthwise in half. Place strips, filling sides up and side by side, on cookie sheet.

2. Twist together gently and loosely, keeping cut sides up.

🌾 GARLIC BREAD

> ½ cup margarine or butter, softened
> 1 clove garlic, finely chopped
> 1 loaf (1 pound) French bread, cut into 15 slices

Heat oven to 400°. Mix margarine and garlic. Spread over bread slices. Reassemble loaf and wrap securely in heavy-duty aluminum foil. Bake 15 to 20 minutes or until hot.   1 LOAF (15 SLICES); ABOUT 140 CALORIES PER SLICE.

To Microwave: Do not wrap loaf in aluminum foil. Divide assembled loaf in half and place halves side by side in napkin-lined basket or on microwavable dinner plate. Cover with microwavable paper towel and microwave on medium (50%) 1 minute 30 seconds to 3 minutes, rotating basket ½ turn after 1 minute, until bread is warm.

HERB-CHEESE BREAD: Add 2 tablespoons grated Parmesan cheese, 2 teaspoons chopped fresh parsley and 1 teaspoon chopped fresh or ½ teaspoon dried oregano leaves to the margarine mixture.   145 CALORIES PER SLICE.

CHEESY PEPPER-ONION BREAD

> 1 loaf (1 pound) French bread
> 1 cup shredded mozzarella cheese (4 ounces)
> ½ cup mayonnaise or salad dressing
> ¼ cup finely chopped red, yellow or green bell pepper
> 1 small onion, finely chopped (about ¼ cup)
> 1 tablespoon chopped fresh or 1 teaspoon dried cilantro
> ½ teaspoon ground cumin

Heat oven to 400°. Cut loaf horizontally to make 3 layers. Mix remaining ingredients. Spread half of the cheese mixture over one layer. Place second layer on top. Spread with remaining cheese mixture. Top with third layer and press firmly. Cut loaf into 16 slices. Wrap bread securely in heavy-duty aluminum foil. Bake 15 to 20 minutes or until hot.   1 LOAF (16 SLICES); 155 CALORIES PER SLICE.

To Microwave: Prepare as directed—except do not wrap in aluminum foil. Cut assembled loaf crosswise in half and place halves side by side in napkin-lined basket or on microwavable dinner plate. Cover with microwavable paper towel and microwave on medium (50%) 2 to 4 minutes, rotating basket ½ turn after 2 minutes, until bread is warm and cheese begins to melt.

FIX-IT-FAST

- Use leftover muffins or popovers for dessert by filling with pudding or ice cream and topping with fresh fruit or your favorite dessert topping.

- Use leftover popovers as an appetizer or snack. Cut lengthwise into fourths and sprinkle with shredded cheese and chopped green chilies. Broil until cheese is melted.

- For a different twist to French toast, use English muffins, bagels, challah bread, croissant halves, nut breads, whole grain or cinnamon-raisin bread instead of French or regular white bread.

- Use refrigerated or frozen doughs to make quick breadsticks.

- Serve biscuits, popovers, pancakes or waffles instead of potatoes, pasta or rice.

- Brush split pita bread or tortillas with melted margarine or butter and sprinkle with herbs. Bake at 400° 6 to 8 minutes.

- Use just about any bread to make croutons— French, Italian, whole wheat, rye, croissants, whatever you have on hand. See page 10 for directions.

- Thickly slice nut breads, then cut into "fingers" or cubes for dipping into chocolate, fruit or other dessert sauces. Or frost fingers or cubes with thinned leftover frosting and roll in nuts for a sweet snack.

- Mix your own flavored butters to make breads special. Mix ½ cup softened margarine or butter with ½ to 1 teaspoon chopped herbs or 1 or 2 finely chopped garlic cloves. For a sweet butter, mix in 1 to 2 tablespoons of your favorite fruit preserves.

- Turn English muffins or bagels into caramel rolls by spreading with softened margarine or butter, sprinkling with brown sugar and nuts, then broiling.

- Mix mayonnaise or salad dressing with Parmesan or shredded cheeses. Spread on bread and broil until puffed and golden.

- When preparing toast for a crowd, use the oven and broil bread on both sides about 4 to 5 inches from heat.

- Spread leftover pancakes with margarine or butter, softened cream cheese, peanut butter or fruit preserves. Top with sugar, chopped nuts, chocolate chips, sliced fruit or another favorite topping. Roll up and enjoy for a quick snack.

PER SERVING OR UNIT

NUTRITION INFORMATION

RECIPE, PAGE

PERCENT U.S. RECOMMENDED DAILY ALLOWANCE

Recipe, Page	Servings per recipe	Calories	Protein (grams)	Carbohydrate (grams)	Fat (grams)	Cholesterol (milligrams)	Sodium (milligrams)	Protein	Vitamin A	Vitamin C	Thiamine	Riboflavin	Niacin	Calcium	Iron
QUICK BREADS															
Apple Muffins, 37															
Baking Powder Biscuits, 38	10	185	3	20	11	0	350	4	0	0	6	4	6	8	2
Banana Bread, 42	48	85	1	12	4	10	95	2	0	0	2	2	2	0	0
Blueberry Streusel Muffins, 37	12	185	3	27	8	25	230	4	2	0	6	6	4	8	4
Buttermilk Biscuits, 38	10	185	3	20	10	0	345	4	0	0	6	4	6	6	2
Buttermilk Pancakes, 41	9	75	2	8	4	30	205	2	0	0	2	4	0	6	0
Cheese-and-Bacon Waffles, 41	12	265	8	18	17	65	290	12	4	0	8	10	6	18	4

RECIPE, PAGE	Servings per recipe	Calories	Protein (grams)	Carbohydrate (grams)	Fat (grams)	Cholesterol (milligrams)	Sodium (milligrams)	Protein	Vitamin A	Vitamin C	Thiamine	Riboflavin	Niacin	Calcium	Iron
								PERCENT U.S. RECOMMENDED DAILY ALLOWANCE							

QUICK BREADS (*continued*)

RECIPE, PAGE	Servings per recipe	Calories	Protein (grams)	Carbohydrate (grams)	Fat (grams)	Cholesterol (milligrams)	Sodium (milligrams)	Protein	Vitamin A	Vitamin C	Thiamine	Riboflavin	Niacin	Calcium	Iron
Cheese Dumplings, 37	10	115	3	14	5	5	215	4	0	0	4	4	4	8	2
Chocolate-Peanut Banana Bread, 42	48	85	1	13	3	10	95	2	0	0	2	2	2	0	0
Cinnamon-Oatmeal Pancakes, 41	9	85	2	9	4	30	235	2	0	0	2	4	0	10	2
Corn Bread, 39	12	100	3	9	6	45	370	4	0	0	2	4	2	8	2
Corn Muffins, 39	14	85	2	8	5	40	320	2	0	0	2	4	0	6	2
Corn Sticks, 39	18	65	2	6	4	30	250	2	0	0	2	2	0	4	0
Corn Waffles, 41	12	165	3	15	11	45	230	4	2	0	4	4	4	10	2
Cornmeal Biscuits, 38	10	150	2	12	10	0	360	2	0	0	4	2	2	8	2
Cornmeal Pancakes, 41	9	80	2	9	4	30	230	2	0	0	2	4	2	10	2
Cranberry Bread, 44	48	100	2	14	4	25	105	2	0	0	2	2	2	0	2
Cranberry-Orange Muffins, 37	12	190	3	27	8	25	230	4	2	2	6	6	4	8	4
Custardy Overnight French Toast, 40	18	130	5	18	4	95	220	8	2	0	6	8	4	4	4
Danish Puff, 44	12	335	4	32	22	70	230	6	14	0	6	4	4	0	4
Date-Nut Muffins, 36	12	230	4	30	12	25	360	4	10	4	16	14	14	10	14
Drop Biscuits, 38	10	190	3	20	11	0	350	4	0	0	6	4	6	10	2
Dumplings, 37	10	105	2	14	4	0	200	2	0	0	4	4	4	6	2
French Puffs, 37	18	130	5	18	4	95	220	8	2	0	6	8	4	4	4
French Toast, 40	18	130	5	18	4	95	220	8	2	0	6	8	4	4	4
Golden Raisin Puff, 44	12	325	4	36	19	70	230	4	14	0	6	4	4	0	4
Herb Dumplings, 37	10	105	2	14	4	0	200	2	0	0	4	4	4	6	2
Lemon-Oat Scones, 40	15	120	3	10	8	40	175	4	4	0	2	4	2	6	2
Macadamia-Coconut Banana Bread, 42	48	95	1	12	5	10	95	2	0	0	2	2	2	0	0
Mexican Double Corn Bread, 39	12	110	3	12	6	45	420	4	4	4	4	4	2	6	2
Mini Banana Breads, 42	20	205	3	28	9	30	230	4	4	2	6	4	2	2	4
Molasses-Bran Muffins, 36	12	190	3	24	10	25	360	4	10	4	12	14	12	10	14
No-Cholesterol Oat Bran Muffins, 35	12	145	4	16	10	0	210	6	0	0	10	4	2	6	4
Nut Waffles, 41	12	210	5	18	13	50	210	6	2	0	8	8	6	12	4
Oat Bran Muffins, 35	12	150	4	16	10	25	200	6	0	0	10	4	2	6	4
Oatmeal-Raisin Muffins, 37	12	200	3	31	8	25	265	4	2	0	6	4	2	10	4
Onion-Cheese Corn Bread, 39	12	115	4	9	7	50	440	6	4	0	2	6	2	10	2

NUTRITION INFORMATION

PER SERVING OR UNIT

RECIPE, PAGE

PERCENT U.S. RECOMMENDED DAILY ALLOWANCE

Recipe, Page	Servings per recipe	Calories	Protein (grams)	Carbohydrate (grams)	Fat (grams)	Cholesterol (milligrams)	Sodium (milligrams)	Protein	Vitamin A	Vitamin C	Thiamine	Riboflavin	Niacin	Calcium	Iron
QUICK BREADS (continued)															
Orange-Cheese Braid, 46	12	280	4	29	16	30	415	6	10	4	10	8	4	6	6
Pancakes, 40	9	100	3	12	4	30	215	4	0	0	4	4	2	10	2
Parsley Dumplings, 37	10	105	2	14	4	0	200	2	0	0	4	4	4	6	2
Popovers, 42	6	115	5	17	3	95	220	8	2	0	6	8	4	6	4
Pumpkin Bread, 44	48	100	2	15	4	25	100	2	42	0	2	2	2	0	2
Raspberry-Chocolate Coffee Cake, 47	12	330	5	45	15	25	265	8	6	2	8	8	6	8	6
Raspberry-Marzipan Coffee Cake, 47	12	290	5	40	13	25	265	8	6	2	8	12	6	10	6
Rhubarb-Pear Bread, 44	48	100	1	13	4	25	100	2	0	0	2	2	2	0	2
Scones, 40	15	130	3	17	6	40	165	4	4	0	4	2	2	4	2
Sour Cream Coffee Cake, 45	16	355	5	47	17	60	375	6	10	0	8	6	6	6	6
Spicy Fruit Scones, 40	15	130	3	17	6	40	165	4	16	0	4	4	4	4	4
Waffles, 41	12	185	4	18	11	50	210	6	2	0	6	6	4	12	4
Wine-and-Cheese Muffins, 36	12	150	4	14	9	35	300	6	2	0	8	6	4	10	4
Zucchini Bread, 44	48	95	1	13	4	25	105	2	0	0	2	2	2	0	2
Zucchini Muffins, 44	24	200	3	28	9	45	205	4	2	0	6	4	4	2	4
YEAST BREADS															
Angel Biscuits, 56	30	145	2	18	7	0	220	2	0	8	4	2	4	2	2
Apricot-Cashew Rounds, 54	48	100	3	17	3	0	155	4	2	0	6	2	4	0	4
Caramel Sticky Rolls, 57	15	385	5	53	18	20	285	8	8	0	16	10	10	4	12
Cheesy Pepper-Onion Bread, 60	16	155	4	16	8	5	230	6	0	2	4	4	2	4	4
Cinnamon-Raisin Bread, 51	32	130	3	28	1	0	210	4	0	0	8	4	6	0	4
Cloverleaf Rolls, 58	12	90	2	15	2	10	120	2	0	0	4	4	4	0	2
Coconut-Praline Coffee Cake, 60	16	170	3	22	8	0	185	4	2	0	8	4	4	4	6
Crescent Rolls, 58	16	70	2	11	2	10	90	2	0	0	4	2	2	0	2
Crusty Hearth Bread, 57	12	160	4	25	5	0	260	6	0	0	8	8	8	8	4
Danish Twist, 59	9	190	3	26	8	60	245	4	6	0	6	6	4	2	4
Fan Tans, 58	12	90	2	15	2	10	120	2	0	0	4	4	4	0	2
Four-Grain Batter Bread, 55	32	85	3	16	1	0	90	4	0	0	6	6	4	2	4
French Bread, 52	24	65	2	12	1	0	95	2	0	0	4	2	4	0	2
Fresh Herb Bread, 51	32	105	3	21	1	0	205	4	0	0	8	4	6	0	4

NUTRITION INFORMATION

PER SERVING OR UNIT

PERCENT U.S. RECOMMENDED DAILY ALLOWANCE

RECIPE, PAGE

YEAST BREADS (continued)

Recipe, Page	Servings per recipe	Calories	Protein (grams)	Carbohydrate (grams)	Fat (grams)	Cholesterol (milligrams)	Sodium (milligrams)	Protein	Vitamin A	Vitamin C	Thiamine	Riboflavin	Niacin	Calcium	Iron
Garlic Bread, 60	15	140	3	17	7	0	250	4	4	0	4	4	2	0	2
Hearty Dark Rye Bread, 54	24	120	3	24	2	0	290	4	0	0	8	6	6	2	8
Herb Batter Bread, 55	16	100	2	17	2	0	145	2	0	0	6	4	6	0	4
Herb-Cheese Bread, 60	15	145	3	17	7	0	260	4	4	0	4	4	2	2	2
Herbed Flatbread, 52	24	75	2	11	3	0	30	2	0	0	4	2	4	0	2
Honey Almond-Apple Puffs, 56	9	180	2	19	11	0	110	2	0	0	4	4	2	0	4
Honey–Whole Wheat Bread, 54	32	115	3	22	2	0	205	4	0	0	8	4	6	0	4
Italian Flatbread, 52	24	75	2	11	3	0	30	2	0	0	4	2	4	0	2
Jumbo Caramel Sticky Rolls, 57	8	720	10	99	33	35	535	14	16	0	30	20	18	10	22
Lattice Coffee Cake, 59	8	240	4	26	9	65	275	4	6	0	6	6	6	2	4
Low-Salt Honey–Whole Wheat Bread, 54	32	115	3	21	2	0	70	4	0	0	8	4	6	0	4
Low-Salt Traditional White Bread, 51	32	105	3	20	1	0	70	4	0	0	8	4	6	0	4
Maple-Nut Bread, 57	12	235	5	33	10	0	270	6	0	0	10	8	8	8	6
Pan Rolls, 59	24	45	1	8	1	5	60	0	0	0	2	2	2	0	0
Parker House Rolls, 59	12	90	2	15	2	10	120	2	0	0	4	4	4	0	2
Pesto Swirl Bread, 51	32	130	3	21	3	0	220	4	0	0	8	4	6	2	6
Quick Coconut-Praline Filling Coffee Cake, 60	16	215	2	30	10	0	235	2	2	0	6	4	4	2	4
Red Pepper Flatbread, 52	24	85	2	12	3	0	30	2	4	12	4	2	4	0	2
Soft Breadsticks, 52	24	65	2	12	1	0	95	2	0	0	4	2	4	0	2
Spicy Corn Rolls, 57	12	150	3	23	5	0	270	4	0	0	8	6	6	8	4
Square Rolls, 59	15	75	2	12	2	10	95	2	0	0	4	2	2	0	2
Traditional White Bread, 51	32	105	3	20	1	0	205	4	0	0	8	4	6	0	4
Whole Wheat Batter Bread, 55	32	110	3	23	1	0	85	4	0	0	12	8	8	2	6

CAKES & PIES

Just about everyone enjoys freshly baked, lusciously frosted cakes and warm, juicy pies. From delicious fruit pies with flaky crusts to the easy pat-in-the-pan crust that requires no rolling, to Impossible Brownie Pie (page 99) that makes its own crust, you'll love the many types of pies you can make. Our cakes are also mouth-watering and so varied! Bake rich chocolate cakes; airy angel food cakes and spicy gingerbread. Or try our recipes for cakes to mix right in the pan or pop into the micro-wave or a conventional oven. And when you bake a cake or pie, you'll have more than forty years of kitchen testing behind you, to make sure the experience is "a piece of cake."

CAKE BASICS

SHORTENING-TYPE CAKES

Shortening-type cakes contain these same ingredients: shortening, margarine or butter; flour; eggs; a liquid; and a leavening agent, such as baking powder or soda. Only the flavorings are different.

A good shortening-type cake is light and has a slightly rounded, smooth, tender top. It is fine grained with an even texture (not crumbly), light, velvety, and slightly moist with a pleasant, sweet flavor.

♦ Always use the size pans called for in the recipe. To check the width of a pan, measure across the top from inside edge to inside edge. Baking a cake in too large a pan will result in a pale, flat, shrunken cake. Too small or too shallow a pan will result in a cake that bulges and loses its shape.

♦ Shiny metal pans reflect heat away from the cake. They produce a tender, light brown crust and are preferred for baking cakes.

♦ Dark nonstick or glass baking pans should be used by following the manufacturers' directions. These pans readily absorb heat and a better result is often achieved if the baking temperature is reduced 25°.

♦ Fill cake pans no more than half full. If you are using a pan with an unusual shape (heart, star, bell), measure the capacity by filling with water, measure the water and use half that amount in batter. (Cupcakes can be made from any remaining batter.)

♦ For shortening-type cakes, such as yellow and white cakes, oven racks should be in the middle of the oven and pans placed in the center of the rack. Layer pans should not touch and there should be at least 1 inch of space between the pans and the oven sides.

Insert a wooden pick near the center of cake after the minimum baking time. If the pick comes out clean, cake is done.

Cool pan on wire rack 5 to 10 minutes. Place towel-covered rack on top of layer. Towel prevents damage to cake top. Invert as a unit; remove the pan.

Place original rack on bottom of layer; turn over both racks as a unit. Cool the layer completely on the rack.

Preceding page: *Best Chocolate Cake (page 68) with Chocolate Frosting (page 85), Orange-glazed Lattice Cherry Pie (page 93)*

PAN PREPARATION

♦ Generously grease bottoms and sides of pans with shortening. (Do not use margarine, butter or oil, as they will not coat as evenly.) Use about 1 tablespoon shortening for each 8- or 9-inch layer. Dust each greased pan with flour (or cocoa for a chocolate cake), shaking pan until bottom and sides are well-coated. Shake out excess flour. For nonstick pans, follow manufacturers' directions.

♦ For cupcakes, line medium muffin cups, 2½ × 1¼ inches, with paper baking cups. The use of liners helps keep cupcakes moist and easy to transport and makes cleanup easy.

♦ For fruitcakes, line pans with aluminum foil, then grease, or line with cooking parchment. Leave short "ears" so the baked cake can be easily lifted out of the pan. Extend the foil up over the pan if you intend to store the cake. When the cake has cooled, the foil can be brought up and over the top of the cake and sealed.

MIXING CAKES

♦ The cake recipes in this cookbook have been tested with portable mixers. Because mixers vary in power, you may need to adjust the speed, particularly during the initial step of blending ingredients.

♦ Our one-bowl method was developed using the electric mixer, but mixing can also be done by hand. Stir the ingredients to moisten and blend them well. Beat 150 strokes for each minute of beating time (3 minutes equals 450 strokes). If a cake is not beaten enough, its volume will be lower.

CAKE YIELDS

♦ The cake and frosting recipes include calories per serving based on the first pan size listed in the recipe.

Size and Kind	Servings
8- or 9-inch layer cake	16
8- or 9-inch square cake	9 to 12
13 × 9 × 2-inch rectangular cake	16
10 × 4-inch tube cake	16 to 24
12-cup bundt cake	16 to 24

CUTTING CAKES

♦ For shortening-type cakes, use a sharp, long, thin knife.

♦ For angel food, chiffon and pound cakes, use a long serrated knife (such as a bread knife) or an electric knife.

♦ If the frosting sticks, dip the knife in hot water and wipe with a damp towel after cutting each slice.

♦ For fruitcake, use a thin, nonserrated or electric knife. For easiest slicing and a mellow flavor, fruitcake should be made three to four weeks ahead of time, then wrapped and stored in the refrigerator.

STORING CAKES

♦ Unfrosted cakes should be cooled completely before storing. They will become sticky if covered while warm.

♦ Foam-type cakes will stay fresh overnight stored in their baking pan and covered with waxed paper. Remove from pan and frost the day it is served.

♦ Cakes with creamy-type frosting can be stored in a cake safe or under a large inverted bowl. Or loosely cover with aluminum foil, plastic wrap or waxed paper.

♦ Cakes with fluffy frosting should be served the same day they are made. If it is necessary to store this type of cake, use a cake safe or inverted bowl, with a knife slipped under the edge so the container is not airtight.

♦ Cakes with whipped cream toppings, cream fillings or cream cheese frostings should be refrigerated.

SUCCESS TIPS

♦ When margarine or butter is specified in the recipe, use margarine or butter sticks, not whipped. Whipped margarines and butter contain considerably more water and may affect the batter.

♦ Do not substitute oil for shortening, margarine or butter, even when those ingredients are to be melted. Recipes formulated with shortening that is solid at room temperature need the solids for proper structure and texture.

♦ Test a cake by inserting a wooden pick or cake tester into the center of the cake. The cake is done if it comes out clean.

♦ Cool cakes to be served from the pan in their pans on wire racks. Some cakes such as snack cakes may be served warm.

♦ Cool layer cakes or bundt cakes in their pans on wire racks 5 to 20 minutes. Remove from pans; cool completely on wire racks.

❦ BEST CHOCOLATE CAKE

This chocolate cake with its rich red-brown color, moist texture and deep fudge flavor is one of our flagship recipes. Unbeatable any time!

> 2 cups all-purpose flour* or cake flour
> 2 cups sugar
> ½ cup shortening
> ¾ cup water
> ¾ cup buttermilk
> 1 teaspoon baking soda
> 1 teaspoon salt
> 1 teaspoon vanilla
> ½ teaspoon baking powder
> 2 eggs
> 4 ounces unsweetened chocolate, melted and cooled

Heat oven to 350°. Grease and flour rectangular pan, 13 × 9 × 2 inches, 2 round pans, 9 × 1½ inches, 3 round pans, 8 × 1½ inches or 12-cup bundt cake pan. Beat all ingredients on low speed 30 seconds, scraping bowl constantly. Beat on high speed 3 minutes, scraping bowl occasionally. Pour into pan(s).

Bake rectangle 40 to 45 minutes, rounds 30 to 35 minutes, bundt cake 50 to 55 minutes or until wooden pick inserted in center comes out clean. Cool rectangle on wire rack. Cool layers and bundt cake 10 minutes. Invert onto wire rack and cool completely. Frost rectangle or fill and frost layers with Chocolate Frosting (page 85) or Caramel Frosting (page 85) if desired.   16 SERVINGS; 250 CALORIES PER SERVING.

If using self-rising flour, omit baking soda, salt and baking powder.

To Microwave: Generously grease 16-cup microwavable bundt cake dish; coat with cornflake crumbs or graham cracker crumbs. Substitute ½ cup vegetable oil for the shortening. Pour batter into dish. Microwave uncovered on medium (50%) 15 minutes, rotating dish ¼ turn every 5 minutes. Microwave uncovered on high 3 to 5 minutes longer or until top springs back and appears slightly moist. Let stand uncovered on flat, heatproof surface (not wire rack) 10 minutes. Invert onto heatproof serving plate.

WHOLE WHEAT–CHOCOLATE CAKE: Substitute 1 cup whole wheat flour for 1 cup of the all-purpose flour.   250 CALORIES PER SERVING.

❦ DOUBLE CHOCOLATE SNACK CAKE

> 1⅔ cups all-purpose flour*
> 1 cup packed brown sugar or granulated sugar
> ¼ cup cocoa
> 1 teaspoon baking soda
> ½ teaspoon salt
> 1 cup water
> ⅓ cup vegetable oil
> 1 teaspoon vinegar
> ½ teaspoon vanilla
> ½ cup semisweet chocolate chips

Heat oven to 350°. Mix flour, brown sugar, cocoa, baking soda and salt with fork in ungreased square pan, 8 × 8 × 2 inches. Stir in remaining ingredients except chocolate chips. Sprinkle chocolate chips over batter.

Bake 35 to 40 minutes or until wooden pick inserted in center comes out clean. Cool on wire rack. Sprinkle with powdered sugar if desired.   9 SERVINGS; 300 CALORIES PER SERVING

Do not use self-rising flour in this recipe.

To Microwave: Mix batter in ungreased round microwavable dish, 8 × 1½ inches. Elevate dish on inverted microwavable pie plate in microwave oven. Microwave uncovered on medium (50%) 15 to 17 minutes, rotating dish ¼ turn every 5 minutes, until top springs back when touched lightly. (Top may appear wet but will continue cooking as cake stands.) Let stand on flat, heatproof surface (not wire rack); cool.

CHOCOLATE-WALNUT SNACK CAKE: Substitute ⅓ cup miniature chocolate chips and ⅓ cup chopped walnuts for the ½ cup chocolate chips. Sprinkle over batter.   295 CALORIES PER SERVING.

MAPLE-NUT SNACK CAKE: Omit cocoa, vanilla and chocolate chips. Stir ½ cup chopped nuts into flour mixture. Stir in ½ teaspoon maple flavoring with the remaining ingredients.   275 CALORIES PER SERVING.

OATMEAL-MOLASSES SNACK CAKE: Omit cocoa, vanilla and chocolate chips. Stir ¾ cup quick-cooking oats, ½ cup raisins and 1 teaspoon ground allspice into flour mixture. Stir in 2 tablespoons dark molasses with the remaining ingredients.   305 CALORIES PER SERVING.

PUMPKIN SNACK CAKE: Omit cocoa, vanilla and chocolate chips. Stir 1 teaspoon ground allspice into flour mixture. Decrease water to ½ cup. Stir in ½ cup canned pumpkin with the remaining ingredients.   255 CALORIES PER SERVING.

🌾 GERMAN CHOCOLATE CAKE

German Chocolate Cake came to Texas in the mid-1800s, not from Germany but by way of a man named Samuel German, who invented a sweet chocolate bar. Below is the grass-roots recipe for the cake that became a favorite in the 1950s.

½ cup boiling water
1 bar (4 ounces) sweet cooking chocolate
2 cups sugar
1 cup margarine or butter, softened
4 egg yolks
1 teaspoon vanilla
2¼ cups all-purpose flour* or 2½ cups cake flour
1 teaspoon baking soda
1 teaspoon salt
1 cup buttermilk
4 egg whites, stiffly beaten
Coconut-Pecan Frosting (right)

Heat oven to 350°. Grease 2 square pans, 8×8×2 or 9×9×2 inches, or 3 round pans, 8×1½ or 9×1½ inches. Line bottoms of pans with cooking parchment paper or waxed paper.

Pour boiling water over chocolate, stirring until chocolate is melted; cool. Mix sugar and margarine in medium bowl until light and fluffy. Beat in egg yolks, one at a time. Beat in chocolate and vanilla on low speed. Mix flour, baking soda and salt. Add alternately with buttermilk, beating after each addition until batter is smooth. Fold in egg whites. Divide batter between pans.

Bake 8-inch squares 45 to 50 minutes, 9-inch squares 40 to 45 minutes, 8-inch rounds 35 to 40 minutes, 9-inch rounds 30 to 35 minutes or until wooden pick inserted in center comes out clean. Cool cakes 10 minutes. Invert on wire rack and cool completely. Fill layers and frost top of cake with Coconut-Pecan Frosting. 16 SERVINGS; 525 CALORIES PER SERVING.

Do not use self-rising flour in this recipe.

Coconut-Pecan Frosting

3 egg yolks
1 cup evaporated milk
1 cup sugar
½ cup margarine or butter
1 teaspoon vanilla
1⅓ cups flaked coconut
1 cup chopped pecans

Beat egg yolks and milk in 2-quart saucepan. Stir in sugar, margarine and vanilla. Cook over medium heat about 12 minutes, stirring occasionally, until thick. Stir in coconut and pecans. Beat until frosting is of spreading consistency.

Carrot Cake (page 76), German Chocolate Cake

Decadent Chocolate Cake with Raspberry Sauce

DECADENT CHOCOLATE CAKE WITH RASPBERRY SAUCE

1 cup semisweet chocolate chips
½ cup margarine or butter
½ cup all-purpose flour* or cake flour
4 eggs, separated
½ cup sugar
½ cup semisweet chocolate chips
2 tablespoons margarine or butter
2 tablespoons corn syrup
Raspberry Sauce (right)

Heat oven to 325°. Grease springform pan, 8 × 2½ inches, or round pan, 9 × 1½ inches. Heat 1 cup chocolate chips and ½ cup margarine in 2-quart heavy saucepan over medium heat until chocolate chips are melted; cool 5 minutes. Stir in flour until smooth. Stir in egg yolks until well blended.

Beat egg whites in large bowl on high speed until foamy. Beat in sugar, 1 tablespoon at a time, until soft peaks form. Fold chocolate mixture into egg whites. Spread in pan.

Bake springform 35 to 40 minutes, round 30 to 35 minutes (top will appear dry and cracked) or until wooden pick inserted in center comes out clean;

cool 10 minutes. Run knife along side of cake to loosen; remove side of springform pan. Invert cake onto wire rack; remove bottom of springform pan and cool cake completely. Place on serving plate.

Heat ½ cup chocolate chips, 2 tablespoons margarine and the corn syrup over medium heat until chocolate chips are melted. Spread over top of cake, allowing some to drizzle down side. Serve with Raspberry Sauce. Garnish with fresh raspberries and sweetened whipped cream if desired.
12 SERVINGS; 325 CALORIES PER SERVING.

Do not use self-rising flour in this recipe.

Raspberry Sauce

1 package (10 ounces) frozen raspberries, thawed, drained and juice reserved
¼ cup sugar
2 tablespoons cornstarch
1 to 2 tablespoons orange- or raspberry-flavored liqueur, if desired

Add enough water to reserved juice to measure 1 cup. Mix sugar and cornstarch in 1-quart saucepan. Stir in juice and raspberries. Heat to boiling over medium heat. Boil and stir 1 minute; strain. Stir in liqueur.

BLACK MIDNIGHT CAKE

One of our editors grew up with the 1956 Betty Crocker's Picture Cook Book and remembers baking this popular cake six times in one week, for family, friends and school functions!

> 2¼ cups all-purpose flour* or cake flour
> 1⅔ cups sugar
> ⅔ cup cocoa
> ¾ cup shortening
> 1¼ cups water
> 1¼ teaspoons baking soda
> 1 teaspoon salt
> ¼ teaspoon baking powder
> 1 teaspoon vanilla
> 2 eggs

Heat oven to 350°. Grease and flour rectangular pan, 13 × 9 × 2 inches, 2 round pans, 9 × 1½ inches or 3 round pans, 8 × 1½ inches. Beat all ingredients 30 seconds on low speed, scraping bowl constantly. Beat on high speed 3 minutes, scraping bowl occasionally. Pour into pan(s).

Bake rectangle 40 to 45 minutes, rounds 30 to 35 minutes or until wooden pick inserted in center comes out clean. Cool rectangle on wire rack. Cool layers 10 minutes; remove from pans and cool completely on wire rack. Frost rectangle or fill and frost layers with Browned Butter Frosting (page 84) or White Mountain Frosting (page 84) if desired.   16 SERVINGS; 245 CALORIES PER SERVING.

*Do not use self-rising flour in this recipe.

 ## POUND CAKE

The first pound cakes were made with a pound each of butter, sugar, flour and eggs.

> 2¾ cups sugar
> 1¼ cups margarine or butter, softened
> 1 teaspoon vanilla or almond extract
> 5 eggs
> 3 cups all-purpose flour*
> 1 teaspoon baking powder
> ¼ teaspoon salt
> 1 cup milk or evaporated milk

Heat oven to 350°. Grease and flour 12-cup bundt cake pan or tube pan, 10 × 4 inches. Beat sugar, margarine, vanilla and eggs in large bowl on low speed 30 seconds, scraping bowl constantly. Beat on high speed 5 minutes, scraping bowl occasionally. Mix flour, baking powder and salt. Beat in alternately with milk on low speed. Spread in pan.

Bake 1 hour 10 minutes to 1 hour 20 minutes or until wooden pick inserted in center comes out clean. Cool 20 minutes; remove from pan and cool completely on wire rack.   24 SERVINGS; 245 CALORIES PER SERVING.

*Do not use self-rising flour in this recipe.

BROWN SUGAR POUND CAKE: Heat oven to 325°. Reduce sugar to ½ cup. Add 2¼ cups packed brown sugar with the sugar. Fold 1 cup chopped pecans into batter. Bake 1 hour 20 minutes to 1 hour 30 minutes.   270 CALORIES PER SERVING.

LEMON POUND CAKE: Substitute 1 teaspoon lemon extract for the vanilla. Fold 2 to 3 teaspoons grated lemon peel into batter.   245 CALORIES PER SERVING.

ORANGE-COCONUT POUND CAKE: Fold 1 can (3½ ounces) flaked coconut (1⅓ cups) and 2 to 3 tablespoons grated orange peel into batter.   260 CALORIES PER SERVING.

TOASTED ALMOND POUND CAKE: Omit vanilla. Add 2 teaspoons ground cinnamon with the flour. Fold 1½ cups chopped blanched almonds, toasted, into batter.   290 CALORIES PER SERVING.

CARAMEL PECAN CAKE

> 3 cups all-purpose flour*
> 2¼ cups packed brown sugar
> ½ cup margarine or butter, softened
> ½ cup shortening
> ¾ cup milk
> 1½ teaspoons baking powder
> ½ teaspoon salt
> 1½ teaspoons vanilla
> 5 eggs
> 1 cup chopped pecans
> 1 tablespoon powdered sugar

Heat oven to 325°. Grease and flour 12-cup bundt cake pan. Beat all ingredients except pecans and powdered sugar on low speed 30 seconds, scraping bowl constantly. Beat on high speed 3 minutes, scraping frequently. Stir in pecans. Pour into pan.

Bake 1 hour 5 minutes to 1 hour 15 minutes or until wooden pick inserted in center comes out clean. Cool 20 minutes. Invert onto wire rack and cool completely. Sprinkle with powdered sugar. Serve with Hot Fudge Sauce (page 161) if desired.   24 SERVINGS; 255 CALORIES PER SERVING.

*If using self-rising flour, omit baking powder and salt.

SILVER WHITE CAKE

This cake is a classic—it's been in every Betty Crocker's basic cookbook since 1950. We use it in our test kitchens to train new employees in the use of different types of flour. The lemon-filled variation is a favorite of the Betty Crocker Dining Room guests—try it in your dining room, too!

    2¼ cups all-purpose flour*
    1⅔ cups sugar
    3½ teaspoons baking powder
    1 teaspoon salt
    1¼ cups milk
    ⅔ cup shortening
    1 teaspoon vanilla or almond extract
    5 egg whites

Heat oven to 350°. Grease and flour rectangular pan, 13 × 9 × 2 inches, 2 round pans, 9 × 1½ inches, or 3 round pans, 8 × 1½ inches. Beat all ingredients except egg whites in large bowl on low speed 30 seconds, scraping bowl constantly. Beat on high speed 2 minutes, scraping bowl occasionally. Beat in egg whites on high speed 2 minutes, scraping bowl occasionally. Pour into pan(s).

Bake rectangle 40 to 45 minutes, 9-inch rounds 30 to 35 minutes, 8-inch rounds 23 to 28 minutes or until wooden pick inserted in center comes out clean or until cake springs back when touched lightly in center. Cool rectangle on wire rack. Cool layers 10 minutes; remove from pans and cool completely on wire rack. Frost cake with Cherry-Nut Frosting (page 84) if desired.   16 SERVINGS; 225 CALORIES PER SERVING.

*Do not use self-rising flour in this recipe.

CHERRY-NUT CAKE: Fold ½ cup chopped nuts and ⅓ cup chopped maraschino cherries, well-drained, into batter.   250 CALORIES PER SERVING.

CHOCOLATE CHIP CAKE: Fold ½ cup miniature or finely chopped semisweet chocolate chips into batter. Frost with Chocolate Frosting (page 85) if desired.   250 CALORIES PER SERVING.

LEMON-FILLED WHITE CAKE: Spread rectangle or fill layers with Lemon Filling (right). Frost with White Mountain Frosting (page 84). Sprinkle cake with about 1 cup flaked or shredded coconut if desired.   310 CALORIES PER SERVING.

Lemon Filling

    ¾ cup sugar
    3 tablespoons cornstarch
    ¼ teaspoon salt
    ⅔ cup water
    1 tablespoon margarine or butter
    1 teaspoon grated lemon peel
    ¼ cup lemon juice
    2 drops yellow food color, if desired

Mix sugar, cornstarch and salt in 1½-quart saucepan. Gradually stir in water. Cook over medium heat, stirring constantly, until mixture thickens and boils. Boil and stir 1 minute; remove from heat. Stir in margarine and lemon peel until margarine is melted. Gradually stir in lemon juice and food color. Press plastic wrap onto filling. Refrigerate about 2 hours or until set.

SILVER WHITE CUPCAKES: Line 30 medium muffin cups, 2½ × 1¼ inches, with paper baking cups. Fill cups about one-half full. Bake 20 to 25 minutes.   30 CUPCAKES; 120 CALORIES PER CUPCAKE.

SILVER WHITE SHEET CAKE: Pour batter into greased and floured jelly roll pan, 15½ × 10½ × 1 inch. Bake about 25 minutes.   24 SERVINGS; 150 CALORIES PER SERVING.

Silver White Cupcakes with Creamy Vanilla Frosting (page 84)

STARLIGHT YELLOW CAKE

Although we have changed its name over the years, the popularity of this basic yellow cake hasn't changed. Its versatility is another reason we always include this recipe in every Betty Crocker basic cookbook.

2¼ cups all-purpose flour*
1½ cups sugar
3½ teaspoons baking powder
1 teaspoon salt
1¼ cups milk
½ cup shortening (half margarine or butter, softened, if desired)
1 teaspoon vanilla
3 eggs

Heat oven to 350°. Grease and flour rectangular pan, 13 × 9 × 2 inches, 2 round pans, 9 × 1½ inches or 3 round pans, 8 × 1½ inches. Beat all ingredients on low speed 30 seconds, scraping bowl constantly. Beat on high speed 3 minutes, scraping bowl occasionally. Pour into pan(s).

Bake rectangle 40 to 45 minutes, 9-inch rounds 30 to 35 minutes, 8-inch rounds 20 to 25 minutes or until wooden pick inserted in center comes out clean or until cake springs back when touched lightly in center. Cool rectangle on wire rack. Cool layers 10 minutes; remove from pans and cool completely on wire rack. Frost with Chocolate Frosting (page 85) if desired.   16 SERVINGS; 205 CALORIES PER SERVING.

If using self-rising flour, omit baking powder and salt.

EGGNOG CAKE: Substitute rum flavoring for the vanilla. Beat in 1 teaspoon ground nutmeg and ¼ teaspoon ground ginger.   210 CALORIES PER SERVING.

LEMON-FILLED YELLOW CAKE: Spread rectangle or fill layers with Lemon Filling (page 72). Frost with White Mountain Frosting (page 84). 295 CALORIES PER SERVING.

MARBLE CAKE: Pour half of the batter into another bowl. Mix 2 ounces unsweetened chocolate, melted and cooled, 1 tablespoon sugar, 2 tablespoons warm water and ¼ teaspoon baking soda. Stir into one batter. Spoon light and dark batters alternately into pan. Cut through batter several times for marbled effect.   230 CALORIES PER SERVING.

PEANUT CAKE: Fold ½ cup finely chopped peanuts into batter.   235 CALORIES PER SERVING.

STARLIGHT YELLOW CUPCAKES: Line 36 medium muffin cups, 2½ × 1¼ inches, with paper baking cups. Fill cups about one-half full. Bake 20 minutes.   36 CUPCAKES; 90 CALORIES PER CUPCAKE.

WHITE CHOCOLATE CHIP CAKE

What is known as "white chocolate" isn't truly chocolate because it does not contain chocolate liquor. Still, the expression "white chocolate" has stuck, and the flavor is featured in many desserts. For an elegant topping, place a paper doily on the cake, after the glaze is set, sprinkle with sifted cocoa (remove the doily carefully to keep the pattern from smudging).

1¼ cups all-purpose flour*
⅔ cup sugar
½ cup buttermilk
¼ cup shortening
½ teaspoon baking soda
½ teaspoon baking powder
¼ teaspoon salt
½ teaspoon vanilla
2 eggs
⅔ cup vanilla milk chips, finely chopped
White Chocolate Glaze (below)

Heat oven to 350°. Grease side and line bottom of round pan, 9 × 1½ inches, or square pan, 8 × 8 × 2 inches, with cooking parchment paper or waxed paper. Beat all ingredients except vanilla chips and White Chocolate Glaze on low speed 30 seconds, scraping bowl constantly. Beat on high speed 2 minutes, scraping bowl occasionally. Stir in vanilla chips. Pour into pan.

Bake 35 to 40 minutes or until wooden pick inserted in center comes out clean. Cool 10 minutes; remove from pan. Peel off paper; cool completely on wire rack. Spread with White Chocolate Glaze, allowing some to drizzle down side.   8 SERVINGS; 340 CALORIES PER SERVING.

If using self-rising flour, omit baking soda and salt.

White Chocolate Glaze

½ cup vanilla milk chips
2 tablespoons light corn syrup
1½ teaspoons water

Heat all ingredients over low heat, stirring constantly, until vanilla chips are melted and mixture is smooth.

LARGE WHITE CHOCOLATE CHIP CAKE: Prepare 2 round or square pans as directed, or grease and flour rectangular pan, 13 × 9 × 2 inches. Double all ingredients. Pour into pans. Bake rounds or squares as directed, rectangle 40 to 45 minutes.   16 SERVINGS.

Cookie–Sour Cream Cake

COOKIE–SOUR CREAM CAKE

Use your favorite cream-filled cookie in this cake. Cookie sizes vary, so use the guideline that it takes about 8 cream-filled chocolate sandwich cookies to make 1 cup coarsely chopped cookies.

 1 cup all-purpose flour*
 ¾ cup sugar
 ½ cup sour cream
 ¼ cup margarine or butter, softened
 ¼ cup water
 ½ teaspoon baking soda
 ½ teaspoon baking powder
 1 egg
 8 cream-filled sandwich cookies

Heat oven to 350°. Grease and flour round pan, 8 × 1½ or 9 × 1½ inches. Beat all ingredients except cookies in medium bowl on low speed 30 seconds, scraping bowl constantly. Beat on high speed 2 minutes, scraping bowl occasionally. Coarsely chop cookies. Stir into batter. Pour into pan.

Bake 30 to 35 minutes or until cake springs back when touched lightly in center. Cool 10 minutes; remove from pan and cool completely on wire rack. Frost with Sweetened Whipped Cream (page 162) and garnish with additional cookies if desired.   8 SERVINGS; 350 CALORIES PER SERVING.

*If using self-rising flour, decrease baking soda to ¼ teaspoon and omit baking powder.

Food Processor Directions: Place all ingredients except cookies in food processor. Cover and process 30 seconds or until smooth. Add whole cookies. Process using quick on-and-off motions until cookies are coarsely chopped.

LARGE COOKIE–SOUR CREAM CAKE: Grease and flour rectangular pan, 13 × 9 × 2 inches. Double all ingredients. Pour into pan. Bake 40 to 45 minutes.   16 SERVINGS.

TOASTED HAZELNUT CAKE

 2½ cups all-purpose flour*
 1½ cups sugar
 ½ cup shortening
 ¼ cup margarine or butter, softened
 1⅓ cups milk
 3 teaspoons baking powder
 ½ teaspoon salt
 2 teaspoons vanilla
 2 eggs
 ⅔ cup hazelnuts, toasted and ground (about ¾ cup plus 2 tablespoons)

Heat oven to 350°. Grease and flour rectangular pan, 13 × 9 × 2 inches, or 2 round pans, 8 × 1½ or 9 × 1½ inches. Beat all ingredients except hazelnuts on low speed 30 seconds, scraping bowl constantly. Beat on high speed 3 minutes, scraping bowl occasionally. Stir in nuts. Pour into pan(s).

Bake rectangle 35 to 40 minutes, rounds 30 to 35 minutes or until wooden pick inserted in center comes out clean. Cool rectangle on wire rack. Cool layers 10 minutes; remove from pans and cool completely on wire rack. Frost with Cream Cheese Frosting (page 84) if desired. Refrigerate any remaining cake.   16 SERVINGS; 240 CALORIES PER SERVING.

*If using self-rising floor, omit baking powder and salt.

WILD RICE—NUT CAKE

One of our home economists duplicated this dessert after sampling it at a restaurant. If you prefer more nuts, 3 cups of chopped nuts and 1 cup of cooked wild rice can be used. Serve it with hot Caramel Sauce (page 161) instead of Maple Whipped Cream if you like. The wild rice grains in the crust give an interesting crunchy texture.

2½ cups all-purpose flour*
2 cups packed brown sugar
1 cup buttermilk
¾ cup margarine or butter, softened
3 eggs
1 teaspoon baking powder
1 teaspoon baking soda
1 teaspoon vanilla
½ teaspoon salt
½ teaspoon ground nutmeg
½ teaspoon maple flavoring
2 cups cooked wild rice, well drained (page 267)
2 cups chopped nuts, toasted, if desired
Maple Whipped Cream (right)

Place oven rack in lowest position. Heat oven to 350°. Generously grease and flour 12-cup bundt cake pan or tube pan, 10 × 4 inches. Beat all ingredients except wild rice, nuts and Maple Whipped Cream in large bowl on low speed 30 seconds, scraping bowl constantly. Beat on high speed 3 minutes, scraping bowl occasionally. Stir in wild rice and nuts. Pour into pan.

Bake 55 to 60 minutes or until wooden pick inserted in center comes out clean. Cool 20 minutes. Invert onto wire rack and cool completely. Serve with Maple Whipped Cream.   24 SERVINGS; 340 CALORIES PER SERVING.

Do not use self-rising flour in this recipe.

Maple Whipped Cream

2 cups whipping (heavy) cream
¼ cup packed brown sugar
½ teaspoon maple flavoring

Beat all ingredients in chilled medium bowl until soft peaks form.

Wild Rice—Nut Cake

LEMON–POPPY SEED CAKE

A great cake for today's busy and healthy lifestyle—it's fast, and because it is eggless, it has no cholesterol.

1¾ cups all-purpose flour*
¾ cup sugar
2 tablespoons poppy seed
1 teaspoon baking soda
½ teaspoon salt
¾ cup water
¼ cup vegetable oil
1 tablespoon grated lemon peel
2 tablespoons lemon juice

Heat oven to 350°. Mix flour, sugar, poppy seed, baking soda and salt with fork in ungreased square pan, 8×8×2 or 9×9×2 inches. Stir in remaining ingredients.

Bake 35 to 40 minutes or until wooden pick inserted in center comes out clean and top is golden brown. Cool on wire rack. Frost with Citrus Frosting (page 84) if desired.   9 SERVINGS; 210 CALORIES PER SERVING.

*Do not use self-rising flour in this recipe.

To Microwave: Grease 6-cup microwavable ring dish; coat with 2 tablespoons graham cracker crumbs. Mix all ingredients in bowl. Pour into ring dish. Microwave uncovered on high 4 to 6 minutes, rotating dish ¼ turn every 2 minutes, until wooden pick inserted in several places comes out clean. Let stand on flat, heatproof surface (not wire rack) 10 minutes. Invert onto heatproof serving plate.

⚜ CARROT CAKE

This recipe is a favorite in the Betty Crocker Kitchens as well as across the country. Carrots are inexpensive and are almost always on hand. Stays moist and freezes well.

1½ cups sugar
1 cup vegetable oil
3 eggs
2 cups all-purpose flour*
1½ teaspoons ground cinnamon
1 teaspoon baking soda
1 teaspoon vanilla
½ teaspoon salt
¼ teaspoon ground nutmeg
3 cups shredded carrots (about 5 medium)
1 cup coarsely chopped nuts

Heat oven to 350°. Grease and flour rectangular pan, 13×9×2 inches. Mix sugar, oil and eggs in large bowl until blended; beat 1 minute. Stir in remaining ingredients except carrots and nuts; beat 1 minute. Stir in carrots and nuts. Pour into pan.

Bake 35 to 45 minutes or until wooden pick inserted in center comes out clean. Cool on wire rack. Frost with Cream Cheese Frosting (page 84) if desired.   16 SERVINGS; 315 CALORIES PER SERVING.

*If using self-rising flour, omit baking soda and salt.

APPLE CAKE: Substitute 3 cups chopped tart apples (about 3 medium) for the carrots. Frost with Caramel Frosting (page 85) if desired.   325 CALORIES PER SERVING.

⚜ ZUCCHINI-SPICE CAKE

2 cups all-purpose flour*
2 cups finely chopped zucchini (about 3 medium)
1¼ cups sugar
1 cup chopped nuts
½ cup vegetable oil
⅓ cup water
1¼ teaspoons baking soda
1 teaspoon salt
1 teaspoon ground cinnamon
1 teaspoon ground cloves
1 teaspoon ground nutmeg
1 teaspoon vanilla
3 eggs

Heat oven to 350°. Grease and flour rectangular pan, 13×9×2 inches. Beat all ingredients on low speed 1 minute, scraping bowl constantly. Beat on medium speed 2 minutes, scraping bowl occasionally. Pour into pan.

Bake 45 to 50 minutes or until wooden pick inserted in center comes out clean. Cool on wire rack. Frost with Caramel Frosting (page 85) if desired.   16 SERVINGS; 240 CALORIES PER SERVING.

*If using self-rising flour, decrease baking soda to ½ teaspoon and omit salt.

RHUBARB CAKE: Substitute ½ package (16-ounce size) frozen cut rhubarb (2 cups), rinsed, drained and chopped, or 1¾ cups finely chopped fresh rhubarb for the zucchini.   240 CALORIES PER SERVING.

OLD-FASHIONED SPICE CAKE

1 can (13 ounces) evaporated milk
1 tablespoon plus 1 teaspoon vinegar
2½ cups all-purpose flour*
1 cup granulated sugar
1 cup raisins, if desired
¾ cup packed brown sugar
⅔ cup shortening
1 teaspoon baking soda
1 teaspoon baking powder
1 teaspoon salt
¾ teaspoon ground cinnamon
¾ teaspoon ground allspice
½ teaspoon ground cloves
½ teaspoon ground nutmeg
3 eggs
Caramel Frosting (below)

Mix 1⅓ cups of the evaporated milk and the vinegar; reserve. (Reserve remaining evaporated milk for frosting.)

Heat oven to 350°. Grease and flour rectangular pan, 13 × 9 × 2 inches, or 2 round pans, 8 × 1½ or 9 × 1½ inches. Beat vinegar mixture and remaining ingredients except Caramel Frosting on low speed 30 seconds, scraping bowl constantly. Beat on high speed 3 minutes, scraping bowl occasionally. Pour into pan(s).

Bake rectangle about 45 minutes, 8-inch rounds 40 to 45 minutes, 9-inch rounds 35 to 40 minutes or until wooden pick inserted in center comes out clean. Cool rectangle on wire rack. Cool layers 10 minutes; remove from pans and cool completely on wire rack. Frost rectangle or fill and frost layers with Caramel Frosting. Sprinkle with chopped nuts or ground nutmeg if desired. Store tightly covered.   16 SERVINGS; 435 CALORIES PER SERVING.

If using self-rising flour, omit vinegar, baking soda, baking powder and salt.

Caramel Frosting

1 cup packed brown sugar
½ cup margarine or butter
Reserved evaporated milk (about ⅓ cup)
2 cups powdered sugar

Heat brown sugar, margarine and evaporated milk to boiling in 2-quart saucepan over medium heat, stirring constantly. Boil and stir 2 minutes; remove from heat. Cool about 10 minutes or until slightly thickened, stirring occasionally. Gradually stir in powdered sugar. If necessary, stir in 2 to 3 teaspoons water until frosting is smooth and of spreading consistency.

APPLESAUCE-SPICE CAKE: Beat in 1 cup applesauce with the shortening.   445 CALORIES PER SERVING.

 # GINGERBREAD

Some say a gingerbread recipe came over on the Mayflower, and it is certain that gingerbread was a favorite dessert of early settlers.

2⅓ cups all-purpose flour*
⅓ cup sugar
1 cup molasses
¾ cup hot water
½ cup shortening
1 egg
1 teaspoon baking soda
1 teaspoon ground ginger
1 teaspoon ground cinnamon
¾ teaspoon salt
Butterscotch-Pear Sauce (below)

Heat oven to 325°. Grease and flour square pan, 9 × 9 × 2 inches. Beat all ingredients except Butterscotch-Pear Sauce on low speed 30 seconds, scraping bowl constantly. Beat on medium speed 3 minutes, scraping bowl occasionally. Pour into pan.

Bake 50 to 55 minutes or until wooden pick inserted in center comes out clean. Serve warm with Butterscotch-Pear Sauce.   9 SERVINGS; 555 CALORIES PER SERVING.

Do not use self-rising flour in this recipe.

Butterscotch-Pear Sauce

1 cup packed brown sugar
½ cup light corn syrup
¼ cup margarine or butter
½ cup half-and-half
2 teaspoons grated lemon peel
1 can (16 ounces) sliced pears, drained

Mix brown sugar, corn syrup, margarine and half-and-half in 1½-quart saucepan. Cook over low heat 5 minutes, stirring occasionally. Stir in lemon peel and pears. Heat until hot.

APPLESAUCE SNACK CAKE

1⅔ cups all-purpose flour*
1 cup packed brown sugar
1½ teaspoons ground allspice
1 teaspoon baking soda
½ teaspoon salt
½ cup applesauce
⅓ cup chopped nuts
½ cup water
⅓ cup vegetable oil
1 teaspoon vinegar
Apple Cider Sauce (below)

Heat oven to 350°. Mix flour, brown sugar, allspice, baking soda and salt with fork in ungreased square pan, 8×8×2 inches. Stir in remaining ingredients except Apple Cider Sauce.

Bake 35 to 40 minutes or until wooden pick inserted in center comes out clean. Cool on wire rack. Serve with warm Apple Cider Sauce. 9 SERVINGS; 390 CALORIES PER SERVING.

*Do not use self-rising flour in this recipe.

Apple Cider Sauce

½ cup packed brown sugar
¼ cup margarine or butter
¼ cup apple cider or orange juice
2 tablespoons whipping (heavy) cream

Heat all ingredients to rolling boil in 1½-quart heavy saucepan over high heat, stirring constantly; reduce heat slightly. Boil 3 minutes, stirring frequently. (Watch carefully—mixture burns easily.) Refrigerate any remaining sauce.

To Microwave: For cake, mix as directed in ungreased round microwavable dish, 8×1½ inches. Elevate dish on inverted microwavable pie plate in microwave oven. Microwave uncovered on medium (50%) 15 to 17 minutes, rotating dish ¼ turn every 5 minutes, until top springs back when touched lightly. (Center top may appear moist but will continue to cook while standing.) Let stand uncovered on flat, heatproof surface (not wire rack) until cool. For sauce, decrease apple cider to 2 tablespoons. Place all ingredients in 4-cup microwavable measure. Microwave uncovered on high 1 minute 30 seconds to 2 minutes or just until boiling; stir. Microwave uncovered on high 2 to 3 minutes longer, stirring every minute, until thickened.

🌾 CHOCOLATE CHIP– DATE CAKE

A family favorite! With its sprinkle-on topping, it needs no frosting.

⅔ cup hot water
½ cup chopped dates
½ teaspoon baking soda
⅓ cup vegetable oil
1 cup all-purpose flour*
½ cup miniature semisweet chocolate chips
¼ cup granulated sugar
¼ cup packed brown sugar
½ teaspoon baking soda
½ teaspoon vanilla
¼ teaspoon salt
1 egg
Chocolate Chip–Nut Topping (below)

Heat oven to 350°. Pour hot water over dates in medium bowl. Stir in ½ teaspoon baking soda. Let stand 5 minutes.

Stir remaining ingredients except Chocolate Chip–Nut Topping into date mixture. Pour into ungreased square pan, 8×8×2 inches. Sprinkle with Chocolate Chip–Nut Topping. Bake about 35 minutes or until wooden pick inserted in center comes out clean. Cool on wire rack. 9 SERVINGS; 355 CALORIES PER SERVING.

*If using self-rising flour, omit baking soda and salt.

Chocolate Chip–Nut Topping

½ cup miniature semisweet chocolate chips
½ cup chopped nuts
2 tablespoons packed brown sugar

Mix all ingredients.

To Microwave: Pour batter into ungreased round microwavable dish, 8×1½ inches; sprinkle with Chocolate Chip–Nut Topping. Elevate dish on inverted microwavable dinner plate in microwave oven. Microwave uncovered on medium (50%) 6 minutes, rotating dish ½ turn every 3 minutes. Microwave uncovered on high 3 minutes 30 seconds to 4 minutes 30 seconds longer, rotating dish ½ turn after 2 minutes, until wooden pick inserted in center comes out clean (Top may appear wet but will continue cooking as cake stands.) Let stand uncovered on flat, heatproof surface (not wire rack) 10 minutes. Cool.

❀ PINEAPPLE UPSIDE-DOWN CAKE

This cake first became popular in the 1920s and was also known as Spider, an old term for a skillet, or Skillet Cake because it was baked in a skillet.

¼ cup margarine or butter
⅔ cup packed brown sugar
1 can (about 16 ounces) sliced pineapple, drained.
Maraschino cherries, if desired
1⅓ cups all-purpose flour*
1 cup granulated sugar
⅓ cup shortening
¾ cup milk
1½ teaspoons baking powder
½ teaspoon salt
1 egg

Heat oven to 350°. Heat margarine in 10-inch ovenproof skillet or square pan, 9×9×2 inches, in oven until melted. Sprinkle brown sugar over margarine. Arrange pineapple slices in skillet. Place cherry in center of each pineapple slice.

Beat remaining ingredients on low speed 30 seconds, scraping bowl constantly. Beat on high speed 3 minutes, scraping bowl occasionally. Pour over fruit in skillet. Bake skillet 45 to 50 minutes, square 50 to 55 minutes or until wooden pick inserted in center comes out clean, Immediately invert onto heatproof plate. Let skillet remain over cake a few minutes. Serve warm and, if desired, with Sweetened Whipped Cream (page 162).   9 SERVINGS; 360 CALORIES PER SERVING.

If using self-rising flour, omit baking powder and salt.

APRICOT-PRUNE UPSIDE-DOWN CAKE: Substitute 1 can (8¾ ounces) apricot halves (9 halves), drained, and 12 pitted cooked prunes for the pineapple.   380 CALORIES PER SERVING.

❀ JEWELED FRUITCAKE

This pretty cake gets its name from the large pieces of candied fruit and whole nuts that stud it throughout. If you like, wrap the fruitcake in cheesecloth; dampen with brandy, rum or wine; cover it tightly and refrigerate. Brush additional brandy on the cake every week, for as long as 2 months.

12 ounces Brazil nuts (about 1½ cups)
8 ounces dried apricots (about 2 cups)
8 ounces pitted dates (about 1½ cups)
5 ounces red and green candied pineapple, cut up (about 1 cup)
1 cup red and green maraschino cherries
¾ cup all-purpose flour*
¾ cup sugar
½ teaspoon baking powder
½ teaspoon salt
1½ teaspoons vanilla
3 eggs

Heat oven to 300°. Line loaf pan, 9×5×3 or 8½×4½×2½ inches, with aluminum foil; grease. Mix all ingredients. Spread in pan.

Bake about 1¾ hours or until wooden pick inserted in center comes out clean. If necessary, cover with aluminum foil last 30 minutes of baking to prevent excessive browning. Remove from pan; cool on wire rack. Wrap in plastic wrap; store in refrigerator.   32 SERVINGS; 155 CALORIES PER SERVING.

If using self-rising flour, omit baking powder and salt.

FOAM-TYPE CAKES

While angel food, sponge and chiffon cakes all depend on beaten egg whites for lightness, they do differ slightly.

◆ Angel food cakes have no added leavening (such as baking powder), shortening or egg yolks. They contain a high proportion of beaten egg whites to flour. Because there are no egg yolks, this type of cake is an excellent treat for those concerned with cholesterol or calories.

◆ Sponge cakes use both the egg whites and yolks. Sometimes additional leavening is called for, but never fat, because fat would break down the foam created by beating. Jelly rolls are sponge cakes.

◆ Chiffon cakes combine the lightness of foam-type cakes and the richness of shortening-type cakes, because they use egg yolks, leavening and vegetable oil or shortening.

SUCCESS TIPS

♦ Cakes in tube pans should be baked on the bottom rack of the oven to bake the cake without overbrowning the top.

♦ Egg whites should be beaten until stiff, straight peaks form. Underbeating or under-folding the egg whites can result in coarse, low-volume cakes. Overbeating or overfolding can break down the egg whites and result in a compact cake. Be sure the bowl and beaters are clean and dry, even a bit of grease or egg yolk will prevent egg whites from beating properly.

♦ Always add another mixture to beaten egg whites by pouring the mixture over the egg whites. Cut down through the mixture, then slide a spatula across the bottom and up the side of the bowl. Rotate the bowl ¼ turn and continue folding just until no streaks remain.

♦ For angel food and chiffon cakes, do not grease and flour the pans. To rise properly, the batter must cling to the side and tube of the pan.

♦ Cakes baked in rectangular, layer or jelly roll pans are done when a wooden pick or cake tester inserted in center comes out clean.

♦ Angel food cakes are done when the cracks feel dry and the top springs back when touched lightly. A cake that pulls away and/or falls out of the pan is underbaked.

♦ Foam-type cakes baked in a tube pan can be removed after cooling by sliding a stiff knife or spatula firmly against the side of pan and moving it in up-and-down strokes. Invert the pan and hit one side against the counter. The cake will slip out.

ANGEL FOOD CAKE

1½ cups powdered sugar
1 cup cake flour
1½ cups egg whites (about 12)
1½ teaspoons cream of tartar
1 cup granulated sugar
1½ teaspoons vanilla
½ teaspoon almond extract
¼ teaspoon salt

Move oven rack to lowest position. Heat oven to 375°. Mix powdered sugar and flour. Beat egg whites and cream of tartar in medium bowl on medium speed until foamy. Beat in granulated sugar on high speed, 2 tablespoons at a time, adding vanilla, almond extract and salt with the last addition of sugar. Continue beating until stiff and glossy. Do not underbeat.

Sprinkle sugar-flour mixture, ¼ cup at a time, over meringue, folding in just until sugar-flour mixture disappears. Push batter into ungreased tube pan, 10 × 4 inches. Cut gently through batter.

Bake 30 to 35 minutes or until cracks in cake feel dry and top springs back when touched lightly. Immediately turn pan upside down onto glass bottle or metal funnel. Let hang about 2 hours or until cake is completely cool. Remove from pan. Spread top of cake with Vanilla Glaze (page 85) if desired.   16 SERVINGS; 130 CALORIES PER SERVING.

CHOCOLATE ANGEL FOOD CAKE: Substitute ¼ cup cocoa for ¼ cup of the flour. Omit almond extract.   130 CALORIES PER SERVING.

COCONUT ANGEL FOOD CAKE: Fold in 1 cup shredded coconut, ½ cup at a time, after folding in sugar-flour mixture.   150 CALORIES PER SERVING.

ANGEL FOOD BASICS

To fold, cut down through center of egg whites, along bottom and up side of bowl; rotate bowl a quarter turn. Repeat.

Use a knife to cut through batter and break large air pockets and to seal batter against side of pan and tube.

Cool cake upside down in pan by placing tube on heatproof funnel or bottle so cake does not touch counter

🌾 JELLY ROLL

The jelly roll was created during the Depression because inexpensive, homemade jelly could be used as a filling. For a delicious change, try using about 1 cup of Prune-Almond Sauce (page 360) as filling.

> 3 eggs
> 1 cup granulated sugar
> ⅓ cup water
> 1 teaspoon vanilla
> ¾ cup all-purpose flour* or 1 cup cake flour
> 1 teaspoon baking powder
> ¼ teaspoon salt
> About ⅔ cup jelly or jam
> Powdered sugar

Heat oven to 375°. Line jelly roll pan, 15½ × 10½ × 1 inch, with cooking parchment paper, aluminum foil or waxed paper; grease aluminum foil or waxed paper generously. Beat eggs in small bowl on high speed about 5 minutes or until very thick and lemon colored. Pour eggs into medium bowl. Gradually beat in granulated sugar. Beat in water and vanilla on low speed. Gradually add flour, baking powder and salt, beating just until batter is smooth. Pour into pan, spreading to corners.

Bake 12 to 15 minutes or until wooden pick inserted in center comes out clean. Immediately

loosen cake from edges of pan and invert onto towel generously sprinkled with powdered sugar. Carefully remove paper. Trim off stiff edges of cake if necessary. While hot, carefully roll cake and towel from narrow end. Cool on wire rack at least 30 minutes. Unroll cake and remove towel. Beat jelly slightly with fork to soften. Spread over cake. Roll up and sprinkle with powdered sugar. 10 SERVINGS; 205 CALORIES PER SERVING.

*If using self-rising flour, omit baking powder and salt.

APPLE BUTTER CAKE ROLL: Add ½ teaspoon ground cinnamon, ½ teaspoon ground cloves and ¼ teaspoon ground allspice with the salt. Omit jelly. Spread Apple Butter Filling (below) over cake. Roll up and sprinkle with powdered sugar and cinnamon. Refrigerate any remaining cake roll. 320 CALORIES PER SERVING.

Apple Butter Filling

> 1 cup whipping (heavy) cream
> 3 tablespoons powdered sugar
> ½ cup apple butter
> 1 cup coarsely chopped walnuts

Beat whipping cream and powdered sugar in chilled small bowl until stiff. Fold in apple butter and walnuts.

LEMON CAKE ROLL: Substitute Lemon Filling (page 72) for the jelly. Serve with Sweetened Whipped Cream (page 162) if desired. 220 CALORIES PER SERVING.

CHOCOLATE ICE-CREAM ROLL: Do not use self-rising flour. Increase eggs to 4. Beat in ¼ cup cocoa with the flour. Spread 1 to 1½ pints ice cream, slightly softened, over cake. Roll up and wrap in plastic wrap. Freeze about 4 hours or until firm. Serve with Hot Fudge Sauce (page 161) if desired. 230 CALORIES PER SERVING.

TRI-COLOR JELLY ROLL: Omit jelly. After unrolling cake, spread ¼ cup apricot preserves lengthwise down one-third of cake, ¼ cup mint jelly on next one-third and ¼ cup strawberry or raspberry jelly on remaining cake. Roll up; sprinkle with powdered sugar. 170 CALORIES PER SERVING.

Apple Butter Cake Roll

🌾 LEMON CHIFFON CAKE

This is the same tried-and-true recipe from our first basic cookbook in 1950.

2 cups all-purpose flour* or 2¼ cups cake flour
1½ cups sugar
3 teaspoons baking powder
1 teaspoon salt
¾ cup cold water
½ cup vegetable oil
2 teaspoons vanilla
2 teaspoons grated lemon peel
7 egg yolks (with all-purpose flour) or 5 egg yolks (with cake flour)
1 cup egg whites (about 8)
½ teaspoon cream of tartar

Move oven rack to lowest position. Heat oven to 325°. Mix flour, sugar, baking powder and salt. Beat in water, oil, vanilla, lemon peel and egg yolks with spoon until smooth. Beat egg whites and cream of tartar in large bowl until stiff peaks form. Gradually pour egg yolk mixture over beaten egg whites, folding with rubber spatula just until blended. Pour into ungreased tube pan, 10 × 4 inches.

Bake about 1¼ hours or until top springs back when touched lightly. Immediately turn pan upside down onto glass bottle or metal funnel. Let hang about 2 hours or until cake is completely cool. Remove from pan. Glaze with Lemon Glaze (page 85) or frost with Citrus Frosting (page 84) if desired.   16 SERVINGS; 220 CALORIES PER SERVING.

If using self-rising flour, omit baking powder and salt.

CINNAMON CHIFFON CAKE: Substitute ¾ cup packed brown sugar, sifted, for ¾ cup of the sugar. Add ½ teaspoon ground cinnamon with the salt and lemon peel.   220 CALORIES PER SERVING.

MAPLE-NUT CHIFFON CAKE: Substitute ¾ cup packed brown sugar, sifted, for ¾ cup of the sugar. Substitute maple flavoring for the vanilla. Omit lemon peel. Fold in 1 cup very finely chopped nuts.   225 CALORIES PER SERVING.

ORANGE CHIFFON CAKE: Omit vanilla. Substitute 2 tablespoons grated orange peel for the lemon peel. Spread top of cake with Orange Glaze (page 85) if desired.   220 CALORIES PER SERVING.

Lemon Chiffon Cake

CHIFFON CAKE

In 1948 Betty Crocker introduced the chiffon cake, hailed as "the cake discovery of the century!" With the help of a mystery ingredient, chiffon cakes combined the lightness of angel food with the richness of butter cake. How it was done—with the addition of salad or vegetable oil. The recipe was the brainchild of Harry Baker, a California insurance salesman, who invented the cake in 1927. He became famous for his cakes in the Los Angeles area and baked them for famous Hollywood restaurants, but would give the recipe to no one.

Harry had listened to Betty Crocker's radio program over the years and decided that she should be the one to share his special cake recipe with other cooks. He traveled to Minneapolis and revealed his secret to Betty Crocker home economists. With his help they added other flavor variations, introducing a new cake idea across the country.

FROSTING BASICS

The crowning glory of many a cake is its frosting. A good frosting has a smooth consistency that holds swirls, but is still soft enough to spread on a cake without running down the sides.

SUCCESS TIPS

♦ Fluffy frostings like White Mountain Frosting (page 84) are not as stable as creamy frostings made with powdered sugar and should be prepared with caution in humid or rainy weather. Because of moisture in the air, beating time will be longer and the amount of water should be reduced slightly. There's no hard-and-fast rule for how much to reduce water, due to varying humidity levels. You'll need to experiment with reducing the water. Serve a cake with fluffy frosting on the day it is made.

♦ Creamy frostings, if too thick, can pull and tear the cake surface being frosted. Thin frosting with a few drops of water or milk, then coat the side of the cake with a thin layer, as shown.

♦ Use a flexible spatula and a light touch when frosting cakes.

FROSTING AND GLAZING CAKES

Brush away any loose crumbs from cooled cake layers. Place a cake layer rounded side down, on a plate that has 4 strips of waxed paper around the edge if desired. Spread ⅓ cup creamy-type or ½ cup fluffy-type frosting to within ½ inch of edge. Top with second layer, rounded side up.

Spread the side of the cake with a very thin layer of frosting to seal in the crumbs. Frost side of cake making a rim about ¼-inch high around top. Spread remaining frosting on top, just to the built-up rim. Remove waxed paper.

Glaze an angel food, bundt, chiffon or pound cake by pouring or drizzling a small amount of glaze on top of cake. Spread glaze if desired, allowing some to drizzle down side. Repeat until all glaze is used.

🌾 WHITE MOUNTAIN FROSTING

This classic American boiled frosting is named for the way it peaks after it is beaten. The method of cooking the egg whites by beating hot syrup into them is known as "Italian meringue."

½ cup sugar
¼ cup light corn syrup
2 tablespoons water
2 egg whites
1 teaspoon vanilla

Mix sugar, corn syrup and water in 1-quart saucepan. Cover and heat to rolling boil over medium heat. Uncover and cook, without stirring, to 242° on candy thermometer or until small amount of mixture dropped into very cold water forms a ball that flattens when removed from water. To get an accurate temperature reading it may be necessary to tilt the saucepan slightly. It takes 4 to 8 minutes for the syrup to reach 242°.

While mixture boils, beat egg whites in medium bowl just until stiff peaks form. Pour hot syrup very slowly in thin stream into egg whites, beating constantly on medium speed. Add vanilla. Beat on high speed about 10 minutes until stiff peaks form. Preparing this type of frosting on a humid day may require a longer beating time. Frosts a 13 × 9-inch cake or fills and frosts two 8- or 9-inch cake layers.   16 SERVINGS; 40 CALORIES PER SERVING.

CHERRY-NUT FROSTING: Stir in ¼ cup cut-up candied cherries, ¼ cup chopped nuts and, if desired, 6 to 8 drops red food color.   60 CALORIES PER SERVING.

CHOCOLATE REVEL FROSTING: Stir in ½ cup semisweet chocolate chips or 1 square (1 ounce) unsweetened chocolate, coarsely grated.   70 CALORIES PER SERVING.

COFFEE FROSTING: Beat 1 teaspoon powdered instant coffee into Satiny Beige Frosting (below).   45 CALORIES PER SERVING.

PEPPERMINT FROSTING: Stir in ⅓ cup coarsely crushed peppermint candy or ½ teaspoon peppermint extract.   50 CALORIES PER SERVING.

SATINY BEIGE FROSTING: Substitute packed brown sugar for the granulated sugar. Decrease vanilla to ½ teaspoon.   45 CALORIES PER SERVING.

🌾 CREAMY VANILLA FROSTING

3 cups powdered sugar
⅓ cup margarine or butter, softened
1½ teaspoons vanilla
About 2 tablespoons milk

Mix powdered sugar and margarine. Stir in vanilla and milk. Beat until smooth and of spreading consistency. Frosts a 13 × 9-inch cake or fills and frosts two 8- or 9-inch cake layers.   16 SERVINGS; 130 CALORIES PER SERVING.

Note: To fill and frost three 8-inch layers, use 4½ cups powdered sugar, ½ cup margarine or butter, softened, 2 teaspoons vanilla and about 3 tablespoons milk.

BROWNED BUTTER FROSTING: Heat butter over medium heat until delicate brown; cool. Mix melted butter with powdered sugar. (We do not recommend margarine for this recipe.)   130 CALORIES PER SERVING.

CHERRY FROSTING: Stir in 2 tablespoons drained, chopped maraschino cherries and 2 drops red food color.   130 CALORIES PER SERVING.

CITRUS FROSTING: Omit vanilla. Substitute lemon or orange juice for the milk. Stir in ½ teaspoon grated lemon peel or 2 teaspoons grated orange peel.   125 CALORIES PER SERVING.

MAPLE-NUT FROSTING: Substitute ½ cup maple-flavored syrup for the vanilla and milk. Stir in ¼ cup finely chopped nuts.   165 CALORIES PER SERVING.

PEANUT BUTTER FROSTING: Substitute peanut butter for the margarine. Increase milk to ¼ to ⅓ cup.   125 CALORIES PER SERVING.

🌾 CREAM CHEESE FROSTING

1 package (8 ounces) cream cheese, softened
1 tablespoon milk
1 teaspoon vanilla
4 cups powdered sugar

Beat cream cheese, milk and vanilla in medium bowl on low speed until smooth. Gradually beat in powdered sugar, 1 cup at a time, until smooth and of spreading consistency. Frosts a 13 × 9-inch cake or fills and frosts two 8- or 9-inch cake layers. Refrigerate any remaining frosting.   16 SERVINGS; 175 CALORIES PER SERVING.

CHOCOLATE FROSTING

⅓ cup margarine or butter, softened
2 ounces unsweetened chocolate, melted and cooled
2 cups powdered sugar
1½ teaspoons vanilla
About 2 tablespoons milk

Mix margarine and chocolate in medium bowl. Stir in powdered sugar. Beat in vanilla and milk until smooth and of spreading consistency. Frosts a 13 × 9-inch cake or fills and frosts two 8- or 9-inch cake layers.   16 SERVINGS; 115 CALORIES PER SERVING.

Note: To frost three 8-inch layers, use ½ cup margarine or butter, softened, 3 ounces unsweetened chocolate, melted and cooled, 3 cups powdered sugar, 2 teaspoons vanilla and about 3 tablespoons milk.

CREAMY COCOA FROSTING: Substitute ⅓ cup cocoa for the chocolate.   105 CALORIES PER SERVING.

MOCHA FROSTING: Stir in 1½ teaspoons powdered instant coffee with the sugar.   115 CALORIES PER SERVING.

FUDGE FROSTING

½ cup granulated sugar
2 tablespoons cocoa
¼ cup milk
2 tablespoons margarine or butter
1 tablespoon light corn syrup
Dash of salt
½ to ¾ cup powdered sugar
½ teaspoon vanilla

Mix granulated sugar and cocoa in 2-quart saucepan. Stir in milk, margarine, corn syrup and salt. Heat to boiling, stirring frequently. Boil 3 minutes, stirring occasionally; cool. Beat in powdered sugar and vanilla. Frosts one 8- or 9-inch cake layer.   8 SERVINGS; 130 CALORIES PER SERVING.

CHOCOLATE GLAZE

½ cup semisweet chocolate chips
2 tablespoons margarine or butter
2 tablespoons corn syrup
1 to 2 teaspoons hot water

Heat chocolate chips, margarine and corn syrup over low heat, stirring constantly, until chocolate chips are melted; cool slightly. Stir in water, 1 teaspoon at a time, until consistency of thick syrup.

Glazes a 12-cup bundt cake or 10-inch angel food or chiffon cake.   16 SERVINGS; 50 CALORIES PER SERVING.

To Microwave: Place chocolate chips, margarine and corn syrup in 2-cup microwavable measure. Microwave uncovered on medium (50%) 1 to 2 minutes or until chocolate can be stirred smooth. Omit water.

VANILLA GLAZE

⅓ cup margarine or butter
2 cups powdered sugar
1½ teaspoons vanilla
2 to 4 tablespoons hot water

Heat margarine in 1½-quart saucepan until melted. Stir in powdered sugar and vanilla. Stir in water, 1 tablespoon at a time, until smooth and consistency of thick syrup. Glazes a 12-cup bundt cake or 10-inch angel food or chiffon cake.   16 SERVINGS; 95 CALORIES PER SERVING.

BUTTER-RUM GLAZE: Substitute 2 tablespoons light rum or 1½ teaspoons rum flavoring for the vanilla. Stir in water, 1 teaspoon at a time.   100 CALORIES PER SERVING.

LEMON GLAZE: Add ½ teaspoon grated lemon peel to melted margarine. Substitute lemon juice for the vanilla and water.   95 CALORIES PER SERVING.

ORANGE GLAZE: Add ½ teaspoon grated orange peel to melted margarine. Substitute orange juice for the vanilla and water.   95 CALORIES PER SERVING.

CARAMEL FROSTING

½ cup margarine or butter
1 cup packed brown sugar
¼ cup milk
2 cups powdered sugar

Heat margarine over medium heat in 2-quart saucepan until melted. Stir in brown sugar. Heat to boiling, stirring constantly. Reduce heat to low. Boil and stir 2 minutes. Stir in milk. Heat to boiling; remove from heat. Cool to lukewarm.

Gradually stir in powdered sugar. Place saucepan of frosting in bowl of cold water. Beat until smooth and of spreading consistency. If frosting becomes too stiff, stir in additional milk, 1 teaspoon at a time. Frosts a 13 × 9-inch cake or fills and frosts two 8- or 9-inch cake layers.   16 SERVINGS; 165 CALORIES PER SERVING.

PIE AND PASTRY BASICS

PANS AND PREPARATION

♦ The right bakeware is the key to making the perfect pie. Choose heat-resistant glass pie plates or dull-finish (anodized) aluminum pans. Never use shiny pans—pie will have a soggy bottom crust.

♦ The most common pie size is 9 inches. We've found that even though pie plates and pans on the market may be labeled 9 inches, they vary in capacity. Our pie recipes were developed with pie plates having a 1½-quart capacity.

♦ Due to the amount of fat in pastry and crusts, pie plates or pans are not usually greased.

♦ Nonstick pie pans can cause pastry to shrink excessively when baking one-crust pie shells. Be sure pastry is securely hooked over the edge of a nonstick pan.

SUCCESS TIPS

♦ A pastry blender is a great help to cut in shortening evenly. If you don't own one, use two knives. With the blades almost touching each other, move knives back and forth in opposite directions in a parallel cutting motion. The side of a fork or a wire whisk can also be used. It's the "cutting in" of the shortening into tiny lumps that gives pastry its flaky texture.

♦ If using a self-rising flour, omit the salt. Pastry made with self-rising flour will be slightly different—mealy rather than flaky.

♦ Anchor a pastry cloth around a board with tape and use a cloth cover (stockinette) for your rolling pin to keep the dough from sticking. Rub flour into both; this will prevent sticking, yet the flour won't be absorbed by the dough.

♦ Prevent an unbaked pie shell from puffing up as it bakes by pricking the pastry thoroughly after it has been placed in the pie plate to allow steam to escape.

♦ For one-crust pies such as pumpkin or pecan where the filling is baked in the shell, do not prick the crust because the filling would seep under the crust during baking.

♦ For two-crust pies such as cherry, blueberry or apple, a Lattice Top (page 89) can be used instead of a plain top crust.

♦ To give a special finished look to a top crust, try one of the following before baking: For a shiny crust, brush with milk; for a sugary crust, moisten with water, then sprinkle with sugar. For a glazed look, brush the crust lightly with a beaten egg or an egg yolk mixed with a little water.

♦ The Pat-in-the-Pan Oil Pastry (below) and Cookie Tart Pastry (page 89) are easy to prepare, requiring no rolling and minimal pastry-making technique. High-quality results can be achieved in a very short time.

♦ Crumb crusts can be shaped evenly by pressing another pie plate of the same diameter firmly into the crust to make it firm and smooth. Do this after pressing crumbs by hand.

STORING PIES

♦ Pies containing eggs should be refrigerated.

♦ Pie shells can be frozen unbaked or baked. Frozen unbaked shells will keep two months and baked shells four months. To thaw baked pie shells, unwrap and let stand at room temperature or heat in 350° oven about 6 minutes. Do not thaw unbaked shells; immediately bake after removing from freezer.

♦ Baked pies can be frozen. They are easiest to wrap if frozen uncovered, then wrapped tightly or placed in freezer plastic bags. Bake pies before freezing to prevent soggy crusts or possible texture breakdown of raw fruit. Frozen baked pies will keep up to four months.

♦ To serve frozen two-crust pies, unwrap and thaw at room temperature 1 hour. Heat in 375° oven on lowest rack for 35 to 40 minutes until warm.

PAT-IN-THE-PAN OIL PASTRY

In 1950 we introduced a Stir-N-Roll Pastry that used vegetable oil instead of shortening and a spoon instead of a pastry blender. Our Pat-in-the-Pan Oil Pastry is even easier because you don't have to roll out the pastry.

> 1⅓ cups all-purpose flour*
> ⅓ cup vegetable oil
> ½ teaspoon salt
> 2 tablespoons cold water

Mix flour, oil and salt until all flour is moistened. Sprinkle with water, 1 tablespoon at a time, tossing with fork until all water is absorbed. Gather pastry into a ball. Press in bottom and up side of pie plate, 9 × 1¼ inches; flute (page 88) edge. Fill and bake as directed in recipe. 8 SERVINGS PIE CRUST; 150 CALORIES PER SERVING.

*If using self-rising flour, omit salt.

FOR BAKED PIE SHELL: Heat oven to 475°. Prick bottom and side thoroughly with fork. Bake 10 to 12 minutes or until light brown; cool.

🌾 CRUMB CRUSTS FOR 9-INCH PIES

Name	Crumbs	Margarine or Butter	Sugar	Temperature and Time
GRAHAM CRACKER				
Regular or cinnamon	1½ cups (about 20 squares)	⅓ cup, melted	3 tablespoons	350°, 10 minutes
COOKIE				
Vanilla or chocolate wafers, gingersnaps	1½ cups crushed	¼ cup, melted	none	350°, 10 minutes
GRANOLA	2 cups crushed	¼ cup, melted	2 tablespoons	350°, 6 to 8 minutes
NUT				
Almond, hazelnut, pecan, peanut, walnuts	1½ cups ground	2 tablespoons, softened	3 tablespoons	400°, 6 to 8 minutes

Heat oven as directed. Mix crumbs, margarine and sugar. Reserve 3 tablespoons mixture for topping if desired. Press remaining mixture firmly against bottom and side of pie plate, 9 × 1¼ inches. Bake as directed; cool.

To Microwave: Prepare as directed—except use microwavable pie plate. Microwave uncovered on high 2 to 3 minutes, rotating pie plate ½ turn every minute, until set; cool.

PASTRY BASICS

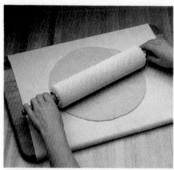

Roll pastry from center to outside edge in all directions, occasionally giving it a quarter turn. For even thickness, lift the rolling pin as it approaches the edge.

Push edge of pastry in gently with sides of hands to keep it circular when rolling out pastry. Lift pastry occasionally to prevent it from sticking to cloth.

Fold pastry into quarters; place in pie plate with point in center. Unfold and gently ease into plate, being careful not to stretch pastry. Trim as directed (page 88).

For two-crust pie, cut slits or special design in pastry before folding. Carefully place folded pastry over filling and unfold. Let top pastry overhang 1 inch beyond edge of pie plate. Fold and roll overhanging pastry under edge of bottom pastry, pressing to seal.

Form a stand-up rim on the edge of the pie plate while pinching the top and bottom edges together. This seals the pastry and makes fluting easier.

Crimp a 2- to 3-inch strip of aluminum foil over the fluted edge to prevent excessive browning. Remove aluminum foil 15 minutes before the end of the baking time.

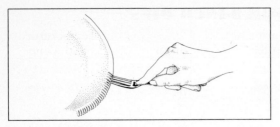

Fork Edge: Flatten pastry evenly on rim of pie plate. Press firmly around with tines of fork. To prevent sticking, dip fork in flour.

Rope Edge: Place side of thumb on pastry rim at an angle. Pinch pastry by pressing the knuckle of your index finger down into pastry toward thumb.

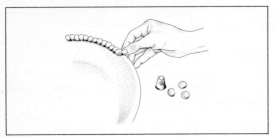

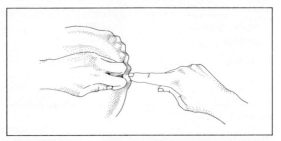

Cutout Edge: Trim overhang even or flatten pastry on rim. Use tiny cookie cutter, thimble or bottlecap to cut ¾-inch circles, leaves, hearts, etc., from pastry scraps. Moisten rim and place cutouts around rim, overlapping if desired. Press into place.

Pinch Edge: Place index finger on inside of pastry rim and knuckles (or thumb and index finger) on outside. Or reverse position if more comfortable. Pinch pastry into V-shape along entire edge. Pinch again to sharpen.

 ## STANDARD PASTRY

One-Crust Pie; 9-Inch

⅓ cup plus 1 tablespoon shortening or ⅓ cup lard
1 cup all-purpose flour*
¼ teaspoon salt
2 to 3 tablespoons cold water

10-Inch

½ cup shortening or ¼ cup plus 3 tablespoons lard
1⅓ cups all-purpose flour*
½ teaspoon salt
3 to 4 tablespoons cold water

Two-Crust Pie; 9-Inch

⅔ cup plus 2 tablespoons shortening or ⅔ cup lard
2 cups all-purpose flour*
1 teaspoon salt
4 to 5 tablespoons cold water

10-Inch

1 cup shortening or ¾ cup plus 2 tablespoons lard
2⅔ cups all-purpose flour*
1 teaspoon salt
7 to 8 tablespoons cold water

Cut shortening into flour and salt until particles are size of small peas. Sprinkle in water, 1 tablespoon at a time, tossing with fork until all flour is moistened and pastry almost cleans side of bowl (1 to 2 teaspoons water can be added if necessary).

Gather pastry into a ball. Shape into flattened round on lightly floured cloth-covered board. (For Two-Crust Pie, divide pastry in half and shape into 2 rounds.)

Roll pastry 2 inches larger than inverted pie plate with floured cloth-covered rolling pin. Fold pastry into fourths; place in pie plate. Unfold and ease into plate, pressing firmly against bottom and side.

FOR ONE-CRUST PIE: Trim overhanging edge of pastry 1 inch from rim of plate. Fold and roll pastry under, even with plate; flute (see pastry edges). Fill and bake as directed in recipe. 8 SERVINGS PIE CRUST; 140 CALORIES PER SERVING FOR 9-INCH PIE CRUST, 180 CALORIES PER SERVING FOR 10-INCH PIE CRUST.

FOR BAKED PIE SHELL: Heat oven to 475°. Prick bottom and side thoroughly with fork. Bake 8 to 10 minutes or until light brown; cool.

FOR TWO-CRUST PIE: Turn desired filling into pastry-lined pie plate. Trim overhanging edge of pastry ½ inch from rim of plate. Roll other round of pastry. Fold into fourths and cut slits so steam can escape.

Place over filling and unfold. Trim overhanging edge of pastry 1 inch from rim of plate. Fold and roll top edge under lower edge, pressing on rim to seal; flute (see pastry edges). Or, if desired, prepare Lattice Top (right).   8 SERVINGS PIE CRUST.

LATTICE TOP: Prepare pastry as directed for Two-Crust Pie (page 88)—except leave 1-inch overhang on lower crust. After rolling circle for top crust, cut into strips about ½ inch wide. (Use a pastry wheel for decorative strips.)

Place 5 to 7 strips (depending on size of pie) across filling in pie plate. Weave a cross-strip through center by first folding back every other strip going the other way. Continue weaving until lattice is complete, folding back alternate strips each time cross-strip is added. (To save time, do not weave strips. Simply lay second half of strips across first strips.) Trim ends of strips.

Fold trimmed edge of lower crust over ends of strips, building up a high edge. Seal and flute (page 88). (A juicy fruit pie with a lattice top is more likely to bubble over than a two-crust pie so a high pastry edge is important.)   8 SERVINGS PIE CRUST; 225 CALORIES PER SERVING FOR 9-INCH PIE CRUST, 360 CALORIES PER SERVING FOR 10-INCH PIE CRUST.

*If using self-rising flour, omit salt. Pie crusts made with self-rising flour differ in flavor and texture from those made with all-purpose flour.

Food Processor Directions: Measure 2 tablespoons water (for One-Crust Pie) or 4 tablespoons (for Two-Crust Pie) into small bowl. Place shortening, flour, and salt in food processor. Cover and process, using quick on-and-off motions, until mixture is crumbly. With food processor running, pour water all at once through feed tube just until dough leaves side of bowl (dough should not form ball). Continue as directed.

 ## BAKED TART SHELLS

Prepare pastry as directed for 9-inch One-Crust Pie (page 88)—except roll into 13-inch circle. Cut into eight 4½-inch circles. Fit circles over backs of medium muffin cups or 6-ounce custard cups, making pleats so pastry will fit closely. (If using individual pie pans or tart pans, cut pastry circles 1 inch larger than inverted pans; fit into pans.) Prick thoroughly with fork to prevent puffing.

Heat oven to 475°. Place on cookie sheet. Bake 8 to 10 minutes or until light brown. Cool before removing from pans. Fill each shell with ⅓ to ½ cup of your favorite filling.   8 TART SHELLS; 140 CALORIES EACH.

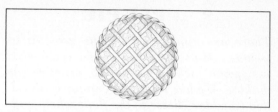

Lattice Top: Place 5 to 7 strips on filling; fold back alternate strips as each cross-strip is added. Strips can be twisted if desired.

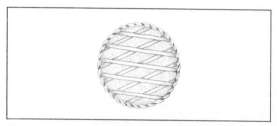

Diamond Top: Lay or weave second half of pastry strips diagonally across first strips of filling.

Spiral Top: Begin from center of pie. Twist one strip and coil it outward on pie, adding length by moistening ends of other strips and pinching. Moisten trimmed edge of bottom crust; place tightly twisted pastry strip around edge, pressing to seal.

COOKIE TART PASTRY

1½ cups all-purpose flour*
¼ cup packed brown sugar
⅔ cup margarine or butter, softened
1 egg

Heat oven to 400°. Mix all ingredients until dough forms. Press firmly and evenly against bottom and side of ungreased 11-inch tart pan. Bake 10 to 12 minutes or until light brown; cool.   8 SERVINGS; 250 CALORIES PER SERVING.

*Do not use self-rising flour in this recipe.

Food Processor Directions: Place all ingredients in food processor. Cover and process, using quick on-and-off motions, until dough forms a ball. Continue as directed.

✻ APPLE PIE

There are apple trees on the grounds at General Mills, and our home economists remember picking apples to practice pie making. We like to add ½ cup finely shredded Cheddar cheese to the flour when making pastry for an extra-special pie. You can also serve this pie with ice cream or a slice of Cheddar cheese. As we said in our 1950 Betty Crocker's Picture Cook Book, "Apple pie without cheese is like a kiss without a squeeze!"

9-Inch

Pastry for 9-inch Two-Crust Pie (page 88)
⅓ to ⅔ cup sugar
¼ cup all-purpose flour*
½ teaspoon ground nutmeg
½ teaspoon ground cinnamon
Dash of salt
8 cups thinly sliced pared tart apples (about 8 medium)**
2 tablespoons margarine or butter

10-Inch

Pastry for 10-inch Two-Crust Pie (page 88)
½ to ¾ cup sugar
⅓ cup all-purpose flour*
1 teaspoon ground nutmeg
1 teaspoon ground cinnamon
Dash of salt
10 cups thinly sliced pared tart apples (about 9 medium)**
3 tablespoons margarine or butter

Heat oven to 425°. Prepare pastry. Mix sugar, flour, nutmeg, cinnamon and salt in large bowl. Stir in apples. Turn into pastry-lined pie plate. Dot with margarine. Cover with top crust that has slits cut in it; seal and flute. Cover edge with 3-inch strip of aluminum foil to prevent excessive browning. Remove foil during last 15 minutes of baking.

Bake 40 to 50 minutes or until crust is brown and juice begins to bubble through slits in crust. 8 SERVINGS; 395 CALORIES EACH FOR 9-INCH PIE, 580 CALORIES EACH FOR 10-INCH PIE.

If using self-rising flour, omit salt.
**Substitute 3 cans (20 ounces each) sliced apples, drained, for the 8 cups of fresh apples and 4 cans (20 ounces each) for the 10 cups of fresh apples.*

To Microwave: Prepare 9-inch pie as directed—except use microwavable pie plate. Microwave uncovered on high 12 to 14 minutes or until filling begins to bubble through slits in crust. Transfer pie to conventional oven (do not preheat). Bake at 450° 12 to 18 minutes or until crust is brown and flaky.

DUTCH APPLE PIE: Prepare 9-inch pie as directed—except make extralarge slits in top crust. Five minutes before end of baking, pour ½ cup whipping (heavy) cream through slits in crust. Serve warm. 415 CALORIES PER SERVING.

FRENCH APPLE PIE: Prepare pastry for 9-inch One-Crust Pie (page 88). Turn apple mixture into pastry-lined pie plate. Omit margarine. Sprinkle apple mixture with Crumb Topping (below). Cover topping with aluminum foil during last 10 minutes of baking. Bake 50 minutes. Serve warm. 460 CALORIES PER SERVING.

Crumb Topping

1 cup all-purpose flour
½ cup packed brown sugar
½ cup firm margarine or butter

Mix all ingredients in medium bowl until crumbly.

✻ APPLE DEEP-DISH PIE

Pastry for 9-inch One-Crust Pie (page 88)
1¼ cups sugar
½ cup all-purpose flour*
1 teaspoon ground cinnamon
½ teaspoon ground nutmeg
¼ teaspoon salt
11 cups thinly sliced pared tart apples (about 10 medium)
1 tablespoon margarine or butter

Heat oven to 425°. Prepare pastry as directed—except roll into 10-inch square. Fold pastry in half and cut slits near center so steam can escape. Mix sugar, flour, cinnamon, nutmeg and salt in large bowl. Stir in apples. Turn into ungreased square pan, 9 × 9 × 2 inches. Dot with margarine. Cover with crust. Fold edges under just inside edge of pan. Bake 50 to 60 minutes or until juice begins to bubble through slits in crust. Serve warm. 12 SERVINGS; 275 CALORIES PER SERVING.

If using self-rising flour, omit salt.

APPLE DUMPLINGS

Apple Dumplings first appeared in the 1904 Christmas Edition Gold Medal Flour Cook Book. The recipe has changed a little over the years, and we've lightened the syrup to cut calories, keeping the same rich flavor.

Pastry for 9-inch Two-Crust Pie (page 88)
6 pared eating apples (each about 3 inches in diameter), cored
3 tablespoons raisins
3 tablespoons chopped nuts
½ cup sugar
½ cup corn syrup
2 tablespoons margarine or butter
¼ teaspoon ground cinnamon
1 cup water

Heat oven to 425°. Prepare pastry as directed— except roll ⅔ of the pastry into 14-inch square. Cut into 4 squares. Roll remaining pastry into rectangle, 14 × 7 inches. Cut into 2 squares. Place apple on each square.

Mix raisins and nuts; fill each apple. Moisten corners of pastry squares. Bring 2 opposite corners up over apple and pinch. Repeat with remaining corners and pinch edges of pastry to seal. Place dumplings in rectangular baking dish, 12 × 7½ × 2 inches, or square pan, 9 × 9 × 2 inches.

Heat remaining ingredients in 2-quart saucepan to boiling; boil 3 minutes. Carefully pour around dumplings. Bake about 40 minutes, spooning syrup over dumplings 2 or 3 times, until crust is golden and apples are tender. Serve warm or cool with cream or Sweetened Whipped Cream (page 162) if desired.   6 DUMPLINGS; 600 CALORIES PER DUMPLING.

CRANBERRY-APPLE PIE

Pastry for 9-inch Two-Crust Pie (page 88)
¼ cup sugar
2 tablespoons quick-cooking tapioca
1 teaspoon apple or pumpkin pie spice
1 can (16 ounces) whole berry cranberry sauce
5 cups coarsely chopped pared tart apples
½ cup coarsely chopped nuts, toasted

Heat oven to 425°. Prepare pastry. Mix sugar, tapioca and pie spice in large bowl. Stir in cranberry sauce, apples and nuts. Turn into pastry-lined pie plate. Dot with margarine. Cover with top crust that has slits cut in it; seal and flute. Cover edge with 2- to 3-inch strip of aluminum foil to prevent excessive browning. Remove foil during last 15 minutes of baking.

Bake 40 to 50 minutes until crust is brown and juice begins to bubble through slits in crust.   8 SERVINGS; 445 CALORIES PER SERVING.

CRANBERRY-PEACH PIE: Substitute 5 cups coarsely chopped fresh or frozen (thawed) peaches for the apples.   425 CALORIES PER SERVING.

BROWN SUGAR PEAR TART

Pecan Crust (below)
3 or 4 medium pears (about 2 pounds), pared
½ cup packed brown sugar
2 tablespoons all-purpose flour*
½ teaspoon ground cinnamon

Prepare and bake Pecan Crust. Heat oven to 375°. Cut each pear lengthwise in half and remove core. Place each pear half, cut side down, on cutting surface. Cut crosswise into thin slices. With spatula, lift each pear half and arrange on crust, separating and overlapping slices (retain pear shape) to cover surface of crust. Mix remaining ingredients. Sprinkle over pears.

Bake 15 to 20 minutes or until crust is golden brown and pears are tender.   8 SERVINGS; 400 CALORIES PER SERVING.

Do not use self-rising flour in this recipe.

Pecan Crust

1⅓ cups all-purpose flour
⅓ cup packed brown sugar
⅓ cup finely chopped pecans
½ teaspoon ground nutmeg
½ teaspoon grated lemon peel
⅔ cup margarine or butter, softened

Heat oven to 375°. Mix all ingredients except margarine. Cut in margarine until crumbly. Press firmly and evenly against bottom and side of ungreased 12-inch pizza pan. Bake 8 minutes; cool.

🌾 BLUEBERRY PIE

In New England blueberry and raspberry pies were common with early settlers, whereas the Pennsylvania Dutch used currants, blackberries, elderberries and gooseberries. Made at the height of the berry season, whether you do the berrying yourself or let your grocer provide the berries, a blueberry pie is one of the highlights of summer.

9-Inch

Pastry for 9-inch Two-Crust Pie (page 88)
¾ cup sugar
½ cup all-purpose flour
½ teaspoon ground cinnamon, if desired
6 cups fresh blueberries*
1 tablespoon lemon juice
1 tablespoon margarine or butter

10-Inch

Pastry for 10-inch Two-Crust Pie (page 88)
1 cup sugar
½ cup plus 1 tablespoon all-purpose flour
¾ teaspoon ground cinnamon, if desired
8 cups fresh blueberries*
2 tablespoons lemon juice
2 tablespoons margarine or butter

Heat oven to 425°. Prepare pastry. Mix sugar, flour and cinnamon in large bowl. Stir in blueberries. Turn into pastry-lined pie plate. Sprinkle with lemon juice. Dot with margarine. Cover with top crust that has slits cut in it; seal and flute. Cover edge with 2- to 3-inch strip of aluminum foil to prevent excessive browning. Remove foil during last 15 minutes of baking.

Bake 35 to 45 minutes or until crust is brown and juice begins to bubble through slits in crust. 8 SERVINGS; 395 CALORIES EACH FOR 9-INCH PIE, 590 CALORIES EACH FOR 10-INCH PIE.

Substitute drained canned blueberries or unsweetened frozen blueberries, thawed, for the fresh blueberries.

BLACKBERRY, BOYSENBERRY, LOGANBERRY OR RASPBERRY PIE: Prepare 9-inch pie as directed —except increase sugar to 1 cup. Substitute fresh berries for the blueberries. Omit lemon juice. 415 CALORIES PER SERVING.

PLUM PIE: Prepare 9-inch pie as directed—except add the cinnamon. Substitute purple plum slices for the blueberries. 425 CALORIES PER SERVING.

🌾 CHERRY PIE

Did George Washington cut down the cherry tree to make gathering cherries for a pie easier? We'll never know, but in later years George still loved cherries. His wife, Martha, wrote about how to store summer cherries for Christmas tarts, keeping them fresh in a barrel of hay, stored under a feather bed. We cannot tell a lie; we love this cherry pie!

9-Inch

Pastry for 9-inch Two-Crust Pie (page 88)
1⅓ cups sugar
½ cup all-purpose flour
6 cups fresh red tart cherries, pitted*
2 tablespoons margarine or butter

10-Inch

Pastry for 10-inch Two-Crust Pie (page 88)
1¾ cups sugar
⅔ cup all-purpose flour
8 cups fresh red tart cherries, pitted*
3 tablespoons margarine or butter

Heat oven to 425°. Prepare pastry. Mix sugar and flour in large bowl. Stir in cherries. Turn into pastry-lined pie plate. Dot with margarine. Cover with top crust that has slits cut in it; seal and flute. Cover edge with 2- to 3-inch strip of aluminum foil to prevent excessive browning. Remove foil during last 15 minutes of baking.

Bake 35 to 45 minutes or until crust is brown and juice begins to bubble through slits in crust. 8 SERVINGS; 505 CALORIES EACH FOR 9-INCH PIE, 735 CALORIES EACH FOR 10-INCH PIE.

Frozen unsweetened pitted red tart cherries, thawed and drained, can be substituted for the fresh cherries. Three cans (16 ounces each) pitted red tart cherries, drained, can be substituted for the 6 cups fresh cherries and 4 cans (16 ounces each) pitted red tart cherries, drained, for the 8 cups fresh cherries.

ORANGE-GLAZED LATTICE CHERRY PIE: Prepare 9-inch pie as directed—except make Lattice Top (page 89). Mix ½ cup powdered sugar, 2 teaspoons finely shredded orange peel and 1 tablespoon orange juice. Spoon over center of warm pie. (Do not allow glaze to run over edge of pie.) 475 CALORIES PER SERVING.

Clockwise from top: Peach Pie (page 94), Apple Deep-Dish Pie (page 90), Blueberry Pie

🌾 RHUBARB PIE

Rhubarb was called "pie plant" because it makes such an excellent filling. Delicious by itself, its pleasant tartness makes a wonderful combination with strawberries. We have found that hydroponically grown rhubarb does not thicken as well as the homegrown variety.

Pastry for 9-inch Two-Crust Pie (page 88)
2 to 2⅓ cups sugar
⅔ cup all-purpose flour
1 teaspoon grated orange peel, if desired
6 cups cut-up rhubarb (½-inch pieces)*
1 tablespoon margarine or butter

Heat oven to 425°. Prepare pastry. Mix sugar, flour and orange peel in large bowl; stir in rhubarb. Turn into pastry-lined pie plate. Dot with margarine. Cover with top crust that has slits cut in it; seal and flute. Sprinkle with sugar if desired. Cover edge with 2- to 3-inch strip of aluminum foil to prevent excessive browning. Remove foil during last 15 minutes of baking.

Bake about 55 minutes or until crust is brown and juice begins to bubble through slits in crust.   8 SERVINGS; 505 CALORIES PER SERVING.

2 packages (16 ounces each) unsweetened frozen rhubarb, completely thawed and drained, can be substituted for the cut-up rhubarb.

STRAWBERRY-RHUBARB PIE: Substitute sliced strawberries for half of the rhubarb and use the lesser amount of sugar.   480 CALORIES PER SERVING.

PIES

Pies have become a uniquely American institution. Early settlers brought over recipes for "pyes" baked in long, deep dishes called "coffins." When times were tight in colonial days, frugal bakers rounded the corners of the coffin and made it shallow, so the pie would stretch further.

Early Americans ate pie for breakfast, pie for lunch and pie for dinner, using fruit and berries in the summer and nuts, dried fruits and root vegetables in the winter. Pies were kept in pie safes, wooden cabinets with pierced tin doors that let the pies cool but kept the flies off.

🌾 PEACH PIE

Make this southern favorite at summer's peak with juicy, ripe peaches.

9-Inch

Pastry for 9-inch Two-Crust Pie (page 88)
⅔ cup sugar
⅓ cup all-purpose flour
¼ teaspoon ground cinnamon
6 cups sliced fresh peaches (6 to 8 medium)*
1 teaspoon lemon juice
1 tablespoon margarine or butter

10-Inch

Pastry for 10-inch Two-Crust Pie (page 88)
1 cup sugar
½ cup all-purpose flour
¼ teaspoon ground cinnamon
8 cups sliced fresh peaches (8 to 10 medium)*
1 teaspoon lemon juice
2 tablespoons margarine or butter

Heat oven to 425°. Prepare pastry. Mix sugar, flour and cinnamon in large bowl. Stir in peaches and lemon juice. Turn into pastry-lined pie plate. Dot with margarine. Cover with top crust that has slits cut in it; seal and flute. Cover edge with 2- to 3-inch strip of aluminum foil to prevent excessive browning. Remove foil during last 15 minutes of baking.

Bake about 45 minutes or until crust is brown and juice begins to bubble through slits in crust. Serve with ice cream and Raspberry-Currant Sauce (page 162) if desired.   8 SERVINGS; 360 CALORIES EACH FOR 9-INCH PIE, 560 CALORIES EACH FOR 10-INCH PIE.

Frozen sliced peaches, partially thawed and drained, can be substituted for the fresh peaches.

APRICOT PIE: Prepare 9-inch pie as directed— except substitute 6 cups fresh apricot halves for the peaches.   375 CALORIES PER SERVING.

PEACH-APRICOT PIE: Prepare 9-inch pie as directed— except substitute ¾ cup packed brown sugar for the granulated sugar. Stir in ¼ cup apricot jam or preserves into peaches and lemon juice before stirring into flour mixture.   400 CALORIES PER SERVING.

Lemon Meringue Pie (page 97), Lemon-Berry Tart

LEMON-BERRY TART

Cookie Tart Pastry (page 89)
½ cup Lemon Curd (page 362) or prepared
   lemon curd
1 package (8 ounces) cream cheese, softened
2 cups berries or sliced fruit

Prepare and bake Cookie Tart Pastry. Beat Lemon Curd and cream cheese until smooth. Spread in crust. Refrigerate at least 1 hour. Arrange berries over lemon mixture just before serving. Sprinkle with powdered sugar if desired.   8 SERVINGS; 405 CALORIES PER SERVING.

 ## COCONUT CREAM PIE

9-inch Baked Pie Shell (page 88)
⅔ cup sugar
¼ cup cornstarch
½ teaspoon salt
3 cups milk
4 egg yolks, slightly beaten
2 tablespoons margarine or butter, softened
2 teaspoons vanilla
¾ cup flaked coconut
1 cup Sweetened Whipped Cream (page 162)
¼ cup flaked coconut

Prepare and bake pie shell. Mix sugar, cornstarch and salt in 2-quart saucepan. Gradually stir in milk. Cook over medium heat, stirring constantly, until mixture thickens and boils. Boil and stir 1 minute. Stir at least half of the hot mixture gradually into egg yolks. Stir into hot mixture in saucepan. Boil and stir 1 minute; remove from heat. Stir in margarine, vanilla and ¾ cup coconut. Pour into pie shell. Press plastic wrap onto filling. Refrigerate about 2 hours or until set.

Remove plastic wrap. Top pie with Sweetened Whipped Cream and ¼ cup coconut. Immediately refrigerate any remaining pie. 8 SERVINGS; 425 CALORIES PER SERVING.

BANANA CREAM PIE: Increase vanilla to 1 tablespoon plus 1 teaspoon. Omit coconut. Press plastic wrap onto filling in saucepan. Cool to room temperature. Slice 2 large bananas into pie shell. Pour filling over bananas. Refrigerate until serving time. Top pie with Sweetened Whipped Cream and garnish with banana slices. Immediately refrigerate any remaining pie.   415 CALORIES PER SERVING.

CHOCOLATE CREAM PIE: Increase sugar to 1½ cups and cornstarch to ⅓ cup. Omit margarine and coconut. Stir in 2 ounces unsweetened chocolate, cut up, after stirring in the milk. Top pie with Sweetened Whipped Cream. Immediately refrigerate any remaining pie.   480 CALORIES PER SERVING.

✻ STRAWBERRY GLACÉ PIE

9-inch Baked Pie Shell (page 88)
1½ quarts strawberries
1 cup sugar
3 tablespoons cornstarch
½ cup water
Few drops red food color, if desired
1 package (3 ounces) cream cheese, softened

Prepare and bake pie shell. Mash enough strawberries to measure 1 cup. Mix sugar and cornstarch in 2-quart saucepan. Gradually stir in water, food color and mashed strawberries. Cook over medium heat, stirring constantly, until mixture thickens and boils. Boil and stir 1 minute; cool.

Beat cream cheese until smooth. Spread in pie shell. Fill shell with remaining strawberries. Pour cooked strawberry mixture over top. Refrigerate about 3 hours or until set.   8 SERVINGS; 320 CALORIES PER SERVING.

PEACH GLACÉ PIE: Substitute 5 cups sliced fresh peaches (about 5 medium) for the strawberries. To prevent peaches from discoloring, use fruit protector as directed on package.   330 CALORIES PER SERVING.

RASPBERRY GLACÉ PIE: Substitute 1½ quarts raspberries for the strawberries.   330 CALORIES PER SERVING.

Strawberry Glacé Pie

MERINGUE BASICS

Meringue can be used to make high, soft, melt-in-your-mouth toppings for pies and tarts. Or it can be used to make a hard, crisp crust to hold your favorite filling. The basic difference between the two is the proportion of sugar to egg whites. The following guidelines will ensure success.

SUCCESS TIPS

♦ Separate eggs very carefully while cold. Make certain no yolk gets into the whites, since even a little bit of yolk or grease will prevent whites from beating properly.

♦ Gradually beat in sugar, about 1 tablespoon at a time. Continue beating until mixture stands in stiff peaks when beaters are lifted. (Meringue should feel smooth, not gritty, when rubbed between your fingers.)

♦ Humidity or rain may cause the sugar to absorb moisture from the air, resulting in a meringue with a sticky, spongy texture. Drops of sugar syrup may form on the surface of the meringue (beading).

♦ Spread soft meringue over hot filling, sealing the meringue right up to the crust all the way around. This prevents shrinking and weeping (the liquid that oozes out of a meringue topping). Swirl or pull meringue up into points for a fluffier look.

♦ A hard meringue shell should be thoroughly dry when properly baked. Underbaking can result in a gummy, limp texture, which makes it difficult to remove from the pie plate.

♦ To dry and crisp the meringue pie shell, cool it in the oven, after it is turned off, for the same amount of time as the bake time.

♦ Cool baked meringue gradually, away from drafts to prevent shrinking.

✻ MERINGUE

3 egg whites
¼ teaspoon cream of tartar
6 tablespoons granulated or packed brown sugar
½ teaspoon vanilla

Beat egg whites and cream of tartar in medium bowl until foamy. Beat in sugar, 1 tablespoon at a time; continue beating until stiff and glossy. Do not underbeat. Beat in vanilla. Tops a 9-inch pie.   8 SERVINGS; 40 CALORIES EACH FOR 9-INCH PIE.

LEMON MERINGUE PIE

9-inch Baked Pie Shell (page 88)
1½ cups sugar
⅓ cup plus 1 tablespoon cornstarch
1½ cups water
3 egg yolks, slightly beaten
3 tablespoons margarine or butter
2 teaspoons grated lemon peel
½ cup lemon juice
2 drops yellow food color, if desired
Meringue (page 96)

Prepare and bake pie shell. Heat oven to 400°. Mix sugar and cornstarch in 2-quart saucepan. Gradually stir in water. Cook over medium heat, stirring constantly, until mixture thickens and boils. Boil and stir 1 minute. Gradually stir at least half of the hot mixture into egg yolks. Stir into hot mixture in saucepan. Boil and stir 1 minute; remove from heat. Stir in margarine, lemon peel, lemon juice and food color. Pour into pie shell.

Prepare Meringue. Spoon onto hot pie filling. Spread over filling, carefully sealing meringue to edge of crust to prevent shrinking or weeping. Bake 8 to 12 minutes or until meringue is delicate brown. Cool away from draft. Immediately refrigerate any remaining pie. 8 SERVINGS; 410 CALORIES PER SERVING.

 CUSTARD PIE

Pastry for 9-inch One-Crust Pie (page 88)
    or Pat-in-the-Pan Oil Pastry (page 86)
4 eggs
2⅔ cups milk
½ cup sugar
1 teaspoon vanilla
½ teaspoon salt
¼ teaspoon ground nutmeg

Place oven rack in lowest position. Heat oven to 450°. Prepare pastry. Beat eggs slightly with hand beater or wire whisk in medium bowl. Beat in remaining ingredients. To prevent spilling, place pastry-lined pie plate on oven rack. Pour filling into pie plate. Bake 20 minutes.

Reduce oven temperature to 350°. Bake 10 to 15 minutes longer or until knife inserted halfway between center and edge comes out clean. Refrigerate about 4 hours or until chilled. Immediately refrigerate any remaining pie. 8 SERVINGS; 270 CALORIES PER SERVING.

 PUMPKIN PIE

9-Inch

Pastry for 9-inch One-Crust Pie (page 88)
2 eggs
½ cup sugar
1 can (16 ounces) pumpkin
1 can (12 ounces) evaporated milk
1 teaspoon ground cinnamon
½ teaspoon salt
½ teaspoon ground ginger
⅛ teaspoon ground cloves

10-Inch

Pastry for 10-inch One-Crust Pie (page 88)
3 eggs
1 cup sugar
2¾ cups canned pumpkin
2¼ cups evaporated milk
1½ teaspoons ground cinnamon
¾ teaspoon salt
¾ teaspoon ground ginger
½ teaspoon ground cloves

Heat oven to 425°. Prepare pastry. Beat eggs slightly with hand beater or wire whisk in medium bowl. Beat in remaining ingredients. To prevent spilling, place pastry-lined pie plate on oven rack. Pour filling into pie plate. Bake 15 minutes.

Reduce oven temperature to 350°. Bake 9-inch pie about 45 minutes longer, 10-inch pie about 55 minutes longer or until knife inserted in center comes out clean. Refrigerate about 4 hours or until chilled. Serve with Sweetened Whipped Cream (page 162) if desired. Immediately refrigerate any remaining pie. 8 SERVINGS; 285 CALORIES EACH FOR 9-INCH PIE, 430 CALORIES EACH FOR 10-INCH PIE.

 PECAN PIE

Pastry for 9-inch One-Crust Pie (page 88)
⅔ cup sugar
⅓ cup margarine or butter, melted
1 cup corn syrup
½ teaspoon salt
3 eggs
1 cup pecan halves or broken pieces

Heat oven to 375°. Prepare pastry. Beat sugar, margarine, corn syrup, salt and eggs with hand beater in medium bowl. Stir in pecans. Pour into pastry-lined pie plate.

Bake 40 to 50 minutes or until set. 8 SERVINGS; 515 CALORIES PER SERVING.

CARAMEL-CHOCOLATE PIE SUPREME

Cookie Crumb Crust (page 87)
30 vanilla caramels
2 tablespoons margarine or butter
2 tablespoons water
½ cup chopped pecans, toasted
2 packages (3 ounces each) cream cheese, softened
⅓ cup powdered sugar
1 bar (4 ounces) sweet cooking chocolate
3 tablespoons hot water
1 teaspoon vanilla
2 cups whipping (heavy) cream
2 tablespoons powdered sugar

Prepare and bake Cookie Crumb Crust as directed using pecan shortbread cookies. Heat caramels, margarine and 2 tablespoons water over medium heat, stirring frequently, until caramels are melted. Pour into crust. Sprinkle with pecans. Refrigerate about 1 hour until chilled. Beat cream cheese and ⅓ cup powdered sugar until smooth. Spread over caramel layer; refrigerate.

Heat chocolate and 3 tablespoons hot water over low heat, stirring constantly, until chocolate is melted. Cool to room temperature. Stir in vanilla. Beat whipping cream and 2 tablespoons powdered sugar in chilled medium bowl until stiff. Reserve 1½ cups. Fold chocolate mixture into remaining whipped cream. Spread over cream cheese mixture. Top with reserved whipped cream. Garnish with chocolate curls if desired. Refrigerate pie at least 1 hour or until firm. Refrigerate any remaining pie.   12 SERVINGS; 455 CALORIES PER SERVING.

 # GRASSHOPPER PIE

Cookie Crumb Crust (page 87)
½ cup milk
32 large jet-puffed marshmallows
¼ cup crème de menthe
3 tablespoons white crème de cacao
1½ cups chilled whipping (heavy) cream
Few drops green food color, if desired

Prepare and bake Cookie Crumb Crust as directed using chocolate wafer cookies. Heat milk and marshmallows in 3-quart saucepan over low heat, stirring constantly, just until marshmallows are melted. Refrigerate about 20 minutes, stirring occasionally, until mixture mounds slightly when dropped from a spoon. (If mixture becomes too thick, place saucepan in bowl of warm water; stir mixture until of proper consistency.) Gradually stir in liqueurs.

Beat whipping cream in chilled medium bowl until stiff. Fold marshmallow mixture into whipped cream. Fold in food color. Pour into crust. Sprinkle with grated semisweet chocolate if desired. Refrigerate about 4 hours or until set.   8 SERVINGS; 385 CALORIES PER SERVING.

Caramel-Chocolate Pie Supreme

ALEXANDER PIE: Substitute dark crème de cacao for the crème de menthe and brandy for the white crème de cacao.   385 CALORIES PER SERVING.

CHERRY CORDIAL PIE: Substitute ½ cup kirsch for the crème de menthe and crème de cacao. Fold few drops red food color into marshmallow–whipped cream mixture if desired.   385 CALORIES PER SERVING.

COFFEE CORDIAL PIE: Substitute water for the milk and add 1 tablespoon instant coffee with the water. Substitute coffee liqueur for the crème de menthe and Irish whiskey for the crème de cacao.   380 CALORIES PER SERVING.

IMPOSSIBLE BROWNIE PIE

Make this pie elegant by serving on a pool of Raspberry-Currant Sauce (page 162) and top with Sweetened Whipped Cream (page 162). It is a child's delight topped with ice cream and Hot Fudge Sauce (page 161).

4 eggs
¼ cup margarine or butter, melted
1 bar (4 ounces) sweet cooking chocolate, melted and cooled
½ cup packed brown sugar
½ cup variety baking mix
½ cup granulated sugar
¾ cup chopped nuts

Heat oven to 350°. Grease pie plate, 9 × 1¼ inches. Beat eggs, margarine and chocolate in medium bowl with hand beater or place in blender or food processor. Beat 30 seconds with hand beater, or cover and blend or process on high speed 10 seconds or until smooth. Add brown sugar, baking mix and granulated sugar. Beat 2 minutes or blend 1 minute on high speed, stopping blender occasionally to scrape sides. Pour into pie plate. Sprinkle with nuts.

Bake about 35 minutes or until knife inserted in center comes out clean. Cool. Serve with ice cream or Sweetened Whipped Cream (page 162) if desired.   8 SERVINGS; 365 CALORIES PER SERVING.

Individual Cream Cheese–Fruit Tarts

INDIVIDUAL CREAM CHEESE–FRUIT TARTS

1 cup variety baking mix
2 tablespoons sugar
1 tablespoon margarine or butter, softened
2 packages (3 ounces each) cream cheese, softened
¼ cup sugar
¼ cup sour cream
1½ cups assorted fresh fruit (raspberries, strawberries, blueberries, grapes or apricot, peach, plum or fig slices)
⅓ cup apple jelly, melted

Heat oven to 375°. Mix baking mix, 2 tablespoons sugar, the margarine and 1 package cream cheese in small bowl until dough forms a ball. Divide into 6 pieces. Press each piece in tart pan, 4¼ × 1 inch, or 10-ounce custard cup (press on bottom and ¾ inch up side). Place on cookie sheet. Bake 10 to 12 minutes or until light brown; cool.

Beat remaining package cream cheese, ¼ cup sugar and the sour cream until smooth. Spoon into tart shells, spreading over bottoms. Top each with about ¼ cup fruit. Brush with jelly.   6 SERVINGS; 325 CALORIES PER SERVING.

FIX-IT-FAST

◆ For a fast dessert using leftover cake, cube or coarsely crumble cake. Layer with fresh fruit, pudding, ice cream and/or whipped cream.

◆ Mix crumbled cake with pudding and serve in ice-cream cones—great for kids.

◆ To make your favorite two-layer cake a little different, fold ½ cup mini chips, coconut, chopped nuts or fruit into batter, or stir in ½ to 1 teaspoon ground spices such as cinnamon or nutmeg.

◆ Change your favorite chocolate cake mix from "ho-hum" to "elegant." Bake cake in 13 × 9 × 2-inch pan, and while cake is hot, insert wooden spoon handle into cake at 1-inch intervals. Soften ¾ cup raspberry or apricot jam by stirring and spread over cake. Cool, then frost with ready-to-spread frosting or whipped cream.

◆ Brush pound cake or angel food cake slices with melted margarine or butter. Roll in coconut or nuts and brown both sides under broiler.

◆ Cut pound cake or sponge cake into fingers. Dip into a glaze, then roll in nuts, coconut, chocolate shot, granola, cereal or chopped candy or cookies.

◆ Make a plain cake fancy by placing a doily on the top and dusting with powdered sugar or cocoa.

◆ Can't wait for the cake to cool? Serve it warm in bowls. Top with ice cream, whipped cream, fruit, liqueur, sour cream, yogurt, crème fraîche or your favorite sauce or pudding.

◆ For a quick torte, bake cake in a 15½ × 10½ × 1-inch jelly roll pan. Cut crosswise into thirds; fill and frost.

◆ Heat ready-to-spread or leftover frosting in the microwave for a fast glaze.

◆ Use a food processor to slice, chop or shred fruits and vegetables quickly for pies and cakes.

◆ Use refrigerator cookie dough to make individual tarts.

◆ Keep pie crust mix on hand or use refrigerated or frozen pie crusts to speed pie baking.

◆ When baking a pie, make two at a time and freeze one for future use.

◆ Use a food processor to make pastry dough or to crush cookie crumbs.

◆ For a free-form and fast fruit pie, roll pastry 4 inches larger than pie plate. Place pastry in plate and fill with fruit filling. Rather than fluting crust, just fold pastry over the fruit toward the center (center will be open). Pleat the top if necessary and bake as directed.

NUTRITION INFORMATION

PER SERVING OR UNIT — RECIPE, PAGE	Servings per recipe	Calories	Protein (grams)	Carbohydrate (grams)	Fat (grams)	Cholesterol (milligrams)	Sodium (milligrams)	Protein	Vitamin A	Vitamin C	Thiamine	Riboflavin	Niacin	Calcium	Iron
CAKES															
Angel Food Cake, 80	16	130	3	29	0	0	80	4	0	0	0	2	0	0	0
Apple Butter Cake Roll, 81	10	320	4	39	17	115	125	6	8	0	6	6	2	6	4
Apple Cake, 76	16	325	4	35	20	50	150	6	0	0	8	4	4	0	4
Applesauce Snack Cake, 78	9	390	3	57	17	5	320	4	4	0	8	4	6	4	10
Applesauce-Spice Cake, 77	16	445	5	71	17	60	340	6	6	0	6	8	4	10	8
Apricot-Prune Upside-down Cake, 79	9	380	4	63	14	30	270	4	16	0	6	6	6	8	8
Best Chocolate Cake, 68	16	250	3	38	11	35	240	4	0	0	4	4	4	2	4

The Percent U.S. Recommended Daily Allowance columns are: Protein, Vitamin A, Vitamin C, Thiamine, Riboflavin, Niacin, Calcium, Iron.

PER SERVING OR UNIT

NUTRITION INFORMATION

RECIPE, PAGE

PERCENT U.S. RECOMMENDED DAILY ALLOWANCE

CAKES (continued)

Recipe, Page	Servings per recipe	Calories	Protein (grams)	Carbohydrate (grams)	Fat (grams)	Cholesterol (milligrams)	Sodium (milligrams)	Protein	Vitamin A	Vitamin C	Thiamine	Riboflavin	Niacin	Calcium	Iron
Black Midnight Cake, 71	16	245	3	34	11	35	240	4	0	0	4	4	4	0	6
Brown Sugar Pound Cake, 71	24	270	3	33	14	60	180	4	8	0	8	6	4	4	8
Caramel Pecan Cake, 71	24	255	3	33	13	55	135	4	4	0	6	4	4	4	8
Carrot Cake, 76	16	315	4	33	20	50	160	6	100	0	8	4	6	2	4
Cherry-Nut Cake, 72	16	250	4	35	11	0	250	6	0	0	6	6	4	8	2
Chocolate Angel Food Cake, 80	16	130	3	29	0	0	80	4	0	0	0	4	0	0	0
Chocolate Chip Cake, 72	16	250	3	37	10	0	250	4	0	0	4	6	4	6	2
Chocolate Chip–Date Cake, 78	9	355	4	44	18	30	200	6	0	0	8	4	6	2	8
Chocolate Ice-Cream Roll, 81	10	230	5	39	6	125	150	6	4	0	4	10	2	8	4
Chocolate-Walnut Snack Cake, 68	9	295	3	45	12	0	250	4	0	0	6	4	6	2	8
Cinnamon Chiffon Cake, 82	16	220	4	30	10	105	250	6	0	0	4	6	4	6	6
Coconut Angel Food Cake, 80	16	150	3	31	1	0	90	4	0	0	0	2	0	0	0
Cookie–Sour Cream Cake, 74	8	350	4	40	20	70	250	4	14	0	4	6	4	4	4
Decadent Chocolate Cake with Raspberry Sauce, 70	12	325	4	39	18	90	140	6	8	2	2	4	2	2	8
Double Chocolate Snack Cake, 68	9	300	3	47	11	0	250	4	0	0	2	4	6	2	10
Eggnog Cake, 73	16	210	3	32	8	55	280	4	4	0	4	6	4	8	2
German Chocolate Cake, 69	16	525	6	60	30	115	470	8	16	0	6	8	0	8	4
Gingerbread, 77	9	555	4	95	19	35	410	6	4	0	10	10	10	16	26
Jelly Roll, 81	10	205	3	45	2	80	120	4	0	0	2	4	2	2	4
Jeweled Fruitcake, 79	32	155	2	25	6	25	50	2	18	0	6	2	2	2	4
Lemon Cake Roll, 81	10	220	3	47	3	80	185	4	2	0	2	4	2	2	2
Lemon Chiffon Cake, 82	16	220	4	29	10	105	250	6	0	0	4	6	2	4	4
Lemon-filled White Cake, 72	16	310	4	54	9	0	310	4	0	0	4	6	4	8	4
Lemon-filled Yellow Cake, 73	16	295	4	52	8	55	340	6	4	0	4	6	4	8	4
Lemon–Poppy Seed Cake, 76	9	210	3	34	7	0	245	4	0	0	6	2	6	2	4
Lemon Pound Cake, 71	24	245	3	34	11	60	170	4	8	0	4	4	2	2	2
Maple-Nut Chiffon Cake, 82	16	225	4	30	9	105	250	6	0	0	4	6	4	6	6
Maple-Nut Snack Cake, 68	9	275	3	41	12	0	250	4	0	0	6	4	6	2	8
Marble Cake, 73	16	230	4	33	9	55	300	6	4	0	4	6	4	8	4
Oatmeal-Molasses Snack Cake, 68	9	305	3	55	9	0	260	4	0	0	10	4	6	4	12

NUTRITION INFORMATION

PER SERVING OR UNIT

RECIPE, PAGE	Servings per recipe	Calories	Protein (grams)	Carbohydrate (grams)	Fat (grams)	Cholesterol (milligrams)	Sodium (milligrams)	Protein	Vitamin A	Vitamin C	Thiamine	Riboflavin	Niacin	Calcium	Iron
CAKES (continued)															
Old-fashioned Spice Cake, 77	16	435	4	68	17	60	340	6	6	0	6	8	4	10	8
Orange Chiffon Cake, 82	16	220	4	29	10	105	250	6	0	0	4	6	2	4	4
Orange-Coconut Pound Cake, 71	24	260	3	35	12	60	180	4	8	0	4	4	2	2	4
Peanut Cake, 73	16	235	5	32	10	55	280	6	4	0	6	6	8	8	4
Pineapple Upside-down Cake, 79	9	360	3	58	14	30	270	4	4	2	6	6	4	8	6
Pound Cake, 71	24	245	3	34	11	60	170	4	8	0	4	4	2	2	2
Pumpkin Snack Cake, 68	9	255	2	44	8	0	280	2	24	0	6	4	6	2	8
Rhubarb Cake, 76	16	240	4	28	13	50	240	6	0	0	8	4	4	4	4
Silver White Cake, 72	16	225	3	33	9	0	250	4	0	0	4	4	4	6	2
Silver White Cupcakes, 72	30	120	2	18	5	0	135	2	0	0	2	2	2	4	0
Silver White Sheet Cake, 72	24	150	2	22	6	0	170	2	0	0	2	2	2	4	0
Starlight Yellow Cake, 73	16	205	3	32	8	55	280	4	4	0	4	6	4	8	2
Starlight Yellow Cupcakes, 73	36	90	1	14	3	25	125	2	0	0	2	2	0	2	0
Toasted Almond Pound Cake, 71	24	290	5	35	15	60	170	6	8	0	6	8	4	4	4
Toasted Hazelnut Cake, 74	16	240	3	33	11	35	340	4	2	0	6	4	4	4	2
Tri-Color Jelly Roll, 81	10	170	3	37	2	80	120	4	0	0	2	4	2	2	2
White Chocolate Chip Cake, 73	8	340	5	48	14	70	200	6	0	0	6	6	4	4	8
Whole Wheat–Chocolate Cake, 68	16	250	3	38	11	35	240	4	0	0	4	4	4	2	6
Wild Rice–Nut Cake, 75	24	340	5	36	20	60	210	6	10	0	8	6	6	6	8
Zucchini-Spice Cake, 76	16	240	4	29	13	50	240	6	4	0	8	4	6	2	6
FROSTINGS															
Browned Butter Frosting, 84	16	125	0	24	4	10	40	0	2	0	0	0	0	0	0
Butter-Rum Glaze, 85	16	100	0	16	4	0	45	0	2	0	0	0	0	0	0
Caramel Frosting, 85	16	165	0	30	6	0	75	0	4	0	0	0	0	0	2
Cherry Frosting, 84	16	130	0	25	4	0	45	0	2	0	0	0	0	0	0
Cherry-Nut Frosting, 84	16	60	1	12	1	0	10	0	0	0	0	0	0	0	0
Chocolate Frosting, 85	16	115	0	17	6	0	45	0	2	0	0	0	0	0	0
Chocolate Glaze, 85	16	50	0	5	3	0	20	0	0	0	0	0	0	0	0
Chocolate Revel Frosting, 84	16	70	1	13	2	0	10	0	0	0	0	0	0	0	2
Citrus Frosting, 84	16	125	0	24	4	0	45	0	2	0	0	0	0	0	0
Coffee Frosting, 84	16	45	0	11	0	0	15	0	0	0	0	0	0	0	2
Cream Cheese Frosting, 84	16	175	1	32	5	15	45	0	4	0	0	0	0	0	0

NUTRITION INFORMATION

PERCENT U.S. RECOMMENDED DAILY ALLOWANCE

RECIPE, PAGE

	Servings per recipe	Calories	Protein (grams)	Carbohydrate (grams)	Fat (grams)	Cholesterol (milligrams)	Sodium (milligrams)	Protein	Vitamin A	Vitamin C	Thiamine	Riboflavin	Niacin	Calcium	Iron
FROSTINGS (*continued*)															
Creamy Cocoa Frosting, 85	16	105	0	17	4	0	45	0	2	0	0	0	0	0	0
Creamy Vanilla Frosting, 84	16	130	0	24	4	0	45	0	2	0	0	0	0	0	0
Fudge Frosting, 85	8	130	0	25	3	0	75	0	2	0	0	0	0	0	0
Lemon Glaze, 85	16	95	0	16	4	0	45	0	2	0	0	0	0	0	0
Maple-Nut Frosting, 84	16	165	0	32	5	0	60	0	2	0	0	0	0	0	0
Mocha Frosting, 85	16	115	0	17	6	0	45	0	2	0	0	0	0	0	0
Orange Glaze, 85	16	95	0	16	4	0	45	0	2	2	0	0	0	0	0
Peanut Butter Frosting, 84	16	125	1	25	3	0	30	2	0	0	0	0	2	0	0
Peppermint Frosting, 84	16	50	0	12	0	0	10	0	0	0	0	0	0	0	0
Satiny Beige Frosting, 84	16	45	0	11	0	0	15	0	0	0	0	0	0	0	2
Vanilla Glaze, 85	16	95	0	16	4	0	45	0	2	0	0	0	0	0	0
White Mountain Frosting, 84	16	40	0	10	0	0	10	0	0	0	0	0	0	0	0
PIES															
Alexander Pie, 99	8	385	3	33	25	80	170	4	18	0	2	6	2	4	4
Apple Deep-Dish Pie, 90	12	275	2	51	8	0	105	2	2	4	6	2	4	0	2
Apple Dumplings, 91	6	600	5	92	25	0	430	6	4	4	14	6	10	2	14
Apple Pie, 9-Inch, 90	8	395	3	59	17	0	340	4	2	4	10	4	8	0	6
Apple Pie, 10-Inch, 90	8	580	5	76	30	0	630	6	4	6	14	6	12	2	6
Apricot Pie, 94	8	375	4	57	15	0	295	6	42	4	10	6	10	2	6
Baked Tart Shells, 89	8	140	1	11	10	0	70	2	0	0	4	2	2	0	2
Banana Cream Pie, 95	8	415	6	45	23	145	300	10	12	2	8	14	4	12	6
Blackberry Pie, 93	6	415	4	65	16	0	290	6	4	18	12	8	10	4	8
Blueberry Pie, 9-Inch, 93	8	395	4	61	16	0	300	6	2	12	14	8	10	0	6
Blueberry Pie, 10-Inch, 93	8	590	6	80	29	0	320	8	4	16	18	10	14	0	8
Brown Sugar Pear Tart, 91	8	400	3	57	19	0	185	4	12	4	10	6	6	4	10
Caramel-Chocolate Pie Supreme, 98	12	455	3	36	32	70	105	4	18	0	2	4	0	4	2
Cherry Cordial Pie, 99	8	385	3	33	25	80	170	4	18	0	2	6	2	4	4
Cherry Pie, 9-Inch, 93	8	505	4	86	17	0	315	6	18	0	12	8	10	2	14
Cherry Pie, 10-Inch, 93	8	735	6	115	30	0	335	8	24	2	16	10	12	2	18
Chocolate Cream Pie, 95	8	480	7	61	24	145	260	10	8	0	6	14	4	14	8
Coconut Cream Pie, 95	8	425	6	42	26	145	320	10	10	0	6	14	4	12	6
Coffee Cordial Pie, 99	8	380	2	32	24	75	165	2	16	0	2	4	2	2	4

NUTRITION INFORMATION

PER SERVING OR UNIT

RECIPE, PAGE

	Servings per recipe	Calories	Protein (grams)	Carbohydrate (grams)	Fat (grams)	Cholesterol (milligrams)	Sodium (milligrams)	PERCENT U.S. RECOMMENDED DAILY ALLOWANCE							
								Protein	Vitamin A	Vitamin C	Thiamine	Riboflavin	Niacin	Calcium	Iron

PIES (continued)

RECIPE, PAGE	Servings	Cal	Prot	Carb	Fat	Chol	Sod	Prot	Vit A	Vit C	Thia	Ribo	Niac	Calc	Iron
Cookie Tart Pastry, 89	8	250	3	23	16	35	190	4	12	0	6	4	4	0	4
Cranberry-Apple Pie, 91	8	445	4	67	19	0	290	6	0	4	12	6	8	2	6
Cranberry-Peach Pie, 91	8	425	5	62	19	0	290	6	8	4	12	6	12	2	6
Custard Pie, 97	8	270	7	27	15	145	280	10	4	0	6	14	4	10	4
Dutch Apple Pie, 90	8	415	4	50	23	20	350	6	8	4	10	6	8	2	6
French Apple Pie, 90	8	460	4	64	22	0	240	4	10	4	10	6	8	2	8
Grasshopper Pie, 98	8	385	3	33	25	80	170	4	18	0	2	6	2	4	4
Impossible Brownie Pie, 99	8	365	6	41	21	135	190	8	6	0	8	8	4	4	10
Individual Cream Cheese–Fruit Tarts, 99	6	325	4	42	17	35	350	6	10	10	8	10	4	6	6
Lemon-Berry Tart, 95	8	405	6	34	28	90	290	8	22	16	8	10	6	4	8
Lemon Meringue Pie, 97	8	410	4	63	17	105	150	6	4	4	4	4	4	0	4
Meringue, 96	8	40	1	9	0	0	25	0	0	0	0	0	0	0	0
One-Crust Pie, 9-Inch, 88	8	140	1	11	10	0	70	2	0	0	4	2	2	0	2
One-Crust Pie, 10-Inch, 88	8	180	2	15	13	0	135	2	0	0	4	2	4	0	2
Orange-glazed Lattice Cherry Pie, 93	8	475	4	79	17	0	310	6	8	2	10	6	8	0	8
Pat-in-the-Pan Oil Pastry, 86	8	150	2	15	9	0	135	2	0	0	4	2	4	0	2
Peach-Apricot Pie, 94	8	400	4	64	15	0	296	6	10	4	10	6	12	2	10
Peach Glacé Pie, 96	8	330	3	50	14	10	100	4	14	10	4	4	8	0	2
Peach Pie, 9-Inch, 94	8	360	4	52	15	0	290	6	10	4	10	6	12	0	6
Peach Pie 10-Inch, 94	8	560	6	73	28	0	310	8	16	6	14	10	18	0	8
Pecan Pie, 97	8	515	5	60	30	105	350	6	8	0	12	6	4	4	14
Plum Pie, 93	8	425	5	68	16	0	290	6	8	10	12	12	12	0	6
Pumpkin Pie, 9-Inch, 97	8	285	6	32	15	80	270	10	100	2	6	12	4	14	8
Pumpkin Pie 10-Inch, 97	8	430	10	53	20	125	450	14	100	4	8	20	6	22	12
Raspberry Glacé Pie, 96	8	330	3	48	15	10	100	4	4	18	6	8	4	2	6
Rhubarb Pie, 94	8	505	5	89	16	0	290	6	2	6	12	6	10	8	6
Strawberry Glacé Pie, 96	8	320	3	47	15	10	100	4	2	100	4	8	4	2	4
Strawberry-Rhubarb Pie, 94	8	480	5	83	16	0	290	6	2	28	12	8	10	4	8
Two-Crust Pie, 9-Inch, 88	8	225	3	22	14	0	275	4	0	0	8	4	6	0	4
Two-Crust Pie, 10-Inch, 88	8	360	4	29	25	0	275	6	0	0	10	4	10	0	6

COOKIES & CANDY

One of the greatest disappointments is to open the cookie jar and find it empty! The luscious recipes in this chapter fit all the roles that cookies play, and are so enticing they'll ensure that the cookie jar doesn't stay empty for long. Whether it's filled with classic Chocolate Chip Cookies (page 107) or cosmopolitan Pizzelles (page 111) your cookie jar will provide good cheer for anyone who lifts the lid.

COOKIE BASICS

COOKIE SHEETS

♦ Use a shiny cookie sheet at least 2 inches narrower and shorter than the oven. The sheet may be open on one to three sides.

♦ If a sheet with a nonstick coating is used, watch carefully—cookies may brown quickly. Follow manufacturers' directions as many suggest reducing the oven temperature by 25°.

♦ Grease the cookie sheet only if specified.

♦ If cookie sheets are thin, consider using two cookie sheets (one on top of the other) for insulation. If cookie sheets are too thin, cookies can bake too rapidly and burn on the bottom.

BAKING

♦ To ensure uniform baking, make cookies the same size and thickness.

♦ Always use a cool cookie sheet. A hot cookie sheet causes dough to soften and spread.

♦ Bake one sheet of cookies at a time on the center rack. Check for doneness at the minimum baking time—just one minute can make a difference.

♦ Unless the recipe states otherwise, remove cookies immediately from the sheet with a wide spatula and place on a wire rack to cool. Cool completely before frosting or storing.

STORING

♦ Store crisp, thin cookies in a container with a loose-fitting cover to keep them crisp. If they soften, recrisp by placing on cookie sheet and warming in a 300° oven for 3 to 5 minutes.

Preceding page, clockwise from left: Chocolate Chip Cookies (page 107), Peachy Pinwheels (page 120–121), Sugar Cookies (page 121), Deluxe Brownies (page 112)

♦ Store unfrosted soft cookies in an airtight container to preserve their moistness. A piece of bread or apple in the container will help keep them soft. Check the bread or apple periodically and change when it gets old.

♦ Store frosted soft cookies in a single layer in an airtight container so the frosting will maintain its shape and the cookies will retain their moistness.

DROP COOKIES

♦ Use two teaspoons (not measuring spoons) to drop dough onto cookie sheet.

♦ If edges are dark and crusty, cookies were overbaked. The problem was a cookie sheet too large for the oven or the use of a dark cookie sheet. If center of cookie is doughy, it was underbaked.

♦ Drop dough about 2 inches apart onto cookie sheet to prevent cookies from baking together when dough spreads.

♦ Excess spreading may be caused by dough being too warm, cookie sheet too hot or oven temperature incorrect. Chill soft doughs. Also, let cookie sheet cool between bakings.

BAR COOKIES

♦ Use the size pan specified in the recipe. Cookies made in a larger pan will be dry and overbaked; in a smaller pan, underbaked.

♦ Cut into bars, squares or triangles when completely cool unless recipe specifies cutting while warm. This helps prevent the bars from crumbling.

MOLDED COOKIES

♦ Rich, soft dough must be chilled before shaping. Work with a small amount at a time, keeping remaining dough refrigerated.

◆ If dough is too soft after chilling, mix in 1 to 2 tablespoons flour. If dough is too dry and crumbly, work in 1 to 2 tablespoons milk, water or softened margarine or butter.

◆ Take time to mold fancy shapes (crescents, candy canes, wreaths, bells) so that cookies are uniform in shape and size. This helps them bake evenly.

REFRIGERATOR COOKIES

◆ Shape dough firmly into a long, smooth roll of the diameter specified in the recipe. Wrap rolled dough in waxed paper, plastic wrap or aluminum foil, twisting ends to seal.

◆ Chill rolled dough until firm enough to slice easily. Use a thin, sharp knife to slice dough.

◆ Rolls of dough can be refrigerated several weeks or frozen in moistureproof and vaporproof wrapping up to twelve months.

ROLLED COOKIES

◆ To prevent dough from sticking, sprinkle surface with flour and rub flour onto rolling pin. Use only enough flour to prevent dough from sticking during rolling. Too much flour and rerolling the dough results in dry, tough cookies.

◆ Roll only part of the chilled dough at a time and keep the remainder refrigerated.

◆ To ensure even baking, roll dough evenly to uniform thickness.

◆ Dip cookie cutter into flour; shake off excess.

PRESSED COOKIES

◆ Test dough for consistency before adding all the flour. Put a small amount of dough in cookie press; squeeze out. Dough should be soft and pliable but not crumbly. If dough seems too stiff, add 1 egg yolk; if too soft, add 1 to 2 tablespoons flour.

◆ Chill dough only if specified in the recipe.

◆ To make pressed cookies, hold cookie press so that it rests on cookie sheet. Raise press from cookie sheet after enough dough has been released to form a cookie.

CHOCOLATE CHIP COOKIES

¾ cup granulated sugar
¾ cup packed brown sugar
1 cup margarine or butter, softened
1 egg
2¼ cups all-purpose flour*
1 teaspoon baking soda
½ teaspoon salt
1 cup coarsely chopped nuts
1 package (12 ounces) semisweet chocolate chips

Heat oven to 375°. Mix sugars, margarine and egg. Stir in flour, baking soda and salt (dough will be stiff). Stir in nuts and chocolate chips. Drop dough by rounded teaspoonfuls about 2 inches apart onto ungreased cookie sheet. Bake 8 to 10 minutes or until light brown. (Centers will be soft.) Cool slightly; remove from cookie sheet. ABOUT 6 DOZEN COOKIES; 90 CALORIES PER COOKIE.

*If using self-rising flour, omit baking soda and salt.

CHOCOLATE CHIP BARS: Press dough in ungreased jelly roll pan, 15½ × 10½ × 1 inch. Bake 15 to 20 minutes or until brown; cool. Cut into 2½ × 1½-inch bars. 48 BARS; 135 CALORIES PER BAR.

JUMBO CHOCOLATE CHIP COOKIES: Drop dough by ¼ cupfuls about 3 inches apart onto ungreased cookie sheet. Bake 12 to 15 minutes or until edges are set. Cool completely; remove from cookie sheet. ABOUT 1½ DOZEN COOKIES; 360 CALORIES PER COOKIE.

CHOCOLATE CHIP COOKIES

The ingenuity of Ruth Wakefield led to the creation of the all-time favorite—the chocolate chip cookie. In 1940 at the Tollhouse Inn in Whitman, Massachusetts, she chopped up a leftover bar of chocolate and added it to her butter cookie dough. A diner, delighted with the cookies, described them to a friend at a Boston newspaper, and the cookies became locally famous. Later that same year the cookies made news from coast to coast on the Betty Crocker radio series "Famous Foods from Famous Places," and the entire country began a love affair with the chocolate chip cookie.

CHOCOLATE DROP COOKIES

1 cup sugar
½ cup margarine or butter, softened
1 egg
2 ounces unsweetened chocolate, melted
   and cooled
⅓ cup buttermilk, milk or water
1 teaspoon vanilla
1¾ cups all-purpose* or whole wheat flour
½ teaspoon baking soda
½ teaspoon salt
1 cup chopped nuts, if desired
Chocolate Frosting (below)

Heat oven to 400°. Mix sugar, margarine, egg, chocolate, buttermilk and vanilla. Stir in flour, baking soda, salt and nuts. Drop dough by rounded teaspoonfuls about 2 inches apart onto ungreased cookie sheet. Bake 8 to 10 minutes or until almost no indentation remains when touched; cool. Frost with Chocolate Frosting.   ABOUT 4½ DOZEN COOKIES; 95 CALORIES PER COOKIE.

Chocolate Frosting

2 ounces unsweetened chocolate
2 tablespoons margarine or butter
3 tablespoons water
About 2 cups powdered sugar

Heat chocolate and margarine over low heat until melted; remove from heat. Stir in water and powdered sugar until smooth.

If using self-rising flour, omit baking soda and salt.

CHOCOLATE-CHERRY DROP COOKIES: Omit nuts. Stir in 2 cups cut-up candied or maraschino cherries.   95 CALORIES PER COOKIE.

COCOA DROP COOKIES: Increase margarine to ⅔ cup. Omit chocolate. Stir in ½ cup cocoa.   95 CALORIES PER COOKIE.

DOUBLE CHOCOLATE DROP COOKIES: Stir in 1 package (6 ounces) semisweet chocolate chips. 110 CALORIES PER COOKIE.

OATMEAL COOKIES

½ cup granulated sugar
½ cup packed brown sugar
¼ cup margarine or butter, softened
¼ cup shortening
½ teaspoon baking soda
½ teaspoon ground cinnamon
½ teaspoon vanilla
¼ teaspoon baking powder
¼ teaspoon salt
1 egg
1½ cups quick-cooking oats
1 cup all-purpose flour*
1 cup raisins or chopped nuts, if desired

Heat oven to 375° Mix all ingredients except oats, flour and raisins. Stir in oats, flour and raisins. Drop dough by rounded teaspoonfuls about 2 inches apart onto ungreased cookie sheet. Bake about 10 minutes or until light brown; cool. ABOUT 2 DOZEN COOKIES; 110 CALORIES PER COOKIE.

If using self-rising flour, omit baking soda, baking powder and salt.

OATMEAL SQUARES: Press dough in ungreased square pan, 8 × 8 × 2 inches. Bake about 25 minutes or until light brown. Cut into about 2-inch squares while warm.   16 SQUARES; 165 CALORIES PER SQUARE.

ALMOND-OATMEAL COOKIES

½ cup granulated sugar
½ cup packed brown sugar
½ cup margarine or butter, softened
½ teaspoon vanilla
1 egg
1½ cups quick-cooking oats
½ cup all-purpose flour*
½ cup ground toasted almonds
½ teaspoon baking soda
¼ teaspoon baking powder
⅛ teaspoon salt
½ cup sliced almonds

Heat oven to 375°. Mix sugars, margarine, vanilla and egg. Stir in oats, flour, ground almonds, baking soda, baking powder and salt. Stir in sliced almonds. Drop dough by rounded teaspoonfuls about 2 inches apart onto ungreased cookie sheet. Bake about 10 minutes or until light brown. Cool 2 minutes; remove from cookie sheet.   ABOUT 3 DOZEN COOKIES; 80 CALORIES PER COOKIE.

If using self-rising flour, omit baking soda, baking powder and salt.

SOUR CREAM— RAISIN COOKIES

Use seedless raisins, not seeded, in this recipe. Seedless raisins are grown without seeds, whereas seeded raisins have had their seeds removed. For variety, try the subtly different flavor of white raisins.

> 1 cup sugar
> ½ cup shortening
> 1 teaspoon vanilla
> 2 eggs
> 2 cups all-purpose flour*
> ½ cup sour cream
> 1 teaspoon baking soda
> ½ teaspoon baking powder
> ¼ teaspoon salt
> ⅛ teaspoon ground nutmeg
> 1⅓ cups raisins

Heat oven to 375°. Mix sugar, shortening, vanilla and eggs. Stir in remaining ingredients except raisins. Stir in raisins. Drop dough by rounded teaspoonfuls about 1 inch apart onto ungreased cookie sheet. Bake 8 to 10 minutes or until light brown. Cool slightly; remove from cookie sheet.   ABOUT 4 DOZEN COOKIES; 75 CALORIES PER COOKIE.

If using self-rising flour, omit baking soda, baking powder and salt.

APPLESAUCE JUMBLES

Jumbles have been popular since colonial days, made with a variety of ingredients reflecting the goods most readily available. This applesauce variation combines all the best parts of jumble history: raisins, nuts and the most popular spice-trade flavorings.

> 3¼ cups all-purpose flour*
> 1½ cups packed brown sugar
> 1 cup chopped walnuts
> 1 cup raisins
> ½ cup shortening
> ¾ cup applesauce
> 1 teaspoon ground cinnamon
> 1 teaspoon vanilla
> ½ teaspoon salt
> ½ teaspoon baking soda
> ¼ teaspoon ground cloves
> 2 eggs
> Browned Butter Glaze (right)

Heat oven to 375°. Mix all ingredients except glaze. (If dough is soft, cover and refrigerate.)

Drop dough by level tablespoonfuls 2 inches apart onto ungreased cookie sheet. Bake 10 minutes or until almost no indentation remains when touched with finger; cool. Spread with Browned Butter Glaze.   4½ TO 5 DOZEN COOKIES; 120 CALORIES PER COOKIE.

Browned Butter Glaze

> ⅓ cup margarine or butter
> 2 cups powdered sugar
> 1½ teaspoons vanilla
> 2 to 4 tablespoons hot water

Heat margarine over low heat until golden brown; remove from heat. Stir in powdered sugar and vanilla. Beat in hot water until smooth.

If using self-rising flour, omit salt and baking soda.

HERMITS

Hermits originated on Cape Cod when clipper ships ruled the economy. Because they kept so well, Hermits could be stored for long sea voyages; today they still last well, even if you are only voyaging to the office or to a picnic.

> 1 cup packed brown sugar
> ¼ cup shortening
> ¼ cup margarine or butter, softened
> ¼ cup cold coffee
> 1 egg
> ½ teaspoon baking soda
> ½ teaspoon salt
> ½ teaspoon ground cinnamon
> ½ teaspoon ground nutmeg
> 1¾ cups all-purpose flour*
> 1¼ cups raisins
> ¾ cup chopped nuts

Heat oven to 375°. Mix brown sugar, shortening, margarine, coffee, egg, baking soda, salt, cinnamon and nutmeg. Stir in remaining ingredients. Drop dough by rounded teaspoonfuls about 2 inches apart onto ungreased cookie sheet. Bake 8 to 10 minutes or until almost no indentation remains when touched; cool.   ABOUT 4 DOZEN COOKIES; 80 CALORIES PER COOKIE.

If using self-rising flour, omit baking soda and salt.

BRAN HERMITS: Omit nuts. Stir in 1¼ cups whole bran cereal with the flour.   75 CALORIES PER COOKIE.

MOLASSES HERMITS: Decrease brown sugar to ¾ cup. Increase shortening to ⅓ cup. Add ¼ cup molasses with the coffee.   90 CALORIES PER COOKIE.

Mint Macaroons (page 111), Salted Peanut Crisps, Cherry Blinks

✹ SALTED PEANUT CRISPS

Keep shelled peanuts fresh by storing in an airtight container in the refrigerator.

> 1½ cups packed brown sugar
> ½ cup margarine or shortening
> ½ cup shortening
> 2 eggs
> 2 teaspoons vanilla
> 3 cups all-purpose flour*
> 2 cups salted peanuts
> ½ teaspoon baking soda
> ¼ teaspoon salt

Heat oven to 375°. Grease cookie sheet lightly. Mix brown sugar, margarine, shortening, eggs and vanilla. Stir in remaining ingredients. Drop dough by rounded teaspoonfuls about 2 inches apart onto cookie sheet. Flatten with greased bottom of glass dipped into sugar. Bake 8 to 10 minutes or until golden brown; cool.   ABOUT 6 DOZEN COOKIES; 85 CALORIES PER COOKIE.

*If using self-rising flour, omit baking soda and salt.

CHOCOLATE CHIP–PEANUT CRISPS: Stir in 1 package (6 ounces) semisweet chocolate chips with the peanuts.   95 CALORIES PER COOKIE.

✹ CHERRY BLINKS

> 1 cup all-purpose flour*
> ½ cup sugar
> ⅓ cup shortening
> ½ teaspoon baking powder
> ¼ teaspoon baking soda
> ¼ teaspoon salt
> 1 egg
> 1 tablespoon plus 2 teaspoons milk
> ½ teaspoon vanilla
> ½ cup raisins or cut-up dates
> ½ cup chopped walnuts
> 1½ cups whole wheat flake cereal, crushed
> Candied or maraschino cherries

Heat oven to 375° Grease cookie sheet. Mix flour, sugar, shortening, baking powder, baking soda, salt, egg, milk and vanilla thoroughly. Stir in raisins and nuts. Drop dough by teaspoonfuls into cereal and roll gently until completely coated. Place 2 inches apart on cookie sheet. Press a cherry into each cookie. Bake 10 to 12 minutes or until light brown.   ABOUT 3 DOZEN COOKIES; 70 CALORIES PER COOKIE.

*If using self-rising flour, omit baking powder, baking soda and salt.

❦ COCONUT MACAROONS

3 egg whites
¼ teaspoon cream of tartar
⅛ teaspoon salt
¾ cup sugar
¼ teaspoon almond extract
2 cups flaked coconut
12 candied cherries, each cut into fourths

Heat oven to 300°. Grease cookie sheet lightly. Beat egg whites, cream of tartar and salt in medium bowl until foamy. Beat in sugar, 1 tablespoon at a time. Continue beating until stiff and glossy. Do not underbeat. Fold in almond extract and coconut.

Drop mixture by teaspoonfuls about 1 inch apart onto cookie sheet. Place a cherry piece on each cookie. Bake 20 to 25 minutes or just until edges are light brown. Cool 10 minutes; remove from cookie sheet. 3½ TO 4 DOZEN COOKIES; 40 CALORIES PER COOKIE.

MINT MACAROONS: Substitute ¼ teaspoon peppermint extract for the almond extract. After beating, fold in 1 package (6 ounces) semisweet chocolate chips, reserving 3½ to 4 dozen chocolate chips. Substitute reserved chips for the cherry pieces. 55 CALORIES PER COOKIE.

❦ FLORENTINES

¾ cup whipping (heavy) cream
¼ cup sugar
½ cup very finely chopped blanched almonds
4 ounces candied orange peel, very finely chopped
¼ cup all-purpose flour*
2 bars (4 ounces each) sweet cooking chocolate

Heat oven to 350°. Grease and flour cookie sheet. Mix whipping cream and sugar until well blended. Stir in almonds, orange peel and flour. (Dough may thicken as it stands.) Drop by rounded teaspoonfuls about 2 inches apart onto cookie sheet. Spread to form 2-inch circles. (Dough may be sticky.)

Bake 10 to 12 minutes or until edges are light brown. Cool 2 minutes; remove from cookie sheet. Heat chocolate until melted. Turn cookies over and spread with chocolate. Dry several hours at room temperature until chocolate becomes firm. ABOUT 4½ DOZEN COOKIES; 55 CALORIES PER COOKIE.

*Self-rising flour can be used in this recipe.

PIZZELLES

You can also use a krumkake iron to make these crisp Italian cookies.

2 cups all-purpose flour*
1 cup sugar
2 teaspoons baking powder
¾ cup margarine or butter, melted and cooled
1 tablespoon anise extract or vanilla
4 eggs, slightly beaten

Grease pizzelle iron. Heat pizzelle iron according to manufacturer's directions. Mix all ingredients. Drop 1 tablespoon batter onto heated pizzelle iron and close iron. Bake about 30 seconds or until golden brown. Carefully remove pizzelle from iron; cool. Repeat with remaining batter. ABOUT 3½ DOZEN COOKIES; 75 CALORIES PER COOKIE.

If using self-rising flour, omit baking powder.

Drop batter onto the center of heated pizzelle iron. The batter will spread as the cookie bakes and fill out the design. When done, carefully loosen pizzelle with a fork or knife point and remove.

FRENCH LACE COOKIES

This elegant cookie can also be served as a rolled variation. While cookies are still warm, roll them around the handle of a wooden spoon. If one should break during rolling, the cookies are too cool; return them to the oven for a minute to soften, then try again.

½ cup light corn syrup
½ cup shortening
⅔ cup packed brown sugar
1 cup all-purpose flour*
1 cup finely chopped pecans

Heat oven to 375°. Grease cookie sheet lightly. Heat corn syrup, shortening and brown sugar to boiling in 2-quart saucepan over medium heat, stirring constantly; remove from heat. Gradually stir in flour and pecans. Drop batter by teaspoonfuls about 3 inches apart onto cookie sheet. (Keep batter warm by placing saucepan over hot water; bake only 8 or 9 cookies at a time.) Bake about 5 minutes or until set. Cool 3 to 5 minutes; remove from cookie sheet. Drizzle with melted chocolate if desired.   ABOUT 4 DOZEN COOKIES; 65 CALORIES PER COOKIE.

*Do not use self-rising flour in this recipe.

DELUXE BROWNIES

Although it's impossible to say how the first brownie was invented—it may have been a fallen chocolate cake—we do know brownies were originally called "Bangor Brownies" because they were "discovered" in Bangor, Maine.

⅔ cup margarine or butter
5 ounces unsweetened chocolate, cut into pieces
1¾ cups sugar
2 teaspoons vanilla
3 eggs
1 cup all-purpose flour*
1 cup chopped walnuts

Heat oven to 350° Grease square pan, 9×9×2 inches. Heat margarine and chocolate over low heat, stirring constantly, until melted; cool slightly. Beat sugar, vanilla and eggs on high speed 5 minutes. Beat in chocolate mixture on low speed. Beat in flour just until blended. Stir in nuts. Spread in pan.

Bake 40 to 45 minutes or just until brownies begin to pull away from sides of pan; cool. Cut into 2-inch squares.   16 BROWNIES: 295 CALORIES PER BROWNIE.

*Do not use self-rising flour in this recipe.

French Lace Cookies, Pizzelles (page 111)

🌾 BUTTERSCOTCH BROWNIES

¼ cup shortening
1 cup packed brown sugar
1 teaspoon vanilla
1 egg
¾ cup all-purpose flour*
½ cup chopped walnuts
1 teaspoon baking powder
¼ teaspoon salt

Heat oven to 350°. Grease square pan, 8 × 8 × 2 inches. Heat shortening in 1½-quart saucepan over low heat until melted; remove from heat. Mix in brown sugar, vanilla and egg. Stir in remaining ingredients. Spread in pan. Bake 25 minutes. Cut into 2-inch squares while warm. 16 BROWNIES; 130 CALORIES PER BROWNIE.

If using self-rising flour, omit baking powder and salt.

BRAZIL NUT–BUTTERSCOTCH BROWNIES: Substitute ¾ cup finely chopped Brazil nuts for the walnuts. 150 CALORIES PER BROWNIE.

DATE-BUTTERSCOTCH BROWNIES: Decrease vanilla to ½ teaspoon. Stir in ½ cup chopped dates with the remaining ingredients. 145 CALORIES PER BROWNIE.

CHEWY FRUIT-AND-WALNUT BARS

1 cup packed brown sugar
½ cup margarine or butter, melted
1 teaspoon grated orange peel
¼ cup orange juice or pineapple juice
1 teaspoon vanilla
2 eggs
2 cups all-purpose flour*
2 teaspoons baking powder
1 package (6 ounces) diced dried fruits and raisins
¾ cup chopped walnuts

Heat oven to 350°. Grease rectangular pan, 13 × 9 × 2 inches. Mix brown sugar, margarine, orange peel, orange juice, vanilla and eggs. Stir in flour and baking powder. Stir in dried fruits and walnuts. Spread batter in pan.

Bake 20 to 25 minutes or until wooden pick inserted in center comes out clean; cool. Sprinkle with powdered sugar if desired. Cut into 2 × 1½-inch bars. 32 BARS; 115 CALORIES PER BAR.

If using self-rising flour, omit baking powder.

RASPBERRY-CHOCOLATE BARS

1½ cups all-purpose flour*
¾ cup sugar
¾ cup margarine or butter, softened
1 package (10 ounces) frozen raspberries, thawed and undrained
¼ cup orange juice
1 tablespoon cornstarch
¾ cup miniature semisweet chocolate chips

Heat oven to 350°. Mix flour, sugar and margarine. Press in ungreased rectangular pan, 13 × 9 × 2 inches. Bake 15 minutes.

Mix raspberries, orange juice and cornstarch in 1-quart saucepan. Heat to boiling, stirring constantly. Boil and stir 1 minute. Cool 10 minutes. Sprinkle chocolate chips over crust. Spoon raspberry mixture over chocolate chips. Bake about 20 minutes or until raspberry mixture is set. Refrigerate until chocolate is firm. Drizzle with additional melted chocolate if desired. Cut into 2 × 1-inch bars. 48 BARS; 70 CALORIES PER BAR.

Self-rising flour can be used in this recipe; omit salt and baking soda.

🌾 LEMON SQUARES

1 cup all-purpose flour*
½ cup margarine or butter, softened
¼ cup powdered sugar
1 cup granulated sugar
2 teaspoons grated lemon peel, if desired
2 tablespoons lemon juice
½ teaspoon baking powder
¼ teaspoon salt
2 eggs

Heat oven to 350°. Mix flour, margarine and powdered sugar. Press in ungreased square pan, 8 × 8 × 2 or 9 × 9 × 2 inches, building up ½-inch edges. Bake 20 minutes. Beat remaining ingredients about 3 minutes or until light and fluffy. Pour over hot crust.

Bake about 25 minutes or until no indentation remains when touched lightly in center; cool. Sprinkle with powdered sugar if desired. Cut into 1½-inch squares. 25 SQUARES; 90 CALORIES PER SQUARE.

Self-rising flour can be used in this recipe; omit salt and baking soda.

LEMON-COCONUT SQUARES: Stir ½ cup flaked coconut into egg mixture. 100 CALORIES PER SQUARE.

 **DATE BARS**

To cut up pitted dates, use a sharp knife or kitchen shears. Rinse knife or shears in cold water when the blade becomes sticky.

Date Filling (below)
1 cup packed brown sugar
1 cup margarine or butter, softened
1¾ cups all-purpose* or whole wheat flour
½ teaspoon salt
½ teaspoon baking soda
1½ cups quick-cooking oats

Prepare Date Filling; cool. Heat oven to 400°. Grease rectangular pan, 13 × 9 × 2 inches. Mix brown sugar and margarine. Mix in remaining ingredients until crumbly. Press half of the crumb mixture evenly in bottom of pan. Spread with Date Filling. Top with remaining crumb mixture, pressing lightly.

Bake 25 to 30 minutes or until light brown; cool slightly. Cut into 2 × 1½-inch bars.   36 BARS; 135 CALORIES PER BAR.

Date Filling

3 cups cut-up pitted dates (1 pound)
¼ cup sugar
1½ cups water

Cook all ingredients over low heat 10 minutes, stirring constantly, until thickened.

If using self-rising flour, omit salt and baking soda.

PUMPKIN-SPICE BARS

4 eggs
2 cups sugar
1 cup vegetable oil
1 can (16 ounces) pumpkin
2 cups all-purpose flour*
2 teaspoons baking powder
2 teaspoons ground cinnamon
1 teaspoon baking soda
½ teaspoon salt
½ teaspoon ground ginger
¼ teaspoon ground cloves
1 cup raisins
Cream Cheese Frosting (right)
½ cup chopped walnuts

Heat oven to 350°. Grease jelly roll pan, 15½ × 10½ × 1 inch. Beat eggs, sugar, oil and pumpkin. Stir in flour, baking powder, cinnamon, baking soda, salt, ginger and cloves. Mix in raisins. Pour batter into pan. Bake 25 to 30 minutes or until light brown; cool. Frost with Cream Cheese Frosting. Sprinkle

with walnuts. Cut into 2 × 1½-inch bars. Refrigerate any remaining bars.   49 BARS; 115 CALORIES PER BAR.

Cream Cheese Frosting

1 package (3 ounces) cream cheese, softened
¼ cup plus 2 tablespoons margarine or butter, softened
1 teaspoon vanilla
2 cups powdered sugar

Mix cream cheese, margarine and vanilla. Gradually beat in powdered sugar until smooth.

If using self-rising flour, omit baking powder, baking soda and salt.

COCONUT CHEESECAKE BARS

1 cup graham cracker crumbs (about 12 squares)
¼ cup finely chopped pecans
3 tablespoons margarine or butter, melted
1 package (8 ounces) cream cheese, softened
½ cup sugar
¼ cup milk
½ cup shredded or flaked coconut, toasted
1 teaspoon vanilla
3 eggs

Heat oven to 325°. Mix cracker crumbs, pecans and margarine thoroughly. Press evenly in bottom of ungreased rectangular baking dish, 11 × 7 × 1½ inches. Bake about 10 minutes or until set.

Beat cream cheese until creamy. Beat in sugar, milk, coconut and vanilla. Beat in eggs, one at a time. Spread mixture over crust. Bake about 30 minutes or until center is set. Cover and refrigerate at least 2 hours. Cut into 2¼ × 1¼-inch bars. Place a pecan half on each bar if desired. Refrigerate any remaining bars.   25 BARS; 100 CALORIES PER BAR.

To Microwave: Prepare crust as directed—except press crumb mixture evenly in rectangular microwavable dish, 11 × 7 × 1½ inches. Elevate dish on inverted microwavable dinner plate in microwave oven. Microwave uncovered on medium (50%) 4 to 6 minutes, rotating dish ¼ turn after 2 minutes, until mixture appears dry.

Prepare filling and spread over crust as directed. Microwave (do not elevate) uncovered on medium (50%) 14 to 19 minutes, rotating dish ¼ turn every 3 minutes, until filling is set. Continue as directed.

🌾 CASHEW TRIANGLES

¼ cup granulated sugar
¼ cup packed brown sugar
½ cup margarine or butter, softened
½ teaspoon vanilla
1 egg, separated
1 cup all-purpose flour*
⅛ teaspoon salt
1 teaspoon water
1 cup chopped salted cashews, macadamia nuts or toasted almonds
1 ounce unsweetened chocolate, melted and cooled

Heat oven to 350°. Mix sugars, margarine, vanilla and egg yolk. Stir in flour and salt. Press dough in ungreased rectangular pan, 13 × 9 × 2 inches, with floured hands. Beat egg white and water. Brush over dough. Sprinkle with cashews and press them lightly into dough.

Bake about 25 minutes or until light brown; cool 10 minutes. Cut into 3-inch squares. Cut each square diagonally in half. Immediately remove from pan; cool. Drizzle with chocolate. Let stand about 2 hours or until chocolate is set. 24 COOKIES; 115 CALORIES PER COOKIE.

*If using self-rising flour, omit salt.

🌾 GINGERSNAPS

You can use either light or dark molasses in this recipe. Light molasses will give you a spicier cookie.

1 cup packed brown sugar
¾ cup shortening
¼ cup molasses
1 egg
2¼ cups all-purpose flour*
2 teaspoons baking soda
1 teaspoon ground cinnamon
1 teaspoon ground ginger
½ teaspoon ground cloves
¼ teaspoon salt
Granulated sugar

Mix brown sugar, shortening, molasses and egg. Stir in flour, baking soda, cinnamon, ginger, cloves and salt. Cover and refrigerate at least 1 hour.

Heat oven to 375°. Grease cookie sheet lightly. Shape dough by rounded teaspoonfuls into balls. Dip tops into granulated sugar. Place balls, sugared sides up, about 3 inches apart on cookie sheet. Bake 10 to 12 minutes or just until set; cool. ABOUT 4 DOZEN COOKIES; 80 CALORIES PER COOKIE.

*If using self-rising flour, decrease baking soda to 1 teaspoon and omit salt.

Clockwise from top left: *Lemon Squares (page 113)*, *Raspberry-Chocolate Bars (page 113)*, *Cashew Triangles*

PEANUT BUTTER COOKIES

½ cup granulated sugar
½ cup packed brown sugar
½ cup peanut butter
¼ cup shortening
¼ cup margarine or butter, softened
1 egg
1¼ cups all-purpose flour*
¾ teaspoon baking soda
½ teaspoon baking powder

Mix sugars, peanut butter, shortening, margarine and egg. Stir in remaining ingredients. Cover and refrigerate at least 3 hours.

Heat oven to 375°. Shape dough into 1¼-inch balls. Place about 3 inches apart on ungreased cookie sheet. Flatten in crisscross pattern with fork dipped into flour. Bake 9 to 10 minutes or until light brown. Cool 2 minutes; remove from cookie sheet. ABOUT 3 DOZEN COOKIES; 80 CALORIES PER COOKIE.

*If using self-rising flour, omit baking soda and baking powder.

PEANUT BUTTER AND JELLY COOKIES: Prepare dough as directed—except shape dough into 1-inch balls. Roll balls in ½ cup finely chopped peanuts. Place about 3 inches apart on lightly greased cookie sheet. Press thumb into center of each. Bake 10 to 12 minutes or until set but not hard. Spoon small amount of jelly or jam into thumbprint. ABOUT 3½ DOZEN COOKIES; 90 CALORIES PER COOKIE.

SNICKERDOODLES

1½ cups sugar
½ cup margarine or butter, softened
½ cup shortening
2 eggs
2¾ cups all-purpose flour*
2 teaspoons cream of tartar
1 teaspoon baking soda
¼ teaspoon salt
¼ cup sugar
2 teaspoons ground cinnamon

Heat oven to 400°. Mix 1½ cups sugar, margarine, shortening and eggs. Stir in flour, cream of tartar, baking soda and salt. Shape into 1¼-inch balls.

Mix ¼ cup sugar and the cinnamon. Roll balls in mixture. Place 2 inches apart on ungreased cookie sheet. Bake 8 to 10 minutes or until set; cool. ABOUT 4 DOZEN COOKIES; 90 CALORIES PER COOKIE.

*If using self-rising flour, omit cream of tartar, baking soda and salt.

BONBON COOKIES

¾ cup powdered sugar
½ cup margarine or butter, softened
1 tablespoon vanilla
Food color, if desired
1½ cups all-purpose flour*
⅛ teaspoon salt
Dates, nuts, semisweet chocolate chips and candied or maraschino cherries
Glaze or Chocolate Glaze (below)

Heat oven to 350°. Mix powdered sugar, margarine, vanilla and few drops food color. Stir in flour and salt until dough holds together. (If dough is dry, mix in 1 to 2 tablespoons milk.)

For each cookie, shape dough by tablespoonful around date, nut, chocolate chips or cherry to form ball. Place about 1 inch apart on ungreased cookie sheet. Bake 12 to 15 minutes or until set but not brown; cool. Dip tops of cookies into Glaze. Decorate with coconut, nuts, colored sugar, chocolate chips or chocolate shot if desired. ABOUT 2 DOZEN COOKIES; 125 CALORIES PER COOKIE.

Glaze

1 cup powdered sugar
1 tablespoon plus 1½ teaspoons milk
1 teaspoon vanilla
Food color, if desired

Mix powdered sugar, milk and vanilla until smooth. Tint with few drops food color.

Chocolate Glaze

1 cup powdered sugar
2 tablespoons milk
1 teaspoon vanilla
1 ounce unsweetened chocolate, melted and cooled

Mix powdered sugar, milk and vanilla until smooth. Stir in chocolate.

*Do not use self-rising flour in this recipe.

CHOCOLATE BONBON COOKIES: Omit food color. Stir in 1 ounce unsweetened chocolate, melted and cooled. 130 CALORIES PER COOKIE.

Clockwise from top: *Berliner Kranzer (page 119), Bonbon Cookies, Russian Teacakes (page 118), Thumbprint Cookies (page 118)*

COOKIE PIZZA

½ cup packed brown sugar
¼ cup granulated sugar
½ cup margarine or butter, softened
1 teaspoon vanilla
1 egg
1¼ cups all-purpose flour*
½ teaspoon baking soda
1 package (6 ounces) miniature semisweet
  chocolate chips
1 cup Sweetened Whipped Cream (page
  162)
¼ cup chopped walnuts
¼ cup flaked or shredded coconut, toasted
½ cup candy-coated chocolate candies

Heat oven to 350°. Mix sugars, margarine, vanilla and egg. Stir in flour and baking soda (dough will be stiff). Stir in chocolate chips. Spread or pat dough in ungreased 12-inch pizza pan or on cookie sheet. Bake about 15 minutes or until golden brown; cool. Just before serving, spread cookie with whipped cream. Sprinkle with walnuts, coconut and chocolate candies. Cut into wedges. Refrigerate any remaining cookie.   16 SERVINGS; 260 CALORIES PER SERVING.

If using self-rising flour, omit baking soda.

Cookie Pizza

RUSSIAN TEACAKES

1 cup margarine or butter, softened
½ cup powdered sugar
1 teaspoon vanilla
2¼ cups all-purpose flour*
¾ cup finely chopped nuts
¼ teaspoon salt
Powdered sugar

Heat oven to 400°. Mix margarine, ½ cup powdered sugar and the vanilla. Stir in flour, nuts and salt until dough holds together. Shape into 1-inch balls. Place about 1 inch apart on ungreased cookie sheet. Bake 10 to 12 minutes or until set but not brown.

Roll in powdered sugar while warm; cool. Roll in powdered sugar again.   ABOUT 4 DOZEN COOKIES; 80 CALORIES PER COOKIE.

Do not use self-rising flour in this recipe.

AMBROSIA BALLS: Omit nuts. Stir in 1 cup flaked coconut and 1 tablespoon grated orange peel.   70 CALORIES PER COOKIE.

SURPRISE CANDY TEACAKES: Decrease nuts to ½ cup. Cut 12 vanilla caramel candies into 4 pieces each, or cut 1 bar (4 ounces) sweet cooking chocolate into ½-inch squares. Shape dough around pieces of caramels or chocolate to form 1-inch balls.   85 CALORIES PER COOKIE.

THUMBPRINT COOKIES

¼ cup packed brown sugar
¼ cup shortening
¼ cup margarine or butter, softened
½ teaspoon vanilla
1 egg, separated
1 cup all-purpose flour*
¼ teaspoon salt
1 cup finely chopped nuts
Jelly

Heat oven to 350°. Mix brown sugar, shortening, margarine, vanilla and egg yolk. Stir in flour and salt until dough holds together. Shape into 1-inch balls.

Beat egg white slightly. Dip each ball into egg white. Roll in nuts. Place about 1 inch apart on ungreased cookie sheet. Press thumb deeply in center of each. Bake about 10 minutes or until light brown; cool. Fill thumbprints with jelly.
ABOUT 3 DOZEN COOKIES; 85 CALORIES PER COOKIE.

If using self-rising flour, omit salt.

BERLINER KRANZER

Charming German wreath-shaped cookies!

1 cup sugar
¾ cup margarine or butter, softened
¾ cup shortening
2 teaspoons grated orange peel
2 eggs
4 cups all-purpose flour*
1 egg white
2 tablespoons sugar
Red candied cherries
Green candied citron

Heat oven to 400°. Mix 1 cup sugar, the margarine, shortening, orange peel and eggs. Mix in flour. Shape dough by rounded teaspoonfuls into ropes, 6 inches long. Form each rope into circle, crossing ends and tucking under. (This shaping method is easier than the traditional method of tying knots.) Place on ungreased cookie sheet.

Beat egg white and 2 tablespoons sugar until foamy. Brush over tops of cookies. Press bits of red candied cherries onto center of knot for holly berries. Add "leaves" cut from green citron. Bake 10 to 12 minutes or until set but not brown; cool.   ABOUT 6 DOZEN COOKIES; 75 CALORIES PER COOKIE.

Self-rising flour can be used in this recipe.

APPLE BUTTER REFRIGERATOR COOKIES

1 cup sugar
1 cup margarine or butter, softened
¼ cup apple butter
1 egg
2½ cups all-purpose flour*
1 cup finely shredded Cheddar cheese (4 ounces)
½ teaspoon baking soda
½ teaspoon apple pie spice

Mix sugar, margarine, apple butter and egg. Stir in remaining ingredients. Cover and refrigerate at least 2 hours.

Divide dough in half. Shape each half into roll, about 1½ inches in diameter and about 8 inches long. Wrap and refrigerate at least 4 hours.

Heat oven to 400°. Cut rolls into ⅛-inch slices. Place about 1 inch apart on ungreased cookie sheet. Bake 7 to 9 minutes or until edges are light brown; cool.   ABOUT 6 DOZEN COOKIES; 55 CALORIES PER COOKIE.

If using self-rising flour, omit baking soda.

VIENNESE ROUNDS

½ cup sugar
¾ cup margarine or butter, softened
1 egg
2 cups all-purpose flour*
½ cup ground pecans
½ cup apricot jam
½ cup semisweet chocolate chips
1 tablespoon shortening

Mix sugar, margarine and egg. Stir in flour and pecans. Shape into roll 12 inches long. Wrap and refrigerate at least 4 hours or until firm.

Heat oven to 350°. Cut roll into ¼-inch slices. Place about 1 inch apart on ungreased cookie sheet. Bake about 15 minutes or until light golden brown; cool. Spread ½ teaspoon jam over each cookie. Heat chocolate chips and shortening over low heat until melted. Drizzle chocolate over cookies. ABOUT 4 DOZEN COOKIES; 80 CALORIES PER COOKIE.

Self-rising flour can be used in this recipe.

VIENNESE SANDWICHES: Decrease apricot jam to ¼ cup. Put about ½ teaspoon jam between 2 cookies to form sandwich. Heat 1 package (6 ounces) semisweet chocolate chips and 2 tablespoons shortening until melted. Dip about half of each cookie sandwich into chocolate mixture.   ABOUT 2 DOZEN COOKIES; 210 CALORIES PER COOKIE.

 SOUR CREAM COOKIES

1 cup sugar
¼ cup shortening
¼ cup margarine or butter, softened
1 teaspoon vanilla
1 egg
2⅔ cups all-purpose flour*
½ cup sour cream
1 teaspoon baking powder
½ teaspoon baking soda
½ teaspoon salt
¼ teaspoon ground nutmeg
Sugar

Heat oven to 425°. Mix 1 cup sugar, the shortening, margarine, vanilla and egg. Stir in remaining ingredients. Divide dough into 3 equal parts. Roll each part ¼ inch thick on lightly floured surface. Cut with 2-inch cookie cutter. Sprinkle with sugar. Place on ungreased cookie sheet. Bake 6 to 8 minutes or until no indentation remains when touched; cool.   4 TO 5 DOZEN COOKIES; 65 CALORIES PER COOKIE.

If using self-rising flour, omit baking powder, baking soda and salt.

🌾 GINGERBREAD PEOPLE

Half the fun of Gingerbread People is in making them—the other half is eating them. Queen Elizabeth of England is credited with creating gingerbread people in the sixteenth century when she ordered cakes spiced with ginger to be baked in the shapes of her friends.

    1 cup packed brown sugar
    ⅓ cup shortening
    1½ cups dark molasses
    ⅔ cup cold water
    7 cups all-purpose flour*
    2 teaspoons baking soda
    2 teaspoons ground ginger
    ½ teaspoon salt
    1 teaspoon ground allspice
    1 teaspoon ground cloves
    1 teaspoon ground cinnamon

Mix brown sugar, shortening, molasses and water. Stir in remaining ingredients. Cover and refrigerate at least 2 hours.

Heat oven to 350°. Grease cookie sheet lightly. Roll about ¼ of the dough ¼ inch thick on floured board. Cut with floured gingerbread cutter or other favorite cutter. Place about 2 inches apart on cookie sheet. Bake 10 to 12 minutes or until no indentation remains when touched; cool. Decorate with colored frosting, colored sugar and candies if desired. ABOUT 2½ DOZEN 2½-INCH COOKIES; 185 CALORIES PER COOKIE.

If using self-rising flour, omit baking soda and salt.

PEACHY PINWHEELS

For the freshest nutmeg flavor, grate your own nutmeg.

    1 cup finely chopped dried peaches
    ¾ cup water
    ½ cup sugar
    ½ teaspoon ground nutmeg
    ½ cup margarine or butter, softened
    ¼ cup shortening
    1 cup sugar
    2 eggs
    1 teaspoon vanilla
    2½ cups all-purpose flour*
    1 teaspoon baking powder
    ¼ teaspoon salt

Mix peaches, water, ½ cup sugar and the nutmeg in 1-quart saucepan. Heat to boiling; reduce heat. Cover and simmer about 35 minutes or until peaches are tender and water is almost absorbed; cool slightly. Mash with fork.

Gingerbread People

Mix margarine, shortening, 1 cup sugar, the eggs and vanilla. Stir in remaining ingredients. Cover and refrigerate at least 1 hour.

Divide dough in half. Roll each half into rectangle, 11 × 7 inches, on floured surface. Spread half of the peach mixture to within ½ inch of edges of each rectangle. Roll up tightly, beginning at long side. Pinch to seal. Wrap and refrigerate at least 4 hours or until firm.

Heat oven to 375°. Cut roll into ¼-inch slices. Place on ungreased cookie sheet. Bake about 10 minutes or until light brown; cool.   ABOUT 5 DOZEN COOKIES; 75 CALORIES PER COOKIE.

*If using self-rising flour, omit baking powder and salt.

SUGAR COOKIES

1½ cups powdered sugar
1 cup margarine or butter, softened
1 teaspoon vanilla
½ teaspoon almond extract
1 egg
2½ cups all-purpose flour*
1 teaspoon baking soda
1 teaspoon cream of tartar
Granulated sugar

Mix powdered sugar, margarine, vanilla, almond extract and egg. Stir in remaining ingredients except granulated sugar. Cover and refrigerate at least 2 hours.

Heat oven to 375°. Grease cookie sheet lightly. Divide dough in half. Roll each half ¼ inch thick on lightly floured surface. Cut into desired shapes with 2- to 2½-inch cookie cutters. Sprinkle with granulated sugar. Place on cookie sheet. Bake 7 to 8 minutes or until edges are light brown; cool. ABOUT 5 DOZEN COOKIES; 65 CALORIES PER COOKIE.

*If using self-rising flour, omit baking soda and cream of tartar.

DECORATED SUGAR COOKIES: Omit granulated sugar. Frost or decorate cooled cookies with Creamy Vanilla Frosting (page 84) tinted with food color if desired. Decorate with colored sugar, small candies, candied fruit or nuts if desired.   80 CALORIES PER COOKIE.

FILLED SUGAR COOKIES: Cook 2 cups raisins, cut-up dates or figs, ¾ cup sugar, ½ cup chopped nuts, if desired, and ¾ cup water, stirring constantly, until mixture thickens; cool. Roll dough ⅛ inch thick. Cut into 24 circles with 2½-inch doughnut cutter that has center removed. Replace center and cut out 24 circles with doughnut cutter. Place whole circles on lightly greased cookie sheet. Top

with raisin mixture, spreading almost to edges. Top with remaining circles. Press edges together with floured fork. Sprinkle tops with sugar. Bake 8 to 10 minutes or until light brown; cool.   2 DOZEN COOKIES; 245 CALORIES PER COOKIE.

PAINTBRUSH SUGAR COOKIES: Omit granulated sugar. After rolling out dough, cut into desired shapes with cookie cutters. (Cut no more than 12 cookies at a time to keep them from drying out.) Mix 1 egg yolk and ¼ teaspoon water. Divide mixture among several custard cups. Tint each with different food color to make bright colors. (If paint thickens while standing, stir in few drops water.) Paint designs on cookies with small paintbrushes. Bake as directed.   60 CALORIES PER COOKIE.

CREAM WAFERS

2 cups all-purpose flour*
1 cup margarine or butter, softened
⅓ cup whipping (heavy) cream
Granulated sugar
Creamy Filling (below)

Mix flour, margarine and whipping cream. Cover and refrigerate at least 1 hour.

Heat oven to 375°. Roll about one-third of the dough at a time ⅛ inch thick on floured cloth-covered board (keep remaining dough refrigerated until ready to roll). Cut into 1½-inch circles. Transfer circles with spatula to waxed paper that is heavily covered with sugar. Turn each circle so that both sides are coated with sugar. Place on ungreased cookie sheet. Prick each circle with fork about 4 times.

Bake 7 to 9 minutes or just until set but not brown; cool. Just before serving, make cookie sandwiches each with about ½ teaspoon Creamy Filling.   ABOUT 5 DOZEN COOKIES; 60 CALORIES PER COOKIE.

Creamy Filling

¼ cup margarine or butter, softened
¾ cup powdered sugar
1 teaspoon vanilla
Few drops food color

Beat margarine, powdered sugar and vanilla until smooth and fluffy. Tint with food color. Stir in few drops water, if necessary, until of spreading consistency.

*Self-rising flour can be used in this recipe.

SCOTCH SHORTBREAD

¾ cup margarine or butter, softened
¼ cup sugar
2 cups all-purpose flour*

Heat oven to 350°. Mix margarine and sugar. Stir in flour. (If dough is crumbly, mix in 1 to 2 table-spoons margarine or butter, softened.) Roll dough ½ inch thick on lightly floured surface. Cut into small shapes about 1½ × 1-inch (leaves, ovals, squares, triangles, etc.). Place ½ inch apart on ungreased cookie sheet. Bake about 20 minutes or until set; cool.   ABOUT 2 DOZEN 1½ × 1-INCH COOKIES; 95 CALORIES PER COOKIE.

Do not use self-rising flour in this recipe.

BROWNIE CUPS

When you make these cups, you may think the amount of filling looks skimpy, but don't add more—the filling puffs up nicely during baking.

½ cup margarine or butter, softened
1 package (3 ounces) cream cheese, softened
¾ cup all-purpose flour*
¼ cup powdered sugar
½ teaspoon vanilla
3 ounces semisweet chocolate
1 tablespoon margarine or butter
⅓ cup granulated sugar
¼ cup chopped walnuts
1 egg

Mix ½ cup margarine and the cream cheese. Stir in flour, powdered sugar and vanilla. Cover and refrigerate at least 1 hour.

Heat oven to 325°. Pat scant 1 tablespoon dough in bottom and up side of each of 24 small muffin cups, 1¾ × 1 inch. Heat chocolate and 1 tablespoon margarine over low heat until melted; remove from heat. Stir in remaining ingredients. Fill each muffin cup about two-thirds full with chocolate mixture (about 1½ teaspoons). Bake about 25 minutes or until edges are light brown; cool. Remove cups from pan.   2 DOZEN COOKIES; 110 CALORIES PER COOKIE.

Self-rising flour can be used in this recipe.

 ROSETTES

Vegetable oil
1 egg
1 tablespoon sugar
¼ teaspoon salt
½ cup all-purpose flour*
½ cup water or milk
1 tablespoon vegetable oil

Heat oil (2 to 3 inches) to 400°. Beat egg, sugar and salt. Beat in flour, water and 1 tablespoon oil until smooth. Heat rosette iron by placing in hot oil 1 minute. Tap excess oil from iron. Dip hot iron into batter just to top edge of iron (do not go over top). Fry about 30 seconds or until golden brown; remove rosette. Invert to cool. (If rosette is not crisp, stir small amount of water or milk into batter.)

Heat iron in hot oil and tap off excess oil before making each rosette. (If iron is not hot enough, batter will not stick.) Sprinkle rosettes with powdered sugar just before serving if desired.   ABOUT 18 ROSETTES; 75 CALORIES PER ROSETTE.

If using self-rising flour, omit salt.

 SPRITZ

1 cup margarine or butter, softened
½ cup sugar
2¼ cups all-purpose flour*
1 teaspoon almond extract or vanilla
½ teaspoon salt
1 egg

Heat oven to 400°. Mix margarine and sugar. Stir in remaining ingredients. Place dough in cookie press. Form desired shapes on ungreased cookie sheet. Bake 6 to 9 minutes or until set but not brown; cool.   ABOUT 5 DOZEN COOKIES; 50 CALORIES PER COOKIE.

Do not use self-rising flour in this recipe.

CHOCOLATE SPRITZ: Stir 2 ounces unsweetened chocolate, melted and cooled, into margarine mixture.   55 CALORIES PER COOKIE.

Poppy Seed-filled Ravioli Cookies, Rosettes (page 122)

POPPY SEED–FILLED RAVIOLI COOKIES

These cookies get their name from their shape—they look like Italian ravioli.

1 cup sugar
½ cup shortening
¼ cup margarine or butter, softened
2 eggs
1 teaspoon vanilla
2½ cups all-purpose flour*
1 teaspoon baking soda
½ teaspoon salt
½ cup poppy seed
½ cup almonds
½ cup milk
2 tablespoons honey
1 teaspoon finely shredded lemon peel
1 tablespoon lemon juice
Honey
Poppy seed

Mix sugar, shortening, margarine, eggs and vanilla. Stir in flour, baking soda and salt. Divide dough into 4 equal parts. Cover and refrigerate 2 hours.

Place ½ cup poppy seed, the almonds, milk, 2 tablespoons honey, the lemon peel and lemon juice in blender or food processor. Cover and blend, or process, until liquid is absorbed.

Heat oven to 400°. Roll one part of dough into rectangle, 12 × 8 inches, on lightly floured surface. Cut dough into 12 rectangles, each 3 × 2 inches. Place 1 teaspoon poppy seed mixture on one end of each rectangle. Using metal spatula or knife dipped into flour, carefully fold dough over filling. Pinch edges to seal. Press edges with fork dipped into flour. Place on ungreased cookie sheet. Bake 8 to 10 minutes or until cookies are light brown. Brush warm cookies with honey. Sprinkle with poppy seed. Remove to rack to cool. Repeat with remaining dough. 4 DOZEN COOKIES; 95 CALORIES PER COOKIE.

*If using self-rising flour, omit baking soda and salt. Decrease flour to 2⅓ cups.

CHOCOLATE-FILLED RAVIOLI COOKIES: Prepare dough as directed. Substitute ¾ cup miniature chocolate chips for the poppy seed and ¾ cup walnuts for the almonds. Omit milk, 2 tablespoons honey, the lemon peel and lemon juice. Process chocolate chips and walnuts in food processor about 30 seconds or until mixture begins to hold together. Place 1 teaspoon packed chocolate mixture on one end of each rectangle. Continue as directed. Brush warm cookies with honey. Sprinkle with finely chopped walnuts. Repeat with remaining dough. 100 CALORIES PER COOKIE.

CANDY BASICS

Making candy at home can be a special event—invite friends and family for a taffy pull or to make popcorn balls. It's also satisfying to personalize candy we take for granted. Making your own gumdrops, lollipops, truffles or taffy can lead to wonderful flavor combinations that are better than "store bought."

♦ Always use the recommended size saucepan. A smaller or larger pan could affect quality and cooking time. If a size is not stated, size is not important.

♦ Don't double the recipe—make another batch. Increasing ingredients changes cooking time.

♦ A cool, dry day is best for making candy. Heat, humidity and altitude can affect quality. On a humid day, cook candy to a temperature a degree or so higher than the recipe indicates.

♦ Consult an altitude table to determine boiling point in your area, then adjust recipe if necessary.

♦ To prevent crystallization or grainy candy, sugar must dissolve completely over low heat; stir down any grains from side of saucepan. After candy has boiled, do not stir until it has cooled as the recipe indicates. To prevent crystals, do not scrape pan or stir candy during cooling.

♦ Use a reliable candy thermometer. Check your candy thermometer for accuracy by placing it in water and bringing it to boiling. The thermometer should read 212°. If the reading is higher or lower, take the difference into account when testing your temperature while making candy.

♦ To get an accurate reading, be sure the thermometer stands upright in cooking mixture and bulb does not rest on bottom of pan. Read it at eye level; watch temperature closely. After 200°, temperature goes up very quickly.

♦ If you don't have a thermometer, use the cold water test. Using a clean spoon, drop small amount of cooking mixture into a cupful of very cold water. Test hardness with fingers (see candy cooking tests chart). If candy does not pass test, continue cooking. Repeat water test with clean water.

CANDY COOKING TESTS

Hardness	Temperature	Cold Water Test
Soft ball	*234° to 240°*	*forms a soft ball that flattens when removed from water*
Firm ball	*242° to 248°*	*forms a firm ball that holds its shape until pressed.*
Hard ball	*250° to 268°*	*forms a ball that holds its shape but is pliable*
Soft crack	*270° to 290°*	*separates into hard but not brittle threads*
Hard crack	*300° to 310°*	*separates into hard, brittle threads*
Caramel	*320° to 350°*	*do not use cold water test; mixture coats metal spoon and forms light caramel-colored mass when poured on a plate*

BOURBON BALLS

3 cups finely crushed vanilla wafers (about 75)
2 cups powdered sugar
1 cup finely chopped pecans or walnuts
¼ cup cocoa
½ cup bourbon
¼ cup light corn syrup
Granulated or powdered sugar

Mix crushed wafers, powdered sugar, pecans and cocoa. Stir in bourbon and corn syrup. Shape mixture into 1-inch balls. Roll in granulated sugar. Cover tightly and refrigerate several days before serving. ABOUT 5 DOZEN CANDIES; 75 CALORIES PER CANDY.

BRANDY BALLS: Substitute ½ cup brandy for the bourbon. 75 CALORIES PER CANDY.

RUM BALLS: Substitute ½ cup light rum for the bourbon. 75 CALORIES PER CANDY.

Soft ball: Forms a soft ball that flattens when removed from water.

Firm ball: Forms a firm ball that holds its shape until pressed.

Hard ball: Forms a hard ball that holds its shape but is pliable.

Soft crack: Separates into hard but not brittle threads.

Hard crack: Separates into hard, brittle threads.

Caramel: Do *not* use cold water test. Mixture coats metal spoon and forms light caramel-colored mass when poured on plate.

CREAMY CARAMELS

½ cup finely chopped pecans
2 cups sugar
2 cups whipping (heavy) cream
¾ cup light corn syrup
½ cup margarine or butter

Butter square pan, 8×8×2 or 9×9×2 inches. Spread pecans in pan. Heat remaining ingredients to boiling in 3-quart saucepan over medium heat, stirring constantly. Cook, stirring frequently, to 245° on candy thermometer or until small amount of mixture dropped into very cold water forms a firm ball that holds its shape until pressed. Spread over nuts in pan; cool. Cut into 1-inch squares. Wrap individually in plastic wrap or waxed paper.   64 CANDIES; 80 CALORIES PER CANDY.

CHOCOLATE CARAMELS: Heat 2 ounces unsweetened chocolate with the sugar mixture.   85 CALORIES PER CANDY.

TOFFEE

1 cup pecans, chopped
¾ cup packed brown sugar
½ cup margarine or butter
½ cup semisweet chocolate chips

Butter square pan, 9×9×2 inches. Spread pecans in pan. Heat brown sugar and margarine to boiling over medium heat, stirring constantly. Boil 7 minutes, stirring constantly. Immediately spread mixture evenly over pecans. Sprinkle with chips.

Cover with cookie sheet. Let stand 1 minute or until chips soften. Spread softened chocolate over candy. While hot, cut into 1½-inch squares. Refrigerate until firm.   36 CANDIES; 75 CALORIES PER CANDY.

To Microwave: Prepare pan as directed. Microwave brown sugar and margarine uncovered in 4-cup microwavable measure on high 5 minutes, stirring every minute. Continue as directed.

🌾 CHOCOLATE FUDGE

2 cups sugar
⅔ cup milk
2 tablespoons corn syrup
¼ teaspoon salt
2 ounces unsweetened chocolate or ⅓ cup cocoa
2 tablespoons margarine or butter
1 teaspoon vanilla
½ cup coarsely chopped nuts, if desired

Butter loaf pan, 9 × 5 × 3 inches. Cook sugar, milk, corn syrup, salt and chocolate in 2-quart saucepan over medium heat, stirring constantly, until chocolate is melted and sugar is dissolved. Cook, stirring occasionally, to 234° on candy thermometer or until small amount of mixture dropped into very cold water forms a soft ball that flattens when removed from water; remove from heat. Add margarine.

Cool mixture to 120° without stirring. (Bottom of saucepan will be lukewarm.) Add vanilla. Beat vigorously and continuously 5 to 10 minutes or until candy is thick and no longer glossy. (Mixture will hold its shape when dropped from spoon.) Quickly stir in nuts. Spread in pan. Cool until firm. Cut into 1-inch squares. 32 CANDIES; 75 CALORIES PER CANDY.

To Microwave: Prepare pan as directed. Stir sugar, milk, corn syrup and salt together in microwavable 3-quart casserole. Add chocolate. Cover tightly and microwave on high 4 to 5 minutes or until bubbly and chocolate is melted. Stir thoroughly, using wire whisk. Microwave uncovered on medium-high (70%) 8 to 12 minutes, stirring every 4 minutes with wire whisk, to 234° on microwave candy thermometer or until small amount of mixture dropped into very cold water forms a soft ball that flattens when removed from water. Continue as directed.

PENUCHE: Substitute 1 cup packed brown sugar for 1 cup of the granulated sugar and omit chocolate. 65 CALORIES PER CANDY.

FUDGE

The word fudge originally meant "nonsense or lies." Some say the term came from a Captain Fudge who told tall tales to his crew. Fudge later came to include the meaning of substituting or making do—you "fudged" a project. Fudge as a delicious confection is thought to have been invented when a resourceful cook botched a batch of caramels and "fudged" the results.

In the late 1800s, fudge was all the rage at women's colleges. First came the classic Vassar College Fudge, followed by the Wellesley College variation with marshmallows, and then the Smith College version that used brown sugar and molasses as well as regular sugar. It was a hit with students because they could "fudge" regulations and make the candy in their dorm rooms.

HAZELNUT FUDGE

2 cups sugar
⅓ cup milk
⅓ cup half-and-half
2 tablespoons light corn syrup
2 tablespoons hazelnut liqueur
2 tablespoons margarine or butter
½ cup chopped hazelnuts, toasted

Butter loaf pan, 9 × 5 × 3 inches. Cook sugar, milk, half-and-half, corn syrup and hazelnut liqueur in 3-quart saucepan over medium heat, stirring constantly, until sugar is dissolved. Cook, stirring occasionally, to 234° on candy thermometer or until small amount of mixture dropped into very cold water forms a soft ball that flattens when removed from water; remove from heat. Add margarine.

Cool mixture to 120° without stirring. (Bottom of saucepan will be lukewarm.) Beat vigorously and continuously 5 to 10 minutes or until candy is thick and no longer glossy. (Mixture will hold its shape when dropped from a spoon.) Quickly stir in hazelnuts. Spread in pan; cool. Cut into 1-inch squares. 32 CANDIES; 75 CALORIES PER CANDY.

AMARETTO FUDGE: Substitute almond-flavored liqueur for the hazelnut liqueur and ½ cup chopped almonds, toasted, for the hazelnuts. 75 CALORIES PER CANDY.

COFFEE FUDGE: Substitute coffee liqueur for the hazelnut liqueur and ½ cup chopped walnuts for the hazelnuts. 75 CALORIES PER CANDY.

PEANUT BRITTLE

1½ teaspoons baking soda
1 teaspoon water
1 teaspoon vanilla
1½ cups sugar
1 cup water
1 cup light corn syrup
3 tablespoons margarine or butter
1 pound shelled unroasted peanuts

Butter 2 cookie sheets, 15½ × 12 inches, and keep warm. Mix baking soda, 1 teaspoon water and the vanilla. Mix sugar, 1 cup water and the corn syrup in 3-quart saucepan. Cook over medium heat, stirring occasionally, to 240° on candy thermometer or until small amount of mixture dropped into very cold water forms a soft ball that flattens when removed from water.

Stir in margarine and peanuts. Cook, stirring constantly, to 300° or until small amount of mixture dropped into very cold water separates into hard, brittle threads. (Watch carefully so mixture does not burn.) Immediately remove from heat. Quickly stir in baking soda mixture until light and foamy.

Pour half of the candy mixture onto each cookie sheet and quickly spread about ¼ inch thick: cool. Break into pieces. ABOUT 6 DOZEN CANDIES; 70 CALORIES PER CANDY.

PRALINES

2 cups packed light brown sugar
1 cup granulated sugar
1¼ cups milk
¼ cup light corn syrup
⅛ teaspoon salt
1 teaspoon vanilla
1½ cups pecan halves (5½ ounces)

Heat sugars, milk, corn syrup and salt to boiling in 3-quart saucepan, stirring constantly. Cook, without stirring, to 236° on candy thermometer or until small amount of mixture dropped into very cold water forms a soft ball that flattens when removed from water. Cool, without stirring, about 1½ hours or until saucepan is cool to touch.

Add vanilla and pecans. Beat about 1 minute or until mixture is slightly thickened and just coats pecans but does not lose its gloss. Drop by spoonfuls onto waxed paper. (Try to divide pecans equally.) Cool 12 to 18 hours or until candies are firm and no longer glossy.

Wrap individually in plastic wrap or waxed paper and store tightly covered at room temperature. ABOUT 1½ DOZEN CANDIES; 225 CALORIES PER CANDY.

GRAPE GUMDROPS

You can cut gumdrops into different shapes, just as you would cookies. Use small cookie or canapé cutters dipped in sugar, or cut them freehand.

Vegetable oil
1 cup sugar
1 cup light corn syrup
¾ cup grape juice
1 package (1¾ ounces) powdered fruit pectin
½ teaspoon baking soda
2 drops blue food color, if desired
Sugar

Line loaf pan, 9 × 5 × 3 inches, with aluminum foil. Brush with oil. Heat 1 cup sugar and the corn syrup to boiling in 1½-quart saucepan over medium-high heat, stirring constantly, until sugar is dissolved. Cook, without stirring, to 280° on candy thermometer or until small amount of mixture dropped into very cold water separates into hard but not brittle threads.

While cooking sugar mixture, heat grape juice, pectin and baking soda to boiling (mixture will be foamy) in 2-quart saucepan over high heat, stirring constantly; reduce heat.

Slowly pour hot sugar mixture in a thin stream into grape juice mixture, stirring constantly (this should take 1 to 2 minutes); remove from heat. Stir in food color. Let stand 2 minutes. Skim off foam.

Pour mixture into pan. Let stand uncovered at room temperature 24 hours. Lift foil from pan and remove foil from sides. Cut into ¾-inch squares with knife dipped into sugar. Roll squares in sugar. Let stand uncovered at room temperature 1 hour. Store gumdrops in airtight container. ABOUT 72 GUMDROPS; 28 CALORIES PER GUMDROP.

ORANGE GUMDROPS: Substitute orange juice for the grape juice and red food color for the blue food color. 28 CALORIES PER GUMDROP.

APPLE-CHERRY GUMDROPS: Substitute apple-cherry drink for the grape juice and red food color for the blue food color. 28 CALORIES PER GUMDROP.

 **DIVINITY**

This confection truly lives up to its name. Before electric mixers this was quite a chore to make. Now you can whip up divinity without using any elbow grease at all. For a special treat, add chopped candied cherries along with the nuts.

2⅔ cups sugar
⅔ cup light corn syrup
½ cup water
2 egg whites
1 teaspoon vanilla
⅔ cup coarsely chopped nuts

Cook sugar, corn syrup and water (use 1 tablespoon less water on humid days) in 2-quart saucepan over low heat, stirring constantly, until sugar is dissolved. Cook, without stirring, to 260° on candy thermometer or until small amount of mixture dropped into very cold water forms a hard ball that holds its shape but is pliable.

Beat egg whites in medium bowl until stiff peaks form. Continue beating while pouring hot syrup in a thin stream into egg whites, beating constantly on medium speed. (For best results, use countertop mixer.) Add vanilla. Beat until mixture holds its shape and becomes slightly dull. (Mixture may become too stiff for mixer.) Fold in nuts.

Drop mixture from buttered spoon onto waxed paper. Let stand at room temperature at least 12 hours, turning candies over once, until candies feel firm. Store in airtight container. ABOUT 4 DOZEN CANDIES; 65 CALORIES PER CANDY.

To Microwave: Mix sugar, corn syrup and water in 8-cup microwavable measure until sugar is thoroughly moistened. Microwave uncovered on high 13 to 15 minutes, stirring once after 5 minutes, to 260° on microwave candy thermometer or until small amount of mixture dropped into very cold water forms a hard ball that holds its shape but is pliable. Continue as directed.

TRUFFLES

6 ounces semisweet chocolate, cut up
2 tablespoons margarine or butter
¼ cup whipping (heavy) cream
1 tablespoon shortening
1 cup semisweet or milk chocolate chips

Heat semisweet chocolate in heavy 2-quart saucepan over low heat, stirring constantly, until melted; remove from heat. Stir in margarine. Stir in whipping cream.

Refrigerate 10 to 15 minutes, stirring frequently, *just* until thick enough to hold a shape. Drop mixture by teaspoonfuls onto aluminum foil-covered cookie sheet. Shape into balls. (If mixture is too sticky, refrigerate until firm enough to shape.) Freeze 30 minutes.

Heat shortening and chocolate chips over low heat, stirring constantly, until chocolate is melted and mixture is smooth; remove from heat. Dip truffles, one at a time, into chocolate. Place on aluminum foil–covered cookie sheet. Immediately sprinkle some of the truffles with finely chopped nuts if desired.

Refrigerate truffles about 10 minutes or until coating is set. Drizzle some of the truffles with a mixture of ¼ cup powdered sugar and ½ teaspoon milk if desired. Refrigerate just until set. Serve at room temperature. Store truffles in airtight container. 15 CANDIES; 155 CALORIES PER CANDY.

ALMOND TRUFFLES: Stir 2 tablespoons almond-flavored liqueur into whipping cream. 165 CALORIES PER CANDY.

APRICOT TRUFFLES: Soak 3 tablespoons chopped apricots in 1 tablespoon brandy 15 minutes. Stir into whipping cream mixture. 160 CALORIES PER CANDY.

CASHEW TRUFFLES: Stir 3 tablespoons chopped cashews into whipping cream mixture. 165 CALORIES PER CANDY.

CHERRY TRUFFLES: Stir 2 tablespoons cherry-flavored brandy into whipping cream. 165 CALORIES PER CANDY.

ORANGE TRUFFLES: Stir 2 tablespoons orange-flavored liqueur into whipping cream. 165 CALORIES PER CANDY.

Chocolate Fudge (page 126), Taffy (page 130), Gumdrops (page 127), Raspberry Truffle Cups

PRALINE TRUFFLE CUPS

These bite-size candy cups make charming gifts. You'll also enjoy using milk chocolate candy coating to line the cups.

6 ounces vanilla-flavored candy coating
24 tiny paper candy cups
6 ounces semisweet chocolate, cut up
2 tablespoons margarine or butter, cut into pieces
⅓ cup whipping (heavy) cream
¼ cup finely ground pecans
1 tablespoon praline liqueur

Heat candy coating in double boiler over hot water until melted. Spread 1 teaspoon coating evenly on bottoms and up sides of paper candy cups. Let stand until hard.

Heat chocolate in heavy 2-quart saucepan over low heat, stirring constantly, until melted; remove from heat. Stir in remaining ingredients. Refrigerate about 35 minutes, stirring frequently, or until mixture is thick and mounds when dropped from a spoon. Spoon mixture into decorating bag with star tip. Pipe mixture into candy-coated cups. Refrigerate about 30 minutes or until chocolate mixture is firm. Peel paper from cups before serving if desired.   24 CANDIES; 95 CALORIES PER CANDY.

CHERRY TRUFFLE CUPS: Omit pecans. Substitute 2 tablespoons cherry liqueur for the praline liqueur. Place candied cherry half in each cup before filling with chocolate mixture.   95 CALORIES PER CANDY.

CRÈME DE MENTHE TRUFFLE CUPS: Substitute ¼ cup finely ground almonds for the pecans and 2 tablespoons crème de menthe for the praline liqueur.   95 CALORIES PER CANDY.

RASPBERRY TRUFFLE CUPS: Omit pecans. Substitute 2 tablespoons raspberry liqueur for the praline liqueur. Place fresh raspberry in each cup before filling with chocolate mixture.   95 CALORIES PER CANDY.

POPCORN BALLS

For holidays or special occasions, tint popcorn balls with a few drops of food color to match the mood. Add the food color with the corn syrup.

½ cup sugar
¼ cup margarine or butter
½ cup light corn syrup
¼ teaspoon salt
8 cups popped popcorn

Heat all ingredients except popcorn to boiling in Dutch oven over medium-high heat, stirring constantly. Boil and stir 2 minutes; remove from heat. Stir in popcorn until well coated; cool slightly.

Dip hands into cold water. Shape mixture into 8 balls, each about 2½ inches in diameter. Place on waxed paper; cool. Wrap individually in plastic wrap, or place in plastic bags and seal.   8 POPCORN BALLS; 200 CALORIES PER BALL.

To Microwave: Mix all ingredients except popcorn in 3- or 4-quart microwavable bowl or casserole. Microwave uncovered on high about 2 minutes or until boiling. Stir until smooth. Microwave uncovered about 1 minute longer or until boiling. Stir in popcorn. Continue as directed.

CARAMEL POPCORN BALLS: Substitute packed brown sugar for the granulated sugar and dark corn syrup for the light corn syrup.   205 CALORIES PER BALL.

CHOCOLATE POPCORN BALLS: Add 2 tablespoons cocoa with the sugar.   205 CALORIES PER BALL.

❀ CANDIED CITRUS PEEL

3 oranges
3 lemons
1½ cups sugar
¾ cup water
½ cup sugar

Cut peel of each orange and lemon into 4 sections with sharp knife. Remove peel carefully with fingers. Scrape white membrane from peel with spoon (back of peel will appear porous when membrane is removed). Cut peel lengthwise into strips about ¼ inch wide. Heat peel and enough water to cover to boiling in 1½-quart saucepan; reduce heat. Simmer uncovered 30 minutes. Drain and repeat simmering process.

Heat 1½ cups sugar and ¾ cup water to boiling in 1½-quart saucepan, stirring constantly, until sugar is dissolved. Stir in peel. Simmer uncovered, stirring occasionally, 45 minutes. Drain in a strainer. Roll peel in ½ cup sugar, and spread on waxed paper to dry. Store peel in airtight container up to 1 week.   12 SERVINGS (ABOUT ¼ CUP EACH); 65 CALORIES PER SERVING.

MINT WAFERS

Many people find mints are refreshing at the end of a meal. Their mixture of sweetness and coolness can be enjoyed any time.

3½ to 4 cups powdered sugar
⅔ cup sweetened condensed milk
Few drops food color, if desired
½ teaspoon peppermint, spearmint or wintergreen extract

Cover cookie sheet with waxed paper. Mix 3½ cups powdered sugar, the milk and food color. Knead in extract and enough additional powdered sugar to make a smooth, creamy mixture. Shape mixture into 1-inch balls. Place about 1 inch apart on cookie sheet. Flatten each ball with fork to about ¼-inch thickness. Let stand uncovered at room temperature about 1 hour or until firm.

Turn candies over and let stand about 1 hour or until tops are firm. Store mints in airtight container.   ABOUT 8 DOZEN CANDIES; 25 CALORIES PER CANDY; ABOUT 25 CALORIES PER CANDY.

CUTOUT MINTS: Divide mixture in half. Shape one half into flattened round on cloth-covered board generously sprinkled with granulated sugar. Roll in sugar to coat. Roll mixture ¼ inch thick. Cut with 1-inch cutters. Place mints on waxed paper. Repeat with remaining mixture. Continue as directed.   ABOUT 8 DOZEN CANDIES.

❀ TAFFY

You don't have to go to the seaside for great saltwater taffy. Salt water isn't even a necessary ingredient; fresh water works wonderfully (no matter what they tell you down on the boardwalk). Use different extracts to create your favorite flavors.

1 cup sugar
1 tablespoon cornstarch
¾ cup light corn syrup
⅔ cup water
2 tablespoons margarine or butter
1 teaspoon salt
2 teaspoons vanilla
¼ teaspoon food color, if desired

Butter square pan, 8 × 8 × 2 inches. Mix sugar and cornstarch in 2-quart saucepan. Stir in corn syrup, water, margarine and salt. Heat to boiling over medium heat, stirring constantly. Cook, without stirring, to 265° on candy thermometer or until small amount of mixture dropped into very cold water forms a hard ball that holds its shape but is pliable; remove from heat. Stir in vanilla and food color. Pour into pan.

When just cool enough to handle, pull taffy with lightly buttered hands until satiny, light in color and stiff. Pull into long strips ½ inch wide. Cut strips into 1½-inch pieces with scissors. (For ease in cutting, wipe scissors with vegetable oil.) Wrap pieces individually in plastic wrap or waxed paper (candy must be wrapped to hold its shape).   ABOUT 4 DOZEN CANDIES; 15 CALORIES PER CANDY.

ALMOND TAFFY: Stir in 2 teaspoons almond extract with the vanilla.   15 CALORIES PER CANDY.

PEPPERMINT TAFFY: Substitute 1 tablespoon peppermint extract for the vanilla. Stir in ¼ teaspoon red food color, if desired, with the peppermint extract.   15 CALORIES PER CANDY.

FIX-IT-FAST

- Fold your favorite crumbled cookies or cookie crumbs into sweetened whipped cream or yogurt. Serve in ice-cream cones or over fresh fruit, pound cake or brownies.

- Make homemade cookie sandwiches by putting two cookies or graham crackers together with your favorite frosting, jam, peanut butter or cream cheese.

- Create brownie or cookie sundaes by placing a brownie or cookie in shallow dish, then topping with scoops of ice cream and your favorite sundae toppings.

- Jazz up brownies by sprinkling batter in pan with chopped nuts, chocolate chips, raisins or shredded coconut before baking.

- For a thick cookie-and-ice-cream shake combine crumbled cookies, vanilla ice cream and milk in a blender container. Cover and blend.

- Use whole or broken cookies to dip into dessert fondues.

- Spread your favorite cracker with peanut butter and top with another cracker. Dip it into melted chocolate chips or chocolate bars, and let stand until firm.

- Brush saltine crackers with softened margarine or butter and sprinkle with cinnamon-sugar mixture. Good cold, even more delicious broiled.

- Use leftover cookies for pie crust. See Cookie Crumb Crust (page 87).

- Alternate fruit, yogurt or pudding and crumbled cookies in parfait glasses for a quick dessert.

- Use favorite dried fruits—apricots, peaches, dates, apples, raisins or diced fruits and raisins—to dip into melted frosting or melted chocolate chips.

- Spread fruit roll-ups with flavored cream cheese, yogurt, peanut butter or melted chocolate. Roll up and cut into 1-inch pieces.

NUTRITION INFORMATION

PER SERVING OR UNIT

RECIPE, PAGE	Servings per recipe	Calories	Protein (grams)	Carbohydrate (grams)	Fat (grams)	Cholesterol (milligrams)	Sodium (milligrams)	Protein	Vitamin A	Vitamin C	Thiamine	Riboflavin	Niacin	Calcium	Iron
COOKIES															
Almond-Oatmeal Cookies, 108	36	80	1	8	5	8	65	2	2	0	0	2	0	0	2
Ambrosia Balls, 118	48	70	0	8	4	0	60	0	2	0	0	0	0	0	0
Apple Butter Refrigerator Cookies, 119	72	55	1	6	3	6	50	0	2	0	0	0	0	0	0
Applesauce Jumbles, 109	54	120	1	20	4	10	50	2	0	0	2	0	2	0	2
Berliner Kranzer, 119	72	75	1	8	4	8	30	0	0	0	0	0	0	0	0
Bonbon Cookies, 116	24	125	1	22	4	0	60	0	2	0	2	2	2	0	0
Bran Hermits, 109	48	75	1	13	2	6	65	0	2	0	2	2	2	0	4
Brazil Nut–Butterscotch Brownies, 113	16	150	2	18	8	18	70	2	0	0	6	2	2	4	4
Brownie Cups, 122	24	110	1	9	8	16	65	2	4	0	0	2	0	0	2
Butterscotch Brownies, 113	16	130	2	18	6	18	70	2	0	0	2	0	2	2	4
Cashew Triangles, 115	24	115	2	10	8	12	100	2	2	0	2	2	2	0	2
Cherry Blinks, 110	36	70	1	10	3	8	50	0	0	0	2	2	2	0	2
Chewy Fruit-and-Walnut Bars, 113	32	115	1	17	5	18	70	2	2	0	2	2	2	2	2

NUTRITION INFORMATION

PER SERVING OR UNIT

RECIPE, PAGE

	Servings per recipe	Calories	Protein (grams)	Carbohydrate (grams)	Fat (grams)	Cholesterol (milligrams)	Sodium (milligrams)	PERCENT U.S. RECOMMENDED DAILY ALLOWANCE							
								Protein	Vitamin A	Vitamin C	Thiamine	Riboflavin	Niacin	Calcium	Iron

COOKIES (*continued*)

	Servings per recipe	Calories	Protein (grams)	Carbohydrate (grams)	Fat (grams)	Cholesterol (milligrams)	Sodium (milligrams)	Protein	Vitamin A	Vitamin C	Thiamine	Riboflavin	Niacin	Calcium	Iron
Chocolate Bonbon Cookies, 116	24	131	1	22	5	0	60	0	2	0	2	2	2	0	2
Chocolate-Cherry Drop Cookies, 108	54	95	1	17	3	6	60	0	2	0	0	0	0	0	0
Chocolate Chip Bars, 107	48	135	1	15	8	5	95	2	2	0	2	0	2	0	2
Chocolate Chip Cookies, 107	72	90	1	10	5	4	65	0	2	0	2	0	0	0	2
Chocolate Chip–Peanut Crisps, 110	72	95	2	10	5	8	50	2	0	0	2	0	4	0	2
Chocolate Drop Cookies, 108	54	95	1	12	5	6	60	0	0	0	2	0	0	0	2
Chocolate-filled Ravioli Cookies, 123	48	100	0	12	5	12	65	2	0	0	2	0	0	0	0
Chocolate Spritz, 122	60	55	0	5	4	5	55	0	2	0	0	0	0	0	0
Cocoa Drop Cookies, 108	54	95	1	12	5	6	65	0	2	0	2	0	0	0	0
Coconut Cheesecake Bars, 114	25	100	2	8	7	45	80	2	4	0	0	2	0	0	2
Coconut Macaroons, 111	48	40	0	6	2	0	30	0	0	0	0	0	0	0	0
Cookie Pizza, 118	16	260	2	27	16	38	120	4	8	0	4	4	2	2	4
Cream Wafers, 121	60	60	0	5	4	2	45	0	2	0	0	0	0	0	0
Date Bars, 114	36	135	1	22	5	0	125	0	4	0	2	0	2	0	2
Date-Butterscotch Brownies, 113	16	145	2	22	6	18	70	2	0	2	2	2	2	2	4
Decorated Sugar Cookies, 121	60	80	1	10	4	5	70	0	2	0	0	0	0	0	0
Deluxe Brownies, 112	16	295	4	31	18	52	105	6	6	0	6	4	4	2	6
Double Chocolate Drop Cookies, 108	54	110	1	14	6	5	65	2	2	0	2	0	0	0	2
Filled Sugar Cookies, 121	24	245	2	39	10	12	140	2	6	0	6	2	4	0	4
Florentines, 111	54	55	1	6	3	5	5	0	0	0	0	0	0	0	0
French Lace Cookies, 112	48	65	0	8	4	0	5	0	0	0	2	0	0	0	2
Gingerbread People, 120	30	185	3	37	3	0	120	4	0	0	8	4	8	4	10
Gingersnaps, 115	48	80	1	12	3	6	60	0	0	0	0	0	0	0	2
Hermits, 109	48	80	1	12	3	6	50	0	0	0	2	0	0	0	2
Jumbo Chocolate Chip Cookies, 107	18	360	4	41	20	16	250	6	8	0	8	4	4	2	8
Lemon-Coconut Squares, 113	25	100	1	13	5	22	85	0	2	0	0	0	0	0	0
Lemon Squares, 113	25	90	1	13	4	22	80	0	2	0	0	0	0	0	0
Mint Macaroons, 111	48	55	0	7	3	0	30	0	0	0	0	0	0	0	0
Molasses Hermits, 109	48	90	1	13	4	6	65	2	2	0	4	2	2	0	4
Oatmeal Cookies, 108	24	110	1	16	5	10	75	2	0	0	4	0	0	0	2
Oatmeal Squares, 108	16	165	2	23	7	15	115	2	2	0	6	2	2	0	4

PER SERVING OR UNIT

NUTRITION INFORMATION

RECIPE, PAGE

PERCENT U.S. RECOMMENDED DAILY ALLOWANCE

Recipe, Page	Servings per recipe	Calories	Protein (grams)	Carbohydrate (grams)	Fat (grams)	Cholesterol (milligrams)	Sodium (milligrams)	Protein	Vitamin A	Vitamin C	Thiamine	Riboflavin	Niacin	Calcium	Iron
COOKIES (continued)															
Paintbrush Sugar Cookies, 121	60	60	1	7	3	8	60	0	2	0	0	0	0	0	0
Peachy Pinwheels, 120–121	54	75	1	11	3	10	40	0	2	0	0	0	2	0	0
Peanut Butter Cookies, 116	36	80	1	9	5	8	65	2	0	0	0	0	2	0	0
Peanut Butter and Jelly Cookies, 116	42	90	2	11	5	8	55	2	0	0	0	0	4	0	0
Pizzelles, 111	42	75	1	9	4	26	45	2	2	0	2	2	0	0	0
Poppy Seed–filled Ravioli Cookies, 123	48	95	1	11	5	12	65	2	0	0	2	2	0	4	2
Pumpkin-Spice Bars, 114	49	115	1	20	3	25	90	2	42	0	2	2	0	2	2
Raspberry-Chocolate Bars, 113	48	70	1	9	4	0	35	0	2	0	0	0	0	0	0
Rosettes, 122	18	75	0	3	7	0	35	0	0	0	0	0	0	0	0
Russian Teacakes, 118	48	80	1	8	5	0	60	0	2	0	2	0	0	0	0
Salted Peanut Crisps, 110	72	85	2	9	5	8	50	2	0	0	2	0	4	0	2
Scotch Shortbread, 122	24	95	1	9	6	0	70	0	4	0	2	0	2	0	0
Snickerdoodles, 116	48	90	1	12	4	10	60	0	0	0	2	0	0	0	0
Sour Cream Cookies, 119	48	65	1	9	3	8	60	0	0	0	2	0	0	0	0
Sour Cream–Raisin Cookies, 109	48	75	1	11	3	14	45	0	0	0	2	0	0	0	0
Spritz, 122	60	50	0	5	3	5	55	0	2	0	0	0	0	0	0
Sugar Cookies, 121	60	65	0	8	3	5	55	0	2	0	0	0	0	0	0
Surprise Candy Teacakes, 118	48	85	1	9	5	0	60	0	2	0	2	0	0	0	0
Thumbprint Cookies, 118	36	85	1	9	5	10	35	0	0	0	2	0	0	0	2
Viennese Rounds, 119	48	80	1	9	5	6	35	0	2	0	2	0	0	0	0
Viennese Sandwiches, 119	24	210	2	23	12	12	75	2	4	0	4	2	2	0	4
CANDIES															
Almond Taffy, 130	48	15	0	4	0	0	45	0	0	0	0	0	0	0	0
Almond Truffles, 128	15	165	1	16	10	6	20	2	2	0	0	0	0	0	2
Amaretto Fudge, 126	32	75	0	14	2	2	12	0	0	0	0	0	0	0	0
Apple-Cherry Gumdrops, 127	72	28	0	7	0	0	10	0	0	0	0	0	0	0	0
Apricot Truffles, 128	15	160	1	16	10	6	20	2	6	0	0	0	0	0	4
Bourbon Balls, 124	60	65	0	11	2	0	20	0	0	0	2	0	0	0	0
Brandy Balls, 124	60	65	0	11	2	0	20	0	0	0	2	0	0	0	0
Candied Citrus Peel, 130	12	65	0	22	0	0	5	0	0	25	0	0	0	2	0

NUTRITION INFORMATION

PER SERVING OR UNIT

RECIPE, PAGE

	Servings per recipe	Calories	Protein (grams)	Carbohydrate (grams)	Fat (grams)	Cholesterol (milligrams)	Sodium (milligrams)	Protein	Vitamin A	Vitamin C	Thiamine	Riboflavin	Niacin	Calcium	Iron

PERCENT U.S. RECOMMENDED DAILY ALLOWANCE spans: Protein, Vitamin A, Vitamin C, Thiamine, Riboflavin, Niacin, Calcium, Iron

CANDIES (continued)

Recipe, Page	Servings per recipe	Calories	Protein (g)	Carbohydrate (g)	Fat (g)	Cholesterol (mg)	Sodium (mg)	Protein	Vitamin A	Vitamin C	Thiamine	Riboflavin	Niacin	Calcium	Iron
Caramel Popcorn Balls, 129	8	205	1	38	6	0	155	2	4	0	0	0	0	2	8
Cashew Truffles, 128	15	165	1	15	11	6	35	2	2	0	0	0	0	0	4
Cherry Truffle Cups, 129	24	95	1	10	6	5	30	0	0	0	0	0	0	0	0
Cherry Truffles, 128	15	165	1	16	10	6	20	2	2	0	0	0	0	0	2
Chocolate Caramels, 125	64	85	0	9	5	12	25	0	2	0	0	0	0	0	0
Chocolate Fudge, 126	32	75	1	14	2	0	20	0	0	0	0	0	0	0	0
Chocolate Popcorn Balls, 129	8	205	2	37	6	0	150	2	4	0	0	0	0	0	6
Coffee Fudge, 126	32	75	0	14	2	2	12	0	0	0	0	0	0	0	0
Creamy Caramels, 125	64	80	0	9	5	12	25	0	2	0	0	0	0	0	0
Crème de Menthe Truffle Cups, 129	24	95	1	10	6	5	30	0	0	0	0	0	0	0	0
Divinity, 128	48	65	0	14	1	0	10	0	0	0	0	0	0	0	0
Grape Gumdrops, 127	72	28	0	7	0	0	10	0	0	0	0	0	0	0	0
Hazelnut Fudge, 126	32	75	0	14	2	2	12	0	0	0	0	0	0	0	0
Mint Wafers, 130	96	25	0	6	0	0	5	0	0	0	0	0	0	0	0
Orange Gumdrops, 127	72	28	0	7	0	0	10	0	0	0	0	0	0	0	0
Orange Truffles, 128	15	165	1	16	10	6	20	2	2	0	0	0	0	0	2
Peanut Brittle, 127	72	70	1	9	4	0	35	2	0	0	0	0	4	0	0
Penuche, 126	32	65	0	14	1	0	0	0	0	0	0	0	0	0	2
Peppermint Taffy, 130	48	15	0	4	0	0	45	0	0	0	0	0	0	0	0
Popcorn Balls, 129	8	202	1	36	6	0	150	2	4	0	0	0	0	0	6
Praline Truffle Cups, 129	24	95	1	10	6	5	30	0	0	0	0	0	0	0	0
Pralines, 127	18	225	1	41	7	2	35	2	0	0	6	2	0	4	6
Raspberry Truffle Cups, 129	24	95	1	10	6	5	30	0	0	0	0	0	0	0	0
Rum Balls, 124	60	65	0	11	2	0	20	0	0	0	2	0	0	0	0
Taffy, 130	48	15	0	4	0	0	45	0	0	0	0	0	0	0	0
Toffee, 125	36	75	0	7	5	0	35	0	2	0	2	0	0	0	0
Truffles, 128	15	155	1	14	10	6	20	2	2	0	0	0	0	0	2

DESSERTS

DESSERTS

Desserts are delicious and satisfying endings to any meal and range from a piece of ripe fruit or a berry cobbler to ice cream with chocolate sauce and cheesecake. The dessert you choose complements the meal—a light dessert is just right after a large meal, while Hot Chocolate Soufflé (page 146) will be enjoyed the most after a more modest dinner. Desserts are also wonderful ways to celebrate special events—a Strawberry Shortcake (page 143) for the Fourth of July or Cherry-Berries on a Cloud (page 157) for a good-bye dinner or party. However you wish to use these recipes, we know you'll enjoy your just desserts!

DESSERT BASICS

This chapter is a collection of those desserts that go beyond Cakes and Pies (page 65) or Cookies and Candy (page 105).

♦ A great variety of fresh fruits are now available to us. Choose fruits at their seasonal peak for the fullest flavors and the most economical prices.

♦ Fruits can be served as snacks or at any meal. Serve whole and uncut, cut up and mixed or baked in delicious cobblers or other dessert specialties.

♦ Orchard fruits, citrus fruits and even those that used to be considered exotic, such as kiwifruit, mangoes and papayas, are now close to staples. Even unusual fruits such as carambolas, tamarinds and prickly pears are becoming easy to find.

♦ Canned and frozen fruits may be used in many recipes that call for fresh fruits not in season.

♦ Baked custards are done when a knife inserted halfway between center and edge of the custard comes out clean. The center of the custard may look soft but will become firm as it cools.

♦ Cheesecakes are baked at low temperatures. This prevents excess shrinkage. The center may look slightly soft, but will set while chilling. Refrigerate cheesecakes for at least 3 hours before serving.

♦ Cheesecakes cut easily when a wet knife is used, cleaning after each cut; or use a piece of dental floss.

♦ When preparing meringue shells, gradually add the sugar so it has time to dissolve while beating.

♦ When making ice cream that includes eggs, we recommend the eggs be cooked in a custard for safety reasons.

Preceding page: Raspberry Swirl Cheesecake (page 148), Gingered Pineapple (page 142), Chocolate Eclairs (page 151)

BAKED APPLES

4 large unpared apples (Rome Beauty, Golden Delicious, Greening)
2 to 4 tablespoons granulated or packed brown sugar
4 teaspoons margarine or butter
½ teaspoon ground cinnamon

Heat oven to 375°. Core apples. Pare 1-inch strip of skin around middle of each apple, or pare upper half of each to prevent splitting. Place apples in ungreased baking dish. Place 1 teaspoon to 1 tablespoon sugar, 1 teaspoon margarine and ⅛ teaspoon cinnamon in center of each apple. Sprinkle with cinnamon. Pour water into baking dish until ¼ inch deep.

Bake 30 to 40 minutes or until tender when pierced with fork. (Time will vary with size and variety of apple.) Spoon syrup in dish over apples several times during baking if desired.   4 SERVINGS; 165 CALORIES PER SERVING.

To Microwave: Prepare apples as directed—except omit water. Place each apple in 10-ounce custard cups or individual casseroles. Microwave uncovered on high 5 to 10 minutes, rotating cups ½ turn after 3 minutes, until apples are tender when pierced with fork.

BAKED HONEY APPLES: Substitute honey for the sugar.   185 CALORIES PER SERVING.

BAKED MINCEMEAT APPLES: Omit sugar, margarine and cinnamon. Fill each apple with 1 to 2 tablespoons prepared mincemeat.   115 CALORIES PER SERVING.

APPLE TART TATIN

2 tablespoons margarine or butter
½ cup packed brown sugar
8 large tart apples (about 3 pounds), pared and cut into eighths
½ package (17½-ounce size) frozen puff pastry, thawed
Apple Chantilly Cream (below)

Heat margarine and brown sugar in 10-inch oven-proof skillet over medium heat, stirring constantly, until melted. Stir in apples. Cook 20 to 25 minutes, stirring frequently, until syrup thickens; remove from heat.

Heat oven to 400°. Roll pastry into 10½-inch square on lightly floured surface. Cut into 10½-inch circle. Fold pastry into fourths; cut slits so steam can escape. Place over apples and unfold; carefully tuck edge down around apples. Bake 15 to 20 minutes or until pastry is brown. Let stand 5 minutes; invert onto heatproof serving plate. Serve with Apple Chantilly Cream. 8 SERVINGS; 410 CALORIES PER SERVING.

Apple Chantilly Cream

1 cup whipping (heavy) cream
1 tablespoon apple brandy or calvados

Beat ingredients in chilled medium bowl until soft peaks form.

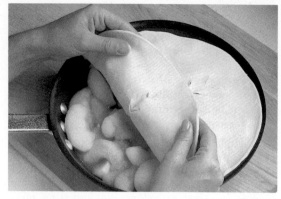

1. Place pastry over apples and unfold; carefully tuck edge down around apples.

2. Bake 15 to 20 minutes or until pastry is brown.

Apple Tart Tatin

☀ APPLESAUCE

4 medium cooking apples, pared and each
    cut into fourths
½ cup water
¼ cup packed brown sugar or 3 to 4 table-
    spoons granulated sugar
¼ teaspoon ground cinnamon
⅛ teaspoon ground nutmeg

Heat apples and water to boiling over medium
heat, stirring occasionally; reduce heat. Simmer
uncovered 5 to 10 minutes, stirring occasionally to
break up apples, until tender. Stir in remaining
ingredients. Heat to boiling. Boil and stir 1 minute. 6 SERVINGS (ABOUT ½ CUP EACH); 90 CALO-
RIES PER SERVING.

To Microwave: Decrease water to ¼ cup. Place
all ingredients in 2-quart microwavable casserole.
Cover tightly and microwave on high 10 to 12
minutes, stirring and breaking up apples every 3
minutes, until apples are soft.

☀ APPLE CRISP

*Apple Crisp is an American classic that
uses our abundance of native apples in a
luxurious-tasting, no-fuss dessert. During
World War II when food rationing was in
effect, this patriotic crisp was featured as
"easy on shortening and sugar."*

4 cups sliced tart apples (about 4 medium)
⅔ to ¾ cup packed brown sugar
½ cup all-purpose flour*
½ cup oats
⅓ cup margarine or butter, softened
¾ teaspoon ground cinnamon
¾ teaspoon ground nutmeg

Heat oven to 375°. Grease square pan, 8×8×2
inches. Arrange apples in pan. Mix remaining ingredients. Sprinkle over apples. Bake about 30
minutes or until topping is golden brown and apples are tender. Serve warm and, if desired, with
cream or ice cream. 6 SERVINGS; 290 CALORIES
PER SERVING.

Self-rising flour can be used in this recipe.

To Microwave: Prepare as directed—except use
ungreased 2-quart microwavable casserole or square
microwavable dish, 8×8×2 inches. Microwave uncovered on high 10 to12 minutes, rotating dish ½
turn after 5 minutes, until apples are tender.

APRICOT CRISP: Substitute 2 cans (17 ounces each)
apricot halves, drained, for the apples and use the
lesser amount of brown sugar. 265 CALORIES PER
SERVING.

CHERRY CRISP: Substitute 1 can (21 ounces) cherry
pie filling for the apples and use the lesser amount
of brown sugar. 325 CALORIES PER SERVING.

PEACH CRISP: Substitute fresh peaches or 1 can
(29 ounces) sliced peaches, drained, for the apples
and use the lesser amount of brown sugar. 285
CALORIES PER SERVING.

PINEAPPLE CRISP: Substitute 2 cans (13½ ounces
each) pineapple chunks, drained, or 2 cans (20
ounces each) crushed pineapple, drained, for the
apples and use the lesser amount of brown sugar.
285 CALORIES PER SERVING.

APPLE-APRICOT
STRUDELS

3 cups chopped all-purpose apples (about
    3 medium)
1 cup chopped dried apricots
½ cup slivered almonds, toasted
⅓ cup granulated sugar
¼ cup dry bread crumbs
1 tablespoon lemon juice
¼ teaspoon ground nutmeg
8 frozen (thawed) phyllo leaves
¼ cup margarine or butter, melted
Powdered sugar

Heat oven to 375°. Mix apples, apricots, almonds,
granulated sugar, bread crumbs, lemon juice and
nutmeg. Fold 1 phyllo leaf in half crosswise and
brush with margarine. (Keep remaining phyllo leaves
covered with a dampened towel to prevent them
from drying out.) Place about ⅔ cup of the apple
mixture in center of phyllo leaf 1 inch from narrow
end of leaf. Fold sides of phyllo toward center,
overlapping sides slightly. Roll up, beginning at
filling end. Place seam side down on ungreased
cookie sheet. Repeat with remaining phyllo leaves
and apple mixture.

Bake 30 to 35 minutes or until golden brown; cool.
Sprinkle with powdered sugar. Serve with Soft
Custard (page 00) if desired. 8 SERVINGS; 280
CALORIES PER SERVING.

Place apple mixture in center of folded phyllo leaf
1 inch from narrow end of leaf. Fold sides of phyllo
toward center, overlapping sides slightly.

Fresh Blueberry Cobbler

FRESH BLUEBERRY COBBLER

½ cup sugar
1 tablespoon cornstarch
4 cups blueberries
1 teaspoon lemon juice
3 tablespoons shortening
1 cup all-purpose flour*
1 tablespoon sugar
1½ teaspoons baking powder
½ teaspoon salt
½ cup milk

Heat oven to 400°. Mix ½ cup sugar and the cornstarch in 2-quart saucepan. Stir in blueberries and lemon juice. Cook, stirring constantly, until mixture thickens and boils. Boil and stir 1 minute. Pour into ungreased 2-quart casserole; keep blueberry mixture hot in oven.

Cut shortening into flour, 1 tablespoon sugar, the baking powder and salt until mixture resembles fine crumbs. Stir in milk. Drop dough by 6 spoonfuls onto hot blueberry mixture.

Bake 25 to 30 minutes or until topping is golden brown. Serve warm and, if desired, with Sweetened Whipped Cream (page 162).   6 SERVINGS; 265 CALORIES PER SERVING.

*If using self-rising flour, omit baking powder and salt.

FRESH CHERRY COBBLER: Substitute 4 cups pitted red tart cherries for the blueberries. Increase sugar in cherry mixture to 1¼ cups and cornstarch to 3 tablespoons. Add ¼ teaspoon ground cinnamon with the cornstarch. Substitute ¼ teaspoon almond extract for the lemon juice.   365 CALORIES PER SERVING.

FRESH PEACH COBBLER: Substitute 4 cups sliced peaches (about 6 medium) for the blueberries. Add ¼ teaspoon ground cinnamon with the cornstarch.   250 CALORIES PER SERVING.

CHERRY CLAFOUTI

3 eggs
1 cup milk
½ cup all-purpose flour
¼ cup granulated sugar
1 teaspoon vanilla
2 cups pitted dark sweet cherries
Powdered sugar

Heat oven to 350°. Grease square baking dish, 8 × 8 × 2 inches. Beat eggs, milk, flour, granulated sugar and the vanilla with hand beater until smooth. Spread cherries in dish. Pour batter over cherries. Bake 45 to 50 minutes or until puffed and golden brown. Sprinkle with powdered sugar. Serve warm. 6 SERVINGS; 170 CALORIES PER SERVING.

CHERRIES JUBILEE

Vanilla ice cream
1/4 cup rum
2 cups pitted dark sweet cherries*
3/4 cup currant jelly
1 teaspoon grated orange peel
1/4 cup brandy

Scoop ice cream into serving-size portions onto cookie sheet; freeze. Pour rum over cherries. Refrigerate 4 hours.

Just before serving, heat jelly in chafing dish or 1 1/2-quart saucepan over low heat until melted. Stir in cherry mixture and orange peel. Heat to simmering, stirring constantly. Heat brandy in small, long-handled pan or metal ladle just until warm. Ignite and pour flaming over cherries. Serve hot over ice cream in dessert dishes. 8 TO 10 SERVINGS; 300 CALORIES PER SERVING.

*1 can (16 ounces) pitted dark sweet cherries, drained and 1/4 cup syrup reserved, can be substituted for the 2 cups cherries. Mix reserved cherry syrup and the rum; pour over cherries.

SPICY FRUIT COMPOTE

1 two-inch cinnamon stick
6 whole cloves
1/4 cup sugar
1/2 cup port, sweet red wine or apple juice
1/2 cup water
2 tablespoons lemon juice
1 package (11 ounces) mixed dried fruit
2 bananas, sliced

Tie cinnamon stick and cloves in cheesecloth bag. Heat cheesecloth bag, sugar, port, water and lemon juice to boiling in 2-quart saucepan. Stir in dried fruit. Heat to boiling; reduce heat. Simmer uncovered 10 to 15 minutes, stirring occasionally, until fruit is plump and tender. Refrigerate uncovered about 3 hours, stirring occasionally, until chilled.

Remove cheesecloth bag. Stir bananas into fruit mixture until coated with syrup. Drain fruit, reserving syrup. Serve fruit with some of the syrup. Serve with sour cream or plain yogurt if desired. 6 SERVINGS; 220 CALORIES PER SERVING.

PEACH MELBA

1 cup sugar
2 cups water
4 peaches, peeled and cut in half*
Raspberry-Currant Sauce (page 162)
Vanilla or pistachio ice cream

Heat sugar and water to boiling in 10-inch skillet; reduce heat. Place peaches, cut sides down, in skillet. Cover and simmer 10 to 15 minutes or until peaches are tender.

Prepare Raspberry-Currant Sauce. Place 2 peach halves in each of 4 dessert dishes. Pour sauce over peaches. Refrigerate until chilled. Top each serving with 1 scoop ice cream. 4 SERVINGS; 540 CALORIES PER SERVING.

*8 canned peach halves, drained, can be substituted for the sugar, water and fresh peaches.

PRALINE-PEACH DESSERT

1/2 cup packed brown sugar
1/2 cup chopped almonds
1/3 cup margarine or butter
3 cups sliced fresh (about 3 medium) or frozen (thawed) peaches
6 slices angel food or pound cake

Heat brown sugar, almonds and margarine in 10-inch skillet to boiling; reduce heat. Stir in peaches. Cover and simmer about 3 minutes or until peaches are hot. Serve warm or cool over angel food cake. 6 SERVINGS; 390 CALORIES PER SERVING.

To Microwave: Place brown sugar, almonds and margarine in microwavable 2-quart casserole. Microwave uncovered on high 1 minute 30 seconds to 2 minutes 30 seconds, stirring every minute, until boiling. Stir in peaches. Microwave uncovered 1 to 2 minutes longer or until peaches are hot. Continue as directed.

MANGO WITH PASSION FRUIT

1 large mango (about 1 pound), thinly sliced
8 pitted dates, cut in half
1 passion fruit
1/2 cup vanilla yogurt or sour cream

Arrange mango and dates on 4 dessert plates. Cut passion fruit in half and scoop out center. Mix passion fruit and yogurt. Serve with fruit. 4 SERVINGS; 110 CALORIES PER SERVING.

SPECIALTY FRUIT

Top: *Quince, Asian pear, red bartlett pear, pomegranate, mango, horned melon.* Middle: *Papaya, green prickly pear, tamarind, sapota or custard apple, red prickly pear.* Bottom: *Manzano or apple banana, passion fruit, coquito nuts, golden raspberries, black currants.*

PEARS HÉLÈNE

1 cup sugar
2 cups water
1 teaspoon vanilla
3 medium pears, pared and cut in half*
Hot Fudge Sauce (page 161)
Vanilla ice cream

Heat sugar and water to boiling in 10-inch skillet; reduce heat. Stir in vanilla. Place pears, cut sides down, in skillet. Cover and simmer about 15 minutes or until pears are tender. Turn pears over. Refrigerate in syrup at least 2 hours or until chilled.

Just before serving, prepare Hot Fudge Sauce. Place 1 scoop ice cream in each of 6 dessert dishes. Top with pear half and 1 tablespoon Hot Fudge Sauce.   6 SERVINGS; 340 CALORIES PER SERVING.

6 canned pear halves, drained, can be substituted for the sugar, water and fresh pears. Refrigerate until chilled.

RHUBARB-STRAWBERRY FOOL

Rhubarb-Strawberry Sauce (below)
1 cup sour cream or plain yogurt
1 cup whipping (heavy) cream
⅓ cup packed brown sugar

Prepare Rhubarb-Strawberry Sauce. Cover and refrigerate about 3 hours or until chilled. Mix sauce and sour cream. Beat whipping cream in chilled medium bowl until stiff. Fold in sauce mixture just until fruit streaks remain. Pour into dessert dishes or serving bowl. Sprinkle with brown sugar. Refrigerate any remaining dessert. 6 SERVINGS (ABOUT ¾ CUP EACH); 380 CALORIES PER SERVING.

Rhubarb-Strawberry Sauce

½ to ¾ cup sugar
⅓ cup water
1 pound rhubarb, cut into 1-inch pieces (about 4 cups)
1 cup sliced strawberries
Few drops red food color, if desired

Heat sugar and water to boiling in 2-quart saucepan, stirring occasionally. Add rhubarb; reduce heat. Simmer uncovered about 10 minutes or until rhubarb is tender and slightly transparent. Stir in strawberries. Heat just to boiling. Stir in food color.

GINGERED PINEAPPLE

1 medium pineapple, pared and cut into chunks*
1 teaspoon finely chopped gingeroot or ½ teaspoon ground ginger
1 medium orange

Sprinkle pineapple with gingeroot. Grate 2 teaspoons orange peel; sprinkle over pineapple. Cut orange in half and remove seeds. Squeeze juice (about ¼ cup) over pineapple. Stir gently. Cover and refrigerate at least 1 hour, stirring once, to blend flavors.   6 SERVINGS; 45 CALORIES PER SERVING.

3 cans (8 ounces each) pineapple chunks in juice, drained, can be substituted for the fresh pineapple.

To cut pineapple into chunks, twist top from pineapple.

1. Cut pineapple into fourths and then cut fruit from rind.

2. Remove core and any eyes. Slice each fourth lengthwise and cut crosswise into chunks.

WATERMELON WITH BLACKBERRIES AND PEAR PUREE

Watermelon is a summer favorite, especially in the South. Mark Twain best summed up the glory of southern watermelon: "When one has tasted it, he knows what the angels eat."

3 slices watermelon, ¾ inch thick each
1½ cups blackberries
Pear Puree (below)

Cut each watermelon slice into 10 wedges. Cut rind from wedges and remove seeds. Arrange wedges on 6 dessert plates. Top with blackberries. Refrigerate about 1 hour or until chilled. Top each serving with Pear Puree.   6 SERVINGS; 100 CALORIES PER SERVING.

Pear Puree

2 medium pears
¼ cup light rum

Pare pears. Cut into fourths; remove cores and stems. Place pears and rum in blender or food processor. Cover and blend on medium, or process, about 1 minute or until smooth.

Clockwise from top: *Watermelon with Blackberries and Pear Puree, Starfruit and Strawberries in Champagne (page 143), Mango with Passion Fruit (page 140)*

Strawberry Shortcakes

🌾 STRAWBERRY SHORTCAKES

This heralds summer in the Betty Crocker Dining Room! Cut shortcakes into different shapes with cookie cutters just for fun. Remember, you can use any fresh, seasonal berry you like.

1 quart strawberries, sliced
½ cup sugar
⅓ cup shortening
2 cups all-purpose flour*
2 tablespoons sugar
3 teaspoons baking powder
1 teaspoon salt
¾ cup milk
Margarine or butter, softened
Sweetened Whipped Cream (page 162)

Mix strawberries and ½ cup sugar. Let stand 1 hour.

Heat oven to 450°. Cut shortening into flour, 2 tablespoons sugar, the baking powder and salt with pastry blender until mixture resembles fine crumbs. Stir in milk just until blended. Turn dough onto lightly floured surface. Gently smooth into a ball. Knead 20 to 25 times. Roll ½ inch thick. Cut with floured 3-inch cutter. Place about 1 inch apart on ungreased cookie sheet.

Bake 10 to 12 minutes or until golden brown. Split crosswise while hot. Spread with margarine. Fill and top with strawberries. Top with Sweetened Whipped Cream. 6 SERVINGS; 570 CALORIES PER SERVING.

*If using self-rising flour, omit baking powder and salt.

PAT-IN-THE-PAN SHORTCAKE: Do not smooth dough into a ball. Pat in greased round pan, 8 × 1½ inches. Bake 15 to 20 minutes.

STARFRUIT AND STRAWBERRIES IN CHAMPAGNE

2 starfruit
¼ cup sugar
2 cups strawberries, cut in half
¾ cup champagne or sparkling Catawba grape juice

Cut starfruit crosswise into ¼-inch slices. Sprinkle with sugar. Let stand 30 minutes. Spoon starfruit and strawberries into 6 dessert dishes. Pour champagne over fruit. 6 SERVINGS; 75 CALORIES PER SERVING.

BLACK WALNUT TORTE

2 cups whipping (heavy) cream
¼ cup packed brown sugar
½ cup finely chopped black walnuts or
  pecans
33 graham crackers (each 2½ inches square)

Beat whipping cream and brown sugar in chilled large bowl until stiff. Fold in walnuts. Spread small amount of whipped cream mixture on each of 3 crackers. Arrange crackers, frosted sides down and with edges touching to form a rectangle, on serving plate. Spread rectangle with about ¼ cup whipped cream mixture. Layer with 3 crackers. Repeat layers 9 times. Gently press torte together. Carefully turn torte on its side with spatula so crackers are vertical. Frost sides and top with remaining whipped cream mixture. Refrigerate at least 6 hours (torte will mellow and become moist). 10 SERVINGS; 305 CALORIES PER SERVING.

CHOCOLATE TORTE: Omit black walnuts. Substitute ½ cup chocolate-flavored syrup for the brown sugar. 295 CALORIES PER SERVING.

HOT FUDGE SUNDAE CAKE

Hot Fudge Sundae Cake has appeared in every basic Betty Crocker's cookbook since 1950. In our first three cookbooks it was called "Hot Fudge Pudding," and in 1969 we changed the name to make it clear that two different textures are formed, as if by magic, while the cake is baking. You can spoon the cake into a dessert dish and then top with the pudding for a true sundae effect!

During World War II, we recommended this pudding/cake as a substitute for more conventional cakes, because it used no eggs or butter, products that were in very short supply due to rationing. Today it will appeal to people concerned with cholesterol. In 1980 we added microwave directions to this recipe, and we all agree that it's just about the perfect cake for the microwave with its rich, dark color and balance of moisture and sugar.

HOT FUDGE SUNDAE CAKE

1 cup all-purpose flour*
¾ cup granulated sugar
2 tablespoons cocoa
2 teaspoons baking powder
¼ teaspoon salt
½ cup milk
2 tablespoons vegetable oil
1 teaspoon vanilla
1 cup chopped nuts, if desired
1 cup packed brown sugar
¼ cup cocoa
1¾ cups very hot water
Ice cream

Heat oven to 350°. Mix flour, granulated sugar, 2 tablespoons cocoa, the baking powder and salt in ungreased square pan, 9 × 9 × 2 inches. Mix in milk, oil and vanilla with fork until smooth. Stir in nuts. Spread in pan. Sprinkle with brown sugar and ¼ cup cocoa. Pour very hot water over batter.

Bake 40 minutes. Spoon warm cake into dessert dishes and top with ice cream. Spoon sauce from pan onto each serving. 9 SERVINGS; 475 CALORIES PER SERVING.

*If using self-rising flour, omit baking powder and salt.

To Microwave: Mix flour, granulated sugar, 2 tablespoons cocoa, the baking powder and salt in 2-quart microwavable casserole. Mix in milk, oil and vanilla with fork until smooth. Stir in nuts. Sprinkle with brown sugar and ¼ cup cocoa. Pour very hot water over batter. Microwave uncovered on medium (50%) 9 minutes; rotate casserole ¼ turn. Microwave uncovered on high 5 to 7 minutes longer or until top is almost dry. Continue as directed.

BUTTERSCOTCH SUNDAE CAKE: Substitute 1 package (6 ounces) butterscotch chips for the nuts. Decrease brown sugar to ½ cup and the ¼ cup cocoa to 2 tablespoons. 430 CALORIES PER SERVING.

MALLOW SUNDAE CAKE: Substitute 1 cup miniature marshmallows for the nuts. 400 CALORIES PER SERVING.

PEANUTTY SUNDAE CAKE: Substitute ½ cup peanut butter and ½ cup chopped peanuts for the nuts. 515 CALORIES PER SERVING.

RAISIN SUNDAE CAKE: Substitute 1 cup raisins for the nuts. 440 CALORIES PER SERVING.

PEPPERMINT CREAM TORTE

Chocolate Ice-Cream Roll (page 81)
2½ cups whipping (heavy) cream, whipped, or 1 carton (12 ounces) frozen whipped topping, thawed
½ cup crushed hard peppermint candies (about 18 candies)

Prepare Chocolate Ice-Cream Roll as directed—except do not fill with ice cream. Reserve 2 cups whipped cream. Fold peppermint candies into remaining whipped cream. Unroll cake and remove towel. Spread cake with peppermint topping. Cut cake lengthwise evenly into 6 strips. Roll up one of the strips and place it cut side up on 10-inch serving plate. Coil remaining strips tightly around center roll. Smooth top with spatula if necessary. Frost top and side of torte with reserved whipped cream. Drizzle with chocolate syrup if desired. Refrigerate at least 2 hours. 12 SERVINGS; 230 CALORIES PER SERVING.

COCONUT CREAM TORTE: Substitute 1 cup flaked coconut for the peppermint candies. 230 CALORIES PER SERVING.

HAZELNUT CREAM TORTE: Substitute ¾ cup finely chopped hazelnuts, toasted, for the peppermint candies; reserve ¼ cup to sprinkle on top. 250 CALORIES PER SERVING.

1. Roll up one of the strips and place on the serving plate. Coil remaining strips tightly around center roll.

2. Smooth top. Frost top and side of torte with reserved whipped topping.

Peppermint Cream Torte

🌾 HOT CHOCOLATE SOUFFLÉ

⅓ cup sugar
⅓ cup cocoa
¼ cup all-purpose flour
1 cup milk
3 egg yolks
2 tablespoons margarine or butter, softened
1 teaspoon vanilla
4 egg whites
¼ teaspoon cream of tartar
⅛ teaspoon salt
3 tablespoons sugar
Best Sauce (below) or Amber Sauce
   (page 154)

Mix ⅓ cup sugar, the cocoa and flour in 1½-quart saucepan. Gradually stir in milk. Heat to boiling, stirring constantly; remove from heat. Beat egg yolks with fork in small bowl. Beat in about one-third of the cocoa mixture. Gradually stir in remaining cocoa mixture. Stir in margarine and vanilla; cool slightly.

Place oven rack in lowest position. Heat oven to 350°. Butter and sugar 6-cup soufflé dish. Make 4-inch band of triple-thickness aluminum foil 2 inches longer than circumference of dish. Butter and sugar one side of band. Extend dish by securing band, buttered side in, around outside edge.

Beat egg whites, cream of tartar and salt in 2½-quart bowl until foamy. Beat in 3 tablespoons sugar, 1 tablespoon at a time; continue beating until stiff and glossy. Do not underbeat. Stir about one-fourth of the egg whites into cocoa mixture. Fold in remaining egg whites. Carefully pour into soufflé dish. Place dish in square pan, 9 × 9 × 2 inches, on oven rack. Pour very hot water into pan until 1 inch deep. Bake 1¼ hours. While soufflé is baking, prepare Best Sauce. Immediately serve with Best Sauce.   6 SERVINGS; 445 CALORIES PER SERVING.

Best Sauce

½ cup powdered sugar
½ cup margarine or butter, softened
½ cup whipping (heavy) cream

Beat powdered sugar and margarine in 1-quart saucepan until creamy. Beat whipping cream in chilled bowl until stiff. Fold whipped cream into sugar mixture. Heat to boiling, stirring occasionally.

Opposite page, clockwise from top: Bittersweet Chocolate Cheesecake with White Truffle Sauce (page 149), Lindy's Cheesecake Squares, Mini Peanut Butter Cheesecakes (page 149)

🌾 LINDY'S CHEESECAKE

1 cup all-purpose flour
½ cup margarine or butter, softened
¼ cup sugar
1 tablespoon grated lemon peel
1 egg yolk
5 packages (8 ounces each) cream cheese, softened
1¾ cups sugar
3 tablespoons all-purpose flour
1 tablespoon grated orange peel
1 tablespoon grated lemon peel
¼ teaspoon salt
5 eggs
2 egg yolks
¼ cup whipping (heavy) cream
¾ cup whipping (heavy) cream
⅓ cup toasted slivered almonds, if desired

Move oven rack to lowest position. Heat oven to 400°. Lightly grease springform pan, 9 × 3 inches; remove bottom. Mix 1 cup flour, the margarine, ¼ cup sugar, 1 tablespoon lemon peel and 1 egg yolk with hands. Press one-third of the mixture evenly on bottom of pan. Place on cookie sheet. Bake 8 to 10 minutes or until golden brown; cool. Assemble bottom and side of pan; secure side. Press remaining mixture all the way up side of pan.

Heat oven to 475°. Beat cream cheese, 1¾ cups sugar, 3 tablespoons flour, the orange peel, 1 tablespoon lemon peel, the salt and 2 of the eggs in large bowl until smooth. Continue beating, adding remaining eggs and 2 egg yolks, one at a time, until blended. Beat in ¼ cup whipping cream on low speed. Pour into pan. Bake 15 minutes. Reduce oven temperature to 200°. Bake 1 hour. Turn off oven and leave cheesecake in oven 15 minutes. Run metal spatula along side of cheesecake to loosen before and after refrigerating. Cover and refrigerate at least 12 hours.

Remove cheesecake from side of pan. Beat ¾ cup whipping cream in chilled bowl until stiff. Spread whipped cream over top of cheesecake. Decorate with almonds. Refrigerate any remaining cheesecake.   20 SERVINGS; 410 CALORIES PER SERVING.

LINDY'S CHEESECAKE SQUARES: Heat oven to 400°. Lightly grease rectangular pan, 13 × 9 × 2 inches. Press crust mixture on bottom of pan. Do not place pan on cookie sheet. Bake 15 minutes; cool. Heat oven to 475°. Pour cream cheese mixture into pan. Bake 15 minutes. Reduce oven temperature to 200°. Bake about 45 minutes or until center is set. Turn off oven and leave cheesecake in oven 15 minutes; cool 15 minutes. Cover and refrigerate at least 12 hours.

Continue as directed—except increase almonds to ½ cup.   20 SERVINGS; 410 CALORIES PER SERVING.

RASPBERRY SWIRL CHEESECAKE

This cheesecake plays off the delicious combination of chocolate and raspberries. The chocolate-lined pastry makes it especially elegant.

Raspberry Sauce (right)*
1 cup all-purpose flour
¼ cup sugar
⅓ cup margarine or butter, softened
1 egg yolk
1 cup semisweet chocolate chips
3 tablespoons whipping (heavy) cream
5 packages (8 ounces each) cream cheese, softened
1¾ cups sugar
3 tablespoons all-purpose flour
¼ teaspoon salt
¼ cup whipping (heavy) cream
5 eggs
2 egg yolks
⅓ cup semisweet chocolate chips, finely chopped

Move oven rack to lowest position. Heat oven to 400°. Lightly grease springform pan, 9 × 3 inches; remove bottom. Prepare Raspberry Sauce. Mix 1 cup flour, ¼ cup sugar, the margarine and 1 egg yolk with hands. (If dough is crumbly, sprinkle with 2 to 3 teaspoons water.) Press one-third of the mixture evenly on bottom of pan. Place on cookie sheet. Bake 8 to 10 minutes or until golden brown; cool. Assemble bottom and side of pan; secure side. Press remaining mixture 2½ inches up side of pan. Cut an 11-inch circle of heavy-duty aluminum foil. Place pan on foil circle; press foil up side to prevent dripping in oven during baking.

Heat 1 cup chocolate chips and 3 tablespoons whipping cream until chocolate chips are melted; cool slightly. Spread over bottom and up side of crust. Increase oven temperature to 475°.

Beat cream cheese, 1¾ cups sugar, 3 tablespoons flour, the salt, ¼ cup whipping cream and 2 eggs in large bowl until smooth. Continue beating, adding remaining eggs and the egg yolks, one at a time, until blended. Stir in finely chopped chocolate chips.

Pour one-half of the batter carefully into crust. Reserve ½ cup Raspberry Sauce for topping. Spread one-half of the remaining Raspberry Sauce by spoonfuls onto batter. Repeat with remaining batter and Raspberry Sauce; swirl through batter with metal spatula. Cover with aluminum foil. Bake 20 minutes.

Remove aluminum foil and reduce oven temperature to 300°. Bake 1 hour. (If cheesecake browns too quickly, cover loosely with aluminum foil during last 30 minutes of baking.) Turn off oven and leave cheesecake in oven 15 minutes. Spread reserved Raspberry Sauce over top of cheesecake; cool 15 minutes. Run metal spatula along side of cheesecake to loosen before and after refrigerating. Cover and refrigerate at least 12 hours.

Remove cheesecake from side of pan. Refrigerate any remaining cheesecake. 20 SERVINGS; 455 CALORIES PER SERVING.

Raspberry Sauce

1 package (10 ounces) frozen raspberries, thawed, drained and juice reserved
¼ cup sugar
2 tablespoons cornstarch

Add enough water to reserved juice to measure 1¼ cups. Mix sugar and cornstarch in 1-quart saucepan. Stir in juice and raspberries. Heat to boiling over medium heat, stirring frequently. Boil and stir 1 minute; strain. Cool completely.

1⅓ cups raspberry jam can be substituted for the Raspberry Sauce. Or 2 cups fresh or frozen raspberries, thawed and well drained, can be substituted for the Raspberry Sauce. Pour one-half of the batter into pan as directed. Sprinkle with one-half of the raspberries. Repeat with remaining batter and raspberries. Swirl through batter with metal spatula. Continue as directed.

AMARETTO-ALMOND SWIRL CHEESECAKE: Substitute Glazed Almonds (below) for the Raspberry Sauce. Stir ¼ cup amaretto into cream cheese mixture. Pour one-half of the batter into crust. Sprinkle with one-half of the Glazed Almonds. Repeat with remaining batter and almonds. Continue as directed. 470 CALORIES PER SERVING.

Glazed Almonds

½ cup sliced almonds
1 tablespoon plus 2 teaspoons packed brown sugar
2 tablespoons granulated sugar

Cook almonds in brown sugar and granulated sugar in 10-inch skillet over low heat, stirring constantly, until sugar is melted and almonds are coated. Spread on waxed paper–covered cookie sheet; cool and break apart.

MINI ALMOND CHEESECAKES

12 vanilla wafers
1 package (8 ounces) plus 1 package
  (3 ounces) cream cheese, softened
¼ cup sugar
2 tablespoons amaretto or ½ teaspoon
  almond extract
2 eggs
¼ cup chopped toasted almonds

Heat oven to 350°. Line 12 medium muffin cups, 2½ × 1¼ inches, with paper baking cups. Place 1 wafer, flat side down, in each cup. Beat cream cheese and sugar in medium bowl until fluffy. Add amaretto. Beat in eggs, one at a time. Fill cups three-fourths full. Sprinkle with almonds. Bake about 20 minutes or until centers are firm; cool 15 minutes. Cover and refrigerate at least 2 hours. Serve with fresh fruit or Raspberry-Currant Sauce (page 162), if desired. 12 SERVINGS; 170 CALORIES PER SERVING.

MINI PEANUT BUTTER CHEESECAKES: Omit amaretto and almonds. Stir in ½ teaspoon vanilla. Top filling in each cup with 1 milk chocolate–covered peanut butter cup. Bake 15 minutes. 195 CALORIES PER SERVING.

BITTERSWEET CHOCOLATE CHEESECAKE WITH WHITE TRUFFLE SAUCE

2 packages (8 ounces each) cream cheese,
  softened
1 teaspoon vanilla
⅔ cup sugar
1 tablespoon all-purpose flour
3 eggs
8 ounces bittersweet chocolate, melted and
  cooled
White Truffle Sauce (right)

Heat oven to 275°. Lightly grease springform pan, 9 × 3 inches. Beat cream cheese and vanilla on medium speed in medium bowl until smooth. Gradually add sugar, beating until fluffy. Beat in flour. Beat in eggs, one at a time. Beat in chocolate; pour into pan.

Bake about 1¼ hours or until center is firm. Cool 15 minutes. Run metal spatula along side of cheesecake to loosen before and after refrigerating. Cover and refrigerate about 3 hours or until chilled. Meanwhile, prepare White Truffle Sauce.

Remove cheesecake from side of pan. Let cheesecake stand at room temperature 15 minutes before cutting. Serve cheesecake with sauce and, if desired, fresh raspberries or strawberries. Refrigerate any remaining cheesecake. 12 SERVINGS; 415 CALORIES PER SERVING.

White Truffle Sauce

1 package (6 ounces) white baking bar,
  chopped
2 tablespoons margarine or butter
½ cup whipping (heavy) cream

Heat baking bar and margarine in heavy 2-quart saucepan over low heat, stirring constantly, until melted (mixture will be thick and grainy); remove from heat. Stir in whipping cream until smooth. Cover and refrigerate about 2 hours or until chilled.

 **CREPES**

Crepes can be frozen up to 3 months. Let crepes cool covered to keep them from drying out. Make 2 stacks of 6 crepes, placing waxed paper between each crepe. Wrap each stack in aluminum foil and freeze. Thaw crepes at room temperature.

1½ cups all-purpose flour*
1 tablespoon sugar
½ teaspoon baking powder
½ teaspoon salt
2 cups milk
2 tablespoons margarine or butter, melted
½ teaspoon vanilla
2 eggs

Mix flour, sugar, baking powder and salt in medium bowl. Stir in remaining ingredients. Beat with hand beater until smooth. Lightly butter 6- to 8-inch skillet. Heat over medium heat until bubbly. For each crepe, pour scant ¼ cup of the batter into skillet. *Immediately* rotate skillet until thin film covers bottom.

Cook until light brown. Run wide spatula around edge to loosen; turn and cook other side until light brown. Stack crepes, placing waxed paper between each; keep covered.

If desired, spread applesauce, sweetened strawberries, currant jelly or raspberry jam thinly over each warm crepe; roll up. (Be sure to fill crepes so the more attractive side is on the outside.) Sprinkle with powdered sugar if desired. 12 CREPES; 105 CALORIES PER CREPE.

If using self-rising flour, omit baking powder and salt.

FRESH FRUIT IN PHYLLO CUPS

Custard Sauce (below)
6 frozen phyllo leaves, thawed
¼ cup margarine or butter, melted
1 tablespoon powdered sugar
3 cups cut-up fresh fruit (berries, peaches, bananas, oranges, kiwifruit, papaya)

Prepare Custard Sauce. Move oven rack to lowest position. Heat oven to 400°. Grease six 10-ounce custard cups or 4-inch ramekins. Place damp towel on work surface, long side facing you. Cover with plastic wrap or waxed paper. Place phyllo sheets on plastic wrap. Cover with plastic wrap. Fold sheets crosswise in half. Unfold sheets one at a time, brushing each with margarine. Remove plastic wrap. Working quickly, fold top sheet crosswise in half. Carefully lift sheet and gently ease into custard cup, folding top edge under to form a loosely ruffled edge. Repeat with remaining phyllo sheets, replacing plastic wrap to keep sheets covered until needed.

Bake 10 to 12 minutes or until golden brown. Cool 5 minutes. Carefully remove to wire rack; cool. Dust with powdered sugar. Place phyllo cups on dessert plates. Divide fruit evenly among cups. Serve with Custard Sauce.   6 SERVINGS; 245 CALORIES PER SERVING.

Custard Sauce

2 eggs, slightly beaten
3 tablespoons sugar
Dash of salt
1¼ cups milk
½ teaspoon vanilla or ¼ teaspoon almond extract

Mix eggs, sugar and salt in heavy 2-quart saucepan. Gradually stir in milk. Cook over low heat 15 to 20 minutes, stirring constantly, until mixture just coats a metal spoon; remove from heat. Stir in vanilla. Refrigerate 30 minutes, stirring occasionally. (If custard curdles, beat vigorously with wire whisk or hand beater until smooth.) Serve warm or chilled. Cover and refrigerate any remaining sauce.

 CHERRY BLINTZES

Crepes (page 149)
1 cup dry cottage cheese
½ cup sour cream
2 tablespoons sugar
1 teaspoon vanilla
½ teaspoon grated lemon peel
¼ cup margarine or butter
1 cup sour cream
1 can (21 ounces) cherry pie filling

Prepare Crepes—except brown only one side. Stack crepes, placing waxed paper between each. Keep crepes covered to prevent them from drying out.

Mix cottage cheese, ½ cup sour cream, the sugar, vanilla and lemon peel. Spoon about 1½ tablespoons of the cheese mixture onto browned side of each crepe. Fold sides of crepe up over filling, overlapping edges; roll up.

Heat margarine in 12-inch skillet over medium heat until bubbly. Place blintzes, seam sides down, in skillet. Cook, turning once, until golden brown. Top each with rounded tablespoon sour cream and about 3 tablespoons pie filling.   6 SERVINGS; 545 CALORIES PER SERVING.

✻ CREAM PUFFS

This favorite has appeared in every Betty Crocker basic cookbook.

1 cup water
½ cup margarine or butter
1 cup all-purpose flour*
4 eggs
Cream Filling (below) or Sweetened
    Whipped Cream (page 162)
Powdered Sugar

Heat oven to 400°. Heat water and margarine to rolling boil in 2½-quart saucepan. Stir in flour; reduce heat. Stir vigorously over low heat about 1 minute or until mixture forms a ball; remove from heat. Beat in eggs, all at once; continue beating until smooth. Drop dough by scant ¼ cupfuls about 3 inches apart onto ungreased cookie sheet.

Bake 35 to 40 minutes or until puffed and golden brown. Cool away from draft. Cut off top one-third of each puff and pull out any filaments of soft dough. Fill puffs with Cream Filling. Replace tops and dust with powdered sugar. Refrigerate until serving time. Refrigerate any remaining puffs. 12 CREAM PUFFS; 205 CALORIES EACH.

*Self-rising flour can be used in this recipe.

Cream Filling

⅓ cup sugar
2 tablespoons cornstarch
⅛ teaspoon salt
2 cups milk
2 egg yolks, slightly beaten
2 tablespoons margarine or butter, softened
2 teaspoons vanilla

Mix sugar, cornstarch and salt in 2-quart saucepan. Gradually stir in milk. Cook over medium heat, stirring constantly, until mixture thickens and boils. Boil and stir 1 minute. Gradually stir at least half of the hot mixture into egg yolks. Stir into hot mixture in saucepan. Boil and stir 1 minute; remove from heat. Stir in margarine and vanilla; cool.

CHOCOLATE CREAM PUFFS: Decrease flour to ¾ cup plus 2 tablespoons. Mix 2 tablespoons cocoa and 1 tablespoon sugar with the flour. Omit Cream Filling. Fill puffs with chocolate or peppermint ice cream and frost with Chocolate Frosting (right). 320 CALORIES PER CREAM PUFF.

CHOCOLATE ECLAIRS: Drop dough by scant ¼ cupfuls onto ungreased cookie sheet. Shape each into finger 4½ inches long and 1½ inches wide with spatula. Bake as directed; cool. Fill with Cream Filling (left). Frost with Chocolate Frosting (below). 260 CALORIES PER ECLAIR.

Chocolate Frosting

1 ounce unsweetened chocolate
1 teaspoon margarine or butter
1 cup powdered sugar
1 to 2 tablespoons hot water.

Heat chocolate and margarine in 1-quart saucepan over low heat until melted; remove from heat. Stir in powdered sugar and hot water. Beat until smooth and of spreading consistency.

CHOCOLATE BELGIAN WAFFLES WITH HAZELNUT CREAM

2 cups variety baking mix
1 cup milk
⅓ cup chocolate-flavored syrup
2 tablespoons vegetable oil
1 egg
½ cup chopped hazelnuts, toasted
Hazelnut Cream (below)

Heat Belgian waffle iron (regular waffle iron can be used; bake times may be slightly shorter). Beat all ingredients except hazelnuts and Hazelnut Cream in medium bowl until smooth. Stir in hazelnuts. Pour batter from cup or pitcher onto center of hot waffle iron. Bake about 5 minutes or until steaming slows. Carefully remove waffle. While waffles are baking, prepare Hazelnut Cream. Serve with waffles and additional chopped toasted hazelnuts if desired. 6 SERVINGS (TWO 4-INCH SQUARES EACH); 515 CALORIES PER SERVING.

Hazelnut Cream

1 cup whipping (heavy) cream
2 tablespoons sugar
1 to 2 tablespoons hazelnut liqueur

Beat all ingredients in chilled bowl until stiff.

CHOCOLATE BELGIAN WAFFLES WITH STRAWBERRY CREAM: Prepare waffles as directed. Substitute Strawberry Cream for the Hazelnut Cream: Beat 1 cup whipping (heavy) cream and 2 tablespoons sugar in chilled bowl until stiff. Fold in 2 cups sliced fresh strawberries or 1 package (16 ounces) frozen sliced unsweetened strawberries, thawed and drained. 510 CALORIES PER SERVING.

🌾 BAKED CUSTARD

3 eggs, slightly beaten
⅓ cup sugar
1 teaspoon vanilla
Dash of salt
2½ cups milk, scalded
Ground nutmeg

Heat oven to 350°. Mix eggs, sugar, vanilla and salt in medium bowl. Gradually stir in milk. Pour into six 6-ounce custard cups. Sprinkle with nutmeg. Place cups in rectangular pan, 13 × 9 × 2 inches, on oven rack. Pour very hot water into pan to within ½ inch of tops of cups.

Bake about 45 minutes or until knife inserted halfway between center and edge comes out clean. Serve warm or chilled. Refrigerate any remaining custards. 6 SERVINGS; 130 CALORIES PER SERVING.

RASPBERRY CUSTARD: Mix ⅓ cup raspberry preserves and 1 tablespoon orange-flavored liqueur. Divide among custard cups. Continue as directed—except mix in 1 teaspoon orange-flavored liqueur with the salt; omit nutmeg. Refrigerate and unmold at serving time. Top with 2 cups fresh raspberries. 200 CALORIES PER SERVING.

PUMPKIN FLAN

¾ cup sugar
¼ cup water
1 cup canned pumpkin
¾ cup sugar
1 teaspoon ground cinnamon
½ teaspoon ground ginger
¼ teaspoon ground allspice
¼ teaspoon ground nutmeg
6 eggs
1 cup half-and-half
1 cup whipping (heavy) cream

Heat oven to 350°. Heat ¾ cup sugar and ¼ cup water to boiling in heavy 2-quart saucepan over low heat, stirring constantly. Boil, without stirring, until syrup is deep golden brown.

Place quiche dish, 9 × 1½ or 10 × 1¼ inches, in hot water until warm (to prevent dish from cracking when pouring hot syrup into it); dry completely. Pour syrup into dish; immediately rotate dish until syrup covers bottom.

Beat remaining ingredients except half-and-half and whipping cream in large bowl until well blended. Beat in half-and-half and whipping cream. Pour over syrup. Place dish in shallow roasting pan on oven rack. Pour very hot water into pan until 1

inch deep. Bake 1 to 1¼ hours or until knife inserted in center comes out clean.

Remove dish from water; cool 15 minutes. Refrigerate about 3 hours or until chilled. Loosen side of flan from dish, using knife; unmold. Refrigerate any remaining flan. 12 SERVINGS; 280 CALORIES PER SERVING.

🌾 VANILLA PUDDING

⅓ cup sugar
2 tablespoons cornstarch
⅛ teaspoon salt
2 cups milk
2 egg yolks, slightly beaten
2 tablespoons margarine or butter, softened
2 teaspoons vanilla

Mix sugar, cornstarch and salt in 2-quart saucepan. Gradually stir in milk. Cook over medium heat, stirring constantly, until mixture thickens and boils. Boil and stir 1 minute. Gradually stir at least half of the hot mixture into egg yolks. Stir into hot mixture in saucepan. Boil and stir 1 minute; remove from heat. Stir in margarine and vanilla. Pour into dessert dishes. Cover and refrigerate about 2 hours or until chilled. 4 SERVINGS (ABOUT ½ CUP EACH); 225 CALORIES PER SERVING.

To Microwave: Decrease milk to 1¾ cups. Mix sugar, cornstarch and salt in 8-cup microwavable measure or 2-quart microwavable casserole. Gradually stir in milk. Microwave uncovered on high 4 to 6 minutes, stirring every 2 minutes, until thickened and boiling. Stir at least half of the hot mixture gradually into egg yolks. Stir into hot mixture in measure. Microwave on medium (50%) 1 to 3 minutes, stirring every minute, until thickened. Continue as directed.

BUTTERSCOTCH PUDDING: Substitute ⅔ cup packed brown sugar for the granulated sugar and decrease vanilla to 1 teaspoon. 300 CALORIES PER SERVING.

CHOCOLATE PUDDING: Increase sugar to ½ cup and stir ⅓ cup cocoa into sugar mixture. Omit margarine. 285 CALORIES PER SERVING.

CRÈME BRÛLÉE

*"Burnt cream" is the everyday transla-
tion for the classic Crème Brûlée, due to its
caramelized sugar topping. It was a popular dish at Monticello, Thomas Jefferson's
Virginia home. It's also a hit in the Betty
Crocker Dining Room, served over fresh
fruit.*

4 egg yolks
3 tablespoons granulated sugar
2 cups whipping (heavy) cream
⅓ cup packed brown sugar
4 cups cut-up fresh fruit

Beat egg yolks in medium bowl on high speed
about 5 minutes or until thick and lemon colored.
Gradually beat in granulated sugar. Heat whipping
cream in 2-quart saucepan over medium heat just
until hot. Gradually stir at least half of the hot
cream into egg yolk mixture. Stir into hot cream in
saucepan. Cook over low heat 5 to 8 minutes,
stirring constantly, until mixture thickens (do not
boil). Pour custard into ungreased pie plate, 9 × 1¼
inches. Cover and refrigerate at least 2 hours.

Set oven control to broil. Sprinkle brown sugar
over custard. Broil with top about 5 inches from
heat about 3 minutes or until sugar is melted and
forms a glaze. Spoon over fruit. Refrigerate any
remaining custard.   8 SERVINGS; 310 CALORIES PER
SERVING.

BREAD PUDDING

2 cups milk
¼ cup margarine or butter
2 eggs, slightly beaten
½ cup sugar
1 teaspoon ground cinnamon or nutmeg
¼ teaspoon salt
6 cups dry bread cubes (8 slices bread)
½ cup raisins, if desired

Heat oven to 350°. Heat milk and margarine over
medium heat until margarine is melted and milk is
hot. Mix eggs, sugar, cinnamon and salt in 4-quart
bowl. Stir in bread cubes and raisins. Stir in milk
mixture. Pour into ungreased 1½-quart casserole.
Place casserole in pan on oven rack. Pour very hot
water into pan until 1 inch deep.

Bake uncovered 40 to 45 minutes or until knife
inserted 1 inch from edge comes out clean. Serve
warm and, if desired, with cream.   8 SERVINGS;
200 CALORIES PER SERVING.

CHOCOLATE POTS DE CRÈME

⅔ cup semisweet chocolate chips
1 cup half-and-half
2 eggs
3 tablespoons sugar
2 tablespoons rum, if desired
Dash of salt

Heat oven to 350°. Heat chocolate chips and
half-and-half in 1½-quart saucepan over medium
heat, stirring constantly, until chocolate is melted
and mixture is smooth; cool slightly. Beat remaining ingredients. Gradually stir into chocolate mixture. Pour into four 6-ounce custard cups or 4 or 5
ovenproof pot de crème cups.

Place cups in baking pan on oven rack. Pour boiling water into pan to within ½ inch of tops of
cups. Bake 20 minutes; cool slightly. Cover and
refrigerate at least 4 hours. Refrigerate any remaining pudding.   4 OR 5 SERVINGS; 315 CALORIES PER
SERVING.

FIG BREAD PUDDING

*The sugar sprinkled on top of the French
bread gives this dessert a crisp, attractive
top.*

½ pound French bread, torn into 1-inch
   pieces
4 ounces fresh or dried figs, cut into fourths
1½ cups milk
1 cup whipping (heavy) cream
¼ cup margarine or butter
½ cup sugar
3 eggs
1 teaspoon vanilla
2 tablespoons sugar

Heat oven to 350°. Grease square baking dish,
8 × 8 × 2 inches. Sprinkle bread pieces and figs
evenly in dish. Heat milk, whipping cream and
margarine over medium heat until margarine is
melted and milk is hot. Beat ½ cup sugar, the
eggs and vanilla in 4-cup measure or medium bowl.
Stir in milk mixture. Pour over bread pieces and
figs. Sprinkle with 2 tablespoons sugar. Place dish
in pan of very hot water (1 inch deep).

Bake 40 to 45 minutes or until knife inserted 1
inch from edge comes out clean. Serve warm with
Sweetened Whipped Cream (page 162) if desired.
9 SERVINGS; 315 CALORIES PER SERVING.

STEAMED PLUM PUDDING

1 cup milk
3 cups soft bread crumbs
½ cup shortening, melted
½ cup molasses
1 cup all-purpose flour*
½ cup chopped raisins
½ cup finely chopped citron
2 teaspoons ground cinnamon
1 teaspoon baking soda
½ teaspoon salt
¼ teaspoon ground allspice
¼ teaspoon ground cloves
Amber Sauce or Sherried Hard Sauce (below)

Generously grease 4-cup mold. Pour milk over bread crumbs in large bowl. Mix in shortening and molasses. Stir in remaining ingredients except Amber Sauce. Pour into mold. Cover with aluminum foil.

Place mold on rack in Dutch oven. Pour in boiling water up to level of rack. Cover and heat to boiling. Keep water boiling over low heat 3 hours or until wooden pick inserted in center comes out clean. (If it is necessary to add water during steaming, lift cover and quickly add boiling water.) Unmold pudding; cut into slices. Serve warm with Amber Sauce. 8 SERVINGS; 555 CALORIES PER SERVING.

*If using self rising flour, decrease baking soda to ½ teaspoon and omit salt.

Amber Sauce

1 cup packed brown sugar
½ cup light corn syrup
½ cup half-and-half
¼ cup butter or margarine

Mix all ingredients in 1-quart saucepan. Cook over low heat 5 minutes, stirring occasionally. Serve warm. ABOUT 2 CUPS.

Sherried Hard Sauce

½ cup margarine or butter, softened
1 cup powdered sugar
1 tablespoon sherry or brandy

Beat margarine in small bowl on high speed about 5 minutes or until fluffy and light in color. Gradually beat in powdered sugar until smooth. Blend in sherry. Refrigerate about 1 hour or until chilled. ABOUT 1 CUP.

PLUM PUDDING

We are partial to this traditional English Christmas dessert, and have included it in many cookbooks, beginning with our first, Miss Parloa's Cook Book of 1880. We still recommend making several and giving them as gifts. In the 1700s raisins were commonly called plums, which is how this Christmas pudding received its name. In England, there is an old saying: "In as many homes as you eat plum pudding in the twelve days following Christmas, so many happy months you will have during the year." For a dramatic presentation, this pudding can be served flaming. Place sugar cubes soaked in lemon extract around the pudding, then light one, and watch the flames circle the pudding.

NO STEAMER?

A steamer can be improvised using a Dutch oven or a large saucepan with a tight-fitting cover. Place a wire rack or trivet inside to raise the mold about 1 inch above the bottom of the pan.

RICE PUDDING

2 eggs or 4 egg yolks
½ cup sugar
½ cup raisins
2 cups milk
½ teaspoon vanilla
¼ teaspoon salt
2 cups hot cooked rice (page 267)
Ground nutmeg

Heat oven to 325°. Beat eggs in ungreased 1½-quart casserole. Stir in sugar, raisins, milk, vanilla, salt and hot rice. Sprinkle with nutmeg. Bake uncovered 50 to 60 minutes, stirring occasionally, until knife inserted halfway between center and edge comes out clean. Serve warm or cold and, if desired, with cream. Refrigerate any remaining pudding. 8 SERVINGS; 130 CALORIES PER SERVING.

ENGLISH TRIFLE

Early English settlers brought trifle to America, and it was sometimes called Tipsy Squire or Tipsy Parson because of the sherry in the recipe. One of our staff members serves a delicious holiday version that substitutes eggnog for the milk and whole cranberry sauce for the strawberries.

½ cup sugar
3 tablespoons cornstarch
¼ teaspoon salt
3 cups milk
½ cup dry sherry or dry white wine
3 egg yolks, beaten
3 tablespoons margarine or butter
1 tablespoon vanilla
2 packages (3 ounces each) ladyfingers
½ cup strawberry preserves
1 pint strawberries, sliced, or 1 package (12 ounces) frozen strawberries, thawed
1 cup whipping (heavy) cream
2 tablespoons sugar
2 tablespoons toasted slivered almonds

Mix ½ cup sugar, the cornstarch and salt in 3-quart saucepan. Gradually stir in milk and sherry. Heat to boiling over medium heat, stirring constantly. Boil and stir 1 minute. Stir at least half of the hot mixture gradually into egg yolks. Stir into hot mixture in saucepan. Boil and stir 1 minute; remove from heat. Stir in margarine and vanilla. Cover and refrigerate about 3 hours or until chilled.

Cut ladyfingers lengthwise in half. Spread each half with strawberry preserves. Layer one-fourth of the ladyfingers, cut sides up, half of the strawberries and half of the pudding in 2-quart serving bowl; repeat. Arrange remaining ladyfingers around edge of bowl in upright position and with cut sides toward center. (It may be necessary to ease ladyfingers gently down into pudding about 1 inch so they remain upright.) Cover and refrigerate.

Beat whipping cream and 2 tablespoons sugar in chilled medium bowl until stiff. Spread over dessert. Sprinkle with almonds. 10 SERVINGS; 390 CALORIES PER SERVING.

English Trifle, Fig Bread Pudding (page 153)

🌾 MERINGUE SHELL

3 egg whites
¼ teaspoon cream of tartar
¾ cup sugar

Heat oven to 275°. Cover cookie sheet with cooking parchment paper or heavy brown paper. Beat egg whites and cream of tartar in medium bowl until foamy. Beat in sugar, 1 tablespoon at a time; continue beating until stiff and glossy. Do not underbeat. Shape meringue on paper into 9-inch circle with back of spoon, building up side.

Bake 1½ hours. Turn off oven and leave meringue in oven with door closed 1 hour. Finish cooling meringue at room temperature. 8 SERVINGS; 75 CALORIES PER SERVING.

HEART MERINGUE: Fold several drops red food color, if desired, into meringue. Form into heart shape, building up side. Fill baked meringue with 1 quart strawberry ice cream and top with 2 cups sliced strawberries. 220 CALORIES PER SERVING.

INDIVIDUAL MERINGUES: Drop meringue by ⅓ cupfuls onto brown paper. Shape into circles, building up sides. Bake 1 hour. Turn off oven and leave meringues in oven with door closed 1½ hours. Finish cooling at room temperature. 8 TO 10 SHELLS; 75 CALORIES PER SERVING.

🌾 LEMON SCHAUM TORTE

Meringue Shell (left)
¾ cup sugar
3 tablespoons cornstarch
¼ teaspoon salt
¾ cup water
3 egg yolks, slightly beaten
1 tablespoon margarine or butter
1 teaspoon grated lemon peel
⅓ cup lemon juice
1 cup whipping (heavy) cream

Bake Meringue Shell. Mix sugar, cornstarch and salt in 2-quart saucepan. Gradually stir in water. Cook over medium heat, stirring constantly, until mixture thickens and boils. Boil and stir 1 minute. Stir at least half of the hot mixture gradually into egg yolks. Stir into hot mixture in saucepan. Boil and stir 1 minute; remove from heat.

Stir in margarine, lemon peel and lemon juice. Cool to room temperature. Spoon into shell. Refrigerate at least 12 hours. Beat whipping cream in chilled medium bowl until stiff. Spread over filling. Refrigerate any remaining dessert. 8 TO 10 SERVINGS; 275 CALORIES PER SERVING.

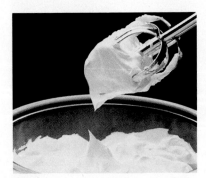

1. Beat egg whites until stiff and glossy.

2. Shape meringue with back of spoon into desired shape.

Heart Meringue

CHERRY-BERRIES ON A CLOUD

A favorite in the Betty Crocker Kitchens! We serve it at parties for staff members and at other department functions—it's also great for showers, teas or other special events. A good do-ahead recipe, the dessert mellows as it chills.

6 egg whites
½ teaspoon cream of tartar
¼ teaspoon salt
1½ cups sugar
2 cups whipping (heavy) cream
2 packages (3 ounces each) cream cheese, softened
½ cup sugar
1 teaspoon vanilla
2 cups miniature marshmallows
Cherry-Berry Topping (below)

Heat oven to 275°. Butter rectangular pan, 13 × 9 × 2 inches. Beat egg whites, cream of tartar and salt in large bowl until foamy. Beat in 1½ cups sugar, 1 tablespoon at a time; continue beating until stiff and glossy. Do not underbeat. Spread in pan. Bake 1½ hours. Turn off oven and leave meringue in oven with door closed at least 2 hours.

Beat whipping cream in chilled large bowl until stiff. Blend cream cheese, ½ cup sugar and the vanilla. Gently fold cream cheese mixture and marshmallows into whipped cream. Spread over meringue. Cover and refrigerate at least 12 hours. Cut into serving pieces; top with Cherry-Berry Topping.   12 SERVINGS; 400 CALORIES PER SERVING.

Cherry-Berry Topping

2 cups sliced strawberries or 1 package (16 ounces) frozen strawberries, thawed
1 can (21 ounces) cherry pie filling
2 teaspoons lemon juice

Mix all ingredients.

POACHED MERINGUE WITH APRICOT SAUCE

Apricot Sauce (right)
Sugar
10 egg whites
½ teaspoon cream of tartar
1 cup sugar

Prepare Apricot Sauce. Grease 12-cup bundt cake pan and sprinkle with sugar. Heat oven to 350°.

Beat egg whites and cream of tartar in large bowl until foamy. Beat in 1 cup sugar, 1 tablespoon at a time; continue beating until soft peaks form. Pour into pan. Gently cut through batter with metal spatula.

Place pan in shallow roasting pan on oven rack. Pour very hot water into pan until 1 inch deep. Bake about 45 minutes or until top is golden brown and meringue is set.

Immediately loosen meringue from edges of pan. Invert onto heatproof serving plate. Cool 30 minutes. Refrigerate no longer than 24 hours. Cut meringue into wedges and serve with Apricot Sauce.   18 SERVINGS; 80 CALORIES PER SERVING.

Apricot Sauce

1 package (6 ounces) dried apricots (about 1 cup)
2 cups water
2 to 3 tablespoons sugar
½ teaspoon ground cinnamon
1 teaspoon lemon juice

Heat apricots, water, sugar and cinnamon to boiling; reduce heat. Cover and simmer about 15 minutes or until apricots are tender. Place apricot mixture and lemon juice in blender. Cover and blend on medium-high speed about 15 seconds, stopping blender occasionally to scrape sides, until smooth. Stir in 1 to 2 tablespoons water, if necessary, until of sauce consistency. Refrigerate about 3 hours or until chilled.

ORANGE BAVARIAN CREAM

So versatile—serve alone in pretty dessert dishes, layer with fruit and crushed vanilla wafers in parfait glasses or serve over slices of Angel Food Cake (page 80) or Pound Cake (page 71).

2 cartons (6 ounces each) orange yogurt
1 package (3½ ounces) vanilla instant pudding and pie filling
1 cup whipping (heavy) cream
Mandarin orange segments, if desired

Beat yogurt and pudding and pie filling (dry) in medium bowl on low speed 30 seconds. Beat in whipping cream on medium speed 3 to 5 minutes, scraping bowl occasionally, until soft peaks form. Garnish with mandarin orange segments. Refrigerate any remaining dessert.   4 TO 6 SERVINGS; 320 CALORIES PER SERVING.

✳ LEMON SOUFFLÉ

¾ cup sugar
1 cup water
¾ cup lemon juice (3 to 4 lemons)
¼ teaspoon salt
2 envelopes unflavored gelatin
4 eggs, separated
2 teaspoons grated lemon peel
¾ cup sugar
2 cups whipping (heavy) cream

Make a 4-inch band of triple-thickness aluminum foil 2 inches longer than circumference of 6-cup soufflé dish. Extend dish by securing band around top edge. (A 2-quart round casserole can be used instead of soufflé dish and foil band.)

Mix ¾ cup sugar, the water, lemon juice, salt and gelatin in saucepan. Beat egg yolks slightly; stir into gelatin mixture. Heat just to boiling over medium heat, stirring constantly; remove from heat. Stir in lemon peel. Place pan in bowl of ice and water, or refrigerate 20 to 30 minutes, stirring occasionally, just until mixture mounds slightly when dropped from a spoon. If mixture becomes too thick, place pan in bowl of hot water; stir constantly until mixture is of proper consistency.

Beat egg whites in large bowl until foamy. Beat in ¾ cup sugar, 1 tablespoon at a time; continue beating until stiff and glossy. Do not underbeat. Fold gelatin mixture into egg whites.

Beat whipping cream in chilled medium bowl until stiff. Fold whipped cream into egg white mixture. Carefully turn into soufflé dish. Refrigerate about 8 hours or until set.

Just before serving, remove foil band. Refrigerate any remaining soufflé.   12 SERVINGS; 260 CALORIES PER SERVING.

BERRY PIROUETTE

1¾ cups boiling water
2 packages (3 ounces each) raspberry-flavored gelatin
1 package (16 ounces) frozen boysenberries or raspberries, partially thawed
1 cup whipping (heavy) cream
1 cup whipping (heavy) cream
1 package (5½ ounces) tube-shaped pirouette cookies (about 24)

Pour boiling water on gelatin in large bowl; stir until gelatin is dissolved. Reserve 3 to 5 berries for garnish. Place remaining berries in blender or food processor. Cover and blend, or process, until smooth. Stir berries into gelatin. Refrigerate about 1 hour or until very thick but not set.

Beat gelatin mixture on high speed about 4 minutes or until thick and fluffy. Beat 1 cup whipping cream in chilled medium bowl until stiff. Fold into gelatin mixture. Pour into springform pan, 9×3 inches. Refrigerate about 3 hours or until set.

Run knife around edge of dessert to loosen; remove side of pan. Place dessert on serving plate. Beat 1 cup whipping cream in chilled medium bowl until stiff. Spread side of dessert with half of the whipped cream. Carefully cut cookies crosswise in half. Arrange cookies, cut ends down, vertically around side of dessert and press lightly. Garnish with remaining whipped cream and berries. Refrigerate any remaining dessert.   12 SERVINGS; 285 CALORIES PER SERVING.

PEACH PIROUETTE: Substitute 1 package (16 ounces) frozen sliced peaches, partially thawed, for the boysenberries and orange-flavored gelatin for the raspberry-flavored gelatin. Reserve 3 peach slices for garnish.   280 CALORIES PER SERVING.

CHERRY AMARETTI DESSERT

Amaretti cookies, a popular Italian almond-flavored sweet, can be found in the gourmet section of the supermarket, gourmet food stores and Italian markets.

2 cups coarsely crushed amaretti cookies or crisp macaroon cookies (about 6 ounces)
1 can (17 ounces) pitted cherries, drained
1 cup whipping (heavy) cream
1 package (3 ounces) cream cheese, softened

Sprinkle 1¼ cups of the cookie crumbs in ungreased square pan, 9×9×2 inches; reserve remaining crumbs. Place cherries in blender or food processor. Cover and blend, or process, until coarsely chopped.

Beat whipping cream and cream cheese in chilled medium bowl until stiff. Fold in cherries. Drop by spoonfuls onto crumbs in pan; carefully spread. Sprinkle with reserved crumbs. Cover and freeze at least 6 hours. Let stand at room temperature 15 minutes before serving. Freeze any remaining dessert.   9 SERVINGS; 225 CALORIES PER SERVING.

PEACH AMARETTI DESSERT: Substitute 1 can (16 ounces) sliced peaches, drained, for the cherries.   215 CALORIES PER SERVING.

CHOCOLATE MOUSSE IN CHOCOLATE CUPS

For lacy chocolate cups drizzle the chocolate randomly over the foil-covered cups. This method comfortably makes 12 chocolate cups.

4 egg yolks
¼ cup sugar
1 cup whipping (heavy) cream
1 cup semisweet chocolate chips
Chocolate Cups (below)
1½ cups whipping (heavy) cream

Beat egg yolks in small bowl on high speed about 3 minutes or until thick and lemon colored. Gradually beat in sugar. Heat 1 cup whipping cream in 2-quart saucepan over medium heat just until hot. Gradually stir at least half of the hot cream into egg yolk mixture. Stir into hot cream in saucepan. Cook over low heat about 5 minutes, stirring constantly, until mixture thickens (do not boil). Stir in chocolate chips until melted. Cover and refrigerate about 2 hours, stirring occasionally, just until chilled. Meanwhile, prepare Chocolate Cups.

Beat 1½ cups whipping cream in chilled medium bowl until stiff. Fold chocolate mixture into whipped cream. Pipe or spoon mixture into cups. Serve with chocolate sauce, Apricot Sauce (157) or Raspberry-Currant Sauce (page 162) if desired. Refrigerate any remaining dessert. 8 SERVINGS; 575 CALORIES PER SERVING.

Chocolate Cups

Wrap the outsides of eight 6-ounce custard cups with aluminum foil. Heat 1⅓ cups semisweet chocolate chips in heavy 1-quart saucepan over low heat, stirring constantly, until melted and smooth; remove from heat. Spread about 1½ tablespoons melted chocolate over foil on bottom and about 1½ inches up side of each cup. Refrigerate about 30 minutes or until chocolate is firm. Carefully remove foil from custard cups, then remove foil from chocolate cups. Refrigerate chocolate cups.

FROZEN FRESH BERRY YOGURT

2 pints strawberries or raspberries
½ cup sugar
8 cups vanilla yogurt

Mash strawberries with sugar. Stir into yogurt. Pour into 2-quart ice-cream freezer and freeze according to manufacturer's directions.* 22 SERVINGS (ABOUT ½ CUP EACH); 110 CALORIES PER SERVING.

A 1-quart ice-cream freezer can be used. Divide ingredients in half.

FROZEN BANANA YOGURT: Substitute 3 cups mashed banana (about 8 medium) for the strawberries. 145 CALORIES PER SERVING.

PEACH SORBET WITH PINEAPPLE

1 package (16 ounces) frozen unsweetened peach slices
¼ cup unsweetened apple juice
6 slices pineapple,* ½ inch thick

Place half of the peaches and 2 tablespoons apple juice at a time in food processor. Cover and process until smooth. Freeze at least 2 hours or until icy. Scoop or spoon over pineapple slices. (If sorbet becomes too firm to scoop, remove from freezer about 1 hour before serving.) 6 SERVINGS; 105 CALORIES PER SERVING.

6 canned pineapple slices in juice, drained, can be substituted for fresh pineapple slices.

Peppermint Ice Cream (page 160) topped with Hot Fudge Sauce (page 161), Chocolate Ice Cream (page 160) topped with Marshmallow Sauce (page 161), Peach Sorbet with Pineapple topped with Raspberry-Currant Sauce (page 162)

FROZEN CHOCOLATE CREAM

Orange Fudge Sauce (page 161)
17 ladyfingers
⅓ cup orange-flavored liqueur
3 tablespoons water
3 cups whipping (heavy) cream
¼ cup orange-flavored liqueur

Prepare Orange Fudge Sauce. Remove 1 cup of the sauce; cool. Cover and refrigerate remaining sauce. Cut ladyfingers lengthwise in half. Place ladyfingers, cut sides toward center, over bottom and upright around side of springform pan, 9 × 3 inches. Mix ⅓ cup liqueur and the water; brush over ladyfingers. Beat whipping cream in chilled large bowl until stiff. Mix the 1 cup Orange Fudge Sauce and ¼ cup liqueur; fold into whipped cream. Spoon into pan and smooth top. Freeze about 8 hours or until firm.

Place in refrigerator at least 1 hour but no longer than 2 hours before serving. Heat refrigerated Orange Fudge Sauce, stirring occasionally, just until warm. Loosen dessert from side of pan; remove side of pan. Cut dessert into wedges; serve with sauce. Refrigerate any remaining dessert.   18 SERVINGS; 250 CALORIES PER SERVING.

FROZEN RUM CREAM: Substitute rum for the orange-flavored liqueur and Hot Fudge Sauce (page 161) for the Orange Fudge Sauce.   240 CALORIES PER SERVING.

═══ ICE CREAM ═══

In 1784 George Washington brought a "Cream Machine for Making Ice" to Philadelphia, then the nation's capital, where many Americans had their first taste of what would become one of our most popular desserts. Later, in Washington, D.C., Dolley Madison reversed the name of the frozen confection and "ice cream" appeared on the White House menu. The ice cream cone is said to have originated at the 1904 St. Louis World's Fair, when an ice-cream vendor ran out of serving cups. He saw a waffle seller next to him and asked to use his extra waffles to form a cone in which to serve the ice cream. A classic was born.

VANILLA ICE CREAM

If you would like to try vanilla bean, omit vanilla extract and add a 3-inch piece of vanilla bean to the milk mixture before cooking. Before cooling, remove bean and split lengthwise. Scrape the seeds into cooked mixture with tip of a small knife; discard bean.

3 egg yolks, beaten
½ cup sugar
1 cup milk
¼ teaspoon salt
2 cups whipping (heavy) cream
1 tablespoon vanilla

Mix egg yolks, sugar, milk and salt in 2-quart saucepan. Cook over medium heat, stirring constantly, just to boiling (do not boil). Refrigerate in chilled bowl 2 to 3 hours, stirring occasionally, until room temperature.

Stir whipping cream and vanilla into milk mixture. Pour into 1-quart ice-cream freezer. Freeze according to manufacturer's directions.   8 SERVINGS (ABOUT ½ CUP EACH); 295 CALORIES PER SERVING.

CHOCOLATE ICE CREAM: Increase sugar to 1 cup. Beat 2 ounces unsweetened chocolate, melted and cooled, into milk mixture before cooking. Decrease vanilla to 1 teaspoon.   370 CALORIES PER SERVING.

CHOCOLATE SANDWICH COOKIE ICE CREAM: Stir 1 cup coarsely broken chocolate sandwich cookies into ice cream.   415 CALORIES PER SERVING.

FRESH PEACH ICE CREAM: Decrease vanilla to 1 teaspoon. Mash 4 or 5 peaches to yield 2 cups. Stir ½ cup sugar into peaches. Stir into milk mixture after adding vanilla.   355 CALORIES PER SERVING.

FRESH STRAWBERRY ICE CREAM: Decrease vanilla to 1 teaspoon. Mash 1 pint strawberries with an additional ½ cup sugar. Stir into milk mixture after adding vanilla. Stir in few drops red food color if desired.   350 CALORIES PER SERVING.

PEPPERMINT ICE CREAM: Decrease vanilla to 1 teaspoon. Stir ½ cup crushed peppermint candy sticks into milk mixture after adding vanilla. Stir in few drops green or red food color.   335 CALORIES PER SERVING.

HAWAIIAN–ICE CREAM DESSERT

1 can (20 ounces) crushed pineapple in syrup
1 package (13¾ ounces) soft coconut macaroons
1 half-gallon vanilla ice cream, softened
½ cup chopped macadamia nuts or almonds, toasted

Heat oven to 400°. Drain pineapple, reserving ¼ cup syrup. Crumble macaroons into ungreased jelly roll pan, 15½ × 10½ × 1 inch. Bake 8 to 10 minutes, stirring occasionally, until golden brown; cool completely.

Reserve about 2 tablespoons macaroon crumbs. Mix remaining crumbs and the pineapple syrup in ungreased springform pan, 9 × 3 inches. Press evenly on bottom and 1 inch up side of pan. Mix ice cream, nuts and pineapple. Spread in pan. Cover and freeze about 8 hours or until firm.

Run knife around edge of dessert to loosen; remove side of pan. Spoon or pipe Sweetened Whipped Cream (page 162) on top of dessert if desired. Sprinkle with reserved macaroon crumbs. 12 SERVINGS; 405 CALORIES PER SERVING.

 MARSHMALLOW SAUCE

⅔ cup sugar
¼ cup water
3 tablespoons light corn syrup
2 cups miniature marshmallows*
¾ teaspoon vanilla
Dash of salt

Heat sugar, water and corn syrup to boiling in 2-quart saucepan; reduce heat. Simmer uncovered 4 minutes, stirring occasionally; remove from heat. Stir in remaining ingredients until marshmallows are melted and mixture is smooth. 1½ CUPS SAUCE; 40 CALORIES PER TABLESPOON.

20 large marshmallows, cut into fourths, can be substituted for the miniature marshmallows.

To Microwave: Mix sugar, water and corn syrup in 2-quart microwavable casserole. Microwave uncovered on high 2 minutes 30 seconds to 3 minutes or until boiling. Stir in remaining ingredients. Microwave uncovered 1 minute longer.

 BUTTERSCOTCH SAUCE

⅔ cup sugar
⅓ cup margarine or butter
⅓ cup buttermilk
2 teaspoons light corn syrup
¼ teaspoon baking soda
1 tablespoon rum or 1 teaspoon rum flavoring, if desired

Heat all ingredients except rum to boiling over medium heat, stirring constantly. Boil 5 minutes, stirring frequently; remove from heat. Stir in rum; cool completely. Refrigerate any remaining sauce. ABOUT ¾ CUP SAUCE; 95 CALORIES PER TABLESPOON.

CARAMEL SAUCE

2 egg yolks, beaten
½ cup packed brown sugar
½ cup granulated sugar
¼ cup margarine or butter
½ cup water
1 teaspoon vanilla

Heat all ingredients to boiling over medium heat, stirring constantly. Boil and stir 1 minute. Serve warm or cold. Refrigerate any remaining sauce. ABOUT 1⅓ CUPS SAUCE; 65 CALORIES PER TABLESPOON.

 HOT FUDGE SAUCE

We can't make this in the test kitchens without everyone craving a taste. Try it over orange or raspberry sherbet as well as ice cream.

1 can (12 ounces) evaporated milk
1 package (12 ounces) semisweet chocolate chips
½ cup sugar
1 tablespoon margarine or butter
1 teaspoon vanilla

Heat milk, chocolate chips and sugar to boiling in 2-quart saucepan over medium heat, stirring constantly; remove from heat. Stir in margarine and vanilla. Serve warm over ice cream. Refrigerate any remaining sauce. ABOUT 3 CUPS SAUCE; 55 CALORIES PER TABLESPOON.

ORANGE FUDGE SAUCE: Substitute 2 teaspoons orange-flavored liqueur or 1 teaspoon orange extract for the 1 teaspoon vanilla. 60 CALORIES PER TABLESPOON.

🌾 LEMON SAUCE

One of our favorites with its clean lemon flavor and multitude of uses.

½ cup sugar
2 tablespoons cornstarch
¾ cup water
1 tablespoon grated lemon peel
¼ cup lemon juice
2 tablespoons margarine or butter

Mix sugar and cornstarch in 1-quart saucepan. Gradually stir in water. Cook over medium heat, stirring constantly, until mixture thickens and boils. Boil and stir 1 minute; remove from heat. Stir in remaining ingredients. Serve warm or cool.   ABOUT 1¼ CUPS SAUCE; 35 CALORIES PER TABLESPOON.

To Microwave: Mix sugar and cornstarch in 4-cup microwavable measure. Gradually stir in water. Microwave uncovered on high 3 to 4 minutes, stirring every minute, until thickened and clear. Stir in remaining ingredients.

🌾 ORANGE SAUCE

1 cup sugar
2 tablespoons cornstarch
1 tablespoon all-purpose flour
¼ teaspoon salt
1¼ cups orange juice
½ cup water
¼ cup lemon juice
1 tablespoon margarine or butter
1 teaspoon grated orange peel
1 teaspoon grated lemon peel

Mix sugar, cornstarch, flour and salt in 1½-quart saucepan. Gradually stir in orange juice, water and lemon juice. Heat to boiling over low heat, stirring constantly. Boil and stir 3 minutes; remove from heat. Stir in remaining ingredients. Serve warm. ABOUT 2⅓ CUPS SAUCE; 35 CALORIES PER TABLESPOON.

To Microwave: Decrease water to ¼ cup. Mix sugar, cornstarch, flour and salt in 4-cup microwavable measure. Gradually stir in orange juice, water and lemon juice. Microwave uncovered on high 5 to 7 minutes, stirring every minute, until thickened and boiling. Stir in remaining ingredients.

🌾 RASPBERRY-CURRANT SAUCE

½ cup currant jelly
1 package (10 ounces) frozen raspberries, thawed and undrained
1 tablespoon cold water
1½ teaspoons cornstarch

Heat jelly and raspberries to boiling in 1-quart saucepan. Mix water and cornstarch. Stir into raspberries. Heat to boiling, stirring constantly. Boil and stir 1 minute; cool. Press through sieve to remove seeds if desired.   ABOUT 1⅓ CUPS SAUCE; 35 CALORIES PER TABLESPOON.

To Microwave: Omit water. Mix jelly and 1 tablespoon cornstarch in 4-cup microwavable measure until well blended. Gradually stir in raspberries. Microwave uncovered on high 5 to 6 minutes, stirring every minute, until boiling.

🌾 SWEETENED WHIPPED CREAM

For 1 cup whipped cream: Beat ½ cup whipping (heavy) cream and 1 tablespoon granulated or powdered sugar in chilled bowl until stiff.   55 CALORIES PER 2 TABLESPOONS.

For 1½ cups whipped cream: Use ¾ cup whipping (heavy) cream and 2 tablespoons granulated or powdered sugar.

For 2⅓ cups whipped cream: Use 1 cup whipping (heavy) cream and 3 tablespoons granulated or powdered sugar.

FLAVORED WHIPPED CREAM: Beat one of the following into 1 cup whipping cream and 2 tablespoons sugar.

1 teaspoon grated lemon or orange peel
1 teaspoon vanilla
½ teaspoon ground cinnamon
½ teaspoon ground ginger
½ teaspoon ground nutmeg
½ teaspoon almond extract
½ teaspoon peppermint extract
¼ teaspoon maple flavoring
½ teaspoon rum flavoring

FIX-IT-FAST

- Dip strawberries, orange wedges, pineapple chunks, apricot halves or other fresh or dried fruit pieces into melted chocolate (milk, semi-sweet, bittersweet or white) or into melted butterscotch chips. For an elegant touch, drizzle dipped fruit with a different melted chocolate. Refrigerate until firm. Serve as a dessert or garnish.

- Offer a fresh fruit buffet for dessert. Serve cut-up fresh fruit (you can pick it up at the salad bar, deli or cut it up yourself). Offer sauces and toppings such as whipped cream or yogurt along with chopped nuts, candy or ice cream.

- Mix pie filling with grated citrus peel, ground spices, lemon or lime juice, liquors or liqueurs. Serve over cake, ice cream or pudding.

- Serve frozen fruits for dessert on hot summer days. Freeze grapes, strawberries, raspberries, pitted cherries or melon cubes on a cookie sheet, then transfer to freezer container.

- Make a luscious sauce with instant pudding mix for fresh fruit or cake. Increase the amount of liquid called for on the package by ½ cup for 4 servings and substitute half-and-half or eggnog for the milk. If desired, substitute 2 to 4 tablespoons liqueur such as crème de cacao, Irish cream, hazelnut or raspberry for part of the liquid.

- Freeze flavored yogurt in small paper cups. Add sticks for frozen pops. This is a nutritious after-school snack or dessert.

- Serve flavored yogurt over fresh fruit or cake. Or stir brown sugar, vanilla, fresh fruit or chocolate drink mix into plain yogurt for a special treat.

- Use leftover cake, instant pudding and fruit to make an easy trifle (see page 155).

- Fill ice-cream cones with pudding or flavored yogurt for dessert on the run.

- Make individual baked Alaskas, using a cookie, brownie or cake. Cut with a cookie cutter into 3-inch rounds for the base. Place on aluminum foil–lined cookie sheet and top with a scoop of ice cream. Freeze until firm. Heat oven to 500°. Prepare Meringue (page 96). Quickly cover each with about 1 inch of meringue, sealing it to foil on cookie sheet. Bake 3 to 5 minutes or until light brown. Serve immediately.

- Serve store-bought ice-cream sandwiches as an impromptu dessert by topping with fresh fruit or ice-cream toppings and whipped cream.

- Make a quick and different sundae using waffles, cookies, brownies, graham crackers or doughnuts on the bottom, topped by your favorite flavor of ice cream or frozen yogurt and ice-cream topping(s).

- Serve liqueur over ice cream, sherbet or frozen yogurt for a special touch. Try pineapple sherbet with sherry, cherry ice cream with amaretto, chocolate ice cream with coffee-flavored liqueur or frozen raspberry yogurt with chocolate truffle liqueur.

- Fill store-bought crepes with fruit, ice cream, pudding or whipped cream.

PER SERVING OR UNIT

NUTRITION INFORMATION

RECIPE, PAGE	Servings per recipe	Calories	Protein (grams)	Carbohydrate (grams)	Fat (grams)	Cholesterol (grams)	Sodium (milligrams)	Protein	Vitamin A	Vitamin C	Thiamine	Riboflavin	Niacin	Calcium	Iron
Amaretto-Almond Swirl Cheesecake, 148	20	470	8	38	32	155	250	12	22	0	4	14	2	6	8
Apple-Apricot Strudels, 138	8	280	5	46	10	0	160	6	46	2	2	6	4	4	8
Apple Crisp, 138	6	290	1	50	11	0	135	2	8	2	4	2	2	2	8
Apple Tart Tatin, 137	8	410	2	45	25	40	175	2	12	4	8	6	4	4	6
Applesauce, 138	6	90	0	24	0	0	5	0	0	2	0	0	0	0	2
Apricot Crisp, 138	6	265	2	42	10	0	140	2	36	2	4	2	4	4	8

PERCENT U.S. RECOMMENDED DAILY ALLOWANCE

NUTRITION INFORMATION

PER SERVING OR UNIT

RECIPE, PAGE	Servings per recipe	Calories	Protein (grams)	Carbohydrate (grams)	Fat (grams)	Cholesterol (milligrams)	Sodium (milligrams)	Protein	Vitamin A	Vitamin C	Thiamine	Riboflavin	Niacin	Calcium	Iron
Baked Apples, 136	4	165	0	34	4	0	45	0	4	4	2	0	0	0	0
Baked Custard, 152	6	130	6	16	4	115	120	10	6	0	2	16	0	12	2
Baked Honey Apples, 136	4	185	0	40	4	0	45	0	4	4	2	0	0	0	0
Baked Mincemeat Apples, 136	4	115	0	30	1	0	20	0	0	4	2	0	0	0	0
Berry Pirouette, 158	12	285	4	32	16	55	85	6	12	8	12	28	10	4	4
Bittersweet Chocolate Cheesecake with White Truffle Sauce, 149	12	415	7	27	34	110	155	10	16	0	2	12	2	6	12
Black Walnut Torte, 144	10	305	3	25	23	65	180	4	14	0	2	6	2	4	2
Bread Pudding, 153	8	200	6	25	9	60	340	8	87	0	8	14	4	10	6
Butterscotch Pudding, 152	4	300	5	46	11	120	215	8	12	0	2	14	0	18	8
Butterscotch Sauce, 161	12	95	0	11	5	0	90	0	4	0	0	0	0	0	0
Butterscotch Sundae Cake, 144	9	430	5	67	16	30	220	8	6	0	6	14	4	16	8
Caramel Sauce, 161	21	65	0	10	3	20	30	0	2	0	0	0	0	0	0
Cherry Amaretti Dessert, 158	9	225	2	20	16	45	80	2	14	0	2	4	0	2	4
Cherry-Berries on a Cloud, 157	12	400	4	55	20	70	140	6	20	24	0	8	0	4	4
Cherry Blintzes, 150	6	545	14	62	27	105	460	20	34	2	12	24	8	20	10
Cherry Clafouti, 139	6	170	6	29	4	110	50	8	6	2	6	14	2	6	4
Cherry Crisp, 138	6	325	1	59	10	0	150	2	18	0	2	2	2	2	10
Cherries Jubilee, 140	8	300	3	49	7	30	65	4	6	2	2	10	0	8	2
Chocolate Belgian Waffles with Hazelnut Cream, 151	6	515	8	46	33	95	530	12	14	0	22	20	10	16	10
Chocolate Belgian Waffles with Strawberry Cream, 151	6	510	9	47	33	95	530	12	14	40	22	22	10	16	12
Chocolate Cream Puffs, 151	12	320	6	42	18	70	150	8	12	0	4	14	2	10	4
Chocolate Eclairs, 151	12	260	5	28	14	110	180	8	12	0	4	10	2	6	4
Chocolate Ice Cream, 160	8	370	4	29	28	165	110	6	20	0	2	10	0	8	4
Chocolate Mousse in Chocolate Cups, 159	8	575	6	39	44	210	35	8	24	0	4	10	0	6	10
Chocolate Pots de Crème, 153	4	315	6	29	18	130	60	8	8	0	2	12	0	8	6
Chocolate Pudding, 152	4	285	7	37	12	120	205	10	12	0	2	16	0	16	8
Chocolate Sandwich Cookie Ice Cream, 160	8	415	4	33	30	165	270	6	20	0	2	10	2	8	4
Chocolate Torte, 144	10	295	3	28	20	65	185	4	14	0	0	6	2	4	2
Coconut Cream Torte, 145	12	230	4	32	10	70	110	6	4	0	2	6	2	2	4

NUTRITION INFORMATION

PER SERVING OR UNIT

PERCENT U.S. RECOMMENDED DAILY ALLOWANCE

RECIPE, PAGE	Servings per recipe	Calories	Protein (grams)	Carbohydrate (grams)	Fat (grams)	Cholesterol (milligrams)	Sodium (milligrams)	Protein	Vitamin A	Vitamin C	Thiamine	Riboflavin	Niacin	Calcium	Iron
Cream Puffs, 151	12	205	5	16	13	110	180	6	12	0	4	10	2	6	2
Crème Brûlée, 153	8	310	3	20	25	190	30	4	20	70	2	10	0	6	4
Crepes, 149	12	105	4	14	4	40	160	6	4	0	4	8	4	6	2
English Trifle, 155	10	390	6	48	17	165	160	8	16	20	2	14	2	12	4
Fig Bread Pudding, 153	9	315	6	33	18	110	260	8	16	0	6	14	2	8	4
Fresh Blueberry Cobbler, 139	6	265	3	49	7	0	300	4	2	10	8	6	6	8	4
Fresh Cherry Cobbler, 139	6	365	4	74	7	0	300	4	26	8	8	6	6	10	4
Fresh Fruit in Phyllo Cups, 150	6	245	6	32	11	75	185	8	12	28	12	16	6	6	4
Fresh Peach Cobbler, 139	6	250	3	45	7	0	295	4	10	4	6	6	8	8	2
Fresh Peach Ice Cream, 160	8	355	3	32	25	165	110	4	24	4	2	10	2	8	0
Fresh Strawberry Ice Cream, 160	8	350	3	30	25	165	110	4	20	36	2	10	0	8	2
Frozen Banana Yogurt, 159	22	145	4	29	2	0	55	4	0	6	2	12	0	12	0
Frozen Chocolate Cream, 160	18	250	2	16	18	90	30	2	12	0	0	4	0	4	2
Frozen Fresh Berry Yogurt, 159	22	110	3	21	2	0	55	4	0	24	2	10	0	12	0
Frozen Rum Cream, 160	18	240	2	14	18	90	30	2	12	0	0	4	0	4	2
Gingered Pineapple, 142	6	45	0	11	0	0	0	0	0	30	4	0	0	0	0
Hawaiian–Ice Cream Dessert, 161	12	405	5	50	22	55	150	6	10	2	8	14	2	12	2
Hazelnut Cream Torte, 145	12	250	5	31	12	70	110	6	4	0	6	6	2	2	4
Heart Meringue, 156	8	220	4	36	7	30	80	6	4	34	0	14	0	8	0
Hot Chocolate Soufflé, 146	6	445	7	36	30	140	340	10	26	0	2	16	2	8	6
Hot Fudge Sauce, 161	48	55	1	7	3	0	10	0	0	0	0	0	0	2	0
Hot Fudge Sundae Cake, 144	9	475	7	71	19	30	220	10	6	0	10	14	6	18	12
Individual Meringues, 156	8	75	1	18	0	0	20	2	0	0	0	2	0	0	0
Lemon Sauce, 162	20	35	0	6	1	0	15	0	0	0	0	0	0	0	0
Lemon Schaum Torte, 156	8	275	2	31	16	130	50	4	14	4	0	6	0	4	0
Lemon Soufflé, 158	12	260	4	26	16	125	85	6	12	2	0	6	0	2	0
Lindy's Cheesecake, 146	20	410	7	26	31	165	300	10	24	0	2	12	2	6	6
Lindy's Cheesecake Squares, 146	20	410	7	26	31	165	300	10	24	0	2	12	2	6	6
Mallow Sundae Cake, 144	9	400	5	72	11	130	230	8	6	0	4	14	4	18	10
Mango with Passion Fruit, 140	4	110	2	23	1	0	20	2	40	26	2	4	2	4	0
Marshmallow Sauce, 161	24	40	0	10	0	0	10	0	0	0	0	0	0	0	0
Meringue Shell, 156	8	75	1	18	0	0	20	2	0	0	0	2	0	0	0
Mini Almond Cheesecakes, 149	12	170	4	10	13	65	120	4	8	0	0	6	0	2	2

NUTRITION INFORMATION

PER SERVING OR UNIT

RECIPE, PAGE	Servings per recipe	Calories	Protein (grams)	Carbohydrate (grams)	Fat (grams)	Cholesterol (milligrams)	Sodium (milligrams)	PERCENT U.S. RECOMMENDED DAILY ALLOWANCE Protein	Vitamin A	Vitamin C	Thiamine	Riboflavin	Niacin	Calcium	Iron
Mini Peanut Butter Cheesecakes, 149	12	195	4	13	14	65	140	6	8	0	0	6	2	2	2
Orange Bavarian Cream, 157	4	320	5	12	23	100	85	6	18	0	2	12	0	14	0
Orange Fudge Sauce, 161	48	60	1	7	3	0	10	0	0	0	0	0	0	2	0
Orange Sauce, 162	32	35	0	8	0	0	20	0	0	4	0	0	0	0	0
Peach Amaretti Dessert, 158	9	215	2	19	16	45	80	2	12	0	2	2	0	2	0
Peach Crisp, 138	6	285	1	49	10	0	140	2	12	2	4	2	4	2	8
Peach Melba, 140	4	540	3	121	7	30	65	4	14	20	4	12	4	10	6
Peach Pirouette, 158	12	280	4	31	16	55	85	6	12	12	12	28	10	4	2
Peach Sorbet with Pineapple, 159	6	125	1	30	0	0	5	0	4	136	6	2	2	0	2
Peanutty Sundae Cake, 144	9	515	11	72	22	30	290	16	6	0	8	14	20	18	12
Pears Hélène, 141	6	340	3	62	10	30	70	4	4	2	2	12	0	10	2
Peppermint Cream Torte, 145	12	230	4	37	8	70	110	4	4	0	2	6	2	2	4
Peppermint Ice Cream, 160	8	335	3	26	24	165	110	4	20	0	2	8	0	8	0
Pineapple Crisp, 138	6	285	1	49	10	0	135	2	8	4	8	2	4	4	8
Poached Meringue with Apricot Sauce, 157	18	80	2	19	0	0	35	2	12	0	0	2	0	0	2
Prailine-Peach Dessert, 140	6	390	6	59	16	0	200	8	14	2	2	10	4	10	6
Pumpkin Flan, 152	10	280	5	33	15	170	60	8	100	0	2	12	0	6	4
Raisin Sundae Cake, 144	9	440	6	83	11	30	230	8	6	0	6	14	4	18	12
Raspberry-Currant Sauce, 162	21	35	0	9	0	0	2	0	0	0	0	0	0	0	0
Raspberry Custard, 152	6	200	7	33	5	115	120	10	8	8	4	18	0	14	4
Raspberry Swirl Cheesecake, 148	20	455	8	40	30	155	250	12	22	0	4	12	2	6	8
Rhubarb-Strawberry Fool, 141	6	380	3	44	23	70	45	4	18	34	2	8	0	14	4
Rice Pudding, 154	8	130	4	23	3	60	115	6	4	0	6	12	2	8	4
Spicy Fruit Compote, 140	6	220	1	58	0	0	10	2	18	8	2	8	6	2	4
Starfruit and Strawberries in Champagne, 143	6	75	0	14	0	0	0	0	0	6	0	2	0	0	2
Steamed Plum Pudding, 154	8	555	5	89	21	25	485	6	6	0	10	10	8	18	24
Strawberry Shortcakes, 143	6	570	6	70	31	55	640	18	16	94	12	14	10	20	8
Sweetened Whipped Cream, 162	8	55	0	2	6	20	5	0	4	0	0	0	0	0	0
Vanilla Ice Cream, 160	8	295	3	16	25	165	110	4	20	0	2	8	0	8	0
Vanilla Pudding, 152	4	225	6	26	11	120	200	8	12	0	2	14	0	16	2
Watermelon with Blackberries and Pear Puree, 142	6	100	1	18	1	0	5	0	10	34	6	2	2	2	2

EGGS & CHEESE

EGGS & CHEESE

Eggs are old friends at breakfast, and we love them at lunch and dinner as well. From easy dishes such as poached or scrambled eggs, to more elegant dishes such as Crab Benedict (page 171) and Vegetable Frittata (page 175), eggs fill the bill. Cheese is a natural to team with eggs as in Classic Cheese Soufflé (page 180) and Quiche Lorraine (page 181). Of course, cheese is a star by itself. Use the cheese chart (page 179) to find new ideas and to learn about new cheeses. Try some of the delicious cheese dishes here for an entrée—Three-Cheese Tortellini (page 183) or a fresh Traditional Cheese Pizza (page 182). With these egg and cheese recipes you'll certainly find some old friends, and discover new ones!

EGG BASICS

The egg is one of the most versatile and nutritious foods available. Eggs are delicious eaten by themselves. Use them in a variety of dishes from appetizers to desserts, where they add nutrients as well as richness, flavor, texture, thickening and/or leavening. Whereas the egg white is mostly water with some protein, the egg yolk contains most of the egg's protein and all of the fat, cholesterol, vitamins and minerals. Chicken eggs are most commonly used, although the eggs of ducks, geese, quail and other poultry are used in other countries and other cuisines.

People with high cholesterol counts may need to limit their intake of egg yolks. As a general guide, two egg whites may be substituted for one whole egg, although the proportion varies as the quantity of eggs becomes larger.

Eggs are marketed according to size, grade (quality) and color. Standards for grade and size of eggs are established by the U.S. Department of Agriculture.

♦ **Size:** Eggs are most often available as extra large, large and medium. All of the recipes in this cookbook were tested with large eggs.

♦ **Grade:** The quality of both the egg and its shell at the time the egg was packed determines the grade. There is little difference in quality between Grades AA and A, and no difference in nutritive content. Grade B eggs are rarely found in the retail market. Gradings are based on thickness of the white, firmness of yolk and size of the interior air pocket. Thick whites, compact, rounded yolks and a small air pocket are characteristics of high-grade, fresh eggs. As eggs get older, the white gradually thins and the yolk flattens.

♦ **Color:** Egg shell color—white or brown—and yolk color—pale or deep yellow—vary with the breed and diet of the hen. White eggs are most in demand, but in some parts of the country brown are preferred. Flavor, nutritive value and cooking performance are the same.

SAFE HANDLING AND STORAGE OF EGGS

Recently, raw eggs contaminated with salmonella bacteria have caused some outbreaks of illness. Scientists suspect salmonella can be transmitted from infected laying hens directly into the interior of the eggs before the shells are formed. People who are particularly vulnerable to salmonella infections include the very young, the elderly, pregnant women (because of risk to the fetus) and people already weakened by serious illness or whose immune systems are weakened. Proper storage and cooking of eggs is necessary to prevent the growth of potentially harmful bacteria. For more information on handling eggs safely, call the USDA Meat and Poultry Hotline at 1–800–535–4555.

♦ Purchase eggs from a refrigerated case and refrigerate at a temperature no higher than 40° immediately on arriving home. You don't need to wash eggs before storing or using them because this is routine in commercial egg processing.

♦ Look for egg shells that are clean and not cracked. If a shell cracks between the market and home, use the egg as soon as possible in a fully cooked dish.

Preceding page: Leek and Mushroom Tart (page 181), Manicotti (page 183)

◆ Store fresh eggs in their carton to help prevent absorption of refrigerator odors. Storing eggs point down helps center the yolk, resulting in more attractive hard- and soft-cooked eggs.

◆ Wash hands, utensils, equipment and work areas with hot, soapy water before and after they come in contact with eggs and dishes where eggs are a main ingredient, such as quiches and custards.

◆ Avoid keeping eggs at room temperature for more than two hours, including time for preparing and serving (not including cooking). If hard-cooked eggs are hidden for an egg hunt, either follow the two-hour rule or don't eat the eggs.

◆ Refrigerate raw and cooked eggs. Use raw eggs in the shell within five weeks and hard-cooked eggs (in the shell or peeled) within one week. Use leftover raw yolks and whites within two days. Unbroken egg yolks store best when covered with a small amount of water.

◆ Freeze raw egg whites in a plastic ice cube tray; remove to a plastic bag for storage. Thaw frozen egg whites in the refrigerator. When measuring, note that 2 tablespoons thawed liquid egg white are equal to 1 fresh large egg white.

◆ Egg yolks require special treatment for freezing. If the yolks are to be used in savory dishes such as scrambled eggs, add ⅛ teaspoon salt for each ¼ cup of egg yolks. If the yolks are to be used in sweet dishes such as custards, add 1½ teaspoons sugar or 1½ teaspoons corn syrup for each ¼ cup of egg yolks.

◆ Hard-cooked egg yolks can be frozen successfully, but hard-cooked egg whites become tough and watery.

COOKING WITH EGGS

◆ Avoid eating raw eggs and foods containing raw eggs. Homemade foods such as ice cream, eggnog and mayonnaise should be avoided unless the eggs in the recipes are cooked. Commercial forms of these foods are safe to serve because they contain pasteurized eggs. Pasteurization destroys salmonella bacteria.

◆ To measure 1 cup, depending on the size of the egg you need 4 to 6 eggs, 8 to 10 whites or 12 to 14 yolks.

◆ Cook eggs thoroughly until both the yolk and white are firm, not runny, to kill any bacteria that might be present.

◆ Keep cooking temperatures medium to low. High heat and overcooking cause egg whites to shrink and become tough and rubbery; yolks become tough and their surface may turn green. Omelets are the exception; over medium-high heat.

◆ Serve cooked eggs and egg dishes immediately after cooking or refrigerate at once for later use. Use within two days.

◆ To refrigerate, divide large amounts of hot-cooked egg-rich dishes into several shallow containers so they will cool quickly.

DONENESS TEST

Cook eggs thoroughly until both the yolk and white are firm, not runny. For food safety reasons, we recommend an internal temperature of 145° to 150°. Cooking at low heat helps to achieve the desired internal temperature without resulting in rubbery eggs. In some recipes, eggs may be somewhat firmer than expected but these cooking times ensure that they will be safe to eat.

⏱ SOFT-COOKED EGGS

You can cook any number of eggs at one time, even combine cooking soft- and hard-cooked eggs.

Place egg(s) in saucepan. Add enough cold water to come at least 1 inch above eggs. Heat rapidly to boiling; remove from heat. Cover and let stand 3 minutes. Immediately cool eggs in cold water several seconds to prevent further cooking. Cut eggs in half. Scoop eggs from shells.   80 CALORIES PER EGG.

⏱ HARD-COOKED EGGS

Hard-cooked eggs are always good to have on hand for quick lunches and garnishes. Use a crayon to mark hard-cooked eggs before refrigerating. Have an unmarked egg? Spin it—if the egg wobbles instead of spinning, it is uncooked.

Place egg(s) in saucepan. Add enough cold water to come at least 1 inch above eggs. Heat rapidly to boiling; remove from heat. Cover and let stand 18 minutes. Immediately cool eggs in cold water to prevent further cooking. Tap egg to crackle shell. Roll egg between hands to loosen shell, then peel. If shell is hard to peel, hold egg in cold water.   80 CALORIES PER EGG.

⏱ POACHED EGGS

Be sure to use a pan large enough to accommodate all the eggs you want to poach at one time. They shouldn't touch while cooking.

Heat water (1½ to 2 inches) to boiling; reduce to simmering. Break each egg into custard cup or saucer. Hold cup or saucer close to water's surface and slip egg into water. Cook about 5 minutes or until whites are set and yolks are thickened. Remove eggs with slotted spoon.   80 CALORIES PER EGG.

To Microwave: Microwave 2 tablespoons water in 6-ounce microwavable custard cup uncovered on high 30 to 60 seconds or until boiling. Carefully break egg into custard cup. Prick egg yolk several times with wooden pick. Cover tightly and microwave on medium (50%) 1 minute to 1 minute 30 seconds or until egg is set and yolk is thickened. Let stand covered 1 minute.

EGGS POACHED IN BROTH: Substitute chicken or beef broth for the water.   85 CALORIES PER EGG.

⏱ FRIED EGGS

Heat margarine, butter or bacon fat (⅛ inch deep) in heavy skillet over medium heat. Break each egg into custard cup or saucer. Slip egg carefully into skillet. Immediately reduce heat to low.

Cook 5 to 7 minutes, spooning margarine over eggs, until whites are set, a film forms over yolks and yolks are thickened. Or gently turn eggs over after 3 minutes and cook 1 to 2 minutes longer or until yolks are thickened.   145 CALORIES PER EGG.

REDUCED-FAT FRIED EGGS: Heat just enough margarine, butter or bacon fat to coat skillet. Cook eggs over low heat about 1 minute or until edges turn white. Add 2 teaspoons water for each egg, decreasing amount slightly for each additional egg. Cover and cook 5 minutes longer or until a film forms over yolks and yolks are thickened.   95 CALORIES PER EGG.

⁂ BAKED (SHIRRED) EGGS

Heat oven to 325° Butter 6-ounce custard cup(s). Break 1 egg carefully into each cup. Sprinkle with salt and pepper and top with 1 tablespoon milk or half-and-half; dot with margarine or butter, softened, or sprinkle with 1 tablespoon shredded Cheddar cheese or grated Parmesan if desired. Bake 15 to 18 minutes or until whites are set and yolks thickened.   120 CALORIES PER EGG.

⏱ SCRAMBLED EGGS

Scrambled eggs shouldn't brown—reduce heat immediately if they start to.

> 2 eggs
> 2 tablespoons milk, cream or water
> ¼ teaspoon salt
> Dash of pepper
> 1½ teaspoons margarine or butter

Stir eggs, milk, salt and pepper thoroughly with fork for a uniform yellow, or slightly for streaks of white and yellow. Heat margarine in 8-inch skillet over medium heat just until hot enough to sizzle a drop of water. Pour egg mixture into skillet.

As mixture begins to set at bottom and side, gently lift cooked portions with spatula so that thin, uncooked portion can flow to bottom. Avoid constant stirring. Cook 3 to 4 minutes or until eggs are thickened throughout but still moist.   1 SERVING; 225 CALORIES PER SERVING.

To Microwave: Microwave margarine uncovered on high in 1-quart microwavable casserole or 4-cup microwavable measure about 30 seconds or until melted. Stir in eggs, milk, salt and pepper. Microwave uncovered 1 minute 30 seconds to 2 minutes, stirring with fork after 1 minute, until eggs are puffy and set but still moist. Stir before serving.

HAM·AND·SPINACH TURNOVERS

> 4 Poached Eggs (page left)
> ½ package (17¼-ounce size) frozen puff pastry, thawed
> 1 package (10 ounces) frozen chopped spinach, thawed and thoroughly drained
> 1 package (2.5 ounces) thinly sliced fully cooked smoked ham
> 4 teaspoons Dijon mustard
> 4 slices process American or Swiss cheese

Heat oven to 425°. Prepare Poached Eggs—except cook 3 minutes; drain thoroughly. Roll pastry into rectangle, 18 × 10 inches, on lightly floured surface. Cut into 4 rectangles, 10 × 4½ inches. Layer spinach, ham, mustard, egg and cheese on one end of each rectangle to within ½ inch of edge. Fold pastry over cheese. Fold edges of pastry, pinching firmly to seal. Bake 15 minutes or until pastry is puffed and deep golden brown.   4 SERVINGS; 510 CALORIES PER SERVING.

SAUSAGE·AND·SPINACH TURNOVERS: Substitute 4 fully cooked sausage patties for the ham. 650 CALORIES PER SERVING.

BAKED EGGS AND ARTICHOKES

Hard-cooked eggs are less difficult to peel if you pierce the large end of the egg with an egg piercer, thumbtack or pin before cooking. The small amount of water that seeps in during cooking makes egg peeling easier and also can keep the egg shell from cracking during cooking.

> 2 cups croutons
> 4 hard-cooked eggs, cut in half
> 1 package (10 ounces) frozen artichoke hearts, thawed and drained
> ¾ cup shredded Swiss cheese (3 ounces)
> 3 tablespoons margarine or butter
> 3 tablespoons all-purpose flour
> ¼ teaspoon salt
> ¼ teaspoon dry mustard
> ⅛ teaspoon pepper
> 1 cup milk
> ½ cup dry white wine*
> 2 slices bacon, crisply cooked and crumbled

Heat oven to 350°. Arrange croutons evenly in ungreased square baking dish, 8×8×2 inches. Arrange eggs and artichoke hearts evenly on croutons. Sprinkle with cheese.

Heat margarine in 2-quart saucepan over medium heat until melted. Stir in flour, salt, mustard and pepper. Cook, stirring constantly, until smooth and bubbly; remove from heat. Stir in milk. Heat to boiling, stirring constantly. Boil and stir 1 minute. Gradually stir in wine. Pour evenly over cheese. Sprinkle with bacon. Bake uncovered about 30 minutes or until center is hot.   4 SERVINGS; 475 CALORIES PER SERVING.

To Microwave: Arrange croutons, eggs, artichoke hearts and cheese in square microwavable dish, 8×8×2 inches, as directed. Place margarine in 4-cup microwavable measure. Microwave uncovered on high 30 to 60 seconds or until melted. Stir in flour, salt, mustard and pepper. Stir in ¾ cup milk. Microwave uncovered on high 1 minute 30 seconds to 2 minutes 30 seconds, stirring every minute, until very thick. Gradually stir in wine pour evenly over cheese. Sprinkle with bacon. Cover loosely and microwave on high 7 to 9 minutes, rotating dish ½ turn after 4 minutes, until center is hot.

*Wine can be omitted. Increase milk to 1½ cups.

BAKED EGGS AND GREEN BEANS: Substitute 1 package (10 ounces) frozen cut green beans, thawed and drained, for the artichoke hearts.   465 CALORIES PER SERVING.

EGGS BENEDICT

> Hollandaise Sauce (page 358)
> 3 English muffins
> Margarine or butter, softened
> 6 thin slices Canadian-style bacon or fully cooked smoked ham
> 1 teaspoon margarine or butter
> 6 Poached Eggs (page 170)

Prepare Hollandaise Sauce; keep warm. Split English muffins; toast. Spread each muffin half with margarine; keep warm. Cook bacon in 1 teaspoon margarine over medium heat until light brown. Prepare Poached Eggs. Place 1 slice bacon on each muffin half. Top with 1 poached egg. Spoon warm sauce over eggs.   6 SERVINGS; 365 CALORIES PER SERVING.

CRAB BENEDICT: Substitute 1½ cups chopped cooked crabmeat for the bacon. Heat in margarine just until hot.   360 CALORIES PER SERVING.

SEAFOOD BENEDICT: Substitute 1½ cups chopped cooked mixed crabmeat, scallops, shrimp and lobster for the bacon. Heat in margarine just until hot.   360 CALORIES PER SERVING.

Eggs Benedict

Tex-Mex Scrambled Eggs, Southwestern Eggs

⏱ SOUTHWESTERN EGGS

Chihuahua cheese takes its name from the Mexican state in which it originated. It has the creamy texture and tang of Cheddar but melts like mozzarella when heated.

1 pound bulk chorizo sausage*
½ cup chopped onion
1 large green bell pepper, cut into 1-inch pieces
1¼ cups Fresh Tomato Salsa (page 20) or prepared salsa
4 eggs
¾ cup shredded Chihuahua or mozzarella cheese (3 ounces)

Cook sausage, onion and bell pepper in 10-inch skillet over medium heat, stirring occasionally, until sausage is brown; drain. Stir in Fresh Tomato Salsa; heat until hot. Spread mixture evenly in skillet. Make 4 indentations in mixture with back of spoon. Break 1 egg into each indentation. Cover and cook over low heat about 12 minutes or until whites are set and yolks are thickened. Sprinkle with cheese. Serve with sour cream if desired.   4 SERVINGS; 380 CALORIES PER SERVING.

**1 pound bulk pork sausage can be substituted for the chorizo sausage.*

⏱ TEX-MEX SCRAMBLED EGGS

6 corn tortillas (6-inch diameter)
3 tablespoons vegetable oil
½ cup chopped green onions (with tops)
6 eggs, beaten
1 cup cubed Mexican-style process cheese spread with jalapeño chilies (about 4 ounces)
1 medium tomato, chopped

Cut each tortilla into 12 wedges. Heat oil in 10-inch skillet just until hot. Cook tortilla wedges in oil over medium-high heat, stirring frequently, until crisp; reduce heat. Add onions. Cook and stir over medium heat 1 minute.

Pour eggs over tortilla mixture. As eggs begin to set at bottom and side, gently lift cooked portions with spatula so that thin, uncooked portion can flow to bottom. Do not stir. Sprinkle with cheese. Cook 1 to 2 minutes longer or until cheese is melted and eggs are thickened throughout but still moist. Top with tomato. Sprinkle with chopped cilantro, oregano or parsley if desired.   4 SERVINGS; 370 CALORIES PER SERVING.

🌾 FRENCH OMELET

2 teaspoons margarine or butter
2 eggs, beaten

Heat margarine in 8-inch omelet pan or skillet over medium-high heat just until margarine begins to brown. As margarine melts, tilt pan to coat bottom.

Quickly pour eggs into pan. Slide pan back and forth rapidly over heat and, at the same time, quickly stir with fork to spread eggs continuously over bottom of pan as they thicken. Let stand over heat a few seconds to brown bottom of omelet lightly. (Do not overcook—omelet will continue to cook after folding.)

Tilt pan and run fork under edge of omelet, then jerk pan sharply to loosen from bottom of pan. Fold portion of omelet nearest you just to center. (Allow for portion of omelet to slide up side of pan.) Turn omelet onto warm plate, flipping folded portion of omelet over so far side is on bottom. Tuck sides of omelet under if necessary.   1 SERVING; 225 CALORIES PER SERVING.

To Microwave: Place margarine in microwavable pie plate, 9 × 1¼ inches. Microwave uncovered on high 30 seconds or until melted. Tilt pie plate to coat bottom completely. Pour eggs into pie plate. Elevate pie plate on inverted microwavable dinner plate in microwave. Cover with waxed paper and microwave 2 minutes to 2 minutes 30 seconds, moving cooked outer edge of omelet to center and gently shaking pie plate to distribute uncooked egg after 1 minute, until center is set but still moist.

FAVORITE FRENCH OMELET: Fold in one or more of the following:

- 2 tablespoons shredded Cheddar, Monterey Jack, Swiss or blue cheese
- 2 tablespoons chopped mushrooms
- 2 tablespoons chopped chives or parsley
- 2 tablespoons crisply cooked and crumbled bacon, finely shredded dried beef or chopped fully cooked ham
- 1 tablespoon canned chopped green chilies

1. Tilt pan and run fork under edge of omelet, then jerk skillet sharply to loosen eggs from bottom of skillet. Fold portion of omelet just to center.

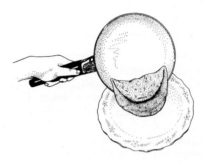

2. Turn omelet onto plate, flipping folded portion of omelet over so it is on the bottom.

⏱ SPICY SHRIMP OMELETS

2 tablespoons peanut or vegetable oil
1 small onion, chopped (about ¼ cup)
½ teaspoon curry powder
⅛ to ¼ teaspoon crushed red pepper
1 clove garlic, finely chopped
¼ cup thin diagonal slices green beans
¼ cup shredded carrot
½ cup fully cooked small shrimp
2 teaspoons soy sauce
2 French Omelets (left)
2 teaspoons chopped fresh cilantro

Heat oil in 8-inch skillet or omelet pan over medium heat. Cook onion, curry powder, red pepper and garlic in oil about 2 minutes, stirring occasionally. Add green beans and carrot. Cook and stir 2 minutes. Stir in shrimp and soy sauce. Heat until hot. Keep warm.

Prepare French Omelets—except before folding, fill each with about ½ cup shrimp mixture. Sprinkle with cilantro.   2 SERVINGS; 480 CALORIES PER SERVING.

🌾 PUFFY OMELET

Beat on high speed until stiff peaks form but the whites aren't dry. A beaten white should more than triple in volume.

- 4 eggs, separated
- ¼ cup water
- ¼ teaspoon salt
- ⅛ teaspoon pepper
- 1 tablespoon margarine or butter

Heat oven to 325°. Beat egg whites, water and salt in medium bowl on high speed until stiff but not dry. Beat egg yolks and pepper on high speed about 3 minutes or until very thick and lemon colored. Fold into egg whites.

Heat margarine in 10-inch ovenproof skillet over medium heat just until hot enough to sizzle a drop of water. As margarine melts, tilt skillet to coat bottom. Pour egg mixture into skillet. Level surface gently; reduce heat. Cook over low heat about 5 minutes or until puffy and light brown on bottom. (Lift omelet carefully at edge to judge color.) Bake uncovered 12 to 15 minutes or until knife inserted in center comes out clean.

Tilt skillet and slip pancake turner or spatula under omelet to loosen. Fold omelet in half, being careful not to break it. Slip onto warm plate. Serve with Italian Tomato Sauce (page 360) if desired. 2 SERVINGS; 210 CALORIES PER SERVING.

🌾 BRUNCH OVEN OMELET

A breakfast favorite in the Betty Crocker Dining Room, especially when served with Canadian-style bacon, fresh fruit and Baking Powder Biscuits (page 38). Great to make for your favorite crowd.

- ¼ cup margarine or butter
- 18 eggs
- 1 cup sour cream
- 1 cup milk
- 2 teaspoons salt
- ¼ cup chopped green onions (with tops)

Heat oven to 325°. Heat margarine in rectangular baking dish, 13 × 9 × 2 inches, in oven until melted. Tilt dish to coat bottom. Beat eggs, sour cream, milk and salt until blended. Stir in onions. Pour into dish.

Bake about 35 minutes or until eggs are set but moist. 12 SERVINGS; 135 CALORIES PER SERVING.

SMALL BRUNCH OVEN OMELET: Use square baking dish, 8 × 8 × 2 inches. Cut all ingredients in half. Bake about 25 minutes. 6 SERVINGS.

Puffy Omelet, Orange-Avocado Salads (page 308)

Vegetable Frittata

🕐 VEGETABLE FRITTATA

3 tablespoons vegetable oil
½ cup sliced zucchini
1 small bell pepper, cut into ¼-inch strips
1 small onion, thinly sliced
1 clove garlic, finely chopped
½ cup coarsely chopped tomato
2 teaspoons chopped fresh or ½ teaspoon dried oregano leaves
2 teaspoons chopped fresh or ½ teaspoon dried basil leaves
8 eggs
½ teaspoon salt
¼ teaspoon pepper
½ cup shredded Fontina or mozzarella cheese (2 ounces)
2 tablespoons grated Romano or Parmesan cheese

Heat oil in 10-inch ovenproof skillet over medium heat. Cook zucchini, bell pepper, onion and garlic in oil 3 minutes, stirring occasionally. Stir in tomato, oregano and basil. Reduce heat to medium-low. Beat eggs, salt and pepper until blended. Stir in Fontina cheese. Pour over vegetable mixture. Cover and cook 9 to 11 minutes or until eggs are set around edge and light brown on bottom. Sprinkle with Romano cheese.

Set oven control to broil. Broil frittata with top about 5 inches from heat about 3 minutes or until golden brown. 6 SERVINGS; 215 CALORIES PER SERVING.

FLORENTINE PIE

Other types of rice such as brown and basmati work nicely for the shell.

1½ cups hot cooked rice (page 267)
¼ cup grated Parmesan cheese
1 tablespoon chopped green onion tops
1 egg white
4 eggs
1 egg yolk
1 cup shredded Swiss cheese (4 ounces)
⅔ cup milk
¼ cup sliced green onions
¼ teaspoon salt
¼ teaspoon ground pepper
¼ teaspoon ground nutmeg
1 package (10 ounces) frozen chopped spinach, thawed and pressed dry

Heat oven to 325°. Grease pie plate, 9 × 1¼ inches. Mix rice, Parmesan cheese, 1 tablespoon green onion tops and the egg white with fork. Press mixture evenly on bottom and up side of pie plate (do not leave any holes). Bake 5 minutes.

Beat eggs and egg yolk with hand beater in medium bowl until very foamy. Stir in remaining ingredients. Pour into rice shell. Bake about 45 minutes or until knife inserted in center comes out clean. Serve with additional Parmesan cheese if desired.   6 SERVINGS; 235 CALORIES PER SERVING.

BREAKFAST POTATO CASSEROLE

1 package (6 ounces) hash brown potato
   mix*
⅓ cup chopped onion
¼ cup chopped green bell pepper
8 slices bacon, crisply cooked and crumbled
1 can (8 ounces) whole kernel corn, drained
1½ cups shredded Cheddar cheese (6 ounces)
1 cup milk
5 eggs, beaten
½ teaspoon salt
Dash of ground red pepper (cayenne)
Paprika

Heat oven to 350°. Cover potatoes with water
and drain as directed on package except omit salt.
Spread potatoes in ungreased rectangular baking
dish, 12 × 7½ × 2 inches. Top with onion, bell pepper, bacon, corn and cheese. Mix remaining ingredients except paprika. Pour over cheese. Sprinkle
with paprika. Bake 35 to 40 minutes or until knife
inserted in center comes out clean.   6 SERVINGS;
350 CALORIES PER SERVING.

*3 cups frozen shredded hash brown potatoes can be substi-
tuted for the potato mix (do not thaw).*

CRAB CROISSANT BAKE

4 large croissants, cut into ½-inch cubes,
   or 4 cups ½-inch cubes French bread
1 cup shredded Jarlsberg, Swiss or mozzarella cheese (4 ounces)
1 package (6 ounces) frozen crabmeat,
   thawed and well drained, or 6 ounces
   imitation crabmeat, cut into ½-inch pieces
2 green onions (with tops), sliced
1½ cups milk
3 eggs
½ teaspoon dry mustard
½ teaspoon salt

Arrange half of the croissant cubes in ungreased
square baking dish, 8 × 8 × 2 inches. Sprinkle with
½ cup of the cheese, the crabmeat and onions.
Arrange remaining cubes over top. Beat milk, eggs,
mustard and salt. Pour over cubes. Cover and refrigerate at least 2 hours but no longer than 24
hours.

Heat oven to 325°. Bake uncovered 1 to 1¼
hours or until knife inserted in center comes out
clean. Sprinkle with remaining ½ cup cheese.
Bake about 2 minutes longer or until cheese melts.
Serve immediately.   6 SERVINGS; 265 CALORIES PER
SERVING.

CHICKEN CROISSANT BAKE: Substitute 1½ cups
diced cooked chicken for the crabmeat.   310 CALO-
RIES PER SERVING.

⏱ SMOKED SALMON ROULADE

*An easy oven omelet that's rolled, quick
and elegant, without the work of individual omelets.*

½ cup all-purpose flour
1 cup milk
3 tablespoons chopped green onion with
   tops
1 tablespoon chopped fresh or 1 teaspoon
   dried dill weed
2 tablespoons margarine or butter, melted
¼ teaspoon salt
4 eggs
1 cup flaked smoked salmon*
1 package (10 ounces) frozen cut asparagus
1½ cups shredded Gruyère or Emmentaler
   cheese (6 ounces)

Heat oven to 350°. Line jelly roll pan, 15½ × 10½ × 1
inch, with aluminum foil. Grease foil generously.
Beat flour, milk, onion, dill, margarine, salt and
eggs until well blended. Pour into pan. Sprinkle
with salmon. Bake 15 to 18 minutes or until eggs
are set.

Meanwhile cook asparagus as directed on package;
drain and keep warm. After removing eggs from
oven, immediately sprinkle with cheese and asparagus. Roll up, beginning at narrow end, using foil
to lift and roll roulade.   6 SERVINGS; 315 CALORIES
PER SERVING.

*1 can (8 ounces) red salmon, drained and flaked, can be
substituted for the smoked salmon.*

HAM ROULADE: Substitute 1 cup coarsely chopped
fully cooked smoked ham for the smoked salmon.
305 CALORIES PER SERVING.

CHEESE BASICS

KINDS OF CHEESE

Learning about the world of domestic and imported cheeses can be a lifelong adventure because new cheeses are often introduced in supermarkets. The variety of flavors, textures and shapes add excitement to eating and cooking alike.

Cheeses vary in fat content, depending on the amount of milk fat used in making them. Low-fat cheeses (fewer than 6 grams of fat per ounce) that are similar in taste to traditional higher fat cheeses are becoming popular. They are often labeled with the word *style* or *flavor*, as in "Cheddar-style" or "Cheddar-flavor."

The U.S. government has created four broad categories of cheese: natural cheese, pasteurized process cheese, cheese food and pasteurized cheese spread.

♦ **Natural cheeses** are made from the milk (whole, skim or, sometimes, raw) or cream of cows, sheep or goats that has been solidified by curdling and the liquid (whey) removed. Some are then aged or ripened. Cheeses not aged (like cottage or cream cheese) are referred to as fresh, or unripened.

It is difficult to categorize natural cheeses because of the many types of cheese and cheese-making methods, the type of milk used and the type of aging or ripening process. Many cheeses fit into more than one category. The Varieties of Natural Cheese chart (page 179) is a guide grouped simply according to hardness.

♦ **Pasteurized process cheese** is a blend of one or more varieties of natural cheese that are ground, blended and heated. The process stops the aging or ripening, resulting in consistent flavor and better keeping quality. The very popular American cheese is a good example of pasteurized process cheese.

♦ **Cheese food** is made of one or more varieties of natural cheese blended either without the aid of heat (cold pack) or with heat (pasteurized process cheese). Dairy products such as cream, milk, skim milk or whey are added, and the food has a higher percentage of moisture than natural or pasteurized process cheese. It is usually sold refrigerated in tubs or jars and often flavorings are added.

♦ **Pasteurized cheese spread** is similar to pasteurized process cheese except it is easy to spread at room temperature. This cheese is higher in moisture and lower in fat than cheese food. Spreads in jars and aerosol cheeses sold at room temperature are good examples.

HANDLING AND STORAGE OF CHEESE

♦ Serve natural cheeses (except such fresh cheeses as cottage cheese) at room temperature to bring out their fullest flavor. Remove cheese from refrigerator and let stand covered about 1 hour before serving. Or microwave firm cheese uncovered on medium-low (30%) about 30 seconds for 8 ounces, rotating ½ turn after half the time. Let stand a few minutes before serving.

♦ All cheese should be wrapped tightly to minimize moisture loss and retain texture, then stored in the refrigerator. Ripened cheeses will continue to age during storage. Mold that forms on natural cheese is harmless but looks unappetizing and may be removed by cutting off approximately ½ inch from each affected area; use the remaining cheese within the week. Changing the wrap each time cheese is used will reduce mold growth.

♦ Fresh, unripened cheeses, such as cottage and cream cheeses, are more perishable because they have a higher water content than hard cheeses. These cheeses do not improve with age and should be used within two weeks of purchase.

♦ Refrigerated cheese is firmer and, therefore, easier to shred than room-temperature cheese. Use a food processor to shred or chop cheese quickly.

♦ Very soft cheese shreds more easily with a shredder that has large holes or if cheese is first placed in the freezer for fifteen minutes.

♦ Mold-ripened or blue-veined cheeses can be cut easily and cleanly in slices at room temperature with dental floss or heavy thread. Crumbling or chopping works best when cheese is cold.

COOKING WITH CHEESE

♦ Four ounces of shredded, crumbled or grated cheese equals 1 cup.

♦ Keep cooking temperature low and the cooking time short. High heat and overcooking cause cheese to become stringy and tough.

♦ Cheese microwaves well, but lower power works best. Soften cream cheese by removing wrapper and microwaving uncovered on medium (50%) until softened. For a 3-ounce package, microwave for 30 to 45 seconds, and for an 8-ounce package, 60 to 90 seconds.

♦ When adding cheese to hot foods, cut it into small pieces so it melts evenly and quickly.

♦ Cheeses with similar flavors and textures can be used interchangeably.

Provolone

Parmesan

Romano

Asiago

Gjetost

Cheshire

Gruyère

Natural Swiss

Jarlsberg

Fontina

White Cheddar

Cheese Curds

Cheddar

Colby

Gouda

Mozzarella

String Cheese (Mozzarella)

Farmer

Brick

Havarti

Bel Paese

Muenster

Port du Salut

Nokkelost

Monterey J.

Roquefort

Gorgonzola

Stilton

Limburger

Blue

Bucheron

Montrachet

Feta

Mascarpone

Boursin

Cream

Camembert

Brie

VARIETES OF NATURAL CHEESE

Texture	Flavor	Use
VERY HARD (grating)		
Asiago	*pungent, sharp*	*cooking, seasoning*
Parmesan	*piquant, sharp*	*cooking, salad, seasoning*
Romano	*piquant, sharp*	*cooking, pasta, seasoning*
HARD		
Cheddar	*mild to very sharp*	*sandwich, cooking, dessert, with fruit*
Cheshire	*rich, robust*	*cooking, with fruit*
Edam, Gouda	*milky, nutty*	*appetizer, dessert*
Gjetost	*caramel, sweet*	*sandwich, snack*
Gruyère	*nutty, slightly sharp*	*cooking, dessert*
Jarlsberg	*buttery, slightly sharp*	*appetizer, sandwich, cooking*
Provolone	*mild to sharp, smoky*	*sandwich, cooking*
Noekkelost	*spicy, creamy*	*appetizer, sandwich, cooking*
Swiss	*mild, nutty, sweet*	*appetizer, sandwich, cooking, dessert*
SEMISOFT		
Blue	*tangy, sharp, robust*	*appetizer, dessert, salad*
Brick	*mild to sharp*	*appetizer, sandwich*
Colby	*mild*	*sandwich, cooking*
Curds	*mild, chewy*	*appetizer, snack*
Fontina	*buttery*	*appetizer, cooking*
Gorgonzola	*piquant, salty*	*dessert, salad*

Texture	Flavor	Use
Havarti	*mellow, mild*	*appetizer, cooking*
Monterey Jack	*creamy, mild*	*appetizer, sandwich, cooking*
Mozzarella, String	*mild, chewy*	*appetizer, sandwich, cooking, snack, pizza*
Muenster	*mild to sharp*	*appetizer, sandwich, dessert*
Port du Salut	*mild to robust*	*appetizer, sandwich, dessert*
Reblochon	*mild*	*appetizer, dessert*
Roquefort	*sharp, salty*	*appetizer, dessert, salad*
Stilton	*piquant, rich*	*dessert, salad, snack*
SOFT		
Bel Paese	*creamy, mild*	*cooking, dessert*
Boursin	*sharp*	*appetizer*
Brie	*mild to pungent*	*appetizer, sandwich, dessert*
Bucheron	*sharp*	*cooking, dessert*
Camembert	*mild to pungent*	*appetizer, sandwich, dessert*
Cottage, dry or creamed	*mild*	*cooking, salad*
Cream	*very mild*	*appetizer, dessert, salad*
Farmer	*mild*	*cooking*
Feta	*salty, sharp*	*cooking, salad*
Liederkranz	*pungent*	*appetizer, dessert*
Limburger	*very pungent*	*appetizer, snack*
Mascarpone	*very mild, sweet*	*dessert*
Montrachet	*creamy, mild*	*appetizer, cooking*
Neufchâtel	*mild*	*appetizer, dessert, salad, spread*
Ricotta	*mild*	*cooking, dessert, pasta*

Classic Cheese Soufflé

CLASSIC CHEESE SOUFFLÉ

¼ cup margarine or butter
¼ cup all-purpose flour
½ teaspoon salt
¼ teaspoon dry mustard
Dash of ground red pepper (cayenne)
1 cup milk
1 cup shredded Cheddar cheese (4 ounces)
3 eggs, separated
¼ teaspoon cream of tartar

Heat oven to 350°. Butter 1-quart soufflé dish or casserole. Make a 4-inch band of triple-thickness aluminum foil 2 inches longer than circumference of dish. Butter one side. Secure foil band by tying with string, buttered side in, around top edge of dish.

Heat margarine in 2-quart saucepan over medium heat until melted. Stir in flour, salt, mustard and red pepper. Cook over medium heat, stirring constantly, until smooth and bubbly; remove from heat. Stir in milk. Heat to boiling, stirring constantly. Boil and stir 1 minute. Stir in cheese until melted; remove from heat.

Beat egg whites and cream of tartar in medium bowl on high speed until stiff but not dry. Beat egg yolks on high speed about 3 minutes or until very thick and lemon colored. Stir into cheese mixture. Stir about ¼ of the egg whites into cheese mixture. Fold cheese mixture into remaining egg whites.

Carefully pour into soufflé dish. Bake 50 to 60 minutes or until knife inserted halfway between center and edge comes out clean. Carefully remove foil band and quickly divide soufflé into servings with 2 forks. Serve immediately.   4 SERVINGS; 330 CALORIES PER SERVING.

SHRIMP SOUFFLÉ: Omit mustard, red pepper and cheese. Add 1 can (4½ ounces) shrimp, rinsed and drained, and 1 tablespoon chopped fresh or 1 teaspoon dried tarragon leaves to sauce before adding the beaten egg yolks.   250 CALORIES PER SERVING.

CHEESE STRATA

⅓ cup margarine or butter, softened
½ teaspoon dry mustard
1 clove garlic, crushed
10 slices white bread (crusts removed)
2 cups shredded sharp Cheddar
   cheese (8 ounces)
2 tablespoons chopped fresh parsley
2 tablespoons chopped onion
1 teaspoon salt
½ teaspoon Worcestershire sauce
⅛ teaspoon pepper
Dash of ground red pepper (cayenne)
4 eggs
2½ cups milk

Mix margarine, mustard and garlic. Spread over each slice bread. Cut each slice into thirds. Line bottom and sides of ungreased square baking dish, 8 × 8 × 2 inches, with enough of the bread slices to cover, buttered sides down.

Mix cheese, parsley, onion, salt, Worcestershire sauce, pepper and red pepper. Spread evenly over bread slices in dish. Top with remaining bread slices, buttered sides up. Beat eggs and stir in milk. Pour over bread. Cover and refrigerate at least 2 hours but no longer than 24 hours.

Heat oven to 325°. Bake uncovered about 1¼ hours or until knife inserted in center comes out clean. Let stand 10 minutes before cutting.   6 SERVINGS; 460 CALORIES PER SERVING.

QUICHE LORRAINE

Pastry for 9-inch One-Crust Pie (page 88)
8 slices bacon, crisply cooked and crumbled
1 cup chredded natural Swiss cheese
    (4 ounces)
⅓ cup finely chopped onion
4 eggs
2 cups whipping (heavy) cream
¼ teaspoon salt
¼ teaspoon pepper
⅛ teaspoon ground red pepper (cayenne)

Heat oven to 425°. Prepare pastry. Ease into quiche dish, 9 × 1½ inches, or pie plate, 9 × 1¼ inches. Sprinkle bacon, cheese and onion in pastry-lined quiche dish. Beat eggs slightly; beat in remaining ingredients. Pour into quiche dish. Bake 15 minutes.

Reduce oven temperature to 300°. Bake about 30 minutes longer or until knife inserted in center comes out clean. Let stand 10 minutes before cutting.   6 SERVINGS; 630 CALORIES PER SERVING.

CHICKEN QUICHE: Substitute 1 cup cut-up cooked chicken or turkey for the bacon and 1 teaspoon chopped fresh or ½ teaspoon dried thyme leaves for the red pepper. Increase salt to ½ teaspoon. 595 CALORIES PER SERVING.

SEAFOOD QUICHE: Substitute 1 cup chopped cooked crabmeat, shrimp, seafood sticks or salmon for the bacon and green onion for the onion. (Pat crabmeat dry.) Increase salt to ½ teaspoon.   575 CALORIES PER SERVING.

IMPOSSIBLE CHILI-CHEESE PIE

2 cans (4 ounces each) chopped green chilies, drained
4 cups shredded Cheddar cheese (16 ounces)
2 cups milk
4 eggs
1 cup variety baking mix

Heat oven to 425°. Grease pie plate, 10 × 1½ inches. Sprinkle chilies and cheese in pie plate. Place remaining ingredients in blender. Cover and blend on high speed about 15 seconds or until smooth. (Or beat remaining ingredients on high speed 1 minute.) Pour into pie plate. Bake 25 to 30 minutes or until knife inserted in center comes out clean. Cool 10 minutes.   8 SERVINGS; 360 CALORIES PER SERVING.

To Microwave: Do not grease pie plate. Decrease milk to 1½ cups. Prepare as directed. Elevate pie plate on inverted microwavable dinner plate in microwave oven. Microwave uncovered on medium-high (70%) 12 to 18 minutes, rotating pie plate ¼ turn every 6 minutes, until knife inserted in center comes out clean. Cool 10 minutes.

LEEK AND MUSHROOM TART

Pastry for 9-inch One-Crust Pie (page 88)
3 tablespoons margarine or butter
2 cups sliced leeks, (about ½ pound)
1 cup coarsely chopped shiitake or other fresh mushrooms (about 3 ounces)
1 cup shredded white Cheddar or Cheddar cheese (4 ounces)
¾ cup shredded mozzarella cheese (3 ounces)
3 eggs
⅔ cup milk
½ teaspoon salt
½ teaspoon ground nutmeg

Heat oven to 475°. Prepare pastry. Ease into tart pan, 9 × 1 inch, or pie plate, 9 × 1¼ inches. Bake as directed; cool.

Reduce oven temperature to 350°. Heat margarine in 10-inch skillet over medium heat. Cook leeks and mushrooms in margarine about 5 minutes. Spread in tart pan. Sprinkle with cheeses. Beat remaining ingredients. Pour over cheeses. Bake about 35 minutes or until set.   6 SERVINGS; 360 CALORIES PER SERVING.

QUICHE

Quiche (pronounced keesh) is a custard pie with cheese that originated in France in Alsace-Lorraine, the region that borders Germany. Some say that it's from the German Küchen that quiche takes its pronunciation. In the 1960s when quiche first became a popular dish in America, its unfamiliar pronunciation stumped many people, including some on our staff who came up with a few amusing pronunciations of their own.

Quiche is great for lunches, brunches, dinner and even appetizers when served in bite-size pieces. Quiche Lorraine is the classic version, and it's one of our favorites, served in the Betty Crocker Dining Room.

You can easily prepare it ahead of time. Sprinkle the bacon, cheese and onion in the unbaked shell, cover and refrigerate. Beat together the remaining ingredients, cover and refrigerate. Stir the egg mixture before pouring into pie plate. Bake as directed—except increase second bake time to about 45 minutes.

🌾 TRADITIONAL CHEESE PIZZA

In our 1956 cookbook, pizza appeared as both an appetizer and a main dish. Our recipe came from a staff member who sampled the delights of pizza on a vacation in Italy. A variety of your favorite toppings can be added to the basic cheese pizza. For each 12-inch pizza, try one or more of the following: ½ pound ground beef or bulk Italian sausage, cooked and well drained; 1 package (3½ ounces) sliced pepperoni; 1 package (6 ounces) sliced Canadian-style bacon; ¼ cup sliced mushrooms, pitted ripe olives, chopped onions or chopped bell pepper.

Crust (right)
1 can (8 ounces) tomato sauce
1 teaspoon Italian seasoning
1 clove garlic, finely chopped
3 cups shredded mozzarella or Fontina cheese (12 ounces)
1 small onion, thinly sliced and separated into rings
¼ cup grated Parmesan cheese

Place oven rack in lowest position. Grease 2 cookie sheets or 12-inch pizza pans. Heat oven to 425°.

Prepare Crust. Mix tomato sauce, Italian seasoning and garlic. Divide dough in half. Pat each half into 11-inch circle on cookie sheet with floured fingers. Sprinkle with mozzarella cheese. Spoon tomato sauce mixture over cheese. Top with onion and Parmesan cheese. Bake one pizza at a time 15 to 20 minutes or until crust is golden brown. 2 PIZZAS (6 SLICES EACH); 205 CALORIES PER SLICE.

Crust

1 package active dry yeast
1 cup warm water (105° to 115°)
2½ cups all-purpose flour
2 tablespoons olive or vegetable oil
1 teaspoon sugar
1 teaspoon salt

Dissolve yeast in warm water in medium bowl. Stir in remaining ingredients. Beat vigorously 20 strokes. Let rest 5 minutes.

PROSCIUTTO-TOMATO PIZZA: Prepare Crust. Top with tomato sauce mixture, onion and Fontina cheese. Before adding Parmesan cheese, sprinkle with 2 tablespoons chopped fresh or 2 teaspoons dried basil leaves, ½ pound prosciutto or fully cooked smoked ham, cut into julienne strips (2 × ¼ × ⅛ inch), and 2 large plum tomatoes, coarsely chopped. 225 CALORIES PER SLICE.

Prosciutto-Tomato Pizza

⏱ THREE-CHEESE TORTELLINI

1 package (7 ounces) dried cheese-filled tortellini
¼ cup margarine or butter
½ cup chopped green bell pepper
2 shallots, finely chopped
1 clove garlic, finely chopped
¼ cup all-purpose flour
¼ teaspoon pepper
1 ¾ cups milk
½ cup shredded mozzarella cheese (2 ounces)
½ cup shredded Swiss cheese (2 ounces)
¼ cup grated Parmesan or Romano cheese

Cook tortellini as directed on package; drain. Heat margarine in 3-quart saucepan over medium heat. Cook bell pepper, shallots and garlic in margarine about 3 minutes. Stir in flour and pepper. Cook, stirring constantly, until mixture is bubbly; remove from heat. Stir in milk. Heat to boiling, stirring constantly. Boil and stir 1 minute; remove from heat. Stir in mozzarella and Swiss cheeses until melted. Add tortellini and stir until coated. Sprinkle with Parmesan cheese. 5 SERVINGS (ABOUT 1 CUP EACH); 390 CALORIES PER SERVING.

🌾 MACARONI AND CHEESE

1 package (7 ounces) uncooked elbow, rotini or ziti macaroni (about 2 cups)
2 tablespoons margarine or butter
1 small onion, chopped (about ¼ cup)
2 tablespoons all-purpose flour
½ teaspoon salt
¼ teaspoon pepper
2 cups milk
8 ounces sharp process American or Swiss cheese, process American cheese loaf or process cheese spread loaf, cut into ½-inch cubes, or shredded Cheddar cheese

Heat oven to 375°. Cook macaroni as directed on package. Heat margarine in 3-quart saucepan over medium heat. Cook onion in margarine about 3 minutes. Stir in flour, salt and pepper. Cook, stirring constantly, until mixture is bubbly; remove from heat. Stir in milk. Heat to boiling, stirring constantly. Boil and stir 1 minute; remove from heat. Stir in cheese until melted. Add macaroni and stir until coated. Pour into ungreased 1½-quart casserole. Bake about 30 minutes or until bubbly and light brown. 6 SERVINGS (ABOUT ¾ CUP EACH); 355 CALORIES PER SERVING.

To Microwave: Mix macaroni, 2 cups hot water, the margarine, onion, salt and pepper in 2-quart microwavable casserole. Cover tightly and microwave on high 5 minutes; stir. Cover tightly and microwave on medium (50%) 4 to 6 minutes or until boiling. Reduce milk to 1¼ cups. Stir in remaining ingredients. Cover tightly and microwave on high 5 to 8 minutes, stirring every 3 minutes, until mixture is bubbly and macaroni is tender. Let stand covered 5 minutes before serving.

🌾 MANICOTTI

We made this recipe easier and faster for our current edition by using uncooked manicotti shells. The secret to tender, evenly cooked shells is to make sure sauce covers the bottom of the pan and the shells.

1 large tomato, chopped (about 1 cup)
1 tablespoon chopped fresh or 1 teaspoon dried basil leaves
2 cans (15 ounces each) tomato sauce
2 cups creamed cottage cheese
¼ cup grated Parmesan cheese
1 clove garlic, finely chopped
1 teaspoon chopped fresh or ½ teaspoon dried thyme leaves
1 small onion, chopped (about ¼ cup)
2 eggs
1 package (10 ounces) frozen chopped spinach, thawed and drained
1 package (8 ounces) manicotti shells (14 shells)
1 cup shredded mozzarella cheese (4 ounces)

Heat oven to 350°. Grease rectangular pan or baking dish, 13×9×2 inches. Mix tomato, basil and tomato sauce. Spread 1½ cups evenly in pan. Mix remaining ingredients except manicotti and mozzarella cheese. Fill uncooked manicotti shells with spinach mixture. Arrange in pan. Pour remaining tomato sauce mixture over manicotti. Cover and bake about 1½ hours or until manicotti shells are tender. Sprinkle with mozzarella cheese. 7 SERVINGS; 380 CALORIES PER SERVING.

❧ CHEESE ENCHILADAS

2 cups shredded Monterey Jack cheese (8 ounces)
1 cup shredded Cheddar cheese (4 ounces)
1 medium onion, chopped (about ½ cup)
½ cup sour cream or plain yogurt
2 tablespoons chopped fresh parsley
¼ teaspoon pepper
6 flour tortillas (7-inch diameter)
1 can (15 ounces) tomato sauce
⅓ cup chopped green bell pepper
1 tablespoon chili powder
1 teaspoon chopped fresh or ½ teaspoon dried oregano leaves
¼ teaspoon ground cumin
1 clove garlic, finely chopped
¼ cup shredded Cheddar cheese (1 ounce)

Heat oven to 350°. Grease rectangular baking dish, 12 × 7½ × 2 inches. Mix Monterey Jack cheese, 1 cup Cheddar cheese, the onion, sour cream, parsley and pepper. Spoon about ½ cup cheese mixture onto each tortilla. Roll tortilla around filling and place seam side down in dish. Mix remaining ingredients except ¼ cup Cheddar cheese. Pour over enchiladas. Sprinkle with ¼ cup Cheddar cheese. Bake uncovered about 20 minutes or until hot and bubbly. Garnish with sour cream and sliced black olives or lime wedges if desired.   6 SERVINGS; 360 CALORIES PER SERVING.

To Microwave: Prepare as directed—except place enchiladas in greased rectangular microwavable dish, 12 × 7½ × 2 inches, and do not sprinkle with ¼ cup Cheddar cheese. Cover with waxed paper and microwave on high 9 to 11 minutes, rotating dish ½ turn after 5 minutes, until hot and bubbly. Sprinkle with ¼ cup Cheddar cheese. Cover and let stand about 3 minutes.

WELSH RABBIT

From our 1950 Betty Crocker's Picture Cook Book: *"The story goes that long ago in Wales the peasants, not allowed to hunt on the estates of noblemen, served melted cheese as a substitute for rabbit, popular prize of the hunt. It became a famous dish at Ye Olde Cheshire Inn, meeting place of England's illustrious penmen. There rare wits from Ben Jonson to Charles Dickens conversed copiously while enjoying the specialty of the house."*

❧ WELSH RABBIT

3 tablespoons margarine or butter
3 tablespoons all-purpose flour
¼ teaspoon salt
¼ teaspoon pepper
¼ teaspoon dry mustard
¼ teaspoon Worcestershire sauce
1 cup milk
½ cup beer or white wine*
1½ cups shredded Cheddar cheese (6 ounces)
4 slices toast, cut into triangles

Heat margarine in 2-quart saucepan over medium heat until melted. Stir in flour, salt, pepper, mustard and Worcestershire sauce. Cook, stirring constantly, until smooth and bubbly; remove from heat. Stir in milk. Heat to boiling, stirring constantly. Boil and stir 1 minute. Gradually stir in beer. Stir in cheese. Heat over low heat, stirring constantly, until cheese is melted. Serve over toast. Sprinkle with paprika if desired.   4 SERVINGS; 390 CALORIES PER SERVING.

*Beer or wine can be omitted. Increase milk to 1½ cups.

ASPARAGUS WELSH RABBIT: Cook 1 package (10 ounces) frozen asparagus spears as directed on package; drain. Arrange on toast before topping with cheese sauce.   415 CALORIES PER SERVING.

Asparagus Welsh Rabbit

FIX-IT-FAST

- Keep hard-cooked eggs on hand to make sandwiches and main dishes or to top salads, vegetables and sauces.

- Extend egg sandwich fillings by adding shredded cheese or chopped vegetables when you're short on hard-cooked eggs.

- To make poached eggs special, use half dry white wine or chicken broth in the poaching liquid.

- For an egg sandwich on the run, serve egg salad or scrambled eggs in a tortilla or pocket bread.

- For a quick, light meal, serve a platter of cheese, fresh fruit and crackers. Select a colorful variety of fruits, and choose local cheeses or try imported cheeses.

- Serve assorted cheeses in chunks and let guests slice as they wish.

- For an interesting snack or dessert, serve baked apples or apple pie with a slice of cheese.

- Purchase cheese already shredded or cubed to cut down on preparation time.

- Fix a quick toasted cheese sandwich in the microwave. Place cheese between 2 slices of toasted bread. Microwave on a microwavable paper towel for about 1 minute on medium (50%).

- Use leftover cheeses to make quick sandwich fillings, to add to salads or to stir into scrambled eggs.

- For a quick appetizer, top a block of cream cheese with one of the following: curry powder and chutney, jalapeño pepper jelly or shrimp sauce with tiny shrimp.

- To vary cottage cheese, stir in one of these easy-to-prepare combinations: shredded carrots and raisins; crushed pineapple and fresh mint; chopped green bell pepper, tomato and onion; sunflower nuts, alfalfa sprouts and chopped carrots; or toasted pine nuts, chopped tomato and basil.

- Mix preserves or jam into cottage cheese. Spread on toast or English muffins and broil.

- Make a quick fondue with cheese soup thinned with wine or beer.

- Use pasteurized process cheese spreads as a base for soups and sauces. Thin with milk, beer or wine; then heat in a saucepan or quickly in the microwave.

NUTRITION INFORMATION

PER SERVING OR UNIT

RECIPE, PAGE	Servings per recipe	Calories	Protein (grams)	Carbohydrate (grams)	Fat (grams)	Cholesterol (milligrams)	Sodium (milligrams)	Protein	Vitamin A	Vitamin C	Thiamine	Riboflavin	Niacin	Calcium	Iron
EGGS															
Baked Eggs and Artichokes, 171	4	475	20	31	23	300	740	30	20	2	12	28	6	34	14
Baked Eggs and Green Beans, 171	4	465	19	29	23	300	710	28	28	6	12	26	4	36	14
Baked (Shirred) Eggs, 170	1	120	6	1	10	275	120	10	8	0	2	10	0	4	4
Breakfast Potato Casserole, 176	6	350	18	28	19	270	345	28	12	12	12	18	10	28	14
Brunch Oven Omelet, 174	12	135	5	2	12	215	470	8	14	0	2	8	0	4	4
Crab Benedict, 171	6	360	16	8	29	470	780	24	30	0	8	14	6	8	12
Crab Croissant Bake, 176	6	265	15	16	16	205	720	22	20	0	16	18	6	20	8
Chicken Croissant Bake, 176	6	310	21	15	18	210	515	32	16	0	18	22	20	20	8
Eggs Benedict, 171	6	365	15	8	30	445	385	22	20	4	20	14	10	6	10
Eggs Poached in Broth, 170	1	85	6	1	6	275	410	8	4	0	2	8	0	2	4

NUTRITION INFORMATION

PER SERVING OR UNIT

PERCENT U.S. RECOMMENDED DAILY ALLOWANCE

RECIPE, PAGE	Servings per recipe	Calories	Protein (grams)	Carbohydrate (grams)	Fat (grams)	Cholesterol (milligrams)	Sodium (milligrams)	Protein	Vitamin A	Vitamin C	Thiamine	Riboflavin	Niacin	Calcium	Iron
EGGS (continued)															
Florentine Pie, 175	6	235	15	17	12	245	490	22	64	6	8	20	2	34	10
French Omelet, 173	1	225	18	1	19	550	225	18	16	0	6	16	0	4	10
Fried Eggs, 170	1	145	6	1	13	275	160	8	10	0	2	8	0	2	04
Ham Roulade, 176	6	305	30	12	19	225	600	30	24	16	22	22	10	36	8
Ham-and-Spinach Turnovers, 170	4	510	22	22	36	310	715	34	82	6	24	26	10	38	18
Hard-cooked Eggs, 169	1	80	6	1	6	275	70	8	4	0	2	8	0	2	4
Poached Eggs, 170	1	80	6	1	6	275	70	8	4	0	2	8	0	2	4
Puffy Omelet, 174	2	210	12	1	17	550	480	18	14	0	6	16	0	6	10
Reduced-Fat Fried Eggs, 170	1	95	6	1	7	275	90	8	6	0	21	8	0	2	4
Sausage-and-Spinach Turnovers, 170	4	650	25	23	51	300	845	38	82	4	26	28	14	38	20
Scrambled Eggs, 170	1	225	13	3	17	550	220	20	16	0	6	20	0	8	10
Seafood Benedict, 171	6	360	16	8	29	470	780	24	30	0	8	14	6	8	12
Smoked Salmon Roulade, 176	6	315	22	12	20	220	405	34	26	10	10	22	16	44	8
Soft-cooked Eggs, 169	1	80	6	1	6	275	70	8	4	0	2	8	0	2	4
Southwestern Eggs, 172	4	380	17	16	28	275	1185	26	34	50	26	20	18	6	
Spicy Shrimp Omelets, 173	2	480	24	21	33	590	620	36	100	4	16	22	6	14	22
Tex-Mex Scrambled Eggs, 172	4	370	18	17	25	410	555	26	28	8	8	16	2	28	16
Vegetable Frittata, 175	6	215	11	5	17	375	10	16	14	20	6	14	0	12	10
CHEESE															
Asparagus Welsh Rabbit, 184	4	405	18	27	25	50	25	26	28	14	14	24	10	42	8
Cheese Enchiladas, 184	6	360	18	19	24	35	780	28	42	38	6	18	4	54	16
Chicken Quiche, 181	6	595	20	17	50	330	510	30	30	0	8	20	14	26	8
Classic Cheese Soufflé, 180	4	330	22	9	26	240	660	22	22	0	6	20	2	30	6
Impossible Chili-Cheese Pie, 181	8	360	20	14	25	200	595	30	18	4	8	26	4	52	8
Leek and Mushroom Tart, 181	6	360	12	21	26	160	610	18	12	4	8	16	6	22	10
Macaroni and Cheese, 183	6	355	18	31	17	75	370	28	12	0	26	24	14	46	8
Manicotti, 183	7	325	22	37	11	135	1090	32	100	52	32	26	20	26	28
Prosciutto-Tomato Pizza, 182	12	225	14	23	9	25	600	20	10	8	18	12	12	20	8
Quiche Lorraine, 181	6	630	16	18	55	320	535	24	30	0	12	20	8	26	8
Seafood Quiche, 181	6	575	17	17	49	335	760	26	40	2	8	18	6	26	8
Shrimp Soufflé, 180	4	250	14	9	17	250	520	20	16	0	4	14	4	13	10
Three-Cheese Tortellini, 183	5	390	16	41	18	30	300	24	8	34	28	22	14	34	8
Traditional Cheese Pizza, 182	12	205	10	22	8	20	400	16	6	2	8	10	8	20	4
Welsh Rabbit, 184	4	390	16	23	25	50	680	24	18	0	12	22	8	12	8

FISH & SHELLFISH

Fish has been gaining popularity as a light entrée that is extremely healthful, full of protein and light on fat, while its versatility and easy preparation fit into our fast-paced lifestyles. People who don't live close to well-stocked lakes or the ocean still have full access to fresh fish and shellfish—in fact our consumption of fish has jumped 25 percent in the last five years! So, whether you're fishing for trout in a clear stream, clamming at the beach or just keeping an informed eye on the fish section in the supermarket, you'll definitely enjoy the range of delicious recipes we have gathered here.

FISH BASICS

Fish is increasingly available in its fresh form, but frozen and canned fish remain the most popular ways to purchase fish and seafood. (Canned tuna is the number one–ranked fish in the United States today.) Smoked fish is also growing in popularity.

Imitation crab and other seafood fish products are prepared from pollock, a mild white-fleshed fish. Real shellfish, a shellfish extract or artificial shellfish flavoring is added to the pollock, along with stabilizers, to create a shellfishlike product that is tasty and less expensive than real shellfish.

SELECTING FRESH FISH

- Eyes should be bright, clear and not sunken.
- Gills should be reddish pink, never brown.
- Scales should be bright with a sheen.
- Flesh should be firm and elastic; it should spring back when touched.
- There should be no odor.

SELECTING FROZEN FISH

- Package should be tightly wrapped and frozen solid with little or no airspace between packaging and fish.
- There should be no discoloration; if the fish is discolored, this may indicate freezer burn.
- There should be no odor.

Preceding page: *Wild Rice–stuffed Northern Pike (page 192), Steamed Mussels (page 203)*

BUYING FISH

How much fish you buy depends on the form you select. Below are the different forms of fish and some general guidelines to use when buying them.

- **Whole fish** is just as it comes from the water. Allow about 1 pound per serving.
- **Drawn fish** is whole, but the internal organs have been removed. Allow about ¾ pound per serving.
- **Pan-dressed fish** is scaled and the internal organs removed. The head, tail and fins have usually been removed. Allow about ½ pound per serving.
- **Steaks** are the cross-sectional slices of a large pan-dressed fish. Steaks are ½ to 1 inch thick. Allow about ¼ pound per serving.
- **Fillets** are the fleshy sides of the fish, cut lengthwise from the fish along the backbone. You may also find butterfly fillets, two fillets held together by the uncut flesh and skin of the belly. Fillets are usually boneless, although in some fish small bones called "pins" may be present. Allow about ¼ pound per serving.

LEAN FISH, FAT FISH

Fish is divided into three classifications: lean, medium-fat and fatty. Fish containing less than 2½ percent fat are considered lean. These fish are mild-flavored with tender, white or pale flesh. Lean fish are best steamed, poached, microwaved or fried. Fish with 2½ to 5 percent fat content are medium-fat fish. These fish are suitable for all cooking methods. Fish with a fat content greater than 5 percent are considered fatty fish and generally have a firmer texture, more pronounced flavor and a deeper color. Fatty fish are best broiled, grilled, microwaved or baked.

Individual fish have different percentages of fat that vary with the season, stage of maturity, locale, species and the diet of each fish. You can substitute one type of fish for another of the same classification when preparing recipes in this chapter.

Lean	Medium-Fat	Fatty
Bass, sea	Anchovy	Butterfish
Bass, striped	Bluefish	Carp
Burbot (freshwater cod)	Catfish	Eel
	Croaker	Herring
Cod	Mullet	Mackerel, Atlantic
Cusk	Porgy	
Flounder	Redfish	Mackerel, Pacific
Grouper	Salmon, pink	Mackerel, Spanish
Haddock	Shark	
Hake	Swordfish	Pompano
Halibut	Trout, rainbow	Sablefish
Lingcod	Trout, sea	Salmon, Chinook
Mackerel, king	Tuna, bluefin	Salmon, coho
Mahimahi (dolphin fish)	Turbot	Salmon, sockeye
Monkfish	Whitefish	Sardines
Orange roughy		Shad
Perch, ocean		Trout, lake
Pike, northern		Tuna, albacore
Pollock		
Red snapper		
Rockfish		
Scrod		
Smelt		
Sole		
Tilefish		
Tuna, skipjack		
Tuna, yellowfin		
Whiting		

As fish are delicate and tender, avoid overcooking, which makes fish dry and tough. Cook until fish flakes easily with a fork. You can test this by inserting a fork at an angle into the thickest part of the fish and twisting gently. For food safety reasons we recommend cooking to an internal temperature of 160°.

FISH DONENESS TEST

To test fish for doneness place fork in the thickest part of the fish. Gently twist fork. The fish will flake easily when done.

MICROWAVING FISH

Arrange fish fillets or steaks, thickest parts to outside edges, in shallow microwavable dish large enough to hold pieces in single layer. Cover tightly and microwave on high as directed below or until fish flakes easily with fork.

Fish	Amount	Time	Stand Time
Fillets, ½ to ¾ inch thick	1 pound	5 to 7 minutes, rotating dish ½ turn after 3 minutes	2 minutes
	1½ pounds	7 to 9 minutes, rotating dish ½ turn after 4 minutes	3 minutes
Steaks, 1 inch thick	1 pound	5 to 7 minutes, rotating dish ½ turn after 3 minutes	3 minutes
	2 pounds	8 to 10 minutes, rotating dish ½ turn after 4 minutes	3 minutes

PANFRIED FISH

1½ pounds lean fish fillets or pan-dressed fish
½ teaspoon salt
⅛ teaspoon pepper
1 egg
1 tablespoon water
½ cup all-purpose flour, cornmeal, dry bread crumbs or grated Parmesan cheese
Vegetable oil or shortening

If fish fillets are large, cut into 6 serving pieces. Sprinkle both sides of fish with salt and pepper. Beat egg and water until blended. Dip fish into egg, then coat with flour.

Heat oil (⅛ inch) in 10-inch skillet until hot. Fry fish in hot oil over medium heat 6 to 10 minutes, carefully turning once until fish flakes easily with fork and is brown on both sides. Drain on paper towels.   6 SERVINGS; 195 CALORIES PER SERVING.

OVEN-FRIED FISH

So easy—no basting, no turning, no constant watching!

1 pound lean fish fillets
¼ cup cornmeal
¼ cup dry bread crumbs
½ teaspoon paprika
¼ teaspoon salt
¾ teaspoon chopped fresh or ¼ teaspoon dried dill weed
⅛ teaspoon pepper
¼ cup milk
3 tablespoons margarine or butter, melted

Move oven rack to position slightly above middle of oven. Heat oven to 500°. Cut fish fillets into 2×1½-inch pieces. Mix cornmeal, bread crumbs, paprika, salt, dill weed and pepper. Dip fish into milk, then coat with cornmeal mixture.

Place fish in rectangular pan, 13×9×2 inches. Drizzle margarine over fish. Bake uncovered about 10 minutes or until fish flakes easily with fork.   4 SERVINGS; 205 CALORIES PER SERVING.

DEEP-FRIED FISH

For most even cooking, don't fry too many pieces of fish at the same time. When fish is done it will rise to the surface of the oil.

Vegetable oil or shortening
1 pound lean fish fillets, about ¾ inch thick
⅓ cup all-purpose flour
¼ teaspoon salt
⅛ teaspoon pepper
2 eggs, slightly beaten
½ cup dry bread crumbs

Heat oil (2 to 3 inches) in deep fryer or Dutch oven to 375°. If fish fillets are large, cut into 8 serving pieces. Mix flour, salt and pepper. Coat fish with flour mixture. Dip into eggs, then coat with bread crumbs. Fry a few pieces at a time about 3 minutes or until fish flakes easily with fork and is deep golden brown. Drain on paper towels.   4 SERVINGS; 300 CALORIES PER SERVING.

BROILED FISH STEAKS

For easy, different flavors when broiling fish, brush with Herb or Garlic Butter (page 361).

4 small fish steaks, about ¾ inch thick (about 1½ pounds)
Salt
Pepper
2 tablespoons margarine or butter, melted

Set oven control to broil. Sprinkle both sides of fish steaks with salt and pepper. Brush with half of the margarine. Broil fish with tops about 4 inches from heat about 5 minutes. Brush fish with margarine. Turn fish carefully and brush with margarine. Broil 4 to 6 minutes or until fish flakes easily with fork.   4 SERVINGS; 340 CALORIES PER SERVING.

To Grill: Grease wire grill. Place fish on grill. Cover and grill fish steaks about 4 inches from medium coals 20 to 25 minutes, turning fish once and brushing with margarine, until fish flakes easily with fork.

BROILED FISH FILLETS: Substitute 1 pound fish fillets, cut into 4 serving pieces, for the fish steaks. Broil with tops about 4 inches from heat 5 to 6 minutes or until fish flakes easily with fork (do not turn).

CREOLE CATFISH

A staple at fish fries, it is always accompanied by hush puppies or Corn Bread (page 39) and Coleslaw (page 313).

2 pounds catfish or other medium-fat fish fillets
⅓ cup chopped green bell pepper
2 tablespoons chopped fresh parsley
1 tablespoon lemon juice
½ teaspoon salt
½ teaspoon ground red pepper (cayenne)
1 medium onion, chopped (about ½ cup)
1 clove garlic, crushed
1 can (28 ounces) whole tomatoes, undrained
3 cups hot cooked rice (page 267)

Heat oven to 450°. If fillets are large, cut into 8 serving pieces. Place in ungreased rectangular baking dish, 11 × 7 × 1½ inches. Mix remaining ingredients except rice; break up tomatoes. Pour over fish.

Bake uncovered 25 to 30 minutes, spooning tomato mixture over fish occasionally, until fish flakes easily with fork. Serve over rice. Garnish with lemon slices sprinkled with chopped parsley if desired.   8 SERVINGS; 220 CALORIES PER SERVING.

COD

Cod has played an important role since colonial days. Plentiful along the Atlantic coastline, it was a mainstay of early American diets, and when salted, it was a particularly valuable commodity both abroad and for inland areas. The cod fish family includes haddock, pollock (Boston bluefish), hake, whiting and scrod, a cod less than 2½ pounds.

There are many theories as to how scrod received its name, and one favorite story of ours concerns the chef at Boston's Parker House, also the home of Parker House rolls and Boston Cream Pie. Rather than wait to hear the catch of the day so he could print his menu, he devised the word scrod *to cover any fish and sent the menu off to the printer.*

VEGETABLE-STUFFED SOLE

½ teaspoon salt
½ teaspoon chopped fresh or ½ teaspoon dried dill weed
¼ teaspoon pepper
6 sole or other lean fish fillets (about 2 pounds)
2 medium carrots, cut into julienne strips
1 green bell pepper, cut into julienne strips
¼ cup dry white wine or apple juice
2 tablespoons margarine or butter
2 tablespoons all-purpose flour
½ teaspoon salt
⅛ teaspoon pepper
1 cup milk
¼ cup dry white wine or apple juice

Heat oven to 350°. Mix ½ teaspoon salt, the dill weed and ¼ teaspoon pepper. Sprinkle over fish fillets. Divide carrot and bell pepper strips among fish. Roll up fish and place seam sides down in ungreased rectangular baking dish, 13 × 9 × 2 inches. Pour ¼ cup wine over fish. Cover with aluminum foil and bake about 40 minutes or until fish flakes easily with fork.

Heat margarine in 1½-quart saucepan until melted. Stir in flour, ½ teaspoon salt and ⅛ teaspoon pepper. Cook over medium heat, stirring constantly, until smooth and bubbly; remove from heat. Stir in milk and ¼ cup wine. Heat to boiling, stirring constantly. Boil and stir 1 minute.

Arrange fish on serving platter. Pour sauce over fish. Garnish with dill weed if desired.   6 SERVINGS; 225 CALORIES PER SERVING.

To Microwave: Place carrot strips in rectangular microwavable dish, 11 × 7 × 1½ inches. Add 1 tablespoon wine. Cover tightly and microwave on high about 4 minutes or until crisp-tender. Remove with slotted spoon. Prepare fish fillets as directed. Arrange seam sides down around sides of dish. Drizzle with 3 tablespoons wine. Cover tightly and microwave on high 10 to 12 minutes, rotating dish ½ turn after 5 minutes, until fish flakes easily with fork. Let stand covered 3 minutes. Remove to warm platter and keep warm.

Microwave margarine in 4-cup microwavable measure uncovered on high 15 to 30 seconds or until melted. Stir in flour, ½ teaspoon salt and ⅛ teaspoon pepper. Gradually stir in milk and ¼ cup wine. Microwave uncovered on high about 4 minutes, stirring every minute, until thickened.

FRUIT-STUFFED TROUT

4 pan-dressed rainbow trout (6 to 8 ounces each) or drawn trout (about 12 ounces each)
Fruit Stuffing (below)
2 tablespoons margarine or butter, melted
1 tablespoon lemon juice

Heat oven to 425°. Grease jelly roll pan, 15½ × 10½ × 1 inch. Stuff fish with Fruit Stuffing. Close openings with skewers or wooden picks if necessary. Place fish in pan. Mix margarine and lemon juice. Drizzle over fish. Bake uncovered 15 to 18 minutes or until fish flakes easily with fork. 4 SERVINGS; 530 CALORIES PER SERVING.

Fruit Stuffing

1 cup unseasoned croutons
⅓ cup diced dried fruits and raisins
2 tablespoons margarine or butter, melted
2 tablespoons dry white wine
¼ teaspoon salt
⅛ teaspoon ground allspice
1 green onion (with top), chopped

Mix all ingredients until liquid is absorbed.

To Grill: Grease wire grill. Place stuffed fish on grill. Cover and grill about 4 inches from medium coals 12 to 15 minutes, turning fish once and brushing occasionally with margarine mixture, until fish flakes easily with fork.

WILD RICE—STUFFED NORTHERN PIKE

Follow the same guidelines for stuffing fish as you would for meat and poultry. You'll find this information in Stuffing Basics (page 282).

Wild Rice Stuffing (below)
2½- to 3-pound pan-dressed northern pike or other lean fish
Lemon juice
Salt
Vegetable oil
¼ cup margarine or butter, melted
2 tablespoons lemon juice
Lemon wedges

Prepare Wild Rice Stuffing. Heat oven to 350°. Rub cavity of fish with lemon juice; sprinkle with salt. Loosely stuff with Wild Rice Stuffing. Close opening with skewers and lace with string. (Spoon any remaining stuffing into buttered baking dish; cover and refrigerate. Place in oven with fish 30 minutes before fish is done.)

Brush fish with oil. Mix margarine and 2 tablespoons lemon juice. Place fish in shallow roasting pan. Bake 50 to 60 minutes, brushing occasionally with margarine mixture, until fish flakes easily with fork. Serve with lemon wedges. 6 SERVINGS; 400 CALORIES PER SERVING.

Wild Rice Stuffing

¾ cup uncooked wild rice
2 cups water
1½ teaspoons chicken bouillon granules
¼ cup margarine or butter
8 ounces mushrooms, sliced (about 2½ cups)
½ cup thinly sliced celery
½ cup chopped onion (about 1 medium)
¼ cup slivered almonds

Heat wild rice, water and bouillon granules to boiling, stirring once or twice; reduce heat. Cover and simmer 40 to 50 minutes or until rice is tender. (Check after 30 minutes to see that rice is not sticking to pan.) Stir in 2 to 3 tablespoons water if necessary. Heat margarine in 10-inch skillet over medium-high heat. Sauté mushrooms, celery, onion and almonds in margarine about 4 minutes. Stir in wild rice.

Fruit-stuffed Trout

Carving a Whole Fish

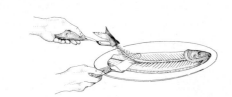

1. Using a sharp knife, cut the top side of fish into serving pieces, just down to the bone. Carefully remove pieces from the rib bones.

2. Carefully remove bones and discard. Cut the lower portion into serving pieces.

 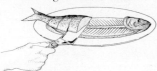

CREAMY TUNA CASSEROLE

8 ounces uncooked noodles
1 can (12½ ounces) tuna, drained
1 can (4 ounces) sliced mushrooms, drained
1 jar (2 ounces) sliced pimientos, drained
1½ cups sour cream
¾ cup milk
¼ teaspoon pepper
¼ cup dry bread crumbs
¼ cup grated Parmesan cheese
2 tablespoons margarine or butter, melted
Chopped fresh parsley

Heat oven to 350°. Cook noodles as directed on package; drain. Mix noodles, tuna, mushrooms, pimientos, sour cream, milk and pepper in ungreased 2-quart casserole. Mix bread crumbs, cheese and margarine. Sprinkle over tuna mixture.

Bake uncovered 35 to 40 minutes or until hot and bubbly. Sprinkle with parsley. 6 SERVINGS; 370 CALORIES PER SERVING.

To Microwave: Cook noodles as directed on package; drain. Decrease milk to ⅔ cup. Mix noodles, tuna, mushrooms, pimientos, sour cream, milk and pepper in 2-quart microwavable casserole. Cover tightly and microwave on medium (50%) 10 minutes; stir. Mix bread crumbs, cheese and margarine. Sprinkle over tuna mixture. Microwave uncovered on medium (50%) 4 to 7 minutes or until hot and bubbly.

SALMON LOAF

2 cans (15½ ounces each) salmon, drained, flaked and liquid reserved
2 eggs
Milk
3 cups coarse cracker crumbs
2 tablespoons lemon juice
2 tablespoons chopped onion
¼ teaspoon salt
¼ teaspoon pepper

Heat oven to 350°. Grease loaf pan, 9×5×3 inches. Mix salmon and eggs. Add enough milk to reserved salmon liquid to measure 1½ cups. Stir liquid mixture and remaining ingredients into salmon mixture. Spoon lightly into pan. Bake 45 minutes. Garnish with lemon wedges if desired. 8 SERVINGS; 285 CALORIES PER SERVING.

To Microwave: Spread mixture evenly in 6-cup microwavable ring dish. Cover with waxed paper and microwave on medium-high (70%) 15 to 20 minutes, rotating dish ½ turn after 10 minutes, until loaf is firm. Remove to serving platter. Cover and let stand 5 minutes.

MONKFISH WITH SOUR CREAM SAUCE

1 pound monkfish or other lean fish fillets
2 tablespoons margarine or butter
4 ounces mushrooms, sliced (about 1⅓ cups)
1 small onion, chopped (about ¼ cup)
1 teaspoon chopped fresh or ½ teaspoon dried thyme leaves
¼ teaspoon salt
⅛ teaspoon white pepper
½ cup dry white wine or chicken broth
½ cup sour cream

If fish fillets are large, cut into 4 serving pieces. Heat margarine in 10-inch skillet over medium heat. Cook mushrooms and onion in margarine about 3 minutes, stirring occasionally. Remove mushrooms and onion from skillet. Place fish fillets in skillet. Sprinkle with thyme, salt and pepper. Stir in wine. Heat to boiling; reduce heat. Cover and simmer 15 to 17 minutes or until fish flakes easily with fork. Remove fish and keep warm.

Heat liquid in skillet to boiling. Boil about 2 minutes or until reduced by half; remove from heat. Gradually stir in sour cream. Stir in mushrooms and onion. Cook over medium heat 1 to 2 minutes, stirring occasionally, until mushrooms are hot. Serve with fish. 4 SERVINGS; 280 CALORIES PER SERVING.

Mahimahi in Fennel Sauce, Sesame Pea Pods (page 389)

⊙ MAHIMAHI IN FENNEL SAUCE

1½ pounds mahimahi or other lean fish
   fillets
2 tablespoons olive oil
2 tablespoons margarine or butter
½ cup chopped fennel bulb
¼ cup chopped onion
¼ teaspoon salt
⅛ teaspoon pepper

Heat oven to 450°. If fish fillets are large, cut
into 6 serving pieces. Arrange fish in ungreased
rectangular baking dish, 12 × 7½ × 2 inches. Heat
oil and margarine in 1-quart saucepan over medium-
high heat. Sauté remaining ingredients in oil about
2 minutes. Spoon over fish. Bake 12 to 17 minutes
or until fish flakes easily with fork.   6 SERVINGS;
130 CALORIES PER SERVING.

To Microwave: Arrange fish fillets, thickest parts
to outside edges, in rectangular microwavable dish,
12 × 7½ × 2 inches. Place remaining ingredients in
4-cup microwavable measure. Cover fennel mixture tightly and microwave on high 2 minutes,
stirring after 1 minute. Spoon over fish. Cover fish
tightly and microwave 8 to 10 minutes, rotating
dish ½ turn after 4 minutes, until fish flakes easily
with fork. Let stand covered 3 minutes.

POMPANO NIÇOISE

1½ pounds pompano or other fatty fish
   fillets
¼ cup pitted ripe olives, cut in half
1 tablespoon chopped fresh or 1 teaspoon
   dried basil leaves
1 tablespoon olive oil
¼ teaspoon salt
1 clove garlic, finely chopped
1 can (14 ounces) artichoke hearts, drained
   and quartered
1 can (16 ounces) whole tomatoes, drained

Heat oven to 450°. If fish fillets are large, cut
into 6 serving pieces. Grease rectangular baking
dish, 12 × 7½ × 1½ inches. Place fish fillets in dish.
Mix remaining ingredients; break up tomatoes.
Pour over fish. Cover with aluminum foil and bake
18 to 22 minutes or until fish flakes easily with
fork.   6 SERVINGS; 275 CALORIES PER SERVING.

To Microwave: Arrange fish fillets, thickest parts
to outside edges, in microwavable rectangular dish,
12 × 7½ × 2 inches. Mix remaining ingredients; break
up tomatoes. Pour over fish. Cover tightly and
microwave on high 10 to 11 minutes, rotating dish
½ turn after 6 minutes, until fish flakes easily with
fork. Let stand covered 3 minutes.

⏱ SALMON WITH ROSEMARY SAUCE

1 teaspoon chopped fresh or ½ teaspoon dried rosemary leaves
4 fresh parsley sprigs
3 peppercorns
¼ lemon
1 can (14½ ounces) ready-to-serve chicken broth
1 pound salmon or other fatty fish fillets
½ cup half-and-half
1 teaspoon cornstarch
1 teaspoon chopped fresh or ¼ teaspoon dried rosemary leaves
½ teaspoon salt

Place 1 teaspoon rosemary, the parsley, peppercorns and lemon in cheesecloth; tie securely. Heat broth and cheesecloth bag to boiling in 10-inch skillet; reduce heat. Cover and simmer 5 minutes. If fish fillets are large, cut into 4 serving pieces. Place fish fillets in skillet; add water, if necessary, to cover. Heat to boiling; reduce heat. Simmer uncovered 5 to 10 minutes or until fish flakes easily with fork. Remove fish to serving platter and keep warm. Reserve ⅓ cup broth mixture. Discard cheesecloth bag and remaining broth mixture.

Salmon with Rosemary Sauce, Spinach Fettuccine (page 262)

Mix half-and-half and cornstarch. Heat half-and-half mixture, reserved broth mixture, 1 teaspoon rosemary and the salt to boiling in skillet over medium heat. Boil and stir 1 minute. Pour over fish. 4 SERVINGS; 225 CALORIES PER SERVING.

To Microwave: Prepare cheesecloth bag as directed above. Reserve ¼ cup chicken broth. Place fish fillets, thickest parts to outside edges, in rectangular microwavable dish, 12 × 7½ × 2 inches. Add remaining chicken broth and cheesecloth bag. Cover tightly and microwave on high 7 to 9 minutes, rotating dish ½ turn after 4 minutes, until fish flakes easily with fork. Let stand covered 3 minutes. Remove fish to serving platter and keep warm. Mix remaining ingredients in 1-quart microwavable bowl. Microwave uncovered on high 2 to 3 minutes or until boiling. Pour over fish.

SALMON-HORSERADISH ROLLS

1¼ pounds salmon or other fatty fish fillets
½ cup whipping (heavy) cream
1 egg white
1 tablespoon prepared horseradish
¼ teaspoon salt
⅛ teaspoon pepper
1 tablespoon chopped fresh chives

Cut fish fillets into 5 equal pieces. Coarsely chop 1 piece. Place chopped fish and 1 tablespoon whipping cream in blender or food processor. Cover and blend, or process, until smooth. Add egg white, horseradish, salt and pepper. Gradually add remaining whipping cream. Cover and blend 30 to 60 seconds, stopping blender occasionally to scrape sides, or process, until thick. Cover and refrigerate about 2 hours or until chilled.

Heat oven to 350°. Pound remaining fish pieces until ¼ inch thick. Spread whipping cream mixture evenly over fish. Roll up and place seam sides down in ungreased rectangular baking dish, 11 × 7 × 1½ inches. Cover with aluminum foil and bake 25 to 30 minutes or until fish flakes easily with fork. Sprinkle with chives. 4 SERVINGS; 315 CALORIES PER SERVING.

To Microwave: Place fish rolls in rectangular microwavable dish, 11 × 7 × 1½ inches. Cover tightly and microwave on high 8 to 10 minutes, rotating dish ½ turn after 5 minutes, until fish flakes easily with fork. Let stand covered 3 minutes.

Snappy Swordfish Kabobs, Three-Grain Medley (page 270)

SNAPPY SWORDFISH KABOBS

Swordfish has firm flesh and a mild flavor. It is a good choice for all methods of cooking fish. Tuna or shark, both similar in texture, make excellent substitutes in these kabobs.

  1 pound swordfish or other medium-fat fish
    fillets
  ¼ cup lime juice
  ¼ cup vegetable oil
  1 tablespoon chopped fresh cilantro
  ½ teaspoon salt
  1 clove garlic, finely chopped
  ½ jalapeño chili, seeded and chopped
  1 cup pineapple chunks*
  2 small zucchini, cut into ½-inch pieces
  1 medium red bell pepper, cut into 1-inch
    pieces

Cut fish fillets into ¾-inch pieces. Mix lime juice, oil, cilantro, salt, garlic and jalapeño chili in glass or plastic container. Gently stir in fish pieces. Cover and refrigerate at least 2 hours, stirring occasionally.

Remove fish; reserve marinade. Thread fish, pineapple, zucchini and bell pepper alternately on eight 11-inch metal skewers, leaving space between each. Place on rack in broiler pan. Brush with reserved marinade. Set oven control to broil. Broil kabobs with tops about 3 inches from heat 4 minutes. Turn kabobs and brush with marinade. Broil 4 to 5 minutes or until fish flakes easily with fork.   4 SERVINGS; 365 CALORIES PER SERVING.

*1 can (8 ounces) pineapple chunks, drained, can be substituted for the fresh pineapple.

○ GINGERED TUNA STEAKS

  ¼ cup margarine or butter, melted
  1 tablespoon dry sherry
  1 tablespoon soy sauce
  1 tablespoon grated gingerroot
  6 small albacore tuna or other fatty fish
    steaks, about 1 inch thick (about 2 pounds)

Mix margarine, sherry, soy sauce and gingerroot. Set oven control to broil. Brush fish steaks with half of the margarine mixture. Broil fish with tops about 4 inches from heat 9 minutes. Turn fish carefully and brush with remaining margarine mixture. Broil about 9 minutes or until fish flakes easily with fork.   6 SERVINGS; 265 CALORIES PER SERVING.

To Microwave: Place fish steaks in rectangular microwavable dish, 12 × 7½ × 2 inches. Pour margarine mixture over fish. Cover tightly and microwave on high 9 to 11 minutes, rotating dish ½ turn after 4 minutes, until fish flakes easily with fork. Let stand covered 3 minutes.

⏱ POACHED WHITEFISH WITH ORANGE SAUCE

Orange Sauce (below)
1½ pounds whitefish or other medium-fat
   fish fillets
3 cups water
2 teaspoons chopped fresh or ¾ teaspoon
   dried tarragon leaves
½ teaspoon salt
⅛ teaspoon pepper
1 small orange, cut into wedges
1 small onion, sliced

Prepare Orange Sauce and keep warm. If fish fillets are large, cut into 6 serving pieces. Heat remaining ingredients to boiling in 10-inch skillet;
reduce heat. Cover and simmer 5 minutes. Place
fish in skillet. Heat to boiling; reduce heat. Simmer uncovered 8 to 10 minutes or until fish flakes
easily with fork. Serve with Orange Sauce.   6 SERV-
INGS; 275 CALORIES PER SERVING.

Orange Sauce

1 tablespoon margarine or butter
1 tablespoon all-purpose flour
1 teaspoon chopped fresh or ¼ teaspoon
   dried tarragon leaves
½ teaspoon grated orange peel
¼ teaspoon salt
1 cup orange juice

Heat margarine in 1½-quart saucepan over low
heat until melted. Stir in flour, tarragon, orange
peel and salt. Cook over low heat, stirring constantly, until smooth and bubbly; remove from
heat. Stir in orange juice. Heat to boiling, stirring
constantly. Boil and stir 1 minute.

To Microwave: Prepare Orange Sauce—except
mix margarine, tarragon, orange peel and salt in
4-cup microwavable measure. Microwave uncovered on high 30 seconds or until margarine is melted.
Stir in flour. Stir in orange juice until smooth.
Microwave uncovered on high 2 minutes 30 seconds to 4 minutes, stirring every minute, until
slightly thickened. Cover and keep warm.

Arrange fish fillets, thickest parts to outside
edges, in rectangular microwavable dish, 12 × 7½ × 2
inches. Sprinkle tarragon, salt, pepper and onion
over fish. Decrease water to 1½ cups; pour over
fish. Arrange orange wedges around fish. Cover
tightly and microwave on high 7 to 9 minutes,
rotating dish ½ turn after 4 minutes, until fish
flakes easily with fork. Let stand covered 3 minutes. Serve with Orange Sauce.

🌾 COLD POACHED SALMON

2 cups water
1 cup dry white wine or water
½ teaspoon salt
1 sprig fresh or ¼ teaspoon dried thyme
   leaves
1 sprig fresh or ¼ teaspoon dried tarragon
   leaves
5 peppercorns
4 fresh parsley sprigs
1 small onion, sliced
1 stalk celery (with leaves), chopped
1 bay leaf
4 small salmon or other fatty fish steaks, 1
   inch thick (about 1½ pounds)
Green Sauce (below)

Heat water, wine, salt, thyme, tarragon, peppercorns, parsley, onion, celery and bay leaf to boiling
in 12-inch skillet; reduce heat. Cover and simmer
5 minutes. Place fish steaks in skillet. Add water,
if necessary, to cover. Heat to boiling; reduce
heat. Simmer uncovered 12 to 15 minutes or until
fish flakes easily with fork.

Carefully remove fish with slotted spatula; drain
on wire rack. Carefully remove skin if desired.
Cover and refrigerate about 4 hours or until chilled.
Serve fish with Green Sauce.   4 SERVINGS; 425
CALORIES PER SERVING.

Green Sauce

1 cup fresh parsley sprigs
1½ cups large curd creamed cottage cheese
1 tablespoon lemon juice
1 tablespoon milk
2 teaspoons chopped fresh or ½ teaspoon
   dried basil leaves
½ teaspoon salt
⅛ teaspoon pepper
4 to 6 drops red pepper sauce

Place all ingredients in blender or food processor.
Cover and blend on high speed about 3 minutes,
stopping blender occasionally to scrape sides, or
process, until smooth.

To Microwave: Arrange fish, thickest parts to
outside edges, in rectangular microwavable dish,
11 × 7 × 1½ inches. Place salt, thyme, tarragon,
peppercorns, parsley, onion, celery and bay leaf on
fish. Pour 1 cup water and ½ cup wine over fish.
Cover tightly and microwave on high 8 to 10 minutes, rotating dish ½ turn after 3 minutes, until
small ends of fish flake easily with fork. Let stand
covered 3 minutes.

⏱ SPICY BREADED RED SNAPPER

1 pound red snapper or other lean fish fillets
1½ cups seasoned croutons, crushed
1 teaspoon dry mustard
½ teaspoon salt
¼ teaspoon ground red pepper (cayenne)
⅛ teaspoon pepper
1 egg
1 tablespoon water
3 tablespoons margarine or butter, melted

Move oven rack to position slightly above middle of oven. Heat oven to 500°. Grease rectangular pan, 13×9×2 inches. If fillets are large, cut into 4 pieces. Mix croutons, mustard, salt, red pepper and pepper. Beat egg and water until well blended. Dip fish into egg, then coat with crouton mixture.

Place fish in pan. Drizzle margarine over fish. Bake uncovered about 10 minutes or until fish flakes easily with fork. 4 SERVINGS; 240 CALORIES PER SERVING.

To Grill: Grease wire grill. Place fish fillets on grill. Grill 3 to 4 inches from medium coals 10 to 12 minutes, turning fish once and brushing with margarine, until fish flakes easily with fork.

SWEET-AND-SOUR TUNA

1 pound yellowfin tuna or other lean fish steaks, 1 inch thick
1 can (8 ounces) pineapple chunks in juice, drained and juice reserved
⅓ cup packed brown sugar
⅓ cup cider vinegar
1 tablespoon grated gingerroot
2 tablespoons soy sauce
½ teaspoon salt
1 carrot, cut diagonally into thin slices
2 cloves garlic, finely chopped
3 tablespoons cornstarch
3 tablespoons cold water
1 green bell pepper, cut into ¾-inch pieces
2 cups hot cooked rice (page 267)

Cut fish steaks into 1-inch cubes. Add enough water to reserved pineapple juice to measure 1½ cups. Heat juice mixture, brown sugar, vinegar, gingerroot, soy sauce, salt, carrot and garlic to boiling in 3-quart saucepan; reduce heat. Cover and simmer 6 minutes or until carrot is crisp-tender.

Mix cornstarch and 3 tablespoons water. Stir into sauce. Stir in fish, pineapple and bell pepper. Heat to boiling, stirring constantly; reduce heat.

Simmer 5 to 7 minutes, stirring occasionally, until fish flakes easily with fork. Serve with rice. 4 SERVINGS; 360 CALORIES PER SERVING.

To Microwave: Cut fish steaks into 1-inch cubes. Omit salt and 3 tablespoons water. Place cornstarch in 3-quart microwavable casserole. Add enough water to reserved pineapple juice to measure 1¼ cups. Stir into cornstarch. Stir in brown sugar, vinegar, gingerroot, soy sauce, carrot and garlic. Cover tightly and microwave on high 6 to 8 minutes, stirring every 2 minutes, until carrot is crisp-tender. Stir in fish, pineapple and bell pepper. Cover tightly and microwave 10 to 14 minutes, stirring every 4 minutes, until fish flakes easily with fork.

SOLE WITH GRAPES

1½ pounds sole or other lean fish fillets
1¼ cups water
⅓ cup dry white wine or apple juice
1 tablespoon lemon juice
½ teaspoon salt
¼ teaspoon pepper
3 green onions (with tops), sliced
½ cup whipping (heavy) cream.
2 tablespoons all-purpose flour
1 cup seedless red or green grapes, cut lengthwise in half

If fish fillets are large, cut into 6 serving pieces. Place fish in 10-inch skillet. Add water, wine, lemon juice, salt, pepper and onions. Heat to boiling; reduce heat. Cover and simmer 5 to 6 minutes or until fish flakes easily with fork. Remove fish to platter with slotted spatula and keep warm.

Mix whipping cream and flour. Stir into skillet. Heat to boiling. Boil about 10 minutes, stirring frequently, until slightly thickened. Stir in grapes. Heat until hot. Spoon sauce over fish. 6 SERVINGS; 315 CALORIES PER SERVING.

To Microwave: Arrange fish fillets, thickest parts to outside edges, in rectangular microwavable dish, 11×7×1½ inches. Sprinkle with lemon juice, salt, pepper and onions. Cover with vented plastic wrap and microwave on high 7 to 8 minutes, rotating dish ½ turn after 4 minutes, until fish flakes easily with fork. Let stand covered. Pour ¾ cup water and ¼ cup wine into 4-cup microwavable measure. Shake whipping cream and flour in tightly covered container. Gradually stir into wine mixture. Microwave uncovered on high 3 to 4 minutes, stirring every minute, until boiling. Stir in grapes. Serve sauce over fish.

HALIBUT ON STEAMED VEGETABLES

1 tablespoon margarine or butter
1 medium onion, sliced and separated into rings
1 small yellow bell pepper, cut into ¼-inch slices
1 small red bell pepper, cut into ¼-inch slices
8 ounces spinach, coarsely chopped (about 6 cups)
4 small halibut or other lean fish steaks, 1 inch thick (about 1½ pounds)*
1 tablespoon chopped fresh or 1 teaspoon dried savory leaves
⅛ teaspoon salt
⅛ teaspoon pepper
4 thin slices lemon

Heat margarine in 10-inch skillet until melted. Layer onion, bell peppers, spinach and fish steaks in skillet (skillet will be full). Sprinkle with savory, salt and pepper. Place lemon slice on each fish steak.

Cover and cook over low heat 15 minutes. Uncover and cook 15 to 20 minutes or until fish flakes easily with fork and liquid is reduced. 4 SERVINGS; 350 CALORIES PER SERVING.

*1 or 2 large fish steaks can be used. Cut into 4 serving pieces.

⏱ SESAME PERCH

1 pound ocean perch or other lean fish fillets
¼ teaspoon salt
2 tablespoons margarine or butter
2 tablespoons vegetable oil
1 tablespoon sesame seed
1 lemon, cut in half
1 tablespoon chopped fresh or 1 teaspoon dried basil leaves
2 tablespoons chopped fresh parsley

If fish fillets are large, cut into 4 serving pieces. Sprinkle both sides with salt. Heat margarine and oil in 10-inch skillet over medium heat until hot. Cook fish about 10 minutes, carefully turning once, until brown on both sides. Remove fish and keep warm.

Cook and stir sesame seed in same skillet over medium heat about 5 minutes or until golden brown; remove from heat. Squeeze lemon over sesame seed. Stir in basil. Pour over fish. Sprinkle with parsley. 4 SERVINGS; 215 CALORIES PER SERVING.

Oriental Fish with Bok Choy

⏱ ORIENTAL FISH WITH BOK CHOY

1 pound orange roughy or other lean fish fillets
½ pound bok choy
1 tablespoon sesame seed
1 tablespoon vegetable oil
1 bunch green onions (with tops), cut into 2-inch pieces
1 small red bell pepper, cut into 1-inch pieces
½ cup chicken broth
½ teaspoon red pepper flakes
1 tablespoon cornstarch
1 tablespoon teriyaki sauce
2 cups hot cooked rice (page 267)

Cut fish fillets into 1-inch pieces. Remove leaves from bok choy. Cut leaves into ½-inch strips and stems into ¼-inch slices. Cook sesame seed in oil in 10-inch skillet over medium heat, stirring occasionally, until golden brown. Add bok choy stems, onions, bell pepper, fish, broth and pepper flakes. Heat to boiling; reduce heat. Cover and simmer about 5 minutes or until fish flakes easily with fork.

Mix cornstarch and teriyaki sauce. Gradually stir into fish mixture. Heat to boiling, stirring constantly. Boil and stir 1 minute. Stir in bok choy leaves and heat until wilted. Serve over rice. 4 SERVINGS; 280 CALORIES PER SERVING.

FISH AND CHIPS

The traditional English way to serve Fish and Chips is to drizzle them with malt or cider vinegar and then sprinkle with salt. In British take-outs it comes wrapped in newspaper, but we suggest using plates!

4 potatoes
Vegetable oil
1 pound cod or other lean fish fillets
⅔ cup all-purpose flour
½ teaspoon salt
½ teaspoon baking soda
1 tablespoon vinegar
⅔ cup water

Cut potatoes lengthwise into ½-inch strips. Heat oil (2 to 3 inches) in deep fryer or Dutch oven to 375°. Fill basket one-fourth full with potatoes. Slowly lower basket into hot oil. (If oil bubbles excessively, raise and lower basket several times.) Use long-handled fork to keep potatoes separated. Fry potatoes 5 to 7 minutes or until golden brown; drain on paper towels. Place potatoes in single layer on cookie sheet and keep warm. Repeat with remaining potatoes.

Cut fish fillets into 2 × 1½-inch pieces. Pat dry with paper towels. Mix flour and salt. Mix baking soda and vinegar. Stir vinegar mixture and water into flour mixture; beat until smooth. Dip fish into batter, allowing excess batter to drip into bowl. Fry 4 or 5 fish pieces at a time (do not use basket) about 3 minutes, turning fish once, until brown. Drain on paper towels.

Set oven control to broil. Broil potatoes 6 inches from heat 2 to 3 minutes or until crisp. 4 SERVINGS; 375 CALORIES PER SERVING.

FISH PATTIES WITH TOMATO SALSA

1 pound fish, cooked and flaked (about 3 cups)
½ cup finely chopped onion
2 tablespoons lemon juice
1 teaspoon chopped fresh or ½ teaspoon dried marjoram leaves
½ teaspoon salt
½ teaspoon dry mustard
2 slices bread, torn into crumbs
2 eggs, beaten
1 tablespoon vegetable oil
Fresh Tomato Salsa (page 20)

Mix all ingredients except oil and Fresh Tomato Salsa. Shape mixture into 8 patties. Cook patties in oil in 10-inch skillet over medium heat about 8 minutes, turning patties once, until golden brown. Serve with Fresh Tomato Salsa. 4 SERVINGS (2 PATTIES EACH); 315 CALORIES PER SERVING.

SHELLFISH BASICS

♦ Live clams, oysters, mussels and scallops should have tightly closed shells. Shells should not be cracked, chipped or broken. To test if open shellfish are alive, tap the shell; live shellfish will close their shells when disturbed. Never cook dead, unshucked clams, oysters, mussels or scallops. Shellfish should have a mild odor.

♦ Shucked clams, oysters and mussels should be plump, surrounded by a clear, slightly opalescent liquid. Clams may range in color from pale to deep orange. Oysters are typically creamy white, but may also be tinted green, red, brown or pink. Mussels are light tan to deep orange.

♦ Shucked sea scallops are about 2 inches in diameter, and bay scallops average about ½ inch in diameter. Shucked scallops have a mild, sweet odor and should look moist; they should not be standing in liquid or on ice. Sea scallops are usually creamy white and may be tinted light orange or pink. Bay scallops are also creamy white and may be tinted light tan or pink.

♦ Live lobsters, crabs and shrimp should have hard shells and moving legs. Discard any that show no movement. A lobster will tightly curl its tail when picked up. Soft-shell crabs are actually hard-shell crabs that have molted and shed their shell, which happens on an average of 3 times per year.

♦ Shrimp may be sold raw (also known as "green" with the heads on); raw in the shell without the heads; raw but peeled and deveined; cooked in the shell or cooked, peeled and deveined. They are usually sold by count or number per pound. These numbers may range from fewer than 10 per pound to more than 100 per pound. Sizes are occasionally expressed in names that range from "colossal" to "tiny." However, neither by count nor by description is size universally defined and regulated.

Counts and descriptions vary and can be confusing, since sometimes shelled shrimp count is based on number per pound before peeling, while other times it is based on number per pound after peeling. Ask at your grocery store for clarification, if necessary.

A general rule of thumb is that raw shrimp in the shell lose one size when peeled and another when cooked, or about ¼ pound when peeled and another ¼ pound when cooked. One pound of raw shrimp will give you about ½ to ¾ pound of cleaned, cooked shrimp. The smaller the shrimp size, the higher the count per pound; the larger the shrimp, the higher the price.

SHELLFISH

Top row: *Lobster, cooked stone crab claws, Dungeness crab, cooked king crab legs.* Second row: *soft-shell crab, cooked snow crab cluster, squid.* Third row: *Oyster, scallops, shucked sea scallops, shucked bay scallops, cockles (clams), New Zealand greenlip mussels, blue mussels.* Bottom row: *Cooked crawfish, raw shrimp with heads on, raw headless shrimp, raw headless prawns.*

BUYING SHELLFISH

Live shellfish can be purchased in the seafood section of the supermarket or at a seafood store. Cooked shellfish can be purchased frozen or in the deli or seafood section of the supermarket. Below are guidelines for amounts to purchase.

♦ For live clams, oysters and mussels, allow about 6 oysters or small hard-shell clams, or 3 large hard-shell clams or 18 mussels or soft-shell clams (steamers) per serving.

♦ Allow about ¼ pound shucked oysters, scallops, clams or mussels per serving. Oysters, clams and mussels can be purchased shucked in their own liquid.

♦ Raw shrimp can be purchased with or without shells. Allow about 1 pound whole shrimp, ½ pound headless, unpeeled shrimp or ¼ pound headless, peeled shrimp per serving.

♦ Allow about 1¼ pounds live or ¼ pound cooked crabmeat or lobster meat per serving.

SHELLFISH DONENESS

Avoid overcooking shellfish, which makes it tough and rubbery.

♦ Raw shrimp is pink and firm when cooked properly. The cooking time depends on the size of the shrimp.

♦ Live oysters, clams and mussels open when they are done.

♦ Shucked oysters, clams and mussels become plump and opaque. Oyster edges will start to curl.

♦ Scallops turn white or opaque and become firm. Again, the size of scallops will determine the cooking time.

♦ Boiled crabs and lobsters turn bright red when properly cooked.

MICROWAVING SHELLFISH

Cut large scallops in half. Rinse shrimp. Place in microwavable dish. Cover tightly and microwave on high as directed below or until scallops are opaque or shrimp are pink.

Shellfish	Amount	Time	Stand Time
Scallops, sea	1½ pounds	6 to 9 minutes, stirring after 4 minutes	3 minutes
Shrimp, peeled and deveined	1 pound	6 to 8 minutes, stirring after 3 minutes	3 minutes
Shrimp, in shells	1 pound	5 to 7 minutes, stirring after 3 minutes	3 minutes

BOILED SHRIMP

Depending on the species and their maturity, shrimp range from as small as 1 inch to as long as 13 inches, at which point they are often called "prawns." If a recipe doesn't specify what size to use, you may want to ask your seafood salesperson.

   4 cups water
   1½ pounds fresh or frozen raw medium
      shrimp (in shells)

Heat water to boiling. Add shrimp. Cover and heat to boiling; reduce heat. Simmer 3 to 5 minutes or until shrimp are pink and firm; drain. Peel shrimp, leaving tails intact. Make a shallow cut lengthwise down back of each shrimp and wash out vein. Chill shrimp and serve with cocktail sauce if desired.   4 SERVINGS (ABOUT ¼ POUND EACH); 100 CALORIES PER SERVING.

DEEP-FRIED SHRIMP

   1½ pounds medium raw shrimp
   Vegetable oil
   ½ cup all-purpose flour
   1 teaspoon salt
   ½ teaspoon pepper
   2 eggs, slightly beaten
   ¾ cup dry bread crumbs

Peel shrimp, leaving tails intact. Make a shallow cut lengthwise down back of each shrimp and wash out vein. Heat oil (2 to 3 inches) in deep fryer or Dutch oven to 325°. Mix flour, salt and pepper. Coat shrimp with flour mixture. Dip into eggs, then coat with bread crumbs. Fry about 2 minutes or until brown; drain on paper towels. 4 SERVINGS; 365 CALORIES PER SERVING.

DEEP-FRIED SCALLOPS: Substitute 12 ounces shucked scallops, drained, for the shrimp. Fry 3 to 4 minutes or until golden brown.   350 CALORIES PER SERVING.

DEEP-FRIED OYSTERS AND CLAMS: Substitute 12 ounces shucked oysters or clams for the shrimp. 320 CALORIES PER SERVING.

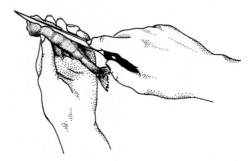

Using a small, pointed knife make a shallow cut along the outside the length of the shrimp. Remove black vein; wash.

STEAMED CLAMS

4 pounds soft-shell clams (steamers)
6 cups water
⅓ cup vinegar
½ cup boiling water

Discard any broken-shell or open (dead) clams. Place remaining clams in large container. Cover with 6 cups water and vinegar; let stand 30 minutes. Scrub clams in cold water.

Place clams in steamer* with boiling water. Steam 5 to 8 minutes or until clams open at least ½ inch, removing clams as they open. Serve hot in shells with melted margarine or butter and cups of chicken broth for dipping if desired.   4 SERVINGS; 50 CALORIES PER SERVING.

*If steamer is not available, place clams in 6-quart Dutch oven. Add 1 inch boiling water; cover tightly.

STEAMED MUSSELS

4 pounds mussels
½ cup boiling water

Discard any broken-shell or open (dead) mussels. Scrub remaining mussels in cold water, removing any barnacles with a dull paring knife. Remove beards by tugging them away from shells (using a kitchen towel may help).

Place mussels in large container. Cover with cool water. Agitate water with hand, then drain and discard water. Repeat several times until water runs clear; drain.

Place half of the mussels in steamer* with boiling water. Steam 3 to 5 minutes or until mussels open, removing mussels as they open. Discard unopened mussels. Repeat with remaining mussels. Serve hot in shells with melted margarine or butter and cups of chicken broth if desired.   4 SERVINGS; 150 CALORIES PER SERVING.

STEAMED OYSTERS: Substitute oysters for the mussels. Do not cover with cool water. Continue as directed. Steam 5 to 8 minutes.   35 CALORIES PER SERVING.

*If steamer is not available, place mussels in 6-quart Dutch oven. Add 1 inch boiling water; cover tightly.

CLAMS

1. Hold a clam with the hinged side against a heavy cloth or oven mitt. Insert a blunt-tipped knife between shell halves. Be sure to work over a bowl or plate to catch juices.

2. Hold the clam firmly and move knife around the clam, cutting the muscle at the hinge. Gently twist the knife to pry open the shell. Cut the clam meat free from the shell.

MUSSELS

To remove the byssal threads (or beard), pull by giving the "beard" a tug (using a kitchen towel may help). If you have trouble removing it, pull gently with pliers.

⏱ BOILED HARD-SHELL CRABS

4 quarts water
16 live hard-shell blue crabs

Heat water to boiling in large kettle or canner. Drop 4 crabs at a time into water. Cover and heat to boiling; reduce heat. Simmer 10 minutes; drain. Repeat with remaining crabs.

To remove meat, grasp body of crab. Break off large claws. Pull off top shell. Cut or break off legs. Scrape off the gills and carefully remove organs located in center part of body. Serve crab hot or cold with cocktail sauce if desired. 4 SERVINGS; 80 CALORIES PER SERVING.

1. Using your thumb, pry off the tail flap, twist off and discard. Turn crab right side up and pry up the top shell. Pull away from the body. Discard.

2. Using a small knife (or your fingers), cut the gray-white gills (called "devil's fingers") from both sides of the crab. Discard gills and internal organs.

3. To remove meat, twist off the crab claws and legs. Using a nutcracker crack shells at the joint. Remove meat with a small fork or nut pick. Break the body and remove any remaining meat in the deeper pockets with a small fork or nut pick.

⏱ BOILED LOBSTER

2 to 4 quarts water
2 live lobsters (about 1 pound each)

Use Dutch oven or stockpot that holds at least 6 quarts. Fill one-third full with water. Heat to boiling. Plunge lobsters headfirst into water. Cover and heat to boiling; reduce heat. Simmer 10 to 12 minutes or until lobsters turn bright red; drain. Place each lobster on its back. Cut lengthwise in half with sharp knife.

Remove stomach, which is just behind head, and the intestinal vein, which runs from the stomach to the tip of the tail. Crack claws. Serve with melted margarine or butter and lemon wedges if desired. 2 SERVINGS; 430 CALORIES PER SERVING.

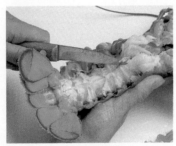

1. Place the lobster on its back. Using a kitchen scissors, cut lengthwise down the body up to the tail, cutting to, but not through the back shell.

2. Cut away the membrane on the tail to expose meat. Discard the intestinal vein running through the tail and the small sac near the head of the lobster. You can serve the green tomalley (liver) and coral roe (only in females) if you like.

3. Twist the large claws away from the body of the lobster. Using a nutcracker, break open the claws. Remove meat from claws, tail and body.

CRAB IN PUFF PASTRY

This elegant dish can also be made less expensively with imitation crabmeat.

- ½ package (17½ ounce-size) frozen puff pastry
- 2 tablespoons margarine or butter
- 2 tablespoons thinly sliced green onions (with tops)
- 2 tablespoons all-purpose flour
- ½ cup milk
- ½ cup whipping (heavy) cream
- 1½ cups chopped cooked crabmeat
- ½ cup dry white wine or chicken broth
- 2 tablespoons chopped fresh parsley
- 1 teaspoon finely shredded lemon peel
- ¼ teaspoon salt
- ⅛ teaspoon pepper

Thaw 1 sheet puff pastry as directed on package. Heat oven to 350°. Unfold pastry and place on lightly floured surface. Roll into 10-inch square. Fold in half and roll to seal edges. Cut crosswise into 4 equal pieces. Place on ungreased cookie sheet. Bake about 20 minutes or until golden brown.

While pastry is baking, heat margarine in 2-quart saucepan over medium heat. Cook onions in margarine about 2 minutes, stirring occasionally. Stir in flour. Cook over medium heat, stirring constantly, until mixture is bubbly; remove from heat. Gradually stir in milk and whipping cream. Heat to boiling, stirring constantly. Boil and stir 1 minute. Stir in remaining ingredients. Heat until hot.

Split each pastry horizontally with fork. Spoon crab mixture over bottom half. Top each with remaining pastry half. Garnish with parsley if desired.   4 SERVINGS; 590 CALORIES PER SERVING.

LOBSTER IN PUFF PASTRY: Substitute lobster for the crabmeat.   585 CALORIES PER SERVING.

SHRIMP IN PUFF PASTRY: Substitute shrimp for the crabmeat.   585 CALORIES PER SERVING.

Curried Scallops (page 208), Artichokes and Shrimp with Lemon Pasta

ARTICHOKES AND SHRIMP WITH LEMON PASTA

Lemon Pasta (page 262)
1 cup plain yogurt
1 tablespoon chopped fresh or 1 teaspoon freeze-dried chives
1 teaspoon finely shredded lemon peel
½ teaspoon salt
¾ pound cooked shrimp or 1 package (12 ounces) frozen cooked shrimp, thawed
1 jar (6 ounces) marinated artichoke hearts, undrained
1 package (3 ounces) cream cheese
1 tablespoon chopped fresh or 1 teaspoon freeze-dried chives

Cook pasta as directed; drain. Mix yogurt, 1 tablespoon chives, the lemon peel, salt, shrimp, artichoke hearts and cream cheese in 2-quart saucepan. Cook over low heat, stirring constantly, until hot and cream cheese is melted. Toss with pasta. Sprinkle with 1 tablespoon chives.   4 SERVINGS; 495 CALORIES PER SERVING.

Crawfish Etouffée

SHRIMP ETOUFFÉE

1 pound fresh or frozen medium raw shrimp (in shells)
¼ cup margarine or butter
3 tablespoons all-purpose flour
1 medium onion, chopped (about ½ cup)
1 small green bell pepper, chopped (about ½ cup)
1 medium stalk celery, sliced (about ½ cup)
1 clove garlic, finely chopped
1 cup water
2 tablespoons chopped fresh parsley
2 teaspoons lemon juice
½ teaspoon salt
¼ teaspoon pepper
⅛ to ¼ teaspoon red pepper sauce
2 cups hot cooked rice (page 267)

Peel shrimp. Make a shallow cut lengthwise down back of each shrimp and wash out vein.

Heat margarine in 3-quart saucepan over medium heat until melted. Stir in flour. Cook about 6 minutes, stirring constantly, until bubbly and brown. Stir in onion, bell pepper, celery and garlic. Cook and stir about 5 minutes or until vegetables are crisp-tender.

Stir in shrimp, water, parsley, lemon juice, salt, pepper and pepper sauce. Heat to boiling; reduce heat. Simmer uncovered about 5 minutes, stirring occasionally, until shrimp are pink. Serve over rice.   4 SERVINGS; 320 CALORIES PER SERVING.

CRAWFISH ETOUFFÉE: Substitute cleaned raw crawfish for the shrimp. (Sizes of crawfish vary depending on region and variety; 40 to 48 crawfish, each about 5 inches long, yield about 1 pound tail meat.)   290 CALORIES PER SERVING.

GARLIC-AND-BEER— MARINATED SHRIMP KABOBS

1 pound fresh or frozen medium raw shrimp (in shells)
¾ cup beer
1 tablespoon vegetable oil
2 teaspoons chopped fresh or ½ teaspoon freeze-dried chives
½ teaspoon red pepper sauce
¼ teaspoon salt
2 cloves garlic, crushed

Peel shrimp. Make a shallow cut lengthwise down back of each shrimp and wash out vein. Mix remaining ingredients in shallow glass or plastic container. Stir in shrimp. Cover and refrigerate at least 1 hour.

Set oven control to broil. Remove shrimp; reserve beer marinade. Thread shrimp about 1 inch apart on 15-inch metal skewers. Place on rack in broiler pan. Broil kabobs about 4 inches from heat about 5 minutes, turning and brushing with marinade once, until shrimp are pink. Serve with melted margarine or butter and lemon wedges if desired.   4 SERVINGS; 120 CALORIES PER SERVING.

LOBSTER NEWBURG IN POPOVERS

Popovers (page 42)
¼ cup margarine or butter
3 tablespoons all-purpose flour
½ teaspoon salt
½ teaspoon dry mustard
¼ teaspoon pepper
2 cups milk
2 cups cut-up cooked lobster
2 tablespoons dry sheery or apple juice

Prepare Popovers. Heat margarine in 3-quart saucepan over medium heat until melted. Stir in flour, salt, mustard and pepper. Cook, stirring constantly, until smooth and bubbly; remove from heat. Stir in milk. Heat to boiling, stirring constantly. Boil and stir 1 minute. Stir in lobster and sherry. Heat until hot. Serve over hot split Popovers.   6 SERVINGS; 290 CALORIES PER SERVING.

CRAB NEWBURG IN POPOVERS: Substitute 2 cups chopped cooked crabmeat or seafood sticks for the lobster.   305 CALORIES PER SERVING.

LOBSTER NEWBURG

Delmonico's was a famous New York City restaurant that had its glittering heyday around the end of the nineteenth century. Mr. Delmonico created Lobster Wenburg to honor a sea captain and loyal customer named Ben Wenburg. After the two men argued, the annoyed Delmonico changed the name of the dish to Lobster Newburg. Whatever its name, this elegant dish is frequently requested in the Betty Crocker Dining Room. You may add any cooked seafood combinations to the traditional Newburg sauce.

Crab in Puff Pastry (page 205), Lobster Newburg in Popovers

⏱ CHINESE OYSTER STEW

1 can (10¾ ounces) condensed chicken broth
1 soup can water
2 tablespoons soy sauce
¼ teaspoon grated gingerroot
1 pint shucked large oysters, undrained
2 cups chopped Chinese cabbage
8 ounces sliced mushrooms (about 2½ cups)
½ cup bean sprouts
4 green onions (with tops), cut into 1-inch pieces

Heat broth, water, soy sauce and gingerroot to boiling in 3-quart saucepan. Add oysters, cabbage, mushrooms and bean sprouts. Heat to boiling; reduce heat. Cover and simmer about 2 minutes or until cabbage is crisp-tender. Ladle stew into bowls and garnish with green onions. 4 SERVINGS; 135 CALORIES PER SERVING.

⏱ CURRIED SCALLOPS

3 tablespoons margarine or butter
1 pound sea scallops, cut in half
3 green onions (with tops), chopped
1 tablespoon all-purpose flour
1 tablespoon curry powder
½ teaspoon salt
½ cup chicken broth
½ cup milk
1 medium tomato, chopped (about ½ cup)
3 cups hot cooked rice (page 267)

Heat 1 tablespoon of the margarine in 10-inch skillet over medium-high heat until melted. Cook scallops in margarine 4 to 5 minutes, stirring frequently, until scallops are white. Remove from skillet; drain skillet.

Heat remaining 2 tablespoons margarine in same skillet. Cook onions, flour, curry powder and salt over medium heat, stirring constantly, until bubbly; remove from heat. Stir in chicken broth and milk. Heat to boiling, stirring constantly. Boil and stir 1 minute. Stir in tomato and scallops. Heat about 3 minutes, stirring occasionally. Serve over rice. 6 SERVINGS; 230 CALORIES PER SERVING.

── FIX-IT-FAST ──

◆ Serve cooked fish with citrus-flavored butters (orange, lemon, lime, grapefruit). Mix ¼ cup margarine or butter, melted, 1 teaspoon grated peel and 2 tablespoons juice instead of preparing a complicated sauce.

◆ Prepare interesting broiled or baked fish quickly, brushing with herb, garlic, chive or onion butter.

◆ Use canned shrimp or minced clams for soups and casseroles.

◆ For a quick dinner with an Italian flavor, bake frozen fish portions (or sticks) as directed on package. Top with pizza sauce and shredded mozzarella cheese. Bake 2 minutes longer or until cheese melts.

◆ Use frozen crab/shrimp mixture, thawed, for a quick seafood cocktail. Serve with cocktail sauce and lemon wedges.

◆ Purchase fish nuggets or fish sticks, and prepare according to package directions. Serve with your favorite dipping sauces—tartar, sweet-and-sour and barbecue.

◆ Looking for a simple super chowder? Add leftover cooked vegetables and cooked fish or seafood to prepared cream-based soup.

◆ Stir any fish or shellfish (canned, frozen or cooked) into your favorite spaghetti sauce or cream sauce and serve over cooked pasta.

◆ Cut fish steaks into 1-inch cubes for kabobs, or freeze on cookie sheet 1 hour. Place in covered container and freeze. Then you can have kabobs on a moment's notice. Thaw slightly before threading on skewers.

◆ Make sandwich spreads with drained canned seafood (shrimp, crab, clams, salmon, tuna). Mix with mayonnaise, onion, celery and a squirt of lemon juice.

◆ Use canned or frozen shrimp or crab in stir-fried dishes. Combine with deli or leftover vegetables and teriyaki sauce.

◆ Try these quick coatings for whole fish or fillets when frying or baking:

Seasoned bread crumbs

Bread crumbs and Parmesan cheese

Bread crumbs and seasoning mix

Bread crumbs and dry salad dressing mix

Cornmeal and chili powder (or Cajun spice)

Crushed cornflakes or other cereal

Crushed corn chips

RECIPE, PAGE	Servings per recipe	Calories	Protein (grams)	Carbohydrate (grams)	Fat (grams)	Cholesterol (milligrams)	Sodium (milligrams)	Protein	Vitamin A	Vitamin C	Thiamine	Riboflavin	Niacin	Calcium	Iron
								PERCENT U.S. RECOMMENDED DAILY ALLOWANCE							

PER SERVING OR UNIT

NUTRITION INFORMATION

FISH

RECIPE, PAGE	Servings	Calories	Protein	Carb	Fat	Chol	Sodium	Protein %	Vit A	Vit C	Thiamine	Riboflavin	Niacin	Calcium	Iron
Broiled Fish Steaks, 190	4	340	43	0	18	85	430	66	26	0	4	6	70	2	6
Cold Poached Salmon, 197	4	425	48	4	23	105	690	72	18	12	10	28	72	8	6
Creamy Tuna Casserole, 193	6	370	15	32	20	45	745	22	16	6	12	14	20	16	10
Creole Catfish, 191	8	220	21	25	4	35	690	32	14	20	8	4	6	4	10
Deep-fried Fish, 190	4	300	25	17	14	170	265	38	4	0	8	12	10	4	6
Fish and Chips, 200	4	375	7	46	18	35	440	10	0	8	8	6	16	8	64
Fish Patties with Tomato Salsa, 200	4	315	33	11	15	195	665	50	28	8	10	12	50	6	12
Fruit-stuffed Trout, 192	4	530	39	15	32	100	315	60	12	2	12	22	76	2	2
Gingered Tuna Steaks, 196	6	265	33	0	13	55	360	50	6	0	12	4	60	14	8
Halibut on Steamed Vegetables, 199	4	350	45	8	15	85	380	68	100	70	10	14	74	10	20
Mahimahi in Fennel Sauce, 194	6	130	20	0	5	35	90	30	0	0	2	6	4	0	0
Monkfish with Sour Cream Sauce, 193	4	280	21	5	13	45	225	32	10	2	4	16	10	6	6
Oriental Fish with Bok Choy, 199	4	280	24	31	7	30	650	36	68	48	14	14	14	8	12
Oven-fried Fish, 190	4	205	21	7	10	35	305	32	12	0	4	8	6	4	2
Panfried Fish, 190	6	195	21	7	9	75	195	32	0	2	4	8	6	2	2
Poached Whitefish with Orange Sauce, 197	6	275	25	9	15	65	295	38	4	26	10	14	48	0	0
Pompano Niçoise, 194	6	275	26	5	17	65	230	38	8	8	8	16	50	4	4
Salmon-Horseradish Rolls, 195	4	315	32	1	20	95	300	50	12	0	12	6	56	16	8
Salmon Loaf, 193	8	285	23	21	11	70	700	36	2	0	2	14	38	26	12
Salmon with Rosemary Sauce, 195	4	225	27	2	11	55	715	42	4	0	10	6	50	14	6
Sesame Perch, 199	4	215	20	1	15	30	205	30	8	2	2	6	6	2	2
Snappy Swordfish Kabobs, 196	4	365	30	12	22	55	450	44	48	44	8	6	48	4	8
Sole with Grapes, 198	6	315	29	8	15	85	345	44	26	2	6	6	48	4	6
Spicy Breaded Red Snapper, 198	4	240	23	11	11	100	595	34	10	0	4	8	6	4	4
Sweet-and-Sour Tuna, 198	4	360	23	65	1	30	185	34	100	32	16	12	14	6	14
Vegetable-stuffed Sole, 191	6	225	28	10	6	45	440	42	100	20	6	12	8	8	4
Wild Rice–stuffed Northern Pike, 192	6	400	37	17	21	55	375	56	14	2	12	28	22	4	8

NUTRITION INFORMATION

PER SERVING OR UNIT

RECIPE, PAGE

SHELLFISH

Recipe, page	Servings per recipe	Calories	Protein (grams)	Carbohydrate (grams)	Fat (grams)	Cholesterol (milligrams)	Sodium (milligrams)	Protein	Vitamin A	Vitamin C	Thiamine	Riboflavin	Niacin	Calcium	Iron
Artichokes and Shrimp with Lemon Pasta, 205	4	495	28	49	23	380	1065	62	12	2	26	24	22	32	24
Boiled Hard-Shell Crabs, 204	4	80	14	0	2	85	175	22	36	0	8	2	10	10	4
Boiled Lobster, 204	2	430	85	1	7	146	150	100	0	0	30	18	50	28	20
Boiled Shrimp, 202	4	100	17	0	3	285	140	26	0	0	2	8	10	26	8
Chinese Oyster Stew, 208	4	135	17	10	3	60	1100	24	42	46	16	32	38	16	48
Crab Newburg in Popovers, 207	6	305	21	25	13	170	685	30	42	2	16	20	16	24	8
Crab in Puff Pastry, 205	4	590	15	24	40	100	615	22	44	4	18	14	16	14	12
Crawfish Etouffée, 206	4	290	11	33	12	55	825	16	12	24	10	8	12	2	14
Curried Scallops, 208	6	230	12	30	7	20	810	18	16	4	8	8	10	8	14
Deep-fried Oysters and Clams, 202	4	320	11	27	18	165	755	16	4	12	12	14	14	8	24
Deep-fried Scallops, 202	4	350	19	27	18	165	865	30	0	2	8	8	10	10	18
Deep-fried Shrimp, 202	4	365	21	25	20	365	830	30	0	4	10	16	16	24	16
Garlic-and-Beer–marinated Shrimp Kabobs, 206	4	120	12	2	6	150	235	16	0	0	2	6	8	16	6
Lobster Newburg in Popovers, 207	6	290	18	24	13	140	640	26	12	0	12	20	12	18	8
Lobster in Puff Pastry, 205	4	585	15	24	40	90	605	22	18	2	16	14	14	10	12
Shrimp Etouffée, 206	4	290	11	33	12	55	825	16	12	24	10	8	12	2	14
Shrimp in Puff Pastry, 205	4	585	15	24	40	105	550	22	20	2	12	12	12	12	16
Steamed Clams, 203	4	50	9	2	1	25	40	12	4	0	0	8	6	2	52
Steamed Mussels, 203	4	150	24	2	4	75	0	36	0	0	0	10	0	2	44
Steamed Oysters, 203	4	35	4	2	1	25	35	6	2	12	4	4	6	4	14

PERCENT U.S. RECOMMENDED DAILY ALLOWANCE (Protein, Vitamin A, Vitamin C, Thiamine, Riboflavin, Niacin, Calcium, Iron)

MEATS

MEATS

Meat has always been the mainstay of our favorite meals, whether it's the Sunday roast, everyday Skillet Hash (page 224) or a weekend barbecue. We love the heartiness of meat, and the many delicious ways it can be cooked. Today, while cherishing all the old classics, people are also interested in branching out in new directions. So we have included a varied selection of recipes such as Pork and Broccoli Risotto (page 238), Moroccan Beef with Couscous (page 223) and many others. However you slice it, meat's a mainstay that's here to stay!

MEAT BASICS

New breeding techniques, supermarket trends such as trimming more fat from meat, diets and concerns for our health are yielding meats lower in fat, calories and cholesterol than ever before. Animals are bred for leaner meat, and meat cuts are trimmed more closely at the supermarket. With more than sixty cuts of beef to choose from, standing in front of the meat counter at your local market can be a puzzling experience for any shopper. So it's helpful to know what you want before you shop. We consulted with the National Live Stock and Meat Board to give you the latest recommendations on cooking meat.

GRADES OF MEAT

Meats bearing a round stamp with the abbreviation "U.S. Inspected and Passed" guarantees the meat is wholesome and has met federal standards of cleanliness during processing. This stamp is placed only on the primal (wholesale) cuts and might be trimmed before purchase.

The U.S. Department of Agriculture's grades of meat quality are found in a shield-shaped stamp. These grades are USDA Prime, Choice, Select, Standard, Commercial and Utility, in descending order of quality. Most meats sold in supermarkets are Choice. Prime is generally available only in special restaurants, although a few supermarkets carry prime meat cuts. Grades below Select are usually used in combination meats such as cold cuts and sausage.

Marbling in meats means the small flecks or streaks of fat that run through the lean meat. The flavor and juiciness of meat are improved by marbling but, of course, the more marbling, the more calories. You may find that the newer types of meat with less marbling cook differently, so be careful not to overcook; lean meat toughens more easily than well-marbled meat.

SERVINGS PER POUND

When buying meat, consider servings per pound. The number of servings per pound varies according to the cut of meat and is based on an average cooked serving of 2½ to 3½ ounces. However, you may wish to plan on more for heartier appetites. The cooked amount can be affected by the cooking method, the size of the bone and the amount of fat left after trimming. Below is a general guide, which is also helpful in figuring cost per serving:

Type of Meat	Servings per Pound
Boneless cuts (ground, boneless chops, loin, tenderloin)	*3 to 4*
Bone-in cuts (rib roasts, pot roasts, country-style ribs)	*2 to 3*
Very bony cuts (back ribs, spareribs, short ribs, shanks)	*1 to 1½*

Preceding page: *Roast Beef with Oven-browned Potatoes (page 215), Tangy Hazelnut Pork Chops (page 237), Brussels Sprouts in Orange Sauce (page 376)*

SELECTING MEATS

After identifying the cuts you wish to purchase, check the appearance of the meat closely.

BEEF

The color of the lean portions should be bright red. Vacuum-packaged beef and the interior of ground beef have a darker, purplish red color because the meat is not exposed to air; as this beef is exposed to the air, its color turns to the familiar bright red.

Ground beef contains meat from beef only (no variety meat), but in varying degrees of leanness from 70 to 90 percent or more. Ground beef that is 70 percent lean usually loses more fat in cooking, whereas 90 percent lean beef will lose more moisture.

VEAL

Very young beef is classified as veal, naturally lean and easy to prepare. It should have a fine grain and be creamy pink in color. Any fat covering should be milky white.

PORK

The lean part of fresh pork should be grayish pink in color and fine grained in texture. For ham, the lean should be firm, fine grained, pink in color and free from excess moisture. The fat cover should be firm and white.

For ham, the lean should be firm, fine grained, pink in color and free from excess moisture. The fat covering should be firm and white. You may notice a rainbowlike appearance to the surface of ham; this iridescence is caused by the refraction of light on the cut ends of the muscle fibers. The color is not harmful nor does it affect quality.

LAMB

Lamb comes from animals less than one year old, and most lamb is marketed when it is about six to eight months old so it will be tender and tasty. Look for meat that is pinkish red and has a velvety texture. There is little marbling and only a thin layer of fat around the outside of the meat. The bones should be porous and reddish, indicating a young animal.

COOKING MEATS

Recommended cooking methods for each cut of meat are featured on the meat chart in each section—Beef, page 216; Veal, page 229; Pork, page 233 and Lamb, page 250. With the recommendations on the meat charts and the step-by-step methods within the chapter you will be able to cook any cut of meat.

There are six basic methods for cooking meat, using two types of heat: *dry* (without liquid), as in roasting, broiling or grilling, panbroiling and panfrying, and *moist* (with steam or liquid), used for braising and cooking in liquid.

Dry heat methods are generally used for tender meat cuts. Grilling is a variation of broiling, and stir-frying and deep-fat frying are variations of panfrying.

Moist heat methods are most often used for less-tender cuts. Some cuts can be prepared by either method, depending on their quality and the cooking time and temperature used.

When you purchase prepackaged meat, the label will help you identify the cuts. See charts later in this chapter for beef, veal, pork and lamb. A label should tell you the type of meat, where the meat comes from on the carcass and the name of the retail cut. Beef round top round roast is a good example.

Recent research on today's lean pork and the latest cooking recommendations offer cooks a choice of doneness or end temperature with selected pork cuts. Selected cuts can be cooked to medium (160°) or well done (170°).

Boneless pork cooked to medium (160°) is faintly pink in the center. At 170°, the meat loses its pink color. Bone-in cuts have a slightly more intense color near the bone when cooked to 160°, but are perfectly safe to eat. Refer to the pork charts that appear with the pork recipes in this chapter for specific cooking recommendations.

STORING AND HANDLING MEATS

After purchase, fresh meats should be immediately stored in the coldest part of the refrigerator. For more specific information, see Guidelines for Refrigerator Storage (page 416) and Guidelines for Freezer Storage (page 418).

It's important in cooking meat to follow safe handling practices.

♦ All surfaces and utensils that come in contact with meat should be washed with hot, soapy water after each use.

♦ Hot foods should be kept hot (above 140°) and cold foods, cold (below 40°).

♦ Meat should be cooked in one step because bacteria can thrive in meat at partially cooked temperatures. If combination cooking is done using a grill with microwave or conventional methods, be sure the grill is hot and ready for the partially cooked meat so cooking can be continued (see page 408).

SEASONINGS FOR MEAT

Natural meat flavors can be enhanced by seasoning before roasting. Fresh or dried herbs, garlic, commercially prepared mixtures or your own special mixture rubbed or sprinkled on the roast will result in delicious aroma and flavor. Try one of the following seasoning mixtures (enough for a 4-pound roast):

CARAWAY: Mix 2 tablespoons caraway seed, crushed, 1 teaspoon salt, ½ teaspoon garlic powder and ¼ teaspoon pepper.

CURRIED ONION: Mix 2 teaspoons curry powder, 1½ teaspoons instant minced onion, ½ teaspoon salt and ¼ teaspoon pepper.

DILL-ROSEMARY SALT: Mix 2 teaspoons dried dill weed, 1 teaspoon salt, ½ teaspoon dried rosemary leaves and ¼ teaspoon pepper.

HERB: Cut 1 or 2 cloves garlic into halves; rub meat with garlic. Mix 1 teaspoon dried sage leaves, 1 teaspoon marjoram leaves and 1 teaspoon salt.

TERIYAKI: Brush meat with 2 tablespoons teriyaki sauce. Mix ½ teaspoon garlic powder and 1 teaspoon cracked black pepper.

Carving a Standing Rib Roast

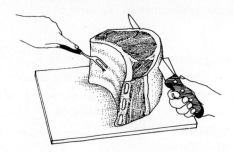

Place roast with large side down on carving board or platter. If necessary, remove wedge-shaped slice from large end so roast will stand firmly. To carve, insert fork below first rib. Slice from outside of roast toward rib side.

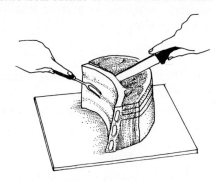

After making several slices, cut along inner side of rib bone with knife. As each slice is released, slide knife under it and lift to plate.

Carving a Blade Pot Roast

Place roast on carving board or platter. With fork in meat, cut between muscles and around the bones. Remove one solid section of pot roast at a time. Turn section so that meat grain runs parallel to carving board. Carve across grain of meat; slices should be about ¼ inch thick.

ROAST BEEF

Select beef roast from those listed in Timetable for Roasting Beef. (If serving Yorkshire Pudding [right], select rib roast or rib eye roast.) Season if desired.

Place beef, fat side up, on rack in shallow roasting pan. The rack keeps meat out of the drippings. (With a rib roast, the ribs form a natural rack.) It is not necessary to baste.

Insert meat thermometer so tip is in thickest part of beef and does not touch bone or rest in fat. Do not add water. Do not cover. Roast in 325° oven (350° for rib eye roast). (It is not necessary to preheat oven.) Roast to 5° below desired degree of doneness (see timetable), using the thermometer reading as final guide.

Cover roast with aluminum foil tent and let stand 15 to 20 minutes before carving. Temperature will rise about 5° and roast will be easier to carve.

To serve au jus, spoon hot beef juices over carved beef. Or serve beef with Oven-browned Potatoes (below), Yorkshire Pudding (right) or Pan Gravy (page 358).

Oven-browned Potatoes

About 1½ hours before beef roast is done, prepare 6 medium potatoes as directed on page 393—except make thin crosswise cuts almost through potatoes, if desired, and decrease boiling time to 10 minutes. Place potatoes in beef drippings in pan, turning each potato to coat completely. Or brush potatoes with margarine or butter, melted, and place on rack with beef. Continue cooking about 1¼ hours, turning potatoes once, until golden brown. Sprinkle with salt and pepper if desired.

Yorkshire Pudding

1 cup all-purpose flour
1 cup milk
½ teaspoon salt
2 eggs

Thirty minutes before rib roast or boneless rib roast is done, mix all ingredients with hand beater just until smooth. Heat square pan, 9 × 9 × 2 inches, in oven. Remove beef from oven. Spoon off drippings and add enough melted shortening to drippings, if necessary, to measure ½ cup.

Increase oven temperature to 425°. Return beef to oven. Place hot drippings in heated square pan. Pour batter into pan. Bake 20 minutes. Remove beef from oven. Bake pudding 15 to 20 minutes longer or until deep golden brown. Cut pudding into squares and serve with beef.   6 SERVINGS.

TIMETABLE FOR ROASTING BEEF
(Oven Temperature 325°)

Cut	Approximate Weight (pounds)	Meat Thermometer Reading	Approximate Cooking Time (minutes per pound)
Eye round	2 to 3	140° (rare)	20 to 22
Rib*	4 to 6	140° (rare)	23 to 25
(small end)		160° (medium)	27 to 30
	6 to 8	140° (rare)	26 to 32
		160° (medium)	34 to 38
Rib eye**	4 to 5	140° (rare)	18 to 20
(small end)		160° (medium)	20 to 22
Round tip	2½ to 4	140° (rare)	30 to 35
(high quality)		160° (medium)	35 to 40
	4 to 6	140° (rare)	25 to 30
		160° (medium)	30 to 35
Tenderloin, whole***	4 to 6	140° (rare)	45 to 60 (total)
Tenderloin, half***	2 to 3	140° (rare)	35 to 45 (total)
Top loin	4 to 6	140° (rare)	17 to 21
		160° (medium)	21 to 25
	6 to 8	140° (rare)	14 to 17
		160° (medium)	17 to 21
Top round	4 to 6	140° (rare)	25 to 30
(high quality)		160° (medium)	30 to 35

*Ribs which measure 6 to 7 inches from chine bone to tip of rib.
**Roast at 350°.
***Roast at 425°.

Beef

• RETAIL CUTS •
WHERE THEY COME FROM
HOW TO COOK THEM

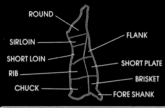

ROUND
SIRLOIN
SHORT LOIN
RIB
CHUCK
FLANK
SHORT PLATE
BRISKET
FORE SHANK

ROUND

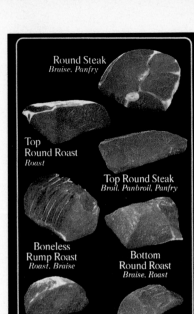

Round Steak
Braise, Panfry

Top Round Roast
Roast

Top Round Steak
Broil, Panbroil, Panfry

Boneless Rump Roast
Roast, Braise

Bottom Round Roast
Braise, Roast

Tip Roast, Cap Off
Roast, Braise

Eye Round Roast
Braise, Roast

Tip Steak
Broil, Panbroil, Panfry

SIRLOIN

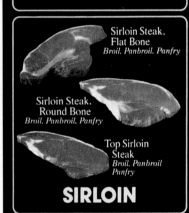

Sirloin Steak, Flat Bone
Broil, Panbroil, Panfry

Sirloin Steak, Round Bone
Broil, Panbroil, Panfry

Top Sirloin Steak
Broil, Panbroil, Panfry

FORE SHANK & BRISKET

Shank Cross Cut
Braise, Cook in Liquid

Brisket, Whole
Braise, Cook in Liquid

Corned Brisket, Point Half
Braise, Cook in Liquid

Brisket, Flat Half
Braise

CHUCK

Chuck Eye Roast
Braise, Roast

Boneless Top Blade Steak
Braise, Panfry

Arm Pot Roast
Braise

Boneless Shoulder Pot Roast
Braise

Cross Rib Pot Roast
Braise

Mock Tender
Braise

Blade Roast
Braise

Under Blade Pot Roast
Braise, Roast

7-Bone Pot Roast
Braise

Short Ribs
Braise, Cook in Liquid

Flanken-Style Ribs
Braise, Cook in Liquid

SHORT LOIN

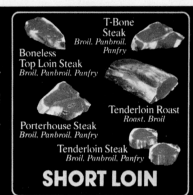

T-Bone Steak
Broil, Panbroil, Panfry

Boneless Top Loin Steak
Broil, Panbroil, Panfry

Porterhouse Steak
Broil, Panbroil, Panfry

Tenderloin Roast
Roast, Broil

Tenderloin Steak
Broil, Panbroil, Panfry

RIB

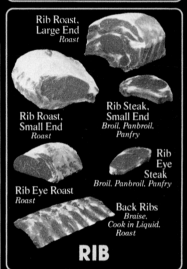

Rib Roast, Large End
Roast

Rib Roast, Small End
Roast

Rib Steak, Small End
Broil, Panbroil, Panfry

Rib Eye Roast
Roast

Rib Eye Steak
Broil, Panbroil, Panfry

Back Ribs
Braise, Cook in Liquid, Roast

FLANK & SHORT PLATE

Flank Steak
Broil, Braise, Panfry

Flank Steak Rolls
Braise, Broil, Panbroil, Panfry

Skirt Steak
Braise, Broil, Panbroil, Panfry

OTHER CUTS

Ground Beef
Broil, Panfry, Panbroil, Roast (Bake)

Cubed Steak
Panfry, Braise

Beef for Stew
Braise, Cook in Liquid

Cubes for Kabobs
Broil, Braise

BEEF ROAST WITH SPICY CHIPOTLE SAUCE

4-pound beef rolled rump roast
4 cloves garlic, slivered
1 can (7 ounces) chipotle peppers in adobo sauce
1 medium onion, cut into fourths
1 cup sour cream

Make 1-inch-deep cuts with tip of sharp knife over entire beef roast. Push garlic slivers in cuts as far as possible. Remove stems from peppers. Place peppers and onion in blender or food processor. Cover and blend, or process, until smooth. Spread half of the pepper mixture over beef. Cover and refrigerate at least 2 hours. Cover and refrigerate remaining pepper mixture.

Heat oven to 325°. Place beef, fat side up, on rack in shallow roasting pan. Insert meat thermometer so tip is in center of thickest part of beef and does not touch fat. Roast to 5° below desired doneness (see Timetable for Roasting Beef). Mix remaining pepper mixture and sour cream. Heat over medium heat to boiling, stirring constantly. Slice beef thinly and serve with pepper sour cream sauce.   16 SERVINGS; 245 CALORIES PER SERVING.

BRAISING BEEF

Cook beef over medium heat in heavy skillet until brown; drain. Season if desired. Pour small amount (¼ to ½ cup) liquid (water, broth, apple, pineapple or vegetable juice) over beef. Cover and cook over low heat on top of range or bake in 325° oven until tender (see Timetable for Braising Beef). Add vegetables near end of cooking if desired. Cooking liquid can be thickened or reduced to make a sauce.

TIMETABLE FOR BRAISING BEEF

Cut	Approximate Weight or Thickness	Approximate Total Cooking Time (hours)
Blade pot roast	3 to 5 pounds	1¾ to 2¼
Arm pot roast	3 to 4 pounds	2 to 3
Boneless chuck roast	2½ to 4 pounds	2 to 3
Short ribs	Pieces (4 × 2 × 2 inches)	1½ to 2½
Round steak	¾ to 1 inch	1 to 1½
	1½ to 2½ inches	2 to 3

NEW ENGLAND POT ROAST

Everyone has a favorite, regional version of pot roast, but we know you'll love our New England classic with succulent vegetables in a nicely spiced sauce.

4-pound beef arm, blade or cross rib pot roast*
1 to 2 teaspoons salt
1 teaspoon pepper
1 jar (5 ounces) prepared horseradish
1 cup water
8 small potatoes, cut in half
8 medium carrots, cut into fourths
8 small onions
Pot Roast Gravy (below)

Cook beef roast in Dutch oven over medium heat until brown; reduce heat. Sprinkle with salt and pepper. Spread horseradish over both sides of beef. Add water. Heat to boiling; reduce heat. Cover and simmer on top of range or bake in 325° oven 2½ hours. Add vegetables. Cover and cook about 1 hour longer or until beef and vegetables are tender. Remove to warm platter; keep warm. Prepare Pot Roast Gravy. Serve with beef and vegetables.   8 SERVINGS; 400 CALORIES PER SERVING.

*3-pound beef bottom round, rolled rump, tip or chuck eye roast can be substituted; decrease salt to ¾ teaspoon.

Pot Roast Gravy

Water
½ cup cold water
¼ cup all-purpose flour

Skim excess fat from broth. Add enough water to broth to measure 2 cups. Shake ½ cup water and the flour in tightly covered container. Gradually stir into broth. Heat to boiling, stirring constantly. Boil and stir 1 minute.

BARBECUE POT ROAST: Decrease pepper to ½ teaspoon. Omit horseradish and water. Prepare Barbecue Sauce (page 360). After browning beef, pour on Barbecue Sauce. Omit gravy. Skim fat from sauce. Spoon sauce over beef and vegetables.   475 CALORIES PER SERVING.

HERBED POT ROAST: Decrease pepper to ½ teaspoon. Omit horseradish. After browning beef, sprinkle with 1 tablespoon chopped fresh or 1 teaspoon dried marjoram leaves, 1 tablespoon chopped fresh or 1 teaspoon dried thyme leaves, 2 teaspoons fresh or ½ teaspoon dried oregano leaves and 3 cloves garlic, crushed. Substitute 1 can (10½ ounces) condensed beef broth for the 1 cup water.   415 CALORIES PER SERVING.

Corned Beef and Cabbage

CORNED BEEF AND CABBAGE

The addition of potatoes, turnips and carrots makes this a New England Boiled Dinner.

> 2-pound well-trimmed corned beef bone-less brisket
> 1 small onion, cut into fourths
> 1 clove garlic, crushed
> 1 small head green cabbage, cut into 6 wedges

Place beef brisket in Dutch oven. Add enough cold water just to cover beef. Add onion and garlic. Heat to boiling; reduce heat. Cover and simmer about 2 hours or until beef is tender. Remove to warm platter; keep warm. Skim fat from broth. Add cabbage. Heat to boiling; reduce heat. Simmer uncovered 15 minutes.   6 SERVINGS; 250 CALORIES PER SERVING.

NEW ENGLAND BOILED DINNER: Decrease simmering time of beef to 1 hour 40 minutes. Skim fat from broth. Add 6 small onions, 6 medium carrots, 3 potatoes, cut in half, and, if desired, 3 turnips, cut into cubes. Cover and simmer 20 minutes. Remove beef to warm platter; keep warm. Add cabbage. Heat to boiling; reduce heat. Simmer uncovered about 15 minutes or until vegetables are tender.   390 CALORIES PER SERVING.

BEEF BRISKET BARBECUE

> 4- to 5-pound well-trimmed beef brisket
> 1 teaspoon salt
> ½ cup ketchup
> ¼ cup vinegar
> ½ cup finely chopped onion
> 1 tablespoon Worcestershire sauce
> 1½ teaspoons liquid smoke
> ¼ teaspoon pepper
> 1 bay leaf, finely crushed

Heat oven to 325°. Rub surface of beef brisket with salt. Place in ungreased rectangular pan, 13 × 9 × 2 inches. Mix remaining ingredients; pour over beef. Cover and bake about 3 hours or until beef is tender. Cut thin diagonal slices across the grain at an angle from 2 or 3 "faces" of beef. Spoon any remaining pan juices over sliced beef if desired.   12 SERVINGS; 300 CALORIES PER SERVING.

To Grill: After rubbing surface of beef with salt, place on 20 × 15-inch piece of heavy-duty aluminum foil. Mix remaining ingredients; pour over beef. Wrap securely in foil. Grill about 5 inches from medium coals about 1½ hours, turning once, until tender.

Carving a Beef Brisket

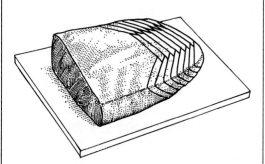

Place beef or corned beef brisket on carving board or platter. Carve across the 2 or 3 "faces" of brisket as shown. Make slices in rotation so that the "faces" will remain equal to each other in size. Cut *thin* slices at right angle, always across the grain.

BROILED OR GRILLED BEEF

Slash outer edge of fat on beef diagonally at 1-inch intervals to prevent curling (do not cut into beef). Set oven control to broil. Place beef on rack in broiler pan. Broil with top at recommended distance from heat about half the time or until brown (see Timetable for Broiling Beef). Beef should be about half done. (Grill beef 4 to 5 inches from low to moderate heat.)

Season brown side if desired. Turn beef; broil until brown. Season if desired.

LONDON BROIL

1-pound high-quality beef flank steak
1 tablespoon margarine or butter
2 medium onions, thinly sliced
¼ teaspoon salt
2 tablespoons vegetable oil
1 teaspoon lemon juice
½ teaspoon salt
¼ teaspoon pepper
2 cloves garlic, crushed

Cut both sides of beef steak in diamond pattern ⅛ inch deep. Heat margarine in 10-inch skillet over medium-high heat. Sauté onions and ¼ teaspoon salt in margarine about 4 minutes or until light brown; keep warm. Mix remaining ingredients; brush half of the mixture over beef.

Set oven control to broil. Broil beef with top 2 to 3 inches from heat about 5 minutes or until brown. Turn beef; brush with remaining oil mixture. Broil 5 minutes longer. Cut beef across grain at slanted angle into thin slices; serve with onions.   4 SERVINGS; 260 CALORIES PER SERVING.

TIMETABLE FOR BROILING BEEF

Cut	Approximate Thickness or Weight	Inches from Heat	Total Cooking Time (minutes) Rare (140°)	Medium (160°)
PORTERHOUSE, T-BONE				
Rib and rib eye	¾ inch	2 to 3	8	12
Steaks	1 inch	3 to 4	10	15
SIRLOIN STEAK				
boneless	¾ inch	2 to 3	10	15
	1 inch	3 to 4	16	21
Tenderloin	1 inch	2 to 3	10	15
Top loin steak	¾ inch	2 to 3	8	12
	1 inch	3 to 4	12	17
CHUCK SHOULDER				
Steak*, boneless	¾ inch	2 to 3	11	14
	1 inch	3 to 4	14	18
Top round steak	1 inch	3 to 4	15	18
Flank steak	1 to 1½ pounds	2 to 3	12	14

*Marinate 6 to 8 hours for best eating quality

Fajitas

 **FAJITAS**

1½-pound beef boneless sirloin steak, about
   1½ inches thick
¼ cup vegetable oil
¼ cup red wine vinegar
1 teaspoon sugar
1 tablespoon chopped fresh or 1 teaspoon
   dried oregano leaves
1 teaspoon chili powder
½ teaspoon garlic powder
½ teaspoon salt
¼ teaspoon pepper
12 ten-inch flour tortillas
2 tablespoons vegetable oil
2 large onions, sliced
2 medium green or red bell peppers, cut
   into ¼-inch strips
1 jar (8 ounces) picante sauce
1 cup shredded Cheddar or Monterey Jack
   cheese (4 ounces)
Guacamole (page 201) or 2 containers (6
   ounces each) frozen guacamole, thawed
¾ cup sour cream

Trim excess fat from beef steak. Prick beef with
fork in several places. Mix ¼ cup oil, the vinegar,
sugar, oregano, chili powder, garlic powder, salt
and pepper in ungreased square baking dish,
8×8×2 inches. Place beef in dish, turning once
to coat both sides. Cover and refrigerate at least 8
hours, turning beef occasionally.

Heat oven to 325°. Wrap tortillas in aluminum
foil. Heat in oven about 15 minutes or until warm.
Remove tortillas from oven; keep wrapped. Remove beef from marinade; reserve marinade. Set
oven control to broil. Broil beef with top about 3
inches from heat about 8 minutes or until brown;
turn. Brush beef with marinade. Broil 7 to 8 minutes longer or until medium doneness. While beef
broils, heat 2 tablespoons oil over medium-high
heat. Sauté onions and bell peppers in oil 6 to 8
minutes or until crisp-tender. Cut beef diagonally
into very thin slices.

For each serving, place beef, onion mixture, picante
sauce, cheese, Guacamole and sour cream in center of tortilla. Fold 1 end up about 1 inch over
beef mixture; fold right and left sides over folded
end.   6 SERVINGS (2 FAJITAS PER SERVING); 870 CALO-
RIES PER SERVING.

⏱ BEEF WITH MARINATED PEPPERS AND GOAT CHEESE

Marinated Peppers (page 314)
1½-pound beef tenderloin or boneless top
   loin steak, about ½ inch thick
2 tablespoons margarine or butter
2 small onions, thinly sliced
½ cup water
1 tablespoon cornstarch
3 cups hot cooked rice (page 267)
¼ cup crumbled soft mild chèvre cheese
   (such as Montrachet)

Prepare Marinated Peppers. Cut beef steak with grain into 2-inch strips. Cut strips diagonally across grain into ¼-inch slices. (For ease in cutting, partially freeze beef about 1½ hours.) Cook and stir beef in margarine in 10-inch skillet over low heat until brown. Drain Marinated Peppers, reserving marinade. Stir reserved marinade and onions into beef. Heat to boiling; reduce heat. Cover and simmer about 10 minutes or until beef is done.

Mix water and cornstarch. Gradually stir into beef mixture. Heat to boiling, stirring constantly. Boil and stir 1 minute. Stir in Marinated Peppers; heat until hot. Serve over rice. Sprinkle with chèvre cheese.   6 SERVINGS (ABOUT 1½ CUPS EACH); 495 CALORIES PER SERVING.

⏱ BEEF MEDALLIONS WITH ROSEMARY SAUCE

1-pound beef tenderloin, about 6 inches long
1 tablespoon margarine or butter
1 tablespoon margarine or butter
½ teaspoon cocoa
⅛ teaspoon salt
1 clove garlic, finely chopped
1 teaspoon chopped fresh or ¼ teaspoon
   dried rosemary leaves
¼ cup dry red wine or beef broth

Cut beef tenderloin into ¾-inch slices. Heat 1 tablespoon margarine in 10-inch skillet over medium-high heat. Sauté beef in margarine over medium-high heat 4 to 5 minutes on each side, turning once, until brown and center is medium rare. Remove beef to warm platter; keep warm.

Cook and stir 1 tablespoon margarine, the cocoa, salt, garlic and rosemary in same skillet until bubbly. Gradually stir in wine. Heat to boiling; boil and stir 1 minute. Serve over beef.   4 SERVINGS; 235 CALORIES PER SERVING.

PORK MEDALLIONS WITH ROSEMARY SAUCE: Substitute 1-pound pork tenderloin for the beef and dry white or rosé wine for the dry red wine. Sauté pork about 6 minutes on each side or until done.   190 CALORIES PER SERVING.

Beef with Marinated Peppers and Goat Cheese, Moroccan Beef with Couscous (page 223)

STIR-FRIED ORANGE BEEF

½ cup cold water
2 tablespoons cornstarch
2 tablespoons soy sauce
1-pound beef boneless sirloin steak
3 tablespoons vegetable oil
¼ teaspoon ground ginger
¼ teaspoon garlic powder
2 tablespoons vegetable oil
3 cups vegetable pieces (sliced mushrooms, broccoli flowerets, cauliflowerets, sliced carrots, celery, onion or bell pepper)
1 cup orange juice
2 cups hot cooked rice (page 267)

Mix water, cornstarch and soy sauce; reserve. Trim fat from beef steak. Cut beef steak with grain into 2-inch strips. Cut strips across grain into ⅛-inch slices. (For ease in cutting, partially freeze beef about 1½ hours.) Heat wok or 12-inch skillet until 1 or 2 drops of water bubble and skitter when sprinkled in wok. Add 3 tablespoons oil and rotate wok to coat side. Add beef, ginger and garlic powder. Stir-fry about 3 minutes or until beef is brown. Remove beef from wok.

Add 2 tablespoons oil to wok and rotate wok to coat side. Add vegetables. Stir-fry 1 minute. Stir in beef and orange juice; heat to boiling. Stir in cornstarch mixture. Cook and stir about 1 minute or until thickened. Serve with rice. 4 SERVINGS; 525 CALORIES PER SERVING.

SWISS STEAK

3 tablespoons all-purpose flour
1 teaspoon dry mustard
½ teaspoon salt
1½-pound beef boneless round, tip or chuck steak, about ¾ inch thick
2 tablespoons vegetable oil
1 can (16 ounces) whole tomatoes, undrained
2 cloves garlic, finely chopped
1 cup water
1 large onion, sliced
1 large green bell pepper, sliced

Mix flour, mustard and salt. Sprinkle one side of beef steak with half of the flour mixture; pound in. Turn beef and pound in remaining flour mixture. Cut beef into 6 serving pieces. Heat oil in 10-inch skillet until hot. Cook beef over medium heat about 15 minutes, turning once, until brown. Add tomatoes and garlic; break up tomatoes. Heat to boiling; reduce heat. Cover and simmer about

1¼ hours or until beef is tender. Add water, onion and bell pepper. Heat to boiling; reduce heat. Cover and simmer 5 to 8 minutes or until vegetables are tender. 6 SERVINGS; 230 CALORIES PER SERVING.

BEEF STEW

This is our all-time favorite beef stew!

1-pound beef boneless chuck, tip or round roast, cut into 1-inch cubes
1 tablespoon vegetable oil or shortening
3 cups hot water
½ teaspoon salt
⅛ teaspoon pepper
2 medium carrots, cut into 1-inch pieces (about 1 cup)
1 large potato, cut into 1½-inch pieces (about 1¼ cups)
1 medium turnip, cut into 1-inch pieces (about 1 cup)
1 medium green bell pepper, cut into 1-inch pieces (about 1 cup)
1 medium stalk celery, cut into 1-inch pieces (about ½ cup)
1 small onion, chopped (about ¼ cup)
½ teaspoon browning sauce, if desired
1 teaspoon salt
1 bay leaf
Parsley Dumplings (page 37)
½ cup cold water
2 tablespoons all-purpose flour

Cook and stir beef in oil in 12-inch skillet or Dutch oven about 15 minutes or until beef is brown. Add 3 cups hot water, ½ teaspoon salt and the pepper. Heat to boiling; reduce heat. Cover and simmer 2 to 2½ hours or until beef is almost tender.

Stir in carrots, potato, turnip, bell pepper, celery, onion, browning sauce, 1 teaspoon salt and the bay leaf. Cover and simmer about 30 minutes or until vegetables are tender. Remove bay leaf.

Prepare Parsley Dumplings. Shake ½ cup cold water and the flour in tightly covered container. Gradually stir into stew. Heat to boiling, stirring constantly. Boil and stir 1 minute; reduce heat. Drop dumpling dough by 10 to 12 spoonfuls onto hot stew (do not drop directly into liquid). Cook uncovered 10 minutes. Cover and cook 10 minutes longer. 6 SERVINGS; 430 CALORIES PER SERVING.

CHICKEN STEW: Substitute 1½- to 2-pound stewing chicken, cut up, for the beef. 440 CALORIES PER SERVING.

Harvest Beef Stew

HARVEST BEEF STEW

2 pounds beef stew meat, cut into 1-inch
  cubes
⅓ cup quick-cooking tapioca
1 tablespoon chopped fresh or 1 teaspoon dried basil leaves
1 tablespoon cumin seed
1 teaspoon salt
4 medium carrots, cut into 1-inch pieces
4 cloves garlic, finely chopped
2 medium onions, cut into eighths
2 cans (16 ounces) tomatoes, undrained
2 ears fresh corn, cut into fourths,* or
  1 package (10 ounces) frozen whole
  kernel corn
8 small new potatoes (about 1 pound),
  cut in half
2 small zucchini, thinly sliced

Heat oven to 325°. Mix all ingredients except
corn, potatoes and zucchini in Dutch oven; break
up tomatoes. Cover and bake 2½ hours, stirring 2
or 3 times during the first 1½ hours. Stir corn and
potatoes into stew. Cover and bake 1 to 1½ hours
longer or until beef and vegetables are tender. Stir
in zucchini. Cover and let stand 10 minutes. 8
SERVINGS (ABOUT 1½ CUPS EACH); 305 CALORIES PER
SERVING.

*4 ears frozen corn, thawed and cut in half, can be
substituted for the fresh corn.*

MOROCCAN BEEF
WITH COUSCOUS

*This dish was inspired by the Moroccan
recipe for Tangia, named after a type of
cooking vessel, the tangia.*

1½ pounds beef boneless chuck, tip or round
  roast, or boneless lamb shoulder cut into
  1-inch cubes
1 cup beef broth or water
⅓ cup chopped fresh or 2 tablespoons dried
  coriander leaves
⅓ cup chopped fresh Italian or regular parsley or 2 tablespoons parsley flakes
1 tablespoon olive or vegetable oil
1 teaspoon ground ginger
½ teaspoon salt
¼ teaspoon pepper
⅛ teaspoon ground red pepper (cayenne)
12 cloves garlic
3 slices lemon, cut in half
2 large tomatoes, seeded and coarsely
  chopped
2 large onions, chopped (about 2 cups)
3 cups hot cooked couscous

Heat oven to 325°. Mix all ingredients except
couscous in ungreased 3-quart casserole. Cover and
bake 2 to 2½ hours or until beef is very tender.
Serve over couscous. 6 SERVINGS (ABOUT 1½ CUPS
EACH); 515 CALORIES PER SERVING.

 # MUSTARD SHORT
RIBS

*This first appeared in our 1969 cookbook
and has been a hit ever since.*

4 pounds beef short ribs, cut into pieces
⅓ cup prepared mustard
1 tablespoon sugar
2 tablespoons lemon juice
1 teaspoon salt
½ teaspoon pepper
2 cloves garlic, crushed
4 medium onions, sliced

Place beef ribs in shallow glass dish. Mix mustard,
sugar, lemon juice, salt, pepper and garlic. Spread
over beef. Top with onions. Cover and refrigerate
at least 12 hours, turning beef occasionally. Remove
beef from marinade; reserve onions and marinade.

Heat oven to 350°. Cook beef in Dutch oven
over medium heat until brown; drain. Add onions,
Pour marinade over beef. Cover and bake about 2
hours or until beef is tender. 6 SERVINGS 625
CALORIES PER SERVING.

Burgundy Beef

BEEF STROGANOFF

1½ pounds beef tenderloin or boneless top loin steak, about ½ inch thick
2 tablespoons margarine or butter
1½ cups beef broth
2 tablespoons ketchup
1 teaspoon salt
1 small clove garlic, finely chopped
8 ounces mushrooms, sliced
1 medium onion, chopped (about ½ cup)
3 tablespoons all-purpose flour
1 cup sour cream or plain yogurt

Cut beef tenderloin across grain into strips, each about 1½ × ½ inch. (For ease in cutting, partially freeze beef.) Cook beef in margarine in 10-inch skillet over low heat, stirring occasionally, until brown. Reserve ⅓ cup of the broth. Stir remaining broth, the ketchup, salt and garlic into skillet. Heat to boiling; reduce heat. Cover and simmer about 10 minutes or until beef is tender.

Stir in mushrooms and onion. Cover and simmer about 5 minutes or until onion is tender. Shake reserved broth and the flour in tightly covered container; gradually stir into beef mixture. Heat to boiling, stirring constantly. Boil and stir 1 minute; reduce heat. Stir in sour cream; heat until hot. Serve over hot cooked noodles or rice if desired.   6 SERVINGS; 405 CALORIES PER SERVING.

BURGUNDY BEEF

A favorite of the Betty Crocker Kitchens staff for years. We heartily recommend it for a do-ahead dinner.

4 pounds beef round steak, 1 inch thick
¼ cup shortening or vegetable oil
5 large onions, sliced
1 pound mushrooms, sliced
3 tablespoons all-purpose flour
2 teaspoons salt
1 teaspoon chopped fresh or ¼ teaspoon dried marjoram leaves
1 teaspoon chopped fresh or ¼ teaspoon dried thyme leaves
¼ teaspoon pepper
1 cup beef broth
2 cups red Burgundy or other dry red wine

Cut beef steak into 1-inch cubes. Heat shortening in Dutch oven until melted. Cook beef in shortening over medium heat until brown; remove. Cook and stir onions and mushrooms in Dutch oven until onions are tender, adding shortening if necessary. Remove mushrooms and onions; cover and refrigerate.

Return beef to Dutch oven. Sprinkle with flour, salt, marjoram, thyme and pepper. Stir in broth and Burgundy. Heat to boiling; reduce heat. Cover and simmer about 1¼ hours or until beef is tender. (Liquid should just cover beef.) If necessary, stir in additional broth and Burgundy (1 part broth to 2 parts Burgundy). Add mushrooms and onions. Heat until hot, stirring occasionally.   12 SERVINGS; 590 CALORIES PER SERVING.

SKILLET HASH

2 cups chopped cooked lean beef or corned beef
4 small potatoes, cooked and chopped (about 2 cups)
1 medium onion, chopped (about ½ cup)
1 tablespoon chopped fresh parsley
½ teaspoon salt
⅛ teaspoon pepper
2 to 3 tablespoons vegetable oil or shortening

Mix beef, potatoes, onion, parsley, salt and pepper. Heat oil in 10-inch skillet over medium heat until hot. Spread beef mixture evenly in skillet. Cook 10 to 15 minutes, turning frequently, until brown.   4 SERVINGS; 395 CALORIES PER SERVING.

RED FLANNEL HASH: Use 1½ cups chopped corned beef and 3 small potatoes, cooked and chopped (about 1½ cups). Mix in 1 can (16 ounces) diced or shoestring beets, drained.   335 CALORIES PER SERVING.

⏱ BEEF AND ARTICHOKE FETTUCCINE

8 ounces uncooked fettuccine or Spinach
    Fettuccine (page 262)
1 jar (6 ounces) marinated artichoke hearts,
    cut in half and marinade reserved
1 small onion, finely chopped (about ¼ cup)
1 cup half-and-half
½ cup grated Parmesan cheese
2 cups julienne strips cooked roast beef
    (about 8 ounces)
Freshly ground pepper
⅓ cup chopped toasted pecans

Cook fettuccine as directed on package. While
fettuccine is cooking, heat reserved marinade in
10-inch skillet over medium heat. Cook onion in
marinade about 4 minutes, stirring occasionally.
Stir in half-and-half; heat until hot. Stir in Parmesan
cheese, artichoke hearts and beef. Heat until hot.

Drain fettuccine; stir into sauce and toss with 2
forks. Sprinkle with pepper and pecans. 6 SERV-
INGS; 320 CALORIES PER SERVING.

⏱ CURRIED BEEF WITH FRUIT

1 package (8 ounces) mixed dried fruit
2½ cups boiling water
3 teaspoons curry powder
½ teaspoon salt
2 cloves garlic, finely chopped
2 tablespoons margarine or butter
2 tablespoons cornstarch
¼ cup orange juice
¾ cup orange juice
3 cups cut-up cooked roast beef
6 green onions, cut into 1-inch pieces
3 cups hot cooked rice (page 267)
⅓ cup slivered almonds

Remove pits from prunes. Pour boiling water over
fruit; let stand. Cook curry powder, salt and garlic
in margarine in 3-quart saucepan over medium
heat 5 minutes, stirring occasionally. Mix cornstarch and ¼ cup orange juice. Stir cornstarch mixture, ¾ cup orange juice and the fruit (with liquid)
into curry mixture. Heat to boiling, stirring constantly. Boil and stir 1 minute. Stir in beef and
onions; heat until hot. Serve over rice. Sprinkle
with almonds.   6 SERVINGS (ABOUT 1½ CUPS EACH);
480 CALORIES PER SERVING.

Beef and Artichoke Fettuccine

MEAT LOAF

1½ pounds ground beef, pork and turkey
1 cup milk
1 teaspoon chopped fresh or ¼ teaspoon dried sage leaves
½ teaspoon salt
½ teaspoon dry mustard
¼ teaspoon pepper
3 slices bread, torn into small pieces*
1 egg
1 clove garlic, finely chopped, or ⅛ teaspoon garlic powder
½ cup ketchup, chili sauce or barbecue sauce
1 small onion, chopped (about ¼ cup)
1 tablespoon Worcestershire sauce

Heat oven to 350°. Mix all ingredients except ketchup. Spread mixture in loaf pan, 8½ × 4½ × 2½ or 9 × 5 × 3 inches, or shape into loaf in rectangular pan, 13 × 9 × 2 inches. Spoon ketchup over top. Bake 1 to 1¼ hours or until done. Remove from pan.   6 SERVINGS; 375 CALORIES PER SERVING.

*½ cup dry bread crumbs or ¾ cup quick-cooking oats can be substituted for the 3 slices bread.

To Microwave: Prepare as directed—except shape into 6 small loaves. Place in rectangular microwavable dish, 11 × 7 × 1½ inches. Cover with waxed paper and microwave on high 14 to 17 minutes, rotating dish ½ turn after 7 minutes. Let stand on flat, heatproof surface (not wire rack) 5 minutes.

INDIVIDUAL MEAT LOAVES: Shape beef mixture into 6 small loaves. Place in rectangular pan, 13 × 9 × 2 inches. Spoon ketchup over top of each loaf. Bake 45 minutes.   375 CALORIES PER SERVING.

SPANISH MEAT LOAF: Omit sage. Substitute ⅔ cup milk and ⅓ cup tomato sauce for the milk. Mix in 8 large pimiento-stuffed olives, sliced. Substitute ⅔ cup tomato sauce for the ketchup. Bake as directed.   380 CALORIES PER SERVING.

VEGETABLE MEAT LOAF: Increase salt to 1 teaspoon. Mix in 1 small green bell pepper, chopped, 1 medium carrot, coarsely shredded, and 1 can (4 ounces) mushroom stems and pieces, drained and chopped. Omit ketchup. Spread beef mixture in loaf pan, 9 × 5 × 3 inches. Bake as directed; drain. Arrange 1 tomato, thinly sliced, down center of meat loaf. Top with 3 slices process American cheese, cut diagonally in half. Bake 3 to 5 minutes or until cheese is melted.   405 CALORIES PER SERVING.

 # CABBAGE ROLLS

To separate cabbage leaves easily, remove core and cover cabbage with cold water. Let stand about 10 minutes and then remove leaves.

12 cabbage leaves
1 pound ground beef
½ cup uncooked instant rice
1 can (15 ounces) tomato sauce
1 teaspoon salt
⅛ teaspoon pepper
⅛ teaspoon garlic salt
1 medium onion, chopped (about ½ cup)
1 can (4 ounces) mushroom stems and pieces, undrained
1 teaspoon sugar
½ teaspoon lemon juice
1 tablespoon cornstarch
1 tablespoon water

Cover cabbage leaves with boiling water. Let stand about 10 minutes or until leaves are limp. Remove leaves; drain.

Heat oven to 350°. Mix ground beef, rice, ½ cup of the tomato sauce, the salt, pepper, garlic salt, onion and mushrooms. Place about ⅓ cup beef mixture at stem end of each leaf. Roll leaf around beef mixture, tucking in sides. Place cabbage rolls, seam sides down, in square baking dish, 8 × 8 × 2 inches. Mix remaining tomato sauce, the sugar and lemon juice. Pour over cabbage rolls. Cover and bake about 45 minutes or until beef mixture is done.

Remove cabbage rolls to platter. Pour liquid from baking dish into 1-quart saucepan. Mix cornstarch and water. Stir into liquid. Heat to boiling, stirring constantly. Boil and stir 1 minute. Pour sauce over cabbage rolls.   4 SERVINGS; 385 CALORIES PER SERVING.

To Microwave: Place cabbage leaves and ¼ cup cold water in 3-quart microwavable casserole. Cover tightly and microwave on high 4 to 5 minutes or until leaves are limp. Continue as directed—except mix remaining tomato sauce, the sugar, lemon juice, cornstarch and water. Pour over cabbage rolls. Cover with vented plastic wrap and microwave on high 15 to 16 minutes, rotating dish ¼ turn after 7 minutes, until beef mixture is done. Let stand covered 1 minute. Remove cabbage rolls to platter. Stir sauce in dish. Pour over cabbage rolls.

STUFFED PEPPERS

6 large green or red bell peppers
1 pound ground beef
2 tablespoons chopped onion
1 cup cooked rice (page 267)
1 teaspoon salt
⅛ teaspoon garlic salt
1 can (15 ounces) tomato sauce
¾ cup shredded mozzarella cheese
(3 ounces)

Cut thin slice from stem end of each bell pepper. Remove seeds and membranes; rinse peppers. Cook peppers in boiling water to cover; about 5 minutes; drain. Cook ground beef and onion in 10-inch skillet, stirring occasionally, until beef is light brown; drain. Stir in rice, salt, garlic salt and 1 cup of the tomato sauce; heat until hot.

Heat oven to 350°. Stuff peppers with beef mixture. Stand upright in square baking dish, 8 × 8 × 2 inches. Pour remaining tomato sauce over peppers. Cover and bake 45 minutes. Uncover and bake 15 minutes longer. Sprinkle with cheese. 6 SERVINGS; 310 CALORIES PER SERVING.

To Microwave: Place peppers, cut sides up, in microwavable pie plate, 9 × 1¼ or 10 × 1½ inches. Cover with vented plastic wrap and microwave on high 3 minutes to 3 minutes 30 seconds or until hot. Mix uncooked ground beef, onion, rice, salt, garlic salt and 1 cup of the tomato sauce. Stuff peppers with beef mixture. Pour remaining tomato sauce over peppers. Cover with vented plastic wrap and microwave on high 12 to 13 minutes, rotating pie plate ¼ turn after 6 minutes, until beef mixture is done. Sprinkle with cheese.

SPAGHETTI AND MEATBALLS

1 tablespoon chopped fresh or 1 teaspoon dried oregano leaves
1 tablespoon chopped fresh or 1 teaspoon dried basil leaves
2 teaspoons chopped fresh or ½ teaspoon dried marjoram leaves
1 teaspoon sugar
½ teaspoon salt
1 large onion, chopped (about 1 cup)
1 clove garlic, crushed
1 can (16 ounces) whole tomatoes, undrained
1 can (8 ounces) tomato sauce
Meatballs (right)
4 cups hot cooked spaghetti

Mix all ingredients except Meatballs and spaghetti in 3-quart saucepan; break up tomatoes. Heat to boiling; reduce heat. Cover and simmer 30 minutes, stirring occasionally.

Prepare Meatballs; drain. Stir meatballs into tomato mixture. Cover and simmer 30 minutes longer, stirring occasionally. Serve over spaghetti and, if desired, with grated Parmesan cheese. 6 SERVINGS; 385 CALORIES PER SERVING.

SPAGHETTI AND BEEF SAUCE: Omit Meatballs. Cook 1 pound ground beef, the onion and garlic in 10-inch skillet, stirring occasionally, until beef is light brown; drain. Stir in remaining ingredients except spaghetti; break up tomatoes. Heat to boiling; reduce heat. Cover and simmer about 1 hour, stirring occasionally. 330 CALORIES PER SERVING.

SPAGHETTI AND CHICKEN SAUCE: Omit Meatballs. Cover and simmer sauce 1 hour. Stir in 1½ cups cut-up cooked chicken or turkey; heat until hot. 230 CALORIES PER SERVING.

MEATBALLS

1 pound ground beef
½ cup dry bread crumbs
¼ cup milk
½ teaspoon salt
½ teaspoon Worcestershire sauce
¼ teaspoon pepper
1 small onion, chopped (about ¼ cup)
1 egg

Heat oven to 400°. Mix all ingredients. Shape into twenty 1½-inch meatballs. Place in rectangular pan, 13 × 9 × 2 inches. Bake 20 to 25 minutes or until no longer pink inside. 4 SERVINGS; 355 CALORIES PER SERVING.

To Panfry: Cook in 10-inch skillet over medium heat about 20 minutes, turning occasionally, until no longer pink inside.

To Microwave: Place meatballs in rectangular microwavable dish, 11 × 7 × 1½ inches. Cover loosely and microwave on high 8 to 10 minutes, rearranging meatballs after 3 minutes, until no longer pink inside. Let stand 3 minutes; drain.

CHILI CON CARNE

1 pound ground beef
1 large onion, chopped (about 1 cup)
2 cloves garlic, crushed
1 tablespoon chili powder
½ teaspoon salt
1 teaspoon ground cumin
1 teaspoon dried oregano leaves
1 teaspoon cocoa
½ teaspoon red pepper sauce
1 can (16 ounces) whole tomatoes, undrained
1 can (15½ ounces) red kidney beans, undrained

Cook ground beef, onion and garlic in 3-quart saucepan, stirring occasionally, until beef is brown; drain. Stir in remaining ingredients except beans; break up tomatoes. Heat to boiling; reduce heat. Cover and simmer 1 hour, stirring occasionally.

Stir in beans. Heat to boiling; reduce heat. Simmer uncovered about 20 minutes, stirring occasionally, until of desired thickness. 4 SERVINGS; 415 CALORIES PER SERVING.

CINCINNATI-STYLE CHILI: For each serving, spoon about ¾ cup beef mixture over 1 cup hot cooked spaghetti. Sprinkle each serving with ¼ cup shredded Cheddar cheese and 2 tablespoons chopped onion. Top with sour cream if desired. 5 SERVINGS; 610 CALORIES PER SERVING.

EASY CHILI CON CARNE: Increase chili powder to 2 tablespoons; omit cumin, oregano, cocoa and pepper sauce. 415 CALORIES PER SERVING.

LASAGNE ROLL-UPS

With its unusual shape, this lasagne is easy to serve, and perfect for buffets.

6 uncooked lasagne noodles
6 uncooked spinach lasagne noodles
1 pound ground beef
1 large onion, chopped (about 1 cup)
1 jar (15½ ounces) spaghetti sauce
1 can (8 ounces) mushroom stems and pieces, undrained
1 carton (15 ounces) ricotta cheese or creamed cottage cheese (about 2 cups)
1 package (10 ounces) frozen chopped spinach, thawed and well drained
1 cup shredded mozzarella cheese (4 ounces)
¼ cup grated Parmesan cheese
1 teaspoon salt
¼ teaspoon pepper
2 cloves garlic, crushed

Heat oven to 350°. Cook noodles as directed on package; drain. Cover noodles with cold water. Cook ground beef and onion in 10-inch skillet, stirring occasionally, until beef is light brown; drain. Stir in spaghetti sauce and mushrooms. Heat to boiling. Pour into rectangular baking dish, 11 × 7 × 1½ inches.

Mix remaining ingredients. Drain noodles. Spread 3 tablespoons of the cheese mixture to edges of 1 noodle. Roll up; cut roll in half. Place cut sides down in beef mixture. Repeat with remaining noodles. Cover and bake about 30 minutes or until hot and bubbly. Serve with grated Parmesan cheese if desired. 8 SERVINGS; 525 CALORIES PER SERVING.

DILLED BEEF AND BULGUR RING

1 teaspoon salt
4 cups cold water
2 to 3 small zucchini (about 6 inches long), cut lengthwise into thin slices
1 pound ground beef
1 cup uncooked bulgur
1 medium onion, chopped (about ½ cup)
2 tablespoons margarine or butter
1 can (10½ ounces) condensed beef broth
1 can (4 ounces) mushroom stems and pieces, drained
½ cup water
2 teaspoons chopped fresh or 1 teaspoon dried dill weed
⅛ teaspoon pepper
2 eggs
1 jar (4 ounces) diced pimientos, drained
⅓ cup slivered almonds

Place salt and water in glass or plastic bowl. Add zucchini; let stand.

Cook ground beef in 3-quart saucepan over medium heat, stirring occasionally, until brown. Remove meat from saucepan; drain. Cook bulgur, onion and margarine in same saucepan over medium heat about 5 minutes, stirring frequently, until onion is tender and bulgur is brown. Stir in remaining ingredients except eggs, pimientos and almonds. Heat to boiling; reduce heat. Cover and simmer 13 to 15 minutes or until liquid is absorbed. Stir in ground beef, eggs, pimientos and almonds.

Heat oven to 350°. Grease 8-cup ovenproof ring mold. Rinse and drain zucchini; pat dry. Line ring mold with zucchini slices. Spoon beef mixture into mold. Bake 30 to 40 minutes or until set. Let stand 10 minutes. Invert onto heatproof serving plate. 8 SERVINGS; 330 CALORIES PER SERVING.

Veal

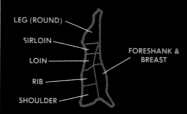

• RETAIL CUTS •
WHERE THEY COME FROM
HOW TO COOK THEM

LEG (ROUND)
SIRLOIN
LOIN
RIB
SHOULDER
FORESHANK & BREAST

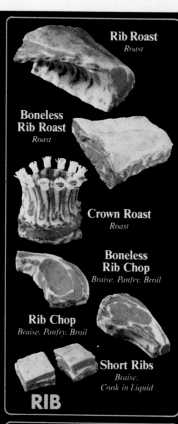

Rib Roast
Roast

Boneless Rib Roast
Roast

Crown Roast
Roast

Boneless Rib Chop
Braise. Panfry. Broil

Rib Chop
Braise. Panfry. Broil

Short Ribs
Braise. Cook in Liquid

RIB

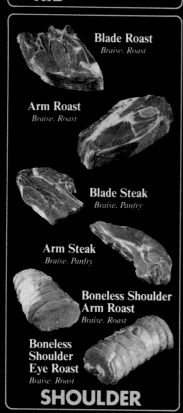

Blade Roast
Braise. Roast

Arm Roast
Braise. Roast

Blade Steak
Braise. Panfry

Arm Steak
Braise. Panfry

Boneless Shoulder Arm Roast
Braise. Roast

Boneless Shoulder Eye Roast
Braise. Roast

SHOULDER

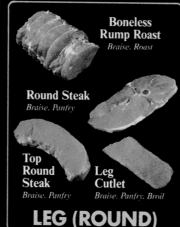

Boneless Rump Roast
Braise. Roast

Round Steak
Braise. Panfry

Top Round Steak
Braise. Panfry

Leg Cutlet
Braise. Panfry. Broil

LEG (ROUND)

Breast
Braise. Roast

Boneless Breast Roast
Braise. Roast

Cross Cut Shank
Braise. Cook in Liquid

Riblet
Braise. Cook in Liquid

Shank
Braise. Cook in Liquid

FORESHANK & BREAST

THIS CHART APPROVED BY
NATIONAL LIVE STOCK & MEAT BOARD

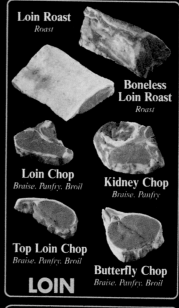

Loin Roast
Roast

Boneless Loin Roast
Roast

Loin Chop
Braise. Panfry. Broil

Kidney Chop
Braise. Panfry

Top Loin Chop
Braise. Panfry. Broil

Butterfly Chop
Braise. Panfry. Broil

LOIN

Sirloin Roast
Roast

Boneless Sirloin Roast
Roast

Sirloin Steak
Braise. Panfry. Broil

Top Sirloin Steak
Braise. Panfry. Broil

SIRLOIN

Veal for Stew
Braise. Cook in Liquid

Ground Veal
Panfry. Broil

Cubes for Kabobs
Braise

Cubed Steak
Braise. Panfry

OTHER CUTS

ROAST VEAL

Select veal roast from those listed in Timetable for Roasting Veal. Season if desired.

Place veal, fat side up, on rack in shallow roasting pan. The rack keeps meat out of the drippings. (With a rib roast, the ribs form a natural rack.) It is not necessary to baste.

Insert meat thermometer so tip is in thickest part of veal and does not touch bone or rest in fat. Do not add water. Do not cover. Roast in 325° oven. (It is not necessary to preheat oven.) Roast to 5° below desired degree of doneness (see timetable), using the thermometer reading as final guide.

Cover roast with aluminum foil tent and let stand 15 to 20 minutes before carving. Temperature will rise about 5° and roast will be easier to carve.

TIMETABLE FOR ROASTING VEAL
(Oven Temperature 325°)

Cut	Approximate Weight (pounds)	Meat Thermometer Reading	Approximate Cooking Time (minutes per pound)
Rib	4 to 5	160° (medium)	25 to 27
	4 to 5	170° (well)	29 to 31
Boneless rump	2 to 3	160° (medium)	33 to 35
	2 to 3	170° (well)	37 to 40
Boneless shoulder	2½ to 3	160° (medium)	31 to 34
	2½ to 3	170° (well)	34 to 37

BROILED OR GRILLED VEAL

Slash outer edge of fat on veal diagonally at 1-inch intervals to prevent curling (do not cut into veal). Set oven control to broil. Place veal on rack in broiler pan. Broil with top at recommended distance from heat until brown (see Timetable for Broiling Veal). Veal should be about half done. (Grill veal 4 to 5 inches from low to moderate heat.)

Season brown side if desired. Turn veal; broil until brown. Season if desired.

TIMETABLE FOR BROILING VEAL

Cut	Approximate Weight (ounces)	Inches from Heat	Approximate Total Cooking Time (minutes) Medium (160°)	Well (170°)
Loin or rib chop				
1 inch	8	4	14	17
1½ inches	11	5	21	25
Arm or blade steak*				
¾ inch	16	4	14	16
Ground veal patties				
½ inch	4	4	8	12
*Marinate at least 6 hours if desired.				

PANBROILING VEAL

Place pork in heated heavy skillet or nonstick skillet. Do not cover. Do not add water. Cook veal until browned on both sides and desired doneness, turning once (see timetable). Cook thicker cuts (⅝- to 1-inch thick) over medium-low to medium heat. Cook thinner cuts (¼-to ½-inch thick) over medium-high heat. Remove drippings as they accumulate. Season veal if desired.

TIMETABLE FOR PANBROILING VEAL
(Medium-Low to Medium Heat)

Cut	Approximate Weight (ounces)	Approximate Total Cooking Time (minutes)	
		Medium (160°)	Well (170°)
Loin or rib chop, ¾ to 1 inch	7 to 8	10	14
Blade or arm steak,* ¾ inch	16	13	15
Ground veal patties,** ½ inch	4	6	9

*Marinate at least 6 hours if desired.
**Medium to medium-high heat.

LEMON VEAL SCALLOPINI

½ cup all-purpose flour
2 teaspoons garlic salt
1 pound veal for scallopini*
¼ cup vegetable oil
2 tablespoons margarine or butter
¼ cup dry white wine or chicken broth
2 tablespoons lemon juice
½ lemon, cut into 4 wedges

Mix flour and garlic salt. Coat veal with flour mixture. Heat 2 tablespoons of the oil in 10-inch skillet over medium-high heat until hot. Sauté half of the veal about 5 minutes, turning once, until brown. Remove veal; keep warm. Repeat with remaining oil and veal.

Drain any remaining oil and overly browned particles from skillet. Add margarine, wine and lemon juice to skillet. Heat to boiling, scraping any remaining brown particles from skillet. Boil until liquid is reduced by about half and mixture has thickened slightly. Pour over veal. Serve with lemon wedges.   4 SERVINGS; 450 CALORIES PER SERVING.

*1 pound veal round steak can be substituted for the veal for scallopini. Cut veal into 8 pieces; pound until ¼ inch thick.

HEART

Heart is flavorful but one of the less tender variety meats. Braising and cooking in liquid are the preferred methods of cooking.   150 CALORIES PER 3-OUNCE SERVING.

To Braise: Cook heart on all sides in small amount of vegetable oil until brown. Add about ½ cup water, beef broth or wine. Sprinkle with salt and pepper. Heat to boiling; reduce heat. Cover and simmer on top of range or in 300° to 325° oven 3 to 4 hours for beef heart, 2½ to 3 hours for lamb, pork or veal heart, or until tender.

To Cook in Liquid: Cover heart with water. Add ½ teaspoon salt for each quart water. Heat to boiling; reduce heat. Cover and simmer 3 to 4 hours for beef heart, 2½ to 3 hours for lamb, pork or veal heart, or until tender.

TONGUE

Purchase tongue fresh, pickled, corned, smoked or canned. Tongue is one of the less tender variety meats, requiring long, slow cooking in liquid. Smoked, corned or pickled tongue may require soaking before cooking. Lamb and pork tongues are usually sold ready-to-serve.   240 CALORIES PER 3-OUNCE SERVING.

To Cook in Liquid: Cover tongue with water. If cooking fresh tongue, add ½ teaspoon salt for each quart water. Heat to boiling; reduce heat. Cover and simmer 3 to 4 hours for beef tongue, 2 to 3 hours for veal tongue or until tender; drain. Immediately place in cold water. Peel skin from tongue; cut away roots, bones and cartilage. If serving tongue cold, reserve cooking liquid. After removing skin, roots, bones and cartilage, allow tongue to cool in reserved liquid.

Liver and Onions, Brussels Sprouts with Mustard Vinaigrette (page 376), Mashed Potatoes (page 394)

LIVER

Beef and pork livers are usually braised or panfried, though sometimes ground for loaves and patties. (If liver is to be ground, cook slowly in 2 to 3 tablespoons vegetable oil about 5 minutes. This makes grinding much easier.) Baby beef, veal and lamb livers are usually panfried or broiled. Have liver sliced ½ to ¾ inch thick. Cut into serving pieces. Remove any membrane from liver before cooking. 135 CALORIES PER 3-OUNCE SERVING.

To Braise: Coat liver with flour. Heat 1 to 2 tablespoons vegetable oil or shortening. Cook liver on each side until brown. Sprinkle with salt if desired. Add ¼ cup water, beef broth or wine. Heat to boiling; reduce heat. Cover and simmer 20 to 30 minutes or until done.

To Panfry: Coat liver with flour. Heat 1 to 2 tablespoons vegetable oil or shortening over medium-high heat. Sauté liver 2 to 3 minutes on each side or until brown.

To Broil: Brush liver with melted margarine, butter or bacon fat. Set oven control to broil. Broil liver with top 3 to 5 inches from heat about 3 minutes on each side or just until brown.

LIVER AND ONIONS

3 tablespoons margarine or butter
2 medium onions, thinly sliced
3 tablespoons vegetable oil or shortening
1 pound liver, ½ to ¾ inch thick
Flour
Salt
Pepper

Heat margarine in 10-inch skillet over medium-high heat. Sauté onions in margarine 4 to 6 minutes or until light brown. Remove from skillet; keep warm.

Heat oil in same skillet until hot. Coat liver with flour. Cook liver in oil over medium heat 2 to 3 minutes on each side or until brown. Sprinkle with salt and pepper. Add onions during last minute of cooking. 4 SERVINGS; 395 CALORIES PER SERVING.

KIDNEYS

Because beef kidney is less tender than other kidneys, cook in liquid or braise. Cook lamb, pork and veal kidneys in liquid, braise or broil. Remove membrane and hard parts from kidney before cooking. 120 CALORIES PER 3-OUNCE SERVING.

To Cook in Liquid: Cover kidney with water. Heat to boiling; reduce heat. Cover and simmer 1 to 1½ hours for beef kidney, 45 to 60 minutes for lamb, pork or veal kidney, or until tender.

To Braise: Cut kidney in half or into pieces. Roll in flour or crumbs seasoned with salt and pepper. Heat vegetable oil in skillet until hot. Cook kidney in oil until brown. Add small amount liquid. Cover and cook 1½ to 2 hours for beef kidney, 45 to 60 minutes for lamb kidney, 1 to 1½ hours for pork or veal kidney, or until tender.

To Broil: Leave lamb kidney whole or cut in half. Cut veal or pork kidney into slices. Brush with margarine or butter, melted, or marinate in Classic French Dressing (page 327). Set oven control to broil. Broil with top 3 to 5 inches from heat about 5 minutes on each side or until done.

Pork

• RETAIL CUTS •
WHERE THEY COME FROM
HOW TO COOK THEM

LEG

SIDE

LOIN

ARM SHOULDER

BLADE SHOULDER

LEG/HAM

Leg Cutlet
Panfry, Braise, Broil, Panbroil

Top Leg (Inside) Roast
Roast, Braise

Smoked Ham
Roast

Smoked Ham Shank Portion
Roast

Smoked Ham Center Slice
Broil, Panbroil, Panfry, Roast

Smoked Ham Rump Portion
Roast

Canned Ham
Roast

Sliced Ham
Panfry, Panbroil, Braise

Boneless Smoked Ham
Roast

SHOULDER

Blade Roast
Roast, Braise

Blade Steak
Braise, Broil, Panbroil, Panfry

Boneless Blade Roast
Roast, Braise

Smoked Shoulder Roll
Roast, Cook in Liquid

Boneless Arm Picnic Roast
Roast, Braise

Smoked Hocks
Braise, Cook in Liquid

Smoked Picnic
Roast, Cook in Liquid

LOIN

Blade Chop
Braise, Broil, Panbroil, Panfry

Rib Chop
Broil, Panbroil, Panfry, Braise

Top Loin Chop
Broil, Panbroil, Panfry, Braise

Loin Chop
Broil, Panbroil, Panfry, Braise

Sirloin Chop
Braise

Butterfly Chop
Broil, Panbroil, Panfry, Braise

Sirloin Cutlet
Braise, Broil, Panbroil, Panfry

Back Ribs
Roast, Broil, Braise, Cook in Liquid

Country-Style Ribs
Roast, Braise, Broil, Cook in Liquid

Tenderloin
Roast, Braise, (Slices: Panfry, Braise)

Center Rib Roast
Roast

Top Loin Roast (Double)
Roast

Blade Roast
Roast, Braise

Boneless Blade Roast
Roast, Braise

Sirloin Roast
Roast

Center Loin Roast
Roast

Smoked Loin Chop
Roast, Broil, Panbroil, Panfry

Boneless Sirloin Roast
Roast

Crown Roast
Roast

Canadian-Style Bacon
Roast, Broil, Panbroil, Panfry

SIDE

Spareribs
Roast, Broil, Cook in Liquid, Braise

Sliced Bacon
Panfry, Broil, Roast (Bake)

OTHER CUTS

Cubed Steak
Braise, Panbroil, Panfry

Pork Pieces
Braise, Cook in Liquid

Cubes for Kabobs
Broil, Braise

Ground Pork
Broil, Panbroil, Panfry, Roast (Bake)

Sausage Links
Braise, Panfry, Roast

ROAST PORK

Select pork roast from those listed in Timetable for Roasting Pork. Season if desired.

Place pork, fat side up, on rack in shallow roasting pan. The rack keeps meat out of the drippings. (With a rib roast, the ribs form a natural rack.) It is not necessary to baste.

Insert meat thermometer so tip is in thickest part of pork and does not touch bone or rest in fat. Do not add water. Do not cover. Roast in 325° oven. (It is not necessary to preheat oven.) Roast to 5° below desired degree of doneness (see timetable), using the thermometer reading as final guide.

Cover roast with aluminum foil tent and let stand 15 to 20 minutes before carving. Temperature will rise about 5° and roast will be easier to carve.

TIMETABLE FOR ROASTING PORK
(Oven Temperature 325°)

Cut	Approximate Weight (pounds)	Meat Thermometer Reading	Approximate Cooking Time (minutes per pound)
Loin			
Center (bone-in)	*3 to 5*	*160°*	*20 to 25*
		170°	*26 to 31*
Boneless rib end— chef's prime	*2 to 4*	*160°*	*26 to 31*
		170°	*28 to 33*
Top (double)	*3 to 4*	*160°*	*29 to 34*
		170°	*33 to 38*
Top	*2 to 4*	*160°*	*23 to 33*
		170°	*30 to 40*
Tenderloin*	*½ to 1*	*160°*	*27 to 29*
		170°	*30 to 32*

*Roast at 425°.
Note: Smaller roasts require more minutes per pound than larger roasts.

PORK

*I*n the War of 1812, Uncle Sam Wilson, a meat packer, shipped hundreds of barrels of pork to American troops. Each was stamped with "U.S." It soon made the rounds that the initials stood for "Uncle Sam" whose pork shipment seemed to be enough to feed the entire army. Soon the expression "Uncle Sam" came to mean the government.

Pork played a role in the naming of Wall Street, too. When settlers first came to the then-rural island of Manhattan, they had to erect a wall to stop the forays of semiwild pigs. They built the wall on the northern edge of lower Manhattan for protection from the pigs, and the street that ran alongside it was called Wall Street.

Carving a Pork Loin Roast

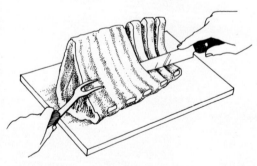

Place roast on carving board or platter; remove backbone from ribs for easy carving. Place roast with the rib side toward carver. With fork inserted in roast, cut slices on each side of rib bones. (Every other slice will contain a bone)

Apricot-Pistachio Rolled Pork, Duchess Potatoes (page 394)

APRICOT-PISTACHIO ROLLED PORK

Impressive for a dinner party with its unusual combination of flavors and crunchy topping.

4-pound pork boneless top loin roast
  (single uncut roast)
½ cup chopped dried apricots
½ cup chopped pistachio nuts
2 cloves garlic, finely chopped
¼ teaspoon salt
¼ teaspoon pepper
¼ cup apricot brandy
¼ cup apricot preserves
Crunchy Topping (right)

To cut pork roast into a large rectangle that can be filled and rolled, cut lengthwise about ½ inch from top of pork to within ½ inch of opposite edge; open flat. Repeat with other side of pork, cutting from the inside edge to the outer edge; open flat to form rectangle. Sprinkle apricots, pistachios, garlic, salt and pepper over pork to within 1 inch of edge. Beginning with short side, tightly roll up pork. Secure with wooden picks or tie with string. Pierce pork all over with metal skewer. Brush entire surface with brandy. Let stand 15 minutes. Brush again with brandy. Cover and refrigerate at least 2 hours.

Heat oven to 325°. Place pork, fat side up, on rack in shallow roasting pan. Roast uncovered 1½ hours. Brush preserves over pork. Sprinkle with Crunchy Topping. Roast 30 to 60 minutes longer or until meat thermometer registers 160°. 12 SERVINGS; 395 CALORIES PER SERVING.

Crunchy Topping

1 tablespoon margarine or butter
¼ cup coarsely crushed cracker crumbs
2 tablespoons chopped pistachio nuts
¼ teaspoon garlic salt

Heat margarine in 2-quart saucepan over medium heat until melted. Stir in remaining ingredients. Cook and stir 1 minute; cool.

Cut lengthwise about ½ inch from top of pork to within ½ inch of opposite edge; open flat. Repeat with other side of pork, cutting loose from inside edge; open flat to form rectangle.

TENDERLOIN WITH BLACK BEAN–TOMATO RELISH

1 tablespoon vegetable oil
1 clove garlic, crushed
1-pound pork tenderloin
1 tablespoon chopped fresh or 1 teaspoon dried oregano leaves
1 medium tomato, finely chopped (about 1 cup)
¼ cup thinly sliced green onions
1 teaspoon chopped fresh or ½ teaspoon dried oregano leaves
½ teaspoon ground cumin
¼ teaspoon salt
¼ teaspoon pepper
1 can (16 ounces) black beans, rinsed and drained

Heat oven to 325°. Mix oil and garlic. Brush over pork tenderloin. Sprinkle with 1 tablespoon oregano.

Place in shallow roasting pan. Insert meat thermometer horizontally so tip is in center of thickest part of pork. Roast uncovered about 45 minutes or until thermometer registers 170°. Remove pork; keep warm.

Heat remaining ingredients over medium heat, stirring occasionally, until hot. Cut pork diagonally into ¼-inch slices. Serve with relish.   4 SERVINGS; 200 CALORIES PER SERVING.

BROILED OR GRILLED PORK

Slash outer edge of fat on pork diagonally at 1-inch intervals to prevent curling (do not cut into pork). Set oven control to broil. Place pork on rack in broiler pan. broil with top at recommended distance from heat about half the time or until brown (see Timetable for Broiling Pork). Pork should be about half done. (Grill pork 4 to 5 inches from low to moderate heat).

Season brown side if desired. Turn pork; broil until brown. Season if desired.

TIMETABLE FOR BROILING PORK
(About 4 Inches from Heat)

Cut	Approximate Thickness or Weight	Meat Thermometer Reading	Total Cooking Time (minutes)
Loin or rib chop (bone-in)	¾ inch	160°	8 to 11
		170°	11 to 14
	1½ inches	160°	19 to 22
		170°	23 to 25
Boneless loin chop– America's cut	1 inch	160°	11 to 13
		170°	13 to 15
	1½ inches	160°	16 to 18
		170°	18 to 20
Blade chop (bone-in)	¾ inch	170°	13 to 15
	1½ inches	170°	26 to 29
Shoulder chop (bone-in)	¾ inch	170°	16 to 18
	1 inch	170°	18 to 20
Pork cube kabobs loin or leg	1 inch	160°	9 to 11
		170°	11 to 13
Tenderloin	1 inch	160°	12 to 14
		170°	16 to 18
	½ to 1 pound	160°	16 to 21
		170°	20 to 25
Country-style ribs*	1-inch slices	tender	45 to 60
Spareribs*		tender	45 to 60
Backribs*		tender	45 to 55

*Broil 5 inches from heat.

TANGY HAZELNUT PORK CHOPS

6 pork rib, loin or shoulder chops, about ¾ inch thick (about 2 pounds)
2 tablespoons Dijon mustard
2 tablespoons mayonnaise or salad dressing
1 tablespoon vegetable oil
½ cup hazelnuts or pecans
1 slice white or whole wheat bread, torn into pieces
4 sprigs fresh parsley or 1 tablespoon parsley flakes
½ teaspoon salt

Slash outer edge of fat on pork chops diagonally at 1-inch intervals to prevent curling (do not cut into pork). Mix mustard, mayonnaise and oil. Place remaining ingredients in blender or food processor. Cover and blend, or process, using quick on- and -off motions, until nuts are finely chopped.

Set oven control to broil. Spread mustard mixture over pork. Coat evenly with nut mixture. Place pork on rack in broiler pan. Broil pork with tops about 6 inches from heat about 10 minutes or until brown; turn. Broil 10 to 15 minutes longer or until pork is no longer pink in center.   6 SERVINGS; 350 CALORIES PER SERVING.

LEMON PORK CHOPS

We used to call this Pork Chops Supreme and it still is a favorite in the Betty Crocker Dining Room. We like to serve it with broccoli, hot Corn Muffins (page 39) and Strawberry Shortcakes (page 143).

4 pork loin or rib chops, about ¾ inch thick
Salt
4 thin onion slices
4 thin lemon slices
4 tablespoons packed brown sugar
4 tablespoons ketchup

Heat oven to 350°. Sprinkle both sides of pork chops with salt. Place pork in ungreased shallow baking pan or dish. Top each with onion slice, lemon slice, 1 tablespoon brown sugar and 1 tablespoon ketchup. Cover and bake 30 minutes. Uncover and bake about 30 minutes longer, spooning sauce onto pork occasionally, until done.   4 SERVINGS; 410 CALORIES PER SERVING.

PANBROILING PORK

Place pork in heated heavy skillet or nonstick skillet. Do not cover. Do not add water. Cook over medium heat, turning once, until desired doneness (see Timetable for Panbroiling Pork). Remove drippings as they accumulate. Season pork if desired.

TIMETABLE FOR PANBROILING PORK
(Medium Heat)

Cut	Approximate Thickness (inches)	Total Cooking Time (minutes)
Loin or rib chop (bone-in)	½	7 to 8
		9 to 10
	1	12 to 14
		15 to 17
Boneless loin chop	½	7 to 8
		9 to 10
	1	10 to 12
		12 to 14
Ground pork patties	½	7 to 9

PANFRYING PORK

Heat small amount vegetable oil in large skillet over medium heat. Add pork and cook uncovered, turning occasionally, until done (see Timetable for Panfrying Pork). Season if desired.

TIMETABLE FOR PANFRYING PORK
(Medium Heat)

Cut	Approximate Thickness (inches)	Total Cooking Time (minutes)
Loin or rib chop (bone-in)	¼	4
	½	5 to 6
		7 to 8
Boneless loin chop	¼	
	½	5 to 6
		7 to 8
Tenderloin	¼	3 to 4
	½	4 to 5

⏱ SESAME PORK WITH GARLIC CREAM SAUCE

Cream cheese is the key to this quick sauce.

1½ pounds pork tenderloin
2 tablespoons vegetable oil
¼ cup sesame seed
1 tablespoon margarine or butter
2 cloves garlic, finely chopped
1 package (3 ounces) cream cheese, cut into cubes
⅓ cup milk
1 tablespoon chopped fresh or 1 teaspoon freeze-dried chives

Cut pork tenderloin crosswise into 12 slices. Flatten slices to ½-inch thickness. Set oven control to broil. Brush pork with oil. Place pork on rack in broiler pan. Sprinkle with half of the sesame seed. Broil pork with tops 3 to 5 inches from heat 6 minutes; turn. Sprinkle with remaining sesame seed. Broil about 5 minutes or until pork is no longer pink in center.

Heat margarine in 10-inch skillet over medium heat. Cook garlic in margarine about 2 minutes, stirring occasionally; reduce heat. Add cream cheese and milk. Cook, stirring constantly, until smooth and hot. Stir in chives. Serve with pork.   6 SERVINGS; 240 CALORIES PER SERVING.

To Grill: After brushing pork with oil, coat with sesame seed. Cover and grill 5 to 6 inches from medium coals 12 to 15 minutes, turning once, until pork is no longer pink in center. Continue as directed.

⏱ PORK AND SQUASH KABOBS

¾-pound pork boneless top loin or tenderloin
⅔ cup apple butter
3 tablespoons vinegar
1 clove garlic, finely chopped
1½ teaspoons chopped fresh or ½ teaspoon dried rosemary leaves, crushed
2 medium onions, cut into eighths
3 small (2½ to 3 inches) pattypan squash, cut into fourths, or 12 one-inch pieces Hubbard squash

Trim excess fat from pork loin. Cut pork into 1½-inch cubes. Mix apple butter, vinegar, garlic and rosemary in glass or plastic bowl. Stir in pork, coating evenly. Cover and refrigerate at least 6 hours. Remove pork from marinade; reserve marinade.

Set oven control to broil. Thread pork alternately with onions and squash on four 11-inch metal skewers, leaving space between each piece. Brush kabobs with reserved marinade. Broil with tops about 3 inches from heat 5 minutes; turn. Brush with marinade. Broil about 5 minutes longer or until pork is no longer pink in center.   4 SERVINGS; 275 CALORIES PER SERVING.

To Grill: Cover and grill kabobs 5 to 6 inches from medium coals 20 to 25 minutes, turning and brushing every 5 minutes with reserved marinade, until pork is no longer pink in center.

PORK AND BROCCOLI RISOTTO

1-pound pork boneless loin or leg
2 teaspoons vegetable oil
3 cups broccoli flowerets
1 medium red bell pepper, chopped (about 1 cup)
2 cloves garlic, finely chopped
1 teaspoon salt
1 tablespoon margarine or butter
1 medium onion, chopped (about ½ cup)
1 cup uncooked regular long grain rice
¼ cup dry white wine
1 cup beef broth
1¼ cups water
¼ cup milk
2 tablespoons grated Parmesan cheese

Trim fat from pork loin. Cut pork into slices, 2 × 1 × ¼ inch. (For ease in cutting, partially freeze pork about 1 hour.) Heat oil in 10-inch skillet over medium-high heat. Sauté pork, broccoli, bell pepper, garlic and salt in oil about 4 minutes or until pork is no longer pink and vegetables are crisp-tender. Remove from skillet; keep warm.

Heat margarine in same skillet over medium heat. Cook onion about 3 minutes. Stir in rice and wine. Cook and stir about 30 seconds or until wine is absorbed. Stir in broth and water. Heat to boiling; reduce heat. Cover and simmer about 15 minutes, stirring occasionally, or until rice is almost tender and mixture is creamy. Stir in milk and pork mixture; heat until hot. Sprinkle with Parmesan cheese.   6 SERVINGS (ABOUT ¾ CUP EACH); 230 CALORIES PER SERVING.

Pork and Broccoli Risotto

SICHUAN PORK

1-pound pork boneless loin or leg
1 tablespoon soy sauce
2 teaspoons cornstarch
½ teaspoon ground red pepper (cayenne)
1 clove garlic, finely chopped
2 tablespoons vegetable oil
3 cups broccoli flowerets or 1 package (16 ounces) frozen broccoli cuts, thawed
2 small onions, cut into eighths
1 can (8 ounces) whole water chestnuts, drained
¼ cup chicken broth
½ cup peanuts
2 cups hot cooked rice (page 267)

Trim fat from pork loin. Cut pork into slices, 2 × 1 × ⅛ inch. Toss pork, soy sauce, cornstarch, red pepper and garlic in glass or plastic bowl. Cover and refrigerate 20 minutes.

Heat wok or 12-inch skillet over high heat until 1 or 2 drops of water bubble and skitter when sprinkled in wok. Add oil and rotate wok to coat side. Add pork. Stir-fry until no longer pink. Add broccoli, onions and water chestnuts. Stir-fry 2 minutes. Stir in broth; heat to boiling. Stir in peanuts. Serve with rice.   4 SERVINGS; 660 CALORIES PER SERVING.

To Microwave: Increase cornstarch to 1 tablespoon. Omit oil. Toss pork, soy sauce, cornstarch, red pepper and garlic in 3-quart microwavable casserole. Cover tightly and refrigerate 20 minutes. Microwave tightly covered on high 9 to 10 minutes, stirring after 4 minutes, until pork is no longer pink. Stir in broccoli, onions, water chestnuts and broth. Cover tightly and microwave 6 to 7 minutes, stirring after 3 minutes, until broccoli is crisp-tender. Stir in peanuts. Serve with rice.

SWEET-AND-SOUR PORK

One of our most favorite dishes. We like to serve it with the oven method hot cooked rice (page 267).

2 pounds pork boneless top loin
Vegetable oil
½ cup all-purpose flour
¼ cup cornstarch
½ cup cold water
½ teaspoon salt
1 egg
1 can (20 ounces) pineapple chunks in syrup, drained and syrup reserved
½ cup packed brown sugar
½ cup vinegar
½ teaspoon salt
2 teaspoons soy sauce
2 carrots, diagonally cut into thin slices
1 clove garlic, finely chopped
2 tablespoons cornstarch
2 tablespoons cold water
1 green bell pepper, cut into ¾-inch pieces
4 cups hot cooked rice (page 267)

Trim excess fat from pork loin. Cut pork into ¾-inch pieces. Heat oil (1 inch) in deep fryer or Dutch oven to 360°. Beat flour, ¼ cup cornstarch, ½ cup cold water, ½ teaspoon salt and the egg with hand beater until smooth. Stir pork into batter until well coated. Add pork pieces, one at a time, to oil. Fry about 20 pieces at a time about 5 minutes, turning 2 or 3 times, until golden brown. Drain on paper towels; keep warm.

Add enough water to reserved pineapple syrup to measure 1 cup. Heat syrup mixture, brown sugar, vinegar, ½ teaspoon salt, the soy sauce, carrots and garlic to boiling in Dutch oven; reduce heat. Cover and simmer about 6 minutes or until carrots are crisp-tender. Mix 2 tablespoons cornstarch and 2 tablespoons cold water; stir into sauce. Add pork, pineapple and bell pepper. Heat to boiling, stirring constantly. Boil and stir 1 minute. Serve with rice.   8 SERVINGS; 645 CALORIES PER SERVING.

⏱ GINGERED PORK WITH PEACHES

1-pound pork tenderloin
1 tablespoon vegetable oil
2 tablespoons soy sauce
2 teaspoons finely chopped gingerroot or
1 teaspoon ground ginger
2 teaspoons cornstarch
⅛ teaspoon pepper
2 cloves garlic, finely chopped
2 tablespoons vegetable oil
½ cup slivered almonds
½ cup chicken broth
3 medium peaches, pared and sliced*
6 green onions (with tops), cut into 1-inch pieces
3 cups hot cooked rice (page 267)

Trim fat from pork tenderloin. Cut pork with grain into 2-inch strips. Cut strips across grain into ¼-inch slices. (For ease in cutting, partially freeze pork about 1½ hours.) Toss pork with 1 tablespoon oil, the soy sauce, gingerroot, cornstarch, pepper and garlic.

Heat 2 tablespoons oil in 10-inch skillet over medium-high heat until hot. Rotate skillet until oil covers bottom. Stir-fry pork and almonds 6 to 8 minutes or until pork is brown. Add chicken broth. Stir about 1 minute or until thickened. Add peaches and onions. Stir about 3 minutes or until peaches are hot. Serve over rice. 6 SERVINGS (ABOUT ¾ CUP EACH); 315 CALORIES PER SERVING.

*1 package (16 ounces) frozen sliced peaches, thawed and drained, can be substituted for the fresh peaches.

🖌 COUNTRY-STYLE RIBS

3 pounds pork country-style ribs
⅔ cup chili sauce
½ cup grape jelly
1 tablespoon dry red wine
1 teaspoon Dijon mustard

Heat oven to 325°. Cut pork ribs into serving pieces if necessary. Place ribs, meaty sides up, in ungreased rectangular pan, 13 × 9 × 2 inches. Cover and bake about 2 hours or until tender; drain.

Heat remaining ingredients, stirring occasionally, until jelly is melted. Pour over ribs. Bake uncovered about 30 minutes, spooning sauce over ribs occasionally, until ribs are hot. Serve sauce over ribs. 6 SERVINGS; 455 CALORIES PER SERVING.

BRAISING PORK

Cook pork over medium heat in heavy skillet until brown; drain. Season if desired. Pour small amount (¼ to ½ cup) liquid (water; broth; apple, pineapple or vegetable juice) over pork. Cover and cook over low heat on top of range or bake in 325° oven until tender (see Timetable for Braising Pork). Add vegetables near end of cooking if desired. Cooking liquid can be thickened or reduced to make a sauce.

TIMETABLE FOR BRAISING PORK

Cut	Approximate Thickness or Weight	Approximate Total Cooking Time
Loin or rib chop (bone-in)	¾ inch	30 minutes
Boneless loin chop	1½ inches	45 minutes
Spareribs		1½ hours
Country-style ribs		1½ to 2 hours
TENDERLOIN Whole	½ to 1 pound	40 to 45 minutes
Slices	½ inch	25 minutes
Shoulder steaks	¾ inch	40 to 50 minutes
Cubes	1 to 1¼ inches	45 to 60 minutes
Blade boston (boneless)	2½ to 3½ pounds	2 to 2½ hours

🖌 MUSTARD SPARERIBS

4½ pounds fresh pork spareribs, cut into serving pieces
Mustard Sauce (below)

Heat oven to 325°. Place pork spareribs, meaty sides up, on rack in shallow roasting pan. Roast uncovered 1 hour. Brush spareribs with Mustard Sauce. Roast about 45 minutes longer, turning and brushing spareribs frequently with sauce, until done. 6 SERVINGS; 605 CALORIES PER SERVING.

Mustard Sauce

½ cup molasses
⅓ cup Dijon mustard
⅓ cup cider vinegar

Mix molasses and mustard. Stir in vinegar.

Clockwise from top: *Mustard Spareribs, Country-style Ribs, Plum-barbecued Spareribs (page 242), Coleslaw (page 313), Corn Muffins (page 39)*

PLUM-BARBECUED SPARERIBS

Great at picnics! Have plenty of Coleslaw (page 313), Corn Bread (page 39) and napkins on hand!

> 4 pounds fresh pork spareribs, cut into serving pieces
> 1 tablespoon salt
> 1 can (16 ounces) whole purple plums, drained and syrup reserved
> 1 tablespoon packed brown sugar
> 3 tablespoons chopped onion
> 2 teaspoons soy sauce
> ¼ teaspoon grated lemon peel
> ¼ teaspoon ground cinnamon
> Dash of ground cloves
> Dash of ground nutmeg
> 3 drops red food color

Place pork spareribs in Dutch oven. Add enough water to cover spareribs (about 3 quarts) and the salt. Heat to boiling; reduce heat. Cover and simmer 40 minutes; drain.

While spareribs are simmering, remove pits from plums. Sieve plums into 2-quart saucepan. Stir in reserved plum syrup and remaining ingredients. Heat to boiling, stirring, constantly. Boil 3 minutes, stirring constantly.

Heat oven to 375°. Place spareribs, meaty sides up, on rack in shallow roasting pan. Spread with ⅔ cup of the plum mixture. Bake uncovered about 45 minutes, brushing with remaining plum mixture 3 times, until spareribs are tender. 4 SERVINGS; 825 CALORIES PER SERVING.

FILLED PORK ROLL

> Sauerkraut-Apple Filling or Cranberry-Squash Filling (right)
> 1 pound ground pork
> ½ pound ground beef
> 2 slices rye or white bread, torn into pieces*
> 1 teaspoon pumpkin pie spice
> ¼ teaspoon pepper
> 1 egg
> ½ cup milk
> 1 small onion, chopped (about ¼ cup)

Heat oven to 325°. Prepare filling of your choice. Mix remaining ingredients thoroughly. Shape mixture into rectangle, 16 × 10 inches, on waxed paper. Spread filling over pork mixture to within 1 inch of edges. Press filling into pork mixture with back of spoon. Roll up, beginning at narrow end, using waxed paper to help roll. Pat ends to seal. Cut roll crosswise in half. Pat cut ends to seal. Place rolls side by side and seam sides down about 3 inches apart on rack in broiler pan. Bake about 1½ hours or until done. 6 SERVINGS; 325 CALORIES PER SERVING.

*⅓ cup dry bread crumbs or ½ cup quick-cooking oats can be substituted for the 2 slices bread.

Sauerkraut-Apple Filling

> 1 can (8 ounces) sauerkraut, drained
> 1 medium apple, chopped (about 1 cup)
> ¼ cup mashed potato mix (dry)
> 2 teaspoons caraway seed

Mix all ingredients.

Cranberry-Squash Filling

> 1 cup whole berry cranberry sauce
> 1 cup chopped pared Hubbard or butternut squash
> 2 tablespoons mashed potato mix (dry)

Mix all ingredients.

To Microwave: Prepare as directed—except place rolls side by side and seam sides down on microwavable rack in microwavable baking dish. Cover loosely and microwave on medium-high (70%) 24 to 28 minutes, rotating dish ½ turn after 10 minutes, until no longer pink in center. Let stand covered 5 minutes.

BAKED HAM

Select ham from those listed in Timetable for Roasting Ham. Place ham, fat side up, on rack in shallow roasting pan. The rack keeps ham out of the drippings. It is not necessary to baste.

Insert meat thermometer so tip is in thickest part of ham and does not touch bone or rest in fat. Do not add water. Do not cover.

Roast in 325° oven. (It is not necessary to preheat oven.) Roast to 135° on meat thermometer (see timetable), using the thermometer reading as final guide.

Ham is easier to carve if allowed to set 10 minutes, covered, until thermometer registers 140°.

GLAZES FOR HAM

For a glazed ham, remove ham 30 minutes before it is done. Pour drippings from pan. Remove any skin from ham. Cut fat surface of ham lightly in uniform diamond shape; insert whole clove in each if desired. Pat or brush on your choice of the following glazes (enough for 4-pound ham). Bake 30 minutes longer.

Brown Sugar Glaze

1 cup packed brown sugar
½ teaspoon dry mustard
1 tablespoon vinegar

Mix all ingredients.

Pineapple Glaze

1 cup packed brown sugar
1 tablespoon cornstarch
¼ teaspoon salt
1 can (8½ ounces) crushed pineapple in syrup, undrained
2 tablespoons lemon juice
1 tablespoon prepared mustard

Mix brown sugar, cornstarch and salt in 1-quart saucepan. Stir in pineapple, lemon juice and mustard. Cook over medium heat, stirring constantly, until mixture thickens and boils. Boil and stir 1 minute.

BROILED OR GRILLED HAM

Slash outer edge of fat on ham diagonally at 1-inch intervals to prevent curling (do not cut into ham). Set oven control to broil. Place ham on rack in broiler pan. Broil with top 4 to 5 inches from heat about half the time or until brown (see Timetable for Broiling Ham). Ham should be about half done. Grill ham 4 to 5 inches from low to moderate heat.

Season brown side if desired. Turn ham; broil until brown. Season if desired.

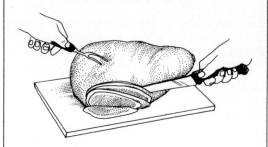

Carving a Whole Ham

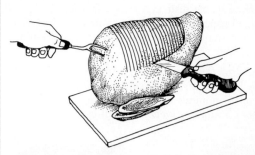

Place ham on carving board or platter with fat side up and shank facing right (or facing left if carver is left-handed.) Cut a few slices from the thin side. Turn ham over so that it rests firmly on the cut side.

Make slices down to bone. Run knife horizontally along bone to release slices.

TIMETABLE FOR ROASTING HAM

(Oven Temperature 325°)

Smoked Cut	Approximate Weight (pounds)	Approximate Cooking Time (minutes per pound)
Ham (fully cooked)		
Boneless		
Whole	8 to 10	15 to 18
Half	5 to 6	18 to 25
Portion	3 to 4	27 to 33
Bone-in		
Whole	10 to 12	15 to 18
Half	7 to 8	18 to 25
Portion	1½ to 3	

TIMETABLE FOR BROILING HAM

Fully Cooked Smoked Cut	Approximate Thickness	Approximate Total Cooking Time (minutes)
Ham Slice	¼ inch	7 to 8
	½ inch	8 to 10
	1 inch	14 to 16
Ham Kabobs 1- to 1½-inch cubes		7 to 8

COOKED SMOKED HAM SLICE

Slash outer edge of fat of fully cooked smoked ham slice (about 1 inch thick) diagonally at 1-inch intervals to prevent curling. Do not cut into ham. 190 CALORIES PER 3-OUNCE SERVING.

To Bake: Heat oven to 325°. Place ham slice in ungreased baking dish. Bake uncovered about 30 minutes or until hot.

To Broil: Set oven control to broil. Broil ham slice with top about 3 inches from heat about 10 minutes or until light brown; turn. Broil about 6 minutes longer or until light brown. Brush with 3 tablespoons jelly or mustard, slightly beaten, during last 2 minutes of broiling if desired.

To Microwave: Place ham slice in rectangular microwavable dish 11 × 7½ × 2 inches. Cover with waxed paper and microwave on medium-high (70%) 8 to 10 minutes, turning ham over after 4 minutes, until hot.

To Panfry: Rub skillet with small piece of fat cut from ham slice. Cook ham over medium heat about 3 minutes or until light brown; turn. Cook about 3 minutes longer or until light brown.

Dijon-Ham Braid

HAM AND SCALLOPED POTATOES

Scalloped Potatoes (page 394)
1½ cups cubed or ½ pound sliced fully cooked smoked ham

Prepare Scalloped Potatoes as directed—except top each of the first 2 layers with half of the ham and half of the onion.   6 SERVINGS; 300 CALORIES PER SERVING.

To Microwave: Prepare Scalloped Potatoes as directed—except place 3 tablespoons margarine or butter, the flour, salt and pepper in 4-cup microwavable measure. Microwave on high 2 minutes, stirring after 1 minute, until very bubbly. Gradually stir in milk. Microwave 5 to 6 minutes, stirring with fork or wire whisk every 2 minutes, until thickened.

Mix potatoes, onion, ham and sauce in 3-quart microwavable casserole. Omit 1 tablespoon margarine. Cover tightly and microwave on medium-high (70%) 21 to 25 minutes, stirring every 6 minutes, until potatoes are tender. Let stand covered 5 minutes.

DIJON-HAM BRAID

½ package (17½-ounce size) frozen puff pastry, thawed (1 sheet)
1 package (3 ounces) cream cheese, cut into cubes
1 tablespoon milk
1 tablespoon Dijon mustard
2 cups chopped fully cooked smoked ham
1 cup frozen green peas
1 egg yolk
1 tablespoon cold water
½ teaspoon poppy seed

Heat oven to 400°. Roll pastry into rectangle, 15 × 10 inches, on lightly floured surface. Place on ungreased cookie sheet. Make 2-inch cuts at 1-inch intervals on long sides of rectangle. Heat cream cheese, milk and mustard in 2-quart saucepan over medium heat, stirring constantly, until smooth. Stir in ham and peas. Spoon ham mixture down center 4 inches of rectangle. Lift pastry over filling, crisscrossing strips over top. Beat egg yolk and cold water; brush over braid. Sprinkle with poppy seed. Bake about 25 minutes or until pastry is puffed and deep golden brown.   6 SERVINGS; 325 CALORIES PER SERVING.

DIJON-CHICKEN BRAID: Substitute 2 cups cut-up cooked chicken for the ham. Stir 1 small onion, chopped (about ¼ cup) and ¼ teaspoon salt into cream cheese mixture.   330 CALORIES PER SERVING.

🌾 HAM LOAF WITH RED CURRANT SAUCE

Red Currant Sauce is a sweet, unusual accompaniment for traditional Ham Loaf, and so easy to make.

1 pound ground ham
¾ pound ground pork
1 cup soft bread crumbs
1 medium onion, chopped (about ½ cup)
1 egg
½ cup milk
Red Currant Sauce (below)

Heat oven to 350°. Mix all ingredients except Red Currant Sauce. Shape mixture into loaf in ungreased rectangular pan, 13 × 9 × 2 inches. Bake 1 to 1¼ hours or until done; remove from pan. Spoon Red Currant Sauce over ham loaf. Serve with any remaining sauce.   8 SERVINGS; 320 CALORIES PER SERVING.

Red Currant Sauce

½ cup red currant jelly
1½ teaspoons grated orange peel
2 tablespoons orange juice
1 tablespoon prepared horseradish

Heat all ingredients, stirring occasionally, until jelly is melted and mixture is smooth.

HAM-AND-BRIE—STUFFED APPLES

We like the mild, sweet taste of Golden Delicious apples to complement the ham and Brie.

4 large apples (about 2 pounds)
1 tablespoon margarine or butter
2 cups diced fully cooked smoked ham
1 cup soft bread crumbs
1 tablespoon chopped fresh chives
¼ teaspoon ground nutmeg
4 ounces Brie or Swiss cheese, thinly sliced
  or shredded
¾ cup dry white wine or apple juice

Cut apples lengthwise in half. Core each and remove pulp, leaving ¼-inch shell. Chop apple pulp; reserve.

Heat margarine over medium-high heat in 3-quart saucepan until melted. Stir in ham, reserved apple pulp, bread crumbs, chives and nutmeg. Cook and stir about 5 minutes until hot. Stir in cheese until melted.

Heat oven to 375°. Place apples, cut sides up, in ungreased rectangular baking dish, 11 × 7 × 1½ inches. Divide filling evenly among apples. Pour wine around apples. Bake uncovered 25 to 30 minutes or until filling is light brown and apples are tender when pierced with fork. Spoon wine in dish over apples several times during baking.   4 SERVINGS; 415 CALORIES PER SERVING.

⏱ SAUSAGE (UNCOOKED, SMOKED OR FRESH)

Fresh sausage should be thoroughly cooked at low to moderate temperatures. It is ready to eat when the center is no longer pink, but turns gray (180° on meat thermometer).   90 CALORIES PER 1-OUNCE LINK OR 210 CALORIES PER 2-OUNCE PATTY.

To Bake: Heat oven to 400°. Arrange pork sausage links or patties in single layer in shallow baking pan. Bake 20 to 30 minutes, turning sausages to brown evenly, until well done. Spoon off drippings as they accumulate.

To Braise and Brown: Place pork sausage links or patties in cold skillet. Add 2 to 4 tablespoons water. Heat to boiling; reduce heat. Cover and simmer 5 to 8 minutes (depending on size or thickness) until done. Uncover and cook, turning sausages to brown evenly, until well done.

To Broil: Place pork sausage links or patties on rack of broiler pan or on grill 3 to 5 inches from heat. Broil until well done, turning to brown both sides.

Sausage in Corn Bread with Salsa–Sour Cream Sauce, Spicy Mexican Torte

SAUSAGE IN CORN BREAD WITH SALSA–SOUR CREAM SAUCE

1 pound pork sausage links
Corn Bread (page 39)
½ cup shredded process sharp American cheese (2 ounces)
3 medium green onions (with tops), chopped (about ¼ cup)
Salsa–Sour Cream Sauce (below)

Heat oven to 400°. Cook sausages in 10-inch ovenproof skillet as directed on package; drain. Prepare Corn Bread—except use skillet and stir in cheese and onions. Pour batter into skillet. Arrange sausages in spoke fashion on top. Bake about 20 minutes or until corn bread is golden brown. Serve in wedges with Salsa–Sour Cream Sauce.   6 TO 8 SERVINGS; 455 CALORIES PER SERVING.

Salsa–Sour Cream Sauce

2 cups prepared salsa
½ cup sour cream

Mix ingredients in 1-quart saucepan. Heat over medium heat until hot.

SPICY MEXICAN TORTE

½ pound chorizo sausage, casings removed
2 medium onions, chopped (about 1 cup)
2 cloves garlic, finely chopped
1 can (4 ounces) chopped green chilies, drained
8 ten-inch flour tortillas*
2 cups shredded Monterey Jack or hot pepper cheese (8 ounces)
1 can (16 ounces) refried beans
1 jar (7 ounces) roasted red peppers, drained

Cook sausage, onions and garlic in 10-inch skillet over medium heat, stirring occasionally, until sausage is done; drain. Stir in green chilies; set aside.

Heat oven to 400°. Grease pie plate, 10 × 1½ inches. Place 2 tortillas in pie plate. Spread half of the sausage mixture over tortillas. Sprinkle with half of the cheese. Place 2 tortillas on cheese. Spread with beans. Place 2 tortillas on beans and place peppers on tortillas. Place 2 tortillas on peppers. Spread with remaining sausage mixture. Sprinkle with remaining cheese. Cover and bake 40 minutes. Uncover and bake 15 minutes or until cheese is melted and center is hot. Cool 10 minutes before cutting. Serve with salsa, sour cream or Guacamole (page 20) if desired.   8 SERVINGS; 350 CALORIES PER SERVING.

Sixteen 6-inch corn tortillas can be substituted for the flour tortillas. Overlap 4 tortillas for each layer.

EASY CASSOULET

This dish thickens as it stands, and you can thin it with a little wine if you wish. It's an excellent company dish, using kitchen staples, and can be made quickly on short notice.

1 pound Polish or smoked sausage, diagonally sliced into 1-inch pieces
1 can (15½ ounces) great northern beans, drained
1 can (15 ounces) kidney beans, drained
1 can (15 ounces) black beans, drained
1 can (15 ounces) tomato sauce
3 medium carrots, thinly sliced
2 small onions, thinly sliced and separated into rings
2 tablespoons packed brown sugar
½ cup dry red wine or beef broth
2 tablespoons chopped fresh or 1½ teaspoons dried thyme leaves
2 cloves garlic, finely chopped

Heat oven to 375°. Mix all ingredients in ungreased 3-quart casserole. Cover and bake 50 to 60 minutes or until hot and bubbly and carrots are tender. 8 SERVINGS (ABOUT 1 CUP EACH); 260 CALORIES PER SERVING.

To Microwave: Place carrots and red wine in 3-quart microwavable casserole. Cover and microwave on high 5 minutes. Place sausage on carrots. Mix remaining ingredients. Pour over top. Cover tightly and microwave on high 18 to 22 minutes, stirring after 12 minutes, until hot and bubbly.

ITALIAN SAUSAGE LASAGNE

Our staff members—and families—love this lasagne!

1 pound bulk Italian sausage
1 medium onion, chopped (about ½ cup)
1 clove garlic, crushed
2 tablespoons chopped fresh parsley
1 teaspoon sugar
1 tablespoon chopped fresh or 1 teaspoon dried basil leaves
1 can (16 ounces) whole tomatoes, undrained
1 can (15 ounces) tomato sauce
12 uncooked lasagne noodles (about 12 ounces)
1 carton (16 ounces) ricotta or creamed cottage cheese (2 cups)
¼ cup grated Parmesan cheese
1 tablespoon chopped fresh parsley
1 tablespoon chopped fresh or 1½ teaspoons dried oregano leaves
2 cups shredded mozzarella cheese (8 ounces)
¼ cup grated Parmesan cheese

Cook sausage, onion and garlic in 10-inch skillet, stirring occasionally, until sausage is brown; drain. Stir in 2 tablespoons parsley, the sugar, basil, tomatoes and tomato sauce; break up tomatoes. Heat to boiling, stirring occasionally; reduce heat. Simmer uncovered about 45 minutes or until slightly thickened.

Heat oven to 350°. Cook noodles as directed on package; drain. Mix ricotta cheese, ¼ cup Parmesan cheese, 1 tablespoon parsley and the oregano. Spread 1 cup of the sauce mixture in ungreased rectangular baking dish, 13 × 9 × 2 inches. Top with 4 noodles. Spread 1 cup of the cheese mixture over noodles; spread with 1 cup of the sauce mixture. Sprinkle with ⅔ cup of the mozzarella cheese. Repeat with 4 noodles, the remaining cheese mixture, 1 cup of the sauce mixture and ⅔ cup of the mozzarella cheese. Top with remaining noodles and sauce mixture. Sprinkle with remaining mozzarella and ¼ cup Parmesan cheese. Cover and bake 30 minutes. Uncover and bake 15 minutes longer or until hot and bubbly. Let stand 15 minutes before cutting. 8 SERVINGS; 510 CALORIES PER SERVING.

GROUND BEEF LASAGNE: Substitute 1 pound ground beef for the Italian sausage. 460 CALORIES PER SERVING.

⏱ FRANKFURTERS AND COOKED SMOKED SAUSAGES

Frankfurters or other cooked smoked sausage links do not require cooking; they need only be heated to serving temperature (140°) if they are to be served hot. Do not pierce with fork.   145 CALORIES PER 1½-OUNCE FRANKFURTER OR 265 CALORIES PER 2½-OUNCE SMOKED SAUSAGE.

To Broil: Set oven control to broil. Brush frankfurters with margarine, butter or shortening. Broil with tops about 3 inches from heat, turning with tongs, until evenly brown.

To Microwave: Pierce frankfurters or sausages and place on paper towel–lined microwavable plate. Cover loosely and microwave on high as directed below.

	Amount	Time
Frankfurters	1	30 to 45 seconds
(10 per pound)	2	1 minute to 1 minute 15 seconds
	4	1 minute 15 seconds to 1 minute 30 seconds
Sausages	2	1 minute 30 seconds to 2 minutes 30 seconds, rearranging after 1 minute
(6 per pound)	4	3 to 4 minutes, rearranging after 2 minutes

To Panfry: Cook frankfurters in small amount of fat over medium heat, turning with tongs, until brown.

To Simmer: Drop frankfurters into boiling water; reduce heat. Cover and simmer 5 to 10 minutes (depending on size) until hot.

FRANKFURTERS

Although frankfurters originated in Frankfurt, Germany, we really think of them at the ballpark. One cold day in 1900 at New York City's Polo Grounds, then home of the New York Giants, a vendor named Harry Stevens couldn't sell his cold fare, and hit on the idea of selling piping hot frankfurters. He hawked them as "dachshund sausages," and when cartoonist Tad Dorgan drew a picture of a dachshund in a roll, "hot dogs" became standard baseball fare.

There is, we must admit, another version of the hot dog story. At the 1904 St. Louis World's Fair, Anton Feuchtwanger lent his customers gloves to hold hot sausages while they ate them. With a dismal return rate on gloves, he consulted with his brother-in-law, a baker, and they created the hot dog in a bun.

BACON

Directions below are for thin-sliced bacon. Thick-sliced bacon will require more time.   110 CALORIES PER 3 SLICES.

To Bake: Heat oven to 400°. Place separated slices of bacon on rack in broiler pan. Bake about 10 minutes, without turning, until brown.

To Broil: Set oven control to broil. Broil separated slices of bacon about 3 inches from heat about 2 minutes or until brown; turn. Broil 1 minute longer.

To Microwave: Place separated slices of bacon on microwavable rack in microwavable dish or on microwavable paper towel–lined dish. Cover with paper towel and microwave on high 45 to 60 seconds per slice. For bacon most similar to conventionally fried, cook in its own fat without using rack or paper towel under bacon.

To Panfry: Place separated slices of bacon in cold skillet. Cook over low heat 8 to 10 minutes, turning bacon to brown evenly on both sides.

BACON CURLS: Cut bacon slices in half. Roll up and secure with wooden picks. Set oven control to broil. Broil with tops 4 to 5 inches from heat 2 minutes; turn. Broil about 2 minutes longer or until crisp.

CANADIAN-STYLE BACON (FULLY COOKED)

To Bake: Heat oven to 325°. Place 2-pound piece Canadian-style bacon, fat side up, on rack in shallow baking pan. Insert meat thermometer so tip is in center of bacon. Bake uncovered 20 to 30 minutes or until thermometer registers 140°. 85 CALORIES PER 2-OUNCE SERVING.

ROAST LAMB

Select lamb roast from those listed in Timetable for Roasting Lamb. The fell (thin, paperlike covering on the outer fat) should not be removed from roasts and legs. It helps these cuts keep their shape and juiciness during cooking. Season if desired.

Place lamb, fat side up, on rack in shallow roasting pan. The rack keeps lamb out of the drippings.

Insert meat thermometer so tip is in thickest part of lamb and does not touch bone or rest in fat. Do not add water. Do not cover. Roast in 325° oven. (It is not necessary to preheat oven.) Roast to 5° below desired degree of doneness (see timetable), using the thermometer reading as final guide.

Cover roast with aluminum foil tent and let stand 15 to 20 minutes before carving. Temperature will rise about 5° and roast will be easier to carve.

To Broil: Set oven control to broil. Broil ¼-inch slices Canadian-style bacon with tops 2 to 3 inches from heat about 3 minutes or until brown; turn. Broil 3 minutes longer.

To Panfry: Place ⅛-inch slices Canadian-style bacon in cold skillet. Cook over low heat 8 to 10 minutes, turning bacon to brown evenly on both sides.

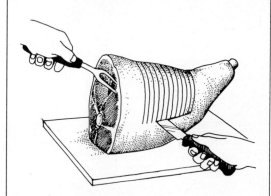

Carving a Leg of Lamb

Place roast on carving board or platter with the shank bone to carver's right (or to left if carver is left-handed.) Cut a few lengthwise slices from the thin side. Turn the leg over so that it rests firmly on the cut side. Make vertical slices to the leg bone, then cut horizontally along bone to release slices.

TIMETABLE FOR ROASTING LAMB
(Oven Temperature 325°)

Cut	Approximate Weight (pounds)	Meat Thermometer Reading	Approximate Cooking Time (minutes per pound)
Leg	7 to 9	140° (rare)	15 to 20
		160° (medium)	20 to 25
		170° (well)	25 to 30
Leg	5 to 7	140° (rare)	20 to 25
		160° (medium)	25 to 30
		170° (well)	30 to 35
Leg, boneless	4 to 7	140° (rare)	25 to 30
		160° (medium)	30 to 35
		170° (well)	35 to 40
Leg, shank half	3 to 4	140° (rare)	30 to 35
		160° (medium)	40 to 45
		170° (well)	45 to 50
Shoulder,* boneless	3½ to 5	140° (rare)	30 to 35
		160° (medium)	35 to 40
		170° (well)	40 to 45

*For presliced, bone-in shoulder, add 5 minutes per pound to times recommended for boneless shoulder.

Lamb

• RETAIL CUTS •
WHERE THEY COME FROM
HOW TO COOK THEM

LEG · LOIN
RIB
SHOULDER · FORESHANK & BREAST

LEG

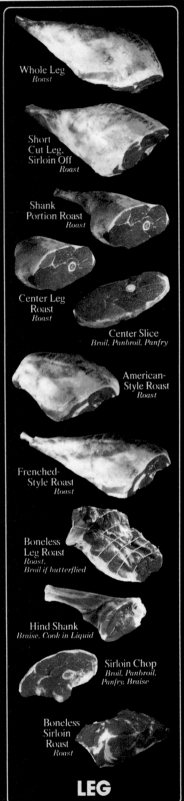

Whole Leg
Roast

Short Cut Leg, Sirloin Off
Roast

Shank Portion Roast
Roast

Center Leg Roast
Roast

Center Slice
Broil, Panbroil, Panfry

American-Style Roast
Roast

Frenched-Style Roast
Roast

Boneless Leg Roast
Roast, Broil if butterflied

Hind Shank
Braise, Cook in Liquid

Sirloin Chop
Broil, Panbroil, Panfry, Braise

Boneless Sirloin Roast
Roast

LOIN

Loin Roast
Roast

Loin Chop
Broil, Panbroil, Panfry

Double Loin Chop
Broil, Panbroil, Panfry

FORESHANK & BREAST

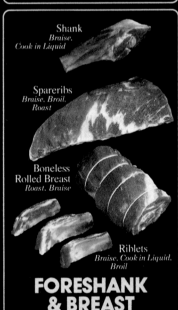

Shank
Braise, Cook in Liquid

Spareribs
Braise, Broil, Roast

Boneless Rolled Breast
Roast, Braise

Riblets
Braise, Cook in Liquid, Broil

RIB

Rib Roast
Roast

Rib Chop
Broil, Panbroil, Panfry, Roast

Frenched Rib Chop
Broil, Panbroil, Panfry

Crown Roast
Roast

SHOULDER

Square-Cut Shoulder, Whole
Roast, Braise

Pre-Sliced Shoulder
Roast, Braise

Boneless Shoulder Roast
Roast, Braise

Neck Slice
Braise, Cook in Liquid

Blade Chop
Braise, Broil, Panbroil, Panfry

Arm Chop
Braise, Broil, Panbroil, Panfry

OTHER CUTS

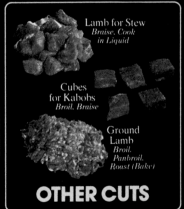

Lamb for Stew
Braise, Cook in Liquid

Cubes for Kabobs
Broil, Braise

Ground Lamb
Broil, Panbroil, Roast (Bake)

BROILED OR GRILLED LAMB

Slash outer edge of fat on lamb diagonally at 1-inch intervals to prevent curling (do not cut into lamb). Set oven control to broil. Place lamb on rack in broiler pan. Broil with top at recommended distance from heat about half the time or until brown (see Timetable for Broiling Lamb). Lamb should be about half done. (Grill lamb 4 to 5 inches from low to moderate heat.)

Season brown side if desired. Turn lamb; broil until brown. Season if desired.

TIMETABLE FOR BROILING LAMB

Cut	Approximate Thickness (inches)	Approximate Weight (ounces)	Inches from Heat	Approximate Total Cooking Time (minutes)
Shoulder chop	1	5 to 9	3 to 4	7 to 11
Rib chop	1	3 to 5	3 to 4	7 to 11
	1½	4½ to 7½	4 to 5	15 to 19
Loin chop	1	3 to 5	3 to 4	7 to 11
	1½	4½ to 7½	4 to 5	15 to 19
Sirloin chop	1	6 to 10	3 to 4	12 to 15
Cubes for kabobs	1 to 1½	——	4 to 5	8 to 12
Ground lamb patties	½ × 4	4	3	5 to 8

⏱ LAMB CHOPS WITH PINEAPPLE

The fresh-tasting combination of mint and pineapple complements lamb beautifully.

3 tablespoons orange juice
2 tablespoons honey
4 lamb loin chops, 1 inch thick (about 1 pound)
1½ cups cubed pineapple*
1 tablespoon chopped fresh or 1 teaspoon dried mint leaves

Set oven control to broil. Mix orange juice and honey; reserve 2 tablespoons. Place lamb chops on rack in broiler pan. Brush lamb with reserved orange mixture. Broil with tops about 5 inches from heat about 6 minutes or until brown; turn. Brush with reserved orange mixture. Broil 6 to 9 minutes or until desired doneness.

Heat remaining orange mixture, the pineapple and mint to boiling, stirring occasionally. Serve with lamb chops.   4 SERVINGS; 425 CALORIES PER SERVING.

1 can (20 ounces) pineapple chunks, drained, can be substituted for the fresh pineapple.

To Grill: Cover and grill lamb 5 to 6 inches from medium coals about 12 minutes, turning and brushing with orange mixture once, until desired doneness.

LAMB CHOPS WITH RASPBERRY-PORT SAUCE

¾ cup port wine or apple juice
2 tablespoons vegetable oil
2 cloves garlic, finely chopped
1 tablespoon chopped fresh or ½ teaspoon dried thyme leaves
½ teaspoon salt
⅛ teaspoon pepper
4 lamb loin chops, 1 inch thick (about 1 pound)
1 cup fresh or frozen raspberries

Mix all ingredients except lamb chops and raspberries in shallow glass or plastic dish or heavy plastic bag. Add lamb, turning to coat. Cover and refrigerate at least 2 hours but no longer than 24 hours, turning lamb occasionally. Remove lamb from marinade; reserve marinade.

Set oven control to broil. Broil lamb with tops about 5 inches from heat about 6 minutes or until brown; turn. Broil 6 to 9 minutes longer or until desired doneness.

Heat reserved marinade and raspberries to boiling in 10-inch skillet over medium heat, stirring occasionally. Cook about 10 minutes, stirring occasionally, until sauce is reduced to half. Serve with lamb.   4 SERVINGS; 415 CALORIES PER SERVING.

Shish Kabobs

🌾 SHISH KABOBS

1 pound lamb boneless shoulder
¼ cup lemon juice
2 tablespoons olive or vegetable oil
2 teaspoons salt
2 teaspoons chopped fresh or ½ teaspoon
   dried oregano leaves
¼ teaspoon pepper
1 green bell pepper, cut into 1-inch pieces
1 medium onion, cut into eighths
1 cup cubed eggplant

Trim excess fat from lamb shoulder. Cut lamb into 1-inch cubes. Place lamb in glass or plastic bowl. Mix lemon juice, oil, salt, oregano and pepper. Pour over lamb. Cover and refrigerate at least 6 hours, stirring occasionally. Remove lamb from marinade; reserve marinade.

Set oven control to 550°. Thread lamb on four 11-inch metal skewers, leaving space between each. Broil with tops about 3 inches from heat 5 minutes; turn. Brush with reserved marinade. Broil 5 minutes longer.

Alternate bell pepper, onion and eggplant on each of four 11-inch metal skewers, leaving space between each piece. Place vegetables on rack in broiler pan with lamb. Turn lamb. Brush lamb and vegetables with marinade. Broil kabobs 4 to 5 minutes, turning and brushing twice with marinade, until brown. 4 SERVINGS; 235 CALORIES PER SERVING.

ROSEMARY LAMB RAGOUT

Ragout is a French word, which means "to restore the appetite." This wonderful lamb stew will certainly please all appetites, from light to hearty.

2 pounds lamb boneless shoulder
2 tablespoons vegetable oil
2½ cups water
1 cup dry white wine or water
3 tablespoons tomato paste
3 teaspoons chicken bouillon granules
1 tablespoon chopped fresh or 1 teaspoon
   dried rosemary leaves, crushed
1 teaspoon chopped fresh or ½ teaspoon
   dried thyme leaves
¼ teaspoon pepper
2 cloves garlic, finely chopped
8 small red potatoes, cut in half
6 small onions, cut into fourths
3 medium carrots, cut into 1½-inch pieces
3 small turnips, cut into fourths
1 package (10 ounces) frozen green peas
¼ cup cold water
2 tablespoons all-purpose flour

Trim excess fat from lamb shoulder. Cut lamb into 1-inch cubes. Cook and stir lamb in oil in Dutch oven over medium-high heat about 20 minutes or until brown; drain. Add 2½ cups water, the wine, tomato paste, bouillon granules, rosemary, thyme, pepper and garlic. Heat to boiling; reduce heat. Cover and simmer about 45 minutes or until lamb is almost tender.

Stir in potatoes, onions, carrots and turnips. Cover and simmer about 20 minutes or until vegetables are almost tender. Stir in peas. Cover and simmer about 10 minutes longer or until vegetables are tender.

Shake ¼ cup water and the flour in tightly covered container. Gradually stir into ragout. Heat to boiling, stirring constantly. Boil and stir 1 minute. 6 SERVINGS (ABOUT 1¼ CUPS EACH); 555 CALORIES PER SERVING.

PORK RAGOUT: Substitute 2 pounds pork boneless loin for the lamb and beef bouillon granules for the chicken bouillon granules. Increase first simmering time to about 1 hour. 605 CALORIES PER SERVING.

GREEK LAMB AND ORZO

Orzo is a type of pasta that resembles rice. Try it in soups, too.

1 pound ground lamb
1 can (16 ounces) stewed tomatoes, undrained
1 stalk celery, cut into ½-inch pieces
½ cup orzo
½ teaspoon salt
¼ teaspoon ground red pepper (cayenne)
Plain yogurt

Cook and stir ground lamb in 10-inch skillet until lamb is light brown; drain. Stir in tomatoes, celery, orzo, salt and red pepper. Heat to boiling; reduce heat. Cover and simmer about 12 minutes, stirring frequently, until tomato liquid is absorbed and orzo is tender. Serve with yogurt. 4 SERVINGS; 285 CALORIES PER SERVING.

To Microwave: Crumble ground lamb into 2-quart microwavable casserole. Cover with waxed paper and microwave on high 5 to 6 minutes, stirring after 3 minutes, until no longer pink; drain. Stir in remaining ingredients except yogurt. Cover tightly and microwave 12 to 14 minutes, stirring every 4 minutes, until orzo is tender. Serve with yogurt.

GREEK BEEF AND ORZO: Substitute 1 pound ground beef for the lamb. 320 CALORIES PER SERVING.

ITALIAN LAMB SHANKS

1 cup Italian Dressing (page 327)
4 lamb shanks (each about 12 ounces)
½ cup grated Parmesan cheese
¼ cup all-purpose flour
2 tablespoons chopped fresh or 1 tablespoon parsley flakes
½ teaspoon salt
¼ teaspoon onion salt
⅓ cup shortening
Grated Parmesan cheese

Pour dressing over lamb shanks in shallow glass dish. Cover and refrigerate at least 5 hours, turning lamb occasionally. Remove lamb from marinade; reserve marinade.

Mix ½ cup cheese, the flour, parsley, salt and onion salt. Coat lamb with cheese mixture, reserving remaining cheese mixture. Heat shortening in 12-inch skillet or Dutch oven until melted. Cook lamb in hot shortening, turning occasionally, until brown; reduce heat. Sprinkle remaining cheese mixture over lamb. Stir in reserved marinade. Cover and simmer about 2½ hours, turning lamb occasionally, until tender. Serve with grated Parmesan cheese. 4 SERVINGS; 785 CALORIES PER SERVING.

ITALIAN CHICKEN: Substitute 2½-pound broiler-fryer chicken, cut up. for the lamb and decrease simmering time to 1 hour. 6 SERVINGS; 495 CALORIES PER SERVING.

VENISON SAUERBRATEN

3- to 3½-pound venison chuck roast
2 onions, sliced
2 bay leaves
12 peppercorns
12 juniper berries, if desired
6 whole cloves
2 teaspoons salt
1½ cups red wine vinegar
1 cup boiling water
2 tablespoons vegetable oil or shortening
12 gingersnap cookies, crushed (about ¾ cup)
2 teaspoons sugar

Place venison roast in glass baking dish. Add onions, bay leaves, peppercorns, juniper berries, cloves, salt, vinegar and boiling water. Cover and refrigerate at least 3 days, turning venison twice a day with tongs. (Never pierce venison with a fork.)

Drain venison, reserving marinade. Heat oil in 10-inch skillet. Cook venison on all sides in hot oil until brown. Stir in marinade. Heat to boiling; reduce heat. Cover and simmer 3 to 3½ hours or until venison is tender. Remove venison and onions from skillet; keep warm. Strain liquid in skillet. Add enough water to measure 2½ cups. Add to skillet. Heat to boiling; reduce heat. Cover and simmer 10 minutes. Stir gingersnap crumbs and sugar into liquid. Cover and simmer 3 minutes. Serve with venison and onions. 10 TO 12 SERVINGS; 500 CALORIES PER SERVING.

Rabbit Stewed in Stout

RABBIT STEWED IN STOUT

4 slices bacon
½ cup all-purpose flour
1 teaspoon salt
¼ teaspoon pepper
¼ teaspoon paprika
3- to 3½-pound rabbit, cut up
8 ounces mushrooms, cut in half
1 jar (16 ounces) whole onions, drained
2 teaspoons chopped fresh or ½ teaspoon
   dried thyme leaves
1 bay leaf
1 bottle (12 ounces) Irish stout or dark
   beer
1 tablespoon cornstarch
2 tablespoons cold water
Chopped fresh parsley

Cook bacon in Dutch oven until crisp. Remove bacon, reserving fat in Dutch oven. Mix flour, salt, pepper and paprika. Coat rabbit pieces with flour mixture. Heat bacon fat until hot. Cook rabbit over medium heat about 15 minutes or until brown on all sides. Add mushrooms, onions, thyme and bay leaf. Pour stout over rabbit and vegetables. Crumble reserved bacon over mixture. Heat to boiling; reduce heat.

Cover and simmer about 1 hour or until thickest pieces of rabbit are tender. Remove rabbit and vegetables to warm platter; keep warm. Remove bay leaf. Heat stout mixture to boiling. Mix cornstarch and water. Stir into stout mixture. Boil and stir 1 minute. Pour sauce over rabbit and vegetables. Sprinkle with parsley.   6 SERVINGS; 515 CALORIES PER SERVING.

JALAPEÑO BUFFALO BURGERS

Meat from buffalo and beefalo, an animal that is a hybrid of beef and buffalo, is increasingly common in supermarkets.

1½ pounds ground buffalo or ground beef
1 medium onion, finely chopped (about
   ½ cup)
2 to 3 jalapeño chilies, seeded and finely
   chopped
1 clove garlic, finely chopped

Mix all ingredients. Shape into 6 patties, each about ½ inch thick. Set oven control to broil. Place patties on rack in broiler pan. Broil with tops about 3 inches from heat 4 to 6 minutes on each side for medium, turning once. Serve with Fresh Tomato Salsa (page 20), taco sauce or chili sauce if desired.   6 SERVINGS; 305 CALORIES PER SERVING.

To Grill: Brush grill with vegetable oil. Grill patties about 4 inches from medium coals 4 to 6 minutes on each side for medium, turning once.

FIX-IT-FAST

- Microwave ground beef or pork in a microwavable colander placed in a casserole; use for main dishes or other meat mixtures. Microwave 1 pound loosely covered on high 5 to 6 minutes, stirring after 3 minutes, until no longer pink. Drain fat from the casserole and continue as directed in recipe.

- To speed the process of making meatballs, pat meat mixture in square or rectangular pan and cut into squares. Cook in the square shape or quickly shape into balls.

- Keep frozen cooked meatballs (homemade or purchased) and prepared spaghetti sauce on hand to heat quickly and serve over your favorite pasta.

- Grill extra steaks, chops or burgers to reheat later in the microwave (or freeze and reheat).

- Buy cooked meats by the chunk, sliced from the deli or in chopped form from the salad bar to use in casseroles, in salads or for sandwiches.

- Prepare a quick main dish using deli foods and meat: Try German potato salad heated with sliced cooked sausages or ham; make a marinated vegetable or pasta salad hearty by adding cooked pork, salami, ham or roast beef; heat baked beans and frankfurters or smoked sausages; or serve whatever combinations appeal to you.

- Prepare a quick beef stroganoff by heating leftover beef mixed with equal amounts cream of mushroom soup and sour cream.

- Heat equal amounts Cheddar cheese soup and beer to use as a sauce for cooked meatballs or cubed cooked ham. Serve over rice or pasta.

- Use prepared spaghetti sauce with cooked meat or sausage as a starting point for pasta and casseroles.

- Heat sliced or cubed meat with leftover gravy and serve over biscuits, corn bread, popovers or baked potatoes.

- Heat leftover sliced or cubed meat in prepared barbecue, pizza or taco sauce and serve in tortillas, pita breads or buns for quick hot sandwiches.

- Keep canned ham on hand for use in casseroles or sandwiches and for broiling or grilling.

- Wrap cooked smoked sausage in frozen (thawed) puff pastry and bake according to the pastry directions for an impressive main dish, or slice for an appetizer.

PER SERVING OR UNIT

NUTRITION INFORMATION

RECIPE, PAGE	Servings per recipe	Calories	Protein (grams)	Carbohydrate (grams)	Fat (grams)	Cholesterol (milligrams)	Sodium (milligrams)	PERCENT U.S. RECOMMENDED DAILY ALLOWANCE							
								Protein	Vitamin A	Vitamin C	Thiamine	Riboflavin	Niacin	Calcium	Iron
BEEF/VEAL															
Barbecue Pot Roast, 217	8	475	40	47	13	105	880	62	100	28	18	24	48	6	30
Beef and Artichoke Fettuccine, 225	6	320	20	28	14	55	190	30	4	2	16	16	16	16	14
Beef Brisket Barbecue, 218	12	300	38	3	13	115	360	58	2	2	4	16	28	2	26
Beef with Marinated Peppers and Goat Cheese, 221	6	495	29	39	24	75	720	44	14	100	18	18	32	6	30
Beef Medallions with Rosemary Sauce, 221	4	235	23	1	14	70	125	34	4	0	4	10	22	0	16
Beef Roast with Spicy Chipotle Sauce, 217	16	245	27	3	12	90	75	42	28	24	4	12	24	2	18
Beef Stew, 222	5	430	26	46	15	60	1350	38	100	36	22	20	34	18	22
Beef Stroganoff, 224	6	405	37	9	24	120	860	56	10	2	10	30	42	6	26
Burgundy Beef, 224	12	590	21	8	50	95	510	32	0	4	8	20	28	2	18

NUTRITION INFORMATION — PER SERVING OR UNIT	Servings per recipe	Calories	Protein (grams)	Carbohydrate (grams)	Fat (grams)	Cholesterol (milligrams)	Sodium (milligrams)	PERCENT U.S. RECOMMENDED DAILY ALLOWANCE							
RECIPE, PAGE								Protein	Vitamin A	Vitamin C	Thiamine	Riboflavin	Niacin	Calcium	Iron

BEEF/VEAL (continued)

RECIPE, PAGE	Servings	Calories	Protein	Carb	Fat	Chol	Sodium	Protein	Vit A	Vit C	Thiamine	Riboflavin	Niacin	Calcium	Iron
Cabbage Rolls, 226	4	385	27	25	20	80	1260	40	26	58	14	14	30	6	30
Chicken Stew, 222	5	440	21	46	19	50	1350	32	100	36	20	16	38	18	14
Chili con Carne, 228	4	415	31	28	21	80	910	46	28	20	18	20	30	8	30
Cincinnati-style Chili, 228	5	610	37	57	26	95	900	56	28	16	28	28	32	28	32
Corned Beef and Cabbage, 218	6	250	15	5	19	55	590	22	2	30	2	8	4	4	12
Curried Beef with Fruit, 225	6	480	28	66	12	65	670	42	100	24	16	22	34	8	36
Dilled Beef and Bulgur Ring, 228	8	330	19	24	17	95	630	28	20	6	10	14	20	4	18
Easy Chili con Carne, 228	4	415	31	28	21	80	910	46	28	20	18	20	30	8	30
Fajitas, 220	6	870	25	35	72	105	880	38	32	62	16	22	26	28	32
Greek Beef and Orzo, 253	4	320	25	7	20	80	540	38	14	14	16	20	30	8	22
Ground Beef Lasagne, 247	8	460	30	32	23	110	680	46	32	28	16	22	20	42	24
Harvest Beef Stew, 223	8	305	28	37	6	70	530	42	100	28	18	16	36	6	26
Herbed Pot Roast, 217	8	415	42	43	8	105	840	64	100	20	18	22	48	6	32
Individual Meat Loaves, 226	6	375	27	15	21	120	750	40	8	6	10	20	26	8	20
Lasagne Roll-ups, 228	8	525	33	49	24	135	1150	50	100	60	28	44	28	52	50
Lemon Veal Scallopini, 231	4	450	23	12	30	80	1210	34	4	0	8	14	24	2	16
London Broil, 219	4	260	24	6	15	70	480	36	2	4	4	10	18	2	16
Meat Loaf, 226	6	375	27	15	21	120	750	40	8	6	10	20	26	8	20
Meatballs, 227	4	355	27	11	21	135	450	40	2	0	8	18	26	4	18
Moroccan Beef with Couscous, 223	6	515	36	77	7	70	390	54	10	24	28	20	42	4	32
Mustard Short Ribs, 223	6	625	64	4	38	190	390	98	0	2	10	24	32	2	38
New England Boiled Dinner, 218	6	390	18	38	19	55	620	28	100	52	16	12	16	6	16
New England Pot Roast, 217	8	400	41	41	7	105	620	62	100	18	18	22	48	6	30
Red Flannel Hash, 224	4	335	14	19	23	50	975	20	0	10	4	8	8	2	12
Skillet Hash 224	4	395	18	17	28	65	935	26	0	10	6	8	10	0	12
Spaghetti and Beef Sauce, 227	6	330	20	31	14	55	550	30	18	24	16	14	24	4	22
Spaghetti and Chicken Sauce, 227	6	230	14	31	5	30	540	22	20	24	14	10	24	4	14
Spaghetti and Meatballs, 227	6	385	23	39	15	90	810	34	20	26	18	18	26	8	24
Spanish Meat Loaf, 226	6	380	27	18	21	115	1225	40	24	32	12	18	30	6	26
Stir-fried Orange Beef, 222	4	525	29	42	27	70	970	44	34	84	20	28	32	14	28

PER SERVING OR UNIT

NUTRITION INFORMATION

RECIPE, PAGE

PERCENT U.S. RECOMMENDED DAILY ALLOWANCE

	Servings per recipe	Calories	Protein (grams)	Carbohydrate (grams)	Fat (grams)	Cholesterol (milligrams)	Sodium (milligrams)	Protein	Vitamin A	Vitamin C	Thiamine	Riboflavin	Niacin	Calcium	Iron
BEEF/VEAL (continued)															
Stuffed Peppers, 227	6	310	21	19	17	65	840	30	30	100	14	14	22	10	26
Swiss Steak, 222	6	230	25	10	10	70	360	38	10	30	8	12	26	2	20
Vegetable Meat Loaf, 226	6	405	29	12	25	130	910	44	78	26	12	24	30	12	22
VARIETY MEATS															
Heart, 231		150	24	0	5	165	55	52	0	2	8	76	16	0	34
Kidneys, 232		120	21	1	3	330	115	46	20	0	10	100	24	0	32
Liver, 232		135	21	3	4	330	60	46	100	30	10	100	44	0	30
Liver and Onions, 232	4	395	27	13	32	435	560	42	100	26	18	100	82	2	48
Tongue, 231		240	19	0	18	90	50	42	0	0	0	16	8	0	16
PORK															
Apricot-Pistachio Rolled Pork, 235	12	395	23	12	27	85	180	36	14	0	48	18	26	2	10
Bacon, 3 slices, 248		110	6	0	9	15	300	12	0	10	8	2	6	0	0
Canadian-style Bacon, 249		85	11	1	4	25	720	24	0	16	24	4	16	0	2
Country-style Ribs, 240	6	455	26	25	27	100	440	40	6	4	54	22	32	2	8
Dijon Chicken Braid, 244	6	330	17	14	22	90	370	26	4	0	8	10	24	2	8
Dijon-Ham Braid, 244	6	325	15	13	23	80	870	24	4	0	28	12	16	2	8
Easy Cassoulet, 247	8	260	18	35	5	30	1260	26	100	34	38	16	16	8	22
Filled Pork Roll with Cranberries and Squash, 241	6	380	27	33	16	115	140	40	20	4	30	24	26	6	14
Filled Pork Roll with Sauerkraut and Apples, 241	6	325	27	18	16	115	350	40	2	6	30	22	26	8	16
Frankfurters and Cooked Smoked Sausages, 248		145	5	1	13	20	500	10	0	20	6	2	4	0	2
Gingered Pork with Peaches, 240	6	315	21	34	10	50	830	32	16	6	58	24	28	4	14
Ground Beef Lasagne, 247	8	460	30	32	23	110	680	46	32	28	16	22	20	42	24
Ham-and-Brie–stuffed Apples, 245	4	415	27	44	15	65	1100	40	10	8	38	20	20	30	6
Ham Loaf with Red Currant Sauce, 245	8	320	23	19	16	95	850	34	0	12	44	20	22	4	8
Ham and Scalloped Potatoes, 244	6	300	16	33	12	30	1010	24	10	14	28	16	18	12	4
Italian Sausage Lasagne, 247	8	510	30	33	28	115	1180	46	32	28	36	24	22	42	22
Lemon Pork Chops, 237	4	410	37	17	20	125	260	56	4	2	86	32	40	2	10
Mustard Spareribs, 240	6	605	39	18	41	160	310	60	0	0	36	30	38	14	24

NUTRITION INFORMATION

RECIPE, PAGE

PER SERVING OR UNIT	Servings per recipe	Calories	Protein (grams)	Carbohydrate (grams)	Fat (grams)	Cholesterol (milligrams)	Sodium (milligrams)	PERCENT U.S. RECOMMENDED DAILY ALLOWANCE							
								Protein	Vitamin A	Vitamin C	Thiamine	Riboflavin	Niacin	Calcium	Iron
PORK (continued)															
Plum-barbecued Spareribs, 242	4	825	42	31	54	215	1170	80	6	0	50	42	50	10	24
Pork and Broccoli Risotto, 238	6	230	13	5	15	45	650	20	10	44	34	18	18	6	10
Pork Medallions with Rosemary Sauce, 221	4	190	24	1	9	75	125	36	4	0	72	18	24	0	8
Pork Ragout, 252	6	605	39	42	22	105	520	58	100	68	84	34	50	6	20
Pork and Squash Kabobs, 238	4	275	13	28	13	45	35	20	0	10	28	12	14	2	4
Sausage in Corn Bread with Salsa–Sour Cream Sauce, 246	6	455	17	27	31	145	1740	26	22	4	28	24	14	28	10
Sesame Pork with Garlic Cream Sauce, 238	6	240	19	2	17	65	110	28	6	0	52	16	18	4	8
Sichuan Pork, 239	4	660	31	59	33	80	890	48	34	64	66	42	46	16	22
Spicy Mexican Torte, 246–247	8	350	15	30	17	310	510	22	44	46	6	10	4	24	8
Sweet-and-Sour Pork, 239	8	645	25	77	26	100	970	38	100	18	60	26	34	4	18
Tangy Hazlenut Pork Chops, 237	6	595	33	4	49	125	380	50	0	0	80	32	36	2	8
Tenderloin with Black Bean–Tomato Relish, 236	4	200	21	17	6	50	470	32	18	10	58	18	20	6	20
LAMB															
Greek Lamb and Orzo, 253	4	285	24	7	17	85	540	36	14	14	20	24	32	8	16
Italian Chicken, 253	6	495	26	5	41	80	680	40	4	0	4	10	36	10	6
Italian Lamb Shanks, 253	4	785	51	8	61	180	1030	78	2	0	18	30	50	16	20
Lamb Chops with Pineapple, 251	4	425	19	28	26	85	50	30	0	10	12	12	22	2	8
Lamb Chops with Raspberry-Port Sauce, 251	4	415	20	10	33	85	320	30	0	6	8	14	22	2	8
Rosemary Lamb Ragout, 252	6	555	37	42	16	110	510	56	10	34	32	28	48	6	24
Shish Kabobs, 252	4	235	24	6	13	80	1150	36	2	32	12	14	26	2	12
GAME															
Jalapeño Buffalo Burgers, 254	6	305	23	3	19	80	60	36	32	32	6	10	22	0	16
Rabbit Stewed in Stout, 254	6	515	48	16	26	250	570	74	0	4	12	20	100	4	18
Venison Sauerbraten, 253	6	500	44	16	28	135	870	68	0	2	6	20	34	2	32

PASTA, GRAINS & LEGUMES

PASTA, GRAINS & LEGUMES

In recent years, pasta, grains and legumes have justifiably moved into a position of importance in our diet. These foods have always played a prominent role in the nutrition and cuisines of many countries, from rice in Asia to lentils in India. Today, we also value the role of complementary proteins, foods that together make a complete protein, such as rice and beans. Our classic Old-fashioned Baked Beans (page 273), when teamed with brown bread, is another excellent example, or the Italian favorite of pasta and cheese. We are realizing that what we have thought of as standard fare can be exciting and inventive. Try Poppy Seed Pasta (page 262), Mexican Kasha (page 269) or Southwestern Black-eyed Peas (page 273), and you'll know this is more than your standby macaroni or rice.

PASTA BASICS

♦ Pasta is available in two forms: dried and fresh. Dried pasta (the most common form) is usually found prepackaged or in serve-yourself bulk form. Fresh pasta can be found in the refrigerated section of the supermarket.

♦ Dried pasta can be stored indefinitely in your pantry. Fresh pasta is perishable and should be covered and refrigerated. If you buy prepackaged fresh pasta, leave it in the original packaging.

♦ When preparing pasta, allow ½ to ¾ cup cooked pasta per side or appetizer serving. If you plan to make pasta your main entrée, allow 1¼ to 1½ cups per serving.

♦ 1 ounce of dried pasta will yield approximately ½ cup of cooked pasta. This yield will vary slightly depending on the shape, type and size of pasta.

PASTA YIELDS FOR DRY PASTA

Uncooked	Cooked	Servings
MACARONI		
6 or 7 ounces (2 cups)	4 cups	4 to 6
SPAGHETTI		
7 or 8 ounces	4 cups	4 to 6
EGG NOODLES		
8 ounces (4 to 5 cups)	4 to 5 cups	4 to 6

Preceding page: *Italian White Beans (page 274), Homemade Pasta (page 262) topped with Italian Tomato Sauce (page 360)*

♦ To measure 4 ounces of spaghetti easily, make a circle with your thumb and index finger, about the size of a quarter, and fill it with pasta.

♦ Always cook pasta uncovered at a fast boil, using plenty of water. This allows the pasta to move freely, promoting even cooking. Be sure water is boiling before adding pasta. Use at least 1 quart water for every 4 ounces of pasta. Stir frequently to prevent sticking.

♦ Do not rinse pasta after draining unless stated in the recipe. Pasta is usually rinsed when it is to be used in salads.

♦ Salting the cooking water is optional and not necessary for the proper cooking of pasta. You might like to add a tablespoon of dried herbs or lemon juice to the water for a slightly different flavor.

♦ Avoid overcooking pasta. Overcooked pasta is mushy and pasty. Follow recipe directions carefully. Pasta should be tender but firm to the bite (*al dente*).

♦ Fresh pasta cooks faster than dried pasta. Remember this rule: The fresher the pasta, the shorter the cooking time.

♦ Couscous (*koose-koose*) is a tiny pasta made from semolina, part of the starchy center of durum wheat. Couscous has been made since ancient times and has a rich culinary tradition in Mediterranean countries.

PASTA

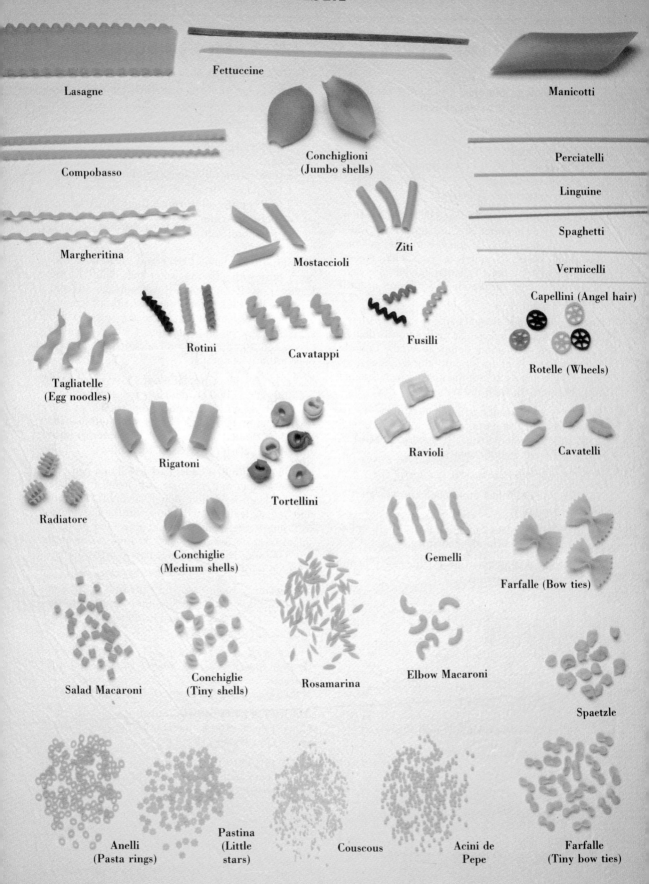

Lasagne

Fettuccine

Manicotti

Conchiglioni (Jumbo shells)

Compobasso

Perciatelli

Linguine

Spaghetti

Vermicelli

Capellini (Angel hair)

Margheritina

Mostaccioli

Ziti

Rotini

Cavatappi

Fusilli

Rotelle (Wheels)

Tagliatelle (Egg noodles)

Rigatoni

Tortellini

Ravioli

Cavatelli

Radiatore

Conchiglie (Medium shells)

Gemelli

Farfalle (Bow ties)

Salad Macaroni

Conchiglie (Tiny shells)

Rosamarina

Elbow Macaroni

Spaetzle

Anelli (Pasta rings)

Pastina (Little stars)

Couscous

Acini de Pepe

Farfalle (Tiny bow ties)

HOMEMADE PASTA

2 cups all-purpose flour*
1 tablespoon chopped fresh or 1 teaspoon
  dried herb, crushed, if desired
½ teaspoon salt
2 eggs
¼ cup water
1 tablespoon olive or vegetable oil
4½ quarts water
¼ teaspoon salt, if desired

Mix flour, herb and ½ teaspoon salt. Make a well in center of flour mixture. Mix in eggs, ¼ cup water and the oil thoroughly. (If dough is too dry, mix in a few drops water. If dough is too sticky, mix in small amount of flour.) Gather dough into ball. Knead on floured surface about 5 minutes or until smooth and elastic.

Divide dough into 4 equal parts. Roll one part at a time into paper-thin rectangle on generously floured surface (keep remaining dough covered). Loosely fold rectangle lengthwise into thirds. See steps below. (If using pasta machine, pass dough through machine until 1/16 inch thick.)

Heat 4½ quarts water to boiling. Stir in ¼ teaspoon salt and the pasta. Cook 3 to 5 minutes or until almost tender; drain.   8 SERVINGS (ABOUT ¾ CUP EACH); 140 CALORIES PER SERVING.

*If using self-rising flour omit the ½ teaspoon salt.

CURRY PASTA: Add 1 tablespoon curry powder to the flour mixture.

LEMON PASTA: Add 2 to 3 teaspoons finely shredded lemon peel to the flour mixture.

POPPY SEED PASTA: Add 1 tablespoon poppy seed to the flour mixture.

1. Cut pasta lengthwise into ¼-inch strips.

2. Unfold strips and place in single layer on towels or hanger at least 30 minutes or until dry.

SPINACH FETTUCCINE

When you cook these vegetable-flavored pastas, the bright colors will fade or even run slightly, for a more pastel effect. This won't affect the taste at all.

8 ounces spinach*
2 eggs
1 tablespoon olive or vegetable oil
1 teaspoon salt
2 to 2¼ cups all-purpose flour**
4½ quarts water
¼ teaspoon salt, if desired

Wash spinach; drain. Cover and cook over medium heat with just the water that clings to the leaves 3 to 10 minutes. Rinse spinach in cold water; drain. Press spinach against side of strainer with back of spoon to remove excess water. Place spinach, eggs, oil and 1 teaspoon salt in blender. Cover and blend on medium speed about 20 seconds or until smooth.

Make a well in center of flour. Mix in spinach mixture thoroughly. (If dough is too dry, mix in a few drops water. If dough is too sticky, mix in small amount of flour.) Gather dough into ball. Knead on floured surface about 5 minutes or until smooth and elastic. Let stand 10 minutes.

Divide dough into 4 equal parts. Roll one part at a time into paper-thin rectangle on generously floured surface (keep remaining dough covered). Loosely fold rectangle lengthwise into thirds. Cut crosswise into ¼-inch strips. Unfold strips and place in single layer on towels at least 30 minutes or until dry. (If using pasta machine, pass dough through machine until 1/16 inch thick.)

Heat water to boiling. Stir in ¼ teaspoon salt and the fettuccine. Cook 3 to 5 minutes or until almost tender; drain.   8 SERVINGS (ABOUT ¾ CUP EACH); 160 CALORIES PER SERVING.

*1 package (10 ounces) frozen spinach can be substituted for the fresh spinach. Cook as directed on package; drain thoroughly.
**If using self-rising flour, omit the 1 teaspoon salt.

CARROT FETTUCCINE: Substitute 1 can (8¼ ounces) sliced carrots, drained, for the cooked spinach.   155 CALORIES PER SERVING.

BEET FETTUCCINE: Substitute 1 can (8 ounces) whole beets, drained, for the cooked spinach.   160 CALORIES PER SERVING.

🌾 EGG NOODLES

2 cups all-purpose* or whole wheat flour
3 egg yolks
1 egg
1 teaspoon salt
⅓ to ½ cup water
3 quarts water
¼ teaspoon salt, if desired

Make a well in center of flour. Mix in egg yolks, egg and 1 teaspoon salt thoroughly. Mix in ⅓ to ½ cup water, 1 tablespoon at a time, until dough is stiff but easy to roll.

Divide dough into 4 equal parts. Roll one part at a time into paper-thin rectangle on generously floured surface (keep remaining dough covered). Loosely fold rectangle lengthwise into thirds. Cut cross-wise into ⅛-inch strips for narrow noodles, ¼-inch strips for wide noodles. (If using pasta machine, pass dough through machine until ¹⁄₁₆ inch thick.) Unfold strips and place in single layer on towels about 2 hours or until stiff and dry.

Break strips into smaller pieces. Heat 3 quarts water to boiling. Stir in ¼ teaspoon salt and the noodles. Cook 5 to 7 minutes or until almost ten-der; drain. (To cook half of the noodles, use 2 quarts water.)   8 SERVINGS (ABOUT ½ CUP EACH); 140 CALORIES PER SERVING.

*If using self-rising flour, omit the 1 teaspoon salt.

CORNMEAL NOODLES: Substitute ½ cup corn-meal for ½ cup of the flour.   120 CALORIES PER SERVING.

BEET FETTUCCINE WITH CAVIAR

The color of caviar—fish roe—ranges from golden yellow to red, to gray, to black. You can use any color in this recipe.

½ recipe Beet Fettuccine (page 262) or 6 ounces uncooked fettuccine
⅓ cup sour cream
¼ cup milk
2 tablespoons grated Parmesan cheese
⅛ teaspoon pepper
1 green onion (with top), thinly sliced
1 tablespoon caviar

Cook fettuccine as directed in recipe or on pack-age; drain. Heat remaining ingredients except cav-iar over low heat, stirring constantly, just until hot. Toss with hot fettuccine. Spoon caviar on top.   4 SERVINGS (ABOUT ⅔ CUP EACH); 235 CALORIES PER SERVING.

🌾 SPAETZLE

Considered both a dumpling and a noodle, this tiny German pasta can be served with meat, poultry or game.

2 eggs, beaten
¼ cup milk or water
1 cup all-purpose flour*
¼ teaspoon salt
Dash of pepper
2 quarts water
1 tablespoon margarine or butter

Mix eggs, milk, flour, salt and pepper (batter will be thick). Heat water to boiling in Dutch oven. Press batter through colander (preferably one with large holes), a few tablespoons at a time, into boiling water. Stir once or twice to prevent sticking.

Cook about 5 minutes or until spaetzle rise to surface and are tender; drain. Toss spaetzle with margarine.   6 SERVINGS (½ CUP EACH); 120 CALORIES PER SERVING.

Do not use self-rising flour in this recipe.

Press batter through a colander with large holes, a few tablespoons at a time into boiling water. If colander has small holes it will be difficult to push the batter through.

Bacon–Green Bean Pasta Toss, Curry Pasta with Cucumber

CURRY PASTA WITH CUCUMBER

Mint has been used since the days of the ancient Greeks and has a distinctive, cool flavor that becomes stronger as it is crushed. In the Greek myth, the nymph Minthe died at the hands of the goddess Persephone. Her soul was said to live on in the hearty and aromatic mint plant.

½ recipe Curry Pasta (page 262) or 6 ounces
    uncooked egg noodles
2 teaspoons vegetable oil
1 small cucumber, chopped
2 green onions, thinly sliced
1½ teaspoons chopped fresh or ½ teaspoon
    dried mint leaves
1 cup plain yogurt
1 tablespoon all-purpose flour
¼ teaspoon salt
½ cup broken walnuts

Cook pasta as directed in recipe or on package; drain. Heat oil in 10-inch skillet over medium heat. Cook cucumber, onions and mint in oil about 3 minutes; remove from heat. Mix yogurt, flour and salt. Stir into cucumber mixture and heat just until hot (do not boil). Toss with hot pasta. Sprinkle with walnuts.   4 SERVINGS (ABOUT ¾ CUP EACH); 310 CALORIES PER SERVING.

BACON–GREEN BEAN PASTA TOSS

½ recipe Poppy Seed Pasta (page 262) or 6
    ounces uncooked vermicelli
4 slices bacon, cut into 1-inch pieces
1 cup frozen French-style green beans
3 green onions (with tops), thinly sliced
⅛ teaspoon pepper

Cook pasta as directed in recipe or on package; drain. Cook bacon in 10-inch skillet until crisp. Remove bacon with slotted spoon and reserve 2 tablespoons fat in skillet. Cook beans and onions in fat 1 to 2 minutes or until beans are crisp-tender. Toss with hot pasta, bacon and pepper.   6 SERVINGS (ABOUT ¾ CUP EACH); 175 CALORIES PER SERVING.

LEMON PASTA WITH CAPERS

½ recipe Lemon Pasta (page 262) or 6 ounces uncooked spaghetti
2 cloves garlic, crushed
½ cup margarine or butter
½ cup dry white wine or apple juice
2 tablespoons capers
1 tablespoon lemon juice
1 tablespoon chopped fresh or 1 teaspoon dried basil leaves
½ teaspoon salt
½ teaspoon freshly ground pepper
2 tablespoons chopped fresh parsley

Cook pasta as directed in recipe or on package; drain. Cook garlic in margarine in 1-quart saucepan over medium heat until garlic is golden brown; remove garlic and discard. Stir in wine, capers, lemon juice, basil, salt and pepper. Heat just until hot. Toss with hot pasta. Sprinkle with parsley. 6 SERVINGS (ABOUT ¾ CUP EACH); 260 CALORIES PER SERVING.

🌾 NOODLES ROMANOFF

These rich noodles come from Eastern Europe and Russia. Garnish with poppy seed for added flavor.

½ recipe Egg Noodles (page 263) or 8 ounces uncooked wide noodles
2 cups sour cream
¼ cup grated Parmesan cheese
1 tablespoon chopped fresh chives
½ teaspoon salt
⅛ teaspoon pepper
1 large clove garlic, crushed
2 tablespoons margarine or butter
¼ cup grated Parmesan cheese

Cook noodles as directed in recipe or on package; drain. Mix sour cream, ¼ cup cheese, the chives, salt, pepper and garlic. Stir margarine into hot noodles. Stir in sour cream mixture. Place on warm platter. Sprinkle with ¼ cup cheese. 8 SERVINGS (ABOUT ⅔ CUP EACH); 210 CALORIES PER SERVING.

CURRY SAUSAGE COUSCOUS

Brilliant green pistachios have been prized in the Middle East for more than 8,000 years.

1½ cups couscous
¼ pound bulk pork sausage
1 medium onion, chopped (½ cup)
¼ cup pistachio nuts, coarsely chopped
½ teaspoon curry powder
½ teaspoon salt
1 clove garlic, finely chopped
1 tablespoon chopped fresh parsley

Prepare couscous as directed on package. Cook pork, onion, nuts, curry powder, salt and garlic in 10-inch skillet, stirring occasionally, until pork is no longer pink; drain. Stir in couscous and parsley. Cook and stir over medium heat about 2 minutes or until mixture is hot. 4 SERVINGS (ABOUT ⅔ CUP EACH); 210 CALORIES PER SERVING.

To Microwave: Prepare couscous as directed on package. Crumble pork into 2-quart microwavable casserole. Cover loosely and microwave on high 2 minutes. Stir in onion, nuts, curry powder, salt and garlic. Cover loosely and microwave on high 1 minute or until pork is no longer pink; drain. Stir in couscous and parsley. Cover loosely and microwave on high 1 minute or until mixture is hot.

Curry Sausage Couscous

GRAINS

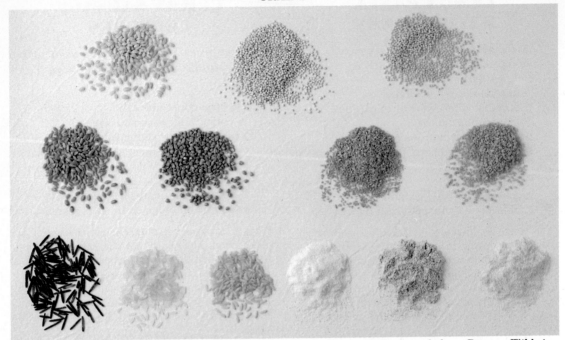

Top: *Pearled barley, quinoa, millet.* Middle: *Wheat berries, kasha, cracked wheat, bulgur.* Bottom: *Wild rice, white rice (regular long grain), brown rice, white cornmeal, blue cornmeal, yellow cornmeal.*

GRAIN BASICS

◆ Regular white rice has been milled to remove the hull, germ and most of the bran. It is available in long, medium and short grains, and long grain is the more common all-purpose rice.

◆ The shorter the grain, the stickier the rice. Medium-grain rice works better in puddings because of its creamier characteristics. Short-grain rice is not widely available.

◆ Parboiled (converted) rice contains the vitamins found in brown rice but is polished like white rice.

◆ Precooked (instant) rice is commercially cooked, rinsed and dried before packaging. It is, therefore, especially quick to prepare.

◆ Brown rice is unpolished with only the outer hull removed. It has a slightly firm texture and a nutlike flavor. Brown rice has more fiber and nutrients because the germ and hull have not been removed.

◆ Wild rice is the seed of an aquatic grass that grows in marshes. It is dark greenish brown in color and has a distinctive, nutlike flavor. As it is expensive, it is sometimes combined with white or brown rice.

RICE COOKING TIME

Type	Time (minutes)	Yield Per 1 Cup Uncooked Rice
Regular	*15*	*3 cups*
Parboiled (converted)	*20 to 25*	*4 cups*
Precooked (instant)	*5*	*2 cups*
Brown	*50*	*4 cups*
Wild rice	*75 to 90*	*3 cups*

◆ You can store cooked rice tightly covered in the refrigerator up to five days or freeze it in a covered container up to six months. To reheat, tightly cover rice and microwave on high. Or place rice in heavy saucepan and add 2 tablespoons water per cup of cooked rice. Cover and cook over low heat about 5 minutes.

◆ Barley, one of the first grains ever cultivated, is commercially hulled to shorten the cooking time that softens the outer seed coat. Pearl barley refers to the milling process in which the grain is husked and polished; it is round like pearls. Pearl barley is the most common variety.

◆ Cornmeal is ground yellow, white or blue corn kernels. Grits is meal that has been coarsely ground from hulled kernels of corn.

♦ Bulgur and cracked wheat are made from whole wheat kernels. Bulgur is wheat kernels that have been parboiled, dried and partially debranned, then cracked into coarse fragments. Cracked wheat is from kernels that are cleaned, then cracked or cut into fine fragments.

♦ Wheat berries are the unprocessed kernels of wheat. They should be presoaked to ensure they are tender enough to eat. Wheat berries are slow to cook, but because they contain the entire wheat kernel, they are high in nutritional value. Look for these in health food stores.

♦ Kasha, also called "buckwheat groats," is the kernel inside the buckwheat seed. It is roasted for a nutlike flavor, then coarsely ground.

♦ Add flavor to rice and grains by cooking in equal parts water and broth (chicken or beef) or juice (apple, orange, tomato).

♦ Millet is a small, round yellow seed that resembles whole mustard seeds. When cooked, this tiny grain has a chewy texture and a mild flavor similar to brown rice.

♦ Quinoa (*keen-wa*) is an ancient grain native to South America. Quinoa is higher in protein than most grains and is actually a complete protein. It has a light texture and mild flavor. You can find quinoa in health food stores.

WHITE RICE

1 cup uncooked regular long grain rice
2 cups water
¼ teaspoon salt, if desired

Heat rice, water and salt to boiling in 1½-quart saucepan, stirring once or twice; reduce heat. Cover and simmer 14 minutes (do not lift cover or stir); remove from heat. Fluff rice lightly with fork. Cover and let steam 5 to 10 minutes.   6 SERVINGS (½ CUP EACH); 120 CALORIES PER SERVING.

OVEN RICE: Heat oven to 350°. Heat water to boiling. Mix rice, water and salt in ungreased 1-quart casserole. Cover and bake 25 to 30 minutes or until water is absorbed.

LEMON RICE: Stir 2 tablespoons margarine or butter, melted, and 2 teaspoons lemon juice into cooked rice.   155 CALORIES PER SERVING.

MUSHROOM RICE: Heat 1 can (4 ounces) sliced mushrooms or mushroom stems and pieces, drained, in 2 tablespoons margarine or butter. Stir into cooked rice.   155 CALORIES PER SERVING.

ONION RICE: Cook 2 tablespoons finely chopped onion in 2 tablespoons margarine or butter over medium heat about 2 minutes. Stir into cooked rice.   155 CALORIES PER SERVING.

PARSLEY RICE: Stir 2 tablespoons chopped fresh parsley into cooked rice.   120 CALORIES PER SERVING.

BROWN RICE

1 cup uncooked brown rice
2¾ cups water
¼ teaspoon salt, if desired

Heat rice, water and salt to boiling in 1½-quart saucepan, stirring once or twice; reduce heat. Cover and simmer 45 to 50 minutes or until tender.   8 SERVINGS (½ CUP EACH); 90 CALORIES PER SERVING.

WILD RICE

1 cup uncooked wild rice
2½ cups water
¼ teaspoon salt, if desired

Place rice in wire strainer. Run cold water through rice, lifting rice with fingers to clean thoroughly. Heat rice, water and salt to boiling, stirring once or twice; reduce heat. Cover and simmer 40 to 50 minutes or until tender. After 30 minutes, check to see that rice is not sticking to pan. Stir in ¼ cup water if necessary.   6 SERVINGS (½ CUP EACH); 100 CALORIES PER SERVING.

WILD RICE

*W*hat we call wild rice has had many other names. Native Americans called it mahnomen, "the precious grain." The French called it folles avoines, or "crazy oats," and settlers called it water oats and water rice as well as wild rice. To be accurate, wild rice isn't truly a rice, but the grain of a tall aquatic grass, found in the northern part of the country. Minnesota is the home of most of our native wild rice, although it is now farmed in paddies in California as well as Minnesota, which makes it available year-round.

Wild rice has a distinctive nutty flavor that stands alone from other rices. Once considered an expensive item, wild rice can be purchased more economically, because it is now grown commercially. Wild rice is highly nutritious, a good source of protein and fiber while providing an excellent source of B vitamins. Because this delicious food is found so close to home, we have always included wild rice recipes in our basic cookbooks—you'll want to add it to your cooking basics as well!

Coconut-Papaya Rice, Herbed Chicken (page 284)

COCONUT-PAPAYA RICE

What we call coconut milk doesn't come from inside the cavity of the coconut, but from soaking the coconut meat and then pressing out the liquid. It's a staple in Southeast Asia, it is as important to their cuisine as cow's milk is to ours.

    1 cup uncooked regular long grain rice
    ¼ cup water
    ¼ teaspoon salt
    ¼ teaspoon ground cinnamon
    ⅛ teaspoon ground nutmeg
    1 can (14 ounces) unsweetened coconut
        milk
    1 ripe papaya (about 1 pound), pared,
        seeded and chopped

Heat rice, water, salt, cinnamon, nutmeg and coconut milk to boiling in 2-quart saucepan, stirring once or twice; reduce heat. Cover and simmer 19 minutes (do not lift cover or stir); remove from heat. Fluff rice lightly with fork. Cover and let steam 5 to 10 minutes.

Mash half of the papaya. Stir mashed papaya and chopped papaya into rice. Heat until mixture is hot, stirring occasionally. 6 SERVINGS (ABOUT ¾ CUP EACH); 350 CALORIES PER SERVING.

CURRIED RICE

    1 cup uncooked regular long grain rice
    2 tablespoons margarine or butter
    1 tablespoon finely chopped onion
    ½ to 1 teaspoon curry powder
    ¼ teaspoon salt
    ¼ teaspoon pepper
    ¼ cup slivered almonds, toasted
    ¼ cup chopped pimiento-stuffed olives or
        ripe olives

Cook rice as directed on page 267. Heat margarine in 10-inch skillet over medium heat. Cook onion in margarine about 2 minutes. Stir in curry powder, salt and pepper. Stir into hot rice. Sprinkle with almonds and olives. 6 SERVINGS (ABOUT ½ CUP EACH); 200 CALORIES PER SERVING.

RICE AND PINE NUTS

    1 cup uncooked brown rice
    1 medium onion, chopped (about ½ cup)
    2 cloves garlic, finely chopped
    2 tablespoons vegetable oil
    2½ cups water
    ½ cup raisins
    1 tablespoon chicken bouillon granules
    ½ teaspoon dry mustard
    ⅛ teaspoon pepper
    1 jar (1 ounce) pine nuts
    ¼ cup chopped fresh parsley

Cook rice, onion and garlic in oil, stirring frequently, in 2-quart saucepan over medium heat about 5 minutes or until onion is tender. Stir in water, raisins, bouillon granules, mustard and pepper. Heat to boiling; reduce heat. Cover and simmer about 45 minutes or until rice is tender and water is absorbed. Stir in pine nuts and parsley. 8 SERVINGS (ABOUT ½ CUP EACH); 185 CALORIES PER SERVING.

Mexican Kasha

MEXICAN KASHA

1 cup medium buckwheat kernels (kasha)
1 egg
2 medium onions, sliced
1 clove garlic, finely chopped
2½ cups water
2 tablespoons margarine or butter
1 teaspoon red wine vinegar
½ teaspoon salt
¼ teaspoon ground cumin
1 medium tomato, chopped (about 1 cup)
1 medium avocado, chopped (about 1 cup)

Mix buckwheat kernels and egg. Cook buckwheat mixture in 10-inch skillet over medium-high heat, stirring constantly, until kernels separate and dry. Stir in onions, garlic, water, margarine, vinegar, salt and cumin. Heat to boiling, stirring constantly; reduce heat. Cover and simmer about 5 minutes or until kernels are tender and liquid is absorbed. Stir in tomato and avocado.   8 SERVINGS (ABOUT ¾ CUP EACH); 120 CALORIES PER SERVING.

MILLET PILAF

4 slices bacon
1 medium onion, thinly sliced
1 medium green bell pepper, chopped (about 1 cup)
1 cup uncooked millet
3 cups water
1 tablespoon chicken bouillon granules
⅛ teaspoon ground ginger
1 medium unpared apple, coarsely chopped (about 1 cup)

Cook bacon in 10-inch skillet until crisp. Remove bacon with slotted spoon, reserving fat in skillet. Crumble bacon and reserve. Cook and stir onion, bell pepper and millet in fat about 5 minutes or until onion is crisp-tender.

Stir in water, bouillon granules and ginger. Heat to boiling; reduce heat. Cover and simmer about 30 minutes or until millet is tender. Stir in apple and heat until hot. Sprinkle with reserved bacon.   6 SERVINGS (ABOUT ¾ CUP EACH); 145 CALORIES PER SERVING.

Fried Polenta, Garlic-and-Beer–marinated Shrimp Kabobs (page 206), Roquefort and Toasted Walnut Salad (page 306)

POLENTA WITH CHEESE

1 cup cornmeal
¾ cup cold water
3¼ cups boiling water
2 teaspoons salt
3 teaspoons margarine or butter
1 cup grated Parmesan cheese
⅓ cup shredded Swiss cheese (1½ ounces)

Heat oven to 350°. Grease 1½-quart casserole. Mix cornmeal and ¾ cup cold water in 2-quart saucepan. Stir in 3¼ cups boiling water and the salt. Cook, stirring constantly, until mixture thickens and boils; reduce heat. Cover and simmer 10 minutes, stirring occasionally; remove from heat. Stir until smooth.

Spread one-third of the mixture in casserole. Dot with 1 teaspoon of the margarine. Sprinkle with ⅓ cup Parmesan cheese. Repeat twice. Sprinkle with Swiss cheese. Bake uncovered 15 to 20 minutes or until hot and bubbly.   6 SERVINGS (ABOUT ¾ CUP EACH); 125 CALORIES PER SERVING.

FRIED POLENTA: Omit margarine, Parmesan cheese and Swiss cheese. Prepare as directed— after simmering 10 minutes, spread in greased loaf pan, 9 × 5 × 3 inches.   Cover and refrigerate at least

12 hours or until firm. Invert pan to unmold. Cut into ½-inch slices. Coat slices with flour. Heat 2 tablespoons margarine or butter in 10-inch skillet until melted. Cook slices over low heat about 5 minutes on each side or until brown. Serve with molasses, jam, maple syrup or sour cream if desired.   65 CALORIES PER SERVING.

CHEESE GRITS

2 cups milk
2 cups water
½ teaspoon salt
¼ teaspoon pepper
1 cup white hominy quick grits
1½ cups shredded Cheddar cheese (6 ounces)
¼ cup sliced green onions (with tops)
2 eggs, slightly beaten
1 tablespoon margarine or butter
¼ teaspoon paprika

Heat oven to 350°. Grease 1½-quart casserole. Heat milk, water, salt and pepper to boiling in 2-quart saucepan. Gradually add grits, stirring constantly; reduce heat. Simmer uncovered, stirring frequently, about 5 minutes or until thick. Stir in cheese and onions.

Stir 1 cup of the hot mixture into eggs. Stir into remaining hot mixture in saucepan. Pour into casserole. Dot with margarine and sprinkle with paprika. Bake uncovered 35 to 40 minutes or until set. Let stand 10 minutes.   8 SERVINGS (⅔ CUP EACH); 225 CALORIES PER SERVING.

THREE-GRAIN MEDLEY

2¼ cups water
1 teaspoon chicken bouillon granules
⅓ cup uncooked wheat berries
⅓ cup pearl barley
¼ cup wild rice
2 tablespoons chopped fresh parsley
1 tablespoon margarine or butter
2 teaspoons finely shredded lemon peel
4 green onions (with tops), thinly sliced
2 cloves garlic, finely chopped

Heat water and bouillon granules to boiling in 1½-quart saucepan. Stir in wheat berries. Cover and simmer 15 minutes. Stir in remaining ingredients. Cover and simmer about 40 minutes or until liquid is absorbed.   6 SERVINGS (½ CUP EACH); 55 CALORIES PER SERVING.

LEGUMES

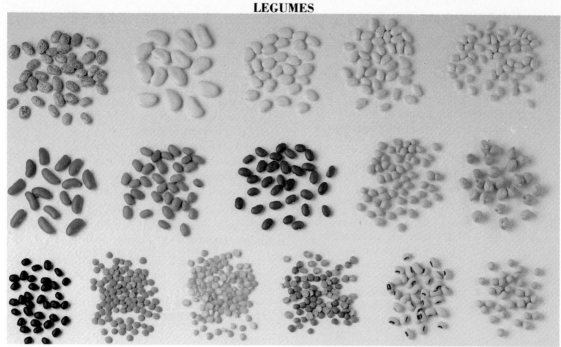

Top: *Pinto beans, lima beans, baby lima beans, great northern beans, navy beans.* Middle: *Kidney beans, brown beans, red beans, soybeans, garbanzo beans.* Bottom: *Black beans, lentils, yellow split peas, green split peas, black-eyed peas, yellow peas.*

LEGUME BASICS

Legumes are dried beans, peas and lentils from pods containing one row of seeds. Because dried beans can be used interchangeably, choose beans of similar size if you can't find the bean called for in a recipe. Experiment with different beans and create new recipes.

♦ Legumes (except lentils) need to be boiled uncovered 2 minutes prior to cooking. This brief boiling period destroys an enzyme present in legumes that can cause some people to become ill.

♦ To prevent the water from foaming when cooking dried beans, add 1 tablespoon of vegetable oil or shortening to the water during the first cooking period.

♦ Dried beans triple in volume as they cook, so be sure to choose a sufficiently large casserole or pan.

YIELDS FOR DRIED BEANS

Bean Quantities	Cooked Quantities
1 cup dried beans	*3 cups*
1 pound dried beans	*6 cups*
1-pound can cooked beans	*about 2 cups*

RED BEANS AND RICE

3 cups water
1 cup dried kidney beans*
2 ounces salt pork (with rind), diced, or 3 slices bacon, cut up
1 medium onion, chopped (about ½ cup)
1 medium green bell pepper, chopped (about 1 cup)
1 cup uncooked regular long grain rice
1 teaspoon salt

Heat water and beans to boiling in 3-quart saucepan. Boil uncovered 2 minutes; reduce heat. Cover and simmer 1 to 1¼ hours or until tender (do not boil or beans will burst).

Drain beans, reserving liquid. Cook salt pork in 10-inch skillet until crisp. Add onion and bell pepper. Cook and stir until onion is softened. Add enough water to bean liquid, if necessary, to measure 2 cups. Add bean liquid, salt pork, onion, bell pepper, rice and salt to beans in 3-quart saucepan. Heat to boiling, stirring once or twice; reduce heat. Cover and simmer 14 minutes (do not lift cover or stir); remove from heat. Fluff with fork. Cover and let steam 5 to 10 minutes.   8 SERVINGS (ABOUT ¾ CUP EACH); 140 CALORIES PER SERVING.

1 can (16 ounces) red kidney beans, drained and liquid reserved, can be substituted for the cooked dried kidney beans.

SPICY SPLIT PEAS

For a colorful combination, try half green and half yellow peas.

3 cups water
¾ cup dried split peas
2 tablespoons margarine or butter
1 teaspoon finely chopped gingerroot or ¼ teaspoon ground ginger
½ teaspoon salt
½ teaspoon ground turmeric
½ teaspoon ground cumin
1 small onion, finely chopped (about ¼ cup)

Heat water and peas to boiling. Boil uncovered 2 minutes; reduce heat. Cover and simmer about 25 minutes or until peas are tender but not mushy; drain. Heat margarine in 10-inch skillet over medium-high heat. Sauté gingerroot, salt, turmeric, cumin and onion about 3 minutes or until onion is tender. Stir in peas until evenly coated.   4 SERVINGS (ABOUT ½ CUP EACH); 190 CALORIES PER SERVING.

GARBANZO BEANS AND VEGETABLES

3 cups water
¾ cup dried garbanzo beans*
2 tablespoons olive or vegetable oil
1 cup sliced mushrooms
2 green onions (with tops), thinly sliced
1 medium carrot, shredded (about ½ cup)
1 clove garlic, finely chopped
1 tablespoon lemon juice
1 teaspoon prepared horseradish
1 teaspoon prepared mustard
¼ teaspoon salt
¼ teaspoon pepper

Heat water and beans to boiling. Boil uncovered 2 minutes; reduce heat. Cover and simmer 1 to 1¼ hours or until beans are tender (do not boil or beans will burst); drain.

Heat oil in 10-inch skillet over medium heat. Cook mushrooms, onions, carrot and garlic in oil about 4 minutes. Stir in beans and remaining ingredients. Cook about 5 minutes or until mixture is hot.   4 SERVINGS (ABOUT ⅔ CUP EACH); 160 CALORIES PER SERVING.

*1 can (16 ounces) garbanzo beans, drained, can be substituted for the cooked dried garbanzo beans.

LENTIL PILAF

3 cups water
1 cup dried lentils
2 tablespoons olive or vegetable oil
3 ounces fully cooked smoked ham, cut into thin strips
¼ teaspoon salt
⅛ teaspoon pepper
1 clove garlic, finely chopped
2 tablespoons chopped fresh parsley
2 tablespoons lemon juice
1 small tomato, seeded and chopped

Heat water and lentils to boiling; reduce heat. Cover and simmer 25 to 30 minutes or until lentils are tender but not mushy; drain.

Heat oil in 10-inch skillet until hot. Add lentils, ham, salt, pepper and garlic. Cook 5 minutes, stirring frequently. Stir in remaining ingredients. Cook and stir 2 minutes or until mixture is hot.   6 SERVINGS (½ CUP EACH); 175 CALORIES PER SERVING.

LENTILS

Lentils are one of the oldest cultivated crops, and references to them date back to 2400 B.C. Lentils are high in protein and provide an excellent substitute for meat when combined with nuts, seeds or grains. They were eaten by the ancient Egyptians, Babylonians, Greeks and Romans. In fact, the first optical lens was named for its resemblance to the lens shape of the lentil.

Though a staple in Indian and Middle Eastern cuisines, lentils are not as prized in Europe. Many Americans first encountered the lentil during World War II when the government recommended eating lentils to stretch our meat supplies. Lentils can be somewhat bland by themselves, but with proper spicing and cooking, they are quite delicious.

Old-fashioned Baked Beans, Garbanzo Beans and Vegetables (page 272), Southwestern Black-eyed Peas

OLD-FASHIONED BAKED BEANS

We based our recipe on Boston baked beans, a dish popular with early Puritans. Because they couldn't cook on their Sabbath— sundown on Saturday to sundown Sunday —they needed a dish that could keep easily on the hearth. Beans with brown bread became a standard Saturday dinner and Sunday breakfast, earning Boston the name "Bean Town."

10 cups water
2 cups dried navy beans
½ cup packed brown sugar
¼ cup molasses
1 teaspoon salt
6 slices bacon, crisply cooked and crumbled
1 medium onion, chopped (about ½ cup)
3 cups water

Heat oven to 350°. Heat 10 cups water and the beans to boiling in Dutch oven. Boil uncovered 2 minutes. Mix in remaining ingredients except 3 cups water. Cover and bake 4 hours, stirring occasionally. Stir in 3 cups water. Bake uncovered 2 to 2¼ hours longer, stirring occasionally, until beans are tender and of desired consistency. 10 SERVINGS (ABOUT ½ CUP EACH); 240 CALORIES PER SERVING.

SOUTHWESTERN BLACK-EYED PEAS

This makes a terrific main dish for two.

2 cups water
¾ cup dried black-eyed peas
1 cup sliced okra
1 small onion, chopped (about ¼ cup)
½ teaspoon salt
2 cloves garlic, crushed
¼ teaspoon red pepper sauce
1 tablespoon vegetable oil
1 tablespoon chopped fresh cilantro
1 small tomato, seeded and chopped

Heat water and peas to boiling in 2-quart saucepan. Boil uncovered 2 minutes; reduce heat. Cover and simmer 30 to 40 minutes, stirring occasionally, until beans are tender (do not boil or peas will burst); drain.

Cook okra, onion, salt, garlic and red pepper sauce in oil in saucepan about 5 minutes or until onion is softened. Stir in cilantro, tomato and peas. Heat until mixture is hot. 6 SERVINGS (ABOUT ½ CUP EACH); 115 CALORIES PER SERVING.

BLACK-EYED PEAS WITH HAM: Add ⅓ cup chopped fully cooked smoked ham while cooking beans. 150 CALORIES PER SERVING.

MEXICAN BLACK BEANS

2¼ cups water
¾ cup dried black beans*
1 tablespoon chopped fresh parsley
1 tablespoon white wine vinegar
1 teaspoon shredded lime or lemon peel
¼ teaspoon red pepper sauce
2 green onions (with tops), thinly sliced
1 medium red or green bell pepper, chopped
   (about 1 cup)

Heat water and beans to boiling in 2-quart sauce-pan. Boil uncovered 2 minutes; reduce heat. Cover and simmer about 1 hour, stirring occasionally, until beans are tender (do not boil or beans will burst); drain. Stir in remaining ingredients. Cook and stir until mixture is hot.   4 SERVINGS (ABOUT ⅔ CUP EACH); 135 CALORIES PER SERVING.

2 cans (15 ounces each) black beans, rinsed and drained, can be substituted for the cooked dried black beans.

ITALIAN WHITE BEANS

2½ cups water
¾ cup dried great northern beans*
½ cup chopped drained marinated sun-dried
   tomatoes
¼ cup sliced ripe olives
1 tablespoon chopped fresh or 1 teaspoon
   dried basil leaves
1 tablespoon olive or vegetable oil
1 clove garlic, crushed

Heat water and beans to boiling in 2-quart sauce-pan. Boil uncovered 2 minutes; reduce heat. Cover and simmer about 45 minutes, stirring occasion-ally, until beans are tender (do not boil or beans will burst); drain. Stir in remaining ingredients. Cook and stir until mixture is hot.   6 SERVINGS (½ CUP EACH); 160 CALORIES PER SERVING.

2 cans (15 ounces each) great northern beans, rinsed and drained, can be substituted for the cooked dried north-ern beans.

——— FIX-IT-FAST ———

♦ Stir leftover grains into packaged pudding mixes, or appetizers such as Mexican Rice Morsels (page 16).

♦ Make the quick, old favorite dessert, Glorified Rice, by folding leftover cooked rice, drained crushed pineapple and chopped maraschino cher-ries into whipped cream.

♦ Save leftover rice for fried rice, to serve with main dishes.

♦ Freeze cooked pasta, grains or legumes. Thaw and add to recipes calling for cooked pasta, grains and legumes.

♦ Use leftover pasta to make pasta salads and in soups.

♦ Make a main-dish pie crust with cooked rice or pasta (see recipe page 175).

♦ Create a quick bean burger by spreading buns with mayonnaise. Top with baked beans and cheese. Broil until cheese melts.

♦ Stir one of the following into cooked pasta, rice or legumes:

   Fresh or dried herbs
   Leftover vegetables
   Crisply cooked bacon or fully cooked smoked
      ham
   Water chestnuts and soy sauce
   Raisins, citrus peel and juice
   Chopped onion, celery and garlic
   Chutney and peanuts
   Salsa
   Barbecue sauce
   Pimiento and olives
   Chopped green chilies
   Shredded cheese

♦ Use rice mix and canned beans for unusual rice-bean combinations—Spanish rice with black beans, for example.

♦ Combine canned black-eyed peas and cooked greens for a quick side dish.

♦ Fry leftover pasta and sprinkle with Parmesan cheese, chili powder, garlic salt, lemon pepper or your favorite spice or flavored salt.

♦ Use rice or grain mixes as a base for casseroles, rice crusts or soups.

NUTRITION INFORMATION

PER SERVING OR UNIT

RECIPE, PAGE

PERCENT U.S. RECOMMENDED DAILY ALLOWANCE

Recipe, Page	Servings per recipe	Calories	Protein (grams)	Carbohydrate (grams)	Fat (grams)	Cholesterol (milligrams)	Sodium (milligrams)	Protein	Vitamin A	Vitamin C	Thiamine	Riboflavin	Niacin	Calcium	Iron
PASTA															
Bacon–Green Bean Pasta Toss, 264	6	175	5	22	7	35	40	8	6	6	22	10	12	2	8
Beet Fettuccine, 262	8	160	5	26	3	70	290	6	0	0	10	6	8	0	8
Beet Fettuccine with Caviar, 263	4	235	7	23	6	25	150	10	6	0	16	8	8	8	6
Carrot Fettuccine, 262	8	155	5	26	3	70	335	6	54	0	10	6	8	0	6
Cornmeal Noodles, 263	8	120	5	22	3	120	140	6	0	0	8	6	6	0	6
Curry Pasta, 262	8	140	4	22	3	70	155	6	0	0	8	6	6	0	6
Curry Pasta with Cucumber, 264	4	310	13	60	13	5	170	18	6	6	46	22	22	10	14
Curry Sausage Couscous, 265	4	210	6	22	7	8	305	8	0	2	10	2	6	0	6
Egg Noodles, 263	8	140	5	22	3	120	140	6	0	0	8	6	6	0	6
Homemade Pasta, 262	8	140	4	22	3	70	155	6	0	0	8	6	6	0	6
Lemon Pasta, 262	8	140	4	22	3	70	155	6	0	0	8	6	6	0	6
Lemon Pasta with Capers, 265	6	260	4	24	16	25	370	6	14	2	20	8	10	2	8
Noodles Romanoff, 265	8	210	5	9	17	40	295	6	12	0	4	6	0	14	2
Poppy Seed Pasta, 262	8	140	4	22	3	70	155	6	0	0	8	6	6	0	6
Spaetzle, 263	6	120	4	15	4	95	140	6	2	0	6	6	4	2	4
Spinach Fettuccine, 262	8	160	6	26	4	70	315	8	38	6	10	10	8	4	10
GRAINS															
Brown Rice, 267	8	90	2	19	0	0	2	2	0	0	4	0	4	0	2
Cheese Grits, 270	8	225	11	20	11	95	335	16	12	0	10	16	4	22	6
Coconut-Papaya Rice, 268	6	350	6	50	15	0	105	8	16	22	12	2	14	4	6
Curried Rice, 268	6	200	3	28	8	0	180	4	2	0	10	8	6	2	6
Fried Polenta Mush, 270	6	65	1	6	4	0	815	0	2	0	2	0	0	0	0
Lemon Rice, 267	6	155	2	27	4	0	45	2	2	0	8	4	4	0	4
Mexican Kasha, 269	8	120	3	14	7	35	180	4	8	4	6	2	4	2	4
Millet Pilaf, 269	6	145	4	28	3	5	335	6	2	28	16	8	4	0	12
Mushroom Rice, 267	6	155	2	27	4	0	45	2	2	0	8	4	4	0	4
Onion Rice, 267	6	155	2	27	4	0	45	2	2	0	8	4	4	0	4
Parsley Rice, 267	6	120	2	27	0	0	2	2	0	0	8	4	4	0	4
Polenta with Cheese, 270	6	125	8	5	8	15	1060	12	4	0	2	4	0	24	0
Rice and Pine Nuts, 268	8	185	3	30	6	0	240	4	2	2	10	2	6	2	4

PER SERVING OR UNIT NUTRITION INFORMATION RECIPE, PAGE	Servings per recipe	Calories	Protein (grams)	Carbohydrate (grams)	Fat (grams)	Cholesterol (grams)	Sodium (milligrams)	Protein	Vitamin A	Vitamin C	Thiamine	Riboflavin	Niacin	Calcium	Iron
GRAINS (continued)															
Three-Grain Medley, 270	6	55	1	8	2	0	125	2	10	4	2	2	2	0	2
White Rice, 267	6	120	2	26	0	0	2	2	0	0	8	4	4	0	4
Wild Rice, 267	6	100	4	21	0	0	2	6	0	0	8	10	8	0	6
LEGUMES															
Black-eyed Peas with Ham, 273	6	115	6	18	3	10	200	8	6	8	16	2	4	2	8
Garbanzo Beans and Vegetables, 272	4	160	4	20	8	0	380	6	82	6	4	6	4	2	8
Italian White Beans, 274	6	160	8	21	6	0	45	10	0	0	14	4	0	8	8
Lentil Pilaf, 272	6	175	13	20	6	10	285	18	4	6	8	6	8	2	16
Mexican Black Beans, 274	4	135	8	25	1	0	10	12	12	56	16	6	4	4	18
Old-fashioned Baked Beans, 273	10	240	10	47	2	5	265	14	0	0	20	6	6	12	22
Red Beans and Rice, 271	8	140	6	16	6	5	300	8	2	22	16	8	6	2	16
Southwestern Black-eyed Peas, 273	6	115	6	18	3	0	190	8	6	8	6	2	2	2	8
Spicy Split Peas, 272	4	190	9	25	6	0	345	14	4	2	18	4	4	2	10

POULTRY

POULTRY

Poultry pleases just about everyone and continues to increase in popularity with every passing day. Economical and relatively low in fat, it is a wise choice. From comforting favorites such as Fried Chicken (page 283), Chicken Pot Pie (page 294) or the Thanksgiving turkey to exotic dishes such as Thai Chicken with Cellophane Noodles (page 293) or Turkey in Lemon Caper Sauce (page 295), poultry is so versatile that it's hard to imagine ever running out of main dish ideas. Poultry can be served as a simple and nutritious turkey salad, as elegant entrées such as Cornish Hens with Glazed Oranges (page 295) and Roast Pheasant in Creamy Mushroom Sauce (page 298) or as a hurry-up dinner. Poultry is your passport to a world of delicious and varied meals.

POULTRY BASICS

Broiler-fryer Chicken: This all-purpose chicken weighs from 3 to 3½ pounds, and your best bargain is buying the whole bird; the bigger the bird, the more meat in proportion to the bone. Allow about ½ pound (bone in) per serving. Cut-up chicken and boneless chicken parts, such as thighs and breasts, will cost more per pound, but offer greater convenience.

Roaster Chicken: This chicken is a little older and larger than the broiler-fryer, weighing 4 to 6 pounds with tender meat that is well suited for roasting.

Stewing Chicken (hen): This chicken weighs 4½ to 6 pounds and provides a generous amount of meat. It is a mature, less tender bird and is best cooked by simmering or in stews and soups.

Rock Cornish Hen (game hen): Small, young, specially bred chickens, weighing 1 to 1½ pounds, these hens have all white meat. Allow ½ to 1 small hen per person. Most supermarkets carry frozen Cornish hens; however, your butcher may be able to special-order fresh hens.

Turkey: Whole turkeys range in size from 4 to 24 pounds, and quality does not vary between fresh and frozen. Whole frozen turkeys can be stored in your freezer at 0° for up to one year, while whole fresh turkeys should be used within one to two days after purchasing. Allow about 1 pound of turkey (bone in) per serving. Fresh turkey breasts, wings, drumsticks, boneless roasts, ground turkey, breast slices and tenderloins are popular turkey selections now widely available in supermarkets. Also available are turkey deli products, such as turkey sausage, salami, pastrami and frankfurters that offer lower fat and lower-calorie alternatives to these traditional items.

Duck: A dark-meat bird that has a high proportion of fat and bone, and is generally roasted. Domesticated duck weighs 4 to 5 pounds; allow about 1 pound of duck (bone in) per serving. Frozen duck is sold in supermarkets—for fresh duck, consult your butcher or a specialty store.

Goose: This dark-meat bird ranges in weight from 4 to 14 pounds, depending on the maturity of the bird. Goose is a fatty bird with a slight "gamey" flavor, and is best roasted. Allow about 1 pound of goose (bone in) per serving. Frozen goose is sold in supermarkets—for fresh goose, consult your butcher or a specialty store.

Pheasant: A small bird that weighs 2 to 3 pounds. Pheasant is generally roasted or braised. Allow about 1 pound of pheasant (bone in) per serving. Frozen pheasant is sold in supermarkets in season, roughly from October through January—for fresh pheasant, consult your butcher or a specialty store.

COOKED POULTRY EQUIVALENTS

Type and Ready-to-Cook Weight	Approximate Cooked Yield
3- to 4-pound broiler-fryer chicken	3 to 4 cups cubed chicken
4½- to 6-pound stewing chicken	4½ to 6 cups cubed chicken
5- to 6-pound boneless turkey roll	10 to 12 cups cubed turkey
12-pound turkey	14 cups cubed turkey

Preceding page: *Mexican Chicken (page 285), Herb-roasted Chicken with Lemon Rice (page 282), Sausage-stuffed Turkey Breast (page 296)*

278

Cutting Up a Whole Chicken

 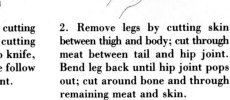 

1. Place breast side up on a cutting surface. Remove wings by cutting into wing joint with a sharp knife, rolling knife to let the blade follow through at curve of the joint.

2. Remove legs by cutting skin between thigh and body; cut through meat between tail and hip joint. Bend leg back until hip joint pops out; cut around bone and through remaining meat and skin.

3. Separate drumsticks from thighs by cutting toward the drumstick at about ⅛ inch from the line of fat that runs crosswise between drumstick and thigh.

 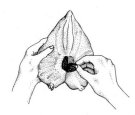 

4. Cut breast from backbone by holding body, neck end down, and cutting down along each side of the backbone through the rib joints.

5. Placing breasts with skin side down, cut just through white cartilage at V of neck to expose end of keel bone (the dark bone at center of breast).

6. Bend back both sides of the breast to pop out keel bone. Cut breasts into halves with knife or kitchen scissors. See illustration #2 (below).

Boning a Chicken Breast

1. Remove skin from a whole chicken breast. Place meaty side down on a clean, dry cutting surface. Cut just through the white cartilage at the V of the neck to expose the end of the keel bone (the dark bone at the center of the breast.)

2. Bend the breast halves back until the keel bone pops away from the meat. Run a finger along each side of the keel bone to loosen it. Pull the bone out; if it comes out in pieces, that is fine.

3. To remove the rib cages, insert the point of the knife under the long rib bone. Cut the rib cage away from the meat. Cut through the shoulder joint to free the entire rib cage.

4. To cut away the wishbone, slip the knife under the white tendons on either side of the breast; loosen and pull out the tendons. Cut the breast into halves.

TIMETABLE FOR MICROWAVING POULTRY

To cook poultry parts, arrange thickest pieces, skin sides up, to outside edge of dish large enough to hold pieces without overlapping. Cover and microwave as directed below until juices run clear.

For boneless whole turkey breast, place skin side down. Cover and begin microwaving on high; continue on medium (50%), turning over after half of cooking time. Microwave until meat thermometer registers 170°.

Type	Weight (pounds)	Power Level	Time
CHICKEN			
Broiler-fryer, cut up	*3 to 3½*	*High*	*15 to 20 minutes, rotating dish ½ turn after 10 minutes*
Breast halves, bone in (two)	*about 1¼*	*High*	*8 to 10 minutes, rotating dish ½ turn after 4 minutes*
Boneless, skinless breast halves (four)	*about 1½*	*High*	*8 to 10 minutes, rotating dish ½ turn after 4 minutes*
Wings	*3 to 3½*	*High*	*12 to 15 minutes, rotating dish ½ turn after 6 minutes*
Legs or thighs	*2*	*High*	*16 to 19 minutes, rotating dish ½ turn after 10 minutes*
ROCK CORNISH HENS			
One	*1 to 1½*	*High*	*10 to 13 minutes, turning over after 10 minutes*
Two	*2 to 3*	*High*	*15 to 20 minutes, turning over after 10 minutes*
TURKEY			
Boneless whole breast	*4 to 5*	*High*	*10 minutes, rotating dish ½ turn*
		Medium (50%)	*40 to 50 minutes; turn breast over after 25 minutes*
Tenderloins (two)	*about 1½*	*High*	*8 to 10 minutes, rotating dish ½ turn after 4 minutes*
Breast slices	*1*	*High*	*3 to 5 minutes, rotating dish ½ turn after 2 minutes*
Ground	*1*	*High*	*6 to 8 minutes, stirring after 4 minutes*

ROAST CHICKEN, DUCK, GOOSE, PHEASANT, ROCK CORNISH HEN AND TURKEY

Remove giblets if present (gizzard, heart and neck). Rinse cavity. Rub cavity of bird lightly with salt if desired. Do not salt cavity if bird is to be stuffed. If stuffing is desired, stuff just before roasting—not ahead of time. (See Rice Stuffing on page 300 and Bread Stuffing on page 300.) Fill wishbone area with stuffing first. Fasten neck skin to back with skewer. Fold wings across back with tips touching. Fill body cavity lightly. (Do not pack—stuffing will expand while cooking.) Tuck drumsticks under band of skin at tail, or tie or skewer to tail.

Place bird, breast side up, on rack in shallow roasting pan. Brush with melted margarine or butter. (If roasting duck or goose, do not brush with margarine. Prick skin with fork.) Do not add water. Do not cover. Follow Timetable for Roasting (below) for approximate roasting time. There is no substitute for a meat thermometer for determining doneness—place in thigh muscle, so thermometer does not touch bone. For turkey, place a tent of aluminum foil loosely over turkey when it begins to turn golden. When two-thirds done, cut band or remove skewer holding legs.

Roast until juices run clear (no pink should remain). Whole birds should reach an internal temperature of 180° when done and the drumstick should move easily when lifted or twisted. When turkey is done, remove from oven and let stand about 15 minutes for easiest serving. Calories per cooked 3-ounce serving:

Chicken	*205 calories*
Duck	*345 calories*
Goose	*260 calories*
Pheasant	*225 calories*
Rock Cornish hen	*115 calories*
Turkey	*175 calories*

TIMETABLE FOR ROASTING

Cut	Ready-to-Cook Weight (pounds)	Oven Temperature	Approximate Roasting Time* (hours)
Chicken	*3 to 3½*	*375°*	*1¾ to 2*
Duck	*3½ to 4*	*350°*	*2*
	5 to 5½	*350°*	*3*
Goose	*7 to 9*	*350°*	*2½ to 3*
	9 to 11	*350°*	*3 to 3½*
	11 to 13	*350°*	*3½ to 4*
Pheasant	*2 to 3*	*350°*	*1¼ to 1½*
Rock Cornish hen	*1 to 1½*	*350°*	*1 to 1¼*
Whole turkey	*6 to 8*	*325°*	*2¼ to 3¼*
	8 to 12	*325°*	*3 to 4*
	12 to 16	*325°*	*3½ to 4½*
	16 to 20	*325°*	*4 to 5*
	20 to 24	*325°*	*4½ to 5½*
Whole turkey (stuffed)	*6 to 8*	*325°*	*3 to 3½*
	8 to 12	*325°*	*3½ to 4½*
	12 to 16	*325°*	*4 to 5*
	16 to 20	*325°*	*4½ to 5½*
	20 to 24	*325°*	*5 to 6½*
Turkey breast	*2 to 4*	*325°*	*1½ to 2*
	3 to 5	*325°*	*1½ to 2½*
	5 to 7	*325°*	*2 to 2½*

Roasting times will be affected by types of oven, actual oven temperature and shape and tenderness of bird. Times given are for unstuffed birds unless noted. Stuffed birds other than turkey require 15 to 30 minutes longer. Begin checking turkey doneness about 1 hour before end of recommended roasting time. For commercially prestuffed turkeys, follow package directions very carefully; do not use this timetable.

STUFFING BASICS

If you enjoy the flavor of moist stuffing with your bird, you can bake the stuffing in a greased, covered casserole the last hour while your bird roasts. If you prefer stuffing your bird, follow these helpful hints:

♦ Only stuff turkey *immediately* before roasting. Stuffing poultry in advance can allow harmful bacteria to multiply and cause food poisoning.

♦ The cavity of the bird should be lightly stuffed because the stuffing expands as it cooks.

♦ Allow approximately ¾ cup of stuffing per pound of ready-to-cook poultry. A 1- to 1½-pound Rock Cornish hen requires about 1 cup stuffing. Allow about ½ cup stuffing per pound of dressed fish (page 192).

♦ Roasting a stuffed bird requires approximately three additional minutes of roasting time per pound of bird.

♦ Stuffing should come to an internal temperature of 165° for food safety reasons. It's wise to check the temperature of both the stuffing and meat in several places.

♦ After you've finished enjoying the bird and stuffing, separate the leftover meat from the stuffing and refrigerate immediately.

Carving Turkey or Chicken

Gently pulling leg away from body, cut through joint between thigh and body. Remove leg. Cut between drumstick and thigh; slice off meat. Make a deep horizontal cut into breast just above wing. Insert fork in top of breast and, starting halfway up breast, carve thin slices down to the cut, working upward. (To carve duckling, cut into quarters or halves with kitchen scissors.)

HERB-ROASTED CHICKEN WITH LEMON RICE

The cream cheese mixture that coats the chicken breast keeps the meat moist during roasting, adding a rich basil flavor.

> 3- to 3½-pound broiler-fryer chicken
> 1 teaspoon finely shredded lemon peel
> 1 package (3 ounces) cream cheese, softened
> 1 tablespoon chopped fresh or 1 teaspoon dried basil leaves
> 2 cups cooked rice (page 267)
> 2 tablespoons chopped fresh parsley
> 1 tablespoon finely chopped lemongrass, if desired

Heat oven to 375°.

Mix rice, parsley, lemongrass and lemon peel. Fill wishbone area with rice mixture. Fasten neck skin to back with skewer. Fold wings across back with tips touching. Fill body cavity with rice mixture. Tie drumsticks or skewer to tail.

Place chicken, breast side up, on rack in shallow roasting pan. Mix cream cheese and basil. Loosen breast skin gently with fingers as far back as possible without tearing skin. Spread cream cheese mixture between breast meat and skin. Cover breast with skin.

Roast uncovered 1 to 1¼ hours or until drumstick moves easily. 6 SERVINGS; 370 CALORIES PER SERVING.

1. Loosen breast skin gently with fingers as far back as possible.

2. Spread cream cheese mixture evenly between breast meat and skin working from back toward the front.

Buttermilk Fried Chicken, Oven-barbecued Chicken, (page 284), Three-Mustard Potato Salad (page 312)

FRIED CHICKEN

Fried chicken used to be served only in the spring when the tender "spring chickens" were available. Now, you can make fried chicken any time with the classic version here, or try one of the delicious variations.

½ cup all-purpose flour
1 teaspoon paprika
½ teaspoon salt
¼ teaspoon pepper
3- to 3½-pound broiler-fryer chicken, cut up
Vegetable oil

Mix flour, paprika, salt and pepper. Coat chicken with flour mixture.

Heat oil (¼ inch) in 12-inch skillet over medium-high heat. Cook chicken in oil about 10 minutes or until light brown on all sides; reduce heat. Cover tightly and simmer about 35 minutes, turning once or twice, until juices run clear. If skillet cannot be covered tightly, add 1 to 2 tablespoons water. Remove cover during last 5 minutes of cooking to crisp chicken.   6 SERVINGS; 385 CALORIES PER SERVING.

BUTTERMILK FRIED CHICKEN: Increase flour to 1 cup, paprika to 2 teaspoons and salt to 1 teaspoon. Dip chicken into 1 cup buttermilk before coating with flour mixture.   440 CALORIES PER SERVING.

MARYLAND FRIED CHICKEN: Coat chicken with flour mixture. Beat 2 eggs and 2 tablespoons water. Mix 2 cups cracker crumbs, dry bread crumbs or 1 cup cornmeal and ¼ teaspoon salt. Dip chicken into egg mixture. Coat with cracker crumb mixture.   545 CALORIES PER SERVING.

OVEN-FRIED CHICKEN

¼ cup margarine or butter
½ cup all-purpose flour
1 teaspoon paprika
½ teaspoon salt
¼ teaspoon pepper
3 pound broiler-fryer chicken, cut up

Heat oven to 425°. Heat margarine in rectangular pan, 13×9×2 inches, in oven until melted. Mix flour, paprika, salt and pepper. Coat chicken with flour mixture. Place chicken, skin sides down, in pan. Bake uncovered 30 minutes. Turn chicken and bake about 30 minutes longer or until juices run clear.   6 SERVINGS; 350 CALORIES PER SERVING.

CRUNCHY OVEN-FRIED CHICKEN: Substitute 1 cup cornflake crumbs for the ½ cup flour. Dip chicken into ¼ cup margarine or butter, melted, before coating with crumb mixture.   350 CALORIES PER SERVING.

OVEN-BARBECUED CHICKEN

3- to 3½-pound broiler-fryer chicken, cut up
¾ cup chili sauce
2 tablespoons honey
2 tablespoons soy sauce
1 teaspoon dry mustard
½ teaspoon prepared horseradish
½ teaspoon red pepper sauce

Heat oven to 375°. Place chicken, skin sides up, in ungreased rectangular pan, 13 × 9 × 2 inches. Mix remaining ingredients. Pour over chicken. Cover and bake 30 minutes. Spoon sauce over chicken. Bake uncovered about 30 minutes longer or until juices of chicken run clear.   6 SERVINGS; 305 CALORIES PER SERVING.

HERBED CHICKEN

2 tablespoons margarine or butter
2 tablespoons olive or vegetable oil
¼ cup finely chopped onion
¼ cup lemon juice
2 tablespoons Worcestershire sauce
1½ teaspoon chopped fresh or ½ teaspoon dried basil leaves
¾ teaspoon chopped fresh or ¼ teaspoon dried marjoram leaves
¾ teaspoon chopped fresh or ¼ teaspoon dried oregano leaves
2 large cloves garlic, finely chopped
3- to 3½-pound broiler-fryer chicken, cut up

Heat oven to 375°. Heat margarine and oil in rectangular pan, 13 × 9 × 2 inches, in oven until margarine is melted. Stir in remaining ingredients except chicken. Place chicken in pan, turning to coat with herb mixture. Arrange chicken pieces skin sides up. Bake uncovered 30 minutes. Turn chicken. Bake about 30 minutes longer or until juices run clear.   6 SERVINGS; 345 CALORIES PER SERVING.

To Microwave: Place margarine and oil in rectangular microwavable dish, 12 × 7½ × 2 inches. Microwave uncovered on high 45 to 60 seconds or until margarine is melted. Stir in remaining ingredients except chicken. Place chicken in dish, turning to coat with herb mixture. Arrange chicken, skin sides up and thickest parts to outside edges, in dish. Cover with waxed paper and microwave on high 16 to 20 minutes, rotating dish ½ turn after 10 minutes, until juices run clear.

 ## BROILED CHICKEN

3- to 3½-pound broiler-fryer chicken, cut into quarters or pieces
2 tablespoons margarine or butter, melted

Fold wing tips across back side of chicken quarters. Set oven control to broil. Brush chicken with 1 tablespoon margarine. Place chicken, skin sides down, on rack in broiler pan. Place broiler pan so top of chicken is 7 to 9 inches from heat. Broil 30 minutes. Sprinkle with salt and pepper. Turn chicken and brush with 1 tablespoon margarine. Broil 15 to 25 minutes longer or until chicken is brown and juices run clear.   6 SERVINGS; 260 CALORIES PER SERVING.

To Grill: Cover and grill chicken, bone sides down, 5 to 6 inches from medium coals 40 to 60 minutes, turning and brushing with margarine, until juices run clear.

BROILED LEMON CHICKEN: Do not brush with margarine or butter. Cut 1 lemon in half. Rub and squeeze lemon over chicken. Brush with 2 tablespoons margarine or butter, melted. Mix ½ teaspoon salt, ½ teaspoon paprika and ⅛ teaspoon pepper. Sprinkle over chicken. Broil as directed. 280 CALORIES PER SERVING.

CHICKEN FRICASSEE

1 cup all-purpose flour
2 teaspoons paprika, if desired
1 teaspoon salt
¼ teaspoon pepper
3- to 3½-pound broiler-fryer chicken, cut up
Vegetable oil
1 cup water
3 tablespoons all-purpose flour
Milk
Herb Dumplings (page 37)

Mix 1 cup flour, the paprika, salt and pepper. Coat chicken with flour mixture. Heat thin layer of oil in 12-inch skillet or Dutch oven. Cook chicken in oil until brown on all sides. Drain fat from skillet; reserve. Add water. Cover and cook over low heat about 45 minutes, adding water if necessary, until juices run clear.

Remove chicken and keep warm. Drain liquid from skillet; reserve. Heat 3 tablespoons reserved fat in skillet. Stir in 3 tablespoons flour. Cook over medium heat, stirring constantly, until mixture is smooth and bubbly; remove from heat. Add enough milk to reserved liquid to measure 3 cups. Pour into skillet. Heat to boiling, stirring constantly. Boil and stir 1 minute. Return chicken to gravy.

Prepare Herb Dumplings. Drop by spoonfuls onto hot chicken (do not drop directly into liquid). Cook uncovered 10 minutes. Cover and cook 20 minutes longer. 6 SERVINGS; 605 CALORIES PER SERVING.

SWEET-AND-SOUR CHICKEN

3- to 3½-pound broiler-fryer chicken, cut up
1 egg, slightly beaten
1 tablespoon cornstarch
2 teaspoons soy sauce
Dash of white pepper
2 tomatoes
1 green bell pepper
Vegetable oil
½ cup all-purpose flour
½ cup water
¼ cup cornstarch
1 tablespoon vegetable oil
½ teaspoon baking soda
1¼ cups sugar
1 cup chicken broth
¾ cup white vinegar
1 tablespoon vegetable oil
Salt
2 teaspoons soy sauce
1 clove garlic, finely chopped
¼ cup cornstarch
¼ cup cold water
1 can (8¼ ounces) pineapple chunks, drained

Remove skin and bones from chicken. Cut chicken into 1-inch pieces. Mix egg, 1 tablespoon cornstarch, 2 teaspoons soy sauce and the white pepper in glass or plastic bowl. Stir in chicken. Cover and refrigerate 20 minutes. Cut each tomato into 8 wedges. Cut bell pepper into 1-inch pieces.

Heat oil (1½ inches) in wok or 12-inch skillet to 350°. Mix flour, ½ cup water, ¼ cup cornstarch, 1 tablespoon oil, the salt and baking soda. Stir in chicken until well coated. Fry about 15 pieces at a time for 3 minutes, turning frequently, until light brown. Drain on paper towels. Increase oil temperature to 375°. Fry chicken again all at one time about 1 minute or until golden brown. Drain on paper towels.

Heat sugar, chicken broth, vinegar, 1 tablespoon oil, 2 teaspoons soy sauce and the garlic to boiling

in 2-quart saucepan. Mix ¼ cup cornstarch and ¼ cup water. Stir into chicken broth mixture. Cook and stir about 10 seconds or until thickened. Stir in tomatoes, bell pepper and pineapple. Heat to boiling. Pour over chicken. 6 SERVINGS; 655 CALORIES PER SERVING.

MEXICAN CHICKEN

3 tablespoons vegetable oil
3- to 3½-pound broiler-fryer chicken, cut up
½ cup all-purpose flour
2½ cups chicken broth
1½ to 2 teaspoons chili powder
½ teaspoon salt
⅛ teaspoon pepper
Dash of ground red pepper (cayenne)
1 medium onion, chopped
1 clove garlic, finely chopped
1 can (28 ounces) whole tomatoes, undrained
1 cup uncooked regular long-grain rice
1 cup frozen corn or 1 can (8 ounces) whole kernel corn, undrained
1 can (8 ounces) kidney beans, undrained

Heat oil in Dutch oven. Coat chicken with flour. Cook in oil over medium heat 15 to 20 minutes or until brown; drain.

Heat oven to 350°. Mix remaining ingredients except rice, corn and beans. Pour over chicken. Cover and bake 30 minutes. Stir in rice, corn and beans. Cover and bake 30 to 40 minutes or until juices of chicken run clear and rice is tender. Serve with tortilla chips if desired. 6 SERVINGS; 435 CALORIES PER SERVING.

To Microwave: Omit oil and flour. Decrease water to 1 cup. Place chicken with thickest parts to outside edge in 3-quart microwavable casserole. Cover tightly and microwave on high 15 minutes, rotating casserole ½ turn after 5 minutes; drain. Mix remaining ingredients except corn and beans; break up tomatoes. Stir into chicken. Cover tightly and microwave on high 25 to 30 minutes, stirring every 8 minutes, until juices of chicken run clear and rice is tender. Drain corn and beans. Stir into chicken mixture. Cover tightly and microwave on high 4 to 6 minutes or until corn and beans are hot. Serve with tortilla chips if desired.

BRUNSWICK STEW

Brunswick Stew comes by way of the southeastern Native-American dish succotash.

3- to 3½-pound broiler-fryer chicken, cut up
2 cups water
½ teaspoon salt
¼ teaspoon pepper
Dash of ground red pepper (cayenne)
2 cans (16 ounces each) whole tomatoes, undrained
1 package (10 ounces) frozen corn or 1 can (17 ounces) whole kernel corn, undrained
1 package (10 ounces) frozen lima beans or 1 can (16 ounces) lima beans, undrained
1 medium potato, cubed (about 1 cup)
1 medium onion, chopped (about ½ cup)
½ cup water
2 tablespoons all-purpose flour

Place chicken, giblets, neck, 2 cups water and the salt in 5-quart Dutch oven. Heat to boiling; reduce heat. Cover and simmer about 40 minutes or until juices run clear.

Skim fat from broth. Remove skin and bones from chicken if desired. Return chicken to broth. Stir in pepper, red pepper, tomatoes, corn, beans, potato and onion. Heat to boiling; reduce heat. Simmer uncovered 45 minutes. Shake ½ cup water and the flour in tightly covered container. Stir into stew. Heat to boiling, stirring constantly. Boil and stir 1 minute. 8 SERVINGS; 390 CALORIES PER SERVING.

CHICKEN WITH WINTER FRUIT

2 tablespoons vegetable oil
3- to 3½-pound broiler-fryer chicken, cut up
2 tablespoons chopped fresh parsley
1 cup pitted prunes (about 18)
⅓ cup dried apricot halves (about 12)
4 medium carrots, cut into ½-inch slices
1 medium onion, thinly sliced
1 cup apple juice
2 tablespoons lemon juice
¼ teaspoon salt
2 cloves garlic, finely chopped
1 can (14½ ounces) ready-to-serve chicken broth

Heat oil in 5-quart Dutch oven until hot. Cook chicken in oil until brown on all sides. Drain fat.

Add parsley, prunes, apricots, carrots and onion. Mix remaining ingredients and pour over chicken. Heat to boiling; reduce heat. Cover and simmer about 45 minutes or until juices of chicken run clear and carrots are crisp-tender. 6 SERVINGS; 415 CALORIES PER SERVING.

To Microwave: Omit oil. Cut carrots into ¼-inch slices. Decrease apple juice to ½ cup. Arrange chicken pieces, thickest parts to outside edge, in 3-quart microwavable casserole. Sprinkle chicken with paprika. Cover tightly and microwave on high 10 minutes. Drain fat. Add parsley, prunes, apricots, carrots and onion. Mix remaining ingredients. Pour over chicken. Cover and microwave on high 10 to 14 minutes longer or until juices of chicken run clear and carrots are crisp-tender.

CHICKEN JAMBALAYA

3- to 3½-pound broiler-fryer chicken, cut up
2 cups water
¾ teaspoon salt
¼ teaspoon pepper
8 pork sausage links
1 cup uncooked regular long-grain rice
1½ teaspoons chopped fresh or ½ teaspoon dried thyme leaves
⅛ to ¼ teaspoon ground red pepper (cayenne)
1 medium onion, chopped (about ½ cup)
1 large clove garlic, finely chopped
1 can (16 ounces) stewed tomatoes, undrained
Chopped fresh parsley

Remove skin from chicken if desired. Place chicken, water, salt and pepper in Dutch oven. Heat to boiling; reduce heat. Cover and simmer 20 minutes. Remove chicken from broth. Strain broth through cheesecloth-lined sieve. Skim fat from broth.

Cook sausage in Dutch oven until brown. Drain fat, reserving 1 tablespoon in Dutch oven. Add chicken. Stir in reserved broth and remaining ingredients except parsley. Heat to boiling, stirring once or twice; reduce heat. Cover and simmer 30 to 40 minutes or until juices of chicken run clear and rice is tender. Sprinkle with parsley. 6 SERVINGS; 350 CALORIES PER SERVING.

Clockwise from top left: Chicken Jambalaya, Baking Powder Biscuits (page 38), Brunswick Stew, Chicken with Winter Fruit

CHICKEN

In the Depression, the phrase "a chicken in every pot" was a measure of comfort and prosperity, something to which everyone aspired. Chicken has always been important to us—for the eggs that they lay and, of course, their delicious and versatile meat. Settlers brought the first chickens to America in the 1700s, and they were considered a delicacy. As the country became more firmly established, so did chickens, and we created our own breeds such as Rhode Island Red and Plymouth Rock.

Different regions created signature chicken dishes—Southern fried chicken, Mid-Atlantic chicken and dumplings, New England chicken pot pies, southwestern chicken burritos and, of course, the countrywide classic, roast chicken. Today, chicken continues to grow in popularity, available in parts or whole, or skinless and boneless.

HONEY-GINGER CHICKEN

2 tablespoons vegetable oil
2 tablespoons margarine or butter
⅓ cup all-purpose flour
1½ teaspoons grated gingerroot or ½ teaspoon ground ginger
¼ teaspoon pepper
3 pounds chicken drumsticks or thighs
⅓ cup honey
⅓ cup chili sauce
⅓ cup soy sauce
½ teaspoon ground ginger

Heat oven to 425°. Heat oil and margarine in rectangular pan, 13×9×2 inches, in oven until melted. Mix flour, 1½ teaspoon gingerroot and the pepper. Coat chicken pieces thoroughly with flour mixture. Place chicken, skin sides down, in pan. Bake uncovered 30 minutes. Turn chicken. Bake 15 minutes. Remove chicken and drain fat. Line pan with aluminum foil. Return chicken to pan.

Mix remaining ingredients. Pour over chicken. Bake 15 minutes, spooning honey mixture over chicken every 5 minutes, until juices run clear. 6 SERVINGS; 500 CALORIES PER SERVING.

To Microwave: Omit oil and margarine. Coat chicken pieces as directed. Arrange chicken, skin sides up and thickest parts to outside edges, in rectangular microwavable dish, 13×9×2 inches. Cover with waxed paper and microwave on high 10 minutes; drain. Mix remaining ingredients. Pour over chicken. Cover with waxed paper and microwave on high 10 to 15 minutes, rotating dish ½ turn every 5 minutes and spooning sauce over chicken, until juices run clear.

CARIBBEAN CHICKEN

The Caribbean flair in this dish comes from black beans, lime, gingerroot and mango. Try substituting papaya for the mango.

4 chicken drumsticks (about 1 pound)
4 chicken thighs (about 1 pound)
2 cans (15 ounces each) black beans, undrained
1 tablespoon grated gingerroot or 1 teaspoon ground ginger
1 teaspoon finely shredded lime peel
2 tablespoons lime juice
½ teaspoon salt
1 clove garlic, finely chopped
1 cup cubed mango or 1 can (8 ounces) peach slices, drained and cut up
2 green onions, thinly sliced (with tops)

Heat oven to 375°. Place chicken pieces, skin sides up, in ungreased rectangular baking dish, 13×9×2 inches. Bake uncovered 40 minutes. Remove excess fat. Mix remaining ingredients. Spoon over and around chicken. Cover and bake 30 minutes longer or until juices of chicken run clear. 4 SERVINGS; 310 CALORIES PER SERVING.

To Microwave: Arrange chicken pieces, skin sides up and thickest parts to outside edges, in rectangular microwavable dish, 12×7½×2 inches. Cover tightly and microwave on high 9 minutes. Remove excess fat. Rotate dish ½ turn. Mix remaining ingredients. Spoon over and around chicken pieces. Cover tightly and microwave on high about 8 minutes longer or until juices of chicken run clear. Let stand 3 minutes.

Chicken with Tomatoes and Leeks (page 291), Madeira-sauced Chicken Wings

MADEIRA-SAUCED CHICKEN WINGS

12 chicken wings (about 2 pounds)
¾ cup water
⅓ cup Madeira*
⅓ cup chopped onion
2 teaspoons finely shredded orange peel
¼ teaspoon salt
2 cloves garlic, finely chopped
2 teaspoons cornstarch
3 slices bacon, crisply cooked and crumbled

Cut each chicken wing at joints to make 3 pieces; discard tips. Cut off excess skin; discard. Place chicken, water, Madeira, onion, orange peel, salt and garlic in glass bowl or plastic bag. Cover bowl or seal bag tightly. Refrigerate at least 2 hours.

Drain chicken, reserving marinade. Set oven control to broil. Place chicken on rack in broiler pan. Place broiler pan so top of chicken is 5 to 7 inches from heat. Broil about 10 minutes, turning once, until juices run clear.

Mix ¼ cup reserved marinade and the cornstarch in 1½-quart saucepan. Stir in remaining marinade. Cook over low heat, stirring constantly, until mixture thickens. Stir in bacon. Serve with chicken wings.   4 SERVINGS; 180 CALORIES PER SERVING.

²⁄₃ cup orange juice can be substituted for the Madeira. Reduce water to ½ cup.

To Microwave: Decrease water to ½ cup (¼ cup if substituting orange juice for the Madeira). Place chicken wings in rectangular microwavable dish, 11 × 7 × 1½ inches. Cover with waxed paper and microwave on high 8 to 10 minutes, rotating dish ½ turn after 4 minutes, until juices run clear; drain. Mix ¼ cup reserved marinade and the cornstarch in 4-cup microwavable measure. Stir in remaining marinade. Microwave uncovered on high 3 to 4 minutes or until thickened and boiling. Continue as directed.

Using scissors or sharp knife, cut each chicken wing at joints to make 3 pieces; discard tips.

CHICKEN CURRY

⅓ cup margarine or butter
1½ teaspoons curry powder
1 small onion, coarsely chopped
1 clove garlic, chopped
¼ cup all-purpose flour
2 teaspoons sugar
½ teaspoon ground ginger
¼ teaspoon dry mustard
¼ teaspoon pepper
1 medium tomato, chopped
1 medium tart apple, chopped
¼ pound fully cooked smoked ham, chopped
¼ cup shredded coconut
2 cups chicken broth
1½ pounds skinless boneless chicken breast
    halves or thighs, cut into ½-inch slices
4 cups hot cooked rice (page 267)

Heat margarine in 3-quart saucepan over medium heat. Cook curry powder, onion and garlic in margarine 2 minutes. Stir in flour, sugar, ginger, mustard, pepper, tomato, apple and ham. Cook 5 minutes, stirring occasionally. Stir in coconut and chicken broth. Heat to boiling; reduce heat. Cover and simmer 1 hour, stirring occasionally.

Rub mixture through sieve. Return liquid to saucepan. Add chicken. Heat to boiling; reduce heat. Cover and simmer 25 to 30 minutes or until juices of chicken run clear. Serve with rice. 6 SERVINGS; 440 CALORIES PER SERVING.

SHRIMP CURRY: Substitute 1½ pounds fresh or frozen medium shrimp (in shells), cleaned and deveined, for the chicken. Increase flour to ⅓ cup. Heat sauce to boiling. Add shrimp. Heat to boiling; reduce heat. Simmer uncovered about 3 minutes, stirring occasionally, just until shrimp are done. 420 CALORIES PER SERVING.

OVEN CHICKEN KIEV

¼ cup margarine or butter, softened
1 tablespoon chopped fresh chives or parsley
⅛ teaspoon garlic powder
3 whole chicken breasts (about 2¼ pounds)
3 cups cornflakes, crushed (about 1½ cups)
2 tablespoons chopped fresh parsley
½ teaspoon paprika
¼ cup buttermilk or milk

Mix margarine, chives and garlic powder. Shape into rectangle, 3 × 2 inches. Cover and freeze about 30 minutes or until firm.

Heat oven to 425°. Grease square pan, 9 × 9 × 2 inches. Remove skin and bones from chicken breasts. Cut chicken breasts in half. Flatten each half to ¼-inch thickness between plastic wrap or waxed paper. Cut margarine mixture crosswise into 6 pieces. Place 1 piece on center of each chicken breast half. Fold long sides over margarine. Fold ends up and secure with wooden pick.

Mix cornflakes, parsley and paprika. Dip chicken into buttermilk. Coat evenly with cornflake mixture. Place chicken, seam sides down, in pan. Bake uncovered about 35 minutes or until juices run clear. Remove wooden picks. 6 SERVINGS; 265 CALORIES PER SERVING.

To Microwave: Prepare chicken as directed. Arrange coated chicken breast halves, seam sides down, on microwavable rack in microwavable dish. Microwave uncovered on high 8 to 10 minutes, rotating dish ½ turn after 4 minutes, until juices run clear. Let stand uncovered 5 minutes.

CHICKEN CORDON BLEU

2 whole chicken breasts (about 1½ pounds)
4 thin slices fully cooked smoked ham or
    prosciutto
4 thin slices Swiss cheese
¼ cup all-purpose flour
¼ teaspoon salt
¼ teaspoon pepper
1 egg, slightly beaten
½ cup dry bread crumbs
3 tablespoon vegetable oil
2 tablespoons water

Remove skin and bones from chicken breasts. Cut chicken breasts in half. Flatten each half to ¼-inch thickness between plastic wrap or waxed paper. Place 1 slice ham and 1 slice cheese on each chicken breast. Roll up carefully, beginning at narrow end. Secure with wooden picks. Mix flour, salt and pepper. Coat rolls with flour mixture. Dip rolls into egg and roll in bread crumbs.

Heat oil in 10-inch skillet over medium heat. Cook rolls in oil 5 to 10 minutes, turning occasionally, until light brown. Add water. Cover and simmer about 10 minutes or until juices run clear. Remove wooden picks. 4 SERVINGS; 445 CALORIES PER SERVING.

To Microwave: Omit vegetable oil and water. Place chicken, seam sides up, on microwavable rack in rectangular microwavable dish, 11 × 7 × 1½ inches. Cover with waxed paper and microwave on high 6 to 8 minutes or until juices run clear. Remove wooden picks.

CHICKEN WITH TOMATOES AND LEEKS

3 slices bacon
4 skinless boneless chicken breast halves (about 1 pound)
2 tablespoons margarine or butter
2 medium leeks, cut lengthwise in half and sliced*
1 can (5 ounces) evaporated milk
2 teaspoons chopped fresh or ½ teaspoon dried tarragon leaves
¼ teaspoon red pepper sauce
4 plum tomatoes or 2 medium tomatoes, chopped

Cook bacon in 10-inch skillet until crisp. Drain bacon, reserving fat in skillet. Cook chicken in fat over medium heat 12 to 14 minutes, turning once, until juices run clear. Remove chicken from skillet; keep warm. Drain fat from skillet.

Cook and stir leeks in margarine in skillet 5 to 7 minutes or until crisp-tender. Stir in milk, tarragon and red pepper sauce. Heat to boiling, stirring occasionally. Boil and stir until slightly thickened. Crumble bacon. Stir bacon, tomatoes and chicken into skillet. Heat over medium heat about 2 minutes, spooning sauce over chicken, until chicken is hot.   4 SERVINGS; 360 CALORIES PER SERVING.

*1 medium onion, thinly sliced, can be substituted for leeks.

⏱ RASPBERRY-PEACH CHICKEN

½ cup fresh or frozen unsweetened raspberries
1 small peach, pared and sliced
2 tablespoons peach brandy or apple juice
2 tablespoons honey
¼ cup all-purpose flour
¼ teaspoon salt
¼ teaspoon pepper
4 small skinless boneless chicken breast halves (about 1 pound)
1 tablespoon vegetable oil

Place raspberries, peach slices, brandy and honey in blender or food processor. Cover and blend on high speed, or process, about 1 minute or until smooth. Heat in 1-quart saucepan until hot; reduce heat. Keep warm.

Mix flour, salt and pepper. Coat chicken breast halves with flour mixture. Heat oil in 10-inch skillet. Cook chicken in oil over medium heat 12 to 14 minutes, turning once, until juices run clear.

Spoon some sauce on serving plate. Place chicken on sauce and drizzle with additional sauce. Garnish with remaining raspberries if desired.   4 SERVINGS; 250 CALORIES PER SERVING.

CHICKEN WITH CASHEWS

2 chicken breasts (about 2¼ pounds)
1 egg white
1 teaspoon cornstarch
1 teaspoon soy sauce
Dash of white pepper
1 large green bell pepper
1 medium onion
1 can (8½ ounces) sliced bamboo shoots, drained
1 tablespoon cornstarch
1 tablespoon cold water
1 tablespoon soy sauce
2 tablespoons vegetable oil
1 cup cashews
¼ teaspoon salt
1 teaspoon finely chopped gingerroot
2 tablespoons vegetable oil
1 tablespoon Hoisin sauce
2 teaspoons chili paste
¼ cup chicken broth
2 tablespoons chopped green onions (with tops)

Remove skin and bones from chicken breasts. Cut chicken breasts in half and cut into ¼-inch pieces. Mix egg white, 1 teaspoon cornstarch, 1 teaspoon soy sauce and the white pepper in glass or plastic bowl. Stir in chicken. Cover and refrigerate 20 minutes. Cut bell pepper into ¾-inch pieces. Cut onion into 8 pieces. Cut bamboo shoots into ½-inch pieces. Mix 1 tablespoon cornstarch, the water and 1 tablespoon soy sauce.

Heat wok or 12-inch skillet until hot. Add 2 tablespoons oil and tilt wok to coat side. Stir-fry cashews about 1 minute or until light brown. Remove cashews from wok. Drain on paper towels. Sprinkle with salt. Add chicken to wok. Stir-fry chicken about 4 minutes or until white. Remove chicken from wok.

Add onion pieces and gingerroot to wok. Stir-fry until gingerroot is light brown. Stir in bamboo shoots. Add 2 tablespoons oil and rotate wok to coat side. Add chicken, bell pepper, Hoisin sauce and chili paste. Stir-fry 1 minute. Stir in chicken broth. Heat to boiling. Stir in cornstarch mixture. Cook and stir about 20 seconds or until thickened. Stir in cashews and green onions.   6 SERVINGS; 335 CALORIES PER SERVING.

CHICKEN EN PAPILLOTE

2 whole chicken breasts (about 1½ pounds)
6 cups chopped fresh spinach
¼ cup shredded provolone cheese (1 ounce)
1 tablespoon chopped sun-dried tomatoes
1 clove garlic, finely chopped
½ lemon
4 twelve-inch-square pieces kitchen parchment paper or aluminum foil

Remove skin and bones from chicken breasts. Cut chicken breasts in half. Flatten each half to ¼-inch thickness between plastic wrap or waxed paper. Cover and cook spinach in 2-quart saucepan over medium heat 2 to 3 minutes or until wilted; drain thoroughly. Reserve 2 tablespoons spinach.

Heat oven to 400°. Mix reserved spinach, the cheese, tomatoes and garlic. Spoon one-fourth of the spinach mixture on one side of each chicken breast half. Fold chicken over filling. Squeeze lemon over chicken. Sprinkle with paprika if desired.

Cut each piece of parchment paper into a 12-inch circle. Spoon one-fourth of the cooked spinach onto half of each circle. Place one stuffed chicken breast half on spinach. Fold other half of paper circle over chicken. Seal edges by turning up and folding together. Twist ends several times to secure packet. Bake on cookie sheet about 15 minutes or until paper puffs up and is light brown. To serve, cut a large X shape on top of each packet and fold back corners.   4 SERVINGS; 180 CALORIES PER SERVING.

To Microwave: Do not use aluminum foil. Arrange sealed packets in circle in microwave oven. Microwave on high 8 to 10 minutes, rearranging packets after 4 minutes, until paper puffs up. Continue as directed.

Seal edges by turning and folding together. Twist ends several times to secure packet.

CHICKEN BREASTS IN MUSTARD SAUCE

Different types of mustard will make subtle and delicious changes in the flavor of this dish. You may want to try a robust grainy German mustard or use a light champagne mustard for more delicate flavor.

2 tablespoons margarine or butter
4 skinless boneless chicken breast halves (about 1 pound)
¼ cup finely chopped onion
2 tablespoons apple brandy or apple juice
1 cup whipping (heavy) cream
2 tablespoons chopped fresh parsley
2 tablespoons Dijon mustard
¼ cup finely chopped walnuts

Heat margarine in 10-inch skillet over medium heat. Add chicken breasts. Cook 12 to 14 minutes, turning after 6 minutes, until juices run clear. Remove chicken and reserve.

Add onion and brandy to skillet. Heat to boiling; reduce heat. Stir in whipping cream, parsley and mustard. Cook and stir over medium heat 5 minutes. Add chicken and walnuts. Heat until hot. 4 SERVINGS; 395 CALORIES PER SERVING.

CHICKEN LIVERS WITH GLAZED APPLES

1 pound chicken livers, each cut in half or into fourths
3 green onions (with tops), sliced
2 tablespoons margarine or butter
½ teaspoon salt
2 medium cooking apples, each cored and cut into eighths
¼ cup packed brown sugar

Cook chicken livers and onions in margarine in 10-inch skillet over medium heat about 6 minutes, stirring occasionally, until livers are brown. Sprinkle with salt. Push to one side of skillet.

Place apples in skillet. Sprinkle with brown sugar. Cook uncovered over medium heat about 8 minutes, stirring occasionally, until apples are tender and glazed. Serve sauce over livers. Garnish with sliced green onion tops if desired.   4 SERVINGS; 205 CALORIES PER SERVING.

Thai Chicken with Cellophane Noodles, Peanutty Chicken Kabobs

🕐 THAI CHICKEN WITH CELLOPHANE NOODLES

1 package (3¾ ounces) cellophane noodles
1 pound skinless boneless chicken breast halves or thighs
2 tablespoons vegetable oil
1 cup thinly sliced carrots
4 serrano chilies, seeded and finely chopped
2 cups shredded Chinese cabbage
1 cup diagonally sliced celery
3 green onions (with tops), cut into 2-inch pieces
⅓ cup fish sauce or soy sauce
2 teaspoons finely shredded lime peel

Cover noodles with cold water. Let stand 20 minutes; drain. Cut into 3- to 4-inch pieces. Cut chicken breast halves into thin slices.

Heat wok or 12-inch skillet until hot. Add oil and tilt wok to coat side. Add chicken, carrots and chilies. Stir-fry about 4 minutes or until chicken is white. Remove from wok.

Add cabbage, celery and onions. Stir-fry 1 minute. Stir in chicken, noodles and remaining ingredients. Stir-fry about 1 minute or until mixture is hot. 4 SERVINGS; 205 CALORIES PER SERVING.

🕐 PEANUTTY CHICKEN KABOBS

The unusual sauce for these kabobs comes from an old standby—the crunchy peanut butter in your cupboard.

1 pound skinless boneless chicken breast halves or thighs
⅓ cup crunchy peanut butter
⅓ cup boiling water
1 tablespoon grated gingerroot or 1 teaspoon ground ginger
1 tablespoon lemon juice
⅛ teaspoon crushed red pepper

Cut chicken into 1½-inch pieces. Mix remaining ingredients. Reserve ¼ cup. Set oven control to broil. Thread chicken cubes on four 11-inch metal skewers, leaving space between each. Brush chicken with half of the reserved peanut butter mixture.

Broil chicken with tops about 4 inches from heat about 5 minutes or until brown. Turn and brush with remaining reserved peanut butter mixture. Broil 5 minutes or until golden brown. Serve with peanut butter mixture and chopped peanuts if desired. 4 SERVINGS; 215 CALORIES PER SERVING.

To Grill: Cover and grill kabobs 4 to 5 inches from medium coals 15 to 25 minutes, turning and brushing with peanut butter mixture, until golden brown.

CHICKEN POT PIE

1 package (10 ounces) frozen peas and
   carrots
⅓ cup margarine or butter
⅓ cup all-purpose flour
⅓ cup chopped onion
½ teaspoon salt
¼ teaspoon pepper
1¾ cups chicken broth
⅔ cup milk
2½ to 3 cups cut-up cooked chicken or
   turkey
Pastry for 9-inch Two-Crust Pie (page 88)

Rinse frozen peas and carrots in cold water to
separate; drain. Heat margarine in 2-quart saucepan over medium heat until melted. Stir in flour,
onion, salt and pepper. Cook, stirring constantly,
until mixture is bubbly; remove from heat. Stir in
broth and milk. Heat to boiling, stirring constantly.
Boil and stir 1 minute. Stir in chicken and vegetables.

Heat oven to 425°. Prepare pastry. Roll two-
thirds of the pastry into 13-inch square. Ease into
ungreased square pan, 9×9×2 inches. Pour chicken
mixture into pastry-lined pan. Roll remaining pastry
into 11-inch square. Cut out designs with cookie
cutter. Place square over filling. Turn edges under
and flute. Bake about 35 minutes or until golden
brown.   6 SERVINGS; 645 CALORIES PER SERVING.

Chicken Pot Pie

CHICKEN A LA KING

½ cup margarine or butter
1 small green bell pepper, chopped (about
   ½ cup)
1 can (4 ounces) mushroom stems and
   pieces, drained and liquid reserved, or 1
   cup chopped mushrooms
½ cup all-purpose flour
½ teaspoon salt
¼ teaspoon pepper
1½ cups milk
1¼ cups chicken broth
2 cups cut-up cooked chicken
1 jar (2 ounces) diced pimientos, drained
Hot cooked rice (page 267), toasted bread
   triangles or patty shells

Heat margarine in 3-quart saucepan over medium-
high heat. Cook bell pepper and mushrooms in
margarine 3 minutes, stirring occasionally. Stir in
flour, salt and pepper. Cook over medium heat,
stirring constantly, until bubbly; remove from heat.
Stir in milk, broth and reserved mushroom liquid.
Heat to boiling, stirring constantly. Boil and stir 1
minute. Stir in chicken and pimientos. Heat until
hot. Serve over rice.   6 SERVINGS; 625 CALORIES
PER SERVING.

CHICKEN RICE CASSEROLE

¼ cup margarine or butter
⅓ cup all-purpose flour
¾ teaspoon salt
⅛ teaspoon pepper
1½ cups milk
1 cup chicken broth
2 cups cut-up cooked chicken or turkey
1½ cups cooked white or wild rice
⅓ cup chopped green bell pepper
¼ cup slivered almonds
2 tablespoons chopped pimiento
1 can (4 ounces) mushroom stems and
   pieces, drained, or 1 cup chopped
   mushrooms

Heat oven to 350°. Heat margarine in 2-quart
saucepan until melted. Stir in flour, salt and pepper. Cook over medium heat, stirring constantly,
until bubbly; remove from heat. Stir in milk and
broth. Heat to boiling, stirring constantly. Boil and
stir 1 minute. Stir in remaining ingredients.

Pour into ungreased 2-quart casserole or rectangular
baking dish, 10×6×1½ inches. Bake uncovered 40 to
45 minutes or until bubbly. Garnish with parsley
if desired.   6 SERVINGS; 310 CALORIES PER SERVING.

CORNISH HENS WITH GLAZED ORANGES

Cornish hens are a compact crossbreed of Cornish game cocks and Plymouth Rock hens, a new breed developed in 1950. These little birds, full of white meat, are elegant and economical.

3 Rock Cornish hens (about 1½ pounds each)
2 tablespoons margarine or butter, melted
Glazed Oranges (below)
½ cup orange juice
1 tablespoon honey
½ teaspoon salt
¼ teaspoon dry mustard
⅛ teaspoon paprika

Heat oven to 350°. Place hens, breast sides up, on rack in shallow roasting pan. Brush with margarine. Roast uncovered 30 minutes.

Prepare Glazed Oranges. Mix remaining ingredients. Roast hens uncovered about 45 minutes longer, brushing occasionally with orange juice mixture, until juices run clear. Cut each hen in half along backbone from tail to neck with kitchen scissors. Serve with Glazed Oranges.   6 SERVINGS; 365 CALORIES PER SERVING.

Glazed Oranges

3 medium oranges
2 tablespoons margarine or butter
¼ cup light corn syrup
1 tablespoon honey

Cut off ends of oranges. Cut each orange into ⅛-inch slices. Heat margarine in 12-inch skillet over medium heat until melted. Stir in corn syrup and honey. Heat to boiling. Add oranges; reduce heat. Simmer uncovered about 25 minutes, spooning sauce frequently over oranges, until oranges are tender and glazed.

To Grill: Cut hens lengthwise in half before grilling. Cover and grill hens, bone sides down, 5 to 6 inches from medium coals 60 to 70 minutes, turning and brushing with orange juice mixture, until juices run clear.

Cornish Hens with Glazed Oranges

⏱ TURKEY IN LEMON CAPER SAUCE

1 pound turkey breast slices
⅓ cup all-purpose flour
¼ teaspoon salt
⅛ teaspoon lemon pepper
2 tablespoons margarine or butter
3 tablespoons olive or vegetable oil
2 tablespoons margarine or butter
3 tablespoons lemon juice
2 teaspoons capers, drained
Chopped fresh parsley
Lemon wedges

Flatten each turkey breast slice to ⅛-inch thickness between plastic wrap or waxed paper. Mix flour, salt and lemon pepper. Coat turkey with flour mixture. Heat 2 tablespoons of margarine and the oil in 12-inch skillet over medium-high heat. Sauté half of the turkey about 3 minutes, turning once, until brown. Remove turkey from skillet and keep warm. Repeat with remaining turkey.

Stir 2 tablespoons margarine, the lemon juice and capers into pan drippings in skillet. Heat to boiling over medium heat, stirring frequently. Pour over turkey. Garnish with parsley and lemon wedges.   4 SERVINGS; 325 CALORIES PER SERVING.

THANKSGIVING

When the pilgrims had the first Thanksgiving in 1621, they probably ate turkey, which was native to America and in plentiful supply. However, it wasn't until the 1800s that turkey became commonplace on the Thanksgiving table.

Thanksgiving wasn't celebrated in any official way until Abraham Lincoln declared in 1863 that the last Thursday in November would be Thanksgiving. We owe this holiday to the determined campaigning of Sarah Josepha Hale, editor of Godey's Lady Book, who worked for more than forty years to have Thanksgiving declared a national holiday.

SAUSAGE-STUFFED TURKEY BREAST

4- to 5-pound fresh or frozen (thawed) boneless whole turkey breast
½ pound Italian sausage, cooked and drained
¾ cup ricotta cheese
¼ cup chopped fresh or 1 tablespoon dried
basil leaves
1 tablespoon pine nuts
⅛ teaspoon pepper
1 egg
1 clove garlic, finely chopped
2 tablespoons margarine or butter, melted
Parmesan Sauce (below)

Heat oven to 425°. Remove excess fat from turkey breast. Place turkey, skin side down, on plastic wrap or waxed paper; unfold. Cover with plastic wrap and flatten to ¾-inch thickness.

Mix remaining ingredients except margarine and Parmesan Sauce. Place mixture lengthwise across center of turkey breast. Bring long sides of turkey up around stuffing. Tie with kitchen string.

Place turkey on rack in shallow roasting pan. Brush with half of the margarine. Cover with aluminum foil. Roast 1 hour; remove foil. Brush turkey with remaining margarine. Roast 45 minutes longer or until golden brown and juices run clear. Let stand 15 minutes. Cut into 16 slices. Serve with Parmesan Sauce. 16 SERVINGS; 235 CALORIES PER SERVING.

Parmesan Sauce
Thin White Sauce (page 357)
¼ cup grated Parmesan cheese
2 tablespoons margarine or butter

Prepare Thin White Sauce—except stir in Parmesan cheese and margarine.

BROILED ORIENTAL TURKEY SLICES

1 pound turkey breast slices
3 tablespoons soy sauce
3 tablespoons honey
1 tablespoon lemon juice
1 tablespoon vegetable oil
1 teaspoon finely chopped gingerroot or
¼ teaspoon ground ginger
2 green onions (with tops), sliced
2 cloves garlic, crushed

Mix all ingredients in glass bowl or plastic bag. Cover bowl or seal bag tightly. Refrigerate at least 4 hours. Remove turkey slices.

Set oven control to broil. Place turkey on rack in broiler pan. Place broiler pan so top of turkey is 4 inches from heat. Broil turkey about 7 minutes, turning once. 4 SERVINGS; 225 CALORIES PER SERVING.

TURKEY AND LEEK CASSEROLE

2 tablespoons margarine or butter
5 medium leeks or 2 medium onions, sliced
2 tablespoons all-purpose flour
½ teaspoon salt
¼ teaspoon ground nutmeg
⅛ teaspoon pepper
1 cup chicken broth
1 cup milk
3 cups cut-up cooked turkey or chicken
½ cup finely chopped fully cooked smoked
ham
1 jar (2 ounces) diced pimiento, drained
3 cups hot cooked noodles
1 cup shredded Swiss cheese (4 ounces)

Heat oven to 350°. Heat margarine in 3-quart saucepan over medium heat. Cook leeks in margarine about 7 minutes, stirring occasionally until softened. Stir in flour, salt, nutmeg and pepper. Cook over medium heat, stirring constantly, until bubbly; remove from heat. Stir in broth and milk. Heat to boiling, stirring constantly. Boil and stir 1 minute. Stir in turkey, ham and pimiento.

Spread about half of the turkey mixture in ungreased square pan, 9 × 9 × 2 inches, or 2½-quart casserole. Spoon noodles over turkey mixture. Top with remaining turkey mixture. Sprinkle with cheese. Bake uncovered 25 to 30 minutes or until cheese is light brown. 8 SERVINGS (ABOUT 1 CUP EACH); 315 CALORIES PER SERVING.

Cold Poached Turkey with Curry Sauce, Almond-crusted Turkey Patties

COLD POACHED TURKEY WITH CURRY SAUCE

Serve this light and fresh turkey dish in hot weather, with such condiments as chutney, raisins and chopped peanuts.

> 2 turkey tenderloins (about 1½ pounds)
> 2 tablespoons lemon juice
> 2 teaspoons chicken bouillon granules
> ⅛ teaspoon crushed red pepper
> 1 small onion, cut into fourths
> 1 clove garlic, cut in half
> Curry Sauce (right)
> Leaf lettuce

Place turkey tenderloins, lemon juice, bouillon granules, red pepper, onion and garlic in Dutch oven. Add just enough water to cover turkey (2½ to 3 cups). Heat to boiling; reduce heat. Cover and simmer about 30 minutes or until juices run clear. Refrigerate turkey in broth until cool. Prepare Curry Sauce.

Line serving platter with leaf lettuce. Slice turkey diagonally across the grain into ¼-inch slices. Arrange turkey in two rows of overlapping slices on serving platter. Spoon some of the Curry Sauce evenly over turkey. Serve with remaining Curry Sauce. Garnish with tomato wedges and cilantro if desired. 6 SERVINGS; 175 CALORIES PER SERVING.

Curry Sauce

> 1 cup plain yogurt
> 1 tablespoon chutney
> 2 teaspoons chopped fresh cilantro
> 1 teaspoon curry powder
> Dash of ground red pepper (cayenne)

Mix all ingredients. Refrigerate.

ALMOND-CRUSTED TURKEY PATTIES

These patties are great with cranberry sauce, Papaya Chutney (page 361) or Raisin Sauce (page 360).

> 1 pound ground turkey
> ¼ cup seasoned dry bread crumbs
> ¼ teaspoon salt
> ¼ teaspoon pepper
> 2 green onions (with tops), chopped
> 1 egg
> ⅔ cup finely chopped almonds, toasted

Heat oven to 375°. Mix turkey, bread crumbs, salt, pepper, onions and egg. Shape into 4 patties, each ¾ inch thick. Coat both sides of patties with almonds. Place patties on rack in broiler pan. Bake about 30 minutes or until patties are no longer pink in center. 4 SERVINGS; 365 CALORIES PER SERVING.

⏱ TURKEY DIVAN

¼ cup margarine or butter
¼ cup all-purpose flour
⅛ teaspoon ground nutmeg
1½ cups chicken broth
½ cup grated Parmesan cheese
2 tablespoons dry white wine
½ cup whipping (heavy) cream
1½ pounds broccoli or 2 packages (10 ounces each) frozen broccoli spears, cooked and drained
6 large slices cooked turkey breast (about ¾ pound)
½ cup grated Parmesan cheese

Heat margarine in 1-quart saucepan over medium heat until melted. Stir in flour and nutmeg. Cook, stirring constantly, until smooth and bubbly; remove from heat. Stir in broth. Heat to boiling, stirring constantly. Boil and stir 1 minute; remove from heat. Stir in ½ cup cheese and the wine. Beat whipping cream in chilled bowl until stiff. Fold cheese mixture into whipped cream.

Place hot broccoli in ungreased rectangular baking dish, 12 × 7½ × 2 inches. Top with turkey. Pour cheese sauce over turkey. Sprinkle with ½ cup cheese. Set oven control to broil. Broil with top 3 to 5 inches from heat until cheese is bubbly and light brown.   6 SERVINGS; 370 CALORIES PER SERVING.

PHEASANT IN CREAMY MUSHROOM SAUCE

2½-pound pheasant, cut into fourths
⅓ cup chopped onion
½ cup apple cider
1 tablespoon plus 1 teaspoon Worcestershire sauce
1 clove garlic, finely chopped
1 can (10¾ ounces) condensed cream of chicken soup
1 can (4 ounces) mushroom stems and pieces, drained, or 1 cup chopped mushrooms
Paprika

Heat oven to 350°. Place pheasant, breast side up, in ungreased square baking pan, 9 × 9 × 2 inches. Mix remaining ingredients except paprika. Pour over pheasant. Sprinkle generously with paprika.

Bake uncovered 1½ to 2 hours, spooning sauce over pheasant occasionally, until done. After baking pheasant 1 hour, generously sprinkle again with paprika.   3 SERVINGS; 600 CALORIES PER SERVING.

DUCKLING WITH ORANGE SAUCE

4- to 5-pound duckling
2 teaspoons grated orange peel
½ cup orange juice
¼ cup currant jelly
1 tablespoon lemon juice
⅛ teaspoon dry mustard
⅛ teaspoon salt
1 tablespoon cold water
1½ teaspoon cornstarch
1 orange, peeled and sectioned
1 tablespoon orange-flavored liqueur, if desired

Heat oven to 350°. Fasten neck skin to back with skewer. Fold wings across back with tips touching. Place duckling, breast side up, on rack in shallow roasting pan. Prick skin all over with fork. Roast uncovered about 2½ hours or until drumstick moves easily, removing excess fat from pan occasionally. If duckling becomes too brown, place piece of aluminum foil loosely over breast. Let stand 10 minutes for easier carving.

Heat orange peel, orange juice, jelly, lemon juice, mustard and salt to boiling. Mix water and cornstarch. Stir into sauce. Cook over medium heat, stirring constantly, until mixture thickens and boils. Boil and stir 1 minute. Stir in orange sections and liqueur. Brush duckling with some of the orange sauce. Serve with remaining sauce.   4 SERVINGS; 445 CALORIES PER SERVING.

BRAISED DUCKLING WITH SAUERKRAUT

2 tablespoons vegetable oil
4- to 5-pound duckling, cut up
1 cup dry white wine or apple juice
⅓ cup coarsely chopped fully cooked smoked ham
1 teaspoon caraway seed
¼ teaspoon pepper
4 to 6 juniper berries, crushed, if desired
1 can (27 ounces) sauerkraut, drained

Heat oil in Dutch oven. Cook duckling in oil over medium-high heat about 15 minutes, turning occasionally, until brown on all sides; drain. Mix remaining ingredients. Pour over duckling. Heat to boiling; reduce heat. Cover and simmer over medium heat 1 to 1¼ hours or until juices run clear.   4 SERVINGS; 565 CALORIES PER SERVING.

Roast Goose with Apple Stuffing

ROAST GOOSE WITH APPLE STUFFING

"Christmas is coming, the goose is getting fat" is the old song still sung during the holiday season. Roast goose can be a festive entrée for Christmas dinner or for any special occasion.

8- to 10-pound goose
2 cups water
1 small onion, sliced
¾ teaspoon salt
6 cups soft bread crumbs
3 tart apples, chopped
2 stalks celery (with leaves), chopped
1 medium onion, chopped
¼ cup margarine or butter, melted
½ teaspoon salt
1 teaspoon ground sage
½ teaspoon ground thyme
¼ teaspoon pepper
½ teaspoon salt
¼ cup all-purpose flour

Trim excess fat from goose. Heat giblets, water, sliced onion and ¾ teaspoon salt to boiling; reduce heat. Cover and simmer about 1 hour or until giblets are done. Strain broth. Cover and refrigerate. Chop giblets. Toss with remaining ingredients except ½ teaspoon salt and the flour.

Heat oven to 350°. Rub cavity of goose with ½ teaspoon salt. Fold wings across back with tips touching. Fill neck and body cavities of goose lightly with stuffing. Fasten neck skin to back with skewer. Fasten opening with skewers and lace with string. Tie drumsticks to tail. Prick skin all over with fork. Place goose, breast side up, on rack in shallow roasting pan.

Roast uncovered 3 to 3½ hours or until drumstick moves easily, removing excess fat from pan occasionally. Place a tent of aluminum foil loosely over goose during last hour to prevent excessive browning. Place goose on heated platter. Let stand 15 minutes for easier carving.

Pour drippings from pan into bowl. Return ¼ cup drippings to pan. Stir in flour. Cook over medium heat, stirring constantly, until smooth and bubbly; remove from heat. Add enough water to reserved broth, if necessary, to measure 2 cups. Stir into flour mixture. Heat to boiling, stirring constantly. Boil and stir 1 minute. Serve goose with apple stuffing and gravy.   8 SERVINGS; 965 CALORIES PER SERVING.

BREAD STUFFING

¾ cup margarine or butter
1½ cups chopped celery (with leaves)
¾ cup finely chopped onion
9 cups soft bread cubes
1 teaspoon salt
½ teaspoon ground sage
1½ teaspoons chopped fresh or ½ teaspoon
   dried thyme leaves
¼ teaspoon pepper

Heat margarine in Dutch oven over medium-high heat. Cook celery and onion in margarine about 2 minutes. Remove from heat. Stir in remaining ingredients.   5 CUPS STUFFING; 200 CALORIES PER ½ CUP.

APPLE-RAISIN STUFFING: Increase salt to 1½ teaspoons. Add 3 cups finely chopped apples and ¾ cup raisins with the remaining ingredients.   7½ CUPS STUFFING; 175 CALORIES PER ½ CUP.

CASSEROLE STUFFING: Place stuffing in ungreased 2-quart casserole. Cover and bake in 375° oven about 30 minutes or until hot.

CORN BREAD STUFFING: Substitute corn bread cubes for the soft bread cubes.   5 CUPS STUFFING; 395 CALORIES PER ½ CUP.

GIBLET STUFFING: Simmer heart, gizzard and neck from chicken or turkey in seasoned water 1 to 2 hours or until tender. Add liver during the last 15 minutes of cooking. Drain giblets. Chop and add with the remaining ingredients.   6 CUPS STUFFING; 180 CALORIES PER ½ CUP.

MUSHROOM STUFFING: Cook and stir 2 cups sliced mushrooms with the celery and onion.   5 CUPS STUFFING; 205 CALORIES PER ½ CUP.

OYSTER STUFFING: Add 2 cans (8 ounces each) oysters, drained and chopped, or 2 cups shucked oysters, drained and chopped, with the remaining ingredients.   6 CUPS STUFFING; 190 CALORIES PER ½ CUP.

RICE STUFFING

2 tablespoons margarine or butter
1 medium stalk celery, chopped (about ½
   cup)
1 small onion, chopped (about ¼ cup)
½ teaspoon salt
⅛ teaspoon pepper
2 cups cooked rice (page 267)
½ cup chopped walnuts
⅓ cup raisins
¼ teaspoon paprika
4 slices bacon, crisply cooked and crumbled

Heat margarine in 10-inch skillet over medium heat. Cook celery, onion, salt and pepper in margarine about 2 minutes. Remove from heat. Stir in rice, walnuts, raisins, paprika and bacon.   4 CUPS STUFFING; 105 CALORIES PER ½ CUP.

FRUITED RICE STUFFING: Omit raisins. Stir in ⅓ cup cut-up prunes and ⅓ cup cut-up dried apricots.   170 CALORIES PER ½ CUP.

——— FIX-IT-FAST ———

♦ Cover and marinate chicken breasts in your favorite salad dressing or sauce overnight in the refrigerator. Try Italian dressing, barbecue sauce, vinaigrette dressing or teriyaki sauce.

♦ Cut up boneless poultry breasts or thighs and combine with cut-up vegetables from the produce section, salad bar or deli for a quick stir-fry.

♦ Use cut-up cooked poultry (frozen or deli) in salads, casseroles, soups and stews.

♦ For an easy poultry salad, combine chopped cooked poultry and equal parts mayonnaise or plain yogurt and your favorite salad dressing.

♦ Use deli fried chicken in casseroles, soups or sandwiches. (Fried chicken adds extra crunch!)

♦ To save time when you sauté poultry, use boneless breasts, chicken thighs or turkey slices.

♦ Combine cooked poultry and frozen and/or deli vegetables, pasta or rice mixes for a quick salad meal.

♦ Arrange sliced cooked poultry and fresh fruit on a platter for a main-dish salad, or toss cut-up cooked poultry with greens.

♦ Bake frozen chicken nuggets or fingers and add to casseroles, or serve with your favorite dipping sauces, such as barbecue or sweet-and-sour sauce.

♦ Prepare frozen chicken or turkey patties as directed on package. Top with spaghetti or pizza sauce and mozzarella cheese. Bake or broil until cheese is melted.

♦ Spruce up roast chicken or turkey. Place cut-up citrus fruits or apple or pear halves in cavity before roasting. Or try packing with fresh herbs.

NUTRITION INFORMATION

PER SERVING OR UNIT

RECIPE, PAGE

PERCENT U.S. RECOMMENDED DAILY ALLOWANCE

RECIPE, PAGE	Servings per recipe	Calories	Protein (grams)	Carbohydrate (grams)	Fat (grams)	Cholesterol (milligrams)	Sodium (milligrams)	Protein	Vitamin A	Vitamin C	Thiamine	Riboflavin	Niacin	Calcium	Iron
CHICKEN															
Broiled Chicken, 284	6	260	28	0	16	90	105	42	4	0	4	10	42	0	6
Broiled Lemon Chicken, 284	6	280	28	0	18	90	310	42	8	0	4	10	42	0	6
Brunswick Stew, 286	8	390	26	23	23	80	890	40	38	42	12	16	44	8	20
Buttermilk Fried Chicken, 283	6	440	31	17	27	90	490	48	12	0	10	16	48	6	10
Caribbean Chicken, 288	4	310	32	26	9	90	760	48	38	16	14	22	30	6	18
Chicken Breasts in Mustard Sauce, 292	4	395	19	5	34	125	225	28	24	2	4	8	24	6	4
Chicken with Cashews, 291	6	335	22	14	22	45	575	34	6	30	6	10	28	2	14
Chicken Cordon Bleu, 290	4	445	40	16	23	170	560	62	6	0	12	18	44	30	10
Chicken Curry, 290	6	440	33	39	16	75	1050	74	12	4	20	16	52	2	14
Chicken Fricassee, 284	6	605	37	45	29	100	910	56	16	0	20	28	58	24	16
Chicken Jambalaya, 286	6	350	32	10	20	100	735	48	18	10	22	20	54	4	18
Chicken a la King, 294	6	625	27	82	24	45	1170	40	100	100	24	44	48	14	76
Chicken Livers with Glazed Apples, 292	4	205	13	21	8	345	305	20	100	10	6	56	12	2	28
Chicken en Papillote, 292	4	180	28	3	6	85	215	42	100	22	8	18	48	14	18
Chicken Pot Pie, 294	6	645	34	40	38	80	1030	52	98	4	20	22	58	6	16
Chicken Rice Casserole, 294	6	310	19	23	15	45	755	30	12	8	10	16	28	10	8
Chicken with Tomatoes and Leeks, 291	4	360	28	8	24	100	240	42	20	10	10	18	50	12	8
Chicken with Winter Fruit, 286	6	415	31	31	19	90	415	46	100	8	8	16	52	4	16
Cornish Hens with Glazed Oranges, 295	6	365	35	26	13	150	375	54	12	36	8	18	64	4	16
Crunchy Oven-fried Chicken, 283	6	350	29	8	22	90	455	44	22	4	20	26	60	2	10
Fried Chicken, 283	6	385	29	7	26	90	265	44	6	0	6	12	46	0	8
Herb-roasted Chicken with Lemon Rice, 282	6	370	30	17	19	105	380	46	8	2	8	14	46	4	12
Herbed Chicken, 284	6	345	28	3	22	90	180	42	6	10	4	10	42	2	8
Honey-Ginger Chicken, 288	6	500	42	25	29	145	1285	64	10	0	10	24	56	2	16
Madeira-sauced Chicken Wings, 289	4	180	18	4	6	50	225	28	0	2	2	6	16	0	4
Maryland Fried Chicken, 283	6	545	35	32	29	180	625	54	8	0	12	20	54	6	16
Mexican Chicken, 285	6	435	33	27	22	90	915	50	26	20	24	22	60	6	22
Oven-barbecued Chicken, 284	6	305	29	14	14	90	830	44	10	4	6	12	46	2	8
Oven Chicken Kiev, 290	6	265	26	13	11	80	330	38	24	10	30	34	72	2	10
Oven-fried Chicken, 283	6	350	29	7	22	90	355	44	14	0	6	12	46	2	8
Peanutty Chicken Kabobs, 293	4	215	21	5	12	45	140	32	0	0	2	4	38	0	4

NUTRITION INFORMATION

PER SERVING OR UNIT

RECIPE, PAGE	Servings per recipe	Calories	Protein (grams)	Carbohydrate (grams)	Fat (grams)	Cholesterol (milligrams)	Sodium (milligrams)	PERCENT U.S. RECOMMENDED DAILY ALLOWANCE Protein	Vitamin A	Vitamin C	Thiamine	Riboflavin	Niacin	Calcium	Iron
CHICKEN (continued)															
Raspberry-Peach Chicken, 291	4	250	25	20	7	80	225	38	4	6	8	12	50	2	8
Roast Chicken, 281	1	205	23	0	12	75	70	34	0	2	2	8	36	0	4
Roast Rock Cornish Hen, 281	1	115	20	0	3	75	55	30	0	0	2	8	36	0	8
Shrimp Curry, 290	6	420	21	49	15	185	1215	30	12	4	24	16	24	18	16
Sweet-and-Sour Chicken, 285	6	655	32	67	29	135	730	48	16	34	12	16	50	2	14
Thai Chicken with Cellophane Noodles, 293	4	205	21	12	9	45	1465	30	100	34	8	10	30	8	12
TURKEY															
Almond-crusted Turkey Patties, 297	4	365	28	9	25	150	265	42	6	2	8	26	30	10	14
Broiled Oriental Turkey Slices, 296	4	225	26	15	7	80	855	40	6	2	6	12	28	2	10
Cold Poached Turkey with Curry Sauce, 297	6	175	27	6	4	80	285	40	0	2	6	16	26	8	8
Sausage-stuffed Turkey Breast, 296	16	235	31	2	10	110	240	46	4	0	6	12	34	8	8
Turkey Divan, 298	6	370	28	12	23	80	590	42	44	60	10	26	26	34	14
Turkey and Leek Casserole, 296	8	315	24	18	15	65	480	36	10	6	12	16	30	18	8
Turkey in Lemon Caper Sauce, 295	4	325	21	8	22	55	310	32	10	2	4	6	28	0	6
GAME FOWL															
Braised Duckling with Sauerkraut, 298	4	565	28	15	43	110	1345	42	4	20	22	24	34	6	34
Duckling with Orange Sauce, 298	4	445	20	24	29	85	140	30	6	28	14	16	24	2	16
Pheasant in Creamy Mushroom Sauce, 298	3	600	94	11	15	90	845	100	30	32	22	38	100	6	32
Roast Goose with Apple Stuffing, 299	8	965	57	69	50	170		86	8	4	22	48	58	12	46
STUFFING															
Apple-Raisin Stuffing, 300	15	175	2	21	10	0	420	2	6	0	6	2	4	2	4
Bread Stuffing, 300	10	200	3	15	15	0	520	4	10	0	6	4	4	4	4
Corn Bread Stuffing, 300	10	395	9	47	19	70	1070	12	18	2	12	18	6	12	10
Fruited Rice Stuffing, 300	8	170	3	23	8	0	200	4	12	0	6	4	4	2	6
Giblet Stuffing, 300	12	180	4	13	13	20	435	4	20	0	6	8	6	2	6
Mushroom Stuffing, 300	10	205	3	16	15	0	520	4	10	0	8	8	8	4	6
Oyster Stuffing, 300	12	190	5	14	13	20	455	6	10	8	8	8	8	6	14
Rice Stuffing, 300	8	105	2	7	8	2	200	2	2	0	8	4	4	0	4
Sausage Stuffing, 300	12	240	5	13	19	0	395	6	8	0	10	6	6	2	4
Vegetable Stuffing, 300	14	155	2	13	10	0	390	2	88	4	6	4	4	4	6

SALADS & SALAD DRESSINGS

═══SALADS & SALAD DRESSINGS═══

You have full creative license when making a salad, from fruit salads to vegetable salads to to main-dish salads for lunch or dinner. We have also included an extensive section of dressings from the classics to new low-calorie dressings. Salads are increasing in popularity because they are healthful and also because they are easy and fit in well with so many different types of meals. Whether you choose hearty South Seas Shrimp Salad (page 322), Sirloin and Mushroom Salad (page 324) or a tossed salad full of fresh produce from the market, you'll enjoy the satisfaction of creating your own salad and dressing it exactly as you please.

GREENS BASICS

Choosing salad greens is often the first step in creating a tossed salad or main-dish salad. Knowing the different types of greens available lets you make inventive and satisfying salads.

♦ Crisphead (or iceberg) lettuce has a mild flavor that makes it the most popular green. Look for solid, compact heads with tight leaves that range from medium-green outer leaves to pale green inside.

♦ Boston (or butterhead) lettuce has a small, rounded head of soft, buttery-feeling leaves that have a delicate flavor.

♦ Bibb (or limestone) lettuce has tender, pliable leaves similar to those of Boston. Bibb is smaller than Boston but has a similar delicate, mild flavor.

♦ Romaine (or cos) has narrow, elongated dark leaves with a crisp texture.

♦ Leaf lettuce—red, bronze or green—has tender leaves that don't form heads. These leafy bunches have a mild, though sometimes nutty, flavor.

♦ Belgian or French endive has closed, narrow, pale leaves with a pleasantly bitter flavor.

SALAD GREENS

Romaine

Bibb and Boston lettuce

Iceberg lettuce

Escarole, curly endive

Leaf lettuce: green, red

Spinach

Arugula

Radicchio, Belgian endive

Preceding page: Cobb Salad *(page 324),* Seafood Pasta Salad *(page 321)*

♦ Curly endive has frilly, narrow leaves with a slightly bitter flavor.

♦ Escarole, also part of the endive family, is a less frilly, broad-leafed endive with dark green leaves.

♦ Radicchio, another member of the endive family, resembles a small loose-leaf cabbage with smooth, tender leaves. The Rosso variety has rose-colored leaves with white veins, and Castelfranco, blander and sweeter, has leaves sprinkled with pink, green and red flecks or swirls.

♦ Watercress has rounded dark-green leaves on leggy stems, with a strong, peppery flavor.

♦ Arugula (or rocket) has small, slender, dark-green leaves with a rich, bitter flavor. Choose smaller leaves for less assertive flavor.

♦ Spinach has smooth, tapered, dark-green leaves, sometimes crumpled at the edges.

♦ Sorrel, also known as sourgrass, looks similar to spinach but its leaves are smaller. Sorrel has a sharp, lemony flavor.

♦ Cabbage comes in a variety of types. Green and red cabbage are the most familiar. Look for compact heads. Savoy cabbage has crinkled leaves and Chinese (or Napa) cabbage has long, crisp leaves.

SELECTING AND STORING SALAD GREENS

♦ Be sure greens are fresh when purchased. Avoid limp or bruised greens and greens with rust spots.

♦ Store greens in the refrigerator until needed. You can keep them in the original wrapping, or place in a plastic bag. Store in the crisper section. Wash them when ready to use.

♦ Be sure to wash greens thoroughly in several changes of cold water, then shake off the excess moisture. For greens that may be sandy, such as spinach, separate leaves with fingers to remove all grit. Toss in a cloth towel, or gently blot dry to remove remaining moisture; refrigerate. Or use a salad spinner to remove excess moisture.

♦ Watercress, parsley and fresh herbs should be refrigerated in screwtop jars filled with water. Make sure the stems are in the water.

♦ Romaine and iceburg lettuce will keep nicely in the refrigerator up to a week. Most other greens wilt within a few days of purchasing.

♦ If you plan to use iceberg lettuce within a day or two, remove the core before washing. Strike the core end against a flat surface; then twist and lift out core. Hold the head, cored end up, under running cold water to separate and clean leaves. Turn right side up and drain thoroughly. Refrigerate in a plastic bag or bowl with an airtight lid.

SERVING SALAD GREENS

♦ Use a variety of greens for complementary textures, flavors and colors. And remember, fresh herbs can perk up even the simplest combinations.

♦ Mix dark greens with light, crisp with tender, and straight with curly. Team pale iceberg lettuce with dark green spinach, romaine with curly endive. Red leaf (bronze) lettuce provides both color and delicate flavor. Red cabbage and radicchio also add color and texture.

♦ Blot any leftover moisture you find in leaf crevices; the drier the leaves, the better. Tear, don't cut, greens into bite-size pieces. Pour dressing on just before serving, using only enough to coat the leaves lightly; then toss. Or serve the salad with dressing on the side so that each person can add the desired amount.

TOSSED SALAD CHART
(serves 4 to 6)

Mix all ingredients in a large salad bowl and toss with your favorite dressing.

SALAD GREENS	SALAD ADDITIONS	GARNISH WITH
Choose one or more to total 5 cups	Choose one or more to total 1 cup	Choose one or more to total ¼ to ⅓ cup
Arugula	Alfalfa sprouts	Cheese
Bibb lettuce	Asparagus	Bacon, crisply
Boston lettuce	Broccoli flowerets	cooked, crumbled
Cabbage	Bell peppers	Croutons
Endive	Carrots	Eggs, hard-cooked
Escarole	Cauliflowerets	Edible flowers
Iceberg lettuce	Cucumbers	French-fried onions
Leaf lettuce	Mushrooms	Fresh herbs
Radicchio	Onions	Nuts
Romaine	Peas	Olives
Spinach	Radishes	Sunflower nuts
Watercress	Tomatoes	Toasted wheat
	Zucchini	germ
	Fruit	
	Meat, poultry or fish, cooked	

SALAD

Salad derives from the Latin word sal, which means salt. The Romans ate vegetables and greens with a dressing made from this precious commodity, salt, which shows how much they valued salads. The custom of mixing greens with oils and herbs began in Italy and Greece, and then spread to Europe. When the Spanish Catherine of Aragon married the English Henry VIII in 1509, the chefs in the palace had to send abroad to find the greens to make her salad! From Spain also comes a proverb advocating four people to make salad dressing: "A spendthrift for oil, a miser for vinegar, a counselor for salt and a madman to stir it up."

We have been adding more salads to the Betty Crocker Cookbook and have more than tripled the number of salad recipes since the first Betty Crocker cookbook in 1950. People are turning to salad not just as a refreshing side dish but as a healthful, varied and delicious main course.

WILTED LETTUCE SALAD

A hot sweet-and-sour dressing gently wilts the greens in this unusual salad.

4 slices bacon, diced
¼ cup vinegar
2 bunches leaf lettuce, coarsely shredded
5 green onions (with tops), chopped (about ⅓ cup)
2 teaspoons sugar
¼ teaspoon salt
⅛ teaspoon pepper

Cook bacon in 12-inch skillet until crisp. Stir in vinegar. Heat until hot; remove from heat. Add lettuce and onions. Sprinkle with sugar, salt and pepper. Toss 1 to 2 minutes or until lettuce is wilted.   4 SERVINGS (ABOUT 1½ CUPS EACH); 170 CALORIES PER SERVING.

DILL WILTED LETTUCE SALAD: Stir ½ teaspoon dried dill weed and ½ teaspoon dry mustard into vinegar.   170 CALORIES PER SERVING.

ROQUEFORT AND TOASTED WALNUT SALAD

Nice to garnish with additional walnut halves and chives!

Toasted Walnut Dressing (below)
1 small head radicchio, torn into bite-size pieces (about 4 cups)
1 head Bibb lettuce, torn into bite-size pieces (about 4 cups)
½ cup crumbled Roquefort or blue cheese (about 2 ounces)
½ cup one-half-inch pieces fresh chives
⅓ cup coarsely chopped walnuts, toasted

Prepare Toasted Walnut Dressing. Toss with remaining ingredients.   6 SERVINGS (ABOUT 1⅓ CUPS EACH); 220 CALORIES PER SERVING.

Toasted Walnut Dressing

⅓ cup olive or vegetable oil
¼ cup coarsely chopped walnuts, toasted
2 tablespoons lemon juice
1 clove garlic
⅛ teaspoon salt
Dash of pepper

Place all ingredients in blender or food processor. Cover and blend on high speed, or process, about 1 minute or until smooth.

STRAWBERRY-SPINACH TOSS

5 cups bite-size pieces spinach
1 cup sliced strawberries
1 cup honeydew melon balls
⅓ cup broken pecans, toasted
⅓ cup julienne strips Gouda or Edam cheese (about 2 ounces)
Ginger-Honey Dressing (below)

Toss all ingredients.   6 SERVINGS (ABOUT 1⅓ CUPS EACH); 115 CALORIES PER SERVING.

Ginger-Honey Dressing

2 tablespoons lime juice
2 tablespoons honey
1 tablespoon vegetable oil
½ teaspoon grated gingerroot or ¼ teaspoon ground ginger

Shake all ingredients in tightly covered container.

Greek Salad, Caesar Salad

GREEK SALAD

Lemon Dressing (below)
5 cups bite-size pieces spinach
4 cups bite-size pieces Boston lettuce
½ cup crumbled feta cheese
¼ cup sliced green onions (with tops)
24 pitted ripe olives
3 tomatoes, cut into wedges
1 cucumber, sliced

Toss all ingredients. 8 SERVINGS; 130 CALORIES PER SERVING.

Lemon Dressing

¼ cup vegetable oil
2 tablespoons lemon juice
½ teaspoons sugar
1½ teaspoons Dijon mustard
¼ teaspoon salt
⅛ teaspoon pepper

Shake all ingredients in tightly covered container.

CAESAR SALAD

Caesar Salad traditionally has a coddled egg in its dressing. However, because it is safest to eat only eggs that are thoroughly cooked, we removed the egg. We bet with all the other delicious ingredients here, you won't miss it.

1 clove garlic, cut in half
8 anchovy fillets, cut up
⅓ cup olive oil
3 tablespoons lemon juice
1 teaspoon Worcestershire sauce
¼ teaspoon salt
¼ teaspoon dry mustard
Freshly ground pepper
1 large or 2 small bunches romaine, torn into bite-size pieces (about 10 cups)
1 cup garlic-flavored croutons
⅓ cup grated Parmesan cheese

Rub large wooden salad bowl with cut clove of garlic. Allow a few small pieces of garlic to remain in bowl if desired. Mix anchovies, oil, lemon juice, Worcestershire sauce, salt, mustard and pepper in bowl. Add romaine and toss until leaves are coated. Sprinkle with croutons and cheese; toss. 6 SERVINGS (ABOUT 1¾ CUPS EACH); 180 CALORIES PER SERVING.

SWEET-AND-SOUR SALAD

⅓ cup coarsely chopped macadamia or hazelnuts
1 tablespoon sugar
3 cups bite-size pieces lettuce
3 cups bite-size pieces romaine
2 medium stalks celery, sliced (about 1 cup)
2 green onions (with tops), thinly sliced (about 2 tablespoons)
1 cup pineapple chunks*
Sweet-and-Sour Dressing (below)

Cook macadamia nuts and sugar over low heat, stirring constantly, until sugar is melted and nuts are coated; cool and break apart. Toss all ingredients. 6 SERVINGS (ABOUT 1⅓ CUPS EACH); 180 CALORIES PER SERVING.

*1 can (8 ounces) pineapple tidbits, drained, can be substituted for the fresh pineapple.

Sweet-and-Sour Dressing

¼ cup olive or vegetable oil
2 tablespoons sugar
2 tablespoons vinegar
1 tablespoon chopped fresh parsley
½ teaspoon salt
Freshly ground pepper
Dash of red pepper sauce

Shake all ingredients in tightly covered container.

MANDARIN SALAD: Substitute sliced almonds for the macadamia nuts and 1 can (11 ounces) mandarin oranges, drained, for the fresh pineapple. 170 CALORIES PER SERVING.

PINEAPPLE SALAD

⅓ cup olive or vegetable oil
2 tablespoons lemon juice
1 tablespoon soy sauce
1 to 2 teaspoons packed brown sugar
1 small pineapple, cut into chunks*
1 tart unpared red apple, diced
3 green onions (with tops), sliced (about 3 tablespoons)
1 small bunch romaine, shredded

Shake oil, lemon juice, soy sauce and brown sugar in tightly covered container. Toss pineapple chunks, apple and onions with dressing. Place romaine in shallow bowl. Mound fruit mixture in center. 6 SERVINGS; 160 CALORIES PER SERVING.

*1 can (20 ounces) pineapple chunks, drained, can be substituted for the fresh pineapple.

 # WALDORF SALAD

Oscar Tschirky, maitre d' at the Waldorf-Astoria Hotel in New York City, created this salad.

2 medium apples, coarsely chopped (about 2 cups)
2 medium stalks celery, chopped (about 1 cup)
½ cup mayonnaise or salad dressing
⅓ cup coarsely chopped nuts

Toss all ingredients. Serve on salad greens if desired. 4 SERVINGS (ABOUT ¾ CUP EACH); 310 CALORIES PER SERVING.

PEAR WALDORF SALAD: Substitute 4 pears, coarsely chopped, for the apples. 360 CALORIES PER SERVING.

WALDORF SALAD SUPREME: Decrease celery to 1 medium stalk and nuts to ¼ cup. Stir in 1 can (8 ounces) pineapple chunks, drained, ½ cup miniature marshmallows and ⅓ cup chopped dates. 380 CALORIES PER SERVING.

ORANGE-AVOCADO SALADS

3 oranges, pared and sliced
2 avocados, sliced
6 thin slices red onion, separated into rings
Salad greens
Orange Dressing (below)

Arrange oranges, avocados and onion on salad greens on 6 salad plates. Serve with Orange Dressing. 6 SERVINGS; 280 CALORIES PER SERVING.

Orange Dressing

⅓ cup vegetable oil
1 teaspoon grated orange peel
¼ cup orange juice
2 tablespoons sugar
2 tablespoons lemon juice
½ teaspoon dry mustard
¼ teaspoon salt

Shake all ingredients in tightly covered container.

ORANGE-JICAMA SALADS: Cut 1 small jicama in half. Cut 1 half into julienne strips. Substitute jicama strips for the onion rings. 275 CALORIES PER SERVING.

Clockwise from top: Waldorf Salad, Tropical Salad (page 311), Melon and Fig Salads (page 310)

MELON AND FIG SALADS

2 cups melon balls or cubes
4 fresh or 8 dried figs, cut into fourths
⅓ cup bottled poppy seed dressing
Bibb lettuce leaves

Mix fruit and poppy seed dressing. Serve on 4 lettuce-lined plates. 4 SERVINGS (ABOUT ½ CUP EACH); 220 CALORIES PER SERVING.

WARM BANANA AND PAPAYA SALAD

Passion fruit is an "ugly duckling" fruit with a leathery, brown skin that has a wrinkled appearance when ripe. The fruit inside is tangy and sweet with dark, edible seeds.

1 passion fruit
1 tablespoon sugar
2 tablespoons margarine or butter
2 small bananas or 1 plantain, cut into ¼-inch slices
1 papaya, pared and cut into ¼-inch slices, or 1 small cantaloupe, cut into ¼-inch slices
¼ cup sweet white wine or apple juice

Cut passion fruit crosswise in half. Scoop pulp and seeds into bowl; discard skin. Heat sugar and margarine in 10-inch skillet over medium-high heat until margarine is melted. Stir in bananas and papaya. Heat about 2 minutes or until warm. Remove to plate; keep warm.

Add wine to skillet. Heat to boiling. Cook about 2 minutes or until reduced slightly. Stir in passion fruit; heat until hot. Serve over bananas and papaya. 4 SERVINGS (½ CUP EACH); 145 CALORIES PER SERVING.

Using a spoon, scoop pulp and seeds from papaya into bowl.

CITRUS SALAD

1 medium grapefruit
1 large orange
1 cup seedless grapes
¼ cup pomegranate seeds
Crème Fraîche (below)
Ground nutmeg

Pare and section grapefruit and orange. Mix grapefruit, orange, grapes and pomegranate seeds. Serve with Crème Fraîche. Sprinkle with nutmeg. 4 SERVINGS (ABOUT ¾ CUP FRUIT EACH); 215 CALORIES PER SERVING.

Crème Fraîche

½ cup whipping (heavy) cream
¼ cup sour cream
1 tablespoon packed brown sugar, if desired

Gradually stir whipping cream into sour cream. Stir in brown sugar. Cover and refrigerate at least 1 hour.

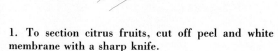

1. To section citrus fruits, cut off peel and white membrane with a sharp knife.

2. Cut along both sides of membrane and remove fruit segment.

TANGERINE-BERRY SALADS

1 small banana
½ cup sour cream or plain yogurt
2 tangerines
1 cup blackberries
½ cup blueberries

Slice banana into blender or food processor. Add sour cream. Cover and blend on high speed, or process, about 1 minute or until smooth. Cut tangerines crosswise into ¼-inch slices. Spoon about ¼ cup banana mixture on individual serving plates. Top with tangerine slices, blackberries and blueberries. 4 SERVINGS; 130 CALORIES PER SERVING.

SORBET AND BERRY SALAD

While we like this fruit and sorbet combination as a salad, it's also terrific as a dessert. This is refreshing served between courses at a formal dinner.

3 medium nectarines, peeled and sliced
⅓ cup water
¼ cup sugar
1 tablespoon lemon juice
1 cup blueberries or blackberries
1 cup strawberries

Place nectarines, water, sugar and lemon juice in blender or food processor. Cover and blend on high speed, or process, until smooth. Pour into loaf pan, 9 × 5 × 3 inches. Cover and freeze about 2 hours or until almost firm.

Break nectarine mixture into chunks into bowl. Beat on low speed about 2 minutes or until smooth. Pour into loaf pan. Freeze about 4 hours or until almost firm.

Scoop nectarine mixture onto individual plates. Arrange berries around mixture. 6 SERVINGS (ABOUT ⅓ CUP EACH); 75 CALORIES PER SERVING.

EASY FRUIT SALAD

1 can (20 ounces) pineapple chunks, drained, and 2 tablespoons juice reserved
1 can (17 ounces) apricot halves, drained
1 can (16 ounces) pitted red tart cherries, drained
1 can (11 ounces) mandarin orange segments, drained
1 cup miniature marshmallows
Fruit Salad Dressing (below)

Mix pineapple, apricots, cherries, orange segments and marshmallows. Toss with Fruit Salad Dressing. Cover and refrigerate at least 12 hours. 8 SERVINGS (ABOUT 1 CUP EACH); 165 CALORIES PER SERVING.

Fruit Salad Dressing

1 cup whipping (heavy) cream
2 tablespoons reserved pineapple juice
Dash of salt

Beat whipping cream in chilled bowl on high speed until soft peaks form. Stir in remaining ingredients.

Sorbet and Berry Salad

TROPICAL SALAD

2 papayas or mangoes, pared and cubed (about 2 cups)
1 cup sliced strawberries
1 cup cubed pineapple*
1 kiwifruit, pared and sliced
2 tablespoons frozen (thawed) limeade concentrate
1 tablespoon vegetable oil
1 tablespoon honey
⅛ teaspoon poppy seed

Mix fruit in bowl. Shake remaining ingredients in tightly covered container. Pour over fruit and toss. 6 SERVINGS (⅔ CUP EACH); 90 CALORIES PER SERVING.

*1 can (8 ounces) pineapple chunks, drained, can be substituted for the fresh pineapple.

PLUM AND PEACH SALAD

2 plums, sliced
2 peaches, sliced
½ cup coarsely chopped walnuts, toasted
¼ cup raspberry preserves
2 tablespoons red wine vinegar or vinegar
1 tablespoon walnut or vegetable oil

Arrange plums and peaches on serving plate. Sprinkle with walnuts. Mix remaining ingredients. Drizzle over fruit. 6 SERVINGS (ABOUT ½ CUP EACH); 135 CALORIES PER SERVING.

POTATO SALAD

2 pounds potatoes (about 6 medium)
1½ cups mayonnaise or salad dressing
1 tablespoon vinegar
1 tablespoon prepared mustard
1 teaspoon salt
¼ teaspoon pepper
2 medium stalks celery, chopped (about 1 cup)
1 medium onion, chopped (about ½ cup)
4 hard-cooked eggs, chopped

Prepare and cook potatoes as directed on page 393; cool slightly. Cut into cubes (about 6 cups). Mix mayonnaise, vinegar, mustard, salt and pepper in large glass or plastic bowl. Add potatoes, celery and onion; toss. Stir in eggs. Cover and refrigerate at least 4 hours.   10 SERVINGS (ABOUT ¾ CUP EACH); 355 CALORIES PER SERVING.

CALIFORNIA POTATO SALAD: Omit eggs. Stir in 1 can (4 ounces) chopped green chilies, drained, with the vegetables. Just before serving, stir in 2 avocados, chopped, and 2 tomatoes, chopped.   400 CALORIES PER SERVING.

GARDEN POTATO SALAD: Stir in ½ cup thinly sliced radishes, ½ cup chopped cucumber and ½ cup chopped green bell pepper. Garnish with tomato wedges.   360 CALORIES PER SERVING.

SCANDINAVIAN POTATO SALAD: Stir in 1 jar (8 ounces) pickled herring, drained and chopped, 1 can (8¼ ounces) julienne beets, drained, and 1 teaspoon dried dill weed.   400 CALORIES PER SERVING.

HOT GERMAN POTATO SALAD

1½ pounds potatoes (about 4 medium), cut in half
3 slices bacon, cut into 1-inch pieces
1 medium onion, chopped (about ½ cup)
1 tablespoon all-purpose flour
1 tablespoon sugar
½ teaspoon salt
¼ teaspoon celery seed
Dash of pepper
½ cup water
¼ cup vinegar

Prepare and cook potatoes as directed on page 393. Cook bacon in 10-inch skillet until crisp. Drain bacon, reserving fat in skillet. Cook and stir onion in fat until tender. Stir in flour, sugar, salt, celery seed and pepper. Cook over low heat, stirring constantly, until mixture is bubbly; remove from heat. Stir in water and vinegar. Heat to boiling, stirring constantly. Boil and stir 1 minute; remove from heat.

Cut warm potatoes into ¼-inch slices. Stir potatoes and bacon into hot mixture. Heat until hot and bubbly, stirring gently to coat potato slices. 6 SERVINGS (⅔ CUP EACH); 195 CALORIES PER SERVING.

To Microwave: Microwave whole potatoes as directed on page 393; reserve. Place bacon in microwavable 2-quart casserole. Cover with microwavable paper towel and microwave on high 3 to 4 minutes or until crisp. Drain bacon, reserving fat in casserole. Stir onion into fat. Cover and microwave on high about 2 minutes or until onion is tender. Stir in remaining ingredients. Cover and microwave on high 3 to 4 minutes, stirring every minute, until mixture thickens and boils. Cut warm potatoes into ¼-inch slices. Stir potatoes and bacon into hot mixture. Cover and microwave on high 1 to 3 minutes or until hot.

THREE-MUSTARD POTATO SALAD

6 medium red potatoes (about 2 pounds)
½ teaspoon beef or chicken bouillon granules
⅓ cup hot water
⅓ cup dry white wine or apple juice
1 clove garlic, finely chopped
Mustard Dressing (below)
3 tablespoons chopped fresh chives or parsley

Prepare and cook potatoes as directed on page 393. Cut potatoes into ¼-inch slices. Dissolve bouillon granules in hot water. Add wine and garlic. Pour over potatoes in large bowl. Cover and refrigerate about 3 hours or until chilled, stirring occasionally. Drain potatoes. Toss gently with Mustard Dressing and chives until coated.   6 SERVINGS (ABOUT ⅔ CUP EACH); 235 CALORIES PER SERVING.

Mustard Dressing

1 tablespoon mustard seed
3 tablespoons olive or vegetable oil
2 tablespoons white vinegar
1 tablespoon Dijon mustard
1 teaspoon dry mustard
1 teaspoon salt
4 to 6 drops red pepper sauce

Shake all ingredients in tightly covered container.

To Microwave: Cut potatoes into ¼-inch slices. Place in 2-quart microwavable casserole. Cover tightly and microwave on high 11 to 13 minutes, stirring after 5 minutes, until tender; drain. Continue as directed.

❧ PEAS AND CHEESE SALAD

A heartland favorite at potluck suppers and backyard picnics with its hearty combination of peas and cheese.

⅓ to ½ cup mayonnaise or salad dressing
½ teaspoon salt
½ teaspoon prepared mustard
¼ teaspoon sugar
⅛ teaspoon pepper
1 package (10 ounces) frozen green peas, thawed and drained
1 cup diced mild Cheddar or Colby cheese
1 medium stalk celery, thinly sliced (about ⅓ cup)
3 sweet pickles, chopped (about ¼ cup)
2 tablespoons finely chopped onion
2 hard-cooked eggs, chopped

Mix mayonnaise, salt, mustard, sugar and pepper in large bowl. Add peas, cheese, celery, pickles and onion; toss. Stir in eggs. Cover and refrigerate about 1 hour or until chilled. Serve on lettuce leaves if desired.   6 SERVINGS (ABOUT ¾ CUP EACH); 240 CALORIES PER SERVING.

KIDNEY BEAN AND CHEESE SALAD: Substitute 1 can (15 ounces) kidney beans, rinsed and drained, for the peas.   240 CALORIES PER SERVING.

❧ COLESLAW

½ cup sour cream or plain yogurt
¼ cup mayonnaise or salad dressing
1 teaspoon sugar
½ teaspoon dry mustard
½ teaspoon seasoned salt
⅛ teaspoon pepper
½ medium head cabbage, finely shredded or chopped (about 4 cups)
1 medium carrot, shredded (about ½ cup)
1 small onion, chopped (about ¼ cup)

Mix sour cream, mayonnaise, sugar, mustard, seasoned salt and pepper. Toss with cabbage, carrot and onion. Sprinkle with paprika or dill weed if desired.   8 SERVINGS (ABOUT ½ CUP EACH); 95 CALORIES PER SERVING.

APPLE-CHEESE COLESLAW: Omit onion. Toss 1 tart apple, chopped, and ¼ cup crumbled blue cheese with the cabbage.   120 CALORIES PER SERVING.

PINEAPPLE-MARSHMALLOW COLESLAW: Omit onion. Toss 1 can (8 ounces) crushed pineapple, drained, and 1 cup miniature marshmallows with the cabbage.   125 CALORIES PER SERVING.

ASPARAGUS AND BLACK BEAN SALAD

Cilantro is also called "Chinese parsley" or "Mexican parsley." It has a fresh, cool citric flavor.

1 pound asparagus, cut into 1-inch pieces*
1 can (16 ounces) black beans, rinsed and drained
1 red bell pepper, cut into ½-inch squares
1 tablespoon finely chopped onion
Cilantro Dressing (below)

Prepare and cook asparagus as directed on page 00. Mix asparagus and remaining ingredients in glass or plastic bowl. Cover and refrigerate at least 4 hours.   6 SERVINGS (½ CUP EACH); 155 CALORIES PER SERVING.

2 packages (10 ounces each) frozen cut asparagus, cooked and drained, can be substituted for the fresh asparagus.

Cilantro Dressing

3 tablespoons olive or vegetable oil
1 tablespoon chopped fresh or 1 teaspoon dried cilantro leaves
2 tablespoons vinegar
½ teaspoon salt
½ teaspoon ground cumin
Dash of pepper
1 small clove garlic, crushed

Shake all ingredients in tightly covered container.

Asparagus and Black Bean Salad

MARINATED PEPPERS

6 large bell peppers
¼ cup olive or vegetable oil
2 tablespoons chopped fresh parsley
2 tablespoons lemon juice
2 tablespoons lime juice
½ teaspoon salt
1 teaspoon chopped fresh or ¼ teaspoon dried oregano leaves
1 teaspoon chopped fresh or ¼ teaspoon dried basil leaves
½ teaspoon chopped fresh or ⅛ teaspoon dried sage leaves
⅛ teaspoon pepper
2 large cloves garlic, finely chopped

Set over control to broil. Broil bell peppers with tops about 5 inches from heat, turning occasionally, until skin is blistered and evenly browned. Place peppers in a plastic bag and close tightly. Let stand 20 minutes.

Remove skin, stems, seeds and membrances from peppers. Cut peppers into ¼-inch strips. Place in glass or plastic bowl. Shake remaining ingredients in tightly covered container. Pour over peppers. Cover and refrigerate at least 4 hours, stirring occasionally.   8 SERVINGS (ABOUT ½ CUP EACH); 85 CALORIES PER SERVING.

MARINATED PEPPERS AND OLIVES: Prepare as directed—except cut peppers into fourths. Stir in 1 cup pitted Greek or black olives, drained, and 4 ounces feta or mozzarella cheese, cubed, with the peppers.   10 SERVINGS (ABOUT ½ CUP EACH); 120 CALORIES PER SERVING.

PARMESAN-BASIL VEGETABLES

⅓ cup grated Parmesan cheese
⅔ cup mayonnaise, salad dressing or plain yogurt
2 tablespoons vinegar
1 tablespoon chopped fresh or 1 teaspoon dried basil leaves
1 clove garlic, finely chopped
2 cups bite-size pieces broccoli flowerets and stems
1½ cups cauliflowerets
1 medium zucchini, cut into cubes
1 medium carrot, thinly sliced
1 small onion, thinly sliced and separated into rings

Mix cheese, mayonnaise, vinegar, basil and garlic in large glass or plastic bowl. Stir in remaining ingredients. Cover and refrigerate at least 2 hours. 6 SERVINGS (ABOUT 1 CUP EACH); 230 CALORIES PER SERVING.

Marinated Peppers and Olives, Parmesan-Basil Vegetables

THREE-BEAN SALAD

This classic is made super simple with canned beans. Colorful and flavorful, it can be assembled in minutes!

1 can (16 ounces) green beans, drained
1 can (16 ounces) wax beans, drained
1 can (15 ounces) kidney beans, drained
4 green onions (with tops), chopped (about ¼ cup)
¼ cup chopped fresh parsley
1 cup Italian Dressing (page 327) or bottled dressing
1 tablespoon sugar
2 cloves garlic, crushed

Mix beans, onions and parsley. Mix Italian Dressing, sugar and garlic. Pour over bean mixture and toss. Cover and refrigerate at least 3 hours, stirring occasionally.   6 SERVINGS (ABOUT ¾ CUP EACH); 135 CALORIES PER SERVING.

FENNEL CUCUMBERS

4 medium cucumbers (about 2 pounds)
¼ cup vegetable oil
2 tablespoons lemon juice
1 teaspoon fennel seed
½ teaspoon salt
1 small onion, finely chopped (about ¼ cup)
Green Mayonnaise (below)

Prepare cucumbers as directed (page 382)—except cut lengthwise in half and remove seeds. Cut each half lengthwise into 4 strips. Cut each strip into pieces, about 2 inches long. Place cucumbers in glass or plastic bowl. Shake oil, lemon juice, fennel seed, salt and onion in tightly covered container. Pour over cucumbers. Cover and refrigerate at least 12 hours, stirring occasionally. Prepare Green Mayonnaise. Drain cucumbers. Serve with Green Mayonnaise.   8 SERVINGS; 280 CALORIES PER SERVING.

Green Mayonnaise

1 cup mayonnaise or salad dressing
¼ cup finely chopped spinach
¼ cup chopped fresh parsley
1 tablespoon fresh or 1½ teaspoons dried dill weed
2 teaspoons tarragon vinegar

Place all ingredients in blender or food processor. Cover and blend on high speed, or process, until smooth. Refrigerate at least 2 hours.

CARROT-RAISIN SALAD

2½ cups shredded carrots (about 3 large)
1 medium stalk celery, sliced (about ½ cup)
½ cup raisins
½ cup mayonnaise or salad dressing
1 teaspoon lemon juice

Mix all ingredients. Serve on salad greens if desired.   5 SERVINGS (½ CUP EACH); 230 CALORIES PER SERVING.

MINTED CUCUMBER AND YOGURT SALAD

1 cup plain yogurt
2 tablespoons finely chopped fresh or ½ teaspoon dried mint leaves
1 tablespoon lemon juice
1 clove garlic, finely chopped
Dash of white pepper
1 medium cucumber, thinly sliced (about 1¼ cups)

Mix all ingredients in medium bowl except cucumber. Cover and refrigerate about 2 hours or until chilled. Just before serving, stir in cucumber. Garnish with additional mint if desired.   4 SERVINGS (ABOUT ½ CUP); 50 CALORIES PER SERVING.

SICHUAN VEGETABLE TOSS

1 package (16 ounces) frozen loose-pack Oriental vegetables
1 jar (7 ounces) tiny ear corn
1 can (8 ounces) sliced water chestnuts, drained
½ cup chopped red bell pepper
Sichuan Dressing (below)

Prepare vegetables as directed on package; drain. Toss all ingredients. Cover and refrigerate at least 2 hours, stirring twice.   8 SERVINGS (ABOUT ½ CUP EACH); 130 CALORIES PER SERVING.

Sichuan Dressing

2 tablespoons vegetable oil
1 tablespoon soy sauce
1 tablespoon dry sherry
1 tablespoon rice wine or balsamic or wine vinegar
1 teaspoon sugar
1 teaspoon sesame oil
½ teaspoon chili oil or ¼ teaspoon ground red pepper
¼ teaspoon salt

Shake all ingredients in tightly covered container.

AVOCADO AND TOMATO SALAD

3 tablespoons vegetable oil
1 tablespoon vinegar
½ teaspoon salt
⅛ teaspoon pepper
3 drops red pepper sauce
2 medium avocados, cubed
6 slices bacon, crisply cooked and crumbled
2 medium tomatoes, cut into ½-inch pieces
1 small onion, chopped (about ¼ cup)
Salad greens

Mix oil, vinegar, salt, pepper and pepper sauce. Pour over avocados and toss. Stir in bacon, tomatoes and onion. Cover and refrigerate at least 2 hours. Just before serving, place on salad greens with slotted spoon. 6 SERVINGS (ABOUT ¾ CUP EACH); 195 CALORIES PER SERVING.

TORTELLINI SALAD

1 package (7 ounces) dried cheese-filled tortellini
¼ cup olive or vegetable oil
¼ cup wine vinegar
2 tablespoons grated Parmesan cheese
1 tablespoon chopped fresh or 1 teaspoon dried basil leaves
2 cups bite-size pieces spinach
¼ cup pine nuts or slivered almonds, toasted
1 medium bell pepper, cut into strips

Cook tortellini as directed on package. Rinse in cold water and drain. Shake oil, vinegar, cheese and basil in tightly covered container. Pour over tortellini. Cover and refrigerate about 2 hours or until chilled. Toss with remaining ingredients. Serve with freshly ground pepper and additional Parmesan cheese if desired. 4 SERVINGS (1¼ CUPS EACH); 250 CALORIES PER SERVING.

BROWN RICE SALAD

½ cup uncooked brown rice
3 tablespoons olive or vegetable oil
2 tablespoons lemon juice
⅛ teaspoon crushed red pepper
1 clove garlic, crushed
1 small cucumber, chopped (about 1 cup)
1 green onion (with top), thinly sliced (about 1 tablespoon)
½ cup cashew pieces

Cook rice as directed on package. Mix oil, lemon juice, red pepper and garlic. Stir cucumber, onion and oil mixture into rice. Cover and refrigerate

about 3 hours or until chilled. Stir in cashews. 4 SERVINGS (ABOUT ½ CUP EACH); 280 CALORIES PER SERVING.

PESTO-MACARONI SALAD

3 cups uncooked medium shell macaroni
1 tablespoon olive or vegetable oil
1 cup Pesto (page 359) or 1 container (8 ounces) pesto
½ cup small pitted ripe olives
¼ cup white wine vinegar
4 Italian plum tomatoes, each cut into 4 wedges
4 cups coarsely shredded spinach
Grated Parmesan cheese, if desired

Cook macaroni as directed on package. Rinse in cold water and drain; toss with oil. Mix pesto, olives, vinegar and tomatoes in large bowl. Arrange 2 cups macaroni and 2 cups spinach on olive mixture; repeat with remaining macaroni and spinach. Cover and refrigerate at least 2 hours. Toss and sprinkle with cheese. 6 SERVINGS (ABOUT 1¼ CUPS EACH); 500 CALORIES PER SERVING.

SHRIMP-PESTO SALAD: Add 1 package (6 ounces) frozen tiny shrimp, thawed, just before tossing salad. 515 CALORIES PER SERVING.

TUNA-PESTO SALAD: Add 1 can (6½ ounces) tuna, drained, just before tossing salad. 530 CALORIES PER SERVING.

ROSAMARINA-FRUIT SALAD

1 cup water
½ cup rosamarina
¼ teaspoon salt, if desired
½ cup whipping (heavy) cream
1 tablespoon sugar
½ cup seedless grapes, halved
½ cup chopped pecans
1 teaspoon shredded lemon peel
1 medium stalk celery, sliced (about ½ cup)
1 can (11 ounces) mandarin orange and pineapple sections, drained

Heat water, rosamarina and salt to boiling in 1-quart saucepan; reduce heat. Simmer 5 to 8 minutes or until almost tender. Rinse in cold water and drain.

Beat whipping cream and sugar in chilled medium bowl until stiff. Stir in rosamarina and remaining ingredients. Cover and refrigerate at least 2 hours. 6 SERVINGS (½ CUP EACH); 230 CALORIES PER SERVING.

Tomato-Pasta Salad, Tabbouleh

TOMATO-PASTA SALAD

1 package (7 ounces) macaroni shells
2 medium tomatoes, chopped (about 2 cups)
2 green onions (with tops), chopped (about 2 tablespoons)
2 cloves garlic, finely chopped
¼ cup chopped fresh parsley
2 tablespoons olive or vegetable oil
½ teaspoon salt
1½ teaspoons chopped fresh or ½ teaspoon dried basil leaves
⅛ teaspoon coarsely cracked pepper

Cook macaroni as directed on package. Rinse in cold water and drain. Stir in tomatoes, onions, garlic, parsley, oil, salt, basil and pepper. Cover and refrigerate about 2 hours or until chilled. 6 SERVINGS (ABOUT ¾ CUP EACH); 145 CALORIES PER SERVING.

TABBOULEH

This traditional Middle Eastern salad has a slightly chewy texture. If you'd like a softer texture, cover the cracked wheat with boiling water instead of cold water and let stand 1 hour.

¾ cup uncooked cracked wheat
1½ cups chopped fresh parsley
3 medium tomatoes, chopped
5 green onions (with tops), thinly sliced (about ⅓ cup)
2 tablespoons chopped fresh or 2 teaspoons crushed dried mint leaves
¼ cup olive or vegetable oil
¼ cup lemon juice
¾ teaspoon salt
¼ teaspoon pepper

Cover cracked wheat with cold water. Let stand 30 minutes; drain. Press out as much water as possible.

Place cracked wheat, parsley, tomatoes, onions and mint in glass or plastic bowl. Mix remaining ingredients. Pour over cracked wheat mixture and toss. Cover and refrigerate at least 1 hour. Garnish with ripe olives if desired. 6 SERVINGS (ABOUT ¾ CUP EACH); 175 CALORIES PER SERVING.

GELATIN BASICS

Gelatin is the basic ingredient in molded salads because it provides structure and form. Recipes can use either unflavored or fruit-flavored gelatin. Unflavored gelatin is unsweetened and flavored gelatin is sweetened.

♦ Gelatin must be completely dissolved for it to jell properly.

♦ To dissolve unflavored gelatin, sprinkle it on cold liquid and allow to stand 1 to 2 minutes to soften. Stir in hot liquid or heat over low heat until gelatin is dissolved.

♦ To dissolve flavored gelatin just add boiling liquid. Because the gelatin is premixed with sugar, it does not need to be softened before dissolving.

♦ If you are using a mold for a gelatin salad, be sure you know the size of your mold. To determine the size, fill it with water and then measure the water.

♦ It is not wise to adjust ingredient amounts to fit an odd-size mold. If your mold is too small, pour any extra gelatin into a small container. Using a mold that is too large can cause the salad to break when it is unmolded.

♦ Before adding solids to a gelatin mixture, the mixture must chill to the consistency of unbeaten egg whites. This can take from 20 to 40 minutes, depending on the quantity of gelatin mixture and the amount of solids added. If the mixture becomes too thick, heat mixture over hot water until it reaches the desired consistency. If the gelatin mixture is too thin, the solids can float to the surface or sink to the bottom.

♦ If you are adding whipped cream or sour cream, chill the gelatin mixture 30 to 40 minutes or until it mounds when dropped from a spoon.

♦ Do not use fresh pineapple, papaya or kiwifruit in gelatin mixtures. They contain an enzyme, protease, that breaks down the gelatin. You can use cooked or canned pineapple.

♦ To unmold a salad, quickly dip the mold in warm water up to the edge of the mold. Loosen edge of gelatin with the tip of a knife. Tip the mold slightly to allow air into the mold and break the vacuum. Rotate the mold so all sides are loose. Place a plate on top of mold. Holding both the mold and plate tightly, invert and shake gently. Carefully remove the mold. Repeat if necessary.

 # PERFECTION SALAD

The original Perfection Salad was a winner in a cooking contest at the turn of the nineteenth century. This adapted favorite appeared in the 1950 Betty Crocker's Picture Cook Book.

> 1 cup boiling water
> 1 package (3 ounces) lemon-flavored gelatin
> 1 cup cold water
> 2 tablespoons lemon juice or vinegar
> 1 teaspoon salt
> 1 cup finely diced celery
> 1 cup finely shredded cabbage
> ⅓ cup chopped sweet pickles
> 2 tablespoons finely chopped pimientos

Pour boiling water on gelatin in medium bowl; stir until gelatin is dissolved. Stir in water, lemon juice and salt. Refrigerate until the consistency of unbeaten egg whites. Stir in remaining ingredients. Pour into 4-cup mold or 6 individual molds. Refrigerate until firm; unmold.   6 SERVINGS; 75 CALORIES PER SERVING.

MOLDED AVOCADO-EGG SALAD

> 2 envelopes unflavored gelatin
> 2 cups cold water
> 1 cup mayonnaise, salad dressing or plain yogurt
> 1 container (6 ounces) frozen avocado dip, thawed
> 4 hard-cooked eggs
> 2 tablespoons chopped green onions (with tops)
> 1 jar (2 ounces) chopped pimientos, drained

Sprinkle gelatin on ½ cup of the cold water in 1-quart saucepan to soften. Heat over low heat, stirring constantly, until gelatin is dissolved. Pour into large bowl. Stir in remaining cold water, the mayonnaise and avocado dip. Beat until smooth. Refrigerate about 5 minutes or until slightly thickened.

Slice 2 eggs. Arrange in single layer in 5-cup ring mold. Chop remaining eggs. Stir eggs, onions and pimientos into gelatin mixture. Pour into mold. Refrigerate about 2 hours or until firm; unmold. Serve with assorted luncheon meats if desired.   6 SERVINGS; 380 CALORIES PER SERVING.

PIÑA COLADA MOLD

1⅔ cups boiling water
2 packages (3 ounces each) pineapple-orange–flavored gelatin
1 can (6 ounces) frozen piña colada concentrate
1 can (20 ounces) pineapple tidbits in juice, drained and juice reserved
½ cup flaked coconut

Pour boiling water on gelatin; stir until gelatin is dissolved. Stir in piña colada concentrate and reserved pineapple juice until concentrate is melted. Refrigerate about 45 minutes or until the consistency of unbeaten egg whites. Stir in pineapple and coconut. Pour into 6-cup mold. Cover and refrigerate about 4 hours or until set; unmold. 8 SERVINGS; 205 CALORIES PER SERVING.

GELATIN

Gelatin comes from the Latin word gelere, "to freeze," and anyone who has used gelatin can vouch for the accuracy of its name. Before the introduction of commercial gelatin in 1890, gelatin was made at home by boiling beef bones, cartilage and tendons and, sometimes, pig's feet. This lengthy process also produced a gelatin that had a distinctive flavor, and so most gelatin was seasoned with herbs and other spices. Today we use packaged gelatin to make molded salads and to add to desserts or to other foods that require a little assistance in "freezing" their shape.

RAINBOW PARTY MOLD

Using frozen raspberries will hasten the thickening process.

1 cup boiling water
1 package (3 ounces) lemon-flavored gelatin
¾ cup sparkling white grape juice, chilled
1 cup chopped fresh, frozen (thawed) or canned (drained) peaches
1½ cups boiling water
1 package (6 ounces) lime-flavored gelatin
2 cups plain or vanilla-flavored yogurt
2 cups boiling water
1 package (6 ounces) raspberry-flavored gelatin
1½ cups sparkling white grape juice, chilled
1 cup fresh or frozen raspberries

Pour 1 cup boiling water on lemon gelatin; stir until gelatin is dissolved. Stir in ¾ cup grape juice. Refrigerate until the consistency of unbeaten egg whites. Stir in peaches. Pour into 12-cup bundt cake pan. Refrigerate until set but not firm.

Pour 1½ cups boiling water on lime gelatin; stir until gelatin is dissolved. Stir in yogurt. Pour over lemon layer. Refrigerate until set but not firm.

Pour 2 cups boiling water on raspberry gelatin; stir until gelatin is dissolved. Stir in 1½ cups grape juice. Refrigerate until the consistency of unbeaten egg whites. Stir in raspberries. Pour over lime layer. Refrigerate about 4 hours or until firm; unmold. (Do not refrigerate longer than 48 hours.) 20 SERVINGS; 125 CALORIES PER SERVING.

SMALL RAINBOW PARTY MOLDS: Use two 6-cup molds. Divide gelatin layers evenly between molds.

1. Before adding lime gelatin layer, the first layer must be set, but not firm. Touch with finger to make sure gelatin is set or shake mold slightly.

2. Refrigerate the raspberry gelatin layer until the consistency of unbeaten egg whites. Then, fold in fruit so added fruit will not float.

AMBROSIA SALAD MOLD

We based this gelatin salad on the popular fruit dessert Ambrosia. We started with the traditional orange and coconut and added pineapple and sour cream for a tempting fruit salad.

1 cup boiling water
1 package (3 ounces) orange-flavored gelatin
1 can (8 ounces) crushed pineapple in juice, drained and juice reserved
½ cup sour cream
2 oranges, pared, sectioned and cut up
½ cup flaked coconut

Pour boiling water on gelatin in large bowl; stir until gelatin is dissolved. Add enough cold water to reserved pineapple juice to measure 1 cup. Stir into gelatin. Refrigerate until gelatin mixture mounds slightly when dropped from spoon.

Beat gelatin mixture and sour cream until light and fluffy. Stir in pineapple, oranges and coconut. Pour into 6-cup mold. Refrigerate until firm. Garnish with additional orange sections if desired. 8 SERVINGS; 120 CALORIES PER SERVING.

MOLDED TANGERINE SALAD

1 envelope unflavored gelatin
1 cup cold water
1 can (6 ounces) frozen tangerine juice concentrate, thawed*
1 package (8 ounces) Neufchâtel or cream cheese, softened
1 can (8 ounces) crushed pineapple in juice, well drained
Watercress
1 kiwifruit, sliced

Sprinkle gelatin on cold water in 1-quart saucepan to soften. Heat over low heat, stirring constantly, until gelatin is dissolved; remove from heat. Stir in tangerine juice concentrate.

Beat cheese in large bowl on medium speed until fluffy. Gradually beat in gelatin mixture on low speed until smooth. Refrigerate about 1 hour or until the consistency of unbeaten egg whites. Stir in pineapple. Pour into 4-cup mold. Refrigerate about 2 hours or until firm. Unmold on serving plate. Garnish with watercress and kiwifruit. 6 SERVINGS; 210 CALORIES EACH.

1 can (6 ounces) frozen orange juice concentrate can be substituted for the tangerine juice concentrate.

FROZEN RASPBERRY SALAD

½ cup boiling water
1 package (3 ounces) raspberry-flavored gelatin
1 package (10 ounces) frozen raspberries, thawed and undrained
1 cup sour cream or plain yogurt
2 packages (3 ounces each) cream cheese, softened
1 can (16 ounces) whole berry cranberry sauce
Salad greens
1 carton (6 ounces) raspberry yogurt

Pour boiling water on gelatin in large bowl; stir until gelatin is dissolved. Stir in raspberries. Mix sour cream and cream cheese. Stir in cranberry sauce. Stir sour cream mixture into gelatin mixture (salad will be lumpy). Pour into square pan, 8 × 8 × 2 or 9 × 9 × 2 inches. Cover and freeze at least 24 hours or until firm.

Remove from freezer about 10 minutes before serving. Cut into serving pieces. Place on salad greens. Serve with yogurt. 9 SERVINGS; 280 CALORIES PER SERVING.

SMOKED FISH SALAD

You can buy smoked whitefish or salmon at your supermarket, favorite deli or local fish market.

2 pounds new potatoes (about 16 small)
2 cartons (6 ounces each) lemon yogurt (about 1⅓ cups)
1 jar (2 ounces) diced pimientos, drained
2 teaspoons chopped fresh or ½ teaspoon dried dill weed
1 teaspoon dry mustard
¼ teaspoon salt
2 pounds smoked whitefish or salmon
3 medium tomatoes, sliced
1 medium onion, thinly sliced
Salad greens

Prepare and cook potatoes as directed on page 390; cool. Cut into ¼-inch slices. Mix yogurt, pimientos, dill weed, mustard and salt in large bowl. Add potatoes and toss. Cover and refrigerate at least 3 hours.

Remove skin and bones from fish. Divide fish into serving pieces. Arrange potato mixture, fish, tomatoes and onion on salad greens. Garnish with fresh dill weed if desired. 8 SERVINGS; 355 CALORIES PER SERVING.

⏱ TUNA-BEAN SALAD

3 cans (15 ounces each) cannellini beans
   or great northern beans, drained
1 jar (2 ounces) diced pimientos, drained
1 large green bell pepper, chopped (about
   1 cup)
1 medium onion, chopped (about ½ cup)
¼ cup chopped fresh parsley
¼ cup olive or vegetable oil
2 tablespoons lemon juice
2 tablespoons capers
¼ teaspoon red pepper sauce
Lettuce leaves
1 can (6½ ounces) tuna in water, drained

Mix beans, pimientos, bell pepper, onion and parsley. Shake oil, lemon juice, capers and pepper
sauce in tightly covered container. Toss with bean
mixture. Spoon onto lettuce. Top with tuna. Serve
with lemon wedges if desired.   5 SERVINGS (ABOUT
1¼ CUPS EACH); 350 CALORIES PER SERVING.

⏱ SEAFOOD-PASTA SALAD

8 ounces uncooked vermicelli
2 cups bite-size pieces cooked seafood or 1
   package (8 ounces) frozen salad-style
   imitation crabmeat, thawed
½ cup coarsely chopped jicama or water
   chestnuts
¼ cup chopped fresh cilantro or parsley
2 medium carrots, shredded (about 1¼ cups)
1 medium cucumber, coarsely chopped
   (about 1 cup)
Ginger Dressing (below)

Break vermicelli in half. Cook as directed on package; drain. Rinse with cold water; drain. Toss
vermicelli, seafood, jicama, cilantro, carrots and
cucumber with Ginger Dressing. Spoon onto salad
greens if desired.   6 SERVINGS; 295 CALORIES PER
SERVING.

Ginger Dressing

⅓ cup mayonnaise or salad dressing
⅓ cup plain yogurt
1 tablespoon soy sauce
1 teaspoon sugar
½ teaspoon ground ginger
Dash of red pepper sauce, hot chili oil or
   hot sesame oil

Mix all ingredients.

CHICKEN-PASTA SALAD: Substitute 2 cups cut-up
cooked chicken or turkey for the seafood.   365
CALORIES PER SERVING.

🦀 CRAB LOUIS

Louis Dressing (below)
4 cups bite-size pieces salad greens
2 cups cut-up cooked crabmeat or 1 package (8 ounces) frozen salad-style imitation crabmeat, thawed*
4 tomatoes, cut into fourths
4 hard-cooked eggs, cut into fourths
Ripe or pimiento-stuffed olives

Prepare Louis Dressing. Divide salad greens among
4 salad bowls or plates. Arrange crabmeat, tomatoes, eggs and olives on lettuce. Pour Louis Dressing over salads.   4 SERVINGS; 435 CALORIES PER
SERVING.

*2 packages (6 ounces each) frozen cooked crabmeat, thawed
and drained, or 2 cans (6½ ounces each) crabmeat, drained
and cartilage removed, can be substituted for the cooked or
imitation crabmeat.*

Louis Dressing

¾ cup chili sauce
½ cup mayonnaise or salad dressing
1 teaspoon finely chopped onion
½ teaspoon sugar
¼ teaspoon Worcestershire sauce
Salt to taste

Mix all ingredients. Refrigerate at least 30 minutes.

Crab Louis

⏱ SOUTH SEAS SHRIMP SALAD

You can make your own five-spice powder by mixing 1 teaspoon ground cinnamon, 1 star anise or 1 teaspoon anise seed, 1 teaspoon fennel seed, ¼ teaspoon peppercorns and ¼ teaspoon ground cloves in a blender. Blend on high speed until finely ground. Store powder in a tightly covered container.

2 cups bite-size pieces spinach
2 cups shredded Chinese cabbage
8 ounces cooked cleaned shrimp (about 1½ cups)
1 cup enoki mushrooms
¼ cup slivered almonds, toasted
1 red bell pepper, cut into ½-inch pieces
1 green onion (with top), thinly sliced (about 1 tablespoon)
2 tablespoons vegetable oil
2 tablespoons rice vinegar or vinegar
2 tablespoons soy sauce
½ teaspoon five-spice powder

Mix spinach, cabbage, shrimp, mushrooms, almonds, bell pepper and onion. Shake remaining ingredients in tightly covered container. Pour over spinach mixture and toss. 4 SERVINGS (ABOUT 2 CUPS EACH); 180 CALORIES PER SERVING.

SOUTH SEAS CHICKEN SALAD: Substitute 1¼ cups cut-up cooked chicken for the shrimp and 2 tablespoons sesame seed, toasted, for the almonds. 195 CALORIES PER SERVING.

MACARONI-SHRIMP SALAD

1½ cups uncooked elbow or spiral macaroni (about 6 ounces)
1 package (10 ounces) frozen green peas
1 cup shredded Cheddar cheese (4 ounces)
¾ cup mayonnaise or salad dressing
8 green onions (with tops), sliced, (about ½ cup)
⅓ cup sweet pickle relish
1 stalk celery, sliced (about ½ cup)
1 can (4½ ounces) tiny shrimp, rinsed and drained
½ head iceberg lettuce, torn into bite-size pieces (about 3 cups)
6 slices bacon, crisply cooked and crumbled

Cook macaroni as directed on package. Rinse in cold water and drain. Rinse frozen peas with cold water to separate; drain. Mix macaroni, peas and remaining ingredients except lettuce and bacon. Cover and refrigerate about 4 hours or until chilled.

Just before serving, mix macaroni mixture, lettuce and bacon. 6 SERVINGS (ABOUT 1½ CUPS EACH); 480 CALORIES PER SERVING.

MACARONI-CHEESE SALAD: Omit shrimp. Increase cheese to 2 cups. 545 CALORIES PER SERVING.

MACARONI-CHICKEN SALAD: Substitute ½ cup cut-up cooked chicken or turkey for the shrimp. 495 CALORIES PER SERVING.

MACARONI-FRANK SALAD: Omit shrimp. Increase cheese to 2 cups. Substitute 3 frankfurters, sliced, for the bacon. 585 CALORIES PER SERVING.

⏱ TURKEY-PASTA SALAD

Spinach Sauce (below)
2 packages (5 ounces each) spiral macaroni
3 cups cut-up cooked turkey or chicken
½ cup sliced ripe olives
1 tablespoon olive or vegetable oil
1 teaspoon vinegar
1 tablespoon pine nuts or slivered almonds

Prepare Spinach Sauce. Cook macaroni as directed on package; drain. Rinse in cold water; drain. Toss macaroni and ½ cup of the Spinach Sauce. Mix turkey, olives, oil and vinegar. Spoon onto center of macaroni mixture. Sprinkle with pine nuts. Serve with remaining Spinach Sauce. 6 SERVINGS (ABOUT 1½ CUPS EACH); 480 CALORIES PER SERVING.

Spinach Sauce

4 cups spinach leaves
1 cup fresh parsley sprigs
¼ cup lemon juice
3 large cloves garlic, cut in half
½ cup grated Parmesan cheese
2 tablespoons olive or vegetable oil
1 tablespoon chopped fresh or 1 teaspoon dried basil leaves
½ teaspoon pepper

Place half each of the spinach, parsley, lemon juice and garlic in blender or food processor. Cover and blend on medium speed about 3 minutes, stopping blender frequently to scrape sides, or process, until spinach is finely chopped. Add remaining spinach, parsley, lemon juice and garlic; repeat. Add remaining ingredients. Cover and blend on medium speed about 2 minutes, stopping blender frequently to scrape sides, or process, until mixture is smooth.

⏱ ORIENTAL CHICKEN SALAD

Cellophane noodles are hard, clear noodles made from mung peas. They become white, puffy and crisp when deep-fried, puffing up to more than twice their original size. Remove them quickly from the oil so they stay white.

Ginger Dressing (below)
Vegetable oil
1 package (3¾ ounces) cellophane noodles (bean threads)*
½ head lettuce, shredded (about 4 cups)
3 cups cut-up cooked chicken or turkey
1 medium carrot, shredded (about ½ cup)
4 green onions (with tops) sliced (about ¼ cup)
1 tablespoon sesame seed, toasted

Prepare Ginger Dressing. Heat oil (1 inch) in Dutch oven to 425°. Fry ¼ of the noodles at a time about 5 seconds, turning once, until puffed; drain.

Pour Ginger Dressing over lettuce, chicken, carrot and onions in large bowl. Toss with half of the noodles. Place remaining noodles on large platter. Spoon salad over noodles. Sprinkle with sesame seed. 6 SERVINGS; 490 CALORIES PER SERVING.

5 cups chow mein noodles can be substituted for the fried cellophane noodles. Toss half of the noodles with chicken-dressing mixture. Continue as directed.

Ginger Dressing

⅓ cup vegetable oil
¼ cup white wine vinegar
1 tablespoon sugar
2 teaspoons soy sauce
½ teaspoon pepper
½ teaspoon ground ginger
¼ teaspoon salt

Shake all ingredients in tightly covered container. Refrigerate at least 2 hours.

Oriental Chicken Salad

CURRIED CHICKEN SALAD

3 cups cold cooked rice (page 267)
2 cups cut-up cooked chicken or turkey
2 medium stalks celery, sliced (about 1 cup)
1 small green pepper, chopped (about ½ cup)
1 can (13¼ ounces) pineapple chunks, drained
1 cup mayonnaise or salad dressing
¾ teaspoon curry powder
¼ teaspoon salt
¼ teaspoon ground ginger
Salad greens
2 medium tomatoes, cut into wedges
6 slices bacon, crisply cooked and crumbled

Mix rice, chicken, celery, bell pepper and pineapple. Mix mayonnaise, curry powder, salt and ginger. Stir into chicken mixture. Cover and refrigerate about 2 hours or until chilled.

Just before serving, spoon chicken mixture onto salad greens. Garnish with tomato wedges and sprinkle with bacon. 6 SERVINGS (ABOUT 1½ CUPS EACH); 555 CALORIES PER SERVING.

✳ SIRLOIN AND MUSHROOM SALAD

1½-pound beef boneless sirloin steak, 1½ inches thick
1 jar (4½ ounces) sliced mushrooms, drained
1 medium green or red bell pepper, cut into thin strips
⅓ cup red wine vinegar
¼ cup vegetable oil
1 teaspoon chopped fresh or ¼ teaspoon dried tarragon leaves
½ teaspoon salt
½ teaspoon Worcestershire sauce
¼ teaspoon pepper
2 cloves garlic, crushed
Salad greens
Cherry or yellow pear tomatoes

Slash outer edge of fat diagonally at 1-inch intervals to prevent curling (do not cut into beef). Set oven control to broil. Place beef on rack in broiler pan. Broil with top about 2 inches from heat about 13 minutes on each side for medium; cool. Cut into ⅜-inch strips. Arrange in ungreased rectangular baking dish, 13 × 9 × 2 inches. Place mushrooms on beef. Top with bell pepper strips.

Mix remaining ingredients except greens and tomatoes. Pour over beef and vegetables. Cover and refrigerate at least 3 hours, spooning marinade over vegetables occasionally. Remove beef and vegetables with slotted spoon onto salad greens. Garnish with tomatoes. 4 SERVINGS; 555 CALORIES PER SERVING.

FRUITED TURKEY SALAD

3 cups cut-up cooked turkey or chicken
¾ cup seedless grape halves
2 medium stalks celery, thinly sliced (about 1 cup)
2 green onions (with tops), thinly sliced
1 can (11 ounces) mandarin orange segments, drained
1 can (8 ounces) sliced water chestnuts, drained
1 carton (6 ounces) lemon, peach or orange yogurt (about ⅔ cup)
2 tablespoons soy sauce

Mix turkey, grapes, celery, onions, orange segments and water chestnuts. Mix yogurt and soy sauce. Pour over turkey mixture and toss. Cover and refrigerate at least 2 hours. 6 SERVINGS (ABOUT 1¼ CUPS EACH); 260 CALORIES PER SERVING.

⏱ ✳ COBB SALADS

Lemon Vinaigrette (below)
6 cups finely shredded lettuce
2 cups cut-up cooked chicken
3 hard-cooked eggs, chopped
2 medium tomatoes, chopped (about 1½ cups)
1 ripe avocado, chopped
¼ cup crumbled blue cheese (1 ounce)
4 slices bacon, crisply cooked and crumbled

Prepare Lemon Vinaigrette. Divide lettuce among 4 salad plates or bowls. Arrange remaining ingredients in rows on lettuce. Serve with Lemon Vinaigrette. 4 SERVINGS; 650 CALORIES PER SERVING.

Lemon Vinaigrette

½ cup vegetable oil
¼ cup lemon juice
1 tablespoon red wine vinegar
2 teaspoons sugar
½ teaspoon salt
½ teaspoon dry mustard
½ teaspoon Worcestershire sauce
¼ teaspoon garlic powder
¼ teaspoon pepper

Shake all ingredients in tightly covered container. Refrigerate at least 1 hour.

Sirloin and Mushroom Salad

CHEF'S SALAD

½ cup julienne strips cooked meat (beef, smoked ham or tongue)
½ cup julienne strips cooked chicken or turkey
½ cup julienne strips Swiss cheese
4 green onions (with tops), chopped (about ½ cup)
1 medium head lettuce, torn into bite-size pieces
1 small bunch romaine, torn into bite-size pieces
1 medium stalk celery, sliced (about ½ cup)
½ cup mayonnaise or salad dressing
¼ cup Classic French Dressing (page 327) or bottled dressing
2 hard-cooked eggs, sliced
2 tomatoes, cut into wedges

Reserve a few strips of meat, chicken and cheese. Mix remaining meat, chicken and cheese, the onions, lettuce, romaine and celery. Mix mayonnaise and French Dressing. Pour over lettuce mixture and toss. Top with reserved meat, chicken and cheese strips, the eggs and tomatoes. 5 SERVINGS; 380 CALORIES PER SERVING.

 # TACO SALADS

For a low-fat variation, substitute ground turkey for the ground beef and nonfat yogurt for the Thousand Island Dressing, and omit the avocado. You reduce the fat by more than 50 percent and the calories by about 35 percent!

Tortilla Shells (right)
1 pound ground beef
⅔ cup water
1 tablespoon chili powder
½ teaspoon salt
¼ teaspoon garlic powder
¼ teaspoon ground red pepper (cayenne)
1 can (15½ ounces) kidney beans, drained (reserve empty can)
1 medium head lettuce, torn into bite-size pieces (about 10 cups)
1 cup shredded Cheddar cheese (4 ounces)
⅔ cup sliced ripe olives
2 medium tomatoes, coarsely chopped
1 medium onion, chopped (about ½ cup)
¾ cup Thousand Island Dressing (page 326) or bottled dressing
1 avocado, thinly sliced
Sour cream

Prepare Tortilla Shells. Cook ground beef in 10-inch skillet, stirring occasionally, until brown; drain. Stir in water, chili powder, salt, garlic powder, red pepper and kidney beans. Heat to boiling; reduce heat. Simmer uncovered 15 minutes, stirring occasionally; cool 10 minutes.

Mix lettuce, cheese, olives, tomatoes and onion in large bowl. Toss with Thousand Island Dressing. Pour ground beef mixture over top and toss. Divide among Tortilla Shells. Garnish with avocado and sour cream. Serve immediately. 8 SERVINGS; 610 CALORIES PER SERVING.

Tortilla Shells

Vegetable oil
8 flour tortillas (10-inch diameter)

Remove label and both ends of reserved kidney bean can. Wash and dry can. Heat oil (1½ inches) in 3-quart saucepan to 375°. (Diameter of saucepan should be at least 9 inches.) Place 1 tortilla on top of saucepan. Place can on center of tortilla with long-handled tongs. Push tortilla into oil by gently pushing can down. Fry tortilla about 5 seconds or until set; remove can with tongs. Fry tortilla 1 to 2 minutes longer, turning tortilla in oil, until tortilla is crisp and golden brown. Carefully remove tortilla from oil and drain excess oil from inside. Turn tortilla shell upside down; cool. Repeat with remaining tortillas.

To Microwave: Crumble ground beef into 2-quart microwavable casserole. Cover loosely and microwave on high 6 to 7 minutes, stirring after 3 minutes, until no pink remains; drain. Reduce water to ¼ cup. Stir in water, chili powder, salt, garlic powder, red pepper and kidney beans. Cover loosely and microwave on high 2 to 3 minutes or until boiling. Continue as directed.

Slowly push tortilla into the hot oil using tongs to gently push can.

COOKED SALAD DRESSING

¼ cup all-purpose flour
2 tablespoons sugar
1 teaspoon dry mustard
¾ teaspoon salt
1½ cups milk
2 egg yolks, slightly beaten
⅓ cup vinegar
1 tablespoon margarine or butter

Mix flour, sugar, mustard and salt in 2-quart saucepan. Gradually stir in milk. Heat to boiling over medium heat, stirring constantly. Boil and stir 1 minute. Gradually stir at least half of the hot mixture into egg yolks. Stir into hot mixture in saucepan. Boil and stir 1 minute; remove from heat. Stir in vinegar and margarine. Cover and refrigerate. ABOUT 2 CUPS DRESSING; 20 CALORIES PER TABLESPOON.

To Microwave: Mix flour, sugar, mustard and salt in 4-cup microwavable measure. Gradually stir in milk. Microwave uncovered on high 2 minutes, stirring every minute. Microwave uncovered 3 to 4 minutes longer, stirring every 30 seconds or until boiling. Gradually stir at least half of the hot mixture into egg yolks. Stir into hot mixture in cup. Microwave 45 seconds to 1 minute 15 seconds or until boiling. Stir in vinegar and margarine.

THOUSAND ISLAND DRESSING

Bits and pieces of seasonings float like islands in this dressing.

1 cup mayonnaise or salad dressing
1 tablespoon chopped fresh parsley
2 tablespoons chopped pimiento-stuffed olives or sweet pickle relish
2 tablespoons chili sauce or ketchup
1 teaspoon finely chopped onion
½ teaspoon paprika
1 hard-cooked egg, chopped

Mix all ingredients. ABOUT 1¼ CUPS DRESSING; 85 CALORIES PER TABLESPOON.

RUSSIAN DRESSING: Omit parsley, olives and egg. Increase chili sauce to ¼ cup and add 1 teaspoon prepared horseradish. 85 CALORIES PER TABLESPOON.

Clockwise from top left: *Berry Vinegar (page 328), Herb Vinegar (page 328), Blue Cheese Dressing, Green Goddess Dressing (page 327)*

BUTTERMILK DRESSING

¾ cup mayonnaise or salad dressing
½ cup buttermilk
1 tablespoon chopped fresh parsley
2 teaspoons finely chopped onion
½ teaspoon salt
Dash of freshly ground pepper
1 clove garlic, crushed

Shake all ingredients in tightly covered container. Refrigerate at least 2 hours. Shake before serving. ABOUT 1¼ CUPS DRESSING; 60 CALORIES PER TABLESPOON.

BLUE CHEESE DRESSING

¾ cup crumbled blue cheese
1 package (3 ounces) cream cheese, softened
½ cup mayonnaise or salad dressing
⅓ cup half-and-half

Reserve ⅓ cup of the blue cheese. Beat remaining blue cheese and the cream cheese on low speed until blended. Add mayonnaise and half-and-half. Beat on medium speed until creamy. Stir in reserved blue cheese. Cover and refrigerate about 3 hours or until chilled. ABOUT 1⅔ CUPS DRESSING; 60 CALORIES PER TABLESPOON.

ITALIAN DRESSING

1 cup olive or vegetable oil
¼ cup vinegar
2 tablespoons finely chopped onion
1 teaspoon sugar
1 teaspoon dry mustard
1 tablespoon chopped fresh or 1 teaspoon dried basil leaves
½ teaspoon salt
2 teaspoons chopped fresh or ½ teaspoon dried oregano leaves
¼ teaspoon pepper
2 cloves garlic, crushed

Shake all ingredients in tightly covered container. Shake before serving. ABOUT 1¼ CUPS DRESSING; 120 CALORIES PER TABLESPOON.

CREAMY ITALIAN DRESSING: Beat ½ cup Italian Dressing and ½ cup mayonnaise or salad dressing with hand beater until smooth. ABOUT 1 CUP DRESSING; 100 CALORIES PER TABLESPOON.

CLASSIC FRENCH DRESSING

Our Classic French Dressing recipe, a simple oil and vinegar base, is reminiscent of traditional French dressing. Our Red French Dressing variation is similar to the creamy, orange-red dressing sold commercially.

1 cup olive or vegetable oil
¼ cup vinegar
¼ cup lemon juice
½ teaspoon salt
½ teaspoon dry mustard
½ teaspoon paprika

Shake all ingredients in tightly covered container. ABOUT 1½ CUPS DRESSING; 80 CALORIES PER TABLESPOON.

LORENZO DRESSING: Mix ½ cup Classic French Dressing and 1 tablespoon chili sauce. ABOUT ½ CUP DRESSING; 80 CALORIES PER TABLESPOON.

RED FRENCH DRESSING: Mix ½ cup Classic French Dressing and ½ cup ketchup. ABOUT 1 CUP DRESSING; 50 CALORIES PER TABLESPOON.

GREEN GODDESS DRESSING

1 cup mayonnaise or salad dressing
½ cup sour cream
⅓ cup finely chopped fresh parsley
3 tablespoons finely chopped fresh chives
3 tablespoons anchovy paste or finely chopped anchovy fillets
3 tablespoons tarragon or wine vinegar
1 tablespoon lemon juice
⅛ teaspoon freshly ground pepper

Mix all ingredients. ABOUT 2 CUPS DRESSING; 60 CALORIES PER TABLESPOON.

ORANGE-PECAN DRESSING

½ cup vegetable oil
½ cup orange juice
2 tablespoons chopped pecans
1 tablespoon honey or sugar
1 teaspoon prepared mustard
½ teaspoon celery salt

Shake all ingredients in tightly covered container. ABOUT 1 CUP DRESSING; 75 CALORIES PER TABLESPOON.

ORANGE-ONION DRESSING: Substitute 2 to 3 teaspoons grated onion for the pecans. Add ¼ teaspoon pepper. 70 CALORIES PER TABLESPOON.

TAHINI DRESSING

Tahini is a popular food from the Middle East made from sesame seeds. It's wonderful as a dip with vegetables, great in sandwiches, and an unusual dressing for vegetables and salads.

½ cup tahini (sesame seed paste)
⅓ cup water
¼ cup vegetable oil
2 tablespoons lemon juice
½ teaspoon salt
1 green onion (with top), chopped (about 1 tablespoon)
2 cloves garlic, crushed
4 to 6 drops red pepper sauce

Place all ingredients in blender or food processor. Cover and blend on high speed, or process, until mixture is smooth. ABOUT 1 CUP DRESSING; 75 CALORIES PER TABLESPOON.

TOFU-TAHINI DRESSING: Reduce tahini to ¼ cup. Add 4 ounces (about ½ cup) tofu. ABOUT 1⅓ CUPS DRESSING; 60 CALORIES PER TABLESPOON.

ORIENTAL DRESSING

⅓ cup rice wine vinegar or vinegar
¼ cup vegetable oil
3 tablespoons soy sauce
2 tablespoons dry sherry
1 tablespoon sesame seed, toasted if
    desired
1 teaspoon grated gingerroot or ¼ teaspoon
    ground ginger
2 drops dark sesame oil, if desired

Shake all ingredients in tightly covered container.
ABOUT 1 CUP DRESSING; 40 CALORIES PER TABLESPOON.

FRESH HERB VINAIGRETTE

½ cup olive or vegetable oil
½ cup vinegar
1 tablespoon finely chopped green onion
1 tablespoon chopped fresh parsley
1 tablespoon chopped fresh herb (tarragon,
    rosemary, basil, oregano, thyme or
    marjoram)

Shake all ingredients in tightly covered container.
ABOUT 1 CUP DRESSING; 60 CALORIES PER TABLESPOON.

NUTTY HERB VINAIGRETTE: Substitute walnut, hazelnut or almond oil for the olive oil. 60 CALORIES PER TABLESPOON.

LOW-CALORIE VINAIGRETTE: Substitute apple juice for the olive oil and reduce vinegar to ⅓ cup. 5 CALORIES PER TABLESPOON.

LOW-CALORIE LEMON-PEPPER DRESSING

This extremely low-calorie dressing packs a lemony pepper punch.

1 cup nonfat plain yogurt
1 tablespoon chopped fresh parsley
1 tablespoon lemon juice
¼ teaspoon pepper
1 clove garlic, crushed

Mix all ingredients. ABOUT 1 CUP DRESSING; 10 CALORIES PER TABLESPOON.

LOW-CALORIE HERB DRESSING: Add 1 teaspoon chopped fresh herb or ¼ teaspoon dried herb, such as tarragon, rosemary, dill weed, oregano or basil. 10 CALORIES PER TABLESPOON.

CREAMY LOW-CAL DRESSING

½ cup skim milk
2 tablespoons lemon juice
1 tablespoon vegetable oil
1½ cups low-fat cottage cheese (12 ounces)
1 small onion, chopped (about ¼ cup)
2 cloves garlic, crushed
½ teaspoon salt
¼ teaspoon pepper
¼ teaspoon paprika

Place all ingredients in blender or food processor in order listed. Cover and blend on medium speed about 1 minute, or process, until smooth. 2 CUPS DRESSING; 15 CALORIES PER TABLESPOON.

HERB VINEGAR

Be creative and substitute one of these delicious, flavored vinegars any time a recipe calls for vinegar.

2 cups white wine or white vinegar
½ cup firmly packed fresh herb (tarragon,
    mint, basil, dill, rosemary, chives or
    oregano)

Shake vinegar and herb in tightly covered glass jar or bottle. Store in cool, dry place 10 days. Strain vinegar. Place one sprig of fresh herb, berries or garlic clove in jar to identify, if desired. 2 CUPS VINEGAR; 2 CALORIES PER TABLESPOON.

BERRY VINEGAR: Substitute 2 cups berries, crushed, for the herb. 6 CALORIES PER TABLESPOON.

GARLIC VINEGAR: Substitute 6 cloves garlic, cut in half, for the herb. 2 CALORIES PER TABLESPOON.

GINGER VINEGAR: Substitute ½ cup peeled, chopped gingerroot for the herb. 2 CALORIES PER TABLESPOON.

LEMON VINEGAR: Substitute peel from 2 lemons for the herb. 2 CALORIES PER TABLESPOON.

NUT-FLAVORED OIL

1 cup walnuts, almonds or hazelnuts
2 cups vegetable oil

Place nuts and ½ cup of the oil in blender or food processor. Cover and blend, or process, until nuts are finely chopped. Place nut mixture and remaining oil in glass jar or bottle. Cover tightly and let stand in a cool, dry place 10 days. Strain oil. Refrigerate up to 3 months. 2 CUPS OIL; 140 CALORIES PER TABLESPOON.

FIX-IT-FAST

♦ Use quick-set directions on package of fruit-flavored gelatin. Pouring into a shallow pan before chilling will help it set even more quickly.

♦ For a super simple fruit salad, toss canned fruit cocktail, drained, and whipped topping.

♦ Arrange fresh or canned fruits and cottage cheese on plate for a quick low-calorie main-dish salad.

♦ Make a quick salad from already prepared deli or salad bar ingredients.

♦ Cook your favorite pasta, drain and rinse in cold water. Stir in bottled salad dressing plus your favorite vegetables, cheeses and meats.

♦ Add leftover cooked rice to salads, or substitute cooked rice for pasta in salads.

♦ Mix marinated artichokes (with marinade), vegetables and olives for a quick salad. To stretch, add torn greens or cooked pasta to the salad.

♦ Mix 1 package (0.50 ounce) salad dressing mix, 2 cups water and 1 cup regular rice. Cook rice according to package directions for salads.

♦ Make salads with convenience products, such as Italian pasta salad mix or pasta primavera salad mix and stir in meat or additional vegetables.

♦ Stir any canned or cooked meat (fish, chicken, beef) into your favorite salad (pasta, rice, potato, vegetable, fruit) to make a main-dish salad.

♦ Toss leftover meats, cheeses, vegetables and fruits with torn greens from the deli or supermarket salad bar.

♦ Mix chilled leftover cooked vegetables with bottled salad dressings for a last-minute salad.

♦ Toss fresh or frozen (thawed and drained) fruits with equal parts apple juice and honey for a quick fruit dressing.

♦ Arrange whole fresh fruits and cheese on platter. Serve with plates, knives and, if desired, a bowl of sour cream or fruit-flavored yogurt for topping fruits of one's choice.

♦ Add instant crunch to any salad by tossing or topping with nuts or chow mein noodles.

PER SERVING OR UNIT

NUTRITION INFORMATION

RECIPE, PAGE	Servings per recipe	Calories	Protein (grams)	Carbohydrate (grams)	Fat (grams)	Cholesterol (milligrams)	Sodium (milligrams)	Protein	Vitamin A	Vitamin C	Thiamine	Riboflavin	Niacin	Calcium	Iron

PERCENT U.S. RECOMMENDED DAILY ALLOWANCE covers Protein through Iron.

SALADS

RECIPE, PAGE	Servings per recipe	Calories	Protein (grams)	Carbohydrate (grams)	Fat (grams)	Cholesterol (mg)	Sodium (mg)	Protein	Vitamin A	Vitamin C	Thiamine	Riboflavin	Niacin	Calcium	Iron
Ambrosia Salad Mold, 320	8	120	2	20	5	5	45	1	2	30	2	2	0	2	0
Apple-Cheese Coleslaw, 313	8	120	2	7	10	10	250	2	4	36	2	2	0	6	0
Asparagus and Black Bean Salad, 313	6	155	7	17	7	0	185	10	30	44	14	6	4	2	10
Avocado and Tomato Salad, 316	6	195	3	9	18	5	155	4	18	24	8	8	10	0	6
Brown Rice Salad, 316	4	280	4	26	19	0	115	6	2	10	8	2	6	2	8
Caesar Salad, 307	6	180	5	8	14	5	325	8	48	42	6	6	4	10	8
California Potato Salad, 312	10	400	4	26	33	0	445	4	10	30	10	4	12	2	6
Carrot-Raisin Salad, 315	5	230	1	20	18	0	155	2	100	8	4	2	2	2	4
Chef's Salad, 325	5	380	16	10	31	145	575	24	56	46	16	16	12	20	12
Chicken-Pasta Salad, 321	6	365	18	35	17	40	300	26	100	12	16	14	28	6	12
Citrus Salad, 310	4	215	2	23	14	50	20	2	16	68	6	6	0	6	2
Cobb Salads, 324	4	650	29	13	55	275	555	44	34	40	16	22	38	10	18
Coleslaw, 313	8	95	1	4	9	5	190	0	2	36	0	2	0	4	0
Crab Louis, 321	4	435	21	21	30	345	1630	32	68	56	16	18	14	8	16

NUTRITION INFORMATION

PER SERVING OR UNIT

RECIPE, PAGE	Servings per recipe	Calories	Protein (grams)	Carbohydrate (grams)	Fat (grams)	Cholesterol (milligrams)	Sodium (milligrams)	Protein	Vitamin A	Vitamin C	Thiamine	Riboflavin	Niacin	Calcium	Iron

SALADS (continued)

RECIPE, PAGE															
Curried Chicken Salad, 323	6	555	17	37	38	45	785	26	10	38	14	10	28	2	12
Dill Wilted Lettuce Salad, 306	4	170	2	6	16	15	195	2	30	16	4	4	2	4	6
Easy Fruit Salad, 311	8	165	1	37	2	0	20	2	14	16	4	2	0	2	4
Fennel Cucumbers, 315	8	280	1	5	29	0	300	0	6	14	2	0	2	2	4
Frozen Raspberry Salad, 320	9	280	4	39	12	35	155	6	10	8	2	6	0	6	2
Fruited Turkey Salad, 324	6	260	21	16	10	65	435	32	6	14	8	14	32	6	
Garden Potato Salad, 312	10	360	5	22	29	110	465	6	4	30	8	4	6	2	4
Greek Salad, 307	8	130	4	7	11	10	290	4	66	40	4	6	2	10	8
Hot German Potato Salad, 312	6	195	3	28	8	10	395	4	0	12	8	2	8	0	2
Kidney Bean and Cheese Salad, 313	6	240	9	11	18	110	605	14	6	2	4	8	0	16	6
Macaroni-Cheese Salad, 322	6	545	17	35	38	45	600	26	26	22	28	18	14	30	12
Macaroni-Chicken Salad, 322	6	495	16	35	33	35	490	24	22	22	28	16	18	16	14
Macaroni-Frank Salad, 322	6	585	19	35	41	55	795	28	26	22	28	20	14	30	14
Macaroni-Shrimp Salad, 322	6	480	15	35	31	40	490	22	22	22	28	14	14	18	14
Mandarin Salad, 308	6	170	2	14	13	0	200	2	10	16	2	4	2	2	4
Marinated Peppers, 314	8	85	1	5	7	0	140	0	8	82	4	2	2	0	6
Marinated Peppers and Olives, 314	10	120	2	5	11	10	340	2	6	66	2	0	0	6	6
Melon and Fig Salads, 310	4	220	1	30	12	0	120	0	28	24	4	2	2	4	2
Minted Cucumber and Yogurt Salad, 313	4	50	3	7	1	5	40	4	0	8	2	6	0	10	0
Molded Avocado-Egg Salad, 318	6	380	7	4	38	185	410	10	14	16	2	6	2	2	6
Molded Tangerine Salad, 320	6	210	4	19	13	40	115	6	22	64	4	6	0	4	2
Orange-Avocado Salads, 308	6	280	2	18	24	0	100	2	10	62	8	6	8	2	4
Orange-Jicama Salads, 308	6	275	2	17	24	0	115	2	10	66	8	6	8	2	4
Oriental Chicken Salad, 323	6	490	25	28	31	65	650	38	100	8	6	8	34	4	8
Parmesan-Basil Vegetables, 314	6	230	5	8	21	5	235	6	84	100	6	8	4	14	6
Pear Waldorf Salad, 308	4	360	3	28	29	0	175	4	2	12	6	4	2	2	4
Peas and Cheese Salad, 313	6	240	9	10	18	110	505	14	12	16	8	8	4	16	6
Perfection Salad, 318	6	75	2	18	0	0	490	2	4	26	0	0	0	0	2
Pesto Macaroni Salad, 316	6	500	12	48	30	5	275	18	82	50	22	16	14	30	32
Piña Colada Mold, 319	8	205	2	41	3	0	95	2	0	8	4	0	0	0	0
Pineapple-Marshmallow Coleslaw, 313	8	125	1	12	9	5	195	0	2	38	2	2	0	4	2

PER SERVING OR UNIT

NUTRITION INFORMATION

RECIPE, PAGE

PERCENT U.S. RECOMMENDED DAILY ALLOWANCE

SALADS (continued)

Recipe, Page	Servings per recipe	Calories	Protein (grams)	Carbohydrate (grams)	Fat (grams)	Cholesterol (milligrams)	Sodium (milligrams)	Protein	Vitamin A	Vitamin C	Thiamine	Riboflavin	Niacin	Calcium	Iron
Pineapple Salad, 308	6	160	1	13	12	0	175	0	24	36	6	4	2	2	4
Plum and Peach Salad, 311	6	135	1	17	8	0	2	2	4	6	2	2	2	0	2
Potato Salad, 312	10	355	5	21	29	110	460	6	4	12	6	4	6	2	4
Rainbow Party Mold, 319	20	125	3	26	0	0	80	4	0	2	0	2	0	2	0
Roquefort and Toasted Walnut Salad, 306	6	220	5	4	21	10	240	8	52	22	4	8	2	10	8
Rosamarina-Fruit Salad, 316	6	230	2	25	14	25	105	4	6	12	12	4	2	2	4
Scandinavian Potato Salad, 312	10	400	9	22	31	130	480	12	4	12	6	6	10	4	8
Seafood Pasta Salad, 321	6	295	13	35	11	50	360	20	100	14	18	12	14	10	10
Shrimp-Pesto Salad, 316	6	515	15	49	31	25	290	22	82	50	22	16	16	32	34
Sichuan Vegetable Toss, 315	8	130	4	19	5	0	205	6	14	48	14	8	8	0	6
Sirloin and Mushroom Salad, 324	4	555	29	3	47	115	345	44	2	54	6	14	28	0	22
Smoked Fish Salad, 320	8	355	29	28	11	0	980	44	12	24	26	12	28	8	12
Sorbet and Berry Salad, 311	6	75	1	18	0	0	2	0	6	32	0	2	2	0	0
South Seas Chicken Salad, 322	4	195	16	6	13	35	600	24	96	100	8	18	22	8	14
South Seas Shrimp Salad, 322	4	180	11	7	13	115	625	16	96	100	8	18	12	20	16
Strawberry-Spinach Toss, 306	6	115	2	13	7	0	45	2	62	56	6	6	2	4	8
Sweet-and-Sour Salad, 308	6	180	1	13	15	0	215	0	10	12	2	2	0	2	2
Tabbouleh, 317	6	175	3	21	10	0	285	4	36	50	8	4	6	2	12
Taco Salads, 325	8	610	22	31	46	65	660	32	28	20	12	16	16	16	16
Tangerine-Berry Salads, 310	4	130	2	19	6	15	15	2	14	42	4	4	2	4	2
Three-Bean Salad, 315	6	135	4	14	8	0	715	4	10	14	4	6	2	4	8
Three-Mustard Potato Salad, 312	6	235	3	32	8	0	455	4	0	34	12	2	12	2	4
Tomato-Pasta Salad, 317	6	145	3	22	5	0	190	4	16	20	8	4	6	2	6
Tortellini Salad, 316	4	250	6	28	13	0	50	10	26	44	22	12	10	6	10
Tropical Salad, 311	6	90	1	17	3	0	5	0	18	100	2	2	2	2	0
Tuna-Bean Salad, 321	5	350	22	41	12	20	280	34	12	90	18	10	24	10	22
Tuna-Pesto Salad, 316	6	530	19	48	31	20	495	28	82	50	22	18	32	32	34
Turkey-Pasta Salad, 322	6	480	29	40	22	65	300	44	62	36	32	24	46	18	24
Waldorf Salad, 308	4	310	2	14	28	0	175	2	2	6	4	0	2	2	2
Waldorf Salad Supreme, 308	4	380	2	37	27	0	170	2	2	10	6	2	4	2	4
Warm Banana and Papaya Salad, 310	4	145	1	24	6	0	70	0	36	46	2	4	2	2	0
Wilted Lettuce Salad, 306	4	170	2	6	16	15	195	2	30	16	4	4	2	4	6

NUTRITION INFORMATION

PER SERVING OR UNIT

RECIPE, PAGE

Recipe, Page	Servings per recipe	Calories	Protein (grams)	Carbohydrate (grams)	Fat (grams)	Cholesterol (milligrams)	Sodium (milligrams)	Protein	Vitamin A	Vitamin C	Thiamine	Riboflavin	Niacin	Calcium	Iron
SALAD DRESSINGS															
Berry Vinegar, 328	32	6	0	2	0	0	0	0	0	14	0	0	0	0	0
Blue Cheese Dressing, 326	30	60	1	0	6	10	90	0	2	0	0	0	0	2	0
Buttermilk Dressing, 326	20	60	0	1	7	0	110	0	0	0	0	0	0	0	0
Classic French Dressing, 327	24	80	0	0	9	0	45	0	0	0	0	0	0	0	0
Cooked Salad Dressing, 326	32	20	1	2	1	15	60	0	0	0	0	0	0	0	0
Creamy Italian Dressing, 327	16	100	0	0	11	5	65	0	0	0	0	0	0	0	0
Creamy Low-Cal Dressing, 328	32	15	1	1	1	9	80	2	0	0	0	0	0	0	0
Fresh Herb Vinaigrette, 328	16	60	0	0	7	0	0	0	0	0	0	0	0	0	0
Garlic Vinegar, 328	32	2	0	1	0	0	0	0	0	0	0	0	0	0	0
Ginger Vinegar, 328	32	2	0	1	0	0	0	0	0	0	0	0	0	0	0
Green Goddess Dressing, 327	32	60	1	1	6	2	175	0	0	0	0	0	0	6	0
Herb Vinegar, 328	32	2	0	1	0	0	0	0	0	0	0	0	0	0	0
Italian Dressing, 327	16	120	0	1	14	0	70	0	0	0	0	0	0	0	0
Lemon Vinegar, 328	32	2	0	1	0	0	0	0	0	0	0	0	0	0	0
Lorenzo Dressing, 327	8	80	0	1	9	0	70	0	0	0	0	0	0	0	0
Low-Calorie Herb Dressing, 328	16	10	1	1	0	0	10	0	0	0	0	0	0	2	0
Low-Calorie Lemon-Pepper Dressing, 328	16	10	1	1	0	0	10	0	0	0	0	0	0	2	0
Low-Calorie Vinaigrette, 328	16	5	0	1	0	0	0	0	0	0	0	0	0	0	0
Nut-flavored Oil, 328	32	140	0	0	16	0	0	0	0	0	0	0	0	0	0
Nutty Herb Vinaigrette, 328	16	60	0	0	7	0	0	0	0	0	0	0	0	0	0
Orange-Onion Dressing, 327	16	70	0	2	7	0	75	0	0	6	0	0	0	0	0
Orange-Pecan Dressing, 327	16	75	0	2	7	0	75	0	0	6	0	0	0	0	0
Oriental Dressing, 328	16	40	0	1	4	0	195	0	0	0	0	0	0	0	0
Red French Dressing, 327	16	50	0	2	5	0	100	0	2	2	0	0	0	0	0
Russian Dressing, 326	20	85	0	1	9	0	105	0	2	0	0	0	0	0	0
Tahini Dressing, 327	16	75	1	2	7	0	75	2	0	0	6	2	2	2	0
Thousand Island Dressing, 326	20	85	0	1	9	15	105	0	2	0	0	0	0	0	0
Tofu-Tahini Dressing, 327	16	60	1	1	6	0	70	0	0	0	2	0	0	2	0

SOUPS, SANDWICHES & SAUCES

SOUPS, SANDWICHES & SAUCES

Soup is a wonderful basic dish—whether simmered on the stove until ready to serve or made quickly in a blender or food processor. Soup can also be an easy first course or a side dish. Try Steak Soup with Winter Vegetables (page 335) or Chicken Noodle Soup (page 339) on a blustery day for warmth not to mention the delicious aroma! Make Chilled Pear-Mint Soup (page 347) for a hot-day dinner or add soups such as Corn Chowder (page 344) and Sweet Potato (page 342) to your menu for a new twist. However you choose to serve it, you'll find that soup can play many roles, from the star of your meal to a satisfying supporting role!

SOUP BASICS

Homemade soup is delicious and easy to prepare. You can make your own with the Chicken and Broth (page 335) and Beef and Broth (right) that follow. Or, you can purchase shortcut alternatives.

♦ Chicken or beef bouillon granules or cubes

♦ Canned condensed chicken or beef broth

♦ Canned ready-to-serve chicken or beef broth

♦ Frozen chicken broth, beef broth or fish stock

♦ Be sure you use the same amount of liquid. For example, 1 can of soup (10¾ ounces) equals about 1⅓ cups homemade broth. Check your liquid measuring cup for measurements given in both cup size and ounces for easy reference. If you're concerned about sodium levels, many products offer reduced- or low-sodium versions. Follow individual package directions for use.

♦ When making your own broth, keep these basics in mind:

No need to peel or trim vegetables; just wash and cut into large pieces.

To remove particles from strained broth and remove the cloudy appearance, you can clarify the broth. Beat 1 egg white, 1 tablespoon water and 1 broken egg shell. Stir into strained broth. Heat to boiling, stirring constantly. Boil 2 minutes. Remove from heat; let stand 5 minutes. Strain through double-thickness cheesecloth.

Control the salt and spices by seasoning to taste (see How to Select and Use Herbs, Spices and Seeds, page 411).

BEEF AND BROTH

2 pounds beef shank cross cuts or soup bones
6 cups cold water
1 teaspoon salt
¼ teaspoon dried thyme leaves
1 carrot, cut up
1 stalk celery with leaves, cut up
1 small onion, cut up
5 peppercorns
3 whole cloves
3 sprigs parsley
1 bay leaf

Remove marrow from center of bones. Heat marrow in Dutch oven over low heat until melted, or heat 2 tablespoons vegetable oil until hot. Cook beef shanks over medium heat until brown on both sides. Add water and heat to boiling. Skim foam from broth. Stir in remaining ingredients and heat to boiling. Skim foam from broth; reduce heat. Cover and simmer 3 hours.

Remove beef from broth. Cool beef about 10 minutes or just until cool enough to handle. Strain broth through cheesecloth-lined sieve; discard vegetables and seasonings. Remove beef from bones. Cut beef into ½-inch pieces. Skim fat from broth. Cover and refrigerate broth and beef in separate containers no longer than 24 hours, or freeze for future use.   ABOUT 3 CUPS COOKED BEEF; 290 CALORIES PER CUP. ABOUT 4 CUPS BROTH; 15 CALORIES PER CUP.

Preceding page: *Muffuletta (page 353), Black Bean Soup (page 345)*

CHICKEN AND BROTH

3- to 3½-pound broiler-fryer chicken, cut up*
4½ cups cold water
1 teaspoon salt
½ teaspoon pepper
1 stalk celery with leaves, cut up
1 medium carrot, cut up
1 small onion, cut up
1 sprig parsley

Remove any excess fat from chicken. Place chicken, giblets (except liver) and neck in Dutch oven. Add remaining ingredients and heat to boiling. Skim foam from broth; reduce heat. Cover and simmer about 45 minutes or until juices of chicken run clear.

Remove chicken from broth. Cool chicken about 10 minutes or just until cool enough to handle. Strain broth through cheesecloth-lined sieve; discard vegetables. Remove skin and bones from chicken. Cut up chicken. Skim fat from broth. Cover and refrigerate broth and chicken in separate containers no longer than 24 hours, or freeze for future use.   ABOUT 3 CUPS COOKED CHICKEN; 335 CALORIES PER CUP. ABOUT 3 CUPS BROTH; 40 CALORIES PER CUP.

3 to 3½ pounds chicken necks, backs and giblets (except liver) can be used to make broth.

FISH BROTH

1½ pounds fish bones and trimmings
4 cups cold water
1½ cups dry white wine
1 tablespoon lemon juice
1 teaspoon salt
½ teaspoon ground thyme or 2 teaspoons fresh chopped thyme leaves
1 large celery stalk, chopped (about ½ cup)
1 small onion, sliced
3 mushrooms, chopped
2 sprigs parsley
1 bay leaf

Rinse fish bones and trimmings with cold water; drain. Mix bones, trimmings and remaining ingredients in Dutch oven. Heat to boiling; skim foam and reduce heat. Cover and simmer 30 minutes.

Strain through cheesecloth-lined sieve. Discard skin, bones, vegetables and seasonings. Use immediately, or cover and refrigerate up to 24 hours, or freeze for future use.   ABOUT 5½ CUPS BROTH; 70 CALORIES PER CUP.

STEAK SOUP WITH WINTER VEGETABLES

1 pound beef boneless sirloin steak, 1 inch thick
2 cans (14½ ounces each) ready-to-serve beef broth
¼ teaspoon pepper
1 cup Brussels sprouts, cut lengthwise in half
1 cup sliced shiitake or domestic mushrooms
2 medium carrots, cut into ½-inch pieces
1 large sweet potato, cubed (about 1 cup)
1 clove garlic, finely chopped
1 teaspoon chopped fresh or ½ teaspoon dried marjoram leaves
1 teaspoon chopped fresh or ½ teaspoon dried thyme leaves

Trim excess fat from beef. Cut steak into 1-inch pieces. Cook beef steak in 3-quart saucepan over medium-high heat about 10 minutes, stirring several times, until brown. Add beef broth and pepper. Reduce heat and simmer 20 to 30 minutes or until beef is tender.

Add remaining ingredients. Heat to boiling; reduce heat. Cover and simmer about 15 minutes or until vegetables are tender.   4 SERVINGS (ABOUT 1½ CUPS EACH); 395 CALORIES PER SERVING.

Clockwise from top left: *Whole Wheat Batter Bread (page 55), Pork and Spaetzle Soup (page 337), Steak Soup with Winter Vegetables*

HAMBURGER MINESTRONE

1 pound ground beef
1 medium onion, chopped (about ½ cup)
1 clove garlic, crushed
1¼ cups water
1 stalk celery, thinly sliced (about 1 cup)
1 small zucchini, sliced (about 1 cup)
1 cup shredded cabbage
½ cup uncooked elbow macaroni or
   broken spaghetti
2 teaspoons beef bouillon granules
1 teaspoon Italian seasoning
1 can (28 ounces) whole tomatoes, undrained
1 can (8 ounces) kidney beans, undrained
1 can (8 ounces) whole kernel corn,
   undrained
Grated Parmesan cheese

Cook ground beef, onion and garlic in Dutch oven, stirring occasionally, until beef is brown; drain. Stir in remaining ingredients except cheese. Break up tomatoes.

Heat to boiling; reduce heat. Cover and simmer about 15 minutes, stirring occasionally, until macaroni is tender. Serve with cheese. 6 SERVINGS (ABOUT 1½ CUPS EACH); 325 CALORIES PER SERVING.

VEGETABLE-BEEF SOUP

Beef and Broth (page 334)
1 ear corn*
2 medium potatoes, cubed (about 2 cups)
1 medium carrot, thinly sliced (about ½ cup)
1 medium stalk celery, sliced (about ½ cup)
1 medium onion, chopped (about ½ cup)
1 cup 1-inch pieces green beans*
1 cup shelled green peas*
¼ teaspoon pepper
2 medium tomatoes, chopped (about
   1½ cups)

Prepare Beef and Broth. Add enough water to broth to measure 5 cups. Return strained beef and broth to Dutch oven. Cut kernels from corn.

Stir corn and remaining ingredients into broth. Heat to boiling; reduce heat. Cover and simmer about 30 minutes or until vegetables are tender. 7 SERVINGS (ABOUT 1½ CUPS EACH); 335 CALORIES PER SERVING.

*1 cup each frozen whole kernel corn, cut green beans and green peas can be substituted for the 1 ear corn, 1-inch pieces green beans and shelled green peas. Add potatoes, carrot,

celery, onion, bouillon granules, pepper and tomatoes to beef broth. Simmer uncovered 15 minutes. Stir in frozen vegetables. Heat to boiling; reduce heat. Cover and simmer about 15 minutes or until vegetables are tender.

BARLEY VEGETABLE-BEEF SOUP: Omit potatoes. Stir ⅔ cup uncooked barley and ½ teaspoon salt into Beef and Broth. Heat to boiling; reduce heat. Cover and simmer 30 minutes. Stir in remaining ingredients. Cover and simmer about 30 minutes or until barley and vegetables are tender. 360 CALORIES PER SERVING.

⏱ CHEESY HAM AND LEEK SOUP

2 tablespoons margarine or butter
1 cup sliced leeks
1 clove garlic, crushed
2 tablespoons all-purpose flour
⅛ teaspoon pepper
1 cup half-and-half
1 can (14½ ounces) ready-to-serve chicken
   broth
1½ cups chopped fully cooked smoked ham
   (about 8 ounces)
1 cup shredded Jarlsberg or Swiss cheese
   (4 ounces)
½ cup pine nuts, toasted
1 tablespoon chopped fresh chives

Heat margarine in 2-quart saucepan over medium heat. Cook leeks and garlic in margarine about 2 minutes. Stir in flour and pepper. Stir in half-and-half and chicken broth. Heat to boiling, stirring constantly. Boil and stir 1 minute. Stir in ham, cheese and pine nuts until cheese is melted and soup is hot. Sprinkle with chives. 4 SERVINGS (ABOUT 1¼ CUPS EACH); 415 CALORIES PER SERVING.

To Microwave: Place leeks, garlic and margarine in 2-quart microwavable casserole. Cover tightly and microwave on high 3 to 4 minutes, stirring after 2 minutes, until leeks are tender. Stir in flour and pepper. Stir in half-and-half and chicken broth. Cover tightly and microwave on high 7 to 9 minutes, stirring after 2 minutes, until mixture is slightly thickened. Stir in ham, cheese and pine nuts. Cover tightly and microwave on high 2 minutes. Sprinkle with chives.

⏱ PORK AND SPAETZLE SOUP

1 pound ground pork
1 egg
½ cup dry bread crumbs
½ teaspoon ground sage
¼ teaspoon salt
¼ teaspoon pepper
1 tablespoon vegetable oil
2 cans (14½ ounces each) ready-to-serve beef broth
¾ cup apple cider or apple juice
½ teaspoon ground sage
1 large unpared all-purpose apple, chopped
Spaetzle (page 263)
¼ cup chopped fresh parsley

Mix ground pork, egg, bread crumbs, ½ teaspoon sage, the salt and pepper. Shape mixture into 1-inch balls. Heat oil in Dutch oven until hot. Cook meatballs in hot oil over medium heat about 10 minutes, turning frequently, until brown.

Add beef broth, apple cider, ½ teaspoon sage and the apple. Heat to boiling; reduce heat. Cover and simmer 10 minutes. Heat to boiling. Prepare Spaetzle batter. Press Spaetzle batter through colander (preferably one with large holes), a few tablespoons at a time, into soup. Stir once or twice to prevent sticking. Cook about 5 minutes or until Spaetzle rise to surface and are tender. Stir in parsley. Heat until hot.   6 SERVINGS (ABOUT ¾ CUP EACH); 350 CALORIES PER SERVING.

COUSCOUS SOUP WITH SAUSAGE

1 tablespoon chopped jalapeño chilies
1 tablespoon olive or vegetable oil
½ teaspoon ground cumin
2 cloves garlic, crushed
1 pound fully cooked smoked sausage, cut crosswise into ¼-inch slices
2½ cups water
1 can (10¾ ounces) condensed chicken broth
½ cup couscous
2 tablespoons chopped fresh or 2 teaspoons dried mint leaves
¼ teaspoon pepper
1 medium tomato, seeded and chopped

Cook chilies, oil, cumin, garlic and sausage in 3-quart saucepan over medium heat about 8 minutes or until sausage is brown; drain.

Add water and chicken broth. Heat to boiling. Stir in couscous, mint and pepper; reduce heat. Cover and simmer 5 minutes. Stir in tomato. Serve with chopped parsley, finely chopped garlic and lemon juice if desired.   4 SERVINGS (ABOUT 1¾ CUPS EACH); 405 CALORIES PER SERVING.

To Microwave: Omit oil. Place chilies, cumin, garlic and sausage in 3-quart microwavable casserole. Cover tightly and microwave on high 2 minutes. Add water and chicken broth. Cover tightly and microwave on high 5 minutes. Stir in couscous, mint and pepper. Cover tightly and microwave on high 3 minutes. Stir in tomato. Let stand covered 5 minutes. Continue as directed.

═ GARLIC ═

*A*mericans *used to be somewhat skeptical of garlic. However, the garlic bulb has been popular throughout history. The Egyptians worshipped garlic, the Romans fed it to their soldiers to make them strong for battle and in the 1500s Europeans considered garlic an aphrodisiac, a cure for baldness, and, of course, protection from werewolves and vampires.*

In the 1960's, garlic became more readily available in supermarkets, a reflection of its rediscovery by Americans. Our 1950 cookbook had only four recipes that called for garlic, and they were all recipes with an "ethnic" background. Our current edition reflects the growth of garlic's popularity, with garlic in salad dressings, meat dishes, sauces, vegetables, and more.

SOUTHWEST CHICKEN SOUP

2 large red bell peppers
1 whole chicken breast (about ¾ pound),
  skinned and boned
1 medium onion, chopped (about ½ cup)
2 cups chicken broth
2 tablespoons lime juice
1 tablespoon chopped fresh cilantro
½ teaspoon salt
¼ teaspoon pepper
2 cloves garlic, crushed
1 cup cubed jicama

Place bell peppers on rack or broiler pan with tops about 5 inches from heat. Broil peppers, turning occasionally, until skin is evenly blistered.

Set oven control to broil. Place bell peppers on rack of broiler pan with tops about 5 inches from heat. Broil peppers, turning occasionally, until skin is blistered and evenly browned (not burned). Remove peppers to a brown bag and close tightly. Let peppers stand 20 minutes.

Place chicken on rack in broiler pan. Place broiler pan so top of chicken is 5 to 7 inches from heat. Broil chicken 15 minutes, turning once, until juices run clear. Cut into ¼-inch strips.

Pare peppers; discard skin. Place peppers and onion in blender or food processor. Cover and blend, or process, until smooth.

Heat pepper mixture, chicken broth, lime juice, cilantro, salt, pepper and garlic to boiling in 2-quart saucepan; reduce heat. Simmer 15 minutes. Stir in chicken and jicama. Heat until hot.   4 SERVINGS (ABOUT 1 CUP EACH); 140 CALORIES PER SERVING.

To Grill: Roast peppers over medium coals, turning occasionally, until skin is blistered and evenly browned (not burned). Continue as directed. Cover and grill chicken 5 to 6 inches from medium coals about 15 minutes. Turn chicken. Cover and grill about 20 minutes longer or until juices run clear. Cut into ¼-inch strips.

Southwest Chicken Soup, Chicken Noodle Soup (page 339)

MULLIGATAWNY SOUP

3-pound broiler-fryer chicken, cut up
4 cups water
1 teaspoon salt
1 teaspoon curry powder
1 teaspoon lemon juice
⅛ teaspoon ground cloves
⅛ teaspoon ground mace
2 tablespoons margarine or butter
1 medium onion, chopped (about ½ cup)
2 tablespoons all-purpose flour
2 medium tomatoes, chopped
1 large all-purpose apple, coarsely chopped
1 medium carrot, thinly sliced
1 medium green bell pepper, cut into ½-inch pieces

Heat chicken, giblets (except liver), neck, water, salt, curry powder, lemon juice, cloves and mace to boiling in Dutch oven; reduce heat. Cover and simmer about 45 minutes or until juices of chicken run clear.

Remove chicken from broth. Cool chicken about 10 minutes or just until cool enough to handle. Remove skin and bones from chicken. Cut chicken into bite-size pieces. Skim fat from broth. Add enough water to broth, if necessary, to measure 4 cups.

Heat margarine in Dutch oven over medium heat. Cook onion in margarine about 2 minutes; remove from heat. Stir in flour. Gradually stir in broth. Add chicken, tomatoes and remaining ingredients. Heat to boiling; reduce heat. Cover and simmer about 10 minutes or until carrot is tender. Garnish with parsley if desired. 6 SERVINGS (ABOUT 1¼ CUPS EACH); 345 CALORIES PER SERVING.

 # CHICKEN NOODLE SOUP

Chicken and Broth (page 335)
2 medium carrots, sliced (about 1 cup)
2 medium stalks celery, sliced (about 1 cup)
1 small onion, chopped (about ¼ cup)
1 tablespoon chicken bouillon granules
1 cup uncooked medium noodles (about 2 ounces)

Prepare Chicken and Broth. Reserve cut-up chicken. Add enough water to broth to measure 5 cups. Heat broth, carrots, celery, onion and bouillon granules to boiling; reduce heat. Cover and simmer about 15 minutes or until carrots are tender. Stir in noodles and chicken. Heat to boiling; reduce heat. Simmer uncovered 7 to 10 minutes or until noodles are tender. Sprinkle with chopped parsley if desired. 6 SERVINGS (ABOUT 1 CUP EACH); 295 CALORIES PER SERVING.

CHICKEN RICE SOUP: Substitute ½ cup uncooked regular long grain rice for the uncooked noodles. Stir in rice with the vegetables. Cover and simmer about 15 minutes or until rice is tender. Stir in chicken and heat until chicken is hot. 315 CALORIES PER SERVING.

TURKEY TORTELLINI SOUP

1 package (7 ounces) dried cheese-filled tortellini
2¼ cups water
2 tablespoons rice wine vinegar or white wine vinegar
2 tablespoons soy sauce
1 can (10¾ ounces) condensed chicken broth
1 to 2 tablespoons finely chopped gingerroot or 1 to 2 teaspoons ground ginger
2 cups sliced bok choy
2 cups cut-up cooked turkey (about 10 ounces)
2 green onions (with tops), sliced
1 cup enoki mushrooms

Cook tortellini as directed on package; drain. Heat water, vinegar, soy sauce, chicken broth and gingerroot to boiling in 3-quart saucepan; reduce heat. Stir in bok choy stems (reserve leaves), turkey and onions. Simmer 15 minutes. Stir in bok choy leaves, mushrooms and tortellini. Simmer just until leaves are wilted and tortellini is hot. 4 SERVINGS (ABOUT 1½ CUPS EACH); 350 CALORIES PER SERVING.

OYSTER SOUP

¼ cup margarine or butter
1 pint shucked oysters, undrained
2 cups milk
½ cup half-and-half
½ teaspoon salt
Dash of pepper

Heat margarine in 1½-quart saucepan until melted. Add oysters. Cook and stir over low heat just until edges curl. Heat milk and half-and-half in 2-quart saucepan. Stir in salt, pepper and oysters. 4 SERVINGS (ABOUT 1 CUP EACH); 260 CALORIES PER SERVING.

Shrimp Gumbo

🌾 SHRIMP GUMBO

¼ cup margarine or butter
2 medium onions, sliced
1 medium green bell pepper, cut into thin strips
2 cloves garlic, crushed
2 tablespoons all-purpose flour
3 cups beef broth
¼ teaspoon salt
¼ teaspoon pepper
½ teaspoon red pepper sauce
1 bay leaf
1 package (10 ounces) frozen cut okra, thawed, or 1 can (16 ounces) okra, drained
1 can (16 ounces) whole tomatoes, undrained
1 can (6 ounces) tomato paste
1½ pounds fresh or frozen raw shrimp (in shells),* thawed
3 cups hot cooked rice (page 267)
¼ cup chopped fresh parsley

Heat margarine in Dutch oven over medium heat. Cook onions, bell pepper and garlic in margarine about 5 minutes. Stir in flour. Cook over medium heat, stirring constantly, until bubbly; remove from heat. Stir in remaining ingredients except shrimp, rice and parsley. Break up tomatoes. Heat to boiling; reduce heat. Simmer uncovered 45 minutes, stirring occasionally.

Peel shrimp. Make a shallow cut lengthwise down back of each shrimp and wash out vein. Stir shrimp into soup. Cover and simmer about 5 minutes or until shrimp are pink. Remove bay leaf. Serve soup over rice and sprinkle with parsley.   6 SERVINGS (ABOUT 1½ CUPS EACH); 220 CALORIES PER SERVING.

1 pound frozen peeled and deveined shrimp, thawed, can be substituted for the 1½ pounds shrimp in shells.

NEW ENGLAND CLAM CHOWDER

Clam chowder has been popular since colonial days, and the original recipe called for cream and clams, the classic New England Clam Chowder. Later, the recipe was modified to use tomatoes in the place of cream, and Manhattan Clam Chowder was born.

¼ cup cut-up bacon or lean salt pork
1 medium onion, chopped (about ½ cup)
2 cans (8 ounces each) minced or whole clams*
1 cup finely chopped potato
½ teaspoon salt
Dash of pepper
2 cups milk

Cook and stir bacon and onion in 2-quart saucepan until bacon is crisp and onion is softened. Drain clams, reserving liquor. Add enough water, if necessary, to clam liquor to measure 1 cup. Stir clams, clam liquor, potato, salt and pepper into bacon and onion. Heat to boiling; reduce heat. Cover and simmer about 15 minutes or until potato is tender. Stir in milk. Heat, stirring occasionally, just until hot (do not boil).   4 SERVINGS (ABOUT 1 CUP EACH); 345 CALORIES PER SERVING.

1 pint shucked fresh clams with liquor can be substituted for the canned clams. Chop clams and stir in with the potatoes.

MANHATTAN CLAM CHOWDER

¼ cup finely chopped bacon or salt pork
1 small onion, finely chopped (about ¼ cup)
1 pint shucked fresh clams with liquor*
2 cups finely chopped potatoes
⅓ cup chopped celery
1 cup water
2 teaspoons chopped fresh parsley
½ teaspoon salt
1 teaspoon chopped fresh or ¼ teaspoon dried thyme leaves
⅛ teaspoon pepper
1 can (16 ounces) whole tomatoes, undrained

Cook bacon and onion in Dutch oven, stirring occasionally, until bacon is crisp and onion is tender. Stir clams and clam liquor, potatoes, celery and water into bacon and onion. Heat to boiling; reduce heat. Cover and simmer about 10 minutes or until potatoes are tender. Stir in remaining ingredients. Break up tomatoes. Heat to boiling, stirring occasionally. 5 SERVINGS (ABOUT 1¼ CUPS EACH); 210 CALORIES PER SERVING.

2 cans (6½ ounces each) minced clams, undrained, can be substituted for fresh clams. Stir in clams with remaining ingredients.

CREAM OF SMOKED SALMON SOUP

1 package (8 ounces) cream cheese, cut into cubes
1 cup milk
2 teaspoons Dijon mustard
1½ teaspoons chopped fresh or ½ teaspoon dried dill weed
2 green onions (with tops), sliced
1 can (14½ ounces) ready-to-serve chicken broth
12 ounces smoked salmon, flaked*

Heat cream cheese, milk, mustard, dill weed, onions and chicken broth in 2-quart saucepan over medium heat until cheese is melted and mixture is smooth. Stir in salmon. Heat until hot. 4 SERVINGS (ABOUT 1 CUP EACH); 380 CALORIES PER SERVING.

1 can (15½ ounces) salmon, drained and flaked, can be substituted for the smoked salmon.

To Microwave: Place all ingredients except salmon in 2-quart microwavable casserole. Cover tightly and microwave on high 8 to 10 minutes, stirring every 2 minutes, until cheese is melted. Stir in salmon. Cover tightly and microwave on high 2 minutes longer.

SPLIT PEA SOUP

1 pound dried split peas (about 2¼ cups)
8 cups water
1 large onion, chopped (about 1 cup)
1 cup finely chopped celery
¼ teaspoon pepper
1 ham bone or 2 pounds ham shanks, or smoked pork hocks
3 medium carrots, cut into ¼-inch slices

Heat peas and water to boiling in Dutch oven. Boil uncovered 2 minutes; remove from heat. Cover and let stand 1 hour.

Stir in onion, celery and pepper. Add ham shanks. Heat to boiling; reduce heat. Cover and simmer about 1½ hours or until peas are tender.

Remove ham shanks; remove ham from bone. Trim excess fat from ham; cut ham into ½-inch pieces. Stir ham and carrots into soup. Heat to boiling; reduce heat. Cover and simmer until carrots are tender and soup is of desired consistency, about 30 minutes. 8 SERVINGS (ABOUT 1½ CUPS EACH); 425 CALORIES PER SERVING.

WILD RICE SOUP

2 tablespoons margarine or butter
2 medium stalks celery, sliced (about 1 cup)
1 medium carrot, coarsely shredded (about 1 cup)
1 medium onion, chopped (about ½ cup)
1 small green bell pepper, chopped (about ½ cup)
3 tablespoons all-purpose flour
¼ teaspoon pepper
1½ cups cooked wild rice (page 267)
1 cup water
1 can (10¾ ounces) condensed chicken broth
1 cup half-and-half
⅓ cup slivered almonds, toasted
¼ cup chopped fresh parsley

Heat margarine in 3-quart saucepan over medium heat. Cook celery, carrot, onion and bell pepper in margarine about 4 minutes. Stir in flour and pepper. Stir in wild rice, water and chicken broth. Heat to boiling; reduce heat. Cover and simmer 15 minutes, stirring occasionally.

Stir in half-and-half, almonds and parsley. Heat just until hot (do not boil). 5 SERVINGS (ABOUT 1 CUP EACH); 280 CALORIES PER SERVING.

🌾 BORSCH

¾ pound beef boneless chuck, tip or round,
  cut into ½-inch cubes
1 smoked pork hock
4 cups water
1 can (10½ ounces) condensed beef broth
1 teaspoon salt
¼ teaspoon pepper
4 cooked medium beets, shredded or cut
  into ¼-inch strips
1 large onion, sliced
2 cloves garlic, chopped
2 medium potatoes, cubed
3 cups shredded cabbage
2 teaspoons dill seed or 1 sprig fresh dill
  weed
1 tablespoon pickling spice
¼ cup red wine vinegar
¾ cup sour cream

Heat beef, pork, water, beef broth, salt and pepper to boiling in Dutch oven; reduce heat. Cover and simmer 1 to 1½ hours or until beef is tender.

Remove pork from soup. Cool pork slightly. Remove pork from bone and cut pork into bite-size pieces. Stir pork, beets, onion, garlic, potatoes and cabbage into soup. Tie dill seed and pickling spice in cheesecloth bag, or place in tea ball and add to soup. Cover and simmer 2 hours.

Stir in vinegar. Simmer 10 minutes. Remove spice bag. Serve sour cream with soup. Sprinkle with chopped fresh dill weed if desired. 6 SERVINGS (ABOUT 1¼ CUPS EACH); 400 CALORIES PER SERVING.

SWEET POTATO SOUP

2 large sweet potatoes (about 1½ pounds),
  cut into large pieces
1 cup chicken broth
¼ cup orange juice
¼ teaspoon salt
¼ teaspoon ground nutmeg
1 cup half-and-half
½ cup chopped pecans

Place steamer basket in ½ inch water (water should not touch bottom of basket). Place sweet potato pieces in basket. Cover tightly and heat to boiling; reduce heat. Steam 10 to 15 minutes or until tender.

Scoop pulp into blender or food processor; discard skin. Add ½ cup chicken broth. Cover and blend, or process, until smooth. Transfer mixture to 2-quart saucepan. Stir in remaining chicken broth, the orange juice, salt and nutmeg. Cover over medium-high heat, stirring constantly, until hot. Stir in half-and-half and pecans. Heat until hot. 4 SERVINGS (ABOUT ¾ CUP EACH); 375 CALORIES PER SERVING.

To Microwave: Arrange potatoes on microwavable paper towel in microwave oven. Microwave uncovered on high 6 to 8 minutes or until tender when pierced with a fork. Scoop pulp into blender or food processor; discard skin. Add ½ cup chicken broth. Transfer mixture to 2-quart microwavable casserole. Stir in remaining chicken broth, the orange juice, salt and nutmeg. Cover tightly and microwave on high 3 to 5 minutes until hot. Stir in half-and-half and pecans. Cover tightly and microwave on high 2 to 3 minutes or until hot.

🌾 HOPPIN' JOHN SOUP

It's a southern tradition to serve black-eyed peas on New Year's Day, to bring good luck throughout the year. The ham hocks give this dish exceptional flavor.

1 cup dried black-eyed peas or dried red
  beans (about 8 ounces)
8 cups water
½ to 1 teaspoon very finely chopped jalapeño
  chili or other hot chili or ¼ to ½ teaspoon crushed red pepper
1 clove garlic, finely chopped
1 ham bone or 1 pound ham shank or
  smoked pork hocks
½ cup uncooked regular long grain rice
1 large onion, chopped (about 1 cup)
1 medium red or green bell pepper, chopped
  (about 1 cup)
1 teaspoon salt
¼ teaspoon pepper
½ pound Swiss chard or mustard greens,
  coarsely chopped (about 4 cups)

Heat peas and water to boiling in Dutch oven. Boil uncovered 2 minutes; remove from heat. Cover and let stand 1 hour.

Stir in chili, garlic and ham bone. Heat to boiling; reduce heat. Cover and simmer 1 to 1½ hours or until peas are tender. Remove ham bone. Remove ham from bone and cut into bite-size pieces. Reserve ham. Stir rice, onions, bell pepper, salt and pepper into soup. Cover and simmer about 25 minutes, stirring occasionally, until rice is tender. Stir in ham and Swiss chard. Cover and simmer until hot. 6 SERVINGS (ABOUT 1½ CUPS EACH); 190 CALORIES PER SERVING.

Clockwise from top: *Sweet Potato Soup, Borsch, Wild Rice Soup (page 341)*

CREAM OF BROCCOLI SOUP

1½ pounds broccoli
2 cups water
1 large stalk celery, chopped (about ¾ cup)
1 medium onion, chopped (about ½ cup)
2 tablespoons margarine or butter
2 tablespoons all-purpose flour
2½ cups chicken broth
½ teaspoon salt
⅛ teaspoon pepper
Dash of ground nutmeg
½ cup whipping (heavy) cream

Prepare broccoli as directed on page 375. Remove flowerets from broccoli. Cut stalks into 1-inch pieces.

Heat 2 cups water to boiling in 3-quart saucepan. Add broccoli flowerets and pieces, celery and onion. Cover and heat to boiling. Boil about 10 minutes or until broccoli is tender (do not drain). Place in blender. Cover and blend until of uniform consistency.

Heat margarine in 3-quart saucepan over medium heat until melted. Stir in flour. Cook, stirring constantly, until mixture is smooth and bubbly; remove from heat. Stir in chicken broth. Heat to boiling, stirring constantly. Boil and stir 1 minute. Stir in broccoli mixture, salt, pepper and nutmeg. Heat just to boiling. Stir in whipping cream. Heat just until hot (do not boil). Serve with shredded cheese if desired.   8 SERVINGS (ABOUT 1 CUP EACH); 120 CALORIES PER SERVING.

CREAM OF CAULIFLOWER SOUP: Substitute 1 head cauliflower (about 2 pounds), separated into flowerets, for the broccoli. Add 1 tablespoon lemon juice with the onion.   120 CALORIES PER SERVING.

🌾 ⏱ CORN CHOWDER

½ pound bacon, cut up
1 medium onion, chopped (about ½ cup)
2 stalks celery, chopped (about ½ cup)
2 tablespoons all-purpose flour
4 cups milk
⅛ teaspoon pepper
1 can (17 ounces) cream-style corn
1 can (16 ounces) tiny whole potatoes, drained and diced
Chopped fresh parsley
Paprika

Cook bacon in 3-quart saucepan until crisp. Drain fat, reserving 3 tablespoons in saucepan. Cook onion and celery in bacon fat about 2 minutes; remove from heat. Stir in flour.

Cook over medium heat, stirring constantly, until mixture is bubbly; remove from heat. Stir in milk. Heat to boiling, stirring constantly. Boil and stir 1 minute. Stir in pepper, corn and potatoes. Heat until hot. Stir in bacon. Sprinkle each serving with parsley and paprika.   6 SERVINGS (ABOUT 1 CUP EACH); 300 CALORIES PER SERVING.

🌾 VICHYSSOISE

Chef Louis Diat of the Ritz-Carlton in New York City created this French classic in 1910. He added milk to the traditional French hot potato soup and then chilled it. It was named Vichyssoise after the French town of Vichy, a fashionable resort.

1 tablespoon margarine or butter
1 medium onion, chopped (about ½ cup)
2 medium potatoes, pared and coarsely chopped (about 2 cups)
½ cup chopped celery
1 can (14½ ounces) ready-to-serve chicken broth
1½ cups milk
⅛ teaspoon pepper
¼ teaspoon salt
¼ teaspoon ground nutmeg
1 cup half-and-half

Heat margarine in 2-quart saucepan over medium heat. Cook onion in margarine about 2 minutes. Add potatoes, celery and chicken broth. Heat to boiling; reduce heat. Cover and simmer about 15 minutes or until vegetables are tender. Place undrained mixture in blender or food processor. Cover and blend on low speed, or process, until smooth.

Stir in remaining ingredients. Refrigerate soup about 5 hours or until thoroughly chilled. Garnish with chopped fresh chives and ground nutmeg if desired.   4 SERVINGS (ABOUT 1¼ CUPS EACH); 240 CALORIES PER SERVING.

To Microwave: Place onion and margarine in 2-quart microwavable casserole. Cover tightly and microwave on high 2 minutes. Add potatoes, celery and chicken broth. Cover tightly and microwave on high 8 to 10 minutes or until boiling; stir. Cover tightly and microwave on high 7 to 9 minutes or until vegetables are tender. Continue as directed.

 HEARTY TOMATO SOUP

2 tablespoons margarine or butter
1 medium onion, finely chopped (about ½ cup)
1 clove garlic, finely chopped
½ teaspoon paprika
1½ teaspoons chopped fresh or ½ teaspoon dried basil leaves
2 packages (3 ounces each) cream cheese, softened
1¼ cups milk
2 cans (10¾ ounces each) condensed tomato soup
2 cans (16 ounces each) whole tomatoes, undrained

Heat margarine in 3-quart saucepan over medium heat. Cook onion and garlic in margarine about 2 minutes; remove from heat. Stir in paprika, basil and cream cheese. Gradually stir in milk and soup. Beat with hand beater until smooth. Stir tomatoes into soup. Break up tomatoes. Heat over medium heat, stirring frequently, until hot. 8 SERVINGS (ABOUT 1 CUP EACH); 200 CALORIES PER SERVING.

GOLDEN ONION SOUP

Parmesan Croutons (below)
¼ cup margarine or butter
1 tablespoon packed brown sugar
1 teaspoon Worcestershire sauce
2 large onions (about ¾ pound each), cut into fourths and sliced
2 cans (10½ ounces each) condensed beef broth
2 soup cans water

Prepare Parmesan Croutons; reserve. Reduce oven temperature to 325°. Heat margarine in Dutch oven until melted. Stir in brown sugar and Worcestershire sauce. Toss onions in margarine mixture.

Bake uncovered about 2½ hours, stirring every hour, until onions are deep golden brown. Stir in beef broth and water. Heat to boiling over high heat. Serve with Parmesan Croutons. 6 SERVINGS (ABOUT 1 CUP EACH); 265 CALORIES PER SERVING.

Parmesan Croutons

¼ cup margarine or butter
3 slices bread, cut into 1-inch cubes
Grated Parmesan cheese

Heat oven to 400°. Heat margarine in rectangular pan, 13 × 9 × 2 inches, in oven until melted. Toss bread cubes in margarine until evenly coated. Sprinkle with cheese. Bake uncovered 10 to 15 minutes, stirring occasionally, until golden brown and crisp.

SENATE BEAN SOUP

2 cups dried navy beans (about 1 pound)
12 cups water
1 ham bone
2½ cups mashed cooked potatoes
2 teaspoons salt
¼ teaspoon pepper
1 large onion, chopped (about 1 cup)
2 stalks celery, chopped (about 1 cup)
1 clove garlic, finely chopped

Heat beans and water to boiling in Dutch oven. Boil uncovered 2 minutes; remove from heat. Cover and let stand 1 hour.

Add ham bone. Heat to boiling; reduce heat. Cover and simmer about 2 hours or until beans are tender. Stir in remaining ingredients. Cover and simmer 1 hour. Remove ham bone. Remove ham from bone and cut into bite-size pieces. Stir into soup. 12 SERVINGS (ABOUT 1 CUP EACH); 95 CALORIES PER SERVING.

BLACK BEAN SOUP

½ cup dried black beans (about 4 ounces)
3 cups water
1 ham bone or 1 pound ham shank or smoked pork hocks
½ teaspoon salt
1 clove garlic, finely chopped
1 small bay leaf
¼ teaspoon crushed red pepper
1 medium carrot, sliced (about ½ cup)
1 medium stalk celery, chopped (about ½ cup)
1 medium onion, chopped (about ½ cup)
2 tablespoons chopped red onion
3 lemon slices, cut in half
3 hard-cooked eggs, finely chopped

Heat beans and water to boiling in Dutch oven. Boil uncovered 2 minutes; remove from heat. Cover and let stand 1 hour.

Add ham bone. Heat to boiling; reduce heat. Cover and simmer about 2 hours or until beans are tender. Stir in salt, garlic, bay leaf, red pepper, carrot, celery and ½ cup onion. Cover and simmer 1 hour.

Remove ham bone and bay leaf. (If desired, place soup in blender. Cover and blend until of uniform consistency.) Trim ham from bone and stir into soup. Serve with red onion, lemon slices and eggs. 6 SERVINGS (ABOUT 1 CUP EACH); 160 CALORIES PER SERVING.

WONTON SOUP

½ pound ground pork
1 green onion (with top), chopped
2 teaspoons soy sauce
½ teaspoon cornstarch
¼ teaspoon ground ginger
24 wonton skins
5 cups water
3 cans (10¾ ounces each) condensed chicken
 broth
3 soup cans water
1 tablespoon soy sauce
1 cup spinach, torn into small pieces, or
 1 cup watercress

Cook pork and green onion, stirring occasionally, until pork is brown; drain. Mix pork mixture, 2 teaspoons soy sauce, the cornstarch and ginger. Place 1 teaspoon filling on center of each wonton skin. Moisten edges with water. Fold each in half to form triangle. Press edges to seal. Pull bottom corners of triangle down and overlap slightly. Moisten one corner with water. Pinch to seal. (Wontons can be covered and refrigerated no longer than 24 hours.)

Heat 5 cups water to boiling in Dutch oven. Add wontons. Heat to boiling; reduce heat. Simmer uncovered 2 minutes (wontons will break apart if overcooked); drain. Heat chicken broth, 3 cans water and 1 tablespoon soy sauce to boiling in 3-quart saucepan. Add spinach. Heat just to boiling. Place 3 wontons and 1 cup hot broth in each soup bowl. 8 SERVINGS (ABOUT 1 CUP EACH); 175 CALORIES PER SERVING.

1. Place filling on center of each wonton skin. Moisten edges with water and fold in half to form a triangle. Press open edges to seal. The water helps to seal the thin pastry.

2. To form wonton, pull bottom corners of triangle down and overlap slightly. Moisten one corner with water and pinch to seal.

♨ ⧗ CHEDDAR CHEESE SOUP

2 tablespoons margarine or butter
1 small onion, chopped (about ¼ cup)
1 medium stalk celery, thinly sliced (about
 ½ cup)
2 tablespoons all-purpose flour
¼ teaspoon pepper
¼ teaspoon dry mustard
1 cup milk
1 can (10¾ ounces) condensed chicken
 broth
2 cups shredded Cheddar cheese (8 ounces)

Heat margarine in 2-quart saucepan over medium heat. Cook onion and celery in margarine about 2 minutes. Stir in flour, pepper and mustard. Stir in milk and chicken broth. Heat to boiling over medium heat, stirring constantly. Boil and stir 1 minute. Stir in cheese. Heat over low heat, stirring occasionally, just until cheese is melted. Sprinkle with paprika if desired. 4 SERVINGS (ABOUT 1 CUP EACH); 355 CALORIES PER SERVING.

POPPY SEED SOUP

1 cup half-and-half
½ cup poppy seed
2 cups (16 ounces) vanilla yogurt
3 tablespoons honey
½ teaspoon ground nutmeg
¼ teaspoon salt

Mix half-and-half and poppy seed. Let stand 15 minutes. Place poppy seed mixture in blender or food processor. Add remaining ingredients. Cover and blend on medium speed, or process, about 3 minutes or until completely mixed. Cover and refrigerate at least 4 hours or until thoroughly chilled. 6 SERVINGS (ABOUT ½ CUP EACH); 225 CALORIES PER SERVING.

⧗ EGG DROP SOUP

3 cups chicken broth
¼ teaspoon salt
Dash of white pepper
1 green onion (with top), chopped
2 eggs, slightly beaten

Heat chicken broth, salt and white pepper to boiling in 3-quart saucepan. Stir onion into eggs. Pour egg mixture slowly into broth, stirring constantly with fork until eggs form threads. 4 SERVINGS (ABOUT ¾ CUP EACH); 70 CALORIES PER SERVING.

AVOCADO SOUP

3 cups chicken broth
1 cup half-and-half
2 large avocados, cut up
1 clove garlic, crushed
1 tablespoon chopped onion
¾ teaspoon salt
¼ teaspoon chopped fresh cilantro
Dash of pepper

Place 1½ cups of the chicken broth and the remaining ingredients in blender or food processor. Cover and blend on medium speed, or process, until smooth. Stir remaining broth into avocado mixture.

Cover and refrigerate about 2 hours or until chilled. Garnish with sour cream and paprika or avocado slices if desired.   6 SERVINGS (ABOUT ¾ CUP EACH); 175 CALORIES PER SERVING.

GAZPACHO

1 can (28 ounces) whole tomatoes, undrained
1 cup finely chopped green bell peppers
1 cup finely chopped cucumbers
1 cup croutons
1 medium onion, chopped (about ½ cup)
2 tablespoons dry white wine
2 tablespoons olive or vegetable oil
1 tablespoon ground cumin
1 tablespoon vinegar
½ teaspoon salt
¼ teaspoon pepper

Place tomatoes, ½ cup bell peppers, ½ cup cucumbers, ½ cup croutons, ¼ cup onion and remaining ingredients in blender or food processor. Cover and blend on medium speed, or process, until smooth. Cover and refrigerate at least 1 hour. Serve remaining vegetables and croutons as accompaniments.   8 SERVINGS (ABOUT ½ CUP EACH); 90 CALORIES PER SERVING.

CHILLED PEAR-MINT SOUP

To cut down on chilling time, start with thoroughly chilled pears. Pears are at their most flavorful and juicy when ripe—a ripe pear yields slightly to gentle pressure.

4 ripe medium pears
¼ cup firmly packed mint leaves
1 cup half-and-half
1 tablespoon sugar
2 tablespoons lime juice

Pare and core pears. Cut into large pieces. Place pear pieces and remaining ingredients in blender or food processor. Cover and blend on high speed, or process, 3 minutes or until smooth. Refrigerate 5 hours or until chilled. Stir before serving. Garnish with mint leaves if desired. Refrigerate any remaining soup.   6 SERVINGS (½ CUP EACH); 120 CALORIES PER SERVING.

Chilled Pear-Mint Soup

SANDWICH BASICS

The definition of a sandwich varies with the person you ask and is not restricted to a filling between two pieces of bread. Almost every cuisine has its own version of a sandwich, from filled Mexican tortillas to Middle Eastern pitas to Italian calzones and Chinese pork buns. The versatile sandwich can be served cold, hot, grilled, baked, fried, layered, stacked, rolled, open-face, with knife and fork, cut in half or quartered.

There are a few basic elements of which sandwiches are usually comprised, and each is delectable even when eaten alone. The tips that follow will help you make the finest sandwich—whether it's one of our recipes, an old favorite or your own newly created masterpiece.

Bread: White, whole wheat, rye, pumpernickel, pita bread, tortillas, hamburger and frankfurter buns, kaiser rolls, nut breads, crackers, sliced vegetables and lettuce leaves can all hold fillings for sandwiches.

♦ Remove the number of bread slices needed per sandwich and lay open in pairs on a flat surface so that when reassembled, the slices fit together perfectly.

♦ To avoid soggy bread, spread each slice completely to the edge with a thin layer of margarine or butter before adding the filling, particularly moist mixtures.

Fillings: Use sliced or chopped, cooked or processed meat, poultry, fish and seafood, cheeses, eggs, vegetables, fruit, peanut butter or preserves.

♦ Spread filling mixtures evenly and to the edge on one of the bread slices; top with matching bread slice.

♦ Filling amounts vary according to individual likes and dislikes. Some like hearty, thick fillings while other prefer them lighter and leaner.

Condiments: Experiment with margarine or butter, mayonnaise or salad dressing, mustards in many flavors, hot or cold sandwich or special sauces and relishes, and herbs and spices.

Garnishes: Make them attractive, complementary to the sandwich, and edible! Fresh herbs, crisp vegetables, fruits at their finest, salsas, relishes and chutneys are good choices. Also crunchy snack foods such as potato chips or pretzels, or coleslaw, fruit, potato or pasta salads in small amounts.

⏱ BARBECUED ROAST BEEF SANDWICHES

Tangy Barbecue Sauce (below)
1 pound thinly sliced cooked roast beef, cut into 1-inch strips (about 3 cups)
6 hamburger buns, split

Prepare Tangy Barbecue Sauce. Stir beef into sauce. Cover and simmer about 5 minutes or until beef is hot. Fill buns with beef mixture.   6 SANDWICHES; 375 CALORIES PER SANDWICH.

Tangy Barbecue Sauce

½ cup ketchup
¼ cup vinegar
2 tablespoons chopped onion
1 tablespoon Worcestershire sauce
2 teaspoons packed brown sugar
¼ teaspoon dry mustard
1 clove garlic, crushed

Heat all ingredients to boiling in 1-quart saucepan over medium heat, stirring constantly; reduce heat. Simmer uncovered 15 minutes, stirring occasionally.

To Microwave: Mix sauce ingredients in 4-cup microwavable measure. Microwave uncovered on high 4 to 6 minutes, stirring after 2 minutes, until sauce is slightly thickened. Stir beef into sauce. Cover tightly and microwave on high 5 to 7 minutes or until beef is hot.

QUICK BARBECUE SANDWICHES: Substitute 1 cup barbecue sauce for the Tangy Barbecue Sauce and 3 packages (3 ounces each) smoked sliced chicken, ham, turkey, beef or pastrami, cut into 1-inch strips, for the beef.   195 CALORIES PER SANDWICH.

HAMBURGERS

The hamburger traces its origins to Hamburg, Germany, but who invented the first, classic hamburger is a contested issue. One school says that Fletcher Davis of Athens, Texas, created a fried ground beef patty topped with mustard and Bermuda onion, served between bread with a pickle on the side, at his lunch counter. In 1904, he and his wife, Cindy, opened a stand at the St. Louis World's Fair, and the hamburger craze was on.

Others contend that Frank Menches, a German American, ran out of pork sausage at the New York Summit County Fair in 1892 and substituted ground beef. And, there is Louie Lassen, who founded Louie's Lunch in New Haven, Connecticut. He saved the beef trimmings from his steak sandwiches, ground them and took them home. One day in 1900 a customer ordered a meal to go and the restaurant was out of steaks. Louie fried up one of his patties, put it between toast, and created the hamburger.

No matter which version of the creation of the hamburger you favor, almost everyone favors hamburgers, served with just the right "fixings."

HAMBURGERS

1 pound ground beef
3 tablespoons finely chopped onions, if desired
3 tablespoons water
½ teaspoon salt
¼ teaspoon pepper
4 hamburger buns, split and toasted

Mix all ingredients except buns. Shape mixture into 4 patties, each about ¾ inch thick. Set oven control to broil. Place patties on rack in broiler pan. Broil with tops about 3 inches from heat 5 to 7 minutes on each side for medium, turning once. (160° on meat thermometer) About 1 minute before hamburgers are done, top each with cheese slice if desired. Broil until cheese is melted. Serve on buns.   4 SERVINGS; 395 CALORIES PER SERVING.

To Grill: Grill patties about 4 inches from medium coals 7 to 8 minutes on each side for medium, turning once, until desired doneness. Brush barbecue or teriyaki sauce on patties before and after turning if desired.

To Microwave: Arrange patties on microwavable rack in microwavable dish. Cover with waxed paper and microwave on high 6 to 7 minutes, for medium, rotating dish ½ turn after 3 minutes, until patties are almost done. Let stand covered 3 minutes.

To Panfry: Cook patties in 10-inch skillet over medium heat about 10 minutes for medium, turning occasionally.

SLOPPY JOES

Sloppy Joes are always favorites, whether served to kids or adults. If you want more "kick" to your sandwich, add a little bit more red pepper sauce.

1 pound ground beef
1 medium onion, chopped (about ½ cup)
⅓ cup chopped celery
⅓ cup chopped green bell pepper
⅓ cup ketchup
¼ cup water
1 tablespoon Worcestershire sauce
½ teaspoon salt
⅛ teaspoon red pepper sauce
6 hamburger buns, split and toasted

Cook and stir ground beef and onion in 10-inch skillet until beef is brown; drain. Stir in remaining ingredients except buns. Cover and cook over low heat 10 to 15 minutes or just until vegetables are tender. Fill buns with ground beef mixture.   6 SANDWICHES; 335 CALORIES PER SANDWICH.

To Microwave: Crumble ground beef into 2-quart microwavable casserole. Add onion, celery and bell pepper. Cover loosely and microwave on high 6 to 7 minutes, stirring after 3 minutes, until very little pink remains in beef; drain. Stir in remaining ingredients except buns. Cover tightly and microwave on high 3 to 5 minutes or until hot; stir.

Chiliburger Pies, Gyros

CHILIBURGER PIES

1½ pounds ground beef
1 can (8 ounces) whole kernel corn, drained
1 can (4 ounces) chopped green chilies, drained
2 teaspoons chili powder
2⅓ cups variety baking mix
3 tablespoons margarine or butter, melted
½ cup milk

Mix ground beef, corn, chilies and chili powder. Shape mixture into 6 patties. Place on rack in broiler pan. Set oven control to broil. Broil with tops 3 to 4 inches from heat 4 minutes on each side.

Heat oven to 400°. Mix remaining ingredients until soft dough forms. Beat vigorously 20 strokes. Smooth dough gently into ball on surface dusted with baking mix. Knead 5 times. Roll ⅛ inch thick. Cut into 12 rounds with floured 4½-inch biscuit cutter. Place beef patties on 6 of the rounds. Top each with another round. Pinch edges together to seal. Place on ungreased cookie sheet. Bake about 15 minutes or until golden brown. 6 SERVINGS; 540 CALORIES PER SERVING.

GYROS

1 pound ground lamb or beef
2 tablespoons water
1 tablespoon lemon juice
½ teaspoon salt
½ teaspoon ground cumin
½ teaspoon dried oregano leaves
¼ teaspoon pepper
2 cloves garlic, crushed
1 small onion, chopped (about ¼ cup)
2 tablespoons vegetable oil
4 pita breads (6-inch diameter)
2 cups shredded lettuce
½ cup plain yogurt
1 tablespoon chopped fresh or 1 teaspoon dried mint leaves
1 teaspoon sugar
1 small cucumber, seeded and chopped (about ¾ cup)
1 medium tomato, chopped (about ¾ cup)

Mix lamb, water, lemon juice, salt, cumin, oregano, pepper, garlic and onion. Shape into 4 thin patties. Cook patties in oil over medium heat 10 to 12 minutes, turning frequently, until done.

Split each bread halfway around edge with knife and separate to form pocket. Place patty in each pocket. Top with lettuce. Mix yogurt, mint and sugar. Stir in cucumber. Spoon onto lettuce and top with tomato. 4 SANDWICHES; 555 CALORIES PER SANDWICH.

PEPPERONI CALZONES

Calzones are a type of folded-over pizza popular in southern Italy.

    Pizza Dough (below)
1 can (8 ounces) tomato sauce
1 can (4 ounces) mushroom stems and pieces, drained
1 tablespoon chopped fresh or 1 teaspoon dried basil leaves
1 tablespoon chopped fresh or 1 teaspoon dried oregano leaves
1 clove garlic, crushed
8 ounces thinly sliced pepperoni
1 small green bell pepper, chopped (about ½ cup)
1 cup shredded mozzarella cheese (4 ounces)
1 egg, beaten

Prepare Pizza Dough. Punch down dough. Divide into 6 equal parts. Roll each part into 7-inch circle on lightly floured surface. Mix tomato sauce, mushrooms, basil, oregano and garlic. Spread over half of each circle to within 1 inch of edge. Top with pepperoni, bell pepper and cheese. Fold dough carefully over filling. Pinch edges to seal securely. Place sandwiches on greased cookie sheet. Let rest 15 minutes.

Heat oven to 375°. Brush sandwiches with egg. Bake about 25 minutes or until golden brown. 6 SANDWICHES; 550 CALORIES PER SANDWICH.

Pizza Dough

    1 package regular or quick-acting active dry yeast
1 cup warm water (105° to 115°)
1 tablespoon sugar
2 tablespoons vegetable oil
½ teaspoon salt
2¾ to 3¼ cups all-purpose flour

Dissolve yeast in warm water in large bowl. Stir in sugar, oil, salt and 1 cup of the flour. Beat until smooth. Mix in enough remaining flour to make dough easy to handle.

Turn dough onto lightly floured surface. Knead about 5 minutes or until smooth and elastic. Place in greased bowl and turn greased side up. Cover and let rise in warm place about 30 minutes or until almost double.

GROUND BEEF CALZONES: Cook and stir 1 pound ground beef, 1 teaspoon salt and 1 medium onion, chopped (about ½ cup), until beef is done; drain. Substitute beef mixture for the pepperoni. 550 CALORIES PER SANDWICH.

REUBEN SANDWICHES

Some say the Reuben originated at the New York deli Reuben's, while others insist that Reuben Kay, a grocer from Omaha, invented the sandwich.

    ⅓ cup mayonnaise or salad dressing
1 tablespoon chili sauce
12 slices rye bread
6 slices Swiss cheese
¾ pound thinly sliced cooked corned beef
1 can (16 ounces) sauerkraut, drained
½ cup margarine or butter, softened

Mix mayonnaise and chili sauce. Spread over 6 slices bread. Place cheese, corned beef and sauerkraut on mayonnaise mixture. Top with remaining bread slices. Spread each top with 1 teaspoon margarine.

Place sandwiches, margarine sides down, in skillet. Spread tops with margarine. Cook uncovered over low heat about 10 minutes or until bottoms are golden brown. Turn and cook about 8 minutes or until golden brown and cheese is melted. 6 SANDWICHES; 610 CALORIES PER SANDWICH.

RACHEL SANDWICHES: Substitute 1½ cups coleslaw for the sauerkraut and thinly sliced cooked turkey or chicken for half of the corned beef. 565 CALORIES PER SANDWICH.

DENVER POCKET SANDWICHES

    1 medium onion, chopped (about ½ cup)
1 small green bell pepper, chopped (about ½ cup)
2 tablespoons margarine or butter
6 eggs
½ cup chopped fully cooked smoked ham or 1 can (6¾ ounces) chunk ham
1 jar (2 ounces) diced pimiento, drained
¼ teaspoon salt
⅛ teaspoon pepper
3 pita breads (6-inch diameter)

Cook and stir onion and bell pepper in margarine in 10-inch skillet over medium heat until onion is softened. Beat eggs slightly. Stir in ham, pimiento, salt and pepper. Pour egg mixture into skillet. Cook over low heat, gently lifting cooked portions with spatula so that thin uncooked portion can flow to bottom. Avoid constant stirring. Cook 3 to 5 minutes or until eggs are thickened throughout but still moist. Cut pita breads in half. Divide egg mixture among pita breads. 6 SANDWICHES; 265 CALORIES PER SANDWICH.

BAKED EGGPLANT SANDWICHES

3 tablespoons vegetable oil
1 medium eggplant (about 1¼ pounds)
6 tablespoons pizza sauce
6 slices mozzarella cheese (about 4 ounces)
2 eggs
¼ cup milk
½ cup Italian-style dry bread crumbs
¼ cup chopped fresh parsley

Heat oven to 400°. Brush 1 tablespoon oil on bottom of rectangular pan, 13 × 9 × 2 inches. Cut eggplant into twelve ½-inch slices. Spoon about 1 tablespoon pizza sauce onto each of 6 eggplant slices. Top each with 1 slice cheese (cut or fold cheese, if necessary, to fit) and with remaining eggplant slices.

Beat eggs and milk. Mix bread crumbs and parsley in shallow dish. Dip each sandwich into egg mixture, then into crumb mixture, turning to coat both sides. Press crumb mixture into and around edges to coat entire sandwich.

Place sandwiches in pan. Drizzle with remaining oil. Cover pan with aluminum foil. Bake 20 minutes. Remove foil and turn sandwiches. Bake 15 to 20 minutes longer or until sandwiches are golden brown and eggplant is tender.   6 SANDWICHES; 215 CALORIES PER SANDWICH.

⏱ SALMON BURGERS

1 can (15½ ounces) salmon, drained and flaked
½ cup crushed buttery crackers
2 tablespoons chopped fresh parsley
½ teaspoon finely shredded lemon peel
1 tablespoon lemon juice
2 green onions, sliced (with tops)
1 egg
2 tablespoons vegetable oil
5 English muffins, split and toasted
Cucumber Sauce (below)

Mix salmon, crackers, parsley, lemon peel, lemon juice, onions and egg. Shape into 5 patties. Heat oil in 10-inch skillet until hot. Cook patties in oil 4 to 5 minutes on each side or until golden brown. Place a patty on each muffin. Serve with Cucumber Sauce.   5 BURGERS; 445 CALORIES PER BURGER.

Cucumber Sauce

⅓ cup finely chopped, seeded and pared cucumber
¼ cup plain yogurt
¼ cup mayonnaise or salad dressing
1 teaspoon chopped fresh or ¼ teaspoon dried tarragon leaves

Mix all ingredients.

Baked Eggplant Sandwiches, Salmon Burgers

⏱ GRILLED FRUIT-AND-CHEESE SANDWICHES

For a change of pace, use flavored cream cheese for the regular cream cheese, and Swiss, for example, in place of the Monterey Jack.

1 cup shredded Monterey Jack cheese (4 ounces)
⅓ cup crumbled blue cheese
2 tablespoons milk
1 package (3 ounces) cream cheese, softened
8 one-quarter-inch slices sourdough bread
1 small ripe pear, thinly sliced
1 small all-purpose apple, thinly sliced
Margarine or butter, softened

Mix Monterey Jack cheese, blue cheese, milk and cream cheese. Spread about 2 tablespoons on each slice bread. Place pear and apple slices on cheese mixture on 4 slices bread. Place remaining slices bread, cheese side down, on pear and apple slices. Spread tops with margarine.

Place sandwiches, margarine sides down, in skillet. Spread tops with margarine. Cook uncovered over medium heat about 5 minutes or until golden brown. Turn and cook 2 to 3 minutes longer or until golden brown.   4 SANDWICHES; 445 CALORIES PER SANDWICH.

⏱ 🌾 SUPER GRILLED CHEESE

8 ounces Monterey Jack, Muenster, provolone or mozzarella cheese, thinly sliced
8 slices white or whole wheat bread
1 small onion, chopped (about ¼ cup)
8 slices bacon, crisply cooked
1 medium tomato, thinly sliced
1 avocado, thinly sliced
Margarine or butter, softened

Place half of the cheese on 4 slices bread. Sprinkle with onion. Top with bacon, tomato, avocado, remaining cheese and bread. Spread top slices of bread with margarine.

Place sandwiches, margarine sides down, in skillet. Spread tops of bread with margarine. Cook uncovered over medium heat about 5 minutes or until golden brown. Turn and cook 2 to 3 minutes or until golden brown and cheese is melted.   4 SANDWICHES; 590 CALORIES PER SANDWICH.

AMERICAN GRILLED CHEESE: Substitute 12 slices process American cheese for the 8 ounces cheese. Omit onion, bacon, tomato and avocado.   475 CALORIES PER SANDWICH.

⏱ 🌾 MUFFULETTA

The Central Grocery in New Orleans created this mammoth sandwich. Its pungent Olive Salad sets it apart from a hero or Submarine Sandwich.

Olive Salad (below)
1 unsliced large round or oval loaf Italian or sourdough bread (8- to 10-inch diameter)
½ pound thinly sliced Italian salami
6 ounces thinly sliced provolone cheese
¼ pound thinly sliced fully cooked smoked ham

Prepare Olive Salad. Cut bread horizontally in half. Remove ½-inch layer of soft bread from inside of each half to within ½ inch of edge. Drain Olive Salad, reserving marinade. Brush reserved marinade over cut sides of bread. Layer salami, one-half of the Olive Salad, the cheese, ham and remaining Olive Salad on bottom half of bread. Cover with top half of bread.   6 SERVINGS; 595 CALORIES PER SERVING.

Olive Salad

1 anchovy fillet, mashed
1 large clove garlic, crushed
⅓ cup olive oil
½ cup chopped pimiento-stuffed olives
½ cup chopped Greek or ripe olives
½ cup chopped mixed pickled vegetables
2 tablespoons chopped fresh parsley
1½ teaspoons chopped fresh or ½ teaspoon crushed dried oregano leaves
⅛ teaspoon pepper

Stir anchovy and garlic into oil in 1-quart glass or plastic bowl until well blended. Stir in remaining ingredients. Cover and refrigerate at least 8 hours, stirring occasionally.

⏱ 🌾 SUBMARINE SANDWICH

This sandwich expands to hold whatever your refrigerator does. It's a hearty creation also called a "Poor Boy," or sometimes a Dagwood, in honor of the towering sandwiches made by the comic-strip character Dagwood Bumstead.

1 loaf (1 pound) French bread
Margarine or butter, softened
4 ounces Swiss cheese slices
½ pound salami, sliced
2 cups shredded lettuce
2 medium tomatoes, thinly sliced
1 medium onion, thinly sliced
½ pound fully cooked smoked ham, thinly sliced
1 medium green bell pepper, thinly sliced
¼ cup creamy Italian dressing

Cut bread horizontally in half. Spread bottom half with margarine. Layer cheese, salami, lettuce, tomatoes, onion, ham and bell pepper on top. Drizzle with dressing. Top with remaining bread half. Secure loaf with wooden picks and cut into 6 pieces.   6 SERVINGS; 590 CALORIES PER SERVING.

CLUB WALDORF SANDWICH LOAF

1-pound unsliced oval loaf Vienna or sourdough bread
Lettuce leaves
1 small onion, thinly sliced
¼ pound thinly sliced fully cooked smoked ham
¼ pound thinly sliced cooked turkey
4 ounces sliced provolone cheese
¼ cup lemon yogurt
¼ teaspoon curry powder
1 medium apple, chopped
1 stalk celery, chopped

Cut bread into sixteen ½-inch slices, not cutting completely through to bottom of loaf. Line every other slice with lettuce, onion, ham, turkey and cheese.

Mix remaining ingredients and spoon onto cheese. To serve, cut loaf between unfilled slices into sandwiches.   8 SANDWICHES; 290 CALORIES PER SANDWICH.

⏱ 🌾 CHICKEN SALAD FILLING

1½ cups chopped cooked chicken or turkey
½ cup mayonnaise or salad dressing
1 medium stalk celery, chopped (about ½ cup)
1 small onion, chopped (about ¼ cup)
¼ teaspoon salt
¼ teaspoon pepper

Mix all ingredients.   ABOUT 2 CUPS FILLING (ENOUGH FOR 4 SANDWICHES); 300 CALORIES PER ½ CUP FILLING.

BEEF SALAD FILLING: Substitute 1½ cups chopped cooked beef for the chicken. Stir in 2 tablespoons sweet pickle relish, drained.   395 CALORIES PER ½ CUP FILLING.

EGG SALAD FILLING: Substitute 6 hard-cooked eggs, chopped, for the chicken.   320 CALORIES PER ½ CUP FILLING.

HAM SALAD FILLING: Substitute 1½ cups chopped fully cooked smoked ham for the chicken. Omit salt and pepper. Stir in 1 teaspoon prepared mustard.   285 CALORIES PER ½ CUP FILLING.

TUNA SALAD FILLING: Substitute 1 can (9¼ ounces) tuna in water, drained, for the chicken. Stir in 1 teaspoon lemon juice.   270 CALORIES PER ½ CUP FILLING.

⏱ SMOKED TURKEY SANDWICH

The marinade from the artichoke hearts provides the base for this sandwich's creamy dressing.

1 jar (6 ounces) marinated artichoke hearts
¼ cup mayonnaise or salad dressing
½ cup chopped bell pepper
1 loaf (1 pound) Italian bread
Romaine or watercress
1 small onion, thinly sliced
¾ pound thinly sliced smoked turkey
1 medium tomato, thinly sliced

Drain artichoke hearts, reserving marinade. Mix mayonnaise and reserved marinade. Chop artichokes coarsely; stir in bell pepper.

Cut bread horizontally in half. Spread cut sides with mayonnaise mixture. Layer romaine, artichoke mixture, onion, turkey and tomato on bottom half. Top with other half. Secure loaf with wooden picks and cut into 6 pieces.   6 SERVINGS; 400 CALORIES PER SERVING.

Ⓞ SHRIMP CLUB SANDWICHES

12 slices white or whole wheat bread, toasted
Mayonnaise or salad dressing
4 lettuce leaves
12 slices tomatoes (about 2 medium)
12 slices bacon, crisply cooked
2 cans (4½ ounces each) large shrimp, rinsed and drained
1 large avocado, thinly sliced

Spread toast with mayonnaise. Place lettuce leaf, 3 slices tomato and 3 slices bacon on each of 4 slices toast. Top with another slice toast. Arrange shrimp on toast. Top with avocado slices. Top with third slice toast. Secure with wooden picks and cut sandwiches diagonally into 4 triangles.   4 SANDWICHES; 520 CALORIES PER SANDWICH.

CLUB SANDWICHES: Substitute 1 pound sliced cooked turkey or chicken for the shrimp and 4 additional lettuce leaves for the avocado.   605 CALORIES PER SANDWICH.

Club Sandwiches

Ⓞ SOUTHWESTERN SHRIMP POCKETS

1 package (10 ounces) frozen cooked shrimp, thawed
2 medium tomatoes, seeded and chopped (about 2 cups)
⅓ cup sliced green onions (with tops)
⅓ cup chopped green bell pepper
1 tablespoon chopped fresh cilantro
1 to 2 tablespoons lime juice
2 teaspoons finely chopped jalapeño chilies
2 cloves garlic, finely chopped
¼ teaspoon salt
3 pita breads (6-inch diameter)
Leaf lettuce

Mix all ingredients except pita breads and lettuce. Cut pita breads in half. Line each half with lettuce. Spoon about ½ cup shrimp mixture into each.   6 SANDWICHES; 150 CALORIES PER SANDWICH.

Ⓞ MEDITERRANEAN SANDWICHES

Throughout the Middle East, hummus, made from garbanzo beans, is common. It makes a wonderful sandwich and also can be served as a delicious dip.

1 can (15 ounces) garbanzo beans
½ cup sesame seed
1 clove garlic, cut in half
3 tablespoons lemon juice
¼ teaspoon salt
16 one-half-inch diagonal slices French bread
2 tablespoons chopped fresh cilantro
½ cup chopped bell pepper
½ medium cucumber, thinly sliced
1 cup alfalfa sprouts

Drain beans, reserving ⅓ cup liquid. Place reserved bean liquid, the sesame seed and garlic in blender or food processor. Cover and blend on high speed, or process, until mixed. Add beans, lemon juice and salt. Cover and blend on high speed, or process, scraping sides, if necessary, until of uniform consistency.

Spread about 2 tablespoons bean mixture on each slice bread. Sprinkle cilantro and bell pepper on 8 of the slices bread. Top with cucumber slices and alfalfa sprouts. Top with remaining slices bread.   4 SERVINGS (2 SANDWICHES PER SERVING); 380 CALORIES PER SERVING.

Brie-and-Cucumber on Rye

🕐 BRIE-AND-CUCUMBER ON RYE

½ seedless cucumber
8 ounces Brie cheese, cut into ¼-inch pieces
¼ cup finely chopped green onions (with tops)
¼ cup oil-and-vinegar dressing
¾ teaspoon chopped fresh or ¼ teaspoon dried dill weed
4 teaspoons margarine or butter, softened
4 slices rye bread
Salad greens

Cut cucumber lengthwise in half. Cut each half into thin slices. Toss cucumber, cheese, onions, dressing and dill weed.

Spread 1 teaspoon margarine on each slice bread. Top with salad greens. Spoon cheese mixture onto greens. Garnish each sandwich with 1 cooked shrimp and fresh dill weed if desired.   4 OPEN-FACE SANDWICHES; 370 CALORIES PER SANDWICH.

ZUCCHINI AND CREAM CHEESE SANDWICHES: Substitute 1 medium zucchini for the English cucumber and 1 package (8 ounces) cream cheese for the Brie cheese.   380 CALORIES PER SANDWICH.

SAUCE BASICS

Sauces of all types are used to enhance the flavor of a dish, whether it's a simple butter sauce or an exquisite vegetable chutney. When you serve sauces with meats, fish, poultry, vegetables and sandwiches, the dishes become even more special. Be inventive—add Pesto (page 359) to soup or peanut sauce (page 360) to plain broiled chicken. Sauces will give you great ideas to perk up the ordinary.

♦ The most common thickener for a sauce is called "a roux," made of fat and flour. Favorite sauces made from a roux are white sauce, velouté sauce and brown sauce. It's important to stir the hot fat and flour mixture and allow it to bubble before adding the liquid. This stirring evenly distributes the flour and encourages the flour to absorb the liquid completely.

♦ Other ways to thicken a sauce are with cornstarch, with egg yolks (as in hollandaise sauce), or by reduction, in which the cooking process "reduces" the volume of liquid by evaporation, resulting in a thickened sauce. Reduction takes the longest amount of time, but will happen more quickly if a pan with a large amount of surface area, such as a 10-inch skillet, is used.

STORING

Using leftover sauces and gravies can liven up even the most uninspired leftovers. Refrigerate leftover sauces immediately in a covered container. You can store them for up to a week, and if you want to keep sauces longer, freeze in small amounts in covered containers.

For food safety reasons, avoid keeping sauces made with egg or cream in the refrigerator for more than three days. For those sauces served hot, reheat slowly and bring to a boil before serving. Allow cold sauces to thaw in the refrigerator. You can freeze hollandaise sauce, but reheat slowly to avoid curdling the sauce. If you want to reheat hollandaise sauce in the microwave, use the low (10%) power setting.

WHITE SAUCE

2 tablespoons margarine or butter
2 tablespoons all-purpose flour
¼ teaspoon salt
⅛ teaspoon pepper
1 cup milk

Heat margarine in 1½-quart saucepan over medium heat until melted. Stir in flour, salt and pepper. Cook over medium heat, stirring constantly, until mixture is smooth and bubbly; remove from heat. Stir in milk. Heat to boiling, stirring constantly. Boil and stir 1 minute.   1 CUP SAUCE; 25 CALORIES PER TABLESPOON.

To Microwave: Place margarine in 4-cup microwavable measure. Microwave uncovered on high 15 to 30 seconds or until melted. Stir in flour, salt, pepper and milk. Microwave uncovered on high 2 to 3 minutes, stirring every minute with wire whisk or fork, until thickened.

CHEESE SAUCE: Stir in ¼ teaspoon dry mustard with the flour. After boiling and stirring sauce 1 minute, stir in ½ cup shredded Cheddar cheese (2 ounces) until melted.   1⅓ CUPS SAUCE; 30 CALORIES PER TABLESPOON.

CURRY SAUCE: Stir in ½ teaspoon curry powder with the flour. Try with chicken, lamb, shrimp or vegetables.   25 CALORIES PER TABLESPOON.

DILL SAUCE: Stir in 1 teaspoon chopped fresh or ½ teaspoon dried dill weed and dash of ground nutmeg with the flour. Nice served with fish.   25 CALORIES PER TABLESPOON.

THIN WHITE SAUCE: Decrease margarine to 1 tablespoon and flour to 1 tablespoon.   15 CALORIES PER TABLESPOON.

THICK WHITE SAUCE: Increase margarine to ¼ cup and flour to ¼ cup.   40 CALORIES PER TABLESPOON.

Constant stirring will help prevent the sauce from lumping. If sauce turns lumpy, strain through a wire sieve before serving.

BROWN SAUCE

2 tablespoons margarine or butter
1 thin slice onion
2 tablespoons all-purpose flour
1 cup beef broth
¼ teaspoon salt
⅛ teaspoon pepper

Heat margarine in 1½-quart saucepan over low heat until melted. Cook and stir onion in margarine until onion is brown; discard onion. Stir flour into margarine. Cook over low heat, stirring constantly, until flour is deep brown; remove from heat. Stir in broth. Heat to boiling, stirring constantly. Boil and stir 1 minute. Stir in salt and pepper. 1 CUP SAUCE; 40 CALORIES PER TABLESPOON.

BORDELAISE SAUCE: Decrease broth to ½ cup and add ½ cup red wine. Stir in ½ teaspoon each chopped fresh parsley, finely chopped onion and crushed bay leaves and ¾ teaspoon chopped fresh or ¼ teaspoon dried thyme leaves with the broth. Serve with steaks, pork chops or hamburgers.   45 CALORIES PER TABLESPOON.

MUSHROOM SAUCE: Stir 1 jar (4½ ounces) sliced mushrooms, drained, and a few drops Worcestershire sauce into sauce. Good with fish, meat or omelets.   50 CALORIES PER TABLESPOON.

PIQUANT SAUCE: Stir in ¼ cup white wine, 1 tablespoon chopped fresh parsley, 1 tablespoon chopped gherkins, 1 tablespoon finely chopped onion and 1½ teaspoons chopped fresh or ½ teaspoon dried chervil leaves with the broth. Try with beef, veal or fish.   50 CALORIES PER TABLESPOON.

VELOUTÉ SAUCE

2 tablespoons margarine or butter
2 tablespoons all-purpose flour
1 cup chicken broth
¼ teaspoon salt
⅛ teaspoon pepper
⅛ teaspoon ground nutmeg

Heat margarine in 1½-quart saucepan over medium heat until melted. Stir in flour. Cook over medium heat, stirring constantly, until mixture is smooth and bubbly; remove from heat. Stir in broth. Heat to boiling, stirring constantly. Boil and stir 1 minute. Stir in remaining ingredients.   ABOUT 1 CUP SAUCE; 20 CALORIES PER TABLESPOON.

ALMOND VELOUTÉ SAUCE: Just before serving, stir in ¼ cup slivered almonds, toasted. Nice with poultry or fish.   30 CALORIES PER TABLESPOON.

PAN GRAVY

2 tablespoons meat drippings (fat and juices)
2 tablespoons all-purpose flour
1 cup liquid (meat juices, broth, water)
¼ teaspoon salt
¼ teaspoon pepper

Place meat on warm platter and keep warm while preparing gravy. Pour drippings from pan into bowl, leaving brown particles in pan. Return 2 tablespoons drippings to pan. (Measure accurately because too little fat makes gravy lumpy.)

Stir in flour. (Measure accurately so gravy is not greasy.) Cook over medium heat, stirring constantly, until mixture is smooth and bubbly; remove from heat. Stir in liquid. Heat to boiling, stirring constantly. Boil and stir 1 minute. Stir in few drops browning sauce if desired. Stir in salt and pepper. ABOUT 1 CUP GRAVY; 20 CALORIES PER TABLESPOON.

CREAMY GRAVY: Substitute milk for half of the liquid. 15 CALORIES PER TABLESPOON.

GIBLET GRAVY: Cook gizzard, heart and neck of fowl in 4 cups salted water 1 to 2 hours or until tender. Add liver the last 30 minutes. Remove meat from neck and finely chop with giblets. Substitute broth from giblets for the liquid. Stir giblets into gravy. Heat until hot. 35 CALORIES PER TABLESPOON.

MUSHROOM GRAVY: Before adding flour, cook and stir 1 cup sliced mushrooms in drippings until light brown. Or use 1 can (4 ounces) mushroom stems and pieces. Drain and use mushroom liquid for part of the liquid in gravy. Stir ½ teaspoon Worcestershire sauce into gravy. 20 CALORIES PER TABLESPOON.

THIN GRAVY: Decrease drippings to 1 tablespoon and flour to 1 tablespoon. 10 CALORIES PER TABLESPOON.

 # HOLLANDAISE SAUCE

Preparing Hollandaise Sauce requires full attention and low heat. If yours curdles, add about 1 tablespoon boiling water to ¾ cup sauce and beat vigorously with a hand beater until smooth.

3 egg yolks
1 tablespoon lemon juice
½ cup firm butter*

Stir egg yolks and lemon juice vigorously in 1½-quart saucepan. Add ¼ cup of the butter. Heat over *very low heat*, stirring constantly with wire whisk, until butter is melted. Add remaining butter. Continue stirring vigorously until butter is melted and sauce is thickened. (Be sure butter melts slowly as this gives eggs time to cook and thicken sauce without curdling.) Serve hot or at room temperature. Cover and refrigerate any remaining sauce. To serve, stir in small amount of hot water. ABOUT ¾ CUP SAUCE; 85 CALORIES PER TABLESPOON.

*Do not use margarine, butter blends or spreads in this recipe.

BÉARNAISE SAUCE: Stir in 1 tablespoon dry white wine with the lemon juice. After sauce thickens, stir in 1 tablespoon finely chopped onion, 1½ teaspoons chopped fresh or ½ teaspoon dried tarragon leaves and 1½ teaspoons chopped fresh or ¼ teaspoon dried chervil leaves. Nice with fish or meat. 90 CALORIES PER TABLESPOON.

MALTAISE SAUCE: After sauce thickens, stir in ½ teaspoon grated orange peel and 2 tablespoons orange juice. Try with green vegetables. 85 CALORIES PER TABLESPOON.

MOUSSELINE SAUCE: Prepare Hollandaise Sauce. Cool to room temperature. Just before serving, beat ¼ cup whipping (heavy) cream in chilled small bowl until stiff. Fold into sauce. This delicate sauce is nice with fish, eggs, artichokes, broccoli or cauliflower. 100 CALORIES PER TABLESPOON.

SWEET-AND-SOUR SAUCE

½ cup sugar
½ cup chicken broth or water
⅓ cup white vinegar
1 teaspoon vegetable oil
1 teaspoon soy sauce
¼ teaspoon salt
1 clove garlic, crushed
2 tablespoons cornstarch
2 tablespoons cold water
1 tomato, cut into thin wedges
1 small green bell pepper, cut into 1-inch pieces
1 can (8¼ ounces) pineapple chunks in syrup, drained

Heat sugar, broth, vinegar, oil, soy sauce, salt and garlic to boiling in 2-quart saucepan over medium-high heat, stirring occasionally. Mix cornstarch and water. Stir into sugar mixture. Cook and stir about 10 seconds or until thickened. Stir in tomato, bell pepper and pineapple. Heat to boiling. ABOUT 2½ CUPS SAUCE; 20 CALORIES PER TABLESPOON.

PESTO

2 cups firmly packed fresh basil leaves
¾ cup grated Parmesan cheese
¾ cup olive oil
2 tablespoons pine nuts
4 cloves garlic

Place all ingredients in blender or food processor. Cover and blend on medium speed, or process, about 3 minutes, stopping occasionally to scrape sides, until smooth.   1¼ CUPS SAUCE; 95 CALORIES PER TABLESPOON.

HERB SAUCE

1½ cups packed parsley sprigs
½ cup marinated sun-dried tomatoes, drained
½ cup olive or vegetable oil
¼ cup packed fresh basil leaves
2 tablespoons lemon juice
¼ teaspoon salt
¼ teaspoon pepper

Place all ingredients in blender or food processor. Cover and blend on high speed, or process, until smooth. Try with hot or cold meats and poultry. ABOUT 1 CUP SAUCE; 80 CALORIES PER TABLESPOON.

MUSTARD SAUCE

1 tablespoon margarine or butter
1 tablespoon all-purpose flour
¼ teaspoon pepper
1 cup milk
3 tablespoons prepared mustard
1 tablespoon prepared horseradish

Heat margarine in 1½-quart saucepan over low heat until melted. Stir in flour and pepper. Cook over medium heat, stirring constantly, until mixture is smooth and bubbly; remove from heat. Stir in milk. Heat to boiling, stirring constantly. Boil and stir 1 minute. Stir in mustard and horseradish. Heat until hot. Serve warm. Nice with smoked sausage, corned beef and cooked cabbage wedges. ABOUT 1 CUP; 20 CALORIES PER TABLESPOON.

HONEY-MUSTARD SPREAD

½ cup mayonnaise or salad dressing
1 tablespoon honey
1 tablespoon Dijon mustard

Mix all ingredients until smooth.   ABOUT ⅔ CUP SPREAD; 85 CALORIES PER TABLESPOON.

MUSHROOM-WINE SAUCE

1 tablespoon margarine or butter
2 cups sliced mushrooms
¼ cup chopped onion
1 teaspoon lemon juice
⅛ teaspoon salt
⅛ teaspoon pepper
⅓ cup dry white wine
⅔ cup whipping (heavy) cream

Heat margarine in 10-inch skillet over medium heat. Cook mushrooms, onion, lemon juice, salt and pepper in margarine about 4 minutes, stirring occasionally. Stir in wine. Cook over medium-high heat about 3 minutes, stirring occasionally, until liquid is reduce by half. Stir in whipping cream and heat to boiling.   ABOUT 1 CUP SAUCE; 55 CALORIES PER TABLESPOON.

TARTAR SAUCE

1 cup mayonnaise or salad dressing
2 tablespoons finely chopped dill pickle
1 tablespoon chopped fresh parsley
2 teaspoons chopped pimiento
1 teaspoon grated onion

Mix all ingredients. Cover and refrigerate about 1 hour or until chilled. Serve with broiled or breaded fish.   ABOUT 1 CUP SAUCE; 100 CALORIES PER TABLESPOON.

APPLESAUCE-HORSERADISH SAUCE

This pungent sauce combines the sweetness of applesauce with the fire of horseradish. Try it with beef, pork, ham or venison.

½ cup unsweetened applesauce
¼ cup sour cream
3 tablespoons grated horseradish or prepared horseradish
1 tablespoon white wine vinegar or white vinegar
1 teaspoon prepared mustard
¼ teaspoon white pepper

Mix all ingredients. Refrigerate at least 1 hour or until chilled. Refrigerate any remaining sauce. ABOUT 1 CUP; 10 CALORIES PER TABLESPOON.

WHIPPED HORSERADISH SAUCE: Substitute ½ cup whipping (heavy) cream, whipped, for the applesauce.   ABOUT 1¼ CUPS SAUCE; 30 CALORIES PER TABLESPOON.

ITALIAN TOMATO SAUCE

2 tablespoons olive or vegetable oil
1 medium onion, chopped (about ½ cup)
1 small green bell pepper, chopped (about ½ cup)
1 large clove garlic, finely chopped
1 can (16 ounces) whole tomatoes, undrained
1 can (8 ounces) tomato sauce
1 tablespoon chopped fresh or 1 teaspoon dried basil leaves
1½ teaspoons chopped fresh or ½ teaspoon dried oregano leaves
¼ teaspoon salt
¼ teaspoon fennel seed
⅛ teaspoon pepper

Heat oil in 3-quart saucepan over medium heat. Cook onion, bell pepper and garlic in oil about 2 minutes. Stir in remaining ingredients. Break up tomatoes. Heat to boiling; reduce heat. Cover and simmer 45 minutes. 2 CUPS SAUCE; 15 CALORIES PER TABLESPOON.

BARBECUE SAUCE

1 cup ketchup
½ cup finely chopped onion
⅓ cup water
¼ cup margarine or butter
1 tablespoon paprika
1 teaspoon packed brown sugar
¼ teaspoon pepper
2 tablespoons lemon juice
1 tablespoon Worcestershire sauce

Heat all ingredients except lemon juice and Worcestershire sauce to boiling over medium heat. Stir in lemon juice and Worcestershire sauce. Heat until hot. ABOUT 2 CUPS SAUCE; 25 CALORIES PER TABLESPOON.

RAISIN SAUCE

½ cup packed brown sugar
2 tablespoons cornstarch
1 teaspoon dry mustard
1½ cups water
¼ teaspoon grated lemon peel
2 tablespoons lemon juice
2 tablespoons vinegar
½ cup raisins

Mix brown sugar, cornstarch and mustard in 1½-quart saucepan. Mix water, lemon peel, lemon juice and vinegar. Gradually stir into sugar mixture. Cook over low heat, stirring constantly, until mixture thickens. Stir in raisins. ABOUT 2 CUPS SAUCE; 20 CALORIES PER TABLESPOON.

To Microwave: Mix brown sugar, cornstarch and mustard in 4-cup microwavable casserole. Mix water, lemon peel, lemon juice and vinegar as directed—except reduce water to 1¼ cups; gradually stir into sugar mixture. Microwave uncovered on high 3 to 5 minutes, stirring every minute, until thickened. Stir in raisins.

PRUNE-ALMOND SAUCE

Not only is this an excellent sauce for pork, ham and poultry, it does double duty as a filling for coffee cakes and muffins, as well as a spread for breads.

1½ cups apple juice
1 package (8 ounces) pitted prunes
2 tablespoons apple brandy, brandy or water
1 teaspoon grated lemon peel
½ cup slivered almonds

Heat apple juice and prunes to boiling; reduce heat. Cover and cook about 20 minutes or until prunes are soft. Drain prunes, reserving ½ cup liquid. Place prunes, reserved liquid, apple brandy and lemon peel in blender or food processor. Cover and blend on high speed, or process, until smooth. Stir in almonds. ABOUT 2 CUPS SAUCE; 40 CALORIES PER TABLESPOON.

To Microwave: Decrease apple juice to ¾ cup. Place apple juice and prunes in 1½-quart microwavable casserole. Cover tightly and microwave on high 6 to 8 minutes, stirring after 4 minutes, until prunes are tender. Continue as directed.

PEANUT SAUCE

1 cup salted peanuts
1 cup flaked coconut
1½ cups milk
¾ teaspoon curry powder
⅛ teaspoon ground red pepper (cayenne)

Place ½ cup peanuts in blender or food processor. Cover and blend on medium speed, or process, until peanuts are coarsely chopped; reserve. Place remaining peanuts and remaining ingredients in blender or food processor. Cover and blend on high speed, or process, until fairly smooth. Transfer mixture to 1-quart saucepan. Heat to boiling; reduce heat. Simmer 5 minutes, stirring occasionally. Stir in reserved peanuts. ABOUT 1¾ CUPS SAUCE; 50 CALORIES PER TABLESPOON.

SAVORY BUTTERS

Beat ¼ cup margarine or butter, softened, and one of the following. ABOUT 35 CALORIES PER TABLESPOON.

GARLIC: ½ teaspoon paprika, ⅛ teaspoon pepper and 2 cloves garlic, crushed.

HERB: 1 to 2 tablespoons chopped fresh or 1 to 2 teaspoons dried herb (basil, chives, oregano, savory, tarragon or thyme), 1 teaspoon lemon juice and ¼ teaspoon salt.

MUSTARD: 1 tablespoon chopped fresh parsley, 2 tablespoons prepared mustard and ¼ teaspoon salt.

SESAME: 1 tablespoon toasted sesame seed, 1 teaspoon Worcestershire sauce and ½ teaspoon garlic salt.

SWEET BUTTERS

Beat ½ cup margarine or butter, softened, and one of the following. ABOUT 40 CALORIES PER TABLESPOON.

ALMOND: 1 tablespoon finely chopped almonds and ½ teaspoon almond extract.

DATE: ¼ cup finely chopped dates.

ORANGE: 1 teaspoon grated orange peel and 1 tablespoon orange juice.

RASPBERRY: ½ cup raspberries, crushed, and 1 tablespoon sugar or ¼ cup raspberry jam.

EGGPLANT-TOMATO CHUTNEY

2 tablespoons olive or vegetable oil
1 medium onion, chopped (about ½ cup)
2 cloves garlic, crushed
1 medium eggplant, pared and cubed
½ teaspoon salt
2 medium tomatoes, seeded and chopped
¼ cup chopped fresh parsley
¼ cup currants
2 tablespoons tarragon vinegar

Heat oil in 12-inch skillet over medium heat. Cook onion and garlic in oil about 2 minutes. Stir in eggplant and salt. Cook over medium heat 15 minutes, stirring occasionally. Add remaining ingredients. Cook 15 minutes longer, stirring occasionally, until vegetables are soft and no excess liquid remains. ABOUT 3½ CUPS SAUCE; 10 CALORIES PER TABLESPOON.

To Microwave: Place onion, garlic and oil in 3-quart microwavable casserole. Cover tightly and microwave on high 3 to 4 minutes or until onion is softened. Add eggplant and salt. Cover tightly and microwave 3 minutes. Add remaining ingredients. Cover tightly and microwave 3 to 5 minutes longer or until vegetables are soft. Let stand 5 minutes. Serve with slotted spoon.

PAPAYA CHUTNEY

1 medium ripe papaya (about 1 pound)
¼ cup white vinegar
¼ cup lemon juice
1 tablespoon chopped fresh cilantro
1 tablespoon vegetable oil
1 tablespoon honey
2 teaspoons grated gingerroot or ¾ teaspoon ground ginger
¼ teaspoon chili powder
⅛ teaspoon ground cinnamon

Pare papaya. Cut papaya in half and scoop out centers. Chop papaya finely. Heat all ingredients to boiling in 10-inch skillet; reduce heat. Cover and simmer 40 minutes, stirring occasionally. Serve warm or cold. ABOUT 1¼ CUPS SAUCE; 20 CALORIES PER TABLESPOON.

Eggplant-Tomato Chutney, Papaya Chutney

MIXED BERRY JAM

1 cup crushed strawberries (about 1 pint whole berries)
1 cup crushed raspberries (about 1 pint whole berries)
4 cups sugar
½ teaspoon grated lemon peel
1 tablespoon lemon juice
1 pouch (3 ounces) liquid fruit pectin

Mix berries and sugar. Let stand at room temperature about 10 minutes, stirring occasionally, until sugar is dissolved. Mix in lemon peel, lemon juice and pectin. Stir 3 to 5 minutes or until slightly thickened. Spoon mixture into freezer containers, leaving ½-inch headspace. Seal immediately. Let stand at room temperature 24 hours. Refrigerate no longer than 3 weeks, or freeze no longer than 1 year. Thaw before serving. ABOUT 5 HALF-PINTS JAM; 40 CALORIES PER TABLESPOON.

ROSY GRAPE JELLY

2 cups cranberry juice cocktail
¾ cup grape juice
1 package (1¾ ounces) powdered fruit pectin
3¼ cups sugar

Mix cranberry juice cocktail, grape juice and pectin in 3-quart saucepan until smooth. Heat to boiling over high heat, stirring constantly. Stir in sugar, all at once. Heat to boiling, stirring constantly. Boil and stir 1 minute; remove from heat. Quickly skim off foam. Immediately pour into hot sterilized jars. Let jars stand 1 hour. Cover with lids. Refrigerate no longer than 3 weeks, or freeze no longer than 6 months. Thaw before serving. ABOUT 5 HALF-PINTS JELLY; 35 CALORIES PER TABLESPOON.

LEMON CURD

1 cup sugar
2 teaspoons finely shredded lemon peel
1 cup lemon juice (about 5 large lemons)
3 tablespoons firm margarine or butter, cut up
3 eggs, slightly beaten

Mix sugar, lemon peel and lemon juice in heavy 1½-quart saucepan. Stir in margarine and eggs. Cook over medium heat about 8 minutes, stirring constantly, until mixture thickens and coats back of spoon (do not boil). Immediately pour into 1-pint container or two 1-cup containers. Cover and refrigerate no longer than 2 months. ABOUT 2 CUPS CURD; 40 CALORIES PER TABLESPOON.

——— FIX-IT-FAST ———

- Add leftover meats and vegetables to canned or prepared dry soup mixes; then spark their flavor with herbs.

- Serve thick cream soups in hollowed-out hard rolls. Use the hollowed-out bread to serve with the soup, as croutons or as "dunking bread." When you finish your soup, you can eat your "bowl."

- Blend or process 1 package (8 ounces) cream cheese, softened, and 1 chilled 16-ounce can fruit for a quick fruit soup. Stir in additional liquid, if necessary, until of desired thickness. Add cinnamon, nutmeg or allspice to taste.

- For another easy fruit soup, blend or process 1 package (16 ounces) frozen fruit without sugar and 1 package (8 ounces) cream cheese, softened. Stir in additional liquid, if necessary, until of desired thickness, and spice to taste.

- Make any soup a pasta soup. For canned or dry mix soups, precook pasta and add just before serving. If making homemade soup, add during the last 15 minutes of cooking.

- Layer luncheon meat and deli salads on bread.

- For a quick pizza sandwich, toast bread or English muffins and top with pizza sauce, cheese and your favorite toppings. Broil until cheese is melted.

- Try a grilled PB&J sandwich. Spread peanut butter and jelly on bread, then spread margarine or butter on outside of sandwich. Cook both sides in a skillet or place sandwich in waffle iron to "grill."

- Substitute plain yogurt or sour cream for half of the mayonnaise when preparing tuna, chicken or egg salad sandwiches; it's just as delicious and has less fat and calories.

- To stretch your sandwich fillings, add chopped vegetables, shredded cheese, chopped nuts, chopped hard-cooked eggs or chopped apples.

- Mix wheat and white bread for a two-tone sandwich. Or try rice cakes, flatbread, pita breads, rusks, thin crackers or raisin bread for sandwiches.

- Use canned soup as a base for sauces, and thin with milk or hot water. Heat and serve over pasta, vegetables, baked potatoes or meat.

- Melt a jar of cheese spread. Thin with milk or water, if necessary, for a fast cheese sauce.

- Use cream cheese as a base for your sauces. Thin with ½ to ¾ cup milk and beat until smooth.

- Use a bit of a strong sauce such as Pesto (page 359) to flavor less-distinctive sauces such as White Sauce (page 357).

PER SERVING OR UNIT NUTRITION INFORMATION RECIPE, PAGE	Servings per recipe	Calories	Protein (grams)	Carbohydrate (grams)	Fat (grams)	Cholesterol (grams)	Sodium (milligrams)	Protein	Vitamin A	Vitamin C	Thiamine	Riboflavin	Niacin	Calcium	Iron
SOUPS															
Avocado Soup, 347	6	175	8	7	14	15	1080	10	8	6	4	10	18	4	4
Barley Vegetable-Beef Soup, 336	7	360	27	44	9	55	865	40	100	16	18	16	28	6	26
Beef and Broth, Beef, per cup, 334		290	41	0	13	125	100	62	0	0	6	18	36	0	28
Broth, per cup, 334		15	3	1	1	0	795	4	0	0	0	2	8	0	2
Black Bean Soup, 345	6	160	14	16	4	150	540	20	70	6	24	10	8	4	10
Borsch, 342	6	400	21	24	25	55	1010	32	18	24	12	10	16	10	32
Cheddar Cheese Soup, 346	6	355	20	9	27	65	935	30	18	2	2	20	10	48	4
Cheesy Ham and Leek Soup, 336	4	415	27	12	29	75	1430	40	16	4	36	22	24	30	10
Chicken and Broth, Chicken, per cup, 335		335	38	0	19	125	115	58	4	0	4	14	58	2	8
Broth, per cup, 335		40	5	1	1	0	775	6	0	0	0	4	16	0	2
Chicken Noodle Soup, 339	6	295	31	7	15	90	670	48	100	2	6	14	54	2	10
Chicken Rice Soup, 339	6	315	31	12	15	90	620	48	100	2	8	14	54	2	10
Chilled Pear-Mint Soup, 347	6	120	2	18	5	15	20	2	2	8	2	4	0	4	0
Corn Chowder, 344	6	300	10	34	15	25	410	16	16	10	10	20	10	20	8
Couscous Soup with Sausage, 337	4	405	20	5	34	70	1115	30	6	8	46	18	32	6	14
Cream of Broccoli Soup, 344	8	120	3	8	9	20	400	4	32	66	4	6	2	4	4
Cream of Cauliflower Soup, 344	8	120	3	9	9	20	390	4	6	68	6	4	4	4	4
Cream of Smoked Salmon Soup, 341	4	380	26	6	28	70	860	40	26	2	2	22	38	32	10
Egg Drop Soup, 346	4	70	7	1	4	140	290	10	4	0	0	6	12	2	4
Fish Broth, per cup, 335		70	3	2	0	10	420	4	0	0	0	0	2	0	2
Gazpacho, 347	8	90	2	11	4	0	370	2	14	60	4	2	4	2	6
Golden Onion Soup, 345	6	265	8	21	17	5	960	12	12	10	4	4	8	8	6
Hamburger Minestrone, 336	6	325	23	27	15	55	720	34	20	26	14	14	24	12	20
Hearty Tomato Soup, 345	8	200	5	20	12	28	830	8	32	50	8	10	8	10	10
Hoppin' John Soup, 342	6	190	16	29	2	15	690	24	40	40	30	12	10	14	30
Manhattan Clam Chowder, 341	5	210	7	17	13	15	610	10	10	14	4	4	10	4	28
Mulligatawny Soup, 339	6	345	33	10	19	90	1020	50	84	24	8	16	56	2	12
New England Clam Chowder, 340	4	345	22	22	19	25	1180	34	4	4	4	18	16	18	38
Oyster Soup, 339	4	260	12	10	19	65	408	18	22	22	10	22	10	26	26
Poppy Seed Soup, 346	6	225	6	17	11	20	150	8	4	0	8	10	0	30	

PER SERVING OR UNIT

NUTRITION INFORMATION

PERCENT U.S. RECOMMENDED DAILY ALLOWANCE

RECIPE, PAGE	Servings per recipe	Calories	Protein (grams)	Carbohydrate (grams)	Fat (grams)	Cholesterol (grams)	Sodium (milligrams)	Protein	Vitamin A	Vitamin C	Thiamine	Riboflavin	Niacin	Calcium	Iron
SOUPS (continued)															
Pork and Spaetzle Soup, 337	6	350	23	30	15	190	730	34	6	2	32	22	26	6	14
Senate Bean Soup, 345	12	95	6	16	1	8	660	8	0	4	10	4	6	2	4
Shrimp Gumbo, 340	6	220	14	21	10	160	870	20	42	58	24	20	22	24	22
Southwest Chicken Soup, 338	4	140	19	9	3	35	1110	28	50	80	6	8	42	2	8
Split Pea Soup, 341	8	425	30	39	17	45	830	44	100	4	60	16	24	4	18
Steak Soup with Winter Vegetables, 335	4	395	24	13	27	80	730	36	100	32	8	20	32	4	22
Sweet Potato Soup, 342	4	375	7	49	18	25	380	10	100	38	18	22	10	10	8
Turkey Tortellini Soup, 339	4	350	32	42	5	55	1070	48	32	20	34	28	48	8	20
Vegetable Beef Soup, 336	7	335	27	38	9	55	720	40	100	18	16	16	28	8	42
Vichyssoise, 344	4	240	9	24	12	30	580	12	10	16	8	18	12	18	4
Wild Rice Soup, 341	5	280	10	26	16	20	480	14	94	22	10	18	16	10	10
Wonton Soup, 346	8	175	13	17	6	22	950	20	8	2	10	8	18	0	4
SANDWICHES															
American Grilled Cheese, 353	4	75	18	26	33	60	1300	28	24	0	14	22	10	46	10
Baked Eggplant Sandwiches, 352	6	215	8	15	14	105	250	12	14	6	8	8	6	16	8
Barbecued Roast Beef Sandwiches, 348	6	375	18	29	19	60	470	28	6	6	14	14	22	6	18
Beef Salad Filling, 354	4	395	13	5	36	50	385	18	2	2	2	4	10	0	10
Brie-and-Cucumber on Rye, 356	4	370	15	14	29	60	720	22	16	12	8	20	4	14	6
Chicken Salad Filling, 354	4	300	16	2	26	45	345	24	2	2	2	4	24	0	4
Chiliburger Pies, 350	6	540	28	35	32	80	780	42	12	6	24	24	34	12	24
Club Sandwiches, 355	4	605	45	42	27	95	695	68	16	14	32	30	52	14	30
Club Waldorf Sandwich Loaf, 354	8	290	17	36	7	30	660	26	2	4	18	14	14	14	10
Denver Pocket Sandwiches, 351	6	360	23	43	11	290	935	34	10	18	18	14	8	2	8
Egg Salad Filling, 354	4	320	10	3	30	410	400	14	8	2	2	12	0	4	8
Grilled Fruit-and-Cheese Sandwiches, 353	4	445	14	27	32	35	660	20	22	2	8	18	6	34	8
Ground Beef Calzones, 351	6	550	28	56	23	115	875	42	14	28	26	26	36	14	28
Gyros, 350	4	555	34	47	30	80	665	52	18	20	8	16	24	8	18
Ham Salad Filling, 354	4	285	14	2	25	30	880	20	0	2	24	8	12	0	2
Hamburgers, 349	4	395	26	22	21	80	530	40	0	0	14	16	30	6	22
Mediterranean Sandwiches, 355	4	380	15	53	13	0	700	22	2	56	24	12	14	8	22

NUTRITION INFORMATION

PER SERVING OR UNIT

RECIPE, PAGE

Recipe, Page	Servings per recipe	Calories	Protein (grams)	Carbohydrate (grams)	Fat (grams)	Cholesterol (milligrams)	Sodium (milligrams)	Protein	Vitamin A	Vitamin C	Thiamine	Riboflavin	Niacin	Calcium	Iron
SANDWICHES (continued)															
Muffuletta, 353	6	595	26	47	33	65	1690	40	4	20	38	22	22	22	16
Pepperoni Calzones, 351	6	550	20	56	27	60	1245	30	14	28	30	24	30	12	20
Quick Barbecue Sandwiches, 348	6	195	15	23	4	35	300	22	0	0	22	10	24	6	8
Rachel Sandwiches, 351	6	565	28	32	37	75	845	42	16	10	10	16	12	34	14
Reuben Sandwiches, 351	6	610	26	31	43	80	1525	40	12	10	8	16	8	34	20
Salmon Burgers, 352	5	445	23	35	23	55	810	36	8	8	16	16	36	30	14
Shrimp Club Sandwiches, 355	4	520	19	46	30	55	665	28	22	20	32	22	28	14	26
Sloppy Joes, 349	6	335	19	27	15	55	590	28	4	16	14	14	24	6	18
Smoked Turkey Sandwich, 354	6	400	25	48	11	40	550	38	14	40	20	18	28	4	18
Southwestern Shrimp Pockets, 355	6	150	12	24	2	115	310	18	16	36	4	4	4	12	6
Submarine Sandwich, 354	6	640	30	48	36	75	1965	46	12	70	48	26	28	22	16
Super Grilled Cheese, 353	4	590	23	33	41	50	995	34	30	12	22	26	18	50	16
Tuna Salad Filling, 354	4	270	15	2	22	35	760	22	2	2	0	2	34	0	4
Zucchini and Cream Cheese Sandwiches, 356	4	380	7	15	33	65	525	10	30	8	6	8	4	8	8
SAUCES															
Almond Velouté Sauce, 357	16	30	1	1	3	0	100	0	0	0	0	0	0	0	0
Applesauce-Horseradish Sauce, 359	16	10	0	1	1	2	10	0	0	0	0	0	0	0	0
Barbecue Sauce, 360	32	25	0	3	1	0	120	0	4	2	0	0	0	0	0
Béarnaise Sauce, 358	12	90	1	0	9	80	80	0	6	0	0	0	0	0	0
Bordelaise Sauce, 357	16	45	1	6	1	0	75	0	0	0	2	0	2	0	0
Brown Sauce, 357	16	40	1	6	1	0	100	0	0	0	2	0	2	0	0
Cheese Sauce, 357	21	30	1	1	2	5	60	0	0	0	0	0	0	2	0
Creamy Gravy, 358	16	15	0	1	1	0	65	0	0	0	0	0	0	0	0
Curry Sauce, 357	16	25	1	1	2	0	60	0	0	0	0	0	0	0	0
Dill Sauce, 357	16	25	1	0	2	0	60	0	0	0	0	0	0	2	0
Eggplant-Tomato Chutney, 361	56	10	0	1	1	0	20	0	0	0	0	0	0	0	0
Garlic Sauce, 361	20	45	0	1	5	15	75	0	2	0	0	0	0	0	0
Giblet Gravy, 358	16	35	3	1	2	15	100	4	0	0	0	2	2	0	2
Hollandaise Sauce, 358	12	85	1	0	9	80	80	0	6	0	0	0	0	0	0
Honey-Mustard Spread, 359	10	85	0	2	9	0	80	0	0	0	0	0	0	0	0

NUTRITION INFORMATION

PER SERVING OR UNIT

RECIPE, PAGE

	Servings per recipe	Calories	Protein (grams)	Carbohydrate (grams)	Fat (grams)	Cholesterol (milligrams)	Sodium (milligrams)	PERCENT U.S. RECOMMENDED DAILY ALLOWANCE							
								Protein	Vitamin A	Vitamin C	Thiamine	Riboflavin	Niacin	Calcium	Iron

SAUCES (continued)

	Servings per recipe	Calories	Protein (g)	Carbohydrate (g)	Fat (g)	Cholesterol (mg)	Sodium (mg)	Protein	Vitamin A	Vitamin C	Thiamine	Riboflavin	Niacin	Calcium	Iron
Italian Tomato Sauce, 360	32	15	0	2	1	0	80	0	2	6	0	0	0	0	0
Lemon Curd, 362	32	40	1	7	2	30	20	0	0	0	0	0	0	0	0
Maltaise Sauce, 358	12	85	1	0	9	80	80	0	6	0	0	0	0	0	0
Mixed Berry Jam, 362	80	40	0	11	0	0	0	0	0	0	0	0	0	0	0
Mousseline Sauce, 358	12	100	1	0	11	85	85	0	6	0	0	0	0	0	0
Mushroom Gravy, 358	16	20	1	1	1	0	95	0	0	0	0	0	0	0	0
Mushroom Sauce, 357	16	50	1	6	2	0	110	0	0	0	2	2	2	0	0
Mushroom-Wine Sauce, 359	16	55	0	1	4	15	30	0	2	0	2	0	0	0	0
Mustard Sauce, 359	16	20	1	1	1	0	55	0	0	0	0	0	0	2	0
Pan Gravy, 358	16	20	1	1	1	0	90	0	0	0	0	0	0	0	0
Papaya Chutney, 361	20	20	0	4	1	0	2	0	8	12	0	0	0	0	0
Peanut Sauce, 360	28	50	2	3	3	0	15	2	0	0	0	0	4	2	0
Pesto, 359	20	95	2	2	9	5	60	2	4	2	0	0	0	8	6
Piquant Sauce, 357	16	50	1	6	1	0	105	0	0	0	2	0	2	0	0
Prune-Almond Sauce, 360	32	40	1	6	1	0	0	0	2	0	0	0	0	0	0
Raisin Sauce, 360	32	20	0	6	0	0	0	0	0	0	0	0	0	0	0
Rosy Grape Jelly, 362	80	35	0	10	0	0	0	0	0	0	0	0	0	0	0
Sweet-and-Sour Sauce, 358	40	20	0	4	0	0	35	0	0	4	0	0	0	0	0
Tartar Sauce, 359	16	100	0	0	11	0	95	0	0	0	0	0	0	0	0
Thick White Sauce, 357	16	40	1	2	3	0	75	0	2	0	0	0	0	2	0
Thin Gravy, 358	16	10	0	0	1	0	85	0	0	0	0	0	0	0	0
Thin White Sauce, 357	16	15	0	1	1	0	50	0	0	0	0	0	0	0	0
Velouté Sauce, 357	16	20	0	1	1	0	100	0	0	0	0	0	0	0	0
Whipped Horseradish Sauce, 359	20	30	0	1	3	10	10	0	2	0	0	0	0	0	0
White Sauce, 357	16	25	1	1	2	0	60	0	0	0	0	0	0	0	0

VEGETABLES

VEGETABLES

Vegetables have come into their own, with a splendid variety in the average supermarket and year 'round availability. Here are recipes for the classics we love, along with recipes that showcase vegetables in bright, new ways. For delicious and unusual dishes, try Leek Rolls with Tarragon Mustard (page 385), Stir-fried Zucchini and Jicama (page 399) and Cajun Okra Slices (page 386). With all these recipes to try, we're sure you won't have to remind people to eat their vegetables!

VEGETABLE BASICS

Today supermarkets, grocery stores and farmers' markets have an array of fresh, frozen and canned vegetables. With just a few exceptions, consumers can have their favorite vegetables year 'round. For fresh vegetables, look under the specific vegetable heading in this chaper for selection, preparation and cooking guidelines. Frozen vegetables should be cooked according to package directions and are available in many interesting combinations. Commercially canned vegetables can be heated, undrained, until hot and then drained before serving.

VEGETABLE DONENESS

Cooking vegetables to the proper doneness can mean the difference between a tasty, inviting side dish or vegetables that are overcooked—too soft—or undercooked—too raw and hard to eat. Vegetables such as potatoes, eggplants, peas, mushrooms and greens should be cooked until tender. Other vegetables, such as broccoli, beans, carrots and bell peppers, should be cooked until crisp-tender. Cooking certain types of vegetables until crisp-tender not only keeps the color of the vegetable bright but also retains more vitamins and minerals than cooking for a longer period. When cooking vegetables, be sure to check them at the minimum cooking time, then add additional time, if necessary, until you reach desired doneness.

VEGETABLE ACCOMPANIMENTS

Below are several ways to enhance vegetables.

CRUMB TOPPINGS

Sprinkle these toppings over hot cooked or creamed vegetables.

Bread Topping: Mix ¼ cup dry bread crumbs, 1½ teaspoons margarine or butter, melted, and dash of salt.

Corn Bread Topping: Mix ¼ cup dry corn bread crumbs, 1½ teaspoons margarine or butter, melted, and dash of salt.

Garlic Bread Topping: Mix ¼ cup dry bread crumbs, 1½ teaspoons margarine or butter, melted, ½ small clove garlic, crushed, and dash of salt.

Herb Bread Topping: Mix ¼ cup dry bread crumbs, 1½ teaspoons margarine or butter, melted, ¾ teaspoon chopped fresh or ¼ teaspoon dried herb leaves and dash of salt.

SEASONED BUTTERS

Heat ¼ cup margarine or butter over low heat until melted, or microwave uncovered in 1-cup microwavable measure on high about 45 seconds or until hot. Stir in one of the following:

- **Almond:** 1 tablespoon chopped toasted almonds.
- **Basil:** 1 teaspoon chopped fresh or ½ teaspoon dried basil leaves.
- **Cheese:** 2 tablespoons grated Parmesan cheese.
- **Chive-Parsley:** 1 tablespoon chopped chives and 1 tablespoon chopped parsley.
- **Curry:** ¼ teaspoon curry powder.
- **Garlic:** ½ small clove garlic, crushed, or ½ teaspoon garlic powder.

♦ *Horseradish:* 1 tablespoon prepared horseradish.

♦ *Lemon:* 1 tablespoon grated lemon peel and 2 tablespoons lemon juice.

♦ *Mustard-Dill:* ¼ teaspoon dry mustard and 1 teaspoon fresh or ¼ teaspoon dried dill weed.

♦ *Sesame-Soy:* 1 tablespoon sesame seed and 2 tablespoons soy sauce.

SAUCES

Adding a sauce to any plain cooked vegetable makes it extra special. Prepare and cook your favorite vegetable as directed and then serve with one of these delicious sauces. Or if you're short on time, drizzle vegetables (raw or cooked) with bottled salad dressings or sauces.

♦ Hollandaise Sauce, page 358.

♦ Cheese Sauce, page 357.

♦ Dill Sauce, page 357.

♦ Mustard Sauce, page 359.

♦ Italian Tomato Sauce, page 360.

ARTICHOKES, GLOBE

4 medium yield 4 servings; 75 calories per serving.

WHEN SHOPPING: Look for plump globes that are heavy in relation to their size. Globes should be compact with inner leaves fresh and green.

TO PREPARE: Remove any discolored leaves and the small leaves at base of artichoke. Trim stem even with base of artichoke. Cutting straight across, slice 1 inch off top and discard top. Snip off points of the remaining leaves with scissors. Rinse artichoke with cold water. Invert in cold water with small amount of lemon juice to prevent discoloration. Or if artichoke is to be filled with seafood or meat mixture and baked, remove some of the center leaves and the choke before cooking. (Choke is the fuzzy growth covering artichoke heart.)

TO BOIL: Heat 6 quarts water, 2 tablespoons lemon juice and 1 clove garlic, cut into fourths, to boiling in large kettle. Add artichokes. Heat to boiling; reduce heat. Boil uncovered 30 to 40 minutes, rotating occasionally, until leaves pull out easily and bottom is tender when pierced with a knife. Remove artichokes carefully with tongs or 2 large spoons and place upside down to drain.

TO STEAM: Place steamer basket in ½ inch water (water should not touch bottom of basket). Place artichokes in basket. Cover tightly and heat to boiling; reduce heat. Steam 20 to 25 minutes or until bottom is tender when pierced with knife.

TO MICROWAVE: Place artichokes, 1 cup water, 1 teaspoon lemon juice and 1 small clove garlic, cut into fourths, in 3-quart microwavable casserole. Cover tightly and microwave on high 14 to 20 minutes, rotating casserole ½ turn after 7 minutes, until leaves pull out easily. Remove artichokes carefully with tongs or 2 large spoons and place upside down to drain.

ARTICHOKES WITH ROSEMARY SAUCE

Don't let the appearance of an artichoke mystify you; they are very easy to eat. Pull out a leaf and draw it between your teeth, scraping off the meaty portion. Continue until all the leaves are gone and you see the small center cone of light green leaves. Pull off, or cut the leaves from the cone, slice off and discard the fuzzy choke and a meaty portion will be visible. Savor this final treat—it's the heart of the artichoke.

> 4 medium globe artichokes
> ½ cup margarine or butter
> 1 teaspoon chopped fresh or ¼ teaspoon dried rosemary leaves, crushed*
> 1 teaspoon lemon juice

Prepare and steam artichokes as directed (left). While artichokes are steaming, heat margarine until melted. Stir in rosemary and lemon juice. Pluck leaves out one at a time. To serve, dip base of leaf into rosemary mixture.   4 SERVINGS; 360 CALORIES PER SERVING.

*Any herb can be substituted for the rosemary.

ARTICHOKES, JERUSALEM

4 medium (about 1 pound) yield 4 servings;
105 calories per serving.

WHEN SHOPPING: Look for smooth, firm tubers with the fewest knobs. Tubers should be light colored and free of blotches, green-tinged areas and sprouts.

TO PREPARE: Scrub artichokes; pare thinly if desired. Leave whole or cut into ¼-inch slices or ½-inch cubes. Place in water with small amount of lemon juice to prevent discoloration.

TO BOIL: Heat 1 inch water (salted, if desired) to boiling. Add artichokes. Cover and heat to boiling; reduce heat. Boil whole artichokes 20 to 25 minutes, slices and cubes 7 to 9 minutes or until crisp-tender; drain.

TO STEAM: Place steamer basket in ½ inch water (water should not touch bottom of basket). Place artichokes in basket. Cover tightly and heat to boiling; reduce heat. Steam 15 to 20 minutes or until crisp-tender.

TO MICROWAVE: Place artichoke slices and ¼ cup water in 1½-quart microwavable casserole. Cover tightly and microwave on high 6 to 7 minutes, stirring after 5 minutes, until crisp-tender. Let stand covered 5 minutes; drain.

HORSERADISH-SAUCED ARTICHOKES

The Jerusalem artichoke is also known as the sunchoke. It is actually not an artichoke but a type of sunflower. Native Americans introduced early settlers to this root vegetable, and they used it in much the same way as they did turnips.

> 1 pound Jerusalem artichokes
> ½ cup sour cream or plain yogurt
> 1 tablespoon all-purpose flour
> 1 tablespoon prepared horseradish
> ¼ teaspoon salt
> ¼ teaspoon pepper
> 1 tablespoon vegetable oil
> 1 medium stalk celery, sliced (about ½ cup)
> 2 cups finely chopped spinach or greens

Prepare and cook cubed artichokes as directed (above). Mix sour cream, flour, horseradish, salt and pepper; reserve. Heat oil in 10-inch skillet over medium heat. Stir in artichokes and celery. Cook 5 minutes, stirring occasionally, until celery is crisp-tender. Stir in spinach. Cook just until spinach is wilted. Stir in sour cream mixture. Heat until hot. 4 SERVINGS (ABOUT ½ CUP EACH); 115 CALORIES PER SERVING.

ASPARAGUS

1½ pounds yield 4 servings; 45 calories per serving.

WHEN SHOPPING: Look for smooth, round, tender, medium-size green spears with closed tips.

TO PREPARE: Break off tough ends where they snap easily. Wash asparagus; remove scales if sandy or tough. (If necessary, remove sand particles with a vegetable brush.) For spears, tie whole stalks in bundles with string, or hold together with band of aluminum foil. Or cut each stalk into 1-inch pieces.

TO BOIL: *Spears:* Heat 1 inch water (salted, if desired) to boiling in deep, narrow pan. Place asparagus upright in pan. Heat to boiling; reduce heat. Boil uncovered 5 minutes. Cover and boil 7 to 10 minutes longer or until stalk ends are crisp-tender; drain. *Pieces:* Heat 1 inch water (salted, if desired) to boiling. Add lower stalk pieces. Heat to boiling; reduce heat. Boil uncovered 6 minutes. Add tips. Cover and boil 5 to 8 minutes longer or until crisp-tender; drain.

TO STEAM: Place steamer basket in ½ inch water (water should not touch bottom of basket). Place asparagus (spears) in basket. Cover tightly and heat to boiling; reduce heat. Steam 6 to 8 minutes or until crisp-tender.

TO MICROWAVE: *Spears:* Place asparagus and ¼ cup water in square microwavable dish, 8 × 8 × 2 inches. Cover tightly and microwave on high 6 to 9 minutes, rotating dish ½ turn after 3 minutes, until crisp-tender. Let stand covered 1 minute; drain. *Pieces:* Place asparagus and ¼ cup water in 1½-quart microwavable casserole. Cover tightly and microwave on high 6 to 9 minutes, stirring after 3 minutes, until crisp-tender. Let stand covered 1 minute; drain.

ASPARAGUS WITH BACON

> 1½ pounds asparagus, diagonally cut into 1-inch pieces*
> 2 tablespoons chopped fresh parsley
> 2 teaspoons lemon juice
> ¼ teaspoon salt
> 2 slices bacon, crisply cooked and crumbled

Prepare and steam asparagus pieces as directed (above). Mix asparagus, parsley, lemon juice and salt. Sprinkle with bacon. 4 SERVINGS (ABOUT ¾ CUP EACH); 35 CALORIES PER SERVING.

*2 packages (10 ounces each) frozen cut asparagus, cooked and drained, can be substituted for the fresh asparagus.

Green Bean Stir-Fry with Hoisin Sauce (page 372), Asparagus and Endive with Orange Sauce

ASPARAGUS AND ENDIVE WITH ORANGE SAUCE

The delicate pale green of the endive offsets the more dramatic green of the asparagus.

2 small heads Belgian endive
½ pound asparagus
⅓ cup half-and-half
¼ cup chicken broth
1 teaspoon finely shredded orange peel
1 tablespoon chopped fresh parsley
2 tablespoons orange juice
¼ teaspoon salt

Wash endive; separate leaves. Prepare and steam asparagus spears as directed (page 370)—except add endive. While vegetables are cooking, heat remaining ingredients to boiling in 1-quart saucepan; reduce heat. Simmer uncovered about 13 minutes or until sauce is reduced by half. Pour over cooked vegetables. Garnish with orange zest if desired.   4 SERVINGS; 50 CALORIES PER SERVING.

BEANS, GREEN AND WAX

1 pound yields 4 serings; 40 calories per serving.

WHEN SHOPPING: Look for bright, smooth, crisp pods. Just-picked beans will feel pliable and velvety.

TO PREPARE: Wash beans; remove ends. Leave beans whole or cut crosswise into 1-inch pieces.

TO BOIL: Place beans in 1 inch water (salted, if desired). Heat to boiling; reduce heat. Boil uncovered 5 minutes. Cover and boil 5 to 10 minutes longer or until crisp-tender; drain.

TO STEAM: Place steamer basket in ½ inch water (water should not touch bottom of basket). Place beans in basket. Cover tightly and heat to boiling; reduce heat. Steam 10 to 12 minutes or until crisp-tender.

TO MICROWAVE: Place beans (pieces) and ½ cup water in 1½-quart microwavable casserole. Cover tightly and microwave on high 9 to 12 minutes, stirring every 5 minutes, until crisp-tender. Let stand covered 5 minutes; drain.

PIQUANT GREEN BEANS

¾ pound green beans*
6 medium radishes, cut into fourths
2 sprigs parsley
¼ teaspoon salt
¼ teaspoon mustard seed
1 tablespoon margarine or butter
2 teaspoons lime juice

Prepare and cook green bean pieces as directed (page 371). Place radishes and parsley in blender. Cover and blend on high speed about 20 seconds, stopping blender frequently to scrape sides, until finely chopped. Cook radish mixture, salt and mustard seed in margarine over medium heat about 5 minutes, stirring occasionally, until hot. Mix radish mixture, beans and lime juice.   4 SERVINGS (ABOUT ⅔ CUP EACH); 60 CALORIES PER SERVING.

1 package (10 ounces each) frozen cut green beans, cooked and drained, can be substituted for the fresh green beans.

GREEN BEAN STIR-FRY WITH HOISIN SAUCE

1 pound green beans
2 tablespoons hoisin sauce
2 tablespoons dry sherry or chicken broth
1 teaspoon cornstarch
1 tablespoon vegetable oil
1 cup bean sprouts

Prepare green bean pieces as directed (page 371). Mix hoisin sauce, sherry and cornstarch.

Heat wok or 12-inch skillet until hot. Add oil and tilt wok to coat side. Add beans and bean sprouts. Stir-fry about 8 minutes or until beans are crisp-tender. Stir in hoisin sauce mixture. Cook and stir about 10 seconds or until thickened.   4 SERVINGS (ABOUT ¾ CUP EACH); 90 CALORIES PER SERVING.

GINGERED WAX BEANS

So simple—the beans absorb the spicy ginger flavor while steaming.

1 pound wax beans
8 thin slices gingerroot
1 tablespoon teriyaki sauce

Prepare and steam whole wax beans as directed (page 371)—except add gingerroot slices. Remove gingerroot after cooking. Mix beans and teriyaki sauce.   6 SERVINGS (ABOUT ⅔ CUP EACH); 35 CALORIES PER SERVING.

BEANS, LIMA

3 pounds (unshelled) yield 4 servings; 160 calories per serving.

WHEN SHOPPING: Look for broad, thick, shiny pods that are plump with large seeds.

TO PREPARE: Wash lima beans. Shell just before cooking. To shell beans, remove thin outer edge of pod with sharp knife or scissors. Slip out beans.

TO BOIL: Heat 1 inch water (salted, if desired) to boiling. Add beans. Heat to boiling; reduce heat. Boil uncovered 5 minutes. Cover and boil 15 to 20 minutes longer or until tender; drain.

TO MICROWAVE: Place lima beans and ½ cup water in 1-quart microwavable casserole. Cover tightly and microwave on high 16 to 18 minutes, stirring every 6 minutes, until tender. Let stand covered 1 minute; drain.

SUCCOTASH

Native Americans taught the early settlers how to make succotash, a name that combines several Narragansett words. This delightful mix was made from fresh vegetables in summer, dried vegetables in winter.

3 pounds lima beans*
4 ears corn*
3 slices bacon, cut up
1 small onion, chopped (about ¼ cup)
½ cup half-and-half
¼ teaspoon salt
⅛ teaspoon pepper

Prepare lima beans as directed (above). Prepare corn as directed (page 380). Cut enough kernels from corn to measure 2 cups; reserve. Heat beans, bacon, onion and enough water to cover to boiling in 3-quart saucepan; reduce heat. Cover and simmer 20 to 25 minutes or until beans are tender. Stir in corn. Heat to boiling; reduce heat. Cover and simmer about 5 minutes or until corn is tender; drain. Stir in half-and-half, salt and pepper. Heat, stirring occasionally, until hot.   6 SERVINGS (ABOUT ⅔ CUP EACH); 190 CALORIES PER SERVING.

2 packages (9 ounces each) frozen lima beans can be substituted for the fresh lima beans and 2 cups frozen corn can be substituted for the fresh corn. Heat beans, bacon, onion and enough water to cover to boiling in 3-quart saucepan; reduce heat. Cover and simmer 5 minutes. Stir in corn. Heat to boiling; reduce heat. Cover and simmer about 3 minutes or until beans and corn are tender. Continue as directed.

BEETS

5 medium (about 1¼ pounds) yield 4 servings; 65 calories per serving.

WHEN SHOPPING: Look for firm, round, smooth beets of a deep red color with fresh unwilted tops.

TO PREPARE: Cut off all but 1 inch of beet tops. Wash beets; leave whole with root ends attached.

TO BOIL: Heat 6 cups water, 1 tablespoon vinegar (to preserve color) and salt (if desired) to boiling. Add beets. Cover and heat to boiling; reduce heat. Boil 40 to 50 minutes or until tender; drain. Run cold water over beets; slip off skins and remove root ends. Slice, dice or cut into julienne strips.

TO STEAM: Place steamer basket in ½ inch water (water should not touch bottom of basket). Place beets in basket. Cover tightly and heat to boiling; reduce heat. Steam 45 to 50 minutes or until tender. Add boiling water during steaming if necessary. Run cold water over beets; slip off skins and remove root ends. Slice, dice or cut into julienne strips.

TO MICROWAVE: Place beets and ½ cup water in 1½-quart microwavable casserole. Cover tightly and microwave on high 18 to 25 minutes, stirring every 5 minutes, until tender. Let stand covered 5 minutes. Run cold water over beets; slip off skins and remove root ends.

HARVARD BEETS

No one knows exactly how these beets received their name, but it's a safe bet that it's connected to the best known of Harvard's colors—crimson.

> 5 medium beets (about 1¼ pounds)*
> 1 tablespoon cornstarch
> 1 tablespoon sugar
> ½ teaspoon salt
> Dash of pepper
> ⅔ cup water
> ¼ cup vinegar

Prepare and cook beets as directed (left). Cut into slices. Mix cornstarch, sugar, salt and pepper in 2-quart saucepan. Gradually stir in water and vinegar. Cook, stirring constantly, until mixture thickens and boils. Boil and stir 1 minute. Stir in beets. Heat.   4 SERVINGS; 45 CALORIES PER SERVING.

*1 can (16 ounces) sliced beets, drained and liquid reserved, can be substituted for the fresh beets. Add enough water to reserved liquid to measure ⅔ cup. Substitute beet liquid for the water.

YALE BEETS: Substitute packed brown sugar for the sugar and ¾ cup orange juice for the ⅔ cup water. Mix in 1 teaspoon grated orange peel with the sugar. Decrease vinegar to 1 tablespoon.   65 CALORIES PER SERVING.

Harvard Beets

GINGER-PEAR BEETS

5 medium beets (about 1¼ pounds)*
1 can (6 ounces) pear nectar
1 teaspoon cornstarch
1 tablespoon honey
1 teaspoon grated gingerroot or ¼ teaspoon ground ginger
¼ teaspoon salt

Prepare and cook beets as directed (page 373). Cut into julienne strips. Mix pear nectar and cornstarch in 1-quart saucepan. Stir in honey, gingerroot and salt. Heat to boiling, stirring constantly. Boil and stir 1 minute. Serve over beets. 4 SERVINGS (ABOUT ¾ CUP EACH); 70 CALORIES PER SERVING.

*1 can (16 ounces) sliced beets, drained, can be substituted for the fresh beets. Heat until hot.

BOK CHOY

1½ pounds yield 4 servings; 20 calories per serving.

WHEN SHOPPING: Look for firm, white stalks and shiny, dark leaves.

TO PREPARE: Wash bok choy; cut off leaves. Cut stems into ¼-inch slices; cut leaves into ½-inch strips.

TO BOIL: Heat 1 inch water (salted, if desired) to boiling. Add bok choy stems. Cover and heat to boiling; reduce heat. Boil 5 minutes. Add bok choy leaves. Cover and boil 2 to 3 minutes or until stems are crisp-tender; drain.

TO STEAM: Place steamer basket in ½ inch water (water should not touch bottom of basket). Place bok choy stems in basket. Cover tightly and heat to boiling; reduce heat. Steam 5 minutes. Add bok choy leaves. Steam 2 to 3 minutes or until stems are crisp-tender.

TO MICROWAVE: Place bok choy stems and 2 tablespoons water in 3-quart microwavable casserole. Cover tightly and microwave on high 4 minutes. Stir in bok choy leaves. Cover tightly and microwave 3 to 4 minutes or until stems are crisp-tender. Let stand covered 1 minute; drain.

BOK CHOY WITH TOFU

Bok choy, also known as Chinese chard, is a favorite in Asian cuisines. It resembles a cross between chard and cabbage.

1 pound tofu
4 medium stalks bok choy
4 green onions (with tops)
2 tablespoons vegetable oil
2 tablespoons vegetable oil
1 can (4 ounces) button mushrooms, drained and liquid reserved
3 tablespoons oyster sauce
1 tablespoon cornstarch
1 tablespoon cold water

Cut tofu into ¾-inch cubes; drain thoroughly. Cut bok choy (stems and leaves) diagonally into ¼-inch slices. Cut onions into 2-inch pieces.

Heat 2 tablespoons oil in wok or 10-inch skillet over medium-high heat until hot. Cook tofu 5 minutes, stirring carefully; remove tofu. Add 2 tablespoons oil, the bok choy and onions to wok. Cook over medium-high heat 2 minutes. Stir in mushrooms.

Add enough water to reserved mushroom liquid to measure ½ cup. Stir mushroom liquid and oyster sauce into vegetables. Heat to boiling. Mix cornstarch and water; stir into vegetable mixture. Cook and stir about 1 minute or until thickened. Stir in tofu and onions. Heat until hot. 8 SERVINGS; 135 CALORIES PER SERVING.

BROCCOLI

The Romans called broccoli the "five fingers of Jupiter," in honor of their chief deity, and they had reason to equate broccoli with mythical, superhuman qualities due to its excellent nutritive values. Thomas Jefferson brought broccoli to America from Italy in the early 1800s and grew it in his garden at Monticello. However, broccoli did not become widely known for many years. Italian immigrants grew broccoli in their home gardens for personal enjoyment, but it wasn't until 1920 that a group of Italian farmers in California decided to test the marketability of the vegetable. They sent a trial shipment to Boston where it was an immediate hit, and from there the popularity of broccoli grew.

BROCCOLI

1½ pounds yield 4 servings; 55 calories per serving.

WHEN SHOPPING: Look for firm, compact dark green clusters. Avoid thick, tough stems.

TO PREPARE: Trim off large leaves; remove tough ends of lower stems. Wash broccoli; peel if desired. For spears, cut lengthwise into ½-inch-wide stalks. For pieces, cut lengthwise into ½-inch-wide stalks, then cut crosswise into 1-inch pieces.

TO BOIL: Heat 1 inch water (salted, if desired) to boiling. Add broccoli (spears or pieces). Cover and heat to boiling; reduce heat. Boil 10 to 12 minutes or until crisp-tender; drain.

TO STEAM: Place steamer basket in ½ inch water (water should not touch bottom of basket). Place broccoli in basket. Cover tightly and heat to boiling; reduce heat. Steam 10 to 11 minutes or until stems are crisp-tender.

TO MICROWAVE: *Spears:* Arrange broccoli, flowerets in center, and 1 cup water in square microwavable dish, 8×8×2 inches. Cover tightly and microwave on high 9 to 11 minutes, rotating dish ¼ turn every 4 minutes, until crisp-tender. Let stand covered 5 minutes; drain. *Pieces:* Place broccoli and 1 cup water in 2-quart microwavable casserole. Cover tightly and microwave on high 9 to 11 minutes, stirring every 4 minutes, until crisp-tender. Let stand covered 5 minutes; drain.

BROCCOLI WITH CHEESE

    1½ pounds broccoli*
    6 ounces process American cheese, sliced
    ⅓ cup milk
    ¼ teaspoon onion salt
    1 drop red pepper sauce, if desired

Prepare and cook broccoli spears as directed (above). Heat remaining ingredients over medium heat 6 to 8 minutes, stirring frequently, until cheese is melted and mixture is smooth. Pour over broccoli.   4 SERVINGS; 210 CALORIES PER SERVING.

*1 package (10 ounces) frozen broccoli spears, cooked and drained, can be substituted for the fresh broccoli.

HERBED BROCCOLI

    1 pound broccoli*
    2 tablespoons olive or vegetable oil
    1 teaspoon chopped fresh or ¼ teaspoon dried basil leaves
    1 teaspoon chopped fresh or ¼ teaspoon dried oregano leaves
    ½ teaspoon salt
    1 clove garlic, crushed
    2 plum tomatoes, chopped

Prepare and cook broccoli pieces as directed (left). Heat oil in 10-inch skillet over medium heat. Add basil, oregano, salt, garlic and tomatoes. Heat about 1 minute, stirring frequently, until hot. Pour over broccoli and mix gently.   4 SERVINGS (ABOUT 1 CUP EACH); 90 CALORIES PER SERVING.

*2 packages (10 ounces each) frozen chopped broccoli, cooked and drained, can be substituted for the fresh broccoli.

BROCCOLI AND PASTA TOSS

For variety, try different pasta shapes, such as wheels, tubes or bows. Chose pasta of similar size so their cooking times will be compatible, if you decide to use varied types of pasta in the same dish.

    1 pound broccoli
    4 ounces uncooked spiral macaroni (about 1½ cups)
    ¾ cup milk
    1 package (3 ounces) cream cheese, softened
    2 teaspoons chopped fresh chives
    2 teaspoons prepared mustard
    ½ teaspoon salt

Prepare and cook broccoli pieces as directed (left). While broccoli is cooking, prepare pasta as directed on package; drain. Heat remaining ingredients, stirring occasionally until smooth. Mix with macaroni and broccoli.   6 SERVINGS (ABOUT ⅔ CUP EACH); 115 CALORIES PER SERVING.

BRUSSELS SPROUTS

1 pound yields 4 servings; 55 calories per serving.

WHEN SHOPPING: Look for unblemished, bright green sprouts with compact leaves.

TO PREPARE: Remove any discolored leaves; cut off stem ends. Wash sprouts; cut large ones in half.

TO BOIL: Heat 1 inch water (salted, if desired) to boiling. Add Brussels sprouts. Cover and heat to boiling; reduce heat. Boil 8 to 10 minutes or until tender; drain.

TO STEAM: Place steamer basket in ½ inch water (water should not touch bottom of basket). Place Brussels sprouts in basket. Cover tightly and heat to boiling; reduce heat. Steam 20 to 25 minutes or until tender.

TO MICROWAVE: Place Brussels sprouts and ¼ cup water in 1½-quart microwavable casserole. Cover tightly and microwave on high 8 to 11 minutes, stirring after 5 minutes, until tender. Let stand covered 5 minutes; drain.

BRUSSELS SPROUTS WITH MUSTARD VINAIGRETTE

    1 pound Brussels sprouts*
    2 tablespoons coarse-grained mustard
    2 tablespoons Nut-flavored Oil (page 328)
      or vegetable oil
    1 green onion (with top), thinly sliced (about
      1 tablespoon)
    1 clove garlic, finely chopped
    ¼ teaspoon salt

Prepare and cook Brussels sprouts as directed (above). Shake remaining ingredients in tightly covered container. Toss with Brussels sprouts. 4 SERVINGS (ABOUT 1 CUP EACH); 110 CALORIES PER SERVING.

2 packages (10 ounces each) frozen Brussels sprouts, cooked and drained, can be substituted for the fresh Brussels sprouts.

BRUSSELS SPROUTS IN ORANGE SAUCE

    1 pound Brussels sprouts*
    2 tablespoons margarine or butter
    2 tablespoons orange-flavored liqueur
      or orange juice
    ¼ teaspoon salt

Prepare and cook Brussels sprouts as directed (above). Heat remaining ingredients until margarine is melted. Heat 1 minute longer. Toss with Brussels sprouts. 4 SERVINGS (ABOUT 1 CUP EACH); 95 CALORIES PER SERVING.

2 packages (10 ounces each) frozen Brussels sprouts, cooked and drained, can be substituted for the fresh Brussels sprouts.

CABBAGE, RED AND GREEN

*1 pound (1 small head) yields 4 servings;
25 calories per serving.*

WHEN SHOPPING: Look for firm heads that are heavy in relation to size. Outer leaves should have good color and be free of blemishes.

TO PREPARE: Remove outside leaves. Wash cabbage; cut into 4 wedges. Trim core to within ¼ inch of leaves, or shred cabbage and discard core.

TO BOIL: *Wedges:* Heat 1 inch water (salted, if desired) to boiling. Add cabbage (and 2 tablespoons vinegar or lemon juice for red cabbage). Cover and heat to boiling; reduce heat. Boil 10 to 17 minutes, turning wedges once, until crisp-tender; drain. *Shredded:* Heat ½ inch water (salted, if desired) to boiling. Add cabbage (and 2 tablespoons vinegar or lemon juice for red cabbage). Cover and heat to boiling; reduce heat. Boil 5 to 8 minutes or until crisp-tender; drain.

TO STEAM: *Wedges:* Place steamer basket in ½ inch water (water should not touch bottom of basket). Place cabbage in basket. Cover tightly and heat to boiling; reduce heat. Steam 18 to 24 minutes or until crisp-tender. *Shredded:* Place steamer basket in ½ inch water (water should not touch bottom of basket). Place cabbage in basket. Cover tightly and heat to boiling; reduce heat. Steam 5 to 7 minutes or until crisp-tender.

TO MICROWAVE: *Wedges:* Place cabbage wedges, core ends at outside edge, and ½ cup water in 2-quart microwavable casserole. Cover tightly and microwave on high 10 to 14 minutes, rotating casserole after 5 minutes, until crisp-tender. Let stand covered 5 minutes; drain. *Shredded:* Place shredded cabbage and ¼ cup water in 2-quart microwavable casserole. Cover tightly and microwave on high 8 to 10 minutes, stirring after 4 minutes, until crisp-tender. Let stand covered 5 minutes; drain.

HOT ORIENTAL SLAW

1 small head cabbage (about 1 pound)
2 tablespoons sugar
1 tablespoon cornstarch
2 tablespoons vinegar
1 teaspoon soy sauce
1 tablespoon grated gingerroot or 1 tea-
    spoon ground ginger
1 clove garlic, finely chopped
1 tablespoon vegetable oil
2 green onions (with tops), thinly sliced
    (about 2 tablespoons)
1 medium carrot, shredded
1 medium bell pepper, chopped (about
    1 cup)

Prepare shredded cabbage as directed (page 376). Mix sugar, cornstarch, vinegar, soy sauce, gingerroot and garlic; reserve.

Heat wok or 12-inch skillet until hot. Add oil and tilt wok to coat side. Add cabbage, onions, carrot and bell pepper. Stir-fry 3 minutes. Stir in vinegar mixture. Cook and stir about 10 seconds or until thickened.   4 SERVINGS (ABOUT ¾ CUP EACH); 75 CALORIES PER SERVING.

Hot Oriental Slaw

🌾 SWEET-SOUR RED CABBAGE

German settlers brought us this hearty cab-bage dish with its tangy sweet-and-sour dressing.

1 medium head red cabbage (about
    1½ pounds)
4 slices bacon, diced
¼ cup packed brown sugar
2 tablespoons all-purpose flour
½ cup water
¼ cup vinegar
¼ teaspoon salt
⅛ teaspoon pepper
1 small onion, sliced

Prepare and cook shredded cabbage as directed (page 376). Cook bacon in 10-inch skillet over medium heat, stirring occasionally, until crisp. Remove bacon with slotted spoon. Drain fat from skillet, reserving 1 tablespoon. Stir brown sugar and flour into fat in skillet. Stir in water, vinegar, salt, pepper and onion. Cook about 5 minutes, stirring frequently, until mixture thickens.

Stir bacon and sauce mixture into hot cabbage in saucepan. Heat until hot. Garnish with additional bacon if desired.   6 SERVINGS; 105 CALORIES PER SERVING.

CABBAGE, CHINESE; CELERY OR NAPA

1 pound (1 medium head) yields 4 servings;
10 calories per serving.

WHEN SHOPPING: Look for crisp, green heads with no signs of browning. The leaves can be firm or leafy.

TO PREPARE: Remove root ends. Wash cabbage; shred.

TO BOIL: Heat ½ inch water (salted, if desired) to boiling. Add cabbage. Cover and heat to boiling; reduce heat. Boil 4 to 5 minutes or until crisp-tender; drain.

TO STEAM: Place steamer basket in ½ inch water (water should not touch bottom of basket). Place cabbage in basket. Cover tightly and heat to boiling; reduce heat. Steam 4 to 5 minutes or until tender.

TO MICROWAVE: Place cabbage and ¼ cup water in 2-quart microwavable casserole. Cover tightly and microwave on high 4 to 7 minutes, stirring after 2 minutes, until crisp-tender. Let stand covered 1 minute; drain.

CABBAGE AND SOUR CREAM

1 medium head Chinese cabbage
½ cup sour cream
1 teaspoon all-purpose flour
1 tablespoon vegetable oil
1 tablespoon margarine or butter
½ teaspoon salt
½ teaspoon ground turmeric
½ teaspoon ground ginger
⅛ teaspoon pepper

Prepare shredded cabbage as directed (page 377). Mix sour cream and flour. Heat remaining ingredients in 12-inch skillet over medium-high heat until margarine is melted. Add cabbage. Cook, stirring constantly, 2 to 3 minutes or until crisp-tender. Stir in sour cream mixture.   6 SERVINGS (ABOUT ¾ CUP EACH); 85 CALORIES PER SERVING.

To Microwave: Prepare cabbage as directed—except omit oil. Place 2 tablespoons water, ¼ teaspoon salt and the cabbage in 3-quart microwavable casserole. Cover tightly and microwave on high 6 to 8 minutes, stirring after 3 minutes, until crisp-tender; drain. Mix sour cream and flour. Stir margarine, salt, turmeric, ginger, pepper and sour cream mixture into cabbage.

CARROTS

*1 pound (6 to 7 medium) yields 4 servings;
50 calories per serving.*

WHEN SHOPPING: Look for firm, nicely shaped carrots of good color.

TO PREPARE: Pare carrots thinly and remove ends. Leave carrots whole, shred or cut into julienne strips or crosswise into ¼-inch slices.

TO BOIL: Heat 1 inch water (salted, if desired) to boiling. Add carrots. Cover and heat to boiling; reduce heat. Boil whole carrots 25 minutes, shredded 5 minutes, julienne strips 18 to 20 minutes, slices 12 to 15 minutes or until tender; drain.

TO STEAM: Place steamer basket in ½ inch water (water should not touch bottom of basket). Place carrots (slender whole or slices) in basket. Cover tightly and heat to boiling; reduce heat. Steam whole carrots 12 to 15 minutes, slices 9 to 11 minutes or until tender.

TO MICROWAVE: Place carrots (strips or slices) and ¼ cup water in 1-quart microwavable casserole. Cover tightly and microwave on high 6 to 8 minutes, stirring after 4 minutes, until tender. Let stand covered 1 minute; drain.

CARROTS WITH COCONUT

1½ pounds carrots (8 to 9 medium)
2 tablespoons margarine or butter
½ teaspoon salt
½ teaspoon ground nutmeg
¼ cup flaked coconut, toasted

Prepare and cook carrot slices as directed (left). Mix carrots, margarine, salt and nutmeg. Sprinkle with coconut.   6 SERVINGS (ABOUT ¾ CUP); 100 CALORIES PER SERVING.

CARROT-FENNEL SOUFFLÉ

2 medium carrots
¼ cup chopped fennel bulb
¼ cup margarine or butter
¼ cup all-purpose flour
1 teaspoon chopped fresh or ¼ teaspoon dried dill weed
¼ teaspoon salt
⅛ teaspoon pepper
1 cup milk
3 eggs, separated
¼ teaspoon cream of tartar

Prepare and steam carrot slices as directed (left)—except add fennel. Place carrot mixture in blender or food processor. Cover and blend, or process, until mixture is smooth.

Heat oven to 350°. Butter 6-cup soufflé dish or 1½-quart casserole. Heat margarine in 1½-quart saucepan over medium heat until melted. Stir in flour, dill weed, salt and pepper. Cook, stirring constantly, until smooth and bubbly; remove from heat. Stir in milk. Heat to boiling, stirring constantly. Boil and stir 1 minute.

Beat egg whites and cream of tartar in large bowl on high speed until stiff and dry. Beat egg yolks in medium bowl on high speed until very thick and lemon colored. Stir into white sauce mixture. Stir in carrot mixture. Stir about one-fourth of the egg whites into sauce mixture. Fold into remaining egg whites.

Carefully pour into soufflé dish. Bake 50 to 60 minutes or until knife inserted halfway between center and edge comes out clean. Carefully remove foil band and quickly divide soufflé into servings with 2 forks. Serve immediately.   4 SERVINGS; 235 CALORIES PER SERVING.

SPINACH SOUFFLÉ: Use 4-cup soufflé dish or 1-quart casserole. Prepare and cook 1 pound spinach as directed (page 383). Substitute ⅛ teaspoon ground nutmeg for the dill weed.   235 CALORIES PER SERVING.

CARROTS AND FIGS

A sweet, subtle combination of figs and caramelized almonds makes these carrots very elegant.

¼ cup slivered almonds
4 teaspoons sugar
½ teaspoon grated orange peel
1 pound carrots (6 to 7 medium)
½ cup dried figs, cut into fourths
1 tablespoon margarine or butter, softened

Cook almonds, sugar and orange peel over low heat, stirring constantly, until sugar is melted and almonds are coated; cool. Break almonds apart; reserve.

Prepare and cook carrot slices as directed (page 378)—except add figs. Mix all ingredients.   4 SERVINGS (ABOUT ¾ CUP EACH); 190 CALORIES PER SERVING.

CAULIFLOWER

2 pounds (1 medium head) yield 4 servings;
60 calories per serving.

WHEN SHOPPING: Look for clean, nonspreading flower clusters (the white portion) and green "jacket" leaves.

TO PREPARE: Remove outer leaves and stalk; cut off any discoloration. Wash cauliflower. Leave whole, cutting cone-shaped center from core, or separate into flowerets.

TO BOIL: Heat 1 inch water (salted if, desired) to boiling. Add cauliflower. Cover and heat to boiling; reduce heat. Boil whole cauliflower 20 to 25 minutes, flowerets 10 to 12 minutes or until tender; drain.

TO STEAM: Place steamer basket in ½ inch water (water should not touch bottom of basket). Place cauliflower in basket. Cover tightly and heat to boiling; reduce heat. Steam whole cauliflower 18 to 22 minutes, flowerets 6 to 8 minutes or until tender.

TO MICROWAVE: *Whole:* Place cauliflower and ¼ cup water in 2-quart microwavable casserole. Cover tightly and microwave on high 12 to 14 minutes, rotating casserole ½ turn after 6 minutes, until tender. Let stand covered 1 minute; drain. *Cauliflowerets:* Place cauliflowerets and ¼ cup water in 2-quart microwavable casserole. Cover tightly and microwave on high 12 to 14 minutes, stirring after 6 minutes, until tender. Let stand covered 1 minute; drain.

CHEESE CAULIFLOWER

1 medium head cauliflower (about 2 pounds)
2 tablespoons margarine or butter
2 tablespoons all-purpose flour
1 teaspoon dry mustard
¼ teaspoon salt
Dash of pepper
1 cup milk
1 cup shredded process sharp American cheese (4 ounces)
5 drops red pepper sauce
Paprika

Prepare and cook cauliflower as directed (left) for cauliflowerets or whole cauliflower. Heat margarine in 1½-quart saucepan over medium heat until melted. Stir in flour, mustard, salt and pepper. Cook, stirring constantly, until smooth and bubbly; remove from heat. Stir in milk. Heat to boiling, stirring constantly. Boil and stir 1 minute. Stir in cheese and pepper sauce. Cook and stir over low heat until cheese is melted. Pour over hot cauliflower. Sprinkle with paprika.   4 SERVINGS; 250 CALORIES PER SERVING.

CURRIED CAULIFOWER: Substitute 1 teaspoon curry powder for the dry mustard and omit red pepper sauce.   250 CALORIES PER SERVING.

Curried Cauliflower

SPICY PEANUT CAULIFLOWER

This spicy peanut sauce combines some of the heady spice blends of African and Asian cooking.

> 1 medium head cauliflower (about 2 pounds)
> ⅓ cup apple juice or water
> ¼ cup peanut butter
> ½ teaspoon ground ginger
> ¼ teaspoon curry powder
> ¼ teaspoon ground cumin

Prepare cauliflower—except cut into 4 wedges and steam as directed (page 379). Heat remaining ingredients over low heat until hot. (Do not allow mixture to boil.) Serve over cauliflower. 4 SERVINGS; 160 CALORIES PER SERVING.

To Microwave: Prepare cauliflower as directed. Place cauliflower and ¼ cup water in 2-quart microwavable casserole. Cover tightly and microwave on high 12 to 14 minutes or until cauliflower is tender. Let stand covered 1 minute; drain. Mix remaining ingredients in 1-cup microwavable measure. Microwave uncovered on high 1 minute to 1 minute 30 seconds, stirring every 30 seconds, until hot. Serve over cauliflower.

CELERY

1 medium bunch (about 1¼ pounds) yields 4 servings; 35 calories per serving.

WHEN SHOPPING: Look for crisp, unblemished stalks and fresh leaves.

TO PREPARE: Remove leaves and trim off root ends. Remove any coarse strings. Wash celery; cut stalks into 1-inch pieces.

TO BOIL: Heat 1 inch water (salted, if desired) to boiling. Add celery. Cover and heat to boiling; reduce heat. Boil 15 to 20 minutes or until crisp-tender; drain.

TO STEAM: Place steamer basket in ½ inch water (water should not touch bottom of basket). Place celery in basket. Cover tightly and heat to boiling; reduce heat. Steam 18 to 20 minutes or until crisp-tender.

TO MICROWAVE: Place celery and 2 tablespoons water in 1½-quart microwavable casserole. Cover tightly and microwave on high 7 to 11 minutes, stirring after 4 minutes, until crisp-tender. Let stand covered 1 minute; drain.

MEDITERRANEAN CELERY

The classic ingredients of Italian cooking are here—olives, olive oil, oregano, tomato and garlic.

> 8 stalks celery (about 1 pound)
> ¼ cup sliced ripe olives
> ¼ cup chopped fresh parsley
> 2 tablespoons olive or vegetable oil
> 1 tablespoon white wine vinegar
> 1½ teaspoons chopped fresh or ½ teaspoon dried oregano leaves
> 1 small tomato, seeded and chopped
> 1 clove garlic, crushed

Prepare and cook celery as directed (left)—except cut into ¼-inch slices and boil 3 to 5 minutes or until crisp-tender. Mix all ingredients. 6 SERVINGS (ABOUT ⅔ CUP EACH); 60 CALORIES PER SERVING.

CORN

4 ears yield 4 servings; 90 calories per serving.

WHEN SHOPPING: Look for bright green, tight-fitting husks, fresh-looking silk, plump but not too large kernels.

TO PREPARE: Refrigerate unhusked corn until ready to use. (Corn is best when eaten as soon after picking as possible.) Husk ears and remove silk just before cooking.

TO BOIL: Place corn in enough *unsalted* cold water to cover (salt toughens corn). Add 1 tablespoon sugar and 1 tablespoon lemon juice to each gallon of water, if desired. Heat to boiling. Boil uncovered 2 minutes; remove from heat. Let stand uncovered 10 minutes before serving.

TO STEAM: Place steamer basket in ½ inch water (water should not touch bottom of basket). Place corn in basket. Cover tightly and heat to boiling; reduce heat. Steam 6 to 9 minutes or until tender.

TO MICROWAVE: Place corn and ¼ cup water in square microwavable dish, 8×8×2 inches. Cover tightly and microwave on high 9 to 14 minutes, rearranging ears after 5 minutes, until tender. Let stand covered 5 minutes.

SESAME CORN

3 ears corn*
3 tablespoons margarine or butter
1 clove garlic, crushed
2 tablespoons sesame seed
2 tablespoons chopped green bell pepper
½ teaspoon salt
1 teaspoon chopped fresh or ¼ teaspoon
  dried basil leaves
⅛ teaspoon pepper

Prepare corn as directed (page 380). Cut enough kernels from ears to measure 1½ cups. Mix all ingredients in 1½-quart saucepan. Cover and cook over medium heat 15 minutes or until corn is tender.   4 SERVINGS; 165 CALORIES PER SERVING.

*1 package (10 ounces) frozen whole kernel corn can be substituted for the fresh corn. Cook 7 minutes or until corn is tender.

CORN AND CHEESE

6 ears corn*
2 tablespoons margarine or butter
1 small onion, chopped (about ¼ cup)
1 jalapeño chili, seeded and finely chopped
  (about 1 tablespoon)
½ teaspoon salt
½ cup shredded Cheddar cheese (2 ounces)

Prepare corn as directed (page 380). Cut enough kernels from corn to measure 3 cups. Heat margarine in 1½-quart saucepan over medium heat. Cook onion and chili in margarine about 2 minutes, stirring occasionally, until onion is softened. Stir in corn and salt. Cover and cook 10 to 15 minutes, stirring occasionally, until corn is tender. Stir in cheese.   6 SERVINGS; 160 CALORIES PER SERVING.

*2 packages (10 ounces each) frozen whole kernel corn can be substituted for the fresh corn. Or 2 cans (12 ounces each) vacuum-packed whole kernel corn, drained, can be substituted for the fresh corn. Heat about 5 minutes or until hot.

To Microwave: Mix corn, 2 tablespoons water, the margarine, onion, chili and salt in 2-quart microwavable casserole. Cover tightly and microwave on high 6 to 9 minutes, stirring after 3 minutes, until corn is tender. Stir in cheese.

Spicy Grilled Corn, Ratatouille (page 383)

SPICY GRILLED CORN

Try different twists on this easy corn-on-the-cob side dish. Omit the taco seasoning and substitute any fresh herb or grated orange or lemon peel, adjusting the amount to suit your taste.

4 ears corn
2 tablespoons margarine or butter
1 tablespoon taco seasoning mix or lemon
  pepper
2 tablespoons water

Husk ears and remove silk. Mix margarine and taco seasoning mix. Spread over corn. Place each ear on double thickness heavy-duty aluminum foil. Sprinkle ears with water. Wrap securely in foil and twist ends. Place ears on medium coals. Cover and grill 15 to 25 minutes, turning once, until tender.   4 SERVINGS; 145 CALORIES PER SERVING.

CORN IN THE HUSK: Omit water. Remove large outer husks. Turn back inner husks and remove silk. Spread margarine mixture over corn. Pull husks back over ears, tying with fine wire. Cover and grill corn 3 inches from medium coals 15 to 25 minutes, turning frequently, until tender.

SCALLOPED CORN

4 ears corn*
2 tablespoons margarine or butter
1 small onion, chopped (about ¼ cup)
½ small green bell pepper, chopped
2 tablespoons all-purpose flour
½ teaspoon salt
½ teaspoon paprika
¼ teaspoon dry mustard
Dash of pepper
¾ cup milk
1 egg, slightly beaten
⅓ cup cracker crumbs
1 tablespoon margarine or butter, melted

Prepare and cook corn as directed (page 380). Cut enough kernels from ears to measure 2 cups. Heat oven to 350°. Heat 2 tablespoons margarine in 1-quart saucepan over medium heat. Cook onion and bell pepper in margarine about 2 minutes, stirring occasionally, until onion is softened; remove from heat. Stir in flour, salt, paprika, mustard and pepper. Cook, stirring constantly, until mixture is bubbly; remove from heat. Gradually stir in milk. Heat to boiling, stirring constantly. Boil and stir 1 minute. Stir in corn and egg. Pour into ungreased 1-quart casserole.

Mix crumbs and 1 tablespoon melted margarine. Sprinkle over corn mixture. Bake uncovered 30 to 35 minutes or until bubbly. 4 SERVINGS; 255 CALORIES PER SERVING.

*1 package (10 ounces) frozen whole kernel corn, cooked and drained, or 1 can (16 ounces) whole kernel corn, drained, can be substituted for the fresh corn.

CHEESE SCALLOPED CORN: Fold ½ cup shredded natural Cheddar cheese into sauce mixture. 310 CALORIES PER SERVING.

CUCUMBERS

*2 medium (about 1 pound) yield 4 servings;
15 calories per serving.*

WHEN SHOPPING: Look for firm cucumbers with dark green coloring. Avoid yellowish cucumbers that are soft and pulpy.

TO PREPARE: Wash cucumbers; pare if desired and seed if desired. Cut into ½-inch slices or ½-inch pieces.

TO STEAM: Place steamer basket in ½ inch water (water should not touch bottom of basket). Place cucumber slices or pieces in basket. Cover tightly and heat to boiling; reduce heat. Steam about 5 minutes or until crisp-tender.

TO MICROWAVE: Place cucumber slices or pieces in 1½-quart microwavable casserole. Cover tightly and microwave on high 4 to 5 minutes, stirring after 2 minutes, until crisp-tender. Let stand covered 1 minute; drain.

CUCUMBER AND KALE SAUTÉ

2 medium cucumbers (about 1 pound)
1 tablespoon olive or vegetable oil
1 small onion, thinly sliced
1 clove garlic, finely chopped
2 cups torn kale pieces
2 teaspoons chopped fresh or ½ teaspoon dried basil leaves
¼ teaspoon salt
Dash of pepper

Prepare cucumbers as directed (above)—except pare; cut lengthwise in half and remove seeds. Cut each half crosswise into ¼-inch slices. Heat oil in 12-inch skillet over medium heat. Cook cucumbers, onion and garlic in oil about 4 minutes, stirring occasionally, until cucumbers are crisp-tender. Stir in remaining ingredients. Cook and stir just until kale is wilted. 4 SERVINGS; 65 CALORIES PER SERVING.

To Microwave: Omit oil. Prepare cucumbers as directed—except place cucumbers, onion, garlic, basil, salt and pepper in 2-quart microwavable casserole. Cover tightly and microwave on high 3 to 4 minutes or until cucumbers are crisp-tender. Stir in kale. Cover tightly and microwave on high 1 to 2 minutes longer or just until kale is wilted.

CUCUMBER AND TOMATO SKILLET

2 medium cucumbers (about 1 pound)
2 tablespoons margarine or butter
1 medium onion, sliced and separated into rings
2 medium tomatoes, cut into wedges
½ teaspoon salt
Dash of pepper
1 tablespoon chopped fresh or 1 teaspoon dried dill weed

Prepare cucumbers as directed (page 382)—except cut into 1-inch pieces. Heat margarine in 12-inch skillet over medium heat. Cook cucumbers and onion in margarine about 5 minutes, stirring occasionally, until cucumbers are crisp-tender. Stir in tomatoes. Sprinkle with salt and pepper. Cook, stirring occasionally, just until tomatoes are hot. Sprinkle with dill.   6 SERVINGS; 55 CALORIES PER SERVING.

EGGPLANT

1½ pounds (1 medium) yield 4 servings;
30 calories per serving.

WHEN SHOPPING: Look for smooth, glossy, taut-skinned eggplant that is free from blemishes or rust spots. Fuzzy green caps and stems should be intact and free of mold.

TO PREPARE: Just before cooking, wash eggplant; pare if desired. Cut eggplant into ½-inch cubes or ¼-inch slices.

TO BOIL: Heat small amount water (salted, if desired) to boiling. Add eggplant. Cover and heat to boiling; reduce heat. Boil 5 to 8 minutes or until tender; drain.

TO SAUTÉ: Heat 3 to 4 tablespoons margarine or butter in 10-inch skillet over medium-high heat. Sauté eggplant in margarine 5 to 10 minutes or until tender.

TO STEAM: Place steamer basket in ½ inch water (water should not touch bottom of basket). Place eggplant (slices) in basket. Cover tightly and heat to boiling; reduce heat. Steam 5 to 7 minutes or until tender.

TO MICROWAVE: *Cubes:* Place eggplant and 2 tablespoons water in 1½-quart microwavable casserole. Cover tightly and microwave on high 8 to 10 minutes, stirring every 2 minutes, until tender; drain. *Slices:* Overlap eggplant in a circle around edge of microwavable pie plate, 9 × 1¼ inches. Place 2 tablespoons water in pie plate. Cover tightly and microwave on high 5 to 7 minutes, rotating pie plate ½ turn after 3 minutes, until tender; drain.

RATATOUILLE

Ratatouille, a dish from France, features chunks of eggplant and tomatoes. Ratatouille is also delicious served cold.

1 medium eggplant (about 1½ pounds)
2 small zucchini (about ½ pound)
1 medium green bell pepper, chopped (about 1 cup)
1 medium onion, finely chopped (about ½ cup)
2 medium tomatoes, each cut into fourths
¼ cup olive or vegetable oil
1½ teaspoons salt
¼ teaspoon pepper
1 clove garlic, crushed

Prepare cubed eggplant as directed (left). Prepare sliced zucchini as directed (page 398). Cook all ingredients in 12-inch skillet over medium heat 10 to 15 minutes, stirring occasionally, until zucchini is tender.   6 SERVINGS (ABOUT 1 CUP EACH); 140 CALORIES PER SERVING.

GREENS: BEET, CHICORY, COLLARDS, ESCAROLE, KALE, MUSTARD, SPINACH, SWISS CHARD OR TURNIP

1 pound yields 4 servings;
25 calories per serving.

WHEN SHOPPING: Look for tender, young, un-blemished leaves of bright green color.

TO PREPARE: Remove root ends and imperfect leaves. Wash several times in water, lifting out each time; drain.

TO BOIL: Cover and cook with just the water that clings to leaves until tender, beet tops 5 to 15 minutes; chicory, escarole, mustard and Swiss chard, 15 to 20 minutes; collards 10 to 15 minutes; spinach 3 to 10 minutes; kale and turnip 15 to 25 minutes; drain.

TO MICROWAVE: Place greens (beet, chicory, escarole or spinach) with just the water that clings to the leaves in 3-quart microwavable casserole. Cover and microwave on high 8 to 10 minutes, stirring after 5 minutes, until tender. Let stand covered 1 minute; drain.

WILTED SPINACH

1 pound spinach
1 medium onion, chopped (about ½ cup)
1 slice bacon, cut up
1 clove garlic, finely chopped
2 tablespoons olive or vegetable oil
½ teaspoon salt
¼ teaspoon pepper
¼ teaspoon ground nutmeg
Juice of ½ lime (about 2 tablespoons)

Prepare spinach as directed (page 383). Cook and stir onion, bacon and garlic in oil in Dutch oven over medium heat until bacon is crisp; reduce heat. Stir in salt, pepper and nutmeg. Gradually add spinach. Toss just until spinach is wilted. Drizzle with lime juice: 4 SERVINGS (ABOUT ½ CUP EACH); 100 CALORIES PER SERVING.

STEAMED GREENS WITH MUSHROOM SAUCE

Use your favorite greens in this down-home dish, or experiment with uncommon types such as dandelion and turnip greens. Choose tender young leaves for the mildest flavor.

¾ pound assorted greens
1 tablespoon margarine or butter
1 cup sliced mushrooms
1 tablespoon all-purpose flour
⅛ teaspoon pepper
⅓ cup water
¼ cup milk
1 tablespoon spicy prepared mustard
½ teaspoon beef bouillon granules

Prepare greens as directed (page 383)—except tear into bite-size pieces. Place steamer basket in ½ inch water (water should not touch bottom of basket). Place greens in steamer basket. Cover tightly and heat to boiling; reduce heat. Steam about 5 minutes or until wilted.

While greens are steaming, heat margarine in 1-quart saucepan over medium heat. Cook mushrooms in margarine about 2 minutes, stirring frequently. Stir in flour and pepper; remove from heat. Stir in water, milk, mustard and bouillon granules. Heat to boiling, stirring constantly. Boil and stir 1 minute. Serve sauce over greens. 4 SERVINGS; 75 CALORIES PER SERVING.

LEEKS

2 pounds (6 medium) yield 4 servings; 140 calories per serving.

WHEN SHOPPING: Look for white bulbs with pliable, crisp green tops. Bulbs less than 1½ inches in diameter are the most tender.

TO PREPARE: Remove green tops to within 2 inches of white part (reserve greens for soup or stew). Peel outside layer of bulbs. Wash leeks several times in cold water; drain. Cut large leeks lengthwise into fourths.

TO BOIL: Heat 1 inch water (salted, if desired) to boiling. Add leeks. Cover and heat to boiling; reduce heat. Boil 12 to 15 minutes or until tender; drain.

TO STEAM: Place steamer basket in ½ inch water (water should not touch bottom of basket). Place leeks in basket. Cover tightly and heat to boiling; reduce heat. Steam 13 to 15 minutes or until tender.

TO MICROWAVE: Place leeks and ¼ cup water in square microwavable dish, 8×8×2 inches. Cover tightly and microwave on high 6 to 7 minutes, rotating dish ½ turn after 3 minutes, until tender. Let stand covered 1 minute; drain.

Leek Rolls with Tarragon Mustard

LEEK ROLLS WITH TARRAGON MUSTARD

We've combined Oriental soy sauce and egg roll skins with leeks—the national symbol of Wales—for a satisfying mix of cultures.

1 pound leeks (3 medium)
2 tablespoons vegetable oil
½ cup chopped mushrooms
¼ teaspoon salt
1 medium carrot, shredded (about ½ cup)
1 clove garlic, finely chopped
1 can (8 ounces) sliced water chestnuts, drained and chopped
12 egg roll skins
Tarragon Mustard (below)

Prepare leeks as directed (page 384)—except slice thinly. Heat oil in 10-inch skillet over medium-high heat. Add leeks, mushrooms, salt, carrot, garlic and water chestnuts. Sauté about 3 minutes or until vegetables are tender.

Place ¼ cup leek mixture on center of each egg roll skin. Fold one corner over filling. Overlap the two opposite corners. Moisten fourth corner with water. Fold over to make into roll.

Place lightly greased rack in Dutch oven. Add water to bottom of rack or use steamer. Place rolls on rack. Cover and steam 20 minutes or until skins are firm. Serve with Tarragon Mustard. 12 ROLLS; 120 CALORIES PER ROLL.

Tarragon Mustard

¼ cup prepared mustard
2 teaspoons sugar
2 teaspoons chopped fresh or ¾ teaspoon dried tarragon leaves

Mix all ingredients until sugar is dissolved.

MUSHROOMS

Top: *Portobello, oyster, crimini.*Middle: *Dried porcini, domestic, dried Chinese (black or wood ear), shiitake.* Bottom: *Dried Morels, brown, enoki.*

MUSHROOMS

1 pound yields 4 servings; 30 calories per serving.

WHEN SHOPPING: Look for creamy white to light brown caps, closed around the stems; if slightly open, gills should be light pink or tan.

TO PREPARE: Rinse mushrooms and trim off stem ends. Do not peel. Cut into ¼-inch slices if desired.

TO SAUTÉ: Heat ¼ cup margarine or butter in 10-inch skillet over medium-high heat. Sauté mushrooms in margarine 6 to 8 minutes or until tender.

TO STEAM: Place steamer basket in ½ inch water (water should not touch bottom of basket). Place medium whole mushrooms in basket. Cover tightly and heat to boiling; reduce heat. Steam 6 to 8 minutes or until tender.

TO MICROWAVE: Place mushrooms (slices) in 1½-quart microwavable casserole. Cover tightly and microwave on high 5 to 6 minutes, stirring after 3 minutes, until tender. Let stand covered 1 minute; drain.

MUSHROOMS AND LEEKS

½ pound mushrooms (regular, enoki or shiitake)
¾ pound leeks (2 medium)
1 tablespoon olive or vegetable oil
2 tablespoons chopped fresh lemongrass*
¼ teaspoon salt
¼ teaspoon pepper
2 large cloves garlic, crushed

Prepare mushrooms as directed (page 385); slice if desired. Prepare leeks as directed (page 384)—except cut into ¼-inch slices. Heat oil in 12-inch skillet over medium heat. Add remaining ingredients. Cook, stirring occasionally, about 5 minutes or until vegetables are tender. 4 SERVINGS (½ CUP EACH); 55 CALORIES PER SERVING.

*2 tablespoons chopped fresh chives and 1 tablespoon lemon juice can be substituted for the lemongrass. Stir in just before serving.

GOLDEN PANFRIED MUSHROOMS

1 pound small mushrooms
1 egg, beaten
½ cup dry bread crumbs
⅓ cup margarine or butter
1 medium onion, chopped (about ½ cup)

Prepare whole mushrooms as directed (page 385). Dip mushrooms into egg, then coat with bread crumbs. Heat margarine in 12-inch skillet over medium heat until hot. Cook mushrooms and onion in margarine 7 to 8 minutes, turning occasionally, until mushrooms are tender and golden brown. Drain on paper towels. 4 SERVINGS; 240 CALORIES PER SERVING.

OKRA

1 pound yields 4 servings; 45 calories per serving.

WHEN SHOPPING: Look for tender, unblemished, bright green pods, less than 4 inches long.

TO PREPARE: Wash okra; remove ends and cut into ½-inch slices.

TO BOIL: Heat 1 inch water (salted, if desired) to boiling. Add sliced okra. Cover and heat to boiling; reduce heat. Boil about 10 minutes or until tender; drain.

TO STEAM: Place steamer basket in ½ inch water (water should not touch bottom of basket). Place whole okra in basket. Cover tightly and heat to boiling; reduce heat. Steam 6 to 8 minutes or until tender.

TO MICROWAVE: Place whole okra and ¼ cup water in 1½-quart microwavable casserole. Cover tightly and microwave on high 5 to 7 minutes, stirring after 3 minutes, until tender; drain. Let stand covered 1 minute; drain.

CAJUN OKRA SLICES

Okra is a popular southern vegetable of African origin.

½ pound okra
2 eggs
1 tablespoon water
¾ cup all-purpose flour
1½ teaspoons Cajun spice blend
½ teaspoon salt
½ cup vegetable oil

Prepare okra slices as directed (left). Mix eggs and water in small bowl. Mix flour, Cajun spice and salt in another small bowl. Dip okra into egg mixture, then coat with flour mixture. Repeat with remaining okra.

Heat oil in 10-inch skillet until hot. Fry okra in oil in single layer over medium-high heat 4 to 5 minutes or until golden brown, turning halfway through cooking. 4 SERVINGS (ABOUT ⅔ CUP EACH); 260 CALORIES PER SERVING.

Cajun Okra Slices, Creole Catfish (page 191)

ONIONS: WHITE, YELLOW OR RED

1½ pounds (8 to 10 small) yield 4 servings; 60 calories per serving.

When Shopping: Look for firm, well-shaped onions with unblemished, papery skins and no sign of sprouting.

To Prepare: Peel onions in cold water (to prevent eyes from watering).

To Boil: Heat several inches water (salted, if desired) to boiling. Add onions. Cover and heat to boiling; reduce heat. Boil small onions 15 to 20 minutes, large onions 30 to 35 minutes or until tender; drain.

To Bake: Place large onions in ungreased baking dish. Pour water into dish to ¼-inch depth. Cover and bake in 350° oven 40 to 50 minutes or until tender.

To Sauté: Cut onions into ¼-inch slices. Heat 3 to 4 tablespoons margarine, butter, olive or vegetable oil in 10-inch skillet over medium-high heat. Sauté onions in margarine 6 to 9 minutes or until tender.

To Steam: Place steamer basket in ½ inch water (water should not touch bottom of basket). Place small white onions in basket. Cover tightly and heat to boiling; reduce heat. Steam 15 to 20 minutes or until tender.

To Microwave: Place onions and ¼ cup water in 2-quart microwavable casserole. Cover tightly and microwave on high 6 to 11 minutes, stirring after 4 minutes, until tender. Let stand covered 1 minute; drain.

BAKED WHOLE ONIONS

6 medium onions (with skins)
¼ cup margarine or butter
2 small cloves garlic, finely chopped
¼ cup dry white wine or chicken broth
¼ cup grated Parmesan cheese
2 tablespoons chopped fresh parsley

Prepare onions—except do not peel and bake onions as directed (above). Cut each onion into fourths about halfway through; separate slightly. Heat margarine in 1-quart saucepan over medium-high heat. Sauté garlic in margarine until golden brown; remove from heat. Stir in wine. Stir in cheese and parsley. Pour over onions. 6 SERVINGS; 150 CALORIES PER SERVING.

FRENCH-FRIED ONIONS

Use Spanish, Bermuda or Vidalia onions for frying. They all have a slightly sweet flavor and make a milder onion ring.

Vegetable oil
¾ cup all-purpose flour
½ cup milk
½ teaspoon salt
1 egg
3 large Spanish or Bermuda onions, cut into ¼-inch slices and separated into rings

Heat oil (1 inch) in deep fryer or Dutch oven to 375°. Beat remaining ingredients except onion rings with hand beater until smooth. Dip each onion ring into batter, allowing excess batter to drip into bowl. Fry a few onion rings at a time in hot oil about 2 minutes, turning once, until golden brown. Drain on paper towels. Keep warm in 300° oven while frying remaining onion rings. 4 SERVINGS; 285 CALORIES PER SERVING.

DELUXE CREAMED ONIONS

1½ pounds small white onions*
2 tablespoons margarine or butter
2 tablespoons all-purpose flour
½ teaspoon salt
⅛ teaspoon pepper
1½ cups half-and-half
2 medium carrots, shredded (about 1½ cups)

Prepare and cook onions as directed (left). While onions are cooking, heat margarine in 1-quart saucepan over medium heat until melted. Stir in flour, salt and pepper. Cook, stirring constantly, until smooth and bubbly; remove from heat. Stir in half-and-half. Heat to boiling, stirring constantly. Boil and stir 1 minute. Stir in carrots. Cook 5 minutes longer. Pour sauce over hot onions. 6 SERVINGS; 175 CALORIES PER SERVING.

2 cans (16 ounces each) whole onions can be substituted for the fresh onions. Heat until hot; drain.

ONIONS, GREEN

3 bunches yield 4 servings; 20 calories per serving.

WHEN SHOPPING: Look for crisp green tops; 2 to 3 inches of white root.

TO PREPARE: Wash onions; remove any loose layers of skin. Leave about 3 inches of green tops.

TO BOIL: Heat 1 inch water (salted, if desired) to boiling. Add onions. Cover and heat to boiling; reduce heat. Boil 8 to 10 minutes or just until tender; drain.

TO STEAM: Place steamer basket in ½ inch water (water should not touch bottom of basket). Place onions in basket. Cover tightly and heat to boiling; reduce heat. Steam 8 to 10 minutes or just until tender.

TO MICROWAVE: Place onions and 2 tablespoons water in 1½-quart microwavable casserole. Cover tightly and microwave on high 1 to 2 minutes or just until tender. Let stand covered 1 minute; drain.

ONIONS AND CARROTS

3 bunches green onions (about 20)
1 tablespoon vegetable oil
1 tablespoon margarine or butter
2 thin slices gingerroot, finely chopped
1 clove garlic, finely chopped
1 medium carrot, shredded (about ⅔ cup)
¼ teaspoon salt
⅛ teaspoon pepper

Prepare green onions as directed (above). Cut diagonally into 1½-inch pieces. Heat oil and margarine in 10-inch skillet over medium-high heat. Sauté onions, gingerroot and garlic about 2 minutes or until onions are crisp-tender. Stir in carrot and salt. Sprinkle with pepper.   4 SERVINGS; 80 CALORIES PER SERVING.

PARSNIPS

1½ pounds (6 to 8 medium) yield 4 servings; 130 calories per serving.

WHEN SHOPPING: Look for firm, nicely shaped, unblemished parsnips that are not too wide.

TO PREPARE: Scrape or pare. Leave whole or cut in half, fourths, ¼-inch slices or strips.

TO BOIL: Heat 1 inch water (salted, if desired) to boiling. Add parsnips. Cover and heat to boiling; reduce heat. Boil whole parsnips or halves 15 to 20 minutes, slices or strips 7 to 9 minutes or until tender; drain.

TO STEAM: Place steamer basket in ½ inch water (water should not touch bottom of basket). Place parsnips (whole or slices) in basket. Cover tightly and heat to boiling; reduce heat. Steam whole parsnips 20 to 25 minutes, slices 8 to 10 minutes or until tender.

TO MICROWAVE: Place parsnips (slices or strips) and ¼ cup water in 1-quart microwavable casserole. Cover tightly and microwave on high 8 to 10 minutes, stirring after 4 minutes, until tender. Let stand covered 1 minute; drain.

PARSNIP CAKES

5 medium parsnips (about 1¼ pounds)
2 tablespoons all-purpose flour
½ teaspoon salt
Dash of pepper
2 tablespoons margarine or butter, softened
1 tablespoon chopped onion
1 egg, beaten
Dry bread crumbs or cracker crumbs
¼ cup shortening

Prepare and cook whole parsnips as directed (left); mash parsnips. Mix parsnips, flour, salt, pepper, margarine, onion and egg. Shape into 8 patties. Coat with bread crumbs. Heat shortening in 10-inch skillet over medium heat until hot. Cook patties in shortening about 5 minutes, turning once, until golden brown.   4 SERVINGS; 315 CALORIES PER SERVING.

PEA PODS, CHINESE

1 pound yields 4 servings; 50 calories per serving.

WHEN SHOPPING: Look for flat pods with a velvety feel. Pods should be crisp and evenly green.

TO PREPARE: Wash pods; remove tips and strings.

TO BOIL: Heat 1 inch water (salted, if desired) to boiling. Add pea pods. Heat to boiling. Boil uncovered 2 to 3 minutes, stirring occasionally, until crisp-tender; drain.

TO STEAM: Place steamer basket in ½ inch water (water should not touch bottom of basket). Place pea pods in basket. Cover tightly and heat to boiling; reduce heat. Steam 5 to 7 minutes or until crisp-tender.

TO MICROWAVE: Place pea pods and ¼ cup water in 1½-quart microwavable casserole. Cover tightly and microwave on high 6 to 7 minutes, stirring after 1 minute, until crisp-tender; drain.

Sesame Pea Pods, Stir-fried Orange Beef (page 222)

SESAME PEA PODS

½ pound Chinese pea pods
1 tablespoon sesame oil
1 medium red or yellow bell pepper, cut
 into thin strips
1 tablespoon sesame seed

Prepare pea pods as directed (page 388). Heat oil in 10-inch skillet over medium-high heat. Add bell pepper and sesame seed. Sauté about 2 minutes or until pepper is crisp-tender. Add pea pods. Sauté about 2 minutes or until hot. 6 SERVINGS (ABOUT ⅔ CUP EACH); 65 CALORIES PER SERVING.

PEAS, GREEN

2 pounds yield 4 servings; 40 calories per serving.

WHEN SHOPPING: Look for plump, tender, bright green pods.

TO PREPARE: Wash and shell peas just before cooking.

TO BOIL: Heat 1 inch water (salted, if desired) to boiling. Add peas. Heat to boiling; reduce heat. Boil uncovered 5 minutes. Cover and boil 3 to 7 minutes longer or until tender. If desired, add ½ teaspoon sugar and a few pea pods or lettuce leaf to boiling water for added flavor; drain.

TO STEAM: Place steamer basket in ½ inch water (water should not touch bottom of basket). Place peas in basket. Cover tightly and heat to boiling; reduce heat. Steam 10 to 12 minutes or until tender.

TO MICROWAVE: Place peas and ¼ cup water in 1-quart microwavable casserole. Cover tightly and microwave on high 9 to 11 minutes, stirring after 5 minutes, until tender. Let stand covered 1 minute; drain.

PEAS AND PROSCIUTTO

Prosciutto is an Italian ham that is salted, cured and aged to achieve its delightful flavor.

2 pounds green peas*
2 teaspoons olive or vegetable oil
¼ pound thinly sliced prosciutto, chopped
1 teaspoon chopped fresh or ½ teaspoon
 dried thyme leaves
⅛ teaspoon pepper
1 clove garlic, finely chopped

Prepare and cook peas as directed (left). Heat oil in 10-inch skillet over medium-high heat. Add prosciutto, thyme, pepper and garlic. Sauté about 3 minutes or until prosciutto is hot. Add peas. Sauté about 2 minutes or until hot. 4 SERVINGS (ABOUT ⅔ CUP EACH); 240 CALORIES PER SERVING.

2½ cups frozen peas, cooked and drained, can be substituted for the fresh peas.

PEAS IN CURRY SAUCE

3 pounds green peas*
2 slices bacon
1 medium onion, chopped (about ½ cup)
1 large clove garlic, finely chopped
¼ cup finely chopped salted peanuts
1 teaspoon finely chopped gingerroot
2 teaspoons all-purpose flour
1 teaspoon curry powder
¼ teaspoon salt
¼ teaspoon dry mustard
⅔ cup milk

Prepare peas as directed (page 389). Cook bacon in 10-inch skillet until crisp. Drain bacon, reserving fat in skillet. Crumble bacon and reserve. Cook peas, onion, garlic, peanuts and gingerroot in fat over medium heat 5 minutes, stirring frequently. Stir in flour, curry powder, salt and mustard; remove from heat.

Stir in milk. Heat to boiling, stirring constantly; reduce heat. Cover and simmer about 5 minutes, stirring occasionally, until peas are tender. Sprinkle with bacon.   6 SERVINGS (ABOUT ½ CUP EACH); 245 CALORIES PER SERVING.

2 packages (10 ounces each) frozen green peas can be substituted for the fresh peas. Rinse with cold water to separate; drain. Add frozen peas with milk.

PEPPERS, BELL

2 medium (about ½ pound) yield 4 servings; 25 calories per serving.

WHEN SHOPPING: Look for well-shaped, shiny, bright-colored peppers with firm sides.

TO PREPARE: Wash peppers; remove stems, seeds and membranes. Leave whole to stuff and bake, or cut into thin slices or rings.

TO SAUTÉ: Heat 1 to 2 tablespoons margarine or butter in 10-inch skillet over medium-high heat. Sauté slices or rings in margarine 3 to 5 minutes or until crisp-tender.

TO STEAM: Place steamer basket in ½ inch water (water should not touch bottom of basket). Place peppers in basket. Cover tightly and heat to boiling; reduce heat. Steam 8 to 10 minutes or until tender.

TO MICROWAVE: Place peppers in 1½-quart microwavable casserole. Cover tightly and microwave on high 4 to 5 minutes, stirring after 2 minutes, until crisp-tender. Let stand covered 1 minute; drain.

SAUTÉED PEPPERS

Try mixing green, yellow, orange, red or purple bell peppers to create a rainbow of colors.

3 medium bell peppers (about ¾ pound)
1 tablespoon chopped fresh parsley
1 tablespoon chopped fresh or 1 teaspoon dried basil leaves
1 tablespoon olive or vegetable oil
¼ teaspoon salt
1 clove garlic, crushed
¼ cup sliced ripe olives

Prepare bell peppers as directed (left)—except cut into 1-inch pieces. Heat parsley, basil, oil, salt and garlic in 10-inch skillet over medium-high heat. Add peppers and olives. Sauté 3 to 5 minutes or until peppers are crisp-tender.   4 SERVINGS; 70 CALORIES PER SERVING.

POTATOES, SMALL NEW

10 to 12 new potatoes (about 1½ pounds) yield 4 servings; 135 calories per serving.

WHEN SHOPPING: Look for nicely shaped, smooth, firm potatoes with unblemished skins, free from discoloration.

TO PREPARE: Wash potatoes; pare narrow strip around centers if desired.

TO BOIL: Heat 1 inch water (salted, if desired) to boiling. Add potatoes. Cover and heat to boiling; reduce heat. Boil 20 to 25 minutes or until tender; drain.

TO STEAM: Place steamer basket in ½ inch water (water should not touch bottom of basket). Place potatoes in basket. Cover tightly and heat to boiling; reduce heat. Steam 18 to 22 minutes or until tender.

TO MICROWAVE: Pierce potatoes of similar size with fork to allow steam to escape. Place potatoes, with larger potatoes to outside edge, and ¼ cup water in 2-quart microwavable casserole. Cover tightly and microwave on high 10 to 12 minutes, stirring after 5 minutes, until tender. Let stand covered 1 minute; drain.

LEMON-CHIVE POTATOES

10 to 12 new potatoes (about 1½ pounds)
2 tablespoons margarine or butter
½ teaspoon grated lemon peel
1 tablespoon lemon juice
2 teaspoons chopped fresh chives
½ teaspoon salt
⅛ teaspoon pepper
Dash of ground nutmeg

Prepare and cook new potatoes as directed (page 390). While potatoes are cooking, heat remaining ingredients just to boiling. Turn hot potatoes into serving dish. Pour lemon butter over potatoes.   4 SERVINGS; 170 CALORIES PER SERVING.

CURRIED NEW POTATOES

New potatoes are small potatoes that have been harvested early. These tiny potatoes range from the size of a silver dollar to 2 to 3 inches in diameter. You can keep the potato skins neat-looking if you peel away a narrow band from around the middle of each potato before cooking.

10 to 12 new potatoes (about 1½ pounds)
½ cup sour cream or plain yogurt
2 tablespoons chutney
2 teaspoons curry
½ teaspoon salt
2 green onions (with tops), thinly sliced (about 2 tablespoons)

Prepare and cook new potatoes as directed (page 390). While potatoes are cooking, heat remaining ingredients until hot (do not boil). Toss with potatoes.   4 SERVINGS; 220 CALORIES PER SERVING.

POTATOES

Round potatoes, red/white—for boiling, steaming

Russet potatoes—for baking, frying, mashing

Sweet potatoes: (clockwise from top): yams, red sweet potatoes, sweet potatoes

POTATOES:
SWEET OR YAMS

4 medium (about 1½ pounds) yield 4 servings;
180 calories per serving.

WHEN SHOPPING: Look for nicely shaped, smooth, firm potatoes with even-colored skins.

TO PREPARE: Choose potatoes of similar size. Scrub potatoes but do not pare.

TO BOIL: Heat enough water to cover sweet potatoes (salted, if desired) to boiling. Add potatoes. Cover and heat to boiling; reduce heat. Boil 30 to 35 minutes or until tender; drain. Slip off skins. Leave potatoes whole, slice or mash.

TO BAKE: Pierce sweet potatoes to allow steam to escape. Bake in 375° oven about 45 minutes, in 350° oven about 1 hour, in 325° oven about 1¼ hours or until tender.

TO STEAM: Place steamer basket in ½ inch water (water should not touch bottom of basket). Place sweet potatoes in basket. Cover tightly and heat to boiling; reduce heat. Steam 25 to 30 minutes or until tender. Slip off skins. Leave potatoes whole, slice or mash.

TO MICROWAVE: Pierce 4 medium sweet potatoes of similar size to allow steam to escape. Arrange potatoes in circle on microwavable paper towel in microwave oven. Microwave uncovered on high 8 to 10 minutes or until tender. Let stand uncovered 5 minutes.

SWEET POTATOES
IN MAPLE SYRUP

In colonial times, often the only sweetener available was maple syrup. Here it adds its distinctive flavor to sweet potatoes.

> 4 medium sweet potatoes (about 1½ pounds)
> ¼ cup coarsely chopped walnuts
> ¼ cup maple-flavored syrup
> 1 tablespoon margarine or butter
> ⅛ teaspoon ground nutmeg
> 1 medium pared eating apple, cut into ½-inch pieces

Prepare and bake sweet potatoes as directed (left). Slip off skins. Cut potatoes into ½-inch pieces. Cook remaining ingredients in 10-inch skillet about 6 minutes or until apple is tender. Add sweet potatoes. Mix carefully until coated.   6 SERVINGS (½ CUP EACH); 190 CALORIES PER SERVING.

Sweet Potatoes in Maple Syrup

CANDIED SWEET POTATOES

Sweet potatoes and yams are both varieties of sweet potatoes, and the two can be used interchangeably. Yams, very popular in the South, have a deep orange color and are somewhat moister when cooked. Sometimes called "Jersey Sweets," sweet potatoes are creamy yellow, and slightly drier than yams.

    6 medium sweet potatoes or yams (about
       2 pounds)*
    ½ cup packed brown sugar
    3 tablespoons margarine or butter
    3 tablespoons water
    ½ teaspoon salt

Prepare and cook sweet potatoes as directed (page 392). Slip off skins. Cut into ½-inch slices. Heat remaining ingredients in 10-inch skillet over medium heat, stirring constantly, until smooth and bubbly. Add sweet potatoes. Stir gently until glazed and hot.   4 SERVINGS; 310 CALORIES PER SERVING.

*1 can (23 ounces) sweet potatoes or yams, drained and cut into ½-inch slices, can be substituted for the fresh sweet potatoes.

ORANGE SWEET POTATOES: Substitute orange juice for the water and add 1 tablespoon grated orange peel.   315 CALORIES PER SERVING.

PINEAPPLE SWEET POTATOES: Omit water. Add 1 can (8¼ ounces) crushed pineapple in syrup, undrained.   355 CALORIES PER SERVING.

SPICY SWEET POTATOES: Stir ½ teaspoon ground cinnamon or ¼ teaspoon ground allspice, cloves, mace or nutmeg into brown sugar mixture in skillet.   310 CALORIES PER SERVING.

POTATOES, WHITE

*6 medium (about 2 pounds) yield 4 servings;
180 calories per serving.*

WHEN SHOPPING: Look for nicely shaped, smooth, firm potatoes with unblemished skins, free from discoloration.

TO PREPARE: *For Boiling:* Scrub potatoes. Leave skins on whenever possible, or pare thinly and remove eyes. Leave whole or cut into large pieces. *For Baking:* Scrub potatoes and, if desired, rub with shortening for softer skins. Pierce with fork to allow steam to escape.

TO BOIL: Heat 1 inch water (salted, if desired) to boiling. Add potatoes. Cover and heat to boiling; reduce heat. Boil whole potatoes 30 to 35 minutes, pieces 20 to 25 minutes or until tender; drain.

TO BAKE: Bake in 375° oven 1 to 1¼ hours, in 350° oven 1¼ to 1½ hours, in 325° oven about 1½ hours or until tender.

TO STEAM: Place steamer basket in ¾ inch water (water should not touch bottom of basket). Place whole potatoes in basket. Cover tightly and heat to boiling; reduce heat. Steam 30 to 35 minutes or until tender.

TO MICROWAVE: *Whole:* Pierce potatoes of similar size with fork to allow steam to escape. Arrange potatoes about 1 inch apart in circle on microwavable paper towel in microwave oven. Microwave uncovered on high 12 to 14 minutes, turning potatoes over after 6 minutes, until tender. Let stand uncovered 5 minutes. *Pieces:* Place potatoes and ½ cup water in 2-quart microwavable casserole. Cover tightly and microwave on high 10 to 12 minutes, stirring after 7 minutes, until tender; drain. Let stand covered 1 minute.

AU GRATIN POTATOES

    6 medium potatoes (about 2 pounds)
    ¼ cup margarine or butter
    1 medium onion, chopped (about ½ cup)
    1 tablespoon all-purpose flour
    1 teaspoon salt
    ¼ teaspoon pepper
    2 cups milk
    2 cups shredded natural sharp Cheddar
       cheese (8 ounces)
    ¼ cup fine dry bread crumbs
    Paprika

Heat oven to 375°. Prepare potatoes as directed (left). Cut into enough thin slices to measure about 4 cups. Heat margarine in 2-quart saucepan over medium heat. Cook onion in margarine about 2 minutes, stirring occasionally. Stir in flour, salt and pepper. Cook, stirring constantly, until bubbly; remove from heat. Stir in milk and 1½ cups of the cheese. Heat to boiling, stirring constantly. Boil and stir 1 minute.

Spread potatoes in ungreased 1½-quart casserole. Pour cheese sauce over potatoes. Bake uncovered 1 hour. Mix remaining cheese and the bread crumbs. Sprinkle over potatoes; sprinkle with paprika. Bake 15 to 20 minutes longer or until top is brown and bubbly.   6 SERVINGS; 390 CALORIES PER SERVING.

SCALLOPED POTATOES

6 medium potatoes (about 2 pounds)
3 tablespoons margarine or butter
1 small onion, finely chopped (about ¼ cup)
3 tablespoons all-purpose flour
1 teaspoon salt
¼ teaspoon pepper
2½ cups milk
1 tablespoon margarine or butter

Heat oven to 350°. Grease 2-quart casserole. Prepare potatoes as directed (page 393). Cut into enough thin slices to measure about 4 cups. Heat 3 tablespoons margarine in 2-quart saucepan over medium heat. Cook onion in margarine about 2 minutes, stirring occasionally. Stir in flour, salt and pepper. Cook, stirring constantly, until smooth and bubbly; remove from heat. Stir in milk. Heat to boiling, stirring constantly. Boil and stir 1 minute.

Spread potatoes in casserole; pour sauce over potatoes. Dot with 1 tablespoon margarine. Cover and bake 30 minutes. Uncover and bake 60 to 70 minutes longer or until potatoes are tender. Let stand 5 to 10 minutes before serving. 6 SERVINGS; 240 CALORIES PER SERVING.

HASH BROWN POTATOES

A classic across the country and the pride of many a short-order cook. Served with eggs, they make any morning special.

4 medium potatoes (about 1½ pounds)
2 tablespoons finely chopped onion
¼ teaspoon salt
⅛ teaspoon pepper
¼ cup margarine or butter

Prepare potatoes as directed (page 393); pare. Shred enough to measure 4 cups. Rinse well; drain and pat dry. Mix potatoes, onion, salt and pepper. Heat margarine in 10-inch skillet until melted. Pack potato mixture firmly in skillet, leaving ½-inch space around edge.

Cook over medium-low heat about 15 minutes or until bottom is brown. Cut potato mixture into fourths; turn over. (Potato mixture can be kept in one piece if desired. Place large plate over skillet and invert potatoes onto plate. Slide potatoes back into skillet.) Add 1 tablespoon margarine if necessary. Cook about 12 minutes longer or until bottom is brown. 4 SERVINGS; 220 CALORIES PER SERVING.

MASHED POTATOES

Duchess Potatoes will have an elegant golden-orange color when made with sweet potatoes, and a distinctive flavor that is slightly sweet.

6 medium potatoes (about 2 pounds)
⅓ to ½ cup milk
¼ cup margarine or butter, softened
½ teaspoon salt
Dash of pepper

Prepare and cook potato pieces as directed (page 393). Shake pan with potatoes over low heat to dry. Mash potatoes until no lumps remain. Add milk in small amounts, beating after each addition (amount of milk needed to make potatoes smooth and fluffy depends on kind of potatoes used).

Add margarine, salt and pepper. Beat vigorously until potatoes are light and fluffy. If desired, dot with margarine or sprinkle with paprika, chopped fresh parsley, watercress or chives. 4 TO 6 SERVINGS; 270 CALORIES PER SERVING.

DUCHESS POTATOES: Prepare as directed—except heat oven to 425°. Beat 2 eggs. Add to potatoes and beat until blended. Drop by spoonfuls onto ungreased cookie sheet, or form rosettes or pipe border around meat or fish with pastry tube. Brush potatoes with melted margarine. Bake 15 minutes or until potatoes are light brown. 10 MOUNDS OR ROSETTES; 135 CALORIES PER MOUND.

FRENCH-FRIED POTATOES

4 medium potatoes (about 1½ pounds)
Vegetable oil
Salt

Prepare potatoes as directed (page 393). Cut lengthwise into strips, ¼ to ⅜ inch wide.

Fill deep fryer or deep saucepan one-half full with vegetable oil. Heat oil to 375°. Fill basket one-fourth full with potatoes. Slowly lower into hot oil. (If oil bubbles excessively, raise and lower basket several times.) Use long-handled fork to keep potatoes separated. Fry 5 to 7 minutes or until potatoes are golden. Drain on paper towels. Repeat with remaining potatoes. Sprinkle with salt. 4 SERVINGS; 240 CALORIES PER SERVING.

Potato Pancake Wedges, Meat Loaf (page 226), Herbed Broccoli (page 375)

POTATO PANCAKE WEDGES

3 medium potatoes (about 1 pound)
¼ cup milk
2 tablespoons all-purpose flour
1 tablespoon finely chopped onion
½ teaspoon salt
⅛ teaspoon pepper
2 eggs, beaten
2 tablespoons margarine or butter

Prepare potatoes as directed (page 393); pare. Shred enough to measure 2 cups. Rinse well; drain and pat dry. Mix potatoes and remaining ingredients except margarine. Heat margarine in 10-inch skillet until melted. Spread potato mixture evenly in skillet. Cook over medium heat about 5 minutes or until bottom is brown. Place large plate over skillet and invert pancake onto plate. Slide pancake back into skillet. Cook about 5 minutes longer or until brown. Cut into wedges. 4 SERVINGS; 195 CALORIES PER SERVING.

RUTABAGAS

*1½ pounds (2 medium) yield 4 servings;
60 calories per serving.*

WHEN SHOPPING: Look for rutabagas that are heavy, well shaped (round or elongated) and smooth.

To PREPARE: Wash rutabagas; pare thinly. Cut into ½-inch cubes or 2-inch pieces.

To BOIL: Heat 1 inch water (salted, if desired) to boiling. Add rutabagas. Cover and heat to boiling; reduce heat. Boil cubes 20 to 25 minutes, pieces 30 to 40 minutes or until tender; drain.

To STEAM: Place steamer basket in ½ inch water (water should not touch bottom of basket). Place rutabaga cubes in basket. Cover tightly and heat to boiling; reduce heat. Steam 25 to 28 minutes or until tender.

To MICROWAVE: Place rutabagas (cubes) and ½ cup water in 1½-quart microwavable casserole. Cover tightly and microwave on high 15 to 18 minutes, stirring every 5 minutes, until tender. Let stand covered 1 minute; drain.

RUTABAGAS AND APPLESAUCE

2 medium rutabagas (about 1½ pounds)
¾ cup applesauce
1 tablespoon chopped fresh parsley
1 tablespoon margarine or butter
1 teaspoon grated lemon peel
½ teaspoon salt

Prepare and cook rutabagas as directed (above); mash. Stir in remaining ingredients. Heat over medium heat, stirring frequently, until hot. 4 SERVINGS (ABOUT ¾ CUP EACH); 110 CALORIES PER SERVING.

SQUASH

Top: *Hubbard, butternut, acorn, stripped marrow, banana.* Middle: *Buttercup, sweet dumpling, turban, delicata, golden nugget.* Bottom: *Yellow crookneck, chayote, yellow straightneck, yellow zucchini, green and yellow pattypan, green zucchini, spaghetti.*

SQUASH, WINTER: ACORN, BUTTERCUP, BUTTERNUT, OR SPAGHETTI

2 pounds yield 4 servings; 90 calories per serving.

WHEN SHOPPING: Look for hard, tough rinds with good yellow-orange color and no soft spots. Squash should feel heavy.

TO PREPARE: Wash squash. For boiling, pare squash if desired; cut into 1-inch slices or cubes. Or cut each squash lengthwise in half; remove seeds and fibers.

TO BAKE: Place squash halves in ungreased rectangular baking dish, 13 × 9 × 2 inches. Sprinkle cut sides with salt and pepper. Dot with margarine or butter. Pour water into dish to ¼-inch depth. Cover and bake in 400° oven 30 to 40 minutes, in 350° oven about 40 minutes, in 325° oven about 45 minutes or until tender. For spaghetti squash, remove strands with two forks.

TO BOIL (for large squash): Heat 1 inch water (salted, if desired) to boiling. Add squash (slices or cubes). Cover and heat to boiling; reduce heat. Boil 15 to 20 minutes or until tender; drain.

TO STEAM: Place steamer basket in ½ inch water (water should not touch bottom of basket). Place squash (slices or cubes) in basket. Cover tightly and heat to boiling; reduce heat. Steam slices 12 to 15 minutes, cubes 7 to 10 minutes or until tender.

TO MICROWAVE: *Acorn, Buttercup and Butternut:* Pierce whole squash with tip of sharp knife in several places to allow steam to escape. Place squash on microwavable paper towel in microwave oven. Microwave uncovered on high 4 to 6 minutes or until squash is hot and rind is firm but easy to cut through; cool slightly. Carefully cut in half; remove seeds. Arrange squash halves, cut sides down, on 10-inch microwavable plate. Cover tightly and microwave on high 5 to 8 minutes or until squash is tender when pierced with tip of sharp knife. Let stand covered 1 minute. *Spaghetti:* Pierce whole squash with tip of sharp knife in several places to allow steam to escape. Place squash on microwavable paper towel in microwave oven. Microwave uncovered on high 18 to 23 minutes, turning squash over after 8 minutes, until tender. Let stand uncovered 10 minutes. Cut in half; remove seeds and fibers. Remove squash strands with two forks.

Spaghetti Squash: Using two forks, scrape squash strands from inside of shell. Cutting squash crosswise will give longer spaghetti-like strands.

GOLDEN SQUASH CASSEROLE

This creamy squash dish can be made one day ahead. Prepare as directed, then cover and refrigerate. Bake uncovered at 325° for 40 to 45 minutes or until hot.

2 pounds Hubbard squash*
2 tablespoons margarine or butter
½ cup sour cream
1 medium onion, finely chopped (about ½ cup)
1 teaspoon salt
¼ teaspoon pepper

Prepare and cook squash pieces as directed (page 396). Heat oven to 325°. Mash squash. Stir in remaining ingredients. Pour into ungreased 1-quart casserole. Bake uncovered 25 to 30 minutes or until bubbly around edge.   6 SERVINGS (ABOUT ¾ CUP EACH); 130 CALORIES PER SERVING.

2 packages (12 ounces each) frozen cooked squash, thawed, can be substituted for the fresh squash.

SQUASH AND APPLE BAKE

2 pounds butternut or buttercup squash
½ cup packed brown sugar
¼ cup margarine or butter, melted
1 tablespoon all-purpose flour
1 teaspoon salt
½ teaspoon ground mace
2 baking apples, cored and cut into ½-inch slices

Heat oven to 350°. Prepare squash as directed (page 396)—except pare and cut into ½-inch slices. Mix all ingredients except squash and apple slices.

Arrange squash slices in rectangular baking dish, 11 × 7 × 1½ inches. Top with apple slices. Sprinkle with sugar mixture. Cover with aluminum foil and bake 50 to 60 minutes or until squash is tender.   6 SERVINGS; 220 CALORIES PER SERVING.

SPAGHETTI SQUASH WITH CILANTRO PESTO

1 medium spaghetti squash (about 2½ pounds)
¾ cup chopped fresh cilantro
¼ cup chopped fresh parsley
¼ cup grated Parmesan cheese
2 tablespoons olive or vegetable oil
½ teaspoon salt
⅛ teaspoon pepper
2 cloves garlic
½ cup coarsely chopped walnuts, toasted

Prepare and bake squash as directed (page 396). While squash is baking, place remaining ingredients except walnuts in blender or food processor. Cover and blend, or process, until mixture is smooth. Remove squash strands with two forks. Stir in cilantro mixture and walnuts. Garnish with chopped tomato if desired.   4 SERVINGS (⅔ CUP EACH); 235 CALORIES PER SERVING.

To Microwave: Prepare and microwave squash as directed (page 396). Continue as directed.

Spaghetti Squash with Cilantro Pesto

Stir-fried Zucchini and Jicama (page 399), Spicy Stuffed Zucchini

SQUASH, SUMMER: CHAYOTE, CROOKNECK, PATTYPAN, STRAIGHTNECK OR ZUCCHINI

Summer squash grow quickly and have tender, edible skins. Winter squash grow more slowly, have thick, hard (inedible) skins, and require longer cooking.

1½ pounds yield 4 servings; 35 calories per serving.

WHEN SHOPPING: Look for squash that are heavy in relation to size. Small squash are more tender. Skin should be smooth and glossy.

TO PREPARE: Wash squash; remove stem and blossom ends but do not pare. If squash are small, cut in half. For larger squash, cut into ½-inch slices or cubes.

TO BOIL: Heat 1 inch water (salted, if desired) to boiling. Add squash. Cover and heat to boiling; reduce heat. Boil slices 5 to 10 minutes, cubes 3 to 6 minutes or until tender; drain.

TO STEAM: Place steamer basket in ½ inch water (water should not touch bottom of basket). Place squash (slices or cubes) in basket. Cover tightly and heat to boiling; reduce heat. Steam 5 to 7 minutes or until tender.

TO MICROWAVE: Place squash and ¼ cup water in 1½-quart microwavable casserole. Cover tightly and microwave on high 8 to 10 minutes (pattypan 9 to 13 minutes), stirring after 4 minutes, until almost tender. Let stand covered 1 minute; drain.

SPICY STUFFED ZUCCHINI

    2 medium zucchini (about ¾ pound)
    1 small yellow squash (about ¼ pound)
    1 tablespoon olive or vegetable oil
    ¾ teaspoon curry powder
    ½ teaspoon salt
    ¼ teaspoon ground cinnamon
    ⅛ teaspoon ground cumin
    1 clove garlic, finely chopped
    ¼ cup raisins

Heat oven to 350°. Prepare zucchini and yellow squash as directed (left)—except cut zucchini lengthwise in half. Scoop centers from zucchini; reserve shells. Chop zucchini pulp and yellow squash.

Heat oil, curry powder, salt, cinnamon, cumin and garlic in 10-inch skillet over medium heat. Add zucchini and yellow squash. Cook 3 minutes, stirring occasionally; remove from heat. Stir in raisins. Place zucchini shells in ungreased rectangular baking dish, 11 × 7 × 1½ inches. Spoon mixture into zucchini shells. Cover with aluminum foil and bake about 30 minutes or until zucchini shells are tender.   4 SERVINGS; 80 CALORIES PER SERVING.

STIR-FRIED ZUCCHINI AND JICAMA

1 medium zucchini (about ½ pound)
½ pound jicama
1 tablespoon vegetable oil
1 teaspoon sesame oil
1 tablespoon sesame seed
1 clove garlic, finely chopped
1 teaspoon salt

Prepare zucchini as directed (page 398)—except cut into julienne strips. Pare jicama and cut into julienne strips.

Heat wok or 12-inch skillet until 1 or 2 drops of water bubble and skitter when sprinkled in wok. Add vegetable oil and sesame oil. Rotate wok to coat side. Add sesame seed and garlic. Stir-fry 30 seconds. Add zucchini and jicama. Stir-fry 2 minutes. Stir in salt. 4 SERVINGS; 75 CALORIES PER SERVING.

TOMATOES

*4 medium (1⅓ pounds) yield 4 servings;
30 calories per serving.*

WHEN SHOPPING: Look for nicely ripened, well-shaped tomatoes. Fully ripe tomatoes should be slightly soft but not mushy and have a rich red color.

TO PREPARE: Wash tomatoes; cut into 8 wedges or ½-inch slices. Peel tomatoes before cutting if desired. To remove skin easily, dip tomato into boiling water 30 seconds, then into cold water. Or scrape surface of tomato with blade of knife to loosen; peel.

TO MICROWAVE: Place tomatoes in 2-quart microwavable casserole. Cover tightly and microwave on high, wedges 7 to 9 minutes, gently stirring after 4 minutes, or slices 5 to 7 minutes, gently stirring after 3 minutes, until hot. Let stand covered 1 minute.

🌾 STEWED TOMATOES

The tomato, once called the "love apple," was considered poisonous. Although available in America since the 1700s, it wasn't readily eaten until the 1800s.

3 large ripe tomatoes (about 1½ pounds)*
1 medium onion, finely chopped (about ½ cup)
2 tablespoons finely chopped green bell pepper
1 tablespoon sugar
½ teaspoon salt
⅛ teaspoon pepper
2 slices bread, toasted and cut into ½-inch cubes

Peel tomatoes as directed (left); cut into small pieces. Mix all ingredients except bread cubes in 2½-quart saucepan. Cover and heat to boiling; reduce heat. Simmer about 10 minutes or until tomatoes are soft. Stir in bread cubes. 4 SERVINGS (ABOUT ¾ CUP EACH); 80 CALORIES PER SERVING.

*1 can (28 ounces) peeled tomatoes, undrained, can be substituted for the fresh tomatoes.

🌾 PANFRIED TOMATOES

For an adventuresome change, use green (unripe) tomatoes, which add a special tang to this dish.

4 firm ripe or green medium tomatoes (about 1½ pounds)
½ cup all-purpose flour
1 teaspoon salt
¼ teaspoon pepper
⅓ cup margarine or butter

Prepare tomato slices as directed (left). Mix flour, salt and pepper. Dip tomato slices into flour mixture. Heat margarine in 10-inch skillet over medium heat until hot. Add tomato slices. Cook, turning once, until golden brown. 4 SERVINGS; 210 CALORIES PER SERVING.

TURNIPS

1 pound (4 medium) yields 4 servings;
30 calories per serving.

WHEN SHOPPING: Look for turnips that are smooth, round and firm, with fresh tops.

TO PREPARE: Cut off tops. Wash turnips; pare thinly. Leave whole or cut into ½-inch pieces.

TO BOIL: Heat 1 inch water (salted, if desired) to boiling. Add turnips. Cover and heat to boiling; reduce heat. Boil whole turnips 25 to 30 minutes, pieces 15 to 20 minutes or until tender; drain.

TO STEAM: Place steamer basket in ½ inch water (water should not touch bottom of basket). Place turnip pieces in basket. Cover tightly and heat to boiling; reduce heat. Steam 15 to 20 minutes or until tender.

TO MICROWAVE: Place turnips (½-inch pieces) and ¼ cup water in 2-quart microwavable casserole. Cover tightly and microwave on high 12 to 14 minutes, stirring every 5 minutes, until tender. Let stand covered 1 minute; drain.

BAKED TURNIP CASSEROLE

Turnips, a mainstay for early settlers, were used in everything from puddings and pies to casseroles and salads.

1 pound turnips (about 4 medium)
1 medium all-purpose apple, pared and sliced
2 tablespoons packed brown sugar
½ teaspoon salt
¼ teaspoon pepper
¼ teaspoon ground nutmeg
1 egg
6 slices bacon, cut up
1 medium onion, chopped (about ½ cup)
1 clove garlic, crushed

Prepare and steam turnip pieces as directed (above)—except place apple slices on top. Mash turnips and apple. Beat in brown sugar, salt, pepper, nutmeg and egg.

Heat oven to 350°. Cook bacon in 10-inch skillet until crisp. Drain bacon, reserving 1 tablespoon fat in skillet. Cook and stir onion and garlic in fat until onion is softened. Mix onion mixture, turnip mixture and bacon. Spoon into ungreased 1-quart casserole. Bake uncovered about 45 minutes or until golden brown. 4 SERVINGS (ABOUT ½ CUP EACH); 140 CALORIES PER SERVING.

FIX-IT-FAST

VEGETABLES

♦ Grill whole or mixed cut-up vegetables in foil packages. Top with margarine or butter and your favorite herb.

♦ Purchase cut-up vegetables from your deli for stir-fry side dishes or salads.

♦ Cook vegetables and pasta in the same pot (cook times should be compatible).

♦ Serve leftover cooked vegetables in salads, soups, casseroles, pasta, dips or spreads.

♦ Use leftover potatoes in potato patties, hash browns, potato salad or chowder.

♦ Puree leftover vegetables; use as a base for hot or cold soups.

♦ For a quick snack or appetizer, cut leftover baked potatoes into ½-inch slices. Top with pizza sauce, your favorite pizza toppings and cheese; broil.

♦ Use a food processor for quickly shredding vegetables for cakes, muffins and quick breads, such as Carrot Cake (page 76) and Zucchini Bread (page 44).

♦ Save small pieces of vegetables and throw-away ends of vegetables to use in soup stock.

♦ Create a quick sauce to serve with hot or cold vegetables. Try salsa or jarred or soft cheese spread thinned with milk or beer.

♦ Toss cooked vegetables with melted margarine or olive oil and salad dressing mix. Stir salad dressing mix (ranch-style) into mashed potatoes.

♦ Create a quick main meal by topping baked potatoes with meat or cheese; taco or spaghetti sauce; chili, ham and cheese sauce; chicken a la king or creamed dried beef.

♦ Toss hot cooked vegetables with soy sauce, teriyaki sauce, chili sauce, barbecue sauce, sweet-and-sour sauce or any of your favorite prepared sauces.

NUTRITION INFORMATION

PER SERVING OR UNIT

RECIPE, PAGE

	Servings per recipe	Calories	Protein (grams)	Carbohydrate (grams)	Fat (grams)	Cholesterol (milligrams)	Sodium (milligrams)	Protein	Vitamin A	Vitamin C	Thiamine	Riboflavin	Niacin	Calcium	Iron
								PERCENT U.S. RECOMMENDED DAILY ALLOWANCE							

VEGETABLES

Recipe, page	Servings	Calories	Protein (g)	Carb (g)	Fat (g)	Chol (mg)	Sodium (mg)	Protein	Vit A	Vit C	Thiamine	Riboflavin	Niacin	Calcium	Iron
Artichokes, Globe, 369	4	75	3	15	1	0	100	4	4	10	6	4	4	5	10
Artichokes, Jerusalem, 370	4	105	1	24	0	2	15	2	0	2	8	10	4	0	2
Artichokes with Rosemary Sauce, 369	4	360	8	36	23	0	510	12	28	26	16	10	10	14	26
Asparagus, 370	4	45	5	6	0	0	5	8	30	46	12	12	8	2	6
Asparagus with Bacon, 370	4	35	3	4	2	2	165	4	14	20	6	6	4	2	4
Asparagus and Endive with Orange Sauce, 371	4	50	3	6	3	5	205	4	26	18	6	6	4	4	4
Au Gratin Potatoes, 393	6	390	15	34	22	45	760	22	18	14	12	18	10	38	4
Baked Turnip Casserole, 400	4	140	5	20	6	75	410	6	0	12	6	4	2	4	4
Baked Whole Onions, 387	6	150	3	11	9	0	155	4	6	10	2	2	0	6	2
Beans, Green and Wax, 371	4	40	2	8	0	0	5	2	14	14	6	6	4	4	6
Beans, Lima, 372	4	160	9	30	1	0	160	14	6	24	10	6	8	2	12
Beets, 373	4	65	2	14	0	0	100	2	0	12	4	0	2	2	6
Bok Choy, 374	4	20	2	4	0	0	110	2	100	62	4	6	4	16	6
Bok Choy with Tofu, 374	8	135	5	5	9	0	65	6	16	14	0	2	2	12	8
Broccoli, 375	4	55	5	9	1	0	45	6	50	100	6	12	4	8	8
Broccoli with Cheese, 375	4	210	14	9	14	40	735	20	48	68	8	26	4	42	8
Broccoli and Pasta Toss, 375	6	115	5	12	6	20	270	6	22	30	6	12	2	12	6
Brussels Sprouts, 376	4	55	4	10	0	0	30	4	20	80	10	6	4	4	8
Brussels Sprouts with Mustard Vinaigrette, 376	4	110	3	10	8	0	260	4	18	70	8	4	2	4	8
Brussels Sprouts in Orange Sauce, 376	4	95	3	10	6	0	225	4	20	58	8	4	2	4	6
Cabbage, Chinese, 377	4	10	1	2	0	0	50	0	44	28	2	2	0	6	2
Cabbage, Red and Green, 376	4	25	1	5	0	0	10	0	0	40	2	0	0	4	2
Cabbage and Sour Cream, 378	6	85	1	2	8	10	240	0	24	12	0	2	0	6	2
Cajun Okra Slices, 386	4	260	6	21	16	105	310	10	12	10	14	12	8	6	8
Candied Sweet Potatoes, 393	4	310	2	57	9	0	460	2	100	30	4	4	4	6	12
Carrot-Fennel Soufflé, 378	4	235	8	12	17	215	365	12	100	2	6	14	2	10	6
Carrots, 378	4	50	1	11	0	0	40	0	100	8	6	4	4	2	2
Carrots with Coconut, 378	6	100	1	13	5	0	275	2	100	8	6	4	4	2	2
Carrots and Figs, 379	4	190	3	32	7	65	65	4	100	6	6	6	6	8	6

NUTRITION INFORMATION

PER SERVING OR UNIT

PERCENT U.S. RECOMMENDED DAILY ALLOWANCE

RECIPE, PAGE	Servings per recipe	Calories	Protein (grams)	Carbohydrate (grams)	Fat (grams)	Cholesterol (milligrams)	Sodium (milligrams)	Protein	Vitamin A	Vitamin C	Thiamine	Riboflavin	Niacin	Calcium	Iron
VEGETABLES (*continued*)															
Cauliflower, 379	4	60	4	11	0	0	35	6	0	100	12	8	6	6	6
Celery, 380	4	35	1	8	0	0	200	2	4	10	4	4	2	8	6
Cheese Cauliflower, 379	4	250	12	16	16	30	650	18	16	94	10	18	6	30	6
Cheese Scalloped Corn, 382	4	310	10	32	17	90	850	16	22	26	16	14	8	16	8
Corn, 380	4	90	2	19	1	0	15	2	2	2	10	2	6	0	2
Corn and Cheese, 381	6	160	5	21	8	10	300	6	8	6	10	4	6	6	2
Cucumber and Kale Sauté, 382	4	65	2	8	4	0	150	2	40	22	4	4	2	4	4
Cucumber and Tomato Skillet, 383	6	55	1	5	4	0	230	0	6	10	2	2	0	2	2
Cucumbers, 382	4	15	1	4	0	0	2	0	0	8	2	0	0	0	0
Curried Cauliflower, 379	4	250	12	16	16	30	650	18	16	94	10	18	6	30	6
Curried New Potatoes, 391	4	220	4	37	6	15	310	6	10	18	12	4	10	4	4
Deluxe Creamed Onions, 387	6	175	3	17	11	25	270	4	100	10	6	6	2	10	4
Duchess Potatoes, 394	10	135	3	15	7	55	195	4	6	8	6	2	4	2	2
Eggplant, 383	4	30	1	7	0	0	5	0	0	0	6	0	2	4	2
French-fried Onions, 387	4	285	6	29	16	55	305	10	2	10	12	10	6	8	6
French-fried Potatoes, 394	4	240	2	27	14	0	280	2	0	14	8	0	8	0	2
Gingered Wax Beans, 372	6	35	1	6	1	0	100	2	0	4	2	4	2	2	4
Ginger-Pear Beets, 374	4	70	1	17	0	0	175	0	0	2	0	0	0	0	2
Golden Panfried Mushrooms, 386	4	240	6	17	18	70	290	8	12	4	10	34	24	2	10
Golden Squash Casserole, 397	6	130	3	13	8	10	425	4	100	8	4	4	2	4	2
Green Bean Stir-Fry with Hoisin Sauce, 372	4	90	2	11	4	0	130	4	10	10	6	6	2	4	4
Greens, 383	4	25	3	4	0	0	90	4	100	26	6	12	4	10	16
Harvard Beets, 373	4	45	1	11	0	0	410	0	0	0	0	0	0	0	6
Hash Brown Potatoes, 394	4	220	3	28	12	0	275	4	8	14	10	2	8	0	2
Herbed Broccoli, 375	4	90	3	7	7	0	285	4	30	48	4	10	4	10	8
Horseradish-sauced Artichokes, 370	5	115	3	14	6	10	145	4	32	6	10	6	4	6	16
Hot Oriental Slaw, 377	6	75	1	13	3	0	75	2	70	58	4	2	2	4	4
Leek Rolls with Tarragon Mustard, 385	12	120	2	21	3	0	150	2	32	4	4	2	2	8	10
Leeks, 384	4	140	3	32	1	0	45	4	4	22	8	4	4	12	26
Lemon-Chive Potatoes, 391	4	170	2	28	6	0	345	4	4	16	10	0	8	0	2

NUTRITION INFORMATION

PER SERVING OR UNIT

RECIPE, PAGE

Recipe, Page	Servings per recipe	Calories	Protein (grams)	Carbohydrate (grams)	Fat (grams)	Cholesterol (milligrams)	Sodium (milligrams)	PERCENT U.S. RECOMMENDED DAILY ALLOWANCE							
								Protein	Vitamin A	Vitamin C	Thiamine	Riboflavin	Niacin	Calcium	Iron

VEGETABLES (*continued*)

Recipe, Page	Servings per recipe	Calories	Protein (grams)	Carbohydrate (grams)	Fat (grams)	Cholesterol (milligrams)	Sodium (milligrams)	Protein	Vitamin A	Vitamin C	Thiamine	Riboflavin	Niacin	Calcium	Iron
Mashed Potatoes, 394	4	270	4	38	12	0	425	6	10	20	12	4	12	4	2
Mediterranean Celery, 380	6	60	0	3	6	0	85	0	6	6	0	0	0	2	2
Mushrooms and Leeks, 386	4	55	1	5	4	0	140	2	2	4	4	14	10	0	4
Okra, 386	4	45	2	9	0	0	10	2	14	18	14	3	4	8	4
Onions, 387	4	60	2	12	0	0	5	2	0	10	6	0	0	4	2
Onions and Carrots, 388	4	80	1	6	6	0	180	2	100	24	4	4	0	4	6
Onions, Green, 388	4	20	1	5	0	0	5	2	29	32	4	6	0	4	8
Orange Sweet Potatoes, 393	4	315	2	59	9	0	460	2	100	38	4	6	4	6	12
Panfried Tomatoes, 399	4	210	3	17	15	0	730	4	40	18	8	6	6	2	4
Parsnip Cakes, 388	4	315	4	31	20	70	415	6	6	12	8	6	6	6	6
Parsnips, 388	4	130	2	31	0	0	20	4	0	24	10	4	4	6	4
Pea Pods, Chinese, 388	4	50	3	9	0	0	5	4	2	56	10	4	2	4	12
Peas in Curry Sauce, 390	6	245	15	37	5	5	180	22	28	74	42	20	26	8	20
Peas, Green, 389	4	40	2	7	0	0	5	2	2	44	8	4	2	2	10
Peas and Prosciutto, 389	4	240	17	32	5	10	370	26	28	78	54	20	28	6	20
Peppers, Bell, 390	4	25	1	5	0	0	5	0	10	100	6	2	2	0	6
Pineapple Sweet Potatoes, 393	4	355	2	69	9	0	460	4	100	34	6	6	6	6	12
Piquant Green Beans, 372	4	60	2	8	3	0	175	2	16	10	4	6	2	4	6
Potato Pancake Wedges, 395	4	195	6	23	9	140	390	8	6	10	8	6	6	4	4
Potatoes, Small New, 390	4	135	3	31	0	0	10	4	0	26	10	4	12	0	6
Potatoes, Sweet or Yams, 392	4	180	3	41	1	0	25	4	100	32	6	14	4	2	4
Potatoes, White, 393	4	180	5	41	0	0	15	6	0	36	12	4	16	0	8
Ratatouille, 383	6	140	2	14	10	0	555	2	22	40	10	4	6	2	6
Rutabagas, 395	4	60	2	14	0	0	35	2	0	34	10	4	4	6	4
Rutabagas and Applesauce, 395	4	110	2	21	3	0	335	2	2	28	8	4	4	6	4
Sautéed Peppers, 390	4	70	1	6	6	0	205	0	12	90	4	2	2	4	8
Scalloped Corn, 382	4	255	7	32	13	75	760	10	18	26	14	12	8	6	8
Scalloped Potatoes, 394	6	240	6	33	10	10	510	8	10	14	12	10	10	12	2
Sesame Corn, 381	4	165	3	16	12	0	380	4	10	8	10	2	4	0	4
Sesame Pea Pods, 389	6	65	3	6	3	0	2	4	18	26	10	2	6	0	4

NUTRITION INFORMATION

PER SERVING OR UNIT

RECIPE, PAGE

	Servings per recipe	Calories	Protein (grams)	Carbohydrate (grams)	Fat (grams)	Cholesterol (milligrams)	Sodium (milligrams)	Protein	Vitamin A	Vitamin C	Thiamine	Riboflavin	Niacin	Calcium	Iron

PERCENT U.S. RECOMMENDED DAILY ALLOWANCE

VEGETABLES (continued)

Recipe, Page	Servings	Calories	Protein (g)	Carbohydrate (g)	Fat (g)	Cholesterol (mg)	Sodium (mg)	Protein	Vit A	Vit C	Thiamine	Riboflavin	Niacin	Calcium	Iron
Spaghetti Squash with Cilantro Pesto, 397	4	235	6	15	18	5	400	8	18	14	10	4	10	14	10
Spicy Grilled Corn, 381	4	145	3	22	7	0	340	4	14	2	10	4	6	0	2
Spicy Peanut Cauliflower, 380	4	160	8	16	8	0	90	12	0	80	10	6	16	6	6
Spicy Stuffed Zucchini, 398	4	80	1	12	4	0	280	2	8	4	4	2	2	2	4
Spicy Sweet Potatoes, 393	4	310	2	57	9	0	460	2	100	30	4	4	4	6	12
Spinach Soufflé, 378	4	235	10	12	17	215	410	14	100	18	8	22	4	16	16
Squash and Apple Bake, 397	6	220	1	40	8	0	460	2	100	16	6	2	6	6	8
Squash, Summer, 398	4	35	2	7	0	0	5	2	6	20	6	4	4	2	4
Squash, Winter, 396	4	90	3	20	1	0	10	4	100	22	14	4	8	6	6
Steamed Greens with Mushroom Sauce, 384	4	75	4	7	4	0	195	6	100	54	6	10	8	14	8
Stewed Tomatoes, 399	4	80	3	18	1	0	345	4	28	26	8	6	6	2	6
Stir-fried Zucchini and Jicama, 399	4	75	1	5	6	0	580	2	4	10	4	2	2	2	2
Succotash, 372	6	190	8	32	5	10	225	12	6	16	14	8	10	4	8
Sweet Potatoes in Maple Syrup, 392	6	190	2	35	5	0	35	2	100	12	4	8	4	2	4
Sweet-Sour Red Cabbage, 377	6	105	2	17	4	5	410	2	0	26	2	2	2	4	4
Tomatoes, 399	4	30	1	9	0	0	15	2	38	24	6	4	4	0	4
Turnips, 400	4	30	1	7	0	0	75	0	0	18	2	2	2	2	0
Wilted Spinach, 384	4	100	3	7	8	0	340	4	100	10	6	12	2	10	16
Yale Beets, 373	4	65	1	16	0	0	410	0	0	18	2	0	0	0	8

SPECIAL HELPS

SPECIAL HELPS

TABLE SETTINGS AND ENTERTAINING

SETTING THE TABLE

♦ Be sure to leave enough room for everyone to be seated comfortably.

♦ Place the flatware about one inch from the edge of the table, arranging it so the pieces used first are farthest from the plate. The forks are placed to the left and the knife and spoons to the right.

♦ If a butter plate is used, it is placed above the forks, with the butter knife either in a horizontal position above the plate or vertical position with the other knives.

♦ If salad is to be served with the main course, the salad plate is placed to the left of the forks. (In this case, the salad fork may be placed at either side of the dinner fork.)

♦ Glasses are arranged above the knife in order of their use. The water glass is usually at the tip of the knife, with beverage and/or wineglasses to the right.

♦ If coffee or tea is served at the table, the cup is placed slightly above and to the right of the spoons.

♦ The napkin is traditionally placed in the center of the dinner plate, unless the first course is already on the table. In that case, the napkin goes to the left of the forks or can be placed under the forks. Creative folded napkins can also be very attractive.

♦ Dessert flatware may be on the table during the meal, or it may be brought to the table with the dessert course. As an alternate position, flatware can be placed across the top of the dinner plate.

Sample Table Setting

♦ Before offering dessert, clear the table of all serving dishes; hot pads; salt and pepper sets; and plates, flatware and glasses that won't be used for the dessert course.

THE BUFFET

♦ Common sense and convenience are the watchwords of a good buffet. To avoid congestion in a small room, start the line so guests finish at the door and can easily leave the room.

♦ Begin at one end of the table with plates, then move on in order to the main dish, vegetables, salad, breads, condiments, flatware and napkins. Placing flatware and napkins at the end of the line allows guests free hands to serve themselves.

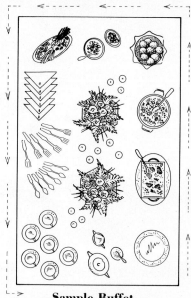

Sample Buffet

ENTERTAINING

♦ While entertaining does not require an occasion, it can be fun to plan the event around a theme. The beginning of football season, an anniversary, trying new recipes, a pumpkin-carving party or TGIF (Thank Goodness It's Friday) are all good reasons to entertain.

♦ Decide on the number of guests and whom you will invite. Think about combinations of personalities—two archenemies at the same party won't be much fun. Really interesting parties often include people with varied backgrounds. Take time to introduce guests to one another.

♦ Schedules are busy these days, so invite guests well in advance. Send invitations ten days to two weeks ahead for casual events, and at least two to three weeks for more formal events. While formal events call for a written invitation, both telephone and written invitations are appropriate for informal get-togethers. Be specific with your invitation regarding time, food and dress. "Friday, the twentieth at seven" is much clearer than "Two weeks from Friday evening."

♦ Have the house in order well before the party so you can focus on food and decorations. Plan enough food and beverages so you won't run out, and be sure to have nonalcoholic beverages available.

♦ Choose a variety of foods, but don't wear yourself out trying to outdo your favorite restaurant! Plan foods to fit the weather, guests' likes and eating habits, serving style and seasonal availability. Prepare as much ahead as possible so you won't have to spend the evening in the kitchen.

MICROWAVE COOKING

MICROWAVE COOKING PRINCIPLES

Temperature of Food: The colder the food, the longer the cooking time. Testing for this book was done with foods taken from their normal storage areas, whether they be freezer, refrigerator or cupboard shelf.

Volume of Food: As the amount of the food increases, so must the cooking time.

Size of Pieces of Food: Small pieces of food cook faster than large pieces, so keep pieces uniform in size to prevent uneven cooking.

Shape of Food: Round or doughnut-shaped foods or foods in round or ring-shaped containers cook most evenly. Irregular-shaped foods need more attention during cooking.

Density of Food: Porous foods (breads, cakes) cook quickly; dense foods (roasts, potatoes) need longer cooking.

Moisture, Sugar, Fat in Food: Microwaves are particularly attracted to these.

Standing Time: This is indicated in recipes where it is important to complete cooking. Food continues to cook while standing.

MICROWAVE TECHNIQUES

Commonly used techniques that ensure even cooking include:

♦ Covering tightly with a lid or plastic wrap (to speed heating), leaving a corner or 2-inch edge of plastic turned back.

♦ Covering loosely with waxed paper or microwavable paper towel (to prevent spatters).

♦ Stirring (moving hot edges to center).

♦ Rotating dish ½ or ¼ turn (for foods that cannot be stirred).

♦ Arranging foods in a circle (for most even cooking).

♦ Turning foods over part way through cooking time (for more even cooking).

♦ Microwaving for the minimum time recommended in the recipe and checking for doneness before adding additional time.

♦ Elevating on an inverted dish (to cook bottom center of very moist food).

♦ Covering uncooked food with a crumb or cracker coating, or brushing on a sauce or glaze (to add color and/or crispness to food that usually browns or becomes crusty when cooked conventionally).

MICROWAVE UTENSILS

Use nonmetal containers: glassware, plastic cookware, dishwasher-safe plastic containers, ceramic plates and casseroles containing no metal, and china with no metal trim. Avoid metal containers except if specifically designed for microwave cooking; they are not suitable for microwaving because arcing (causing a flash, as in welding) can occur. Use containers of the size recommended in the recipes for best results.

SAFETY

The microwave is one of the safest appliances in the home. Strict limits on the level of energy emitted have been established by the government for the safety of microwave cooking.

♦ Closely supervise children operating the microwave. Make sure they can read directions and reach the controls and into the oven easily. Never permit them to lean or swing on the door.

♦ Use potholders to prevent burns when handling containers and utensils that are in contact with hot food. Heat from the food can transfer to the container and make it uncomfortably hot.

♦ Avoid steam burns by uncovering hot containers away from the face and hands. Slowly lift the farthest edge of a cover to release steam; carefully open popcorn and cooking bags away from the face.

♦ Never microwave items such as wet clothes, wet paper or paraffin wax, as the appliance was not designed for such purposes.

♦ Never follow any directions or recommendations that conflict with the microwave oven manufacturer's instructions.

SPECIAL RECOMMENDATIONS

Aluminum Foil and Metal Containers: Follow microwave manufacturer's recommendations regarding use. Never use dishes with metal trim, metal twist ties or foil-lined carry-out containers.

Baby Food and Milk Bottles: Use medium (50%) power setting. Remove baby food to microwavable bowl. Thoroughly shake liquids and stir solid food to distribute the heat evenly after microwaving. Taste-test to be sure it's not too hot.

Deep-frying: Not recommended. Most microwavable utensils can't withstand hot oil temperatures, particularly if chipped or scratched. Maintaining a specific fat temperature is difficult.

Eggs in Shells or Whole, Cooked, Peeled Eggs: Not recommended. Eggs can burst during microwaving.

Foods with Skins: Pierce skin in several places before microwaving to avoid bursting.

Home Canning: Not recommended. Uniformly safe temperatures are difficult to reach.

Jelly or Other Sugary Fillings: Reheat carefully, because fillings with lots of sugar heat faster than surrounding pastry. Break open and let stand to cool if necessary.

Liquids: Briskly stir liquids (particularly tall, narrow containers such as mugs) before heating to incorporate air. This prevents abrupt boil-overs.

Newspaper and Recycled Paper Bags: Not recommended. Both ignite easily.

Pasta: Do not add oil to water—lack of oxygen in water could cause an abrupt boil-over.

Plastic Bags: Pierce or slit microwavable plastic bags to allow steam to escape.

Plastic Wrap: Use only those types designed for microwave use and fold back a small corner or 2-inch edge to allow steam to escape. Avoid direct food contact.

Popcorn: Use corn designed for microwaving or pop in a microwave popper.

Sealed Containers: Never use tightly closed glass jars or airtight containers in the microwave because they can explode.

GRILLING

Once reserved for summer days, grilled foods are now enjoyed year-round. In addition to following the manufacturer's directions for use, care and cleaning of your grill, follow these tips to help you grill foods to perfection. Several recipes in this book include grilling directions appropriate for a charcoal or other grill.

♦ The type of grill, outdoor temperature and wind can affect cooking times. Check the food and fire often for best results.

♦ Whether a gas, electric or charcoal grill is used, it's important to keep the heat as even as possible throughout the grilling period.

♦ If you're not getting a "sizzle," the fire may be too cool. Regulate the heat by spreading the coals or raking them together, opening or closing the vents or adjusting the control on a gas or electric grill. Raising or lowering the cooking grill or covering it will also help control the heat.

♦ To enhance flavors, use wood chips to add a smoky flavor to grilled foods. Soak hickory, mesquite, green hardwood or fruitwood chips in water for thirty minutes, drain and toss on the hot coals.

♦ For a different flavor and aroma, sprinkle the hot coals with soaked and drained dried herbs, fresh herbs or garlic cloves.

♦ Long-handled barbecue tools allow for safe distance between you and intense heat, while the handles stay cool. Use a brush for adding sauces or marinades before or during grilling. But once the food is cooked, the brush should not be used to add additional sauce; this prevents transferring any bacteria from the uncooked food to the cooked food. Wash the brush in hot, soapy water and dry thoroughly.

♦ Be careful not to transfer germs from raw meat to cooked meat. Do not carry raw hamburgers to the grill on a platter, then serve cooked meat on the same, unwashed platter.

Combine the features of your grill with those of your microwave to speed cooking. A rule of thumb to follow: Foods should be microwaved only half of their total microwave time if they are to finish cooking on the grill. Plan preparation time so that foods can go directly from the microwave to the grill. Have coals ready by the time foods are partially microwaved.

HIGH-ALTITUDE COOKING

People who live in a high-altitude area—3,500 feet or higher—face some unique cooking challenges. Air pressure is lower, so liquid evaporates faster and water has a lower boiling point. Recipes must be adjusted for both conventional and microwave cooking. Unfortunately, trial and error is the only way to make improvements because no set rules apply. The following guidelines will be of help:

♦ Foods that require boiling, such as vegetables or eggs, take longer to cook.

♦ Meats cooked in boiling liquid or steam can sometimes take up to 50 to 100 percent longer. Large meat cuts, such as roasts cooked in the oven also need more time. Use a meat thermometer and record the time required as a future guide.

♦ Most baked goods leavened with baking powder or baking soda (not yeast) will be improved by one or more of the following adjustments: increased temperature (25°), increased liquid, decreased leavening, decreased sugar, and/or a larger pan size. For very rich recipes such as pound cakes, decreasing the fat will improve results. Quick breads and cookies usually require fewest adjustments.

♦ Yeast bread dough rises more rapidly at high altitudes and can overrise easily. Allow dough to rise for a shorter time, just until doubled. Flour dries out more quickly at high altitudes. Use the minimum amount the recipe calls for, or ¼ to ½ cup less than the total amount.

♦ Many mixes that require adjustment for high altitudes have specific directions right on the package. Be sure to look for them.

♦ Boiled candy and cooked frostings (sugar mixtures) become concentrated more rapidly because of the faster evaporation of water. Watch cooking closely to prevent scorching. Reduce recipe temperature by 2° for every 1,000 feet of elevation. Or use the cold water test for candy (page 124).

♦ Deep-fried foods often result in overbrowned but undercooked foods. To ensure the outside and inside of food are done at the same time, reduce temperature of the oil by 3° for every 1,000 feet of elevation and increase frying time if necessary.

If you are new to a high-altitude area, call the State Extension Office for help in solving specific problems and for recipe booklets. Recipes are also available from Colorado State University, Fort Collins, Colorado 80521.

CANNING INFORMATION

Canning can be a safe, economical way to preserve food at home. Not only is it a way to put up favorite foods but many people enjoy the reward of canning and preserving produce from their garden or local farmers' market.

It's extremely important to follow proper canning procedures to ensure safe canned goods. Pressure canning meat, poultry, seafood and vegetables is the only recommended method for canning, according to the United States Department of Agriculture (USDA). *Clostridium botulinum* is the bacterium that can remain present in canned foods if not properly processed. The bacteria can be destroyed only if food is processed for the correct length of time in a pressure canner. It is not acceptable to use a boiling water canner.

If *clostridium botulinum* survive and grow inside a sealed jar of food, they can produce a poisonous toxin. When consumed, even in small amounts, this toxin may be fatal. If you are unsure about the safety of certain home-canned foods, boiling food 10 minutes at altitudes below 1,000 feet will destroy these toxins. Add one additional minute per 1,000 feet of additional elevation.

For additional canning information, procedures and recipes, refer to the USDA "Complete Guide to Home Canning," Agriculture Information Bulletin #539, contact the USDA or your local extension agent.

HERBS, SPICES AND SEEDS

Herbs and spices are nature's gifts to cooks. The chart on page 411 is a general guide to selecting herbs, spices and aromatic seeds compatible with a variety of foods.

Because herbs are meant to enhance flavors, using small amounts, then tasting before adding more is recommended. Some herbs have a dominant flavor and can be used by themselves or in combination with milder ones. Milder herbs can be blended into wonderful flavor combinations. The world of herbs is yours to explore—experiment and enjoy!

To use fresh herbs instead of dried, use three to four times more fresh herbs than dried. Start by adding 1 teaspoon of fresh herbs or ¼ teaspoon of dried herbs for every four servings.

Thyme

Sage

Tarragon

Lemon Grass

Mint

Basil

Dill Weed

Parsley

Rosemary

Cilantro

Garlic

Bay Leaves

Oregano

Mustard Seed

Saffron

Cardamom Pods

Whole Nutmeg

Whole White Pepper

Whole Cloves

Cinnamon Sticks

Celery Seed

Whole Allspice

Whole Coriander

Crushed Red Pepper

Caraway Seed

Whole Black Pepper

Fennel Seed

Poppy Seed

HOW TO SELECT AND USE HERBS, SPICES AND SEEDS

HERBS	FLAVOR AND USE
Basil (leaves, ground)	Sweet, with clovelike, pungent tang Eggs, meats, salads, sauces, soups, stews, tomato dishes
Bay leaves (leaves, ground)	Pungent, aromatic Meats, pickling, sauces, soups, stews, vegetables
Cilantro (Chinese parsley, Italian parsley)	Aromatic, parsleylike Mexican, Chinese and Italian dishes, garnishes
Dill weed (whole, dried)	Pungent, tangy Breads, cheese, fish, salads, sauces, vegetables
Lemon grass (leaves)	Delicate, light Asian dishes, soups, stews, salads, sauces
Mint (leaves, flakes)	Strong, sweet with cool aftertaste Beverages, desserts, fish, lamb, sauces, soups
Oregano (leaves, ground)	Strong, aromatic with pleasantly bitter undertone Cheese, eggs, fish, Italian dishes, meats, sauces, soups, vegetables
Parsley (leaves, freeze-dried)	Slightly peppery Garnishes, herb mixtures, sauces, stews, soups
Rosemary (leaves)	Fresh, sweet flavor Casseroles, fish, lamb, salads, seafood, soups, vegetables
Sage (leaves, rubbed, ground)	Aromatic, slightly bitter Dressings, fish, meats, poultry, salads, sausages, soups, stuffings
Tarragon (leaves)	Piquant, reminiscent of anise Eggs, meats, pickling, poultry, salads, sauces, tomatoes
Thyme (leaves, ground)	Aromatic, pungent Chowders, fish, meats, poultry, stews, stuffings, tomato dishes

SPICES	FLAVOR AND USE
Allspice (whole, ground)	Reminiscent of a combination of cloves and cinnamon Cakes, cookies, fruits, pies, stews
Chili powder (ground—blend of chili peppers, and other spices)	Spicy, hot Cocktail sauces, cottage cheese, eggs, Mexican dishes, soups, stews, vegetables
Cinnamon (stick, ground)	Aromatic, pungent, sweet Cakes, cookies, fruit desserts, pies, pickling, puddings

SPICES	FLAVOR AND USE
Cloves (whole, ground)	Aromatic, strong, pungent, sweet Desserts, fruit, meats, pickling, stews, vegetables, sauces
Crushed red pepper (dried pepper flakes)	Hot pungent flavor Meats, casseroles, soups, stews
Curry powder (ground—blend of many ground spices)	Pungent, hot to mild Eggs, fish, meats, sauces, vegetables
Garlic (whole, minced, powdered, dehydrated)	Pungent aroma and taste Fish, meats, salads, sauces, sausages, soups, vegetables
Ginger (whole, cracked, bits, ground)	Pungent, spicy Fish, fruits, meats, sauces, sausages, soups, vegetables, desserts
Nutmeg (whole, ground)	Fragrant, sweet with spicy undertone Beverages, cakes, cookies, puddings, sauces, vegetables
Pepper (whole, ground)	Hot, biting, very pungent Meats, casseroles, soups, salads, vegetables, pickling
Saffron (strands, powdered)	Softly bitter, distinctive flavor Poultry, rice, rolls, sauces, seafood, Spanish dishes

SEEDS	FLAVOR AND USE
Caraway (whole, seeds)	Intense, aromatic Cabbage, cheese, meats, pickling, rye bread, sauerkraut, soups, stews
Cardamom (whole pod, seeds, ground)	Pungent with slight menthol flavor Coffee, custard, curry, fruit, sausages, Scandinavian breads
Celery seed (whole, ground)	Concentrated celery flavor Dressings, meats, pickling, salads, sauces, soups, stuffings
Coriander (whole, ground)	Mildly fragrant, like a cross between lemon peel and sage Breads, cakes, cookies, curry powder, sausages, seafood, Mexican and Spanish dishes, pastries
Cumin (whole, ground)	Pungent, savory, slightly bitter Cheese, pickling, pork, sauerkraut
Fennel seed (whole, ground)	Aromatic, sweet, resembles licorice Breads, fish, Italian dishes, sauces, sausages, soups, sweet pickles
Mustard (whole seed, ground)	Hot, pungent with dry aftertaste Casseroles, meats, pickling, relishes, salads, vegetables
Poppy seed (whole)	Pleasant, nutlike Breads, cakes, cookies, desserts

NUTRITION BASICS

New information linking certain foods with the cause or prevention of health problems is changing the way we cook and the kinds of foods we choose for our daily meals. We are becoming more interested in foods that provide complex carbohydrates and fiber and eating less of foods that are high in fat, sugar, and sodium. The key to healthful eating remains the same, however: Eat a balanced diet that includes appropriate nutrients.

NUTRIENTS IN FOOD

Protein: Protein occurs naturally in foods of animal and plant origin, and is necessary for growth and maintenance of body tissues. Careful combinations of whole grains, vegetables, and legumes can provide the protein we need less expensively and without contributing as much fat as some sources of animal protein.

Carbohydrates: Carbohydrates, the body's main source of energy, are of two types: simple and complex.

Simple carbohydrates include sugars found naturally in foods and sweeteners. Whether a sugar is added to food or occurs naturally in food, it is used in the same way by the body.

Complex carbohydrates are found in vegetables, fruits, dried beans and peas, and whole grain foods and cereal products. An increased use of complex carbohydrate foods as a substitute for foods high in fat is an important factor in reducing the risk of some health problems, among them heart disease, obesity and certain cancers. Complex carbohydrates also contain fiber.

Fiber is the nondigestible portion of foods derived from plants. Soluble fiber, which dissolves easily in water, has been shown to play a role in helping to lower blood cholesterol when part of a low-fat diet. Some foods high in soluble fiber include whole-grain oats, oat bran, whole-grain barley, apples, oranges and legumes. Information suggesting a link between some soluble fiber foods such as oat bran with the lowering of cholesterol levels in the blood has increased their popularity as a food ingredient.

Insoluble fiber, which does not dissolve in water, is best known for promoting regularity. Wheat, corn bran, whole grains, vegetables and nuts are good sources of insoluble fiber.

Fat and Cholesterol: Fat, found in many foods, supplies energy, provides essential fatty acids and aids in the transport of fat-soluble vitamins A, D, E, and K through the body. Our bodies make cholesterol, and we also get it from some foods we eat. Cholesterol is involved in manufacturing certain hormones and is an essential part of the nervous system and the brain.

The concern today about the relationship of dietary fat and cholesterol to heart disease has prompted recommendations that total fat intake be limited to 30 percent or less of daily calories and that cholesterol not exceed 300 milligrams per day.

There are three types of fat: saturated, monounsaturated, and polyunsaturated. Saturated fat is thought to be a major contributor to elevated blood cholesterol levels. Therefore, recommendations are that saturated fats contribute no more than 10 percent of daily calories. Saturated fats are primarily found in animal sources such as meat, eggs and dairy products. Fats and oils that contain primarily monounsaturated and polyunsaturated fats are liquid at room temperature and found most commonly in vegetable or plant sources.

Sodium: Common table salt is a combination of sodium and chloride, both of which are needed to help regulate the balance of water in the body. We get sodium naturally in foods and also from salt used in food preparation and at the table.

Vitamins: Vitamins are compounds that are necessary for growth and development and the maintenance of health. They are found in varying amounts in the food we eat. The vitamins most easily lost during cooking are the B vitamins (thiamine, riboflavin, niacin, B_6, and B_{12}) and vitamin C. Cooking foods, especially vegetables, in only a small amount of water saves the greatest amount of these vitamins. (Very little water is required when vegetables are steamed or cooked in the microwave.)

Minerals: Minerals also are important to the body because they contribute to a rigid skeleton, are needed to help nerves and muscles function and are oxygen carriers.

The most prevalent minerals are calcium, phosphorus, sodium, potassium and magnesium. The trace minerals—those needed in smaller amounts—are iron, zinc, manganese, copper and iodine. Calcium and iron are consumed at less than adequate levels by many, especially teenage girls and adult women.

Calcium deficiency is a contributing factor in the development of osteoporosis.

WATER—THE FORGOTTEN NUTRIENT

Water makes up about 70 percent of the human body and is involved in so many body functions, maintenance of water balance is crucial. Balance is attained when we ingest at least as much water as we lose. Drinking six to eight or more cups of liquids—including juices and broths—per day helps provide some of the water that is needed to maintain water balance. Sodium and potassium are the minerals principally responsible for the body's water balance.

UNDERSTANDING THE BASIC FOOD GROUPS

Food Group	Recommended Daily Amounts	1 Serving	Nutrient Contributions
Milk, yogurt and cheese	Children under 9 years: 3 servings Teenagers 10 to 18 years: 4 servings Adults: 2 servings	1 cup milk or yogurt or 1 ounce cheese or 1/2 cup cottage cheese or 1/2 cup ice cream	Calcium Phosphorus Protein Riboflavin Vitamin A Vitamin D
Meat, fish, poultry and legumes	2 servings	2 to 3 ounces cooked lean meat, fish or poultry or 1/2 cup cooked dried beans or 1 egg or 2 tablespoons peanut butter	Iron Niacin Phosphorus Protein Folic acid Vitamin B_6 Vitamin B_{12}*
Breads and cereals (whole grain, enriched and fortified	4 servings	1 slice bread or 1 ounce ready-to-eat cereal or 1/2 cup cooked cereal, rice or pasta	Carbohydrate Iron Niacin Riboflavin Thiamine Magnesium
Vegetables and fruits	4 servings Include one good source of vitamin C daily; frequently include deep yellow or dark green vegetables	1 cup raw vegetables or 1/2 cup fruit, fruit juice or cooked vegetables or 1 medium or 2 small fruits	Carbohydrate Vitamin A Vitamin C
Combination foods	Count as servings from the food groups from which they are made	1 cup soup or 1 cup macaroni and cheese, lasagna or stew or one-eighth of a 15-inch pizza or 1 sandwich or 1 taco	Same nutrients as the foods they contain
Fats, sweets and alcohol	Number of servings depends on the individual's calorie needs		Fatty acids Vitamin E

*Animal products only.

FOOD SAFETY

Food safety is an increasing concern, from safe packaging to sanitary food preparation at home and in restaurants.

Some bacteria can be useful, such as the bacteria that cause fermentation in cheese and beer. Other bacteria can cause foods to spoil—to rot or turn bad—while even others can cause food poisoning. The major difference between the last two is the temperature at which they grow.

Those that cause food to spoil can grow at refrigerator temperatures. However, at least they make themselves known by making the food look or smell unpleasant, an obvious clue to throw it out.

Most food poisoning bacteria don't grow at refrigerator temperatures, but thrive at room temperatures (60° to 90°). These are pathogens (*salmonella*, *staphylococcus*, *listeria*, *clostridium perfringens* and *clostridium botulinum*), the type of bacteria that if consumed may lead to illness, disease or death. Most of them can't be seen, smelled or tasted.

The majority of food poisoning bacteria can be controlled by cooking and refrigeration. The first rule of food safety is to keep food *hot* or *cold*. The second rule is to keep everything in the kitchen *clean*, because most bactria get into food through careless handling.

KEEPING FOOD HOT OR COLD

♦ The most perishable foods are those containing eggs, milk—such as creamed foods and cream pies—seafood, meat and poultry. When you shop, pick up your meat and poultry selections last. Take them straight home and refrigerate.

♦ Don't allow hot or cold foods to remain at room temperature for more than 2 hours, including preparation time; bacteria thrive in lukewarm food. A standard rule, recommended by the U.S. Department of Agriculture, is to keep hot foods hot (above 140°) and cold foods cold (below 40°).

♦ Once food has been cooked, keep it hot until serving or refrigerate as soon as possible. If it will not raise the refrigerator temperature above 45°, hot food can be placed immediately in the refrigerator.

♦ Follow these rules to serve hot foods safely:

Cook meat and poultry thoroughly, following the "doneness" temperatures given.

Use a meat thermometer.

Don't interrupt cooking. Cook meat and poultry to final doneness at one time, because partial cooking may encourage bacterial growth before cooking is complete.

Thoroughly reheat leftovers. Cover when reheating to retain moisture and ensure thorough heating in the center. Bring gravies to a rolling boil before serving.

Never leave food out longer than 2 hours!

KEEPING THE KITCHEN CLEAN

♦ Germs are a natural part of the environment. Keep countertops, appliances, utensils and dishes sanitary by cleaning with water and soap or other cleansers.

♦ Wash hands thoroughly with soap and water. Wear protective plastic gloves, or just don't handle food, if you have any kind of cut or infection on your hands.

♦ Be careful not to transfer germs from raw meat to cooked meat. For example, do not carry raw hamburgers to the grill on a platter, then serve cooked meat on the same, unwashed platter.

♦ Do not use wooden cutting boards for raw meat or poultry. A hard plastic cutting board is less porous, safer for meats, and easily cleaned or washed in a dishwasher. Wash boards with a mixture of 2 teaspoons chlorine bleach and 1 teaspoon vinegar to 1 gallon of water after each use.

♦ Wash the meat keeper and crisper drawer of your refrigerator often and keep containers for storing refrigerated food very clean.

♦ Use disposable paper towels when working with or cleaning up after raw foods.

FOOD SAFETY TIPS

Eggs: Storage for "do-ahead" recipes should not exceed 48 hours. Foods containing cooked eggs (such as cheesecakes, cream fillings, custards, quiches and potato salads) must be served hot or cold (depending on the recipe), with leftovers refrigerated immediately. Store cooked dishes no longer than 48 hours. See also Safe Handling and Storage of Eggs (page 168) and Cooking with Eggs (page 169).

Ground Meat: Cook thoroughly—it's handled often in preparation and germs can get mixed into it. Make sure ground beef is at least medium doneness (160° and brownish pink in the center) before you serve it. Don't eat raw ground meat—it's not safe! Meat loaves should reach at least 170° in the center, particularly if they contain pork.

Ham: Know what kind of ham you're buying; some are fully cooked but others need cooking. Check the label. If you have any doubts, cook it.

Luncheon Meat, Frankfurters: Refrigerate; use within a week. If the liquid that accumulates around frankfurters is cloudy, discard them.

Poultry: Cook all poultry products as long as directions require. Stuff poultry just before ready to cook. This will keep any bacteria in the raw poultry from contaminating the starchy dressing. Stuffing poultry loosely will allow it to be thoroughly cooked. The center should reach 165°. Refrigerate cooked poultry, stuffing and giblets as soon as possible in separate containers.

Sauces: Leftover marinades and sauces that have been in contact with raw meat should be heated to boiling and boiled 1 minute before serving.

Canned Foods: Do not buy or use food from leaking, bulging or dented cans or jars with cracks or loose or bulging lids. If you are in doubt about a can of food, don't taste it! Return it to your grocer and report it to your local health authority.

Milk: Fresh milk products are highly perishable; refrigerate them as soon after purchase as possible. Unopened evaporated milk and nonfat dry milk may be stored in a cool area for several months. Unopened dry whole milk, which contains fat, should be refrigerated; use within a few weeks.

KEEP FOOD SAFE AT BUFFETS

Serve food in small dishes, refilling frequently from stove or refrigerator. Or keep food hot in electric skillet or chafing dish or on hot tray. Don't depend on warming units with candles. Refrigerate salads made with seafood, poultry or meat. Chill both food and dish before serving. Serve cold foods over crushed ice.

PACK SAFE LUNCHES

♦ Wash fruits and vegetables before packing.

♦ Use fully cooked foods (bologna, frankfurters, canned meats and poultry); they keep well.

♦ Wash vacuum bottles and rinse with boiling water after each use. Be sure hot foods are boiling hot when poured into vacuum bottles.

♦ Lunch boxes insulate better than lunch bags.

Note: For a free copy of the brochure "A Quick Consumer Guide to Safe Food Handling," write to Publications, Room 1165-S, USDA, Washington, DC 20250.

FREEZER AND REFRIGERATOR STORAGE

WRAPPING FOODS

Facilitate proper storage by using durable packaging and wrapping materials. Freezer wraps and containers should be airtight, moistureproof and vaporproof. These materials keep moisture in the food and prevent freezer burn. Good materials are heavy-duty aluminum foil, heavyweight plastic wrap and airtight freezer bags or containers. If you wrap foods, be sure to press out the air and then wrap tightly. More delicate foods, such as certain types of cookies or popovers, may need to be put in a box or sturdy container for protection. Gently wrap the food and then place in an airtight box or container. If desired, foods such as chicken pieces or strawberries can be frozen in a single layer, until frozen hard; then placed in an airtight bag. You can use small quantities of these items as needed.

LABELING FOODS

Be sure to label all packages and containers before freezing. Include the following information: name of recipe, storage time ("use before" date), number of servings and any directions for preparing after freezing. Use an adhesive label or freezer tape and a grease pencil or felt-tipped pen for marking to avoid smudges.

NOT FOR FREEZING

Some foods are not recommended for freezing because the quality of the thawed product is poor. Foods such as cooked egg whites become tough, mayonnaise or salad dressings may separate, salad greens become soggy, raw tomatoes will become limp and watery, and raw apples and grapes become mushy.

FREEZER TEMPERATURE

To freeze and store food, your freezer should be kept at 0° or lower. At this temperature, and below, foods freeze faster with less cellular damage. They are also more likely to retain good flavor and texture. We recommend you purchase a freezer thermometer and check it often to make sure your freezer maintains a temperature of 0° or lower.

GUIDELINES FOR REFRIGERATOR STORAGE

Keep refrigerator temperature at 40° or slightly lower. Always store produce in tightly covered containers or plastic bags to retain moisture and prevent transfer of odors to or from other foods. Remove foods from refrigerator at the time you are ready to use them.

Foods	Length of Time	Storage Precautions
BREADS	5 to 7 days	Refrigerate during hot, humid weather
CONDIMENTS (barbecue sauce, horseradish, ketchup)	12 months	
DAIRY PRODUCTS		
Buttermilk, sour cream, yogurt	2 weeks	Check the freshness date on the container before purchase
Cheese		
Cottage	10 to 30 days	Refrigerate tightly covered
Cream	2 weeks	
Hard	3 to 4 weeks	Wrap tightly; discard if moldy
Sliced	2 weeks	
Spread	1 to 2 weeks	Refrigerate covered after opening
Cream, whipping (heavy), half-and-half	3 to 5 days	Refrigerate tightly closed
Milk		
Reconstituted dry	5 days	Refrigerate evaporated and condensed tightly covered after opening
Skim	5 days	
Whole	5 days	
EGGS		
Whole	1 week	Can be refrigerated longer, but expect loss of some quality and flavor
Yolks, whites	2 to 4 days	Cover yolks with cold water; refrigerate yolks and whites covered
FATS, OILS		
Butter	2 weeks	Refrigerate tightly covered
Margarine	1 month	
Mayonnaise, salad dressings	6 months	Refrigerate after opening
FRUITS		
Apples	1 month	Refrigerate ripe apples uncovered
Apricots, avocados, grapes melons, peaches, pears, plums	3 to 5 days	Store at room temperature until ripe and then refrigerate
Berries, cherries	2 to 3 days	Do not wash or remove stems before refrigerating
Cranberries	1 week	Refrigerate covered
Citrus	2 weeks	Store uncovered in refrigerator
Dried	6 months	Refrigerate during hot, humid weather
Pineapple	2 to 3 days	Use soon after puchase; no further ripening occurs during storage

Foods	Length of Time	Storage Precautions
MEATS, POULTRY, SEAFOOD		
Meats, fresh		*Cover lightly and refrigerate*
Chops	*3 to 5 days*	
Ground	*1 to 2 days*	
Roasts	*3 to 5 days*	
Steaks	*3 to 5 days*	
Variety	*1 to 2 days*	
Meats, processed		
Cold cuts (unopened)	*2 weeks*	
Cold cuts (opened)	*3 to 5 days*	
Cured bacon	*1 week*	
Frankfurters	*1 week*	
Ham, canned		
Half	*3 to 5 days*	
Slices	*3 to 4 days*	
Whole	*1 week*	
Poultry and seafood	*1 to 2 days*	*Refrigerate in plastic wrap or waxed paper*
Pickles, olives	*1 month*	
Stuffing	*1 to 2 days*	*Remove from fowl; refrigerate immediately*
VEGETABLES		
Asparagus	*2 to 3 days*	*Don't wash before refrigerating*
Broccoli, Brussels sprouts, green onions, summer squash	*3 to 5 days*	*Store in refrigerator crisper, plastic bags or containers*
Cabbage, carrots, parsnips, radishes, rutabagas	*2 weeks*	*Remove tops of root vegetables; refrigerate in plastic bags*
Cauliflower, celery, cucumbers, eggplant, green beans, green peppers	*1 week*	*Store in refrigerator crisper, plastic bags or containers*
Corn, sweet	*1 day*	*Refrigerate unhusked and uncovered*
Green peas, lima beans	*3 to 5 days*	*Refrigerate in pods*
Lettuce, greens	*3 to 5 days*	*Wash, drain well and refrigerate in crisper; produce stored in vacuum-pack containers (airproof) lasts three to six times longer*
Tomatoes	*1 week*	*Refrigerate uncovered*
WINE *(opened)*	*1 to 2 days*	*Pour any remaining wine into a small container so there's less contact with air; refrigerate white wine; store red airtight at room temperature*

GUIDELINES FOR FREEZER STORAGE

Purchased frozen foods should be kept in the original packages. Always thaw frozen meats, poultry and seafood in the refrigerator or according to microwave manufacturer's directions.

Foods	Length of Time	Storage Precautions
BREADS, BAKED	*2 to 3 months*	
CAKES, AND COOKIES, BAKED	*3 to 4 months*	
DAIRY PRODUCTS		
Cream, whipping (heavy)	*2 to 3 months*	*Texture changes, after thawing*
Ice cream, sherbet	*2 to 4 months*	*Cover surface with foil to reduce formation of ice crystals*
EGGS		
Whole	*Not recommmended*	
Whites	*1 year*	*Use promptly after thawing*
Yolks	*3 months*	*Add ⅛ teaspoon salt or ½ teaspoon sugar for each ¼ cup yolks.*
FATS, OILS		
Margarine, butter	*2 months*	
FRUITS OR JUICES	*8 to 12 months*	*Wrap, label and date package*
MEATS, SEAFOOD, POULTRY		
Meats, fresh		
Chops	*4 to 6 months*	
Ground	*2 to 3 months*	
Roasts	*8 to 12 months*	
Steaks	*6 to 12 months*	
Meats, cooked	*1 to 3 months*	
Meats, processed		
Cured bacon and frankfurters	*1 month*	*Freeze in vacuum wrap and overwrap for storage over 2 weeks*
	1 to 2 months	
Cured or smoked pork	*1 to 2 months*	*Cured pork loses color and flavor during food storage*
Fish, fresh		
Fatty	*2 to 3 months*	*Freeze covered in single layer on tray*
Lean	*4 to 6 months*	*Dip each piece quickly in ice cold water to form glaze; freeze uncovered to let film harden, 5 to 10 minutes; repeat until thick glaze is formed; wrap, label and freeze*
Fish, frozen		
Breaded, cooked	*2 to 3 months*	
Seafood, fresh		
Shrimp	*4 to 6 months*	*Wrap airtight*
Other shellfish	*2 to 4 months*	
Seafood, cooked		
Scallops or lobster	*1 to 2 months*	
Shellfish	*3 to 4 months*	
Poultry, fresh		
Cut up	*4 to 6 months*	
Whole	*6 to 8 months*	
Poultry, cooked	*1 month*	*Wrap airtight; it dries out quickly*
PIES, BAKED OR PIE SHELLS	*4 months*	*Do not freeze custard or cream pies or pies with a meringue topping*
Unbaked pie shells	*2 months*	
NUTS, SHELLED	*3 months*	
VEGETABLES	*8 months*	

INDEX